A HISTORY AND DESCRIPTION

OF

WINCHESTER

WINCHESTER, FROM ST. GILES HILL.

W.H. Bartlett

C. Cousen

A

HISTORY AND DESCRIPTION

OF

WINCHESTER

BY

B. B. WOODWARD, B.A., F.S.A.

WITH SEVENTEEN STEEL ENGRAVINGS

LAURENCE OXLEY
Broad Street, Alresford, Hampshire

1974

ISBN 0950134759

Printed and Bound in Great Britain
by
THE SCOLAR PRESS LTD
59/61 East Parade
Ilkley
Yorkshire

Publisher's Note

This edition of the History of Winchester by B. B. Woodward was first published in Winchester about 1860 and is still considered the most informative book on the old capital. It deals at great length with the Cathedral, the College, St. Cross and the historical aspects of Winchester. Authorities used are quoted in the many footnotes.

The book has now become rare and expensive, mainly because the delightful steel engravings are frequently taken from the book for framing. The plates were originally drawn by two experienced artists, William H. Bartlett (1809-54) and James C. Armytage (1820-97) and they show Winchester scenes as they were in the mid-19th century.

Bernard Bolingbroke Woodward, B.A., F.S.A., was born in 1816 and died 1869. He was librarian to Queen Victoria at Windsor Castle 1860. He wrote many historical works including (with Wilks and Lockhart) the history of Hampshire, in three volumes.

CONTENTS.

———◆———

LIST OF PLATES.

———◆———

THE
CITY AND BOROUGH
OF
WINCHESTER.

WINCHESTER,[1] in old times the metropolis of England, but now of Hampshire only, and far surpassed, both as to population and importance, by Portsmouth and Southampton,[2] is situated in the centre of its county, in lat. 51° 5′ north, and long. 1° 18′ west. It stands in the pleasant valley of the Itchen, which, having taken a southward direction a little higher up, here widens considerably, and presents the appearance of a noble amphitheatre—worthy, and perhaps to some extent the cause, of the ancient renown of the city which adorns it. ^{Situation of Winchester.}

The rich alluvial level of this valley, which attains the breadth of some half a mile immediately below Winchester, is overlooked on the east by the steep escarpment of St. Giles' Hill, and by St. Catharine's Hill,[3] with its crown of beeches, and deeply-gashed sides; and from the opposite quarter by West Hill, Cromwell's Battery, and other downs; and along it through many channels the Itchen, with its gurgling, crystal waters, hastens to the sea.[4]

As far as Wharf Bridge, where the navigation commences, the main stream keeps to the eastern edge of this valley; and from that point to the southern limit of the borough, the artificial river skirts the foot of the hills, whilst the other turns aside, ^{The River Itchen.}

---

(1) The present name of this city is only a modification of its Saxon name *Wintanceaster*, which was derived from the Roman *Venta* (*Belgarum*). The alleged British original of the latter appellation, *Caer Gwent*,—being supported by no better authorities than the exceedingly questionable " Historia Britonum," ascribed to Nennius, and the undoubtedly fictitious work of Geoffrey of Monmouth, bearing the same title,—cannot, we think, be received. The mediæval names of Winchester were no more than Latinizations of its Saxon designation: *Wincestria, Wintonix, Wentana*, are the principal forms which occur in MSS. and on coins, in every conceivable variety of spelling. The familiar synonym, *Winton.*, is an abbreviation of the second form, or of the derived adjective, after the custom of ancient calligraphers.

(2) Population of Winchester, 13,704; of Southampton, 35,305; and of Portsmouth, 72,096. Census, 1851.

(3) St. Giles' and St. Catharine's Hills are sometimes called Morning Hill and Evening Hill, from a mistake respecting the meaning of those phrases as used in Winchester College. The latter is also known as College Hill.

(4) See Duthy's " Sketches of Hampshire;" §§ iii. and v.; and Leland's Itinerary, vol. iii. fols. 71—73.

and wanders through pasturage and meadow to St. Cross. Above Winchester there are nine streams besides the river. Broad Ditch, Black Ditch, and Swift Lake, are names given to three of them; but the "Hyde Burn" (if modern changes in orthography and feeling have not caused this name to be quite forgotten) is the most illustrious.[1] Then by six channels near Durngate, and two others of less account to the west of them, the waters enter the *enceinte* of the old city.[2] Here, between the East Soke and Winchester itself, is the Itchen, which is crossed by the bridge at Durngate Mill, the Soke Bridge, Wharf Mill, and Wharf Bridge. Four smaller streams, by open or concealed courses, flow through the lower part of the city, and after giving names to the Upper, Middle, and Lower Brooks,[3] on the northern side of High Street, unite, and making an abrupt turn, flow down the southern side of the street,[4] till within a few yards of the river.[5] Three or four channels opening to the south—one of them being the identical "sweet and fishful rivulet" which Bishop Athelwold led through the enclosure of St. Swithin's Priory,[6] and another the mill-stream of St. Mary's Abbey—convey the waters by the back of Wolvesey Palace to the southern limit of the city, where, escaping by a low archway, they wash the eastern walls of Wykeham's College, turn the College Mill, and at last, under the name of the Barton Mill-stream, rejoin the Itchen halfway between Winchester and the Hospital of De Blois.[7]

(1) See p. 3, note 4, *ante*.

(2) Trussell (MS. History of Winchester, fol. 82) states that the Hyde Burn supplied the ditch outside the walls on the western side of the city, and round the castle, with water, until the siege of the castle by the partisans of Stephen, in the year 1141, when the channel was dammed up, and the supply of water cut off by the besiegers, for the purpose of forcing the Empress Maud to surrender. Milner (vol. i. p. 162, Ed. 3) adopts this statement, but quotes "Trussel" as the only authority. Trussell, however, who seems to have been but poorly acquainted with matters only a little removed from his own times (vide Arch. Journal, vol. vii. p. 381, note), is too "apocryphal" an authority for events of five hundred years before them; especially since it would be necessary to suppose that the ditch was inordinately deep, for any water to run into it from the stream that passes through Hyde Abbey precinct. And Trussell admits that this statement was questioned by others, and, at one time, regarded as "improbable" by himself.

In addition to which, it may be observed, that a Letter Patent of the 4th of Edward I., 1275-6, addressed to the Prior of St. Swithin's, speaks of the preservation of the king's ditch, without North-gate, and of renewing the stock of fishes in it, for the king's use. Whence it would appear that the ditch was not dry, although this alleged direct supply from the river had been cut off. (Rot. Pat. 4 Edw. I., m. 31, apud Gale, p. 7.)

In former times there was a rivulet, running past

Fulflood Farm to the neighbourhood of Hyde Abbey Mill; from which the city ditch might have derived some of its supply. We shall speak of the land-springs near the city subsequently.

(3) The fourth, which is nearest the Itchen, used to irrigate and adorn the grounds of Eastgate House, the residence of the Mildmays.

(4) Godson's map of Winchester, 1750, and Buck's "East Prospect of the City of Winchester," 1736, show that a considerable stream flowed along the south side of High Street at that time. When we speak of *New Minster*, it will be necessary to notice the process by which Wavell (vol. ii. p. 55) and Milner (vol. i. p. 155, &c., and vol. ii. p. 244) have—out of an occasional torrent, such as still may be seen sweeping down High Street, after a heavy summer rain-fall—made a "stream" proceeding "from the waters surrounding the castle."

(5) The city walls, between the Soke Bridge and the present gate of Wolvesey Palace grounds, were strengthened by a ditch in front of them, supplied from the river: at the south-eastern angle it is called *Lady's Lake*; and is now being filled up, October, 1856.

(6) This is the *Lock Pond*; anciently called the *Lurte Burne*, as I am informed by the Rev. W. H. Gunner.

(7) Of one branch of the *Lurte Burne*, which is conducted through the Close, by a subterranean channel, and, crossing College Street, passes under *Commoners*, and falls into the Barton Mill-stream, we shall speak in

From various eminences, along both sides of the valley, fine views of the city and its immediate environs may be obtained. That from St. Catharine's Hill is very interesting, as it presents what may be called a profile of the site. But the most favourable situation for studying the topography of Winchester is St. Giles' Hill Looking from this elevated point, we can see every part of the ancient city, exhibited almost as distinctly as in a map, with the luxuriant water-meadows northward as far as the Worthies, and to the south beyond St. Cross; and above, the broad, turf-covered downs, with here and there a clump of fir-trees; and West Hill, directly opposite, upon which a new town is rising.[1] The parallelogram bisected by High Street, which so faithfully records the Roman origin of the city, may still be distinctly traced; although the suburbs that have grown up on every hand at different periods, have so greatly enlarged its area, and altered its figure.

The episcopal moiety of Winchester has in a remarkable manner preserved its antique aspect, as compared with the municipal portion. The massive and venerable cathedral, in whose exterior can be seen, even at this distance, such diverse styles of architecture, stands there, embosomed in the stately lime-trees of the cemetery and the Close, which more than ever deserves its old name—"Paradise." Southward is Wykeham's splendid school, where so much more than the *trivium* and *quadrivium*, even in the most approved forms of them, is wrought into the minds of the learners. Its tall and graceful tower rears itself, with something akin to consciousness of worth, above the thick screen of foliage that hides the extensive collegiate buildings. In front of it is all that remains of the palace at Wolvesey, which Wren's taste, and Morley's and Trelawney's magnificence raised; and of the castle there, the work of an earlier prelate, who lived in troublous times. And hard by there yet stands a portion of the city wall—the only fragment which retains aught of its original appearance. The long narrow suburb at our feet, inclosed between the hill and the river, which is part of the East Soke, wears the same aspect that it did a hundred years and more ago. And the towers of St. Peter's and St. John's Churches have an air of reverend age, strangely contrasting with the upstart look of novelty in two or three other churches within sight.

On the other hand, from Eastgate Street, with its white-fronted shops and steam-worked brewery—across the Brooks, where the poorer classes most numerously dwell, to the better-class houses of the streets above them, and the "Terraces" and "Places" that crowd West Hill—and away to the left, beyond the Cathedral, as far as the fantastic *châlet* you can barely descry in Painter's Fields—secular Winchester seems to be undergoing a process of complete rejuvenescence. The remaining antiques are as conspicuous from their alien environment, as the few recent structures in the

Aspect of Winchester from St. Giles' Hill.

The ancient part of the city.

The modern city.

---

another place. There is, also, a small stream, which has every appearance of being artificial, running from Barton Mill through the quadrangle of St. Cross' Hospital, and rejoining the Itchen beyond the boundary of the borough. The numerous canals, cut for the purpose of irrigating

the water-meadows, ought not to be omitted in this sketch of the *hydrography* of Winchester.

(1) Compare Buck's "East Prospect," and a similar, but not so large or detailed a view, in Stukeley's "Itinerarium Curiosum," pl. 88.

c 2

Bishop's city appear. There is the low tower of the "mother church" of St. Law-rence amongst the house-tops;[1] and there the cupola of the Guild-hall, where the curfew bell tolls, and Sir William Paulet's clock projects over the carriage-way; there, too, is West-gate, and near it, scarcely discernible, the County Hall; to the north you may also see the Church of St. Bartholomew Hyde, but there are no vestiges of the abbey visible from this position. Besides these, and one or two really ancient houses, which a practised eye detects in spite of the modern tiling, we may perhaps reckon that grand building, planned but never finished by Wren for Charles II., and now half modernized; the Duchess of Portsmouth's House; and the Nunnery. St. John's House may be styled ancient; but scarcely so the noble County Hospital.

Recently erected public buildings.

And all else is new: St. Maurice's Church, with its many pinnacles; St. Thomas', with its lofty spire, and Holy Trinity, near Whitebread Mead; St. Peter's Chapel, and the Chapel of the Independents;—all are of recent erection, and some quite new. There is the Museum, where but lately the New Jail was; and a newer Jail, for county as well as city, stands on the very summit of the opposite height, and raises its campanile like a beacon, to be seen far and near. St. John's Almshouses are new; and Lamb's Almshouses, and St. Mary's Abbey. The Corn Exchange, the Gas Works, the Union House, the Chapels of the Cemetery, and, last of all, the London and South-western Railway, which runs along the other side of the valley, coming into view just within the north-western boundary of the borough, lost behind the upper part of the city, re-appearing on an embankment over the trees of the Close, and finally plunging out of sight at the back of St. Cross;—this, which is the chief material source of the renovation we observe in the laical moiety of Winchester, is itself new.

The view to the South;

Far away to the left the Church of St. Cross shows itself, half concealed amidst its umbrageous elms; and beside it, as if guarding the entrance from the sea, St. Catharine's intrenched down juts boldly out into the valley. And, if we mount a little higher, the green and sheltered vale between the downs, called Chilcombe, with its little Norman church, comes into view; and beyond the beeches on the summit of St. Catharine's Hill we can trace the Itchen valley to Southampton, and descry in the distant horizon the uplands of the Isle of Wight, and the tall towers of Osborne House rising where its spreading woods are thickest.

and the East.

Palm Hall, behind us, stands nearly on the spot where St. Giles' Chapel once stood: its old grave-yard you may still discern. St. Mary Magdalen's Hospital would be in sight were it yet standing. Wide-spreading downs, just fringed on the verge of the horizon with signs of corn-land and woods, occupy the rest of the landscape.

Boundaries of Winchester "Borough:"

The limits of the Borough of Winchester, as fixed by the Boundary Act of 1832,[2] inclose an irregular polygonal area of 1043 acres.[3] From a stone placed about a

---

(1) This "low tower" has been *recently* rebuilt, and therefore is not properly an "antique."

(2) 2 & 3 Will. IV. c. 64. The same boundaries were appointed to the municipal borough by the Municipal Corporation Act, 5 & 6 Will. IV. c. 76.

(3) Census, 1851.

furlong from the north end of Hyde Street, on the road to Basingstoke, the line runs in a south-east direction to Winnall Church, on the other side of the Itchen; thence southward to a house on the Alresford Road, about a furlong from Bub's Cross; and thence straight to Bar End Gate, in Chilcombe: turning to the south-west, it next crosses the navigation and the river, to the bifurcation of the roads to Southampton and Gosport, below St. Cross, which is its farthest extension to the south; thence returning to the north-west, it is carried to the side of a lane leading from Compton Down; and from that point it runs due north, through Cock Lane Gate, to the Three Horseshoes public-house on Week Road, a little way beyond Fulflood Farm; and, finally, through the Jolly Farmer public-house on the Andover Road, just over the railway bridge, it goes north-westward to the point it started from. The extreme length of the tract contained within this boundary line exceeds two miles; and its greatest breadth is a little more than one mile.

Municipal and parliamentary Winchester differs wholly in its boundaries from the Winchester of history. The earliest limits of this were, necessarily, the walls of the city; but when, in process of time, suburbs arose on this side and that, the jurisdiction of the two independent authorities which governed the city—the corporation and the bishop—was extended over the suburbs, under the name of the East and West Soke Liberty, and the Soke Liberty; the former being connected with the episcopal city, and the latter with the municipal. *and of the ancient city and Liberties.*

The City Liberty, according to the Boundary Maps published by the Municipal Corporation Commission, was bounded by a line proceeding from Westgate, along the Romsey Road, to a point nearly opposite to the Roman Catholic burial-ground, whence it followed the intrenchment called "the City Ditch," on the west of Oram's Arbour, crossed the two branches of the Week Road, and turning northward, ran almost parallel to the Basingstoke Road, which it crossed midway between the turnpike gate and the present boundary stone; and thence ran to the walls just opposite St. Peter's Street, parallel to the road, but so as to exclude St. Bartholomew's Church, and all the abbey grounds east of the Hyde Burn.[1] It also included a small portion of the land outside the city walls over against Whitebread Mead, between the Upper and Middle Brooks. Within the city, the line dividing the two jurisdictions ran from the south walls near Christ's Hospital, along the boundary wall of the Cathedral Precinct and Cemetery, to the walls next the river between the parish of St. Peter Colebrook, and the grounds of the Wolvesey Palace. The city and castle walls were the boundary of the municipal borough on the south-west and north-east. *The City Liberty.* *Boundary line within the walls.*

Of the Soke we must speak subsequently; here, however, we may say, that it comprised the parishes of St. Michael and St. Swithin, with part of St. Faith's, and of St. Thomas', part of Chilcombe, the Vill of Milland, the parishes of St. Peter *The Soke.*

(1) Godson's and Milne's maps both represent the boundary as returning obliquely from the farthest point attained in a north-eastward direction to the Basingstoke Road, and following it to Northgate.

Cheesehill, and St. John (to which now the name of the Soke is in common exclusively applied), and a portion of the parish of St. Bartholomew Hyde.

Thus, whilst the new boundary excludes some portions of the parishes of St. Peter and St. John in the East Soke, it includes a larger tract from the parish of Week than was before contained in the liberty, with portions of the parishes of Winnall, Chil-combe, and St. Faith, and the extra-parochial precinct of St. Cross. And this is the most extensive area which ever bore the name of Winchester.[1]

Topographical description of Winchester.

West-gate.

Leaving the recently erected suburb on West Hill behind us, we will commence our topographical notice with the West-gate; and speak of the environs after having surveyed the ancient city. This gateway was one of the chief entrances of the place; and in spite of modernisations and restorations, and the commonplace houses which have been built so oppressively close to it, on the outer side it still wears much of its original look. It is a square tower, with a wide archway through it for carriages, and a narrow one beside it, on the north, for pedestrians. The gates and the portcullis have long ago disappeared; but the grooves in the ashlar, for the latter to slide in, remain; and the machicolations are still tolerably perfect. Two string-courses, with ornamented mouldings, run across the western front; which is also enriched with two panels, containing shields within quatrefoils, on which are now painted the arms of England and of Winchester, under hood-mouldings, with corbels. Two other corbels are seen between the panels and the flat buttresses on either side. Below the panels are two loopholes, now closed. The whole of the upper part is gone; and the gateway itself was preserved, at the time when the others were removed, solely (it is stated) because the chamber in it belonged to the dwelling-house adjoining it on the south. This chamber is now used as a muniment-room by the corporation; and a staircase leads to it inside the archway on the south; beneath which is (or was) what Milner calls "a dungeon." The windows lighting the chamber, and many other parts of the gateway are comparatively modern; but the building itself is said to be "a valuable specimen of military architecture of the time of Henry III."[2]

The High Street.

On entering the gate the High Street,[3] which runs completely through the city,

---

(1) Milner (vol. i. p. 157) states that, in the reign of Henry I., the suburbs of Winchester extended "on the north to Worthy; on the west, to Week; on the south, to St. Cross; and on the east, to St. Magdalen's Hill." His only authority is, as usual, "Trussel;" but that worthy alderman's MS. history contains no such statement. Wavell (vol. ii. pp. 47, 48) says, "almost as far as Week parish," and to Hyde Barton, on the west and north; which is more probable.

(2) Arch. Inst., Winchester Volume, "Architectural Notes, &c.," by Mr. J. H. Parker, p. 1.

About fifty years ago, on the outside of the wall, close to this gate on the north (where the back part of the Feathers Inn now is), might be seen a handsome Norman arch, with broad zigzag, and embossed mould-ings, standing on plain shafts and capitals, and having a zigzag moulding running horizontally above it, which was all that existed of a chapel, which Milner calls the Chapel of "St. Mary in the Ditch;" referring to Pontissara's Register as the authority for the name (vol. ii. pp. 210, 307.). Wavell (wrongly) "supposes" it to have been the Chapel of St. Anastatius (vol. ii. p. 240), and he is followed by Godson. Trussell (fol. 26 v°) speaks of this chapel as in ruins when he wrote; but does not mention its name. "The Chapel of our Lady of Westgate" is also named by Wavell (vol. ii. p. 241); but he relates that it was "said to have stood on the south side of the gate." This name occurs in Wykeham's second Register. No traces of this chapel can be discovered at the present time.

(3) The most ancient name of this street, with which we are acquainted, is *Cyp Street*, or "Cheap Street" (Cod. Dipl. No. 1291). At a later period it was called

THE WEST GATE.

Winchester

lies before us, yet not in so straight a line that we may see from one end of it to the other. The upper part of this street has a somewhat rapid slope for a carriage road, but the lower half is nearly level. Its entire length (which is also the greatest extent of the ancient city) is four furlongs and about thirty yards.[1] Narrow streets open on both hands immediately within the gate; that to the right, called Castle Hill, leads by a steep incline to the plateau on which in old times the castle stood, where now are the Barracks and the County Hall; that on the left formerly ran obliquely to the next street, but now it is continued almost to the north walls, under the name of Castle or Tower Street.[2]

Trafalgar Street, a little lower down, runs to the south, and was formerly much longer. It now extends but a very short way beyond St. Clement's Street, which is parallel to the great thoroughfare of Winchester.[3] On the other side of High Street, lower down still, is Bridney Street,[4] leading to Staple Garden; and next to it Jewry Street, leading to the North-gate.[5] At the corner of Jewry Street there stands the George Inn, which, according to Milner, "existed on the same spot as early, at least, as the reign of Edward IV." [6] Below Trafalgar Street lies Southgate Street, at the end of which was the South-gate; and yet further east, St. Thomas' Street, still so called, although the Church of St. Thomas, which was in it, has been totally destroyed, and a new one built in Southgate Street. The Dolphin Inn, at the west corner of this street, retains the projecting upper stories, by which, in old times, the accommodation of householders was increased at the expense of a grievous interference with the convenience of the streets, and the healthiness of the towns. Traces of a similar antiquity may be perceived in the house of Messrs. Jacob and Johnson, and by the side of Hammond's Passage, higher up.

At the opposite corner of St. Thomas' Street stands the Guild-hall, commonly called the Town-hall.[7] The present edifice (which Wavell, with pardonable enthusiasm, calls

The Guild-hall.

Magnus Vicus, Altus Vicus, and *Summus Vicus.* (Liber Winton., &c.)

(1) Measured upon Gale's map of Winchester, 1836. The extreme width of the city, measured in the same way, from North-gate to South-gate, was three furlongs and about sixty-five yards. The width, measured from Durngate to the archway through which the brooks pass, at the back of Wolvesey, is about three furlongs and a hundred and thirty-five yards, according to Gale's map. This irregularity in the parallelogram is not, however, very noticeable. The entire area included within the walls is about a hundred and thirty-eight acres.

(2) Below the opening of this street, and on the same side of the way, there used to stand a church, originally dedicated to St. Paul; but afterwards known as St. Peter's of Whitebread. (MS. Tarrages of Winchester. Brit. Mus. Add. MSS. 6133.) Mr. C. Bailey, the present Town Clerk, whose house occupies this site, informs me that he has found great quantities of human bones in his garden.

(3) This street was formerly called *Bowling Green Street,* and earlier still *Gar Street* (or *Gerestret,* in Liber Winton.), which is considered by J. Y. Akerman, Esq., Sec. S. A., to be equivalent to "Spearmakers' Street." It was shortened in the beginning of the present century.

(4) I am indebted to Mr. Bailey for the knowledge of the ancient name of this street.

(5) Between Bridney Street and Jewry Street, in the time of Henry V. and VI., stood the *Fish-shambles* (MS. Tarrages, before quoted), or *Western Pentice.* (Black Book of Winchester. Brit. Mus. Add. MSS. 6036.)

(6) Vol. ii. p. 212. This inn is mentioned in the MS. Tarrages, above referred to; but not before Elizabeth's reign.

(7) This is said to have been originally the hall of "the Guild of Merchants of Winchester." The other guilds, so long as they were in existence, had their halls in other parts of the city. The burghmotes and assemblies, recorded in the Black Book, before the reign of Henry VIII., are frequently said to have been held in the *Guild-hall,* which was in another part of the city.

" beautiful ")[1] was erected in the year 1711.[2] The front is supported by five Tuscan pillars, almost hidden by the shop-windows, which have been brought forward to the same level between them.   Above the centre one is a statue of Queen Anne, with this inscription, *"Anno Pacifico Anna Regina*, 1713,"[3] which was presented to the city by George Brydges, Esq., who sat in seven successive parliaments as one of its representatives.   The clock, which is protended from the top of the building almost to the middle of the street, and by night is illuminated with gas, was also presented to the city, and at the same time, by Sir William Paulet, who then sat in parliament with Mr. Brydges.   The entrance to the hall is by a somewhat inconvenient staircase in St. Thomas' Street.   The principal chamber is fitted up as a court of justice and for holding council meetings, &c., and is in appearance sufficiently neat and substantial, but not so lofty or spacious as becomes a city of the rank of Winchester.[4]   The other chamber, used by the grand jury, is very small.   In the cupola of the building hangs the Curfew bell, which is still rung at eight o'clock every evening.

Over against the Guild-hall, on the other side of High Street, is a square block, now forming two large business houses, and insulated by St. Peter's Street, and the Royal Oak Passage leading into it.   The side next this passage is a good example of the most solid " post and pan " building ; and the projecting stories very nearly touch the opposite house at the top.[5]

Still descending High Street, and passing by on the south the narrow opening of Little Minster Street (near which, till lately, was the White Hart Inn, known as such, at least from the time of Henry V.), we come, on the same side of the way, to a

(1) Vol. ii. p. 144. But Milner thinks it " would not be an inelegant structure on the outside were not the bold Tuscan pillars, on which it stands, totally buried amidst the vulgar shop-fronts, &c." (vol. ii. p. 213.) It was originally open beneath, and a market was held there ; but it is difficult to say in what respect the appearance of insecurity it must then have had would have been more " elegant " than its present condition.

(2) Before the erection of this town-hall the business of the corporation was transacted at St. John's House, near East-gate, which was given to the city for that purpose, by Henry VIII. Mr. H. Moody, author of the " Sketches of Hampshire," &c., and curator of the Museum, tells me that it is built upon property belonging to a charity ; and that the rents of the shops are paid to the Hospital, or Almshouses of St. John. No rent, however, is paid for the hall. (Mun. Corp. Comm. Report, 1835.)

(3) It is about this inscription that Milner makes such a schoolboy parade of his Latinity. Happily the loyalty of the excellent burgess was indisputable, or he might, on the ground of this venial sciolism (which does not in the least obscure his meaning), have been claimed as a crypto-Jacobite !

(4) In the magistrates' room are portraits of Bishop Morley, Sir Thomas White, Ralph Lamb, George Bemerton, twice mayor, and Launcelot Thorpe, mayor ; most of whom were considerable benefactors of the city, and will be mentioned subsequently. Before the establishment of the muniment-room over West-gate, several " monuments " and " records " were preserved here, which will come under our notice again.

(5) In the Liber Winton. this is called *Domus Godebiete* (p. 532), and *Terra Godebiete* (p. 543) ; and in the Records of both the see and the city it occurs as *Gotebyete*. Rudborne (apud Angl. Sacr., vol. i. p. 241) names it *"privilegium quoddam vocatum God-begete."* It is still called *Good-be-got*, or *God-be-gate ;* and Mr. H. Moody remembers to have heard it named " the Isle of Godbegot."   The interior of the existing building presents little or nothing worthy of attention ; the mantlepieces, stairs, &c., being ordinary specimens of the style of the seventeenth century. It was the old Meat Market, or Shambles ; whence came the old name of the adjoining street, *Fleshmongers' Street*, and the designation of the church of St. Peter *in Macellis*, immediately behind it. Both the church and the shambles are mentioned in the Liber Winton. Some further account of this house and land will be given subsequently.

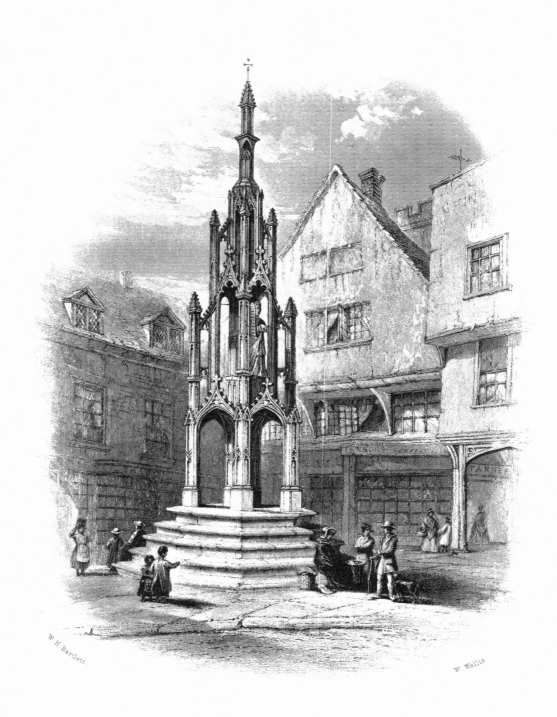

W H Bartlett.

W Wallis

MARKET CROSS, WINCHESTER.

covered passage, for pedestrians only, which is the end of Great Minster Street;[1] almost opposite to which is a pump, standing beside the carriage-way. The house beside this passage, which falls back a little from the line of those above it, is one with projecting upper stories and an aspect of genuine antiquity; this look is shared by the next house below it, which returns at right angles to it, and jutting out beyond the line of shops higher up, forms the commencement of the Pent-house; and in the nook thus formed the City Cross stands.

This "light and elegant" structure is elevated on an octagonal platform, reached *The City Cross.* by five steps, which are continued round it; and on these the market-women used to sit with their country produce, whence it was called the "Butter Cross." The centre shaft is square and panelled, and its entire height is about forty-three feet. The basement is vaulted, and has four flat-pointed arches with smaller square panelled shafts, surmounted by ogee mouldings with crockets and finials. These shafts are carried up to the next stage, and form flying buttresses to the canopy over the figure of a saint, much dilapidated, supposed by Milner, from the palm branch and the book (if it be a book), which it bears, to represent St. Lawrence or St. Amphibalus. The shafts of the canopy are, in like manner, carried up one stage higher, and serve as flying buttresses in their turn to the shaft of the shrine and cross which ornamented its summit. "The detail has been almost entirely destroyed by injudicious repairs," a fate which menaced the entire structure in the year 1770, when it was sold by the paving commissioners to a Mr. Dummér, who was about "to remove it to his grounds at Cranbury." The citizens, however, by a well-organised *émeute* (as Milner intimates) cancelled the bargain, and preserved the cross "for the honour and ornament of their city."[2]

The Pent-house, or Piazza, is a line of shops, extending from the Cross more than *The Pent-house.* half the way to Market Street. The fronts of these houses project quite across the footway, and are carried on a row of Tuscan pillars of various sizes, so that the shops are darkened and public traffic impeded, without the least compensation from the design or the appearance of the obstruction. Before the Market-house was built the sale of provisions from the country was carried on under this Pent-house, as well as at the Cross, and the inconvenience must have been great indeed. The houses forming this piazza, and some of the shop-fronts (one of which, at least, in the memory of those living, had an *open* front, whilst occupied by a draper), are as old as the end of the sixteenth, or beginning of the seventeenth, century. Some have gables, with

(1) This is the only direct means of communication between the city and the cathedral; and it is to be regretted that it has not been improved. In the year 1844 an admirable design for a carriage-way from this corner to the west front of the cathedral was published by Mr. Owen B. Carter; and the practicability of the improvement was discussed; but it was not carried out, and seems now to have been forgotten.

(2) Arch. Inst. Winchester Volume; "Archit. Notes,

&c.," p. 20. Milner (vol. ii. pp. 214, 215) assigns it to the reign of Henry VI.; Mr. J. H. Parker (*u. s.*) says generally "the fifteenth century."

Wavell (vol. i. p. 277) merely compliments "the diligence and resolution of some of our worthy citizens," as the cause of the preservation of "this curious piece of antiquity."

The lower part of the cross has been judiciously strengthened by iron ties.

barge-boards and moulded ridge-tiles overlooking the street; and but one story above the ground-floor; but most of them have been in good part modernised.[1] Parchment Street enters High Street from the north, a little lower down; and the parish church of St. Mary Kalendar used to stand exactly opposite the end of this Pent-house.

The Square.   Parallel with the principal street, on the south, between it and the grave-yard of the cathedral, there runs a small back street, called the Square; at the western end of which is one entrance to the Precinct. And hereby stands the present Butchers' Market, or Shambles, over which are the rooms of the Mechanics' Institution.[2] At the opposite extremity is another gate into the grave-yard, and a street leading into

Market Street. *The Market-house.*   High Street (opposite Upper Brooks), called Market Street,[3] from the Market-house, which adjoins it on the east. This convenient building consists of an oblong quadrangle, open in the centre, with entrances in Market Street and High Street, over the latter of which is inscribed the name of Sir Pawlet St. John, Bart., and the date of his mayoralty, 1772, when it was projected and commenced.

This back street[4] is continued behind Bishop Morley's College, and separated from the cemetery by a railing alone, as far almost as the east end of the cathedral, where it joins Colebrook Street. One footway passes from a gate into the grave-yard, under the tower of St. Maurice's Church, and through a covered passage communicating with it, into High Street, nearly opposite Middle Brooks; above which may be seen the Bell Inn, which was a hostel in the reign of Henry V., and occupied the site of the Church of St. Mary in the Wold. And another, from a second gate, passes through a covered passage into Colebrook Street, over Bishop Athelwold's Burn, which here runs along a concealed channel between the double row of houses, called Paternoster Row.

The Fair ground.   Lower Brooks on the north, through a narrow covered way, and Colebrook Street on the south, enter High Street not far from each other. From this part to the Soke Bridge the great thoroughfare is exceedingly spacious (about forty yards across in the broadest part), having been almost doubled in width, near the end of the last century, by the removal of a range of buildings—one of which was the city jail—that occupied a long strip of ground in what is now the middle of the street.[5] The police-

---

(1) Wavell (vol. ii. p. 20), and Milner (vol. i. p. 112; referring to "Trussel's MSS.," which do not contain any mention of the matter), state that the six mints established in Winchester by Athelstan stood on the site of this Pent-house. The MS. Tarrages, before referred to, say that this *Pentice* was then (4 Hen. V.) called the *Draperie* in the king's Exchequer, and before that *the Kynge's Mynte*. One house under this Pent-house bore the undesirable name of *Hell*; and a tenement near the entry of Minster Street was called *Heaven!*

(2) This was formerly the site of a watch-house; before that, of the theatre; and earlier still, as Trussell's MS. history (fol. 73 v°) and Godson's map show, of the corn-market.

(3) Milner says (vol. ii. p. 216) that in the latter part of the last century, "in digging at the south end of [Market] Street, and the east end of the Square, the workmen met with the foundation of a tower of prodigious strength. This probably made part of the Conqueror's Palace, so often mentioned."

(4) Along this line formerly ran the Temple ditch. (Trussell, fol. 73 v°; Black Book, fol. 31 v°; Records in Cath. Lib. vol. i. 120).

(5) Godson's map and Buck's "East Prospect" both show the original condition of this part of High Street. The southern branch, from its crossing the site of the old *grave-yard* of the monastery, used to be called *the Abbey Litten.*   [In

station, which stands at the corner of Colebrook Street, was originally built in the year 1800 for the City Bridewell, after the alterations last mentioned, as an inscription on the front records. The public fire-engines are kept here.

Below this building, on the same side of the street, is a footway, called the Abbey Passage[1] leading into Colebrook Street (in which is situated the Central National School) ; and a little beyond it St. Mary's Abbey House, a modern building, in the pseudo-antique style, with battlements and turrets. The stream formed by the union of the brooks, which is brought under the roadway by a covered channel, here reappears, and flows in front of the houses as far as St. John the Baptist's Almshouses, which occupy the corner of Colebrook Street, where it turns southward, and passes through the grounds of the Abbey House.

Colebrook Street runs completely round to the south of High Street, from the police-station to St. John's Almshouses. There is a postern entrance to the Close, nearly opposite the Abbey Passage, which marks the boundary between the cathedral precincts and the *enceinte* of Wolvesey Castle. And to the east of it, on the other side of the street, the Abbey Mill[2] is still turned by the stream which runs from Durngate ; not far from which are the Silk Mills. The Church of St. Peter's Colebrook used to stand near the south-eastern corner of the area inclosed by this street ; and some inscriptions on stone tablets record the fact of the repair of the " church walls " by the overseers, many years after the church itself had disappeared. Colebrook Place, and another longer and narrower *cul-de-sac*, run from this street to the boundary of the grounds of Wolvesey Palace. Nell Gwynne's house, sadly dilapidated, stands not far from the east end of the cathedral.

(marginal note: Colebrook Street.)

On the north side of High Street, exactly opposite the Abbey House, is a narrow passage, called Busket Lane,[3] which is all the remains of the ancient Buck Street. It is not a thoroughfare, but only communicates with the tenements in the rear of the

(marginal note: Busket Lane.)

In the old times there stood in the western part of the slip of land between the two streets, the Chapel of the Holy Trinity, which Richard of Inkpenne founded ; further east was the Church or Chapel of St. Mary of the Linen Web ; and near it, the " Linen-cloth Hall," afterwards called *Chapman's-hall ;* of which we shall speak subsequently. The Almshouses of St. John the Baptist occupied the eastern extremity of this tract ; and the brook which flowed in considerable volume on the north side of it, here spread to a greater width, leaving but a narrow way on each side, from the Abbey and from High Street, to the Soke Bridge.

This valuable piece of ground was freely given by a former proprietor of the abbey, Thomas Weld, Esq., for the benefit and improvement of the city, about the year 1799. The land on which the police-station stands was, " at the request of the magistrates," freely given at the same time. (Milner, vol. ii. p. 218, note.) The annual fairs, on the first Monday in Lent, and the 23rd and 24th of October, are now held on this open space.

(1) This was formerly an open footpath " on sufferance," through the abbey grounds.

(2) " The Mill of *Wintine* " (Tarrages, fol. 28 v°).

(3) *Busket* seems to be a condensation of *Buck Street*— a name which occurs with many varieties of spelling (as is usual) in the old documents since the Conquest. The Liber Winton. calls it *Bucchestret.* Can this name be derived from the use of the clear runnels which passed through it for washing clothes ? The " *buck*-basket " in which Shakspere's too-gallant knight was carried so shamefully to Datchet Mead (" Merry Wives of Windsor," act iii. sc. 3) will occur to all our readers as affording some countenance to this derivation. A " common washing-place " is mentioned in the Black Book (fol. 81). *Buck Street* led by a somewhat acute-angled course into the middle of Lower Brooks ; and a streamlet of water flowed beside it for the greater part of the way. Churches dedicated to All Saints, and to St. John in the Latin Gate, are spoken of as being situated in this street. (Reg. Pontiss.; Petition to Henry VI.)

houses next the street. St. John's House and Chapel,[1] with Lamb's Almshouses behind them, adjoin Busket Lane on the east. The grand chamber in St. John's House is a spacious and lofty apartment, nearly one-and-twenty yards long and thirteen wide, well adapted for assemblies, concerts, public meetings, banquets, sales, &c., as is the smaller chamber which opens into it. It contains the fine full-length portrait of Charles II., painted by Sir Peter Lely, and presented by the king to the corporation of Winchester. Portraits of Colonel Brydges, of Avington, by whose munificent bequest the hall was fitted up; Sir Henry St. John Mildmay, M.P., 1808; and the first Marquis of Winchester, also adorn this room. The lower part of the building contains kitchens, offices, and rooms for stores, &c. There is only one entrance, by a small porch next the street, both to the chapel and the rooms.

A fine new street, named High Street East, or Eastgate Street,[2] opens to the north, immediately beyond St. John's House; and a little way past the farther entrance of Colebrook Street, where East-gate[3] used to stand, is the Soke Bridge.[4] A pleasant footpath beside the river, in the farther part scarcely raised above the level of its eddying and limpid waters, conducts southward to Wharf Mill, and, by the outside of the old city wall, to Wolvesey Palace and Winchester College. On the north, just above the Soke Bridge, the City Mill stands over the stream.[5]

The new street we spoke of is but in part complete;[6] but it is being built with tolerable regularity, and in a pretty good modern style of street architecture. Union Street runs from this Eastgate Street to North Walls, against the end of Lower Brooks; and Lawn Street leads from the middle of Union Street by a sharp turn to the east, through Boundary Street, to Eastgate Street. When finished, these streets will greatly raise the importance of this part of the city; and already it wears something of the aspect of a manufacturing town, from the tall chimneys which are rising in this quarter.

(1) Trussell says, that this property was granted to the corporation of Winchester by Henry VIII. in the thirty-second year of his reign, "to bee by them ymployd for the place of election of Maior and officers att tymes accustomed, and for their generall magazine, and other publick occasions" (fol. 103).

(2) Eastgate House, long the property of the Mildmay family (respecting whom see Duthy's "Sketches," pp. 299, &c.), with its pleasure-grounds, used to occupy the line of this street. It was removed in 1846-7. Buck's "East Prospect," and Godson's map, show the condition of this part of the city in the last century. The earlier history of it will be noticed when we speak of the conventual establishments of Winchester.

(3) Buck's "East Prospect," so often referred to, contains a good view of this gate.

(4) The present bridge was erected in the year 1814: from the application of the name *New Bridge* to it, in the "Tarrages of Winchester," before quoted, it seems to have been rebuilt also in about 1400. Legend ascribes

the original structure to St. Swithin, during his tenure of the see, about 855; but it is more probable that the Romans constructed the first bridge over the Itchen here, at the time their *Venta Belgarum* was built.

(5) This footpath beside the river is still known as *the Weirs*, from the fishing dams which used to cross the stream here. A memorandum in the first fly-leaf of the Tarrages speaks of a "little fish-mill or weare upon the river, on the south side of the bridge:" and one may still be seen over the waste-water, at the back of the mill. This City Mill is one in *Coitburie*, which was specifically granted to the city in King John's Charter, A.D. 1215 (Rot. Chart. vol. i. p. 217). In the Tarrages, the marginal annotation of Elizabeth's time states that it was "a capper's mill;" and it is called the "Fulling Mill at Coyteburi," in the Black Book of Winchester (fol. 15 v°). A stone in the front of the mill states that it was rebuilt in the year 1744.

(6) The boundary of St. John's parish here accurately shows the line of the old wall.

Durngate Mill,[1] and the bridge leading to Winnall, are at the point where the new street and North Walls meet. This last-named road has rows of cottages, with small gardens before them, on one side, in this part; but higher up, for the most part, the lofty enclosures of gardens,[2] and rural fences, with a very few houses planted here and there. The houses in the Lower,[3] Middle,[4] and Upper Brooks[5] stand more thickly the nearer you approach High Street. A branch of the new system of streets runs from Lower Brooks into Lawn Street; and a narrow lane, called Cossack Lane,[6] crosses from Middle to Lower Brooks, almost opposite the new street. All these are intersected by a line of streets, running parallel to High Street, and at no great distance from it, called, between Lower and Middle Brooks, Silver Hill, and St. George's Street[7] for the rest of the way, which extends to Jewry Street. These streets are now almost entirely inhabited by people of the operative and the indigent classes; but some houses of considerable antiquity and interest remain,[8] to show that in the old times this quarter was not tenanted by so special a population. The newly-built Church of the Holy Trinity stands near the north end of Middle Brooks, but the principal entrance is from the Upper Brooks. The Baptist Chapel is on Silver Hill, and that of the Wesleyan Association in the Upper Brooks.

Proceeding westward we come to Parchment Street,[9] parallel with the Brooks, and extending from High Street to North Walls. There is a large nursery-ground at the northern part of this street; and in it are situated the County Hospital,[10] the Post-office,

(marginal notes: Durngate. North Walls. The Brooks. St. George's Street. Parchment Street.)

(1) This has been wrongly named *Dean-gate*. Leland supposed that *Bourne-gate* was the true name (Itin. vol. iii. fol. 70); but in all ancient authorities it is called *Durn-gate*, or *Derne-gate*, which name signifies that it was, as Leland said, a postern-gate.

(2) Parts of the old city walls may be discovered at places along the north side of this road.

(3) This is the ancient *Tanners' Street;* so called even in the tenth century.

(4) Formerly *Wongar Street*. In the Liber Winton. this name is spelt *Wenegene* (p. 539) and *Wunegre* (p. 553).

(5) The old name of this street, which, by the help of a blunder of the scribe in the list of churches in Pontissara's Register (fol. 157), can be traced with certainty as far back as the thirteenth century, was *Shulworth*. The blunder referred to, which was detected by the Rev. W. H. Gunner, and obligingly pointed out to me, consists in the substitution of "*M*" for "*Sh*." Wavell (vol. ii. p. 240) and Milner (vol. ii. p. 307) have out of this mis-spelt "Muldworstret," not only manufactured a *Mulward Street*, which never existed, but also a third St. Swithin's Church. The Anglo-Saxon *Scyldwyrhtene Strœt* (see note 7, *infra*) was the present *St. George's Street*, and *Silver Hill*. It is uncertain to which of them the name in the Liber Winton. (p. 553) refers.

(6) In the Tarrages (fol. 24) this lane is named *Buttles* (i.e. St. Botolph's) Lane; and "the Fryers' Wall"

is noted as being next it. Milner calls it *Ruell Street*, from the Chapel of St. Rowald, which Speed's map places at the south corner of its entrance into Lower Brooks; the Tarrages, however (fol. 20), place the lane next St. Ruell's Church, between the east part of Parchment Street and the west part of Shilworth Street.

(7) This parallel to High Street originally extended westward as far as Bridney Street. Between the latter and Jewry Street, it can be traced in Gale's map (1836); and Godson's map shows it as an open way. This was the ancient *Scyldwyrhtene Strœt*—"Shieldmakers' Street" (Cod. Dipl. No. 1291), afterwards known (?) as *Sildwortene Stret* (Liber Winton., p. 553). The name of the lower portion, "Silver Hill" (which is as old as the reign of Edward VI., Black Book, fol. 70 v°), seems to be the last remaining trace of this ancient appellation.

(8) On the western side of Middle Brooks the remains of a building of the middle of the fifteenth century may be seen. Dilapidated as they are, there yet has been preserved more of the original form and appearance than is usual in Winchester. The carved oak tracery of the windows may be seen on the inner side.

(9) The Liber Winton. does not name this street; but in Pontissara's Register it is called *Vicus Pergamenorum*.

(10) Clobery House formerly occupied this spot. The "Saxon doorway" spoken of by Milner (vol. ii. 217) has long ago disappeared.

St. Peter's Street.

the Wesleyan and the Primitive Methodist Chapels, and a temporary Military Hospital. St. Peter's Street, anciently called Fleshmongers' Street,[1] lies next above Parchment Street. All the houses in it are of the better class. On the west side is the one built by Sir Christopher Wren for the Duchess of Portsmouth.[2] Near it, to the north, may be seen the entrance to the Roman Catholic Chapel of St. Peter;[3] and on the opposite side of the way a spacious house (the front of which is of the earlier part of the seventeenth century) is at present used as a Benedictine Nunnery.

Jewry Street.

The Corn Exchange.

Farther towards the west is Jewry Street,[4] now the principal thoroughfare to the Railway-station, and an excellent business street. The Corn Exchange is situated near the northern extremity, where it makes a bend westward, so as to reach the Northgate. This building, which was erected by a company formed for the purpose in 1838, is substantial and spacious, but not of sufficient elevation for effect, with a rotunda, which is very convenient for the corn-market, and the sale of agricultural implements, &c.; and large rooms for other purposes connected with its main design. The front entrance is covered by a bold portico; and over the centre is a campanile, with louvre windows. There are good vaults beneath it, and an extensive yard,

(1) In the charter (Cod. Dipl. No. 1291), already several times referred to, this is spelt *Flæscmangere Stræt*, and in the Liber Winton. (pp. 539, 552) *Flesmangere Stret*. The origin of this name has been pointed out above (see p. 16, note 5). It was first called St. Peter's Street, according to Milner (vol. ii. pp. 213, 251), by the restorer of Roman Catholic worship in Winchester, Roger Corham, Esq., who, "having built a house on the site of the ancient Church of St. Peter de Macello, in the centre of the street, affixed a stone on the front of it, with the following inscription, which is still visible there :—'THIS IS ST. PETER'S STREET.'"

Milner should have known that the site of St. Peter's in Macellis was between the Royal Oak Passage and St. George's Street. The stone may yet be seen in the passage leading to St. Peter's Chapel; but it is inscribed with no more than "ST. PETER'S STREET."

(2) This house is frequently called Nell Gwynne's; and the initials "E. G." upon the cistern-head of the rain-water pipe, on the south side (which once reminded on-lookers of a worthy fellow-citizen, and certainly a good plumber), are pointed out in proof of the house having belonged to Mistress Eleanor Gwynne—a fact which amusingly illustrates the growth of local traditions.

(3) In the middle of the west side of this street is a plain Norman doorway, which was brought from the ruins of the Hospital of St. Mary Magdalen, when they were removed in 1778, and placed here by Dr. Milner to adorn the entrance to St. Peter's Chapel, of which he was the officiating minister. Over it is inscribed :—

"D. O. M.

ÆDIFICAT :   A.D.   MCLXXIV.
RE-ÆDIFICAT :   MDCCXCII."

"Alluding" (he says, vol. ii. p. 253) "to the date of its first erection on Magdalen Hill, and to that of its second position in the place which it now occupies." In a note to this passage Milner says, "There being a necessity on such an occasion of mentioning some one year, we have fixed upon that put down above as the probable date of the said work." But there was no "necessity" for putting up the inscription at all; and there was so strong a probability of this earlier date being mistaken for that of *the first erection of the chapel* to which the doorway leads—the later date being, in fact, that of its rebuilding—that it ought not to have been placed there.

(4) This street was named *Jail Street* from about 1750 to 1830. Before and since that period it has borne its present name. Leland says that it was "caullyd the *Jury*, by cause the Jues did inhabite it, and had theyr Synagoge there." (Itin. vol. iii. fol. 71.) There is no doubt that the Jews' quarter was in this part of the city; but the existence of a synagogue is extremely doubtful. The oldest name of this street was *Alwarene Stret* (as it occurs in the Liber Winton.), or *Alwarde Strete*,—the *Judaismus*, or *Jewry*, could scarcely in the Middle Ages have been a thoroughfare of so much importance as this. Probably it was that part of the present street which turns out of the straight line, and runs to North-gate; which, within the memory of persons now living, was a narrow and insignificant lane. The continuation of the direct line of street to the walls, now closed, was formerly the principal approach to the North-gate. The *Judaismus* is called *Vicus Judæorum* in Edington's Register, about 1350; and *Jewerye Strete* in the Black Book, temp. Hen. IV. (fol. 14). When the name of *Alwarde Strete* was disused, is not known.

where horses, cattle, &c., are on market-days exhibited for sale. The horse-fairs and cattle-shows take place here.

Nearer High Street, on the site of the old jail, and in part consisting of its buildings, are some fine-looking shops, and an extensive coach-manufactory. The central portion of this prison has been converted into the Museum; next to which stands the handsome and spacious chapel and school-rooms, recently erected by the Independent Dissenters of Winchester. The Theatre stands on the opposite side of the way.[1]

At the back of the Museum and the chapel is Staple Garden Lane,[2] which runs from High Street, northward, to a lane which enters Jewry Street by the side of the Corn Exchange.[3] The Winchester Gas-works are situated here. They were erected in 1832; but have been greatly enlarged since that time. There are three gasometers, holding, collectively, sixty thousand cubic feet of gas; one of them is situated in Water Lane, on the other side of the river, and the gas is transmitted to it from these works.

Staple Garden Lane.

Tower Street[4] extends from West-gate to a continuation of the lane at the end of Staple Garden Lane; and into this, also, the original street runs obliquely. Another lane, near the north end, crosses the line of the wall and ditch to Sussex Street. The old Hermit's Tower has been modernised into an ornamental summer-house, in the grounds of the dwelling-house at the north-western angle of the city.[5] And on the eastern side of the street are the School-rooms of St. Thomas' parish.

Tower Street.

(1) A more particular account of these buildings, &c., will be given in another part of this description of Winchester.

(2) Leland says, in his "Itinerary" (vol. iii. fol. 71), "The Staple Houses for wolle, at Winchestre, lay from the West Gate yn a bak way to the North Gate;" and hence the present name of this lane. Wavell (vol. ii. p. 87) states that "all that part of the city lying between the West and North-gates, as low as Jury, now called Goal Street," was purchased by the corporation "for the more commodious stowage" of the wool, &c., which were the commodities of the staple. Trussell (fol. 111) says, "the Beam and Skales remayne in the storehouse to this day."

In the Liber Winton. this lane is named *Bredene Stret* (p. 537) and *Brudene Stret* (p. 550). The latter is used in the Inquest, temp. Edw. I., printed in Arch. Journal, vol. vii. p. 374, &c. In the petition of the citizens to Henry VI. it is called *Burden Strete.* The Tarrages, and other authorities, name it *Bridling Street.*

(3) Possibly the *Scowertene,* or *Scowrtene Stret,*— "Shoemakers' Street,"—of the Liber Winton. (pp. 538, 550), as the name occurs between those of *Burdene Stret* and *Alwarene Stret.* It was afterwards called *Schortene Streta* (Rot. Pip., 4 Rich. I., apud Madox' Hist. Exch. p. 794), *Sortene Stret* (Rot. Chart., vol. i. p. 55 b), and *Shortene Stret* (Inquest, temp. Edw. I., Arch. Journal, vol. vii. p. 374, &c.) And as no *Judaismus* occurs in the Liber Winton., or the Inquest, and not only

Aaron the Jew is said to have had a house in this street, but Bona the Jewess, and (in the Pipe Roll, *u. s.*) Isaac the Jew, are described as householders here, this may have been the original name of *the Jewry.* (See p. 22, note 4).

(4) The maps of Speed and Godson, with Buck's "East Prospect," show with great clearness the condition of this part of the city between about 1600 and 1800. The Tarrages (temp. Eliz.) speak of the hop-yards here. In 1824 (Duthy's "Sketches," p. 187) the Corporation sold the land on which the city wall, between West-gate and the Hermit's Tower, stood; and immediately afterwards the walls were levelled and the ditch partly filled up, and laid out as gardens to the houses built along the line of the ancient ramparts; and Tower Street dates from this *improvement.* In the Liber Winton. (p. 537) occurs a *Snithelinga Stret,* or *Snidelinge Stret* (p. 549), called in the Inquest, temp. Edw. I. (Arch. Journal, vol. vii. p. 376), *Snythelinge Stret.* From its position in both surveys contained in the former record, this "Tailors' Street" appears to have been the older part of *Tower Street.*

(5) Milner, in his map and in his History (vol. i. pp. 162, 166, 190; vol. ii. p. 210), has placed a "royal palace" in this north-western corner of the city. In the map and in his second volume he calls it Henry II.'s Palace: but in his first volume he says that it was built in Stephen's reign, burnt down during the contest between his partisans and those of the empress, in 1141,

St. Clement's
Street.
Southgate
Street.

Castle Hill, on the other side of West-gate has been mentioned; as well as Trafalgar Street,[1] which lies next it to the east. St. Clement's Street,[2] the southern parallel to High Street, runs as far as Little Minster Street. Southgate Street,[3] which follows in the order of our survey, is part of the principal thoroughfare from the North-gate to the opposite gate of the city. The houses in this street are all of the better class; and some might be called mansions. The Judge's Lodgings are conspicuous on the west side of the way; and next to them the new Church of St. Thomas. Offices of the Barracks occupy the remainder of that side.

St. Swithin's
Street.

St. Thomas'
Street.

Just within the line of the old walls, St. Swithin's Street runs down to the south gate of the Close. A narrow lane, for foot-passengers only, called St. Thomas' Passage, also communicates with the next street, now known as St. Thomas',[4] but in which are only the grave-yard belonging to the church so dedicated, and the parochial school-house. The Asylum for Girls is situated here. A lane[5] running eastward from the middle of this street leads directly to the west entrance of the cathedral grave-yard, at which point Symond's Street,[6] coming from the south,—and so named from Symond's, or Christ's Hospital, which stands at the corner of St. Swithin's

Symond's
Street

rebuilt by Henry II. in the very beginning of his reign, and probably "burnt down" or "fallen into ruins" before the time of Henry III. But the only authority appealed to for the existence of this palace is Trussell (who, however, only speaks ambiguously of "the king's pallace" as being in the "north parte of the cittie," fol. 81); William of Malmsbury speaks of no such palace being burnt in his account of the civil war; and the story of the rebuilding is based upon passages from Robert of Gloucester and Knighton, all referring to repairs and improvements at the castle (as Warton stated, though Milner rejected his explanation), as is demonstrated by the Liberate Rolls, and other records of the reign of Henry III., &c.; no authority at all is cited in support of the statement that this palace was destroyed before the middle of the thirteenth century; and we can discover no reference to any such palace in the published records of the reign of John.

Milner asserts that the city ditch, at the north-western angle, "was a stew for the king's fish," and makes it an appendage to "the palace built by Henry II.," which thus disappears from his History at the outset of the reign of Henry III., whilst the only authority quoted is that patent letter addressed in the Prior of St. Swithin's Convent, in the reign of Edward I.

Mr. C. Bailey informs me that in the municipal records of Winchester he finds the Hermit's Tower of Godson's map, &c., designated "King Arthur's Wine-cellar."

(1) See page 15, note 3.

(2) At the north-western angle, formerly the intersection of Southgate Street by this street, St. Clement's Church used to stand. Its remains were visible when Milner wrote (vol. ii. p. 211). The Church of St.

Alphege stood at the corner of this lane, next Calpe Street. (Tarrages, fol. 31 v°.)

(3) *Goldestret* is the old name of this street (Liber Winton.; Inquest, temp. Edw. I.; Petition of Citizens to Henry VI., &c.) See Buck's "East Prospect," for a view of the South-gate. The Prior and Convent of St. Swithin (51 Hen. III.) undertook to keep this gate and King's-gate in repair, with drawbridges outside, and three "kernells" on each side, "congruous" with the wall.

Both this and Gar Street, according to the Tarrages, opened on the south, within the city walls, upon a pasture called *Bemonde*, or *Bewmonds* (fols. 32, 33).

(4) In former times this street was called *Calpe*, or *Caupe Street* (Liber Winton.; Inquest, temp. Edw. I., &c.) Of which appellation Skene, in his "Exposition" (s. v. *Caupe*), says that "it signifies ane gift, sik as horse, or uther thing, qwhilk an man in his awin lifetime, and *liege poustie*, gives to his maister, or to ony uther man that is greatest in power and authoritie, and speciallie to the head and chiefe of the clann, for his maintenance and protection." No account or tradition of its application here has been handed down to us.

(5) Close beside this lane, on the north, in Gold Street, stood the Church of All Saints. (Tarrages, fol. 31 v°.) Traces of the church and the grave-yard were discovered by J. Lampard, Esq., whose garden now occupies this site.

(6) *Symond's Street* was, at the time of the second survey contained in the Liber Winton., called *Mensterstret*; and is so named in the Tarrages, in the reign of Henry V.

The King's Head Inn, in Little Minster Street, has preserved much of its original external aspect.

Stree', —joins Little and Great Minster Streets, coming from High Street. Great Minster Street, now divided from the cemetery by a wall and railing, is the most eastward, and communicates with the Square, as we have seen. A short passage crosses from the one to the other, opposite the Square. The Refuge for the Destitute is in Little Minster Street.

The eastern side of Symond's Street is the high wall of the Cathedral Precinct, which is continued along the north side of St. Swithin's Street as far as the Close gate. A little to the west of this is King's-gate, with the parish church of St. Swithin over it.[1] The gateway has, beside a road for carriages, a way for foot-passengers, flagged, and divided from the road by a breast-high wall between the piles supporting the church above, on each side of it. Its architecture is not of a kind to require any special notice. The whole of this south-eastern corner of the city, as far as the boundaries of Colebrook Parish, and the old city wall, is occupied by the cathedral, with its cemetery, and the residences of its dignified clergy—Bishop Morley's College, Cheyney Court, Wolvesey Palace, and the remains of Wolvesey Castle, which we shall soon speak of more particularly.[2] And now we leave the ancient city, and extend our observations to its environs, within the boundaries of the parliamentary and municipal borough.

At the north-western corner of this polygonal area, just where the road from Easton, Avington, and the villages near them, enters it, stands the Church of St. Martin in Winnall,[3] from which the road runs southward to the East-gate of Winchester. A branch parts from it at a very short distance, and takes its course along the bank of the river. It is called Winnall simply, or Wales Street,[4] before it reaches Durngate Mill; and afterwards, Water Lane.[5]

The other and higher road, which is at first the less considerable of the two, is known by the name of Beggars' Lane,[6] as far as Bub's Cross,[7] where the Alresford Road enters it at right angles; and then as St. John's Street[8] it is continued down the

Margin notes: King's-gate. Environs of Winchester. Winnall. St. John's Street.

---

(1) In 1846 the road and footway through King's-gate was altered and improved. Before that time there was but one path for foot-passengers. Of the church we shall speak elsewhere. Leland (Itin., vol. iii. fol. 71) says that " S. Michael's Gate, in Winchestre, is spoken of of ancient wryters, but that name is now out of use. Ther is a chirch of S. Michael by the Kinge's Gate, whereon I conjecture that the Kinge's Gate was sumtyme caullid S. Michael's Gate, or els the South Gate." The different ways in which the name of this gate is spelt in the ancient records are too numerous for insertion here. Milner (vol. ii. p. 148) rightly rejects Wavell's story of this gate (vol. i. p. 208); since it is spoken of in the Liber Winton., and by its present name.

(2) See the next section, on " The Cathedral," &c.

(3) The account of this church will be given in the description of " The Winchester Division," which follows the present part.

(4) This name I have found in a deed of 27 Hen. VI.,

amongst the Wolvesey Records. In Godson's map it is called *Welsh Street;* and by Milner,—after a MS. Survey of the Soke (temp. Eliz.), which then belonged to J. Duthy, Esq.,—*Waley Street.*

(5) Milner, speaking of this lane, says (vol. ii. p. 228), " It abounds with the ruins of churches." None of his lists of churches, however, refer any one to Water Lane; and, after a very strict inquiry, I have been unable to hear of so much as the vestiges of any ecclesiastical buildings in it.

(6) The whole of this tract appears to have been called *Milland,* in the fourteenth century, from its vicinity to Durngate Mill. *Beggares Strete* is mentioned at the same time; and also a *Brouke Lane.* A hill, said to be near these places, is called *La Lynche.*

(7) Milner, on the authority of the MS. Survey of the Soke, says this was also called *Bubby's Cross* (vol. ii. p. 235).

(8) There are several remarkable ancient houses in

hill to Bridge Street. Stare Lane joins the two roads from Winnall Church, not far from this separation. Red House Lane[1] runs down from Bub's Cross to the water's edge behind Durngate Mill; and there is a footway from Water Lane to St. John's Church. The Almshouses, which are the last remains of the once splendid Hospital of St. Mary Magdalen, are situated on the sloping ground, a little to the north of Red House Lane.[2] From the Alresford Road, a little further to the east, a road runs parallel to this[3] as far as the head of Bridge Street, by which the declivity of St. John's Street can be avoided.

Bridge Street.   Bridge Street runs from the Soke Bridge to the very foot of St. Giles' Hill, where it terminates in three footpaths: one, turning sharply to the south, crosses the lower part of the hill to a road leading from Wharf Bridge to the Alresford Road; the centre one climbs the face of the escarpment of the hill, and conducts to the ground upon which St. Giles' Fair[4] is still held; and the third turns first to the north, and then, running eastward up the hill, leads to Palm Hall, and the Cemetery near it, and northward to the Alresford Road.

Cheesehill Street.   From Bridge Street only one highway runs southward, the name of which, as it has now long been spelt, is Cheesehill Street.[5] A lane leading to a footpath, which joins the one that crosses the foot of St. Giles' Hill, opens to the east; and the street ends at the four cross-ways, called Bar-End. There are several houses in it, noticeable for the quaintness of their architecture; and some, with modern fronts, are still substantially ancient. That next St. Peter's Church has a window (closed by a shutter only) looking into the church, enabling the occupants to take part in the divine services without quitting their own abode. From several of the gardens which run down to the river's edge, foot-bridges have been thrown over to the Weirs, affording an additional and agreeable means of access.[6]

this street: one, almost opposite the church, was used as a barracks, "before the appropriation of the King's House to that purpose" (Ball's "Walks through Winchester," p. 191); another, near the western end of Bridge Street, was the prison belonging to the Cheyney Court, in former times (Godson's map; and local information). Godson places the stocks opposite this prison.

(1) Speed, whose authority is as little as can be, on account of the numerous mistakes contained in his small map, calls this *Tens Lane.* In the copy of this map in the Winchester volume of the Arch. Instit., in Mr. Smirke's paper "On the Hall and Round Table at Winchester," p. 60, the rudely-executed sign of a bridge over the Lower Brooks has been mistaken for the reference to this name. The Rev. W. H. Gunner considers this to have been an extension of the *Procession Way,* which ran under the walls (Tarrages, Memorandum on flyleaf) to Durngate; and Bub's Cross to have been one of the stations visited by the processions which passed along it.

(2) The history of this famous hospital will be given subsequently. These cottages stand on the site of a Roman cemetery.

(3) In several deeds of the fourteenth century this lane is called *Holelane,* and *Hollnlane;* and persons residing near, remember it as *Hollow Lane,* and also as *Pillory Lane.* Godson marks a *Quaker's Burying-place* beside this lane. *Bridge Street* was called *Hole Strete.*

(4) St. Giles' Fair is possessed of such historical importance, that a special account of it will be given later in this work; and the former aspect of the summit of this hill, which is now only ploughed land or pasture, will then be described.

(5) The old spelling is always *Cheshul* or *Chusul.* The word seems to be connected with the Anglo-Saxon *ceosel,* and may have relation to the nature of the ground which bears the name, which (formed from the wreck of the chalk) might have been originally a pebbly hill, or bank beside the stream.

(6) In the Liber Winton. (p. 557) four houses are mentioned, *extra portam de est,* which brought an additional rent to the bishop, *pro via retro.* There is a small island formed in the stream, in such a way as to suggest the existence of a mill below Cheesehill Street, at some early period.

The road to the left at Bar-End[1] divides before reaching the limits of the borough, Bar-End. and one branch ascends St. Giles' Hill, and joins the high road to Alresford. The chalk-pit beside it has long been worked, and is mentioned in many old deeds.[2] The lower branch turns into the valley, and falls into the Petersfield Road. The continuation of Cheesehill Street runs straight through Bar-End Gate to the foot of St. Catharine's Hill, and then, bending eastward, crosses the down, following pretty closely (as it would seem) the line of the old Roman road to Porchester.[3] Wharf Hill descends on the west from Bar-End to the river; the roadway parting at the bottom of the slope, and conducting on one hand to Wharf Mill, and on the other, more to the south, to Wharf or Black Bridge; and by a lane, ending in a footpath across the fields, to St. Catharine's Hill, the Twyford Road and St. Cross, and by Tun Bridge over the navigation, across the water-meadows to Barton Mill and St. Faith's.

There are two streams at Wharf Mill,[4] and the one nearest the east turns a wheel, Wharf Mill. by which the water from a spring, rising just beneath Bar-End, is forced through a pipe under the river, for the supply of the College and of Wolvesey. The waste water is employed to turn a saw-mill, and some other similar machinery. Black Black Bridge. Bridge[5] lies a little lower down the stream, with wharves on each side below it—College Wharf alone on the western bank; but on the other, beside several known by no distinctive name, one called the Domum Wharf, where used to stand the Domum Tree, celebrated in Wykehamical legend.[6]

It is at this place that the Itchen navigation[7] commences; and the other stream[8] turns westward from College Wharf, and, with a winding course, passes through the Milland "de la Barton," to the stillness and shade of St. Cross. New Bridge[9] is thrown over the navigable river from one of the eastern wharves, and Tun Bridge at the foot of St. Catharine's Hill. Hard by are the water-meads, which the Wyke-

(1) Called *Est-barre* (towards Chiltecumbe) in a record of the time of Edward I., in the Cathedral Library.

(2) Part of St. John's Church is built of the hard chalk quarried beneath St. Giles' Hill; and amongst other buildings in Winchester, a substantial crypt, or cellar, beneath part of the house in St. Thomas' Street, now occupied by C. Wooldridge, Esq. Chalk was also used in the construction of the Roman water-conduit discovered near Eastgate Street, in 1849.

Several deeds in the Chartulary of St. Denys' Priory (Brit. Mus. Add. MSS. 15,314), recording gifts of stalls and shops on St. Giles' Hill, make particular mention of the chalk and flint which was obtained there, as giving additional value to the property. The escarpment facing Bridge Street has the appearance of a long unworked chalk-pit.

(3) Of the traces of this road full mention will be made under the head of Chilcombe Parish, and also in the "General Appendix."

(4) This is called in old documents, *Segier's*, *Seagryme's*, and *Segrim's* Mill.

(5) In Leland's time (Itin. vol. iii. fol. 73), and long afterwards, this bridge was only a timber one; and owed its name to its being built of "tarred wood" (Walcot's "William of Wykeham and his Colleges," p. 262). It is now a substantial structure of stone.

(6) See the section on "St. Mary Winton College" for an account of this legend.

(7) When treating of the "Trade" of Winchester, a fuller notice of this navigation, and from the earliest times, will be given.

(8) Godson's map calls the part flowing from the wharf to the side of the path to Barton, *the Old River*; but the Rev. W. H. Gunner informs me that the Wykehamists know it as *the Old Barge River*; and that in ancient deeds belonging to St. Elizabeth's College it is called *Magna Riparia*. In a future page the probability that this branch is the *original* "navigation" will be discussed.

(9) Bathers from the College, as I learn from the Rev. W. H. Gunner, have detected the remains of another bridge not far from this, and call it *Old* New Bridge.

hamists have named " Dalmatia ;" and beyond them, other noted spots, on which here we do not dwell.[1]

College Walk. The road which crosses Black Bridge makes a sharp turn to the north, where it reaches the wall of the Warden's Garden ; and being joined, against the gate of Wolvesey Palace grounds, by a footpath from Wharf Mill, takes a westerly direction beside the old city walls, over the brooks,[2] where they leave the Close, and in front of St. Mary Winton College, under the name of College Street, to King's-gate. A branch of it continues in a straight line along the south side of the Warden's Garden to the College Mill, and there terminates.[3]

Prior's Barton. From this point a footpath, known to anglers, and loved by all who can enjoy the tranquillity of our rich English meadow scenery, follows the course of the river to Barton Mill ; and thence is continued along the margin of a rivulet to the Hospital of St. Cross. Crossing the water at this mill, and pursuing the road from Tun Bridge, we pass the Manor-house of Prior's Barton,[4] with its extensive outbuildings, to which one of the channels of the stream has been led ; and reach the road from King's-gate, which a little way further to the south turns into the high road from the South-gate of Winchester to Southampton.

Sparkford. *St. Faith's.* At the angle formed by the junction of these two roads the Church of St. Faith's,[5] in old time, stood ; and the burial-ground of the parish still remains. The village of St. Cross, and the Hospital, are but a short distance hence to the south ; and a lane immediately opposite, which is now open but a short way towards the north-west, shows where the road from St. Cross to the thickly-peopled suburb without West-gate used to be.[6] The Southampton Road lies in the level bottom of the valley ; and to the west the ground rises with a gradual but varying slope ; along the middle of which, and parallel to the old turnpike, the South-western Railway runs (for the most part upon an embankment of no great elevation) from the immediate proximity of the city to the point where it leaves the boundaries of the borough. The lane from Compton Down and Cromwell's Battery passes under it to the highway at St. Cross Gate.[7]

(1) See p. 27, note 6.

(2) One of these runnels issues from the Precinct at the back of Cheyney Court, and originally flowed along the city ditch to the *Warden's Stream* (as it now passes beside the street and part of the way through a barrel-drain), giving off a branch exactly opposite the western end of Wykeham's building.

(3) The brook that washes the eastern side of the College is known there as the *Warden's Stream*. Beside it, in former times, was a continuation of the footpath to Barton Mill, but now closed for the greater privacy and convenience of the residents of the College.

St. Elizabeth's College stood in the Warden's Meadow (*Pratum S. Stephani*; 30 Edw. I.), between the Old Barge River and the road to the College Mill. The general plan of its buildings is at all times discernible ; and, after long-continued drought, the entire outline may

be traced. St. Stephen's Chapel is said to have stood nearer to Black Bridge.

(4) In the Black Book of Winchester (fols. 5, 13, &c.) this mill is said to be a fulling-mill, and is called *La Kyngesmille juxta* (or *atte*) *le Berton*, or *Priorys berton*. Elsewhere it is called *Crupestre Mill*.

No part of the *old* Manor-house now remains.

(5) This was one of the churches suppressed by Bishop Fox. It will be noticed again when we particularly describe the Hospital and Church of St. Cross.

(6) Milner (vol. ii. p. 191) says that "the society of St. Cross probably made their procession by 'this road' to the venerable church-yard of St. James."

(7) The existence of several footpaths in this part may be alluded to in a note ; because, in many instances, these are all that remain of obsolete roads, which are of great interest to the investigator of ancient topography.

The suburb extending from King's-gate reaches about half way towards St. Faith's Southern
suburb. Cemetery; but, with the exception of here and there a house of older date than the majority (and none of them can well be called ancient), nothing in it requires particular notice.[1] That without South-gate does not extend so far from the city; and there are wider spaces occupied by gardens and shrubberies.[2] A lane runs from one of these roads to the other, about three hundred yards away from the city walls.[3] Nearer to them is a footpath, passing through inclosed passages by St. Michael's Church at the east end, and beside the grounds of the Friary[4] at the west, into Culver Close;[5] which has another outlet on the north into Canon Street[6]—a mere lane running along the edge of the old city ditch from South-gate to King's-gate.

Directly opposite Canon Street, Barnes' Lane[7] (or St. James' Lane) opens to the west. The new suburb commences here in the end of Painter's Fields[8] next this lane, which, crossing the railroad by a bridge that is on a level with the Parade-ground of the Barracks, leads directly to West Hill. Few parts of Winchester are so agreeable West Hill.

(1) Nearly opposite St. Michael's Church Passage was the Carmelite Monastery; and nearer to the corner of College Street, the Church of All Saints in the Vineyards, as appears by the Chartulary of St. Denys' Priory (fol. 122), behind which, on the site of Commoners, was the *Susterns Spital*, or *Hospitium Monachorum* (Liber Winton.)

(2) From a document in Edington's Register (Pars. II. fol. 59, &c.), for the knowledge of which I am indebted to the Rev. W. H. Gunner, it appears that in the year 1351 the road between the South-gate and St. Cross was, " *a bonis honestisque personis in multitudine copiosa,*" inhabited " *per dimidium miliare et amplius* " to the south of the Austin Friars' house; which would extend this suburb as far as Milner has alleged (vol. i. p. 157).

Between South-gate Road and the railway lie Painter's Fields, in which are a few recently-built houses, indicative of the tendency of the new town to follow the line of internal communication from which it originated.

(3) In documents in the Muniment-room of the College, this lane is described as leading to *Flemmynges-halle*, and is called *Flemmynges-halle Lane*, and *Mill Lane. Hoyvile's Garden,* or *Havilgardyn,* lay between it and the Friary.

(4) Or *Priory;* the site of the Convent of the Augustine Friars.

(5) There is (or was) a pond in this pasture, respecting which I have received the following communication from the Rev. W. H. Gunner:—

"Within the memory of man, a spring, called St. Martin's Well, rose just below the South-gate, in the town ditch, and flowed down it into the stream near the College. It was stopped up (as I was told) when the gate was removed, by the rubbish, and shortly after burst out again in the garden in Culver Close; and in wet weather flooded it, and found its way through the

houses into Kingsgate Street. The only measure adopted by the inhabitants on such occasions, to draw the water off, was to dig a channel through the yard of the inn, then called the Blue Boar, now the Crown; until the owner, seeing that a proper system of drainage was required, compelled the inhabitants to construct one, by refusing to allow them to bring the water through his premises any longer. . . . The spring still occasionally rises at its new outlet, but never floods now."

These facts are exceedingly interesting and valuable, from the light they throw upon the source of supply to the *water-ditches* round the upper part of the city and the castle.

(6) The oldest name of this street was *Seve Tuichena* (Liber Winton., p. 560), or *Seuetwychene* (Records in Cath. Lib.) It was afterwards called *Paillardes Twychen* (Tarrages, fol. 39). *Twycina,* or *twycene* (A. S.), signifies "a place where two ways meet;" but its application in this instance is not obvious; nor is the meaning of the remainder of the name, in either form, clear. Godson's name—*Barrowstichin*—which Milner too lightly adopted, has been reasonably, though unintentionally, ridiculed by the etymology proposed in the last edition of the History (vol. ii. p. 192, note). The present name dates from the latter part of the last century.

Wavell (vol. i. pp. 207, 208) says there used to be a foot-bridge over the ditch, and a way into the city, a little below South-gate, from Canon Street.

Another lane outside King's-gate, mentioned in the Cathedral Library Records, was called *Gyrgelane;* and another, lying (apparently) north and south, is spoken of as leading to St. Nicholas'.

(7) Godson's and Gale's maps show the changes in the direction of this lane before the new town was begun; but no map has been published since the laying out of the streets, &c., in this quarter.

(8) Called *Pantersfeld* in some old documents.

as this. The close proximity of the city, the easy access to the railway-station, the clear air of the downs, the magnificent prospect—which stretches to the Worthies on the north, and over the intermediate hills to Southampton and the Island on the south ; the Barracks, the Cathedral, and St. Giles' Hill, with the vale of Chilcombe, being the principal objects in front ; and away from the city, to the west, woods and downs, and the fields of Week and Lainston :—these, together with the numberless accessories, which add so greatly to the comfort of modern suburban residences—such as sufficient space for gardens and offices, and shops in convenient situations, where all the necessaries and most of the luxuries of life may readily be procured—these advantages make West Hill the best quarter of Winchester.

The Cemetery.   On the western side of the railroad, and the south of St. James' Lane, is the Ceme-tery[1]—a piece of ground about seven acres in extent, delightfully situated on the sunny slope of West Hill, and laid out with the greatest taste. A low wall separates the con-secrated from the unconsecrated portion ; and there is a chapel in each division. The grounds are open to the public all day, and afford a very agreeable promenade, with a charming view of the valley beyond St. Catharine's Hill and St. Cross, as far as Twyford and Bambridge.

The Romsey Road   Near the summit of the hill, on the south side of the Romsey Road, is the Catholic Burying-ground, which was walled in and provided with a lodge and porter, in the year 1829, by a gentleman named Farquharson.[2] Next to it, on the east, is the Soldiers' Burial-ground. On the opposite side of the road stands the New County and City Prison, and County Police-station, which was completed in 1850.[3] Nearer Winchester, below the burial-grounds last mentioned, are the Water-works.

Upper High Street.   In front of West-gate, where the Romsey Road branches off from the road to Week and Stockbridge (now called Upper High Street[4]), is the Monument, or Obelisk, erected by the Natives' Society in 1759, and rebuilt in 1821,[5] on the spot where the markets were held when the city was visited by the plague in 1666. The Win-chester Union-house stands on the south side of the Week Road, a little beyond the

(1) The Company was incorporated by Act of Parlia-ment in 1840 ; in which year the grounds were opened. The capital was £5000, in £10 shares. Nearly all the interments for the city now take place here, the cathedral and other grave-yards being closed.

(2) Near this cemetery, in former times, stood the Church of St. James, called in the list in Pontissara's Register (fol. 157)—*de Albo Monasterio ;* whence Mil-ner (vol. ii. p. 206), by the help of Tanner (Not. Mon. Nasmith's Ed. "Hampshire," xxxv. 4), has inferred the existence of a Cistercian monastery—forgetting that "minster" most frequently signified no more than *church.* The procession in "*Ramis palmarum*" used to visit it. Milner also remarks, that "it appears to have been considered as a place of peculiar devotion at the Reformation, by the Catholics of Winchester, and the neighbourhood, who accordingly chose it for their bury-ing-ground." But there is nothing to countenance this statement.

(3) A fuller notice of this prison will be given subse-quently.

(4) This was formerly called *Wode Street,* as appears by several deeds in the College Muniment-room, and St. Denys' Priory Chartulary (fol. 119 v°). I am in-debted to the Rev. W. H. Gunner for the knowledge of this fact. It was also called *Vicus S. Walarici.*

(5) The Natives' Society is one of the charitable in-stitutions of the city (to be spoken of in another section) which held its first meeting in 1669 ; whence arose the error in the date of the visitation, to which it owed its origin, inscribed upon this monument, which Milner corrects (vol. ii. pp. 22, 207). Hard by this spot the Churches of SS. Valericus, Anastasius (or Anastasia), and Leonard, used to stand.

W.H. Bartlett.

S. Bradshaw.

VIEW FROM ST. CATHERINE'S HILL.

Winchester & the Valley of the Itchen.

bridge over the railway. It is built on part of a piece of land called Oram's Arbour; Oram's Arbour. which, though much reduced by the encroachments of the railway-cutting, this Union-house, &c., and now let by the corporation as a pasture, is still fondly regarded by the citizens, as rightfully their *Campus Martius*, and place of public amusement.[1] It is bounded towards the west by a considerable earth-work, or trench, part of which is Bar-ditch. now filled up, and turned into a roadway; which was also the limit of the city liberty here.[2]

Behind West Hill, on the Week Road, in the bottom of the valley, lies Fulflood Fulflood Farm. Farm; and a lane runs from near it, under the railway, close to the station (of which we shall speak hereafter), to the end of Swan Lane,[3] and Northgate Street, or Road. And at the same point, another lane, called Sussex Street, comes from outside West- Sussex Street. gate, parallel to the old city wall. In this lane the houses, which were built before the railway was constructed, at the same time with those in Tower Street, behind it, are almost all of an inferior class, and mark the end of the new town in this direction.[4]

From the end of Sussex Street the Andover Road rises to the north-west, and Andover Road.

---

(1) Godson's map, which shows the extent of this piece of public ground, before the recent invasions, entitles it simply *the Arbour;* and states that the freeholders of the county used to meet there to choose their representatives in parliament. In the Tarrages, so frequently cited (fol. 34), "a great crofte of the citie called *Erberie*" is entered; and in the margin of fols. 33 v° and 34, several crofts are said to form part of *the Harbor;* whence it would appear to have been much more extensive at first, and to have been encroached upon very early. Mr. Moody informs me that it is called *Oram's Arbour*, from having been leased to persons of that name about a hundred years ago.

(2) Milner thinks this entrenchment was "cast up by the royal garrison of the castle and city in 1644" (vol. ii. pp. 13, 207); whilst Wavell ascribes it to Stephen's army, in the campaign against the Empress Maud, in 1141 (vol. ii. p. 54).

But in the Tarrages (4 Hen. V., or A.D. 1417), the whole course of this earth-work, which was then more extensive, is traced, and it is called the *Barditch* (fols. 34 to 38 v°). The description of the property called the *Hawkhey* (fol. 35) also enables us to identify it with the *Domus-havoc*, in the Liber Winton. (p. 537), there said to be "*inter II. fossatum;*" which carries back the record of this trench to the time of Henry I., if not to that of Edward the Confessor. This fact, and the circumstance of its being one of the boundaries of the city liberty, render it not improbable that it may be the last vestige of the aboriginal *Venta Belgarum*, which preceded the Romanised *Venta*—now the city of Winchester.

(3) This road from Fulflood Farm follows the lowest part of the valley, and marks the course of the rivulet we have mentioned above (p. 10, n. 2). *Fulflood*, which, spelt *Fuleflot*, and *Fuleflod*, occurs in the Liber Winton. (pp. 547, 548), would seem to have been the name of this stream. A "Parish of Fulfloude" is mentioned in the Inquisitiones Nonarum (fols. 106, 107), temp. Edw. III.

(4) From the oft-quoted Tarrages (fols. 35 to 38 v°), we learn some interesting particulars respecting the tract included within the road to Fulflood, the Barditch, and the present Sussex Street. And from the descriptions of the several roads, it appears that the Church of St. Mary in the Vale stood not far from the railway-station—perhaps a little to the east of it. From this spot there was, according to Godson's map—and the line is laid down in Gale's also—a narrow lane, called *Old Gallows' Lane;* and "the gallows in the west parte of the Kynge's hie-way leading to Whitchurch," or "upon Barditch nighe" that way, are named in the Tarrages. *Valebarne* is said to be close to this spot.

In ancient deeds, this *Valebarne* often occurs along with the *Hawkhey*, or *Hawkesheyes*, which (together with a "Culver-house") was situated on the west side of Sussex Street, not far from the present road to the railway-station, and in what is called (Rot. Lit. Claus., vol. i. pp. 10, 507, &c.) *la Parrok* (and sometimes *Paroki*, and *Parrocæ*, in the plural), or "the Park." From these published Close Letters, it appears that there were four *Mews* for the king's hawks here in John's time (Ibid. p. 553); and that the chapel there (no doubt St. Mary's in the Vale), was portion of the same estate (Ibid.); the *hayas*, or "hedges," around them are spoken of (Ibid. pp. 10, 363); and whereas the mention of the *Parroc* in the sixth year of this reign (Ibid., p. 10) says nothing of any *Mews* there, in the sixteenth year (Ibid., p. 206)

crosses the railway just within the boundary of the borough. A lane (in which are situated two good suburban villas, in well-planted grounds) branches off from it near the bottom of the slope, to the Basingstoke Road, which runs straight from the North-gate[1] to the utmost limits of parliamentary Winchester in that direction. About midway in this space, a lane crosses from this road to that branch of the Andover Road before mentioned ; and thence is continued by a footpath to the Andover Road itself. Opposite it is a way leading past St. Bartholomew's Church and the gateway of Hyde Abbey, down to the Hyde Burn, and over a bridge to the cottages which have been erected on the site of Hyde Abbey Church, since the removal of the Bridewell. A footpath, called Nuns' Walk (or, according to Milner, Monks' Walk),[2] passes by the north side of St. Bartholomew's Church, across the brook, and along a raised causeway, to the farm still called Abbot's Barton, which lies beyond the line that bounds our present survey.

Hyde Street, in the part nearest the city, wears almost as antique a look as the Soke ; but beyond the road leading to the church, the houses are principally new, and some of them quite modern in style. Hyde Abbey School, which enjoyed considerable celebrity in its time, is remembered by its school-house, which was not long ago used as the County Museum (before that institution was put on its present footing, and lodged in a part of the former jail, in Jewry Street), and now serves as a temporary military hospital. The lofty tennis-wall of the play-ground attached to an existing and most respectable academy almost on the same spot, called Hyde House School, frequently excites the wonder and curiosity of passing railway-travellers. Of the famous abbey from which the name of this suburb is derived, and of the relics (rather than ruins) of it which remain to this time, mention will be made in another section of this part of our work.

Between the site of Hyde Abbey and the river Itchen, below Winnall, lie the water-meadows, intersected by the numerous runnels formerly described, and varied now with a few osier-beds. This is the spot chosen by the Euhemeri of our country as the scene of the legendary duel, in which that most renowned champion, Guy Earl

Left margin notes:

Basingstoke Road.

Hyde Street.

Denemarche Meadow.

directions are given to the mayor and bailiffs of Winchester to prepare *Mews* at the *Parocæ*, for the reception and "mewing" of the king's birds—notices of the purchase of which at Yarmouth, in Norfolk, and St. Botolph's Fair, at Lincoln, occur in the same page.

This last-cited Close Letter seems to contain the true explanation of the verdict upon the land called *le Muwes*, contained in the Inquest before referred to (Arch. Journal, vol. vii. pp. 375, 378, 382, 383) ; for King John did establish the *Mews* here, as the jury in this case found ; or rather *re*-establish them, since there can be no doubt that a *Domus havoc*, or *Mews*, existed here two hundred years before the time of John (Liber Winton., p. 537). Amongst the Charter Rolls, we may add, is one, dated 5 John, which grants certain lands to Math. de Wallop,

Warden of Winchester Castle, for the service of mewing at his own cost the king's birds, "*quas ponemus infra castellum Winton. ad mutandum*" (Rot. Chart., vol. i. p. 126).

Deeds in the Muniment-room of Winchester College, temp. Edw. I. and 12 and 19 Hen. VI. (for the particulars of which I am indebted to the Rev. W. H. Gunner), amply confirm this view of the position of *la Parrok*, the *Hawkesheyes*, and the Church of St. Mary in the Vale.

(1) Some notion of the appearance of this gate may be obtained from Buck's "East Prospect." The bridge which crossed the ditch outside it still remains under the road, and may be seen from the garden of the Swan Inn.

(2) Vol. ii. p. 250.

of Warwick, slew the Danish giant Colbrond, to the infinite relief of this oppressed land, and of Athelstan, its perplexed monarch. Hyde Mead was the old name of the place; but it has lately been better known as Denemarche, or Denmark Meadow.[1]

And thus is concluded our general survey of the City and Borough of Winchester. We shall proceed in the next section to the particular description of the Cathedral and the part of the city appertaining to it; then, after treating of the churches, the college, and the other religious and educational buildings and institutions, the municipal and commercial sections of the subject will be introduced; and, finally, the general history of the place, with such miscellaneous notices as could not well be inserted under any special title.

Plan of the following sections.

(1) Space does not admit the insertion of this goodly ballad, which our readers will find in Ellis's " Early English Metrical Romances " (pp. 225, 233, Bohn's Ed.) almost at full length; and an abridgment would deprive it of all its strength and flavour. But a few remarks must be made upon the rationalisers who have converted this passage in the Romance of Guy of Warwick into an improbable, yet commonplace, piece of local history.

The Annales Wintonienses (Angl. Sacr., vol. i. p. 289) of course take no notice at all of the duel, though they record the gift of the three manors to St. Swithin's. The ballad does not indicate any particular spot as the scene of the combat. Henry Knighton says it took place in the vale of Chilcombe. Rudbourne (who wrote a hundred years later) assigns it to Hyde Mead, "*qui olim Denemarch appellatus est*" (Angl. Sacr., vol. i. p. 212); and states that the very weapon with which the giant's head was cut off by the victor was kept in the Treasury of the Cathedral, "*usque ad hodiernum diem.*" Milner (vol i. p. 110, &c.), who contends for the historical character of the tale, appeals to a turret in the north wall of the city, from which the king watched the fight, thence called " Athelstan's Chair;" to a representation of the battle in stone, formerly existing in the wall; and to two mutilated statues of a very tall man and a little man, fighting, " said to have existed " in the chapel at Guy's Cliff. He also states that " Trussel testifies " to the preservation of the axe in the cathedral in the time of James I.

Trussell himself (fols. 51 v°, 52) quotes an account of this "Duell" by Dr. Harmar (Warden of Winchester College, 1596—1613), but says that Harmar himself knew not " where hee had yt." It was in Latin, and the worthy Alderman gives a part of it in the original, and then translates the whole; and in this narrative it is said that the " hatchett" " is reserued in the vestry there, *ut ferunt.*" Speaking from his own knowledge, he says (fol. 50), " A watch-tower opposite to the place of fight in the wall of the cittie, and where the picture of a great and a litell man, cutt in stone, remayneth att this day, is called Colbrond's Chayer." He also speaks of the alleged place of combat as " a meddowe grownd, att this day called Hide Meade, neer another ground called Denmarck Mead" (fol. 50).

Milner very confidently refers to Harpsfield; but the references to Colman and Giraldus Cambrensis, in the margin of that author's account of this legend, are too vague to be accepted as evidence in its favour.

And, in fine, the only foundation for this resolute attempt to pass legend off as history, is the original name of the spot selected—*Denemede* (Rot. de Oblat. et Fin., p. 238); which signified no more than " the meadow in the valley," and in the reign of John, and long afterwards, was a surname in Winchester.

Godson's map represents, as occupying the fabled scene of this duel, a mound, with a tree on it, no traces of which are visible now.

THE

CATHEDRAL AND ITS PRECINCT;

WITH

WOLVESEY.

ECCLESIASTICAL institutions and structures naturally take precedence of others in the description of a city. And of them, in Winchester, the Cathedral, with the Close and Cemetery, and the Episcopal Palace and grounds of Wolvesey, rank foremost.

Situation and boundaries of the Precinct, &c.

This district occupies the south-eastern corner of the area within the walls; and the boundary proceeding from them, a little to the east of King's-gate, goes along the north side of St. Swithin's Street, and the east side of Symond's and Great Minster Streets, the south side of the Square and the wall of the cemetery to the south-west corner of Colebrook Street, where it nearly touches the Lady Chapel, and thence runs at the back of the houses in Colebrook Street to the city walls, where they begin to turn away from the bank of the river, and follows them to near King's-gate again. The greatest length of the space thus enclosed is very nearly three furlongs; and the greatest breadth rather more than a furlong and a half; the least, rather less than a furlong.[1] Excepting the cemetery, the whole is inclosed by a wall.

Entrances to the Precinct.

There are six entrances into the cemetery, the principal being those opposite the west end of the cathedral,[2] at the corner of the Square, and opposite Market Street. The chief entrance into the Close is by the great gateway[3] at the end of St. Swithin's Street, near King's-gate; a narrow passage and small gate gives access to it from Colebrook Street; and there is a way from the cemetery by the southern side of the west end of the cathedral, called the Slype.[4] The passage to the postern gate into

(1) Measured upon Gale's map. The area of the Precinct, with Wolvesey, is nearly thirty-five acres, or about a quarter of that of the whole city.

(2) Called *Minstre Gate* in Cal. Rot. Pat., 23 Edw. III., 3ᵃ pars., m. 16, or Records in Cath. Lib., vol. i., No. 120.

(3) This is a plain and solid arched gateway, with "doors of prodigious strength" says Milner (vol. ii. p. 148). The royal arms, painted on a large square

tablet, are placed over it on the outside. In the rising of the citizens against the Prior and Convent of St. Swithin's, in 1264, this gate, with the houses near the wall, and King's-gate and St. Swithin's Church, were burnt by the insurgents (Ann. Winton. *s. ann*).

(4) Before the opening of this passage (which was at first cut through the great buttress, on the south-side of the angle), the southern aisle of the cathedral, from the west door to the door which originally led to the

WINCHESTER CATHEDRAL.

(From the North West.)

Colebrook Street is prolonged eastward, and is the means of communication between the Close and the grounds of Wolvesey Palace; but the main entrance is through a gateway in the city wall, opposite the road leading round the end of the Warden's Garden to Wharf Bridge.

All that part of the Precinct which lies to the north of the cathedral (except a small piece of ground lying between the choir and the north transept[1]), and of the wall running from the west end of it to Great Minster Street, is occupied by the cemetery, and is commonly known by the name of Cathedral Yard. Along the entire length of this grave-yard runs a noble alley of limes, elms, and other trees; crossed by others from the gate into the Square, and to Market Street; which form magnificent and appropriate avenues of access to the Minster. There are several other single lines of trees in the same area, which is thus rendered a place of most agreeable resort, for coolness, and fragrancy, and shade in the summer; although it is difficult to get an unimpeded view of the cathedral on this side, from such a distance as to allow of the study of it as a whole, or of a comparison of the several parts.[2]

Cathedral Yard.

Before the formation of the cemetery in St. James's Fields this was the *Campo Santo* of Winchester; but it has recently been closed by the Secretary of State. During the present year (1856), also, some houses which stood within the limits of

---

western cloister, was used as a common thoroughfare. There is a stone archway, which was, originally, the eastern entrance of the Slype, but was built into the south wall of it, some years ago, when the width of the passage was doubled. Over it is inscribed the following notification of the closing of the old way, and the opening of the new one, together with the date of the change, and a not very lucid direction to passengers:—

"CESSIT COMMUNI PROPRIUM JAM PERGITE QUA FAS. 1632."

Beneath it, under a hand pointing originally to a door in the south aisle of the cathedral, is this:—

"S $\overset{ACR}{\underset{ERV}{A}}$ $\overset{S}{\underset{F}{IT}}$ $\overset{ILL}{\underset{IST}{A}}$ $\overset{CH}{\underset{F}{ORO}}$."

And under it another hand points downwards to the entrance to the Slype. In like manner, on the pier of the cathedral, between the southmost of the three western doors and the archway cut through the great buttress in making the new passage, is this equally enigmatical inscription, under a hand with a rod pointing to the cathedral door:—

"ILL $\overset{}{\underset{H}{AC}}$ PREC $\overset{}{\underset{VI}{ATOR}}$

AMBULA."

Under it is a hand pointing to the gate of the Slype.

Britton applies this name (which is not a Hampshire provincialism, since it is the designation of a passage

near New College, Oxford) to the "dark cloister" between the south transept and the chapter-house.

(1) Godson's map is very unsatisfactory here, on account of an unwise fashion of giving imaginary bird's-eye views of the principal buildings in a city, instead of accurate ground-plans, which prevailed in his time. Nevertheless, by comparing it with Buck's "East Prospect," we find that a wall ran along the north side of the cathedral as far as the west end, cutting off a portion of the present grave-yard, and that it was planted with trees and shrubs to the east of the transept. I have been informed that during the French war this space, to the west of the transept, was used as a parade-ground for the Hampshire militia. The level here was considerably higher than it now is—the soil, to the depth of a yard, having been removed not many years since, because it was thought to make the cathedral damp. The floor of the church is still lower than the surface of the ground outside. The doorway in the western side of the north transept shows this, only half the height of the shafts being exposed. On the buttresses the line of the former level may still be seen.

(2) Buck's "East Prospect" represents these fine trees in their youth. Speed's map shows that there were a few a hundred years before that time. Some are beginning to show such symptoms of age as to suggest the need of planting others, to take their places when they are gone, and beautify the cathedral-yard for coming generations. The same remark applies to the trees in the Close, which appear to be older than those in the cemetery.

this cemetery, on the western side, have been removed; and now, although several houses in the Square have doors into Cathedral Yard, Bishop Morley's College (of which we shall speak in another place) is the only dwelling-house in this part of the Precinct. The greater part of the cemetery (we may observe) was originally included within the area of New Minster; the conventual buildings connected with the cathedral, then called Old Minster, lay to the south of it.[1]

The Cathedral.

Winchester Cathedral,[2] though not so elaborately ornamented as many others, is one of the most interesting of these splendid structures, in which are embodied the noblest aspects of the religion of our forefathers. Its appearance, particularly from the south, is not prepossessing, on account of the slight elevation of its massive square tower above the rest of the building, and the great length of the western roof, unbroken either by pinnacle or turret. From the east, and from the west, it is the low tower principally which detracts from its general effect.

Its plan and dimensions.

The plan of the cathedral is simple; and it now consists of a nave with aisles; a central tower; north and south transepts, each with aisles on both sides and at the ends; a choir; a presbytery with aisles; three "chantry aisles" (as Britton names them) to the east of the choir; a Lady chapel, with a smaller chapel on each side of it; and three crypts. The cloisters formerly adjoined the nave on the south; and the chapter-house was separated from the end of the south transept by a narrow passage only. The extreme external length of the building, from east to west, is (according to Mr. Garbett's plan)[3] five hundred and fifty-six feet; the width, from north to south of the transepts, two hundred and thirty feet; and across the west end, a hundred and eighteen feet. The transepts are ninety-seven feet wide, externally, from east to west. The extreme internal length is five hundred and twenty-seven feet; the width within the north and south walls of the transepts, two hundred and eight feet; the width of the nave, eighty-eight feet; and the width of each transept, eighty-one. The ground covered by it exceeds an acre and a half in extent. The height of the tower is about a hundred and forty feet; that of the summit of the pinnacles at the east and west ends, a hundred and thirty feet. The greatest interior height of the nave from the floor is seventy-seven feet.[4] The orientation of the body of the church is E.S.E., or about 23° south of the east cardinal point, which agrees with the sun-rising of none of its real or legendary dedications.

Both within and without, the styles of architecture most conspicuous in this

---

(1) Full accounts of these conventual buildings, and of the existing remains of them, as well as of New Minster, will be given hereafter.

(2) To prevent the unnecessary crowding of the notes with references, I would here mention that, in addition to the historians of Winchester, already so often quoted, "The History and Antiquities of the Cathedral Church of Winchester," by Lord Clarendon and Samuel Gale, 1683 and 1715, and Warton's "Description of the City, &c.," have been referred to; but that I am chiefly indebted to

Britton's "History and Antiquities of the See and Cathedral Church of Winchester," and to "The Architectural History of Winchester Cathedral," by the Rev. Professor Willis (Arch. Instit., Winchester Volume), and to the latter especially. Mr. Cresy's paper upon the Cathedral, in the Winchester volume of the Archæological Association, has also been used.

(3) Britton's Winchester Cathedral, Pl. I.

(4) That the reader may be able to compare this building with others of its kind, the following particulars,

cathedral are the Perpendicular and the Norman; but good examples of the inter-mediate styles abound, and also of all the variations of those which are most prevalent. The western front presents a fine specimen of Perpendicular architecture. It consists of a great nine-light window,[1] filling the whole width of the nave, with a smaller one, square-headed, and of six lights, above it; two side-windows, with four lights each; a large central doorway, divided by a clustered shaft into two cinquefoiled arches; and two smaller side ones. The nave is flanked by two slender octagonal towers, termi-nating above in spire-like pinnacles;[2] and the gable is surmounted by a tabernacle containing the figure of St. Swithin (?). Plain buttresses, reaching nearly to the level of the top of the centre window, support the two towers; and between and in front of them, at the basement, is a recessed and richly-vaulted porch, with an open battlement above it, and a somewhat pointed Tudor-arch, with plain mouldings and no shafts, on each side of which is an elegant canopied niche. Lesser buttresses, gabled at the top, with square panelled and crocketted pinnacles, support the extreme angles of the front, and similar porches of smaller dimensions fill up the space between them and the great buttresses of the towers. The entire front, including the towers, is panelled; across it, over the great window, runs an open battlement; and a plain parapet, supported by a table, surmounts a similar battlement (which is thus converted into a species of arcade) over the aisles.

The western front.

The south side of the nave, which was originally screened by the cloisters and conventual buildings, is almost entirely devoid of ornament. Eleven windows in the

The south side of the nave.

taken from the plates of Britton's "Cathedral Anti-quities," and other authorities, are subjoined :—

Names of Cathedrals.	Length from E. to W.	Length from N. to S.
	Feet.	Feet.
Winchester	556	230
York	525	249
Ely	525	190
Lincoln	524	250
Canterbury	516	156
Westminster	511	203
Durham	502	171
Peterborough	476	203
Salisbury	474	230
Gloucester	435	154
Worcester	425	145
Wells	415	155
Norwich	411	191

(1) "The design of the west window is singularly sim-ple, reducing itself to the merest stone grating" (Willis, p. 65). It is divided into three equal compartments by two large mullions, which, with two smaller between them, run quite from top to bottom; and the parts at the sides

are made into arches, and subdivided through their whole length also by two smaller mullions. Horizontally, it is crossed by five transoms (the topmost tier being intercepted by the curvilinear tracery of the side com-partments), and the head of each division cinquefoiled with a small leaf on the point of each cusp, as are those in the panelling of all the front, except the gable. The heads of the side-lights in the lateral compart-ments exhibit the only approach to tracery throughout the window; being arched, and filled with an elongated quatrefoil, and not crossed by the transom, which is level with the spring of their arch,—precisely resembling the tracery of Wykeham's windows.

The external jambs of all the west windows have two great casement-mouldings; but, while in the side windows both are carried over the arch-head, in the great win-dow, the outer one is stopped by a cap-moulding at the impost point, and only the inner one is carried higher (Willis, pp. 63, 64).

The small square-headed window in the gable is really nothing more than six panels glazed, there being no drip-stone or mouldings of any kind round it.

(2) Since Milner complained of the dilapidated ap-pearance of this front (vol. ii. p. 72), the pinnacle at the southern angle of the nave, and the open battlements over the porches, have been restored in plaster.

aisle[1] (all alike, except the one near the west end) having between them only flat buttresses, not reaching to the ground; the lower part of the wall, broken only by the two doorways formerly leading into the cloisters, and two smaller doorways nearer the west end (all now closed, a new one being opened opposite the centre of the cloister square[2]); eleven windows, all alike, and having only flat buttresses between them, in the clerestory; both aisle and clerestory finished with no more than a plain parapet and corbel-table beneath it;—such are the monotonous details of this part of the cathedral.

The north side. On the north side, although the clerestory is the same as that of the south side, the windows of the aisle (with two exceptions[3]) the same, the parapets of both members the same, and there is a doorway[4] only under the window farthest to the west, the character of the whole is altered by the buttresses of the aisle, which are bold, though plain, and rise by several stages in square, panelled, and crocketted pinnacles above the roof to the level of top of the clerestory windows.

The tower; Passing from the nave, with its various examples of the Perpendicular style, we

(1) These windows are the work of William of Wykeham. They are of three lights, and of a peculiar but elegant form; the window itself being a drop-arch, but the openings, with the mouldings and the gables (which are terminated by corbel heads), the middle and larger segment of a drop-arch, divided perpendicularly into three parts, as may be seen by the panelling in the interior. The heads of the side lights are made pointed arches, and the tracery between the mullions (which run quite to the top) is an elongated quatrefoil, or octofoil, in the centre, over a cinquefoil arch. In the windows of the aisle a transom is substituted for the sill, and the lights are carried down lower, and cinquefoiled under the transom. The greater number of windows on the north side are identical in design with these.

(2) Of these closed doorways, the first is under the window next the west end, and shows merely the outline of a pointed arch, reaching to the water-table under the window,—it was, in all probability, exactly like the existing doorway on the north side; the second, under the next window, shows only the outline of an obtuse-headed arch; the third (which was the door into the west cloister), under the third window, but nearer the right hand buttress, shows the remains of a round-headed arch, with billet-mouldings and impost, having within it a smaller and narrower flat-pointed arch, without shafts or imposts; and the fourth, which stands in the corner against the transept, and led into the eastern cloister, is under a square hood-moulding close beneath the water-table, with the arms of the see, and of Wykeham in the spandrels, and angels' heads against the upper angles of the hood-moulding, and a stoup quite in the corner. Amongst the stones used to stop the second doorway, are some with the arms of the see, knots, &c., carved on them in small size and low relief.

(3) Milner first pointed out the difference between these two windows and Wykeham's windows. The one nearest the west end on the south side, and the two side windows in the west front, differ in the same particulars. They are all four-light windows, the two side mullions being the largest, and carried completely to the top, and the side lights being wider than the two in the centre. There are two transoms in each, under which are cinquefoiled arches. In the heads of the side lights, which are arched and divided into two by a very slender mullion standing on the upper transom, is a quatrefoil; and the heads of the two centre lights being arched, perpendiculars are carried from the points of the arches to the top, and the openings are feathered. The windows in the aisles differ from those in the front only in the form of the opening, which in the latter is a regular drop-arch; but in the former, the middle and larger segment of one, so that the mouldings, &c., are angular where the spring of the arch should be. Professor Willis observes respecting them, that they "are singularly heavy, and from the extreme depth of their exterior mouldings, have a most cavernous and gloomy appearance" (p. 59). There is a set-off in the wall immediately above the two windows on the north side, the level of which coincides with the base of the lower and panelled battlement in the front. The water-table, and consequently the sill of these two windows, is lower than those of the others in the aisle. Wykeham's buttresses differ from those at the angles of the west end, and the second and third on the north side, in having one set-off less; they all originally had gables at the top, and heavy pinnacles, as may yet be seen at the corners; but Wykeham's lighter and more elegant pinnacles have been substituted for the gables, &c., on the other two. The basement moulding under the second window of the north side dips at right angles to a lower level westward, and differs from that on the remainder of the aisle.

(4) It is a Decorated arch with plain mouldings and no shafts; the drip-stone ends in corbel heads.

come to the tower and transepts, which present as many illustrations of Norman architecture.[1] The coping of the tower is not more than five and thirty feet above the ridge of the transept-roof, and still less above that of the nave. The upper part of it is about fifty feet square. It is divided by a string-course into two stories; the lower of which is quite plain, except that there are engaged shafts at the angles (as there are at those of the upper story, and of the parapet also), and small round-headed windows, looking out just above the slope of the roofs of the lower parts of the church. On each side of the upper story are three very elegant narrow, round-headed windows (now closed with louvre-boardings), forming a rich arcade in the middle of the face of the tower;[2] and the whole is crowned with a plain parapet, over a simple zigzag string-course. The south-eastern corner is a little elevated, to cover the entrance from the spiral staircase to the roof. And the clock is now placed in the centre of the southern side.

In both transepts, though the gables are not so high as those of the nave, the clerestory parapets are on the same level; but the side aisles are lower than those of the nave and the presbytery;—the eastern aisle of the south transept so much so, that the tops of the arches of the triforium are seen over the roof. Only the flat Norman buttresses appear, except in the western clerestory of the north transept, where they are manifestly Perpendicular. A central buttress runs up to the level of the angles of both gables; and at all the angles, but that of the eastern aisle in the south transept, and the western one of the north transept, the buttresses are carried a little way higher than the roof as plain square towers.[3] All the parapets are quite plain, with a series of small arches, resting on corbels, under each; except above the western clerestory of the north transept, where there is a cornice with bosses of the Perpendicular character; and on the east aisle of the south transept, where the parapet rests on a row of common plain corbels. Above the east aisle of the north transept the parapet is not marked by any cornice or table at all. The parapet, with no more than a water-table under it, is carried across the gable of the northern transept, so as to form an *alura* above the buttresses, in front of the circular window there. Two string-courses of alternate billet-moulding are carried entirely round the

(marginal note) and the transepts.

---

(1) The *history* of the building, which will be given after the description of it, will contain the grounds on which this part is called Norman, rather than Saxon, which some antiquaries have declared it to be.

(2) This "arcade" consists of three arches, with the plain moulding, fillet, and billet-moulding, so common in Norman work; springing at the sides from an abacus, which is continued to the angle of the tower, and supported on shafts with plain capitals and bases. The windows within these consist of two receding arches, with capitals, bases, and shafts, the outer arch-mould and shaft having the zigzag moulding, and the inner one the same plain round moulding as the arcade.

(3) At the eastern corner of the north transept may

be seen, above the window of the triforium, where the coping of the wall at the end of the aisle abuts upon the clerestory, a portion of a circular arch with a shaft. Whereupon Professor Willis (p. 37) remarks, that this, " with other marks, show that the north wall of the side aisle was to have been carried up vertically, as for the side of a tower. Moreover, the northernmost clerestory window is inserted under an arch, which was meant to open into the tower. Whether the tower ever existed, and has been removed, or whether it was only projected and prepared for, I cannot tell. But traces of similar towers may be found, more or less distant, at each angle of the transept—namely, two towers flanking the north gable, and two the south."

transepts under the windows of the aisles, and under those of the triforium ; but they cannot be traced the whole way round the southern transept. The gable of this transept is curiously panelled with interlacing Norman arches.

Each clerestory has four windows, and each aisle and triforium three,—with a fourth at the ends of those in the north transept, and two in the transverse parts of each. But in the south transept, the dark cloister,[1] and the lean-to roof of the cathedral library over it, hide most of them. Both north and south clerestories have two windows each ; and in the gable of the north transept is a remarkable rose-window of Perpendicular workmanship ;[2] but in the southern gable there are only two small and narrow lights.

Most of the windows still show circular arches with billet-moulding, and the plain shafts supporting the abaci which formed their imposts ; and some few retain their Norman character entire.[3] The greater number of the openings, however, have had two and three-light Decorated windows[4] inserted ; and sometimes the sill has been lowered considerably, and the string-course taken away.[5] Here and there, Decorated windows of larger size have required the removal of the Norman arches.[6] Several windows in the triforia of both transepts have been stopped.

Under the string-course in the west aisle of the north transept, and in the compartment nearest the nave, is a plain, round-headed doorway, the shafts supporting which are half buried by the elevation of the ground outside that part of the church. A narrow doorway opens into the dark cloister from the south transept under the west central window of the terminal aisle ; and through the window itself is a doorway to the library and the choristers' school-room.

The presbytery. Next beyond the transepts, to the east, is that part of the cathedral called the presbytery, extending to the third buttress from them, on each side in the aisles, and to the great eastern window and gable above ; and the predominant character is Perpendicular. Although there are but three compartments, there are four windows on each side, in the aisle as well as in the clerestory ; those furthest west being placed

---

(1) Britton (p. 100) says, " it was originally intended to cover" this passage, "with a sloping roof, now raised over" the library. But it is hardly probable that, between the south transept and the chapter-house, such a roof would have been tolerated. The vaulting of the passage seems to be Norman ; and there are signs of Norman work at the eastern end ; although the entrances are by much more recent arches. The library and choristers' school-room are certainly of modern construction.

(2) In the centre of this rose-window is a hexagon with cusps ; and the sides are produced so as to give six circular-headed rays ; each of which, as well as the triangular spaces between them, is divided into two by small mullions. This window is hidden from view in the interior by the new ceiling of the transept.

(3) Some of these windows in the eastern clerestories are of two lights.

(4) Three-light decorated windows, inserted within the Norman arches, may be seen under the northern gable, and in the eastern aisle of the same transept ; and in the northern and western aisle two-light windows of the same style. In some, the tracery is of a good flowing character ; in others, it partakes of the transitionary character to the Perpendicular.

(5) As in the terminal aisle of the north transept.

(6) The eastmost window in the terminal aisle of the north transept, the window nearest the presbytery in the eastern aisle of the same transept, and two of the windows in the eastern aisle of the south transept, may be cited as examples. Some of them are of three lights, with intersecting tracery ; others of five, with exceedingly rich geometrical patterns, as, for example, the central window in eastern aisle of the south transept.

WINCHESTER CATHEDRAL.

(The East End.)

within the outer line of the transept aisles, the walls of which are cut obliquely away, so as to admit the light to the windows, which would else only look into the aisles and triforia of the transept.   Professor Willis characterises these windows, which are of four lights, as "noble," and "in the best Perpendicular style."[1]   From the peculiar form of the heads of these windows, it is evident that they are an "imitation of Wykeham's."[2]   All the buttresses here rise above the roof, and are crowned with square, panelled pinnacles, set diagonally, and ogee canopies, crocketted, and terminating with finials.   The first two on each side (from the transepts) have four breaks; but the third is much larger, with two breaks only, and, in fact, forms part of the chantry aisles beyond.   Flying buttresses, "consisting of a sloping [and crocketted] straight line above, and a segmental curve beneath, the spandrel being pierced," spring from these buttresses, and abut upon the clerestory walls.[3]   The parapet is plain, with a cornice and bosses under it.

The windows of the clerestory are Perpendicular, and of four lights, within Decorated arches; the drip-stone ending in corbels.[4]   The parapet, over a cornice with bosses, is surmounted by a panelled and pierced battlement on the north side; but on the other side is plain.   A polygonal form is given to the east end, by the inclination of the walls of the last compartment in that direction towards each other. The central gable is rather acute, and is richly panelled, with crockets running up the   The east end. coping, and a tabernacle surmounted by a finial, and containing a statue of Bishop Fox, resting upon his emblem, the pelican, at the apex.   Three of the panels in the centre are pierced and glazed, forming a small square-headed window; and under it is a door opening upon an *alura*, behind a crenellated panelled and pierced parapet, over a cornice with bosses, at the base of the gable, and just above the east window. On each side the gable is flanked by octagonal turrets, crowned with ogee, crocketted canopies, terminated by a finial, and finely panelled.   Like the aisle windows, this eastern one is a noble specimen of Perpendicular work.   It is of seven lights, and the form of the head resembles that of the aisle windows, and of Wykeham's windows.[5] "The north corbel of the hood-mould of this end window is a most characteristic portrait bust of a bishop, evidently Fox, from the resemblance to his head above." Between the cornice and the hood-mould the panelling is continued; there are two smaller flying-buttresses, springing from the walls between the " chantry aisles," to

(1) Archit. Hist., pp. 46, 47.

(2) Ibid., p. 79.   The central mullion in these windows dichotomizes at the level of the spring of the arch, and makes an arch on each side of it ; the general tracery is of the kind so much like panelling ; there is one transom, and the heads of the lights are cinquefoiled under it, as they are also under the tracery.

(3) Bloxam's Gothic Architecture, p. 289.   Professor Willis (p. 49) observes that these flying buttresses are proved to be " subsequent insertions into the walls of the clerestory," by " the jointing of the masonry."   They

" have also the pelican of Fox carved upon them."

(4) Willis's Archit. Hist., p. 48.   These windows are crossed by one transom, and have the ordinary panel-like tracery, under which the lights are cinquefoiled ; and they are the same under the transom.

(5) The four central mullions are carried to the top of the window ; and there are two transoms across them, at the spring of the arch and higher, the lights being cinquefoiled under them ; but arches are made of the two lights on each side, with tracery resembling that of the late Decorated style.

the eastern faces of the octagonal turrets; and the lower part of the east window is lost behind the roof of the central chantry aisle.

The retro-choir.   From the great buttresses just mentioned, and including them, all the retro-choir, with the exception of the portion of the Lady Chapel, which projects beyond the chapels on each side of it, is Early English work, and is ascribed to Godfrey de Lucy. There are three buttresses between those great ones and the eastern angles of the "chantry aisles," small and plain, in but two stages. An unornamented string-course, or water-table, is carried along the whole of this part, and continued round the buttresses, being intercepted only at the angles of the Lady Chapel. Above this, in each compartment, is an arcade of four narrow, pointed arches; the two in the centre of each group being pierced and glazed, making thus pairs of lancet windows. Over the whole is a plain table with corbels, and a level parapet. Eastward of the great buttress, on the south side, is a small entrance-door, reached by a short flight of steps.

The Portland and Langton Chapels;   But the two chapels are decorated with a triple series of arcades; the lowest, resting on the water-table before named, consists of pointed arches, supported by clustered shafts, and is continued from the last buttress of the "chantry aisles" (interrupted, however, by small three-light Perpendicular windows,[1] the arches of which are carried into the second arcade on each side), the span of the arches differing in different parts of the work, and other irregularities appearing. The second tier stands on a plain table, as does the third, above it, and both of them consist of trefoil-headed arches, on single shafts; those of the second series being smaller than the arches below them, and those of the upper tier smaller still. There are no buttresses, nor any distinct parapet, the coping occurring almost immediately above the highest arcade. In the angles between these chapels and the chantry aisles there are staircases, which are carried up as small and plain octagonal turrets, above the level of the adjoining parts.

and the Lady Chapel.   The end of the Lady Chapel exhibits in the lowest portion of the walls an arcade (or panelling) of pointed arches, without mouldings, but filled with tracery in the Decorated style.[2] In each side, and at the east end, is a splendid seven-light Perpendicular window, under hood-mouldings, somewhat resembling those of Wykeham's windows, with corbel-heads at each termination.[3] Over each window is a cornice with

---

(1) The openings of these windows are of the same character as the arcade into which they are inserted; and are either of the early English, or Transition to the Decorated period, or have been constructed in imitation of that style. The tracery of the windows seems to be early Perpendicular; the heads of the three principal lights being long cinquefoils; and the panel-like tracery next above them turned into two small arches, with a quatrefoil in the apex of the whole. And there can be little doubt that this part of the windows is later than the shafts and mouldings of the openings.

(2) On the south and east sides, a small buttress divides this panelling into two compartments. On the north side it is broken by a doorway, which "is supposed to have opened into a sextry" (Britton, p. 97). The jamb between each pair of arches terminates midway to the base in a corbel; and the mullion dividing each arch descends a still shorter distance, and is similarly ended. The tracery of the panel is of an elegant, flowing character; but see the History of the Cathedral, *infra.*

(3) Professor Willis observes (p. 39) that the tracery of these windows is of "a peculiar kind of subordination, or rather interpenetration, of patterns, well worth a careful study." The mullions are all of the same size;

WINCHESTER CATHEDRAL.

(The Nave — looking East)

bosses, supported by a series of small arches on corbels, and above it is a panelled and pierced battlement, which is also crenellated at the east end. Each angle is strengthened by two buttresses, having three set-offs, and ornamented on the faces of the two lower stages with ogee crocketted canopies and finials. These buttresses terminate abruptly at the level of the battlements with what appear to be the bases of panelled pinnacles, and most probably were originally left thus incomplete.

Close to the ground, at intervals, all round this end of the cathedral, may be seen the openings by which the crypts are faintly lighted; and there is one entrance to them, of modern date, close to the transepts on each side.

Returning now to the western end of the nave, we will commence at that point our survey of the interior of this magnificent pile. Immediately upon entering the central doorway, the long vista of nave, choir, and presbytery, as far as the grand eastern window, appears; the effect being enhanced rather than diminished by the interposition of the choir-screen and reredos. From this point of view the structure appears remarkably homogeneous, and at first would be taken for a fine instance of Perpendicular architecture solely. The circular arches, beneath the lantern, at first seem the only exceptions; but the eye is soon caught by the massive character of the piers on each side of the nave, which betrays their Norman origin, notwithstanding the later style of their shafts and ornaments. But these features do not mar the harmony of the impression produced on the mind; they rather, indeed, act as "accidentals" in a musical composition, and prevent the possibility of the feeling of monotony. *The interior.*

The grandeur of the *coup d'œil* is considerably augmented by the circumstance that the vaulting-shafts rise from the very floor, and are not broken by any rings or bands, so that the eye follows them upwards tardily, as if they were more lofty than they actually are, to the capitals, whence the tracery of the groined roof springs. The great elevation of the pier-arches, which have usurped so much of the vertical space as to leave room for an interrupted gallery merely, instead of the customary triforium, conduces to the same result.

From within, the principal western window appears larger than it does on the outside of the cathedral, since it not only fills up the entire width of the nave, but the mullions are also carried down to the floor, and the wall below the sill is divided into a double series of panels, so that, in effect, the whole of the end of the nave seems to be occupied by this window; and the arch between the two large mullions, containing the double central doorway, and rising to the sill of the window, looks like a disturbance of its regularity,[1] and an encroachment on its proper extent.[2] It is filled with *The west window.*

the two in the centre being carried straight to the top, and the side compartments made into arches of three lights each. There is a transom midway below the spring of the arch; and the heads of the lights under it, and below the tracery, and of the panel-like sections of the tracery, are all cinquefoiled.

1) Willis, p. 64.

(2) The mouldings of the inside of the arch of this window are not of precisely the same character as those without, but more closely resemble those of Wykeham's windows, with their brace-mouldings, boutells, and wide cavettos, and are as unquestionably Perpendicular as the mullions and transoms themselves. But the doorway below, and the other two in the aisles (which are double-

stained glass, some of which is considered to be of Bishop Edington's time ; but it is in a very fragmentary condition, and " only two or three of the original figures, and a few circles of a still earlier date, remain."[1] Two small doors, under cinquefoiled arches, with ogee hood-mouldings, included in the lowest panels, next the pier on each side, conduct to spiral stairs within the octagonal turrets that flank the west end, and afford access to the galleries, roofs, and parapets.

The nave;

Between the west end of the church and the great piers supporting the lantern on each side of the nave (a length of two hundred and sixty-five feet) are twelve arches, one of which is included in the choir ; the nave proper, consequently, consists of eleven compartments, and comprises ten piers, with the half-pier, or respond, at the west end, and half the piers of the arch within the choir screen.   All these compartments, with very few and trifling exceptions, which will be noted, are alike, and the description of one will serve for the whole.

its piers—

Vertically, instead of three parts, the compartment is divided into two only, the triforium being reduced, as was just now stated, to a mere gallery, which seems to be only an appendage to the clerestory.   The plan of the piers was originally not much unlike that of the pillars in the transepts, but the square edges have been " chamfered off, and worked either into a casement or a swelled chamfer ;" new bases set upon a plinth, consisting of " successive portions of octagons," in the place of the Norman plinth, which was " disposed in successive squares ;" the shafts reduced considerably in size ; and both shafts and mouldings carried up to new capitals, at the level of the floor of the Norman triforium, which was entirely done away with.[2] By this means the pier-arches, which are " struck from four centres," have an exceedingly light and elegant appearance, in spite of the magnitude of the piers supporting them.[3] Hooks

feathered), are either Decorated, or of the Transition from that to the Perpendicular ; and the niches beside it in the porch, and the arches of the arcade there (which are divided by a central mullion, and have smaller mullions rising perpendicularly from the apex of each lesser arch), are of the same period.

Each panel is made into a cinquefoiled arch, and the points of the cusps are " decorated each with a small leaf " (Willis, p. 62).

Between the double doorway and the arch including it is a species of tympanum, which is ornamented with narrower panels than those on the wall beside it, but otherwise of the same character.

(1) Winston's " Notice of the Painted Glass in Winchester," &c. ; Arch. Inst., Winchester Volume, p. 3.

(2) Willis, pp. 68—73. The professor points out eight piers (including and beginning at the half-pier at the west end) on the south side of the nave, in which the ashlar of the original Norman construction was left on the lower part, and chiselled into the new form determined on by Wykeham ; but in all the rest the old rubble-work of the pillar alone remains, the ashlar being new (p. 73).

Cresy (Arch. Assoc., Winchester Volume, pp. 389, 390) says :—" The three columns on the east and west sides of the original Saxon [Norman] piers remain unaltered . . . The nave being vaulted as well as the side aisles, a different arrangement was required for the pier ; and hence the addition made on their north and south sides, to effect which the large column is put somewhat in advance, and the square angles or faces at the sides have been cut away, and converted into a splay, hollowed out into OG's, in conformity with the practice of the time ; these sweep round the arches below and above."

During the last repairs of the cathedral, the ninth pier from the west end, on the south side of the nave, adjoining Edington's chantry, was, on account of its ruinous condition, removed and rebuilt, shafts of cast-iron being substituted for those of stone, to give greater security to the work. The iron shafts are coloured like the rest, and do not attract attention by any peculiarity of appearance.

(3) Mr. Carter has directed my attention to the piers in Titchfield Church, as exemplifying Wykeham's style when he was unfettered by earlier constructions. And

and brackets are inserted into the face of the piers, at about three-quarter height, for the suspension of arras on grand occasions in former times.

Immediately above the pier-arch is the triforium gallery, which projects so as to be *triforium—* level with the face of the piers on each side ; and under it is a cornice, with " large and very finely-sculptured bosses" (seven in each compartment), the subjects being various ; and amongst them are the cardinal's hat, deer couchant, the lily, man on horseback, roses, masks, busts, &c. &c.[1] The parapet of the gallery is panelled with small pierced trefoil-headed arches ; and the spandrels of the arch below are panelled to correspond with the rest of Wykeham's work.

The clerestory occupies all the space above this gallery ; and it has the appearance *clerestory—* of a very fine Perpendicular window, " divided at mid-height by a transom, and recessed under a deeply-moulded archway."[2] But only the upper part of the centre is in reality the window, the remainder being panelled-work of a bold and handsome character. Two narrow openings, cut through the panels below the window, give access to the triforium gallery from the roof of the aisle. Behind this panelling, under the present clerestory window, there may still be seen the Norman main arch of the triforium ; but the sub-arches, which were unquestionably exactly like those now to be seen in the transept, have been removed, along with the whole of the Norman clerestory ; the parapet of the gallery of which was as high above the floor as the sill of the existing clerestory window. [3]

Each compartment is bounded by two vaulting-shafts, which rise to the level of *and vaults.* the clerestory window-sill, and send out from above the capital nine diverging ribs to the ridge-rib, by which the whole vault is divided into a series of bisected and interlacing lozenges, as the basis for all the other groining. The bosses are numerous, and bear similar sculptures to those on the cornice beneath the triforium gallery.[4] Careful observers may note here a remarkable violation of harmony in the construction of the vault. In consequence of the vaulting-shafts not being carried high enough, the arch formed by the principal oblique rib is not concentric with the arch of the clerestory window and panelling, but cuts across it at the haunch ; and the vault is, in consequence, so much reduced in height, that the windows seem almost

no greater contrast can be imagined than that between the slender pillars, with their four engaged shafts, of the architect's own performance, and the solid piers, with their manifold shafts, chamfers, and casements, of his renovation of the Norman cathedral.

(1) Britton, p. 103 ; Milner, vol ii. p. 73.

(2) Willis, pp. 70—72. Each compartment of the clerestory is divided perpendicularly by four mullions ; the two external ones being much larger than the others, and forming the sides of the opening of the clerestory window. The panels under the transom are arched with cinquefoiled heads ; and the heads of the panels, of which there is one on each side the window, precisely

resemble the heads of the side-lights in the windows. (See p. 38, n. 1).

(3) Willis (p. 71). The professor shows, side by side, the original state, deduced from a comparison of the remains of it with the transepts ; the present state ; and the intermediate state, which, in fact, exhibits the amount of Norman work still existing in each compartment. " From the gallery of the present triforium, the stuffing or filling in with chalk of the Saxon [Norman] wall is evident ; and the mortar which so firmly holds the mass together forms a concrete of great strength " (Cresy, *u. s.,* p. 388).

(4) Britton, Pls. I., v. and x.

changed into dormers, the intersection of the ribs in front of each being very little above the level of the inner moulding of the apex of the window-arch.[1]

At the ninth pier, counting from the west, the level of the floor of the nave is raised six steps; and between the ninth and the tenth, by four more, the level of the floor of the choir is gained. On each side of the choir-screen, under the last arch of the nave, is an ascent of ten steps from the aisle. Beside these steps on the north, may be seen, unaltered, the shafts and capitals of the original Norman pier, with the upper part of Wykeham's shafts standing on the abacus of each.[2]

The aisles;

The proportions of the aisles to the nave, and to the piers which separate the one from the other, as well as to certain dimensions of the entire church, may be noticed here. The whole interior width of the western portion of the edifice was said to be eighty-eight feet, and that of the nave thirty-two feet; whilst the clear width of the aisle is only thirteen feet. From east to west the thickness of the piers is ten feet; but from north to south it is twelve; and the width of the arches between them only fourteen feet. The exterior wall is eleven feet in thickness. In height there is a greater difference between the aisles and the nave than there is in breadth; the ridge-rib of the groining of the nave being seventy-seven feet from the pavement, whilst the summit of the vault of the aisle is but thirty feet.[3]

their windows—

Internally, the west end of the aisles resembles that of the nave; the mullions of the windows being carried down to the floor, and the space between the sill and the floor being divided by a transom. The panels also are precisely like those under the great west window, and the doorway is included within a larger plain arch, filling up the whole width between the principal mullions; the tympanum and the spandrels being panelled as in the other example. The mouldings of the interior of these side windows are, too (as was noticed respecting those of the central window),

---

(1) This fact was observed by the late Mr. Garbett; and Mr. Carter, to whom he pointed it out, obligingly communicated it to me. Mr. Garbett ascribed this remarkable deviation from the original plan (indicated by the height of the clerestory windows) either to the failure of the funds devoted to the reconstruction of the nave, or, more probably, to the fear that if the plan were carried out the flying buttresses, concealed in the roof of the aisle, would not endure the stress to which they must be subjected. (See Britton, Pl. xxvii.)

It was the opinion of the late Mr. Garbett that the whole of the roof of the nave, "with the exception of about fifty feet in length from the west end," was Norman (Britton, p. 57). We have no means of judging of the correctness of this opinion, beyond the improbability of the accomplishment of such a reconstruction as that commenced by Wykeham without the removal of the roof. (See also Wykeham's Will; Lowth's Life, App., pp. xxxvi—xxxviii., and Reg. Wykeham, II., fol. 233 b.)

The part of the roof nearest the west end is, plainly, more modern than the rest; and, from the appearance of

the older portion at the junction, it must be concluded that a conflagration was the cause of the rebuilding of it. But the vault and walls show no signs of fire, nor is any such destruction recorded. Another unrecorded change made in the western part of the cathedral, by the total removal of two great Norman towers which once flanked it (and which will be mentioned in the "History," *infra*), makes the fact of such a conflagration quite credible.

(2) Willis, pp. 66, 70; Britton, Pl. xi. "Norman shafts still remain above the present vault," and "in the southern side aisle part of the lower extremity of a Norman shaft appears . . . having been, probably, covered by some shrine or altar work." The preservation of the shafts mentioned in the text is ascribed to their being covered by the constructions appended to the rood loft. The buttresses to the clerestory are also Norman. (See p. 38, *supra*). These facts abundantly confirm Professor Willis's views of the "transformation" of the cathedral by Wykeham (pp. 66. 67).

(3) These dimensions are principally taken from Britton, Pls. i., v., xxiv. and xxvii.

of a decidedly Perpendicular character, and therein different from the mouldings of the exterior. This remark applies to the mouldings of the first window in the south aisle, and to those of the first two in the north aisle, which were also said to be externally very nearly like the side windows of the west end.[1]

Each bay, or compartment, of the aisles presents a similar appearance to those in the clerestory of the nave; since the mullions and transoms (the sill of the window being extended across the panel on each side as a transom) divide the space in the same manner; and the heads of the panels are exactly like those already described. *panelling—* But the space beneath the windows, which at the west end is divided into two series of panels, in the aisle forms but one. In the aisles, the vaulting-shafts attached to the *and vaults.* walls are of the same height as those on the piers; and from each spring nine ribs, which divide the vault into squares (there being no ridge-rib), and form lozenges in the centre of each square. The arc of the engaged rib is concentric with the arch of the panelling and the window, and the effect contrasts in a very noticeable manner with that observed in the clerestory of the nave.

The whole of the square between the first pier on the north side of the aisle, and *The "Tribune."* the west end and north wall, is occupied by a gallery, which rises to the level of the lowest transom of the adjoining window. It is supported upon two flattened arches, springing without imposts from the shafts of the pier, and panelled on the face and in the spandrels in the same manner as the walls, but with much narrower arches. The central boss of the groining beneath bears the arms of Wykeham. It is now used as the consistory court and muniment-room of the diocese.[2] Beneath this gallery is the small door into the cemetery, spoken of in a former page,[3] which shows within, as well as without, the well-known characteristics of the Decorated style. Before it are two antique (or even ancient) iron gates, which were removed hither from the top of the steps leading out of the north transept to the aisle of the presbytery.

Few traces of the original doors on the south side, noticed above,[4] can be seen in the interior. In "the west windows of the aisles, and the first window in the south aisle, counting from the west," is some of "the earliest Perpendicular glass in the cathedral, consisting, however, chiefly of the heads of canopies." "The next in date in Winchester Cathedral is the glass in the other windows of the aisles of the nave, and in the clerestory windows of the nave. This is a little later than the glass in the west window." "Much more glass remains on the north than on the south side of the cathedral."[5]

---

(1) See p. 38, n. 3. "The points of the cusps in Edingdon's work are decorated each with a small leaf. In Wykeham's work they are each plain" (Willis, p. 62). This holds good for both panelling and windows; and there is a marked difference in the characters of the bases of the shafts in the two architects' works, as Professor Willis has shown (ibid.).

(2) Milner (vol. ii. p. 118) calls this gallery "the Tribune," and introduces a gorgeous description of some occasional ceremonials of the Church of Rome, in connection with it.

(3) See p. 38, n. 4.

(4) See p. 38, n. 2.

(5) Winston, *u. s.*, p. 3.

The font ;

Under the sixth arch (from the west end) on the north side of the nave, upon a platform raised two steps above the floor, stands the very curious and ancient font, which was for so long a time what Milner designates it—"*crux antiquariorum.*" If it have ceased to be so, it is entirely owing to the acumen of that venerable and learned prelate himself, for he alone has propounded a coherent hypothesis respecting the subjects of its singularly rude but forcible sculptures; and his hypothesis is now very generally accepted.[1]

its sculptures—

The bowl of this font is a square, thick block of very dark-coloured marble, and is covered with sculpture. The basin is circular, and of sufficient size for the complete immersion of an infant. Around it is "a twisted band, or ribbon, alternating with radiating lines." " In two of the angles are doves drinking out of a vase,[2] from which rises the cross; . . . . the other two are filled with foliage. One of the sides is ornamented with three circular bands, fastened together, and containing birds, apparently doves or pigeons, pecking at grapes. . . . . The next side is of the same general design; but in the centre circle is a wild beast,[3] . . . . and the birds, who have no grapes, have open flapping wings, not closed in rest as those of the first side. The claws of the animals and birds on this side are strongly marked.

" On the third side are represented [two] women leading men to a bishop, at whose feet one man kneels; his costume would seem to indicate an Anglo-Saxon.[4] That these are people of distinction is made clear by the falcon, or hawk, which one of them bears on his wrist. The church from which the bishop proceeds is in the Norman style, with a roof formed of circular tiles, and a door remarkable for its lock and ornamental hinges. On the fourth side a bishop is represented holding a small figure by the hand, and apparently telling it to be of good cheer; whilst another figure with an axe kills or knocks down three men at a blow.[5] Farther on stands the same bishop, with his crozier resting on a recumbent figure, apparently the same youth, who holds a cup in his hand on the extreme left, the bishop grasping him by the arm.[6] And, lastly, three men are seen in a boat, two of whom are in attitudes expressive of grief, whilst the third has his hands raised."[7]

(1) Milner, vol. ii. pp. 113—118.

(2) Milner says, " breathing into phials surmounted with crosses" (p. 113).

(3) Called by Milner (ibid.) " a salamander."

(4) The kneeling figure seems to be receiving a bag of money from the bishop; the second man is also holding a bag of money; and the females might as accurately be described as led by the men to him. Mr. Owen B. Carter pointed out to me that the ornaments suspended around the necks of some of these figures appear exactly to resemble the well-known jewel of King Alfred.

Both the costume of the figures and the architecture of the church are well deserving of notice; but the arrangement of the females' hair, their wide sleeves, the form of the mitre, with other points, belong to the early part of the twelfth century.

(5) Only three heads are represented, and a mantle appears to cover the prostrate bodies; and the man with the axe seems rather to be preparing to strike. Between him and the bishop is another person, not accounted for by Milner. There is an upright division between this group of figures and the next to the right.

(6) In front of the bishop, and above the figure spoken of here, appear the upper parts of two other figures, recumbent, with their hands raised; and the head of that mentioned in the text is directly beneath the rudder of the ship, or boat, which occupies the remainder of the side.

(7) One of the men in the boat (which has a mast and stays, and dragons' heads at the prow and the stern) has his arm over the tiller; and the form of the vessel is precisely similar to that which is seen on so many seals of our seaport towns of the twelfth century.   [This

This bowl stands upon a large central shaft, rudely ornamented with rings or bands round it at intervals; and on four smaller shafts (two of them twisted), inclining inwards at the angles, with corolla-like capitals, and very simple mouldings for bases, the whole standing on another square block of marble, which is ornamented with a double row of radiating lines.[1]

Little doubt can be entertained respecting the emblematic nature of the sculptures —and their signification. on the upper surface of the bowl, and on the first and second sides described above; nor that they refer to the rite of baptism. The Holy Spirit, the change from unregeneracy to regeneracy, and the sustenance of the regenerate spirit, are plainly typified by the beaked and clawed birds and animal, the doves, the grapes, and the vessels surmounted by the cross; but concerning the two other sculptures there has been much doubt, and some controversy. The earliest conjecture hazarded which requires notice here was by Mr. Gough,[2] who thought that the font was of the age of St. Birinus, and that it represented the history of that saint. Milner has satisfactorily refuted this exceedingly untenable hypothesis.[3] His own explanation is, that it represents various scenes from the legendary life of St. Nicholas of Myra; which, since he was the patron of children, would most appropriately ornament a font. And, it may be remarked, although the legends as related by Milner do not completely agree with the sculptures, the discrepancy is not greater than is common in such cases; and might be in good part explained, did we know where the font was made, by the version of the stories prevalent at that place.[4]

Milner considers the subject of the sculpture first described above to be the rescue of the three daughters of "a man of noble birth, but reduced to poverty," from a life of shame; but only two females appear, there not being "sufficient space to exhibit the nuptials of the third daughter." In the crowded groups on the other side of the font he detects four legends of this celebrated saint: the stilling of a storm during a voyage to Egypt; the restoration of life to one of the seamen who had been killed by falling from the mast, and the healing of many sick persons at Alexandria; the rescue of three young men from the axe of the executioner at Myra; and the preservation from drowning of a nobleman's son, who was on a voyage with his father to Myra, to present a golden cup in the cathedral there, in fulfilment of a vow,—which occurred after the death of the saint, and is represented on the font in

---

This description is taken from the "Handbook to the Byzantine and Romanesque Court in the Crystal Palace," by M. Digby Wyatt and J. B. Waring, pp. 118, 119.

(1) The dimensions of this font are as follow:—Entire height, 3 feet 2 inches; length of side of bowl, 3 feet 3 inches; depth of bowl, 1 foot 6½ inches; diameter of basin, 2 feet 4 inches at top, and 1 foot 7 inches at bottom; depth of basin, 1 foot 3 inches; height of central shaft, 1 foot 6 inches; height of smaller shafts, 1 foot 4 inches.

(2) Vetusta Monumenta, vol. ii: explanation accompanying two engravings of these sculptures. See also Lord Clarendon and Gale's "Antiquities, &c.," and Warton's "Description, &c."

(3) Vol. ii. pp. 113, 114.

(4) Milner (p. 115) refers to the *Portiforium, seu Breviarium, in usum Sarum*, the "Golden Legend," and the "Lives of the Saints" by Surius, where the account is translated from Symeon Metaphrastes. See also "Emblems of Saints," by the Very Rev. Dr. Husenbeth, p. 105.

H

two scenes, in the first of which the youth appears in the water, and in the second under the safe conduct of the bishop.[1]

Its date.   From the dress of the figures in these sculptures, as well as from the architecture of the church represented in one of them, and the general style of the ornaments, this font is now regarded as the workmanship of the middle of the twelfth century.[2] There are two others very similar in character to it in this county; one at East Meon, and the other in the Church of St. Michael, Southampton, which will be described in future pages of this work. Another exists in Lincoln Cathedral.[3]

Of the chantries of Wykeham and Edington we shall speak in a subsequent section of the present part.

The transepts;   The choir at Winchester, as in other Norman cathedrals, is situated beneath the central tower; and the choir-screen is in a line with the western wall of the transept, inclosing (as we before remarked) one pier and one arch of the nave. With the exception of this arch, and the compartments in the aisle beside it, all which are Wykeham's work,[4] the chapel of the Holy Sepulchre, the stalls of the choir, and some screens, &c., evidently modern, this part of the cathedral, from north to south, is Norman. It is in the transepts that the oldest and rudest work is to be seen; and the first glance round the north transept—although a new ceiling has taken the place of the thickly-laid rafters of the old roof, and only the faintest vestiges of the original polychromy remain—is singularly awe-inspiring; so faithfully does the style of the architecture mirror the religion of the rugged descendants of the sea-kings, in which were strength and completeness of conviction, indeed, but neither grace nor tenderness.

—their piers;   It has already been said that the transepts have not only east and west aisles,

(1) "In the year 1817," says Mr. Cresy, "when at Bari, on the south-eastern coast of Italy, the author made a drawing of a stone tablet placed against the east end of the Church of St. Nicholas containing precisely the same legend. This church, or royal priory, was erected by King Roger, the Norman, and within it were deposited the remains of this celebrated Bishop of Myra in 1087, who was held in high estimation by the Normans settled on the coast of Italy" (Arch. Assoc., Winchester Volume, p. 379). Mr. Cresy proceeds to state that, on account of this similarity between the sculptures on this font and that in the Norman churches in southern Italy, "we may assume it to have been brought from Bari, or its neighbourhood." But the thoroughly English character of the sculptures is so apparent as to forbid the indulgence of this hypothesis, even if the material of which the font is formed should not be, as Mr. Carter tells me, marble from the *lias* of England.

(2) Britton (p. 107) ascribes this font to Walkelyn's time, as does Mr. Cresy (*u. s.* p. 378). The opinion of Gough, that it was of the age of Birinus, does not require refutation.

(3) All these fonts have been repeatedly engraved and described. For further remarks on Winchester font, reference may be made to Carter's "Ancient Architecture" (P.V.D. xxxii. 29). A small but accurate model of it was constructed for the Camden (or Ecclesiological) Society, from drawings to scale, by Mr. O. B. Carter; and a full-sized model of it is in the Byzantine Court of the Crystal Palace.

At the foot of the first pier from the western entrance, on the north side of the aisle, is the base of a small font or stoup, the material of which very closely resembles that of the great font—if it be not Purbeck marble. It shows only that the bowl stood upon a round stem, with four small attached shafts opposite the angles of the base, and that it was most probably in the Early English style.

(4) The termination of the aisles in the west side of each transept is effected by arches resembling the pier-arches of the nave, but much narrower, in consequence of the vast size of the tower-piers; with a triforium gallery (as in the nave) over each, behind which rises the crown of the Norman triforium arch, and all above it remains in its original condition.

but terminal aisles also; and that above the former are triforia and clerestories.[1]
Between the tower-piers and the north and south walls of the transepts, there are, on
each side, three piers, or four compartments; and of these, the two adjoining to the
tower-piers in each transept are continuous with the aisles of the nave and the choir;
and the two next the north and south walls open into the terminal aisles. So many
alterations have taken place in this part of the cathedral, that only two piers in each
transept retain their original appearance.[2] Those supporting the tower, and the two
next them in each direction, display much better workmanship than the others, and,
apparently, have been rebuilt. They are also (as it would seem) of larger dimensions
than those at first erected; the tower-piers very much larger, for they now measure
fifteen feet ten inches in length from east to west, and twelve feet eight inches in
breadth from north to south;[3] whilst the piers next to them exceed their original
measurement by at least three feet from north to south, though in the other direction
they have not been increased.[4] A very remarkable addition has been made to the piers
at the angles of the transept; the faces opposite the side walls having been extended
towards the end of the transept in each case, so as to make room for a second engaged
shaft on it, and thereby to enable it to carry an arch twice the width of that which at
first crossed the aisle there.[5] The piers in the centre of the terminal aisles differ
from all the others in being plain, round columns, four feet four inches in diameter,
and have the aspect of being additions to the first plan of this part of the cathedral.[6]

(1) Instead of a triforium gallery, there is a mere
platform, unfurnished even with a parapet, over the terminal aisles of the transept.

(2) Each of these is "a massive square pier, with large
shafts in recesses at the angles, and other large shafts attached to the faces, one carrying the sub-arch, and another
the vaulting-shaft, rising from the ground." (Rickman's
"Gothic Architecture," p. xix., fifth edition.)

(3) Willis, pp. 29—32. The plan of these piers—which,
according to Professor Willis (p. 29), "are the largest
tower-piers in England in proportion to the spans of the
arches that rest on them"—is simple; each consists of a
square, with a broad and shallow segmental shaft, and a
smaller one on each side of it, towards the body of the
church, and on the opposite side responds agreeing (in
the eastern piers) with the Norman piers in the transept,
or (in the western) with Wykeham's of the nave. The
west piers on their western faces have the responds of
Wykeham's arches, and vaulting-shafts at the inner
angles; and the east piers on their eastern faces the
responds of the decorated arches of the presbytery, together with parts of the original Norman responds (consisting of a wide shaft, and a smaller one on each side of
it), which, not interfering with the later additions, were
not removed. A rectangular addition has been made to
the sides of these squares for the purpose of increasing the
strength of them, by which the arches opening into the
transepts are made considerably narrower than those

spanning the body of the church, and there are three
shafts of equal size on the face of each to carry those
arches, and engaged shafts at the angles, which run up to
the lowest string-course round the interior of the lantern
on one side, and to the wall-plate of the transept wall on
the other. The bases of the shafts supporting the tower-
arches stand upon plinths, rising about four feet from the
floor of the presbytery. The capitals are all of a very plain
Norman type, and the arches are semicircular and recessed,
with plain soffits and rectangular edges, but on the east
and west sides (there not being sufficient space for the
completion of the outer arch) the edge is brought down
perpendicularly upon the abacus of the smaller shafts. This,
however, is hidden now by the wooden vaulting inserted
by Charles I.

(4) This lateral expansion gives these piers the aspect
of being portions of a wall in which the adjoining arches
have been formed. "It will be observed," says Professor
Willis, "that the pier in its new form is considerably
stronger than before, although the same number of
shafts are disposed upon the respective faces" (p. 29).

(5) "The evidences of this change are shown by the
joints of the masonry, and by the capital and its abacus,
in a way that when once pointed out cannot be mistaken"
(Willis, p. 26).

(6) Next the aisles there are attached to these columns
rectangular pilasters, with engaged shafts to support the
vault of the gallery or platform above.

—their arches and decoration·

Almost all the capitals of the columns in the transept are of a very common Norman type.[1] The arches were all, originally, semicircular; but, in consequence of the alterations made necessary by the rebuilding of the tower, the first and second from the tower-piers, on each side, have been changed into stilted or horse-shoe arches. Excepting those supporting the platforms at the ends of the transepts, which have a single soffit only, they are double-recessed, and all have plain square edges, without the least appearance of ornament, or even of finish, polychromatic decoration alone being designed by the architect of the oldest portion of the cathedral.[2]

Few of the windows remain in precisely their first condition; but where they have not been altered, we see circular-headed and splayed openings, recessed within plain arches, supported by shafts of the same character,[3] and standing on a semi-hexagonal string-course, which, originally, was carried quite round the walls of each transept (and most probably along those of the whole building), and, as a band, round the columns of the responds also.[4] Beneath the string-course was an arcade of semicircular arches.[5] The vaults of the compartments on the western sides of the transept, and of the two in the centre of each end, are "plain groined vaults, but those of the eastern compartments are ribbed."[6]

Beside the doorway in the western wall of the north transept (which is now stopped up), and the entry into the south transept from the dark cloister, there are doorways in both transepts to spiral staircases in the eastern angles, and a modern opening to the crypts in the south-eastern corner of the north transept. A wooden

(1) "A plain cushion capital, with the abacus most common in this style" (Rickman, p. xxi.) The capitals of the round columns under the platforms, at the end of the transept, are plain and round with thin square abaci (Willis, p. 36).

(2) Vestiges of this polychromy can even now be discovered in the north transept. "In particular," says Milner (vol. ii. p. 111), "against the west wall, at the extremity of the transept, are still seen the traces of a colossal figure of . . . . St. Christopher carrying Christ. Over this subject is clearly discernible that of the Adoration of the Magi." And Mr. J. G. Waller observes (Arch. Assoc., Winchester Volume, p. 268), "there is in one corner a boldly-outlined figure of a king," and "that the soffits of the arches . . . . are painted with patterns of very early character." This satisfactorily explains the want of finish so apparent in the whole of this the most ancient part of the cathedral; it was not intended to remain as we see it, but to be plastered, and covered with Byzantine or Romanesque decorations.

(3) The abaci of these shafts are prolonged to the vaults on each side, and the same is to be noted respecting those of the arches over the windows in the triforia and clerestories.

(4) No band encompasses the shafts which serve for responds to those mentioned p. 51, as constructed on

the enlarged faces of the piers at the angles of the transepts, to carry a wide arch in the direction of east and west on each side. It is wanting also in a few others.

(5) There is no arcade under the windows of the eastern walls of the transepts; it was removed "when altars were attached to the walls" (Cresy, p. 373). And that at the northern end of the transept was restored during the last repairs of the cathedral.

(6) Willis, p. 25. Several of the capitals of the arcade are of a more elaborate character than those already spoken of; being "sculptured to represent busts of kings" in one part (Britton, p. 84). And in some of the shafts of the responds carved stones have been introduced, but in such a way as not to appear parts of any different system of decoration from that which has been described above.

Britton observes that there is "a curious piscina" in the western isle of the north transept; and calling attention to a canopied niche in the side of a pier of the eastern aisle, remarks, that "from other ornaments of this compartment of the aisle we may infer that it was formerly fitted up as a private oratory or chantry chapel" (pp. 84, 91). Milner asserts (vol. ii. p. 111) the existence of seven of these chapels in the north transept, and marks the presumed sites of their altars on his "Ichnography of the Cathedral Church."

W.H.Bartlett.

F.Challis.

WINCHESTER CATHEDRAL.

INTERIOR OF NORTH TRANSEPT.

staircase, occupying half one of the central compartments at the end of the south transept, gives access to the choristers' schoolroom and the cathedral library through the doorway mentioned above.[1]

All the aisles in the south transept are inclosed in part by solid masonry, and in part by screens of wood and stone.[2] The two southmost compartments of the west aisle are now used as the chapter-house and vestry for the dean and canons, and that next the body of the church as the treasury.[3] The terminal aisle serves as a sort of porch or lobby.[4] On the east, the compartment in the centre, denominated Silkstede's Chapel, is used by the lay clerks; and the northern compartment, called the Venerable Chapel, is the minor canon's vestry. The tracery of the screens of these last-named chapels is very rich and elegant.[5] In the north transept, until the last

—aisles and chapels;

(1) See p. 40.

(2) The terminal aisle is inclosed by panelled screens of oak, of a very recent date, to the levels of the capitals of the columns; and similar wood-work fills up the lower part of the central arch of the west aisle, in which is the entrance to the chapter-house. The whole of this aisle is, however, separated by masonry from the transept; and at the end next the aisle of the nave may be seen two semicircular arches, exhibiting the common round Norman mouldings and cavettos, within very good nail-head, billet, and indented mouldings, standing on fluted pilasters, with flat escalloped, and channelled capitals. The centre pilaster is carried up from the junction of the arch-mouldings through a string-course above. Two other arches (closely resembling them) decorate the face of the masonry between the piers of the first compartment of the aisle; but the two circular segments composing each have been put together so as to make pointed arches; and the inner arch-mouldings are a species of zigzag. All these arches and pilasters have evidently been removed from some other place and inserted here without much regard to their congruence with each other, or with the position assigned them. The arches and capitals are, most probably, late Norman; but the pilasters are of a much newer style, and there is nothing to indicate either the time or the reason for their insertion in the walls in which they now are.

(3) Milner calls this "the ancient sacristy, or sextry," and appears to regard it as part of the first plan of the cathedral. In the chapter-house, he says, "Against the west wall we see certain ancient presses bearing upon them the device of Silkstede, the original use of which seems to have been to keep the great habits of the monks, or large outside garments," and that they "are still made use of for containing the surplices of the choristers and singing-men" (vol. ii. pp. 77, 78). The muniments of the chapter are kept here, and a model of the enormous framework of timber set up by the late Mr. Garbett, to sustain the weight of the clerestory and roof when he restored the piers of the nave near Edington's chantry.

A portrait of Bishop Morley, exactly like that in the Town-hall, hangs in the chapter-house.

(4) A wooden bench of curiously rude construction, and as rudely ornamented, stands in this lobby. From its general appearance, Professor Willis says (p. 54) "it might be coëval with the transept itself." There is also a sort of chafing-dish of equally rough workmanship.

(5) Milner designates the southmost compartment the "Calefactory" (u. s.). The wooden screens inclosing it on both sides are of panelled oak, and part of it is converted into open-work by leaving the panels out of their frames. The screen of Silkstede's Chapel does not reach to the capitals of the columns, and is divided into four compartments, and surrounded by a cornice with bosses. There is a richly-foliated doorway, under an ogee crocketted canopy, with a finial, in the compartment to the north; and the lower part of the others beneath a transom is merely panelled, leaving a plain plinth, or base, of about two feet deep. The upper part of each compartment is open-work, and is arched, with pierced quatrefoils in the spandrels; each arch being divided by two mullions, and filled up above with quatrefoil tracery. On the cornice are carved the letters of the Christian name of the prior after whom the chapel is named— THOMAS; "yet so that M. A., the monogram of his patroness, the Blessed Virgin, are distinguished from the rest; together with a skein of silk [or, as Britton (p. 83) says, the letter S], as a rebus upon his surname" (Milner, vol. ii. p. 78). The lock of this chapel is a very curious one from its rude simplicity and its ornaments.

In the Venerable Chapel the screen not only fills up the whole archway, but the highly-ornamented canopies extend beyond the sweep of the arch. There are eight of these canopies with crockets and finials, and the upper part of the screen has as many compartments. The lower part has three compartments, flanked by two smaller ones. In the centre is the entrance, under a finely-canopied double arch. And the openings in the tracery of the other portions are defended by very "elaborate and beautiful iron-work" (Willis, pp. 53, 54). It

repairs of the cathedral, the western aisle was inclosed;[1] but it is evident that the original design of the architect left all these aisles open, as those in the north transept are at the present time.

—triforia;　　On both sides of the transepts the triforium exhibits three complete compartments, in each of which a plain and square-edged semicircular arch has two similar sub-arches beneath it. Most of the capitals of the columns supporting these arches are of the very plainest Norman type—"a square block, with the lower angles rounded off, so as to resemble a common wooden bowl;"[2] but others are like those on the columns of the piers, and some present only a bifid appearance. A few of them show rude attempts at ornament.[3] One compartment of the western sides has been destroyed in the formation of the terminal arch of the aisles of the nave,[4] and on the opposite sides the plain arch with the double sub-arch has been reconstructed on a smaller scale, over a corbel table on a level with the middle of the shafts of the other compartments. There are no sub-arches in the compartments communicating with the platform at the north end.[5] The roofs over the triforia require no special remark; and the windows at the north end exactly resemble those of the aisles below.[6]

—clerestories;　　A plain string-course runs completely round the walls over the arches of the triforia and the terminal windows, above which rises the parapet of the *alura* of the clerestory. There are four compartments on each side, but the only common features are the rather narrow and plain splayed Norman archways, with small columns, the capitals of which are midway between the bases and imposts of the arches.[7] There are engaged-shafts on the faces of the first and second piers (reckoning from the tower-piers) reaching to the top of the wall; but the corresponding shafts, with pier-edges between the terminal and the next compartments of the triforia, at the front of the platform at each end, are abruptly discontinued a little above the capitals of the adjoining columns,

---

is separated by a similar screen, only without canopies, from Silkstede's Chapel. From the situation of this chapel, and from its being profusely ornamented and well secured, Milner (*u. s.*) "is led to believe that the blessed sacrament used to be kept there for the benefit of the sick, and for private communions."

(1) During the repairs this inclosed aisle was used as a workshop for the stonemasons engaged in the alterations and restorations, and the low Norman doorway was opened for their passage to and fro. But the inclosure would seem to date, at least, from the consecration of the chapels contained in the aisle.

(2) Rickman, p. 74. Some of the central columns have higher bases than others; and some of the joints are much longer than is usual.

(3) Cresy says that the ornament referred to "bears a strong resemblance to the Grecian" (Pl. XXIII); but it still more strongly bears marks of having been taught the Normans by Byzantine (rather than Grecian) architects.

(4) See p. 46.

(5) Britton, Pl. XII.; Winkle's Cathedrals, Pl. XLVIII.

(6) A square pilaster, or interior buttress, with square edges in the angles it makes with the wall, is carried up from the platform, between these windows, and to the base of the gable, in a narrower and shallower form. Three rectangular edges fill up each corner also.

(7) Next the tower two compartments in each transept have been rebuilt, and the first arch has been reduced in span, but the arches of the terminal compartments are wider than the two central arches, and are rather flattened in consequence. The columns, spoken of in the text, support small open arches in each jamb of the central window-archways, but only on one side in the other two. This description applies to the window-arches of the ends of the transepts on the level of the clerestory, which have the small arch in but one jamb. The abaci of the window-arches are of the common Norman type, and are prolonged in each direction to the nearest pier. The capitals of the small columns are of the two kinds seen in the clerestory.

and it is plain, from the construction of the clerestory immediately above, that it was never intended to carry them up to the roof like the others.[1]

Nothing can now be seen above the level of the side walls, for during the last alterations of the cathedral a flat wooden ceiling, painted in imitation of " the early Tudor style," was put up, by which the great rose window in the gable of the north transept, and the bare timbers of the roof, formerly exposed, have been concealed from view.[2]

—and roofs.

Between the two great tower-piers on the north side of the choir is a very interesting chapel, known as the Chapel of the Holy Sepulchre. Milner, who determined its purpose, and gave it this name, describes it as " a dark chapel, that has hitherto been overlooked ;" and gives a very brief account of the paintings, which, he says, " from the rudeness of their style, are known to be proportionably ancient."[3] Next the choir, the wall of this chapel seems to be level with the face of the piers, but towards the transept it projects as far as the level of the shafts supporting the arches which open into the aisles. Externally, it is divided into two compartments by a flat buttress, rising nearly to the height of a cornice or string-course under the parapet. At each end of the front is another similar but narrower buttress. In each compartment is a large arched opening, but the lower part of that to the west has been stopped with masonry (pierced in one part with a quatrefoil), in which is a narrow and plain Early English doorway near the western end. There are two compartments in the interior also, each having a plain ribbed vault ; but that in the western compartment has been destroyed to make way for a spiral stair to the organ-loft above, and holes have been cut through the other vault for the passage of the arms of the levers used in blowing the organ.[4]

Chapel of the holy sepulchre ;

---

(1) The engaged-shafts in the central piers of the transepts on both sides remain in their pristine condition ; and instead of being carried up uninterruptedly, the portions crossing the triforia and clerestory are each set back from the level of the portions beneath them, producing an exceedingly unpleasing effect. In the clerestory there is a small arch (with a pair of smaller open arches under it) carried across the whole space between the terminal window-arches and those nearest to them on both sides ; so that the pier-edges and engaged-shafts at the front of the platform could not have been designed to rise above the string-course over the triforium, and most probably would not have been carried so high, for the masonry of the walls above the terminations of those shafts has been disturbed, as if some construction had crossed the transepts there. It may confirm this view to remark that a slender engaged-shaft rises from the abacus of the round column under the platform at each end, which would not have been required if there were no superstructure. (See Willis, pp. 24, 25.)

(2) " The roof of the transept, northward of the tower, being of a construction very different from that of the nave and southern part of the transept, we must conclude that the decay of the Norman roof in that situation was

more rapid, and that it required renewal before the other parts ; for we cannot suppose that Walkelyn would have left this part incomplete" (Garbett, *apud* Britton, p. 57). In the south transept the appearance of the roof quite confirms the story related of the bishop's "too greedy" use of William's "too liberal" grant of timber from Hempage Wood, to assist the rebuilding of the cathedral. (See " History," *infra*.)

The ascent from the triforia to the clerestory, and thence to the *alura* across the north gable, is by a stair in the massive buttress flanking the gable.

Professor Willis (pp. 26—28) explains the alteration of the piers and arches at the angles of the transept, the greater width of the window-arches of the terminal compartments of the clerestory, and other similar indications, noticed above, by the addition of square flanking towers to the *plan* of the transept, after the building " had risen to the height of the pier-arches," a change which was never fully carried out.

(3) Vol. ii. pp. 100, 101.

(4) Britton (Pl. i.) indicates the position of an altar at the eastern end of this chapel ; but as the chapel is now occupied by the apparatus for blowing the organ, a stove,

—and its
paintings.

"The most complete, and perhaps the finest portion [of the paintings which decorated this chapel], is on the east end of the vault. It is a colossal head and bust of
Christ, grandly conceived; it is nimbed, and holding the book of the Gospels in the
hand, on which is written, in Longobardic capitals, 'SALVS POPVLI EGO SVM.' The
right hand . . . . is gone, through the destruction of the plaster. . . . . About the
figure, and filling up the spandrels of a cuspated border, with which it is inclosed,
are the remains of evangelistic symbols."[1] On the wall, beneath this figure of the
Saviour, is represented the Descent from the Cross, and under it the Entombment.
The Nativity is depicted on another segment of the vault, with an elegant flower ornament inclosing two medallions containing the heads of patriarchs, prophets, or apostles.
Under it, on the wall, is the Entry into Jerusalem and the Raising of Lazarus.[2]
Lower still, within a semicircular border, intended to represent an arch (in the spandrels of which were two other medallions, now defaced) are two subjects, the Descent
into Hell and the Appearing to Mary Magdalene in the Garden. In another part of
the vault is the Annunciation. "The other compartments on the roof are too mutilated
to be made out. They seem to have consisted of the Appearance of the Angels to the
Shepherds, and other subjects immediately connected with the Birth. An impost on
the north wall seems to have had painted on it the Dispute with the Doctors;" and
little more can be satisfactorily made out; it is, "however, curious that traces of an
entire series of paintings, of previous execution, are seen beneath, where the plaster
has fallen."[3] Upon the roof of this chapel stands the organ.[4]

Choir-screen,
stalls, &c.

Towards the west, the choir is separated from the nave by an elegant screen, corresponding in its style with the lower part of the west front of the cathedral, in two
niches of which stand bronze figures of James I. and Charles I.[5] At the back of this

and a staircase, it is impossible to verify this. If it were
the Chapel of the Holy Sepulchre, however, it seems unlikely that the side next the choir should be closed; and
the arched openings on the other side are plainly not coeval with the rest of the structure, being flattened rather
than four-centred arches. The doorway, and the string-
course immediately above it, which is carried round all
these buttresses, are most probably parts of its first plan.
The canopies and wood-work over the stalls of the choir
are of a date subsequent to this chapel.

The internal dimensions, for which I am indebted to
Mr. O. B. Carter, are, length, 21 feet; width, 9 feet
3 inches; and height to summit of vault, 13 feet.

(1) Arch. Assoc., Winchester Volume, pp. 265, 266;
and Pl. x.

(2) Ibid., p. 266; and Pl. XI.

(3) Ibid., p. 265. From these "Observations on the
paintings in Winchester Cathedral," by John Green
Waller, which were written before the destruction spoken
of in the text, I will quote the following account of other
paintings in this chapel:—

"The other designs, on the north wall, appear to have
been devoted to the Apocalyptic visions and prophecies,

and, it is to be regretted, are too much mutilated for us to
decide correctly as to the several subjects. The upper
part appears to have had 'The Last Judgment,' and this
portion shows very distinct indications of the previous
layer of paintings before noticed. Beneath the arch
. . . . are the scanty remains of a composition, apparently
the sufferings of the martyrs and saints. . . . . The Crucifixion probably occupied part of the west wall. There
are still remains of figures on horseback to be traced
through the smearing of limewash; but the greater part
of the plaster of this wall has been destroyed. The
subject beneath appears to relate to the murder of Abel"
(pp. 267, 268).

(4) For an account of this splendid instrument see the
Official Catalogue of the Great Exhibition. It has, however, now but fifty-four stops; the largest pipe (CCCC)
is thirty-two feet long, and the smallest (C) three quarters
of an inch; it has now four rows of keys, and other alterations have been made to adapt it to its present use.

(5) This screen is the work of the late Mr. Garbett,
and it replaced one of the composite order, "said to have
been designed by Inigo Jones," but of which Britton
(p. 80) remarks "it is a bad and unsightly object. It

screen are the stalls of the choir, which extend on each side, eastward, as far as " the western corner of the eastern tower-piers;" where they "are terminated on the north side by a rich pulpit of wood, which bears the name of its donor, 'Thomas Silkstede, Prior,' on different parts of it. The wood-work of the stalls is exceedingly rich and beautiful. It has, however, been subjected to various alterations, that may be easily detected upon examination. They are of early Decorated work, and their canopies and gables bear considerable resemblance to that of the tomb of Edward Crouchback, in Westminster Abbey, as Milner has most truly observed. . . . . The desks and stools in front of the upper range bear the initials of Henry VIII., of Bishop Stephen Gardiner, Dean W. Kingsmill, and the date 1540."[1] Opposite the pulpit, on the south side of the choir, but at the eastern corner of the tower-pier, is the episcopal throne,[2] almost in front of which, where the higher level of the presbytery is reached by three broad steps from the choir, stands the gilt eagle or lectern.

A wooden vaulted ceiling now fills up the tower to the level of the first gallery; *Interior of the tower.* and in the centre of the four compartments of fan-tracery is the emblem of the Trinity surrounded by a chronogram of the year in which this ceiling was inserted.[3] There can be no doubt, from the construction and decoration of the interior, that it

may be said to be in the Grecian or Roman style; indeed, it may be pronounced anything but in place and in harmony." Before the erection of this "offensive screen" there must have been one of a different character, which had been set up after the Reformation, but nothing is known respecting it. In the period preceding the Reformation, the rood-screen, with the rood-loft above it, occupied this place, and extended to the next piers towards the west, as we may conclude from the old Norman work which still shows on the eastern face of the piers on the northern side. On this loft stood " the great cross, with the two images of Mary and John, richly clothed in gold and silver," as well as the beam on which they were placed, which the annals of Winchester say Bishop Stigand constructed out of the gifts of Queen Emma to Winchester Cathedral. (See Willis, pp. 16, 52.)

There are shields within quartrefoils in the spandrels of the arch over the doorway of this screen, instead of panelling, as in the western porch. And the bronze figures are even more out of place here than they are in Inigo Jones's classical screen.

(1) Willis, p. 52; Milner, vol. ii. p. 82; Britton, Pl. xiv. pp. 76, 92, 98. The canopies represented in numerous monumental brasses figured in Boutell's valuable work on that subject, and still more frequently in ecclesiastical seals, almost to the end of the fifteenth century, are of the same character precisely as those in the choir of Winchester Cathedral.

The Rev. C. Walters, who has examined these stalls very minutely, is of opinion that the pinnacles are not of the same date as the canopies; and it is very observable that they are inserted *behind* the bases of the gables,

whilst in the monumental brasses, almost universally, the pinnacles are placed in *front* of the point of junction. I am further informed by Mr. Walters that much of this wood-work is mere *deal*, and that the whole is so thickly coated with dark brown paint that it is not easy to distinguish the original oak from the newer and viler wood.

In the carvings of the *misereres* are many grotesque designs; but the general impression produced is that of great richness and variety. Over the stalls is a gallery; the ascent on the north side being by a staircase carried through the ceiling of the Chapel of the Holy Sepulchre, and on the south by stairs from the transept behind the stalls. Before the last alterations, a " boarded partition" filled up the whole of the tower-arch above the stalls (Britton, p. 92).

(2) The present throne was designed by Mr. Garbett, its style is in harmony with the stalls. Its predecessor (the gift of Bishop Trelawney) was, as Britton calls it (p 80), " Romanised," and completely inconsistent with the character and architecture of the edifice in general.

(3) Milner (vol. i. p. 83) notes amongst the ornaments of this wooden ceiling " the arms, initials, and devices of King Charles I.; of his royal consort, Henrietta Maria; and of the Prince of Wales; as likewise the arms of Scotland and Ireland apart; with those of Laud, Archbishop of Canterbury; of Curle, bishop of this see and of Young, dean of the cathedral. . . . . Also a curious medallion of the royal pair, with their faces in profile and their legend round it." In the angles of the tower, the tracery used to spring from gaudily-painted busts of James I. and Charles I. (with mottoes attached to them), instead of corbels; but in the recent restorations these

ɪ

was intended for a lantern to the choir; and that the insertion of floors, and the use of it as a bell-turret are departures from the original design. The first story on each side exhibits an arcade of four narrow, recessed, Norman arches, the outer ones opening to the small, circular-headed windows, which externally appear beside the adjoining roofs.[1] In the upper story are seen the long windows described above, beneath circular arches, with a gallery running round it beneath them.[2] This is now the clock and bell chamber.

The crypts   Beneath the presbytery and its aisles, extending from the eastern tower-piers to the first piers of the retro-choir, is the great crypt. The architecture is of the same rude Norman style as that of the transepts. It consists of a central apartment, with an apsidal termination eastwards, and divided in two by a longitudinal row of five columns; and of two aisles, which have square eastern ends, but are also continued round the semicircular end of the other portion.[3] Beyond this, and opening into it, a second crypt, of less width even than the central part of the first crypt, but, like it, divided longitudinally by a row of five columns, and having an apsidal termination, reaches to the end of the retro-choir.[4] A third crypt (not wider than the second), the vaulting of which rests on two columns, rectangular in its plan, and far more recent in its architecture, forms the substructure of the present Lady Chapel. The way to this crypt is broken through the semicircular end of the second.[5] They all have loops in their external walls, but only the first and third receive any light from without.[6] There are three entrances from the exterior of the cathedral, and one from the north transept; but originally the access was by stairs at the western extremities of the

were removed, and clusters of dwarf pillars substituted for them. The chronogram reads thus :—

" sInt DoMVs hVjVs pIl reges nVtrItII, regInæ nVtrIces pIæ."

The larger letters, which are also distinguished from the others by their colour, MDCVVVVVIIIIIIIII., are equivalent in Roman notation to 1634, the date of the work.

(1) See p. 39. This arcade stands upon a plain string-course over a zigzag moulded cornice. Each compartment consists of four recessed arches with round, zigzag, and other mouldings, on shafts with plain capitals, &c. Under the small windows are doorways leading to the roofs above the vaults of the nave and the presbytery, and to the ceilings and clerestory galleries of the transepts. Staircases in the angles give access to the upper story.

(2) Ibid., and note 2. Each arch has plain round and double-billet mouldings, and is supported by plain shafts and capitals, the abaci next the angles being carried out to meet these; and on the piers between the windows are blank arches of the same character, but narrower. These shafts are not carried down to the parapet of the gallery, but at rather less than a third of the entire height of the arch, they rest on the abaci of other shafts (prolonged at the angles as those above are), which carry zigzag arch moulds across the piers, covering two sub-arches. The capitals are all of the plainest Norman types.

(3) The columns in this crypt are solid and cylindrical, with plain bases, very shallow capitals, and thin, square abaci. The vaulting is of the simplest character; and the arches rest on square pilasters of the same character as the columns. The " central apartment," as Britton (p. 87) calls it, is connected with the aisles by a series of arched openings opposite the loops in the latter. The " Holy Hole" used to communicate with the apsidal end of the centre of this crypt.

(4) In this crypt, whilst the columns and their capitals, the groining and the masonry, are plainly Norman, they are not so solid and rude as those of the first crypt. There is a ring round the neck of the columns, and the capital is little more than a double-based segment of a sphere, with the largest base cut square. The loops show that it was constructed before the retro-choir, which has now rendered them useless, and it receives only a glimmering of light from the other crypts.

(5) The columns of this crypt are less substantial than those of the second; they stand on octagonal plinths, and the capitals are of an inverted bell-shape, but octagonal also. The vaulting-arches are pointed, and there are groining ribs. There is a doorway into this crypt from the open air, on the north side.

(6) See p. 43. The foundations of De Lucy's work have blocked up the loops of the second crypt.

aisles of the presbytery.[1]   At the present time these crypts are filled to about half the height of the columns with earth and rubbish, which have accumulated round the brick graves built on the floor, or have been purposely piled about the columns to add to their stability ; and several walls and square piers have been erected in them.[2]

Eastward from the tower piers extends the presbytery, eighty feet in length, to the wall beneath the great east window, and forty in width.   On each side there are four compartments, of which the eastmost, instead of preserving the line of the others, converge, " so as to give the irregular polygonal form" to that end of the main edifice, which has been noticed before.[3]   This portion of the cathedral is substantially of the Decorated style ; but the screens between the piers, the mullions, and tracery of the clerestory windows (as already remarked), the entire east window, the wooden vaulted and groined roof, and the most conspicuous and beautiful object, not only in the presbytery, but in the cathedral itself—the reredos—are all Perpendicular in character.

The presbytery ;

Here, as in the nave, the compartment shows but two vertical divisions ; and there are galleries under the upper windows having their parapets elegantly pierced in quatrefoils, communicating by passages through the walls with the galleries of the transepts.   The piers are composed of clustered columns, with plain bases and capitals, and the arch-mouldings are plain, except that at the union of the outermost mouldings, above the capitals of the piers, are grotesque animals, and heads, which serve as corbels.[4]   The screens between the piers are about three quarters of the height of the columns ; and each is divided into two compartments.   In the hollow of the cornice, which is surmounted by the Tudor flower and decorated with escutcheons and quatrefoils, are the mottoes of Bishop Fox, Cardinal Beaufort, and another benefactor of the cathedral.[5]   And as these screens are now glazed, each compartment is, in fact, a handsome square-headed window of four lights.[6]   There is an entrance from the aisle through the eastern compartments of the screens nearest the choir ; and on the top of

—its screens ;

(1) See p. 43.   That on the south side is still used.

(2) Willis, p. 51 ; where it is remarked that the reason for raising the graves above the floor, and for covering up the lower parts of the pillars and walls, is the fact that "the water lies so near the surface" of the soil here. The extension of "the raised platform above the crypt under the central tower, and beyond it to the second pillar westward," is noted by the professor (ibid.). Britton (Pl. II. p. 87) marks the place of a well in the eastern extremity of the south aisle, in the first crypt.

There is also shown in Britton's plan of the crypts (Pl. II.) the vault beneath the Chapel of the Guardian Angels, which is lighted by a loop in the eastern wall of the chapel.

(3) Willis, p. 43.   See p. 41, *supra.*

(4) These piers are of Purbeck marble, and consist each of four principal shafts at the angles, and four smaller ones on the sides, of a square, but the bases are octagonal ; none of the columns are disengaged, and there are merely deep hollows between them.   The longest diameter of

each is three feet four inches, yet the span of the arches is very nearly the same as those of the nave ; that of the two converging arches at the east end, behind the reredos, is wider.   The mouldings of those arches also differ from those of the eastern arches of the presbytery.

(5) The initials of Bishop Fox, with his motto, "*Est Deo Gracia*" (in black letter) ; the arms, initials, and motto, "In Domino Confido" (in Roman capitals), of Cardinal Beaufort ; the initials "W. F.," and the motto "Sit Laus Deo" (in Roman capitals) ; the date 1525 ; and the arms and name of Edward the Confessor,—are specified by Milner (vol. ii. p. 89) as the principal ornaments of these screens.

(6) Properly, each of these "windows" consists of a Tudor arch, with quatrefoils (pierced and glazed) in the spandrels ; the four lights are made into two sub-arches of the same character, with a large quatrefoil in the apex of the principal arch ; and each light, again, has a double-feathered trefoil head, with a smaller quatrefoil in the apex of each sub-arch.

each stands a mortuary chest, containing the relics of some of the most celebrated kings and prelates, who were in ancient times interred in this church.[1]

—its vault;

The groining ribs, nine in number, spring from corbels inserted in the wall between the windows of the clerestory; and the principal three of each group meeting those from the opposite side, at the ridge-rib, form (as in the vaults of the nave) intersecting and bisected lozenges.[2] The bosses are very numerous, and are richly painted and gilt; amongst the devices carved on them, Milner notices the arms and badges of the families of Lancaster and Tudor, the arms of Castile, and even of the various sees held successively by Bishop Fox. "The part of the vaulting," he adds, "from the altar to the east window bears none but pious ornaments; the several implements of our Saviour's passion," including Peter's Denial, and the Betrayal in the Garden of Gethsemane, "the faces of Pilate and his wife, of the Jewish high priest, with a great many others," which are deservedly commended for the variety and originality of their designs.[3]

—the reredos.

Behind the platform of the high altar, which is raised four steps above the floor of the presbytery,[4] the magnificent reredos, or altar-screen, rises nearly to the height of the corbels, from which the vaulting ribs spring. No description can do justice to this exquisite specimen of Perpendicular workmanship, which "is executed in a fine, white, soft stone," and is crowded with canopied niches, "pilaster but-tresses," pierced and crocketted pinnacles, and tabernacle-work, with a projecting canopy in the centre of most elaborate design, and surmounted by a triple frieze of running leaves, quatrefoils, and Tudor flowers.[5] On each side of the altar is an elegant

(1) Few things in this noble cathedral produce a deeper impression on the mind of a stranger than these mortuary chests, giving, as they do, the strangest air of reality to characters and events in the history of our country, which are far more indistinct and shadowy than those of a thousand years earlier in the stories of Rome and Greece. These remarkable and interesting relics, with the tomb of William Rufus, which stands behind the lectern, will be described subsequently.

The greater part of the floor of the presbytery (which is of white marble with smaller squares of black inserted at the angles) is occupied by quite modern pews and benches.

(2) Britton, Pl. i. and xxviii. The corbels present only the common device of angels holding shields.

(3) Milner, vol. ii. p. 88.

(4) According to Milner (ibid., p. 85), the carved rails in front of the altar were executed, in the time of Charles I., by Bishop Curle (ibid., p. 11).

(5) Britton, Pl. x. and p. 92. The only other altar-screens in this country comparable with this are those in Christchurch Abbey Church (which will be described in the second volume of this work), St. Alban's, and St. Mary's Overy (now St. Saviour's), Southwark. This screen may be regarded as consisting of three compart-

ments, each having a triple series of canopied niches. In the centre of the principal compartment is the space indi-cating the position of the grand crucifix, with a bracket beneath it, and the projecting canopy over its head; a canopied niche under each arm of the cross, and a bracket at the foot of each, level with the one just named; and two smaller canopied niches above each arm without any traces of bracket or pedestal. The lower part is occupied by West's painting and the present altar. On each side, completing this central compartment, is a polygonal pro-jecting part, the canopies to the niches in which are a little lower than those about the crucifix. Each of the lateral compartments is divided into two parts, that next the centre is considerably recessed, but the other is on a level with the projecting parts of the centre. The arrange-ment of the latter is precisely the same as that of the corresponding central portion; and the upper part of the recessed division agrees with it generally, except that there is a series of smaller niches, or panels, on each side of the principal niches; but instead of the lowest niche, there is a doorway into the feretory behind, over which is an elaborate turreted canopy. Slender, square-edged pinnacled, "pilaster-buttresses" (as Britton designates them), either singly or in small groups, are interposed be-tween the compartments and their several divisions. [It

doorway into the feretory behind.[1] The situation of the great crucifix is indicated by a blank cruciform space in the centre of the screen, beneath which is placed, as an altar-piece, West's painting of the Raising of Lazarus.[2] The back of this beautiful work is closely panelled in the upper part with narrow cinquefoiled arches, and the lower part is almost as richly decorated as the front.[3]

The feretory (called by Milner the "capitular chapel"[4]) is narrower than the presbytery, and is flanked by the chantries of Bishops Fox and Gardiner, both of which open into it; its floor is higher than that of the altar by three steps; and half its space appears to have been occupied with a raised platform, with an ascent of three more steps at each end and an arcade in front.[5] Here formerly stood the shrine of

The feretory.

It is impossible to describe more minutely this exquisite piece of architectural sculpture. Milner (vol. ii. p. 87) applies the term "lace-work" to it, and the appropriateness of the word is the exact measure of the undesirableness of attempting a more detailed description. It is, according to all competent judges, from the gallery under the clerestory windows of the presbytery that the best view of this screen is to be obtained; and perhaps the reason may be, that, with the exception of the doorways and their canopies, the lower part received many injuries at the Reformation, and many more when Inigo Jones (as the Rev. C. Walters reasonably conjectures) attempted to efface the indications of them, whilst the upper part has retained all its pristine finish and beauty.

Before the late restorations, a prodigious canopy of wood-work adorned with festoons and every variety of Jacobean ornament, and a great deal of gilding, covered all the middle part of this splendid reredos. It was the work of Bishop Curle, who, for some unknown reason, introduced Fox's well-known pelican, from which some rashly concluded that he was the guilty author of the whole monstrosity. However, not only the style, but the initials of Charles I. upon it, showed its real age. The curious may now see it in the triforium of the north transept in a becoming state of ignominy and neglect. The niches, with similar taste, were formerly filled with "sham urns" (as Britton, p. 80, indignantly calls them), which were removed with the canopy (Milner, vol. ii. p. 88).

In the inventory of the ornaments of the cathedral, contained in Dugdale's Monasticon (last ed. vol. i. pp. 193, 194), reprinted from the Appendix to Strype's Memorials of Archbishop Cranmer (p. 24), on the authority of a MS. in the library of Benet College, Oxford, may be found an account of the costly ornaments of this screen when it was first erected. A shorter account is given by Milner (vol. ii. p. 85). In front of the Mediæval Court of the Crystal Palace is a head of Christ, discovered by Mr. Digby Wyatt, amongst other fragments, in the feretory, which he regards as very probably part of the life-size figure of the Saviour which belonged to the great crucifix placed in the centre of this screen (Hand-book, pp. 36, 47).

Various opinions have been entertained respecting the date of this noble work of art. Mr. Garbett ascribed it to Cardinal Beaufort, but Britton to Bishop Waynflete (Britton, pp. 66, 93). Professor Willis (p. 50) assigns it generally to "the latter end of the fifteenth century;" and Mr. Cresy (*u. s.* p. 396) says that it was "commenced in the time of Cardinal Beaufort, and finished about 1500, or a little later;" and the latter opinions seem to be confirmed by the date "1510," which, together with the initials "I. R.," have been discovered in the plinth (Hand-book to Mediæval Court, p. 46).

What preceded this lofty reredos we do not know, but it was in all probability a low screen, which allowed the shrines in the feretory to be seen from the choir.

(1) These doorways are good four-centred arches, with hollow mouldings, ornamented in harmony with the whole screen, running round them, nearly to the floor, without any shafts or imposts. In the spandrels of the north door the Annunciation is represented, and in those of the south door the Visitation; Britton says (p. 93), "in a very bad style." From their condition before the restorations, we may conclude that the whole of this screen was originally coloured (Milner, vol. ii. p. 87).

(2) This picture was purchased by Dean Ogle and the chapter in the latter part of the last century. Milner (ibid., pp. 84, 85) severely condemns it; and we must admit that his criticism is not entirely unjust.

(3) Britton (Pl. XXII. and p. 98) gives a good view of the eastern side of one of the doorways, including the canopy above it. The whole stands in a sort of arched recess, the spandrels of which are pierced. The mouldings of the arch of the doorway are quite plain, and the spandrels exhibit "two slips of foliage very finely executed."

(4) Vol. ii. p. 98.

(5) "Its upper surface is now three feet above the floor, but was originally much higher; steps at each end gave access to this upper surface; and in front there are the remains of a hollow place, which from the piers and other indications that remain on the floor, evidently had an arcade in front of it, over which the pavement of the platform extended so as to make its breadth about ten feet in the whole" (Willis, p. 50)

St. Swithin, with those of other canonized patrons of the Church.   It is in a ruinated condition now, and is used only as a place for the deposit of fragments of sculpture belonging to the reredos, the arcade in the retro-choir, and other parts of the cathedral, which are the wreck of the iconoclasm at the Reformation.   The eastern side of this feretory is a low wall, on which stand three Decorated piers, supporting two arches, which assist in carrying the great window with its gable and octagonal turrets. The rest of the weight is sustained by the first piers of the retro-choir, which stand obliquely at the back of the outermost of these three.[1]

The east window, says Mr. Winston, "must, when perfect, have been truly magnificent," and even in its present condition it is an admirable work of art of its kind. "In point of execution, it is as nearly perfect as painted glass can be."[2] Milner says that in the upper row, on each side of "certain traces of the usual emblems of the blessed Trinity" (the place of which is supplied by a figure of St. Bartholomew), are figures of our Saviour and of the Virgin; in the adjoining compartments are angels with trumpets, the arms of the see, or of Bishop Fox, whose motto, "EST DEO GRACIA," is also there.   In the next tier appears St. Ethelwold (?) and two prophets, one (probably Joel) having round his head the legend "CONTREMUIT TERRA MOTI SUNT CŒLI."   In the lowest range are St. Swithin, St. Peter, and St. Paul, with ancient prophets, "one of whom bears the name of 'MALACHIAS' on the border of his mantle."[3]   The other windows of the presbytery are filled with figures of angels, prophets, apostles, and eminent saints with their various emblems, and with legends by which their names may be ascertained.[4]

(1) The plan of these piers is an octagon with the alternate faces chamfered, and four shafts attached to the others; the diameter is two feet ten inches, and the capitals, bases, and arch-moulds are of a good bold character. The north-eastern arch of the presbytery greatly resembles these, but that on the opposite side is of a later character, and is more like the arches of the remainder of the presbytery.

"A mass of masonry now connects" the piers at the north-eastern corner, but at the south-eastern corner "an additional pier has been erected, joining together the piers" there, and "receiving the arch" adjoining on the west. According to Professor Willis, the small eastern arches were first built, then the north-eastern, afterwards the rest of the presbytery, and finally the south-eastern arch, probably in the room of one built at the same time as the north-eastern arch, but which had failed. There are clear signs of a break in the upper wall of the presbytery, against the northern end of the reredos. (See Willis, pp. 43—45.)

Originally the cathedral terminated towards the east in an apse flanked by two square towers. This is manifest from the plan of the crypts; and an apsidal Lady-chapel, of a little later date, extended beyond the east end of the whole building. In Gardiner's chantry may still be seen the base of one of the cylindrical piers which divided the presbytery of the Norman cathedral from its environing aisles, and it stands directly on one of the piers of the crypt below (Willis, p. 43).

(2) Arch. Inst., Winchester Volume, "Short Notice of Painted Glass, &c," p. 6.

(3) Vol. ii. pp. 87, 88.

(4) "The glass in the east window of the choir of Winchester Cathedral is perhaps a little earlier than 1525, and is the work of Bishop Fox." "The only part of the glass now in its original position consists (as I think) of the two figures which occupy the two southernmost of the lower lights, and of that in all the tracery-lights, except the top central one and the three immediately below it. The top central light is filled principally with some glass of Wykeham's time, and all the rest of the windows with glass of Fox's time, removed from other windows." "Bishop Fox's glass seems originally to have extended into some of the side windows of the clerestory of the choir, the heads of some of his canopies still retaining their original positions in these windows. The easternmost window on the north side of this clerestory was evidently at one time filled with his glass.   The tracery-lights still remain" (Winston, u. s., pp. 6, 7).

"In the heads of the three westernmost windows, on

Of the aisles of the presbytery, which are wider than those of the nave, nothing The aisles of the presbytery. more needs to be said than that the walls are covered with the richest cinquefoil-headed panelling, and mouldings, and that the vaults are " fine pieces of stone lierne-work." [1]

The retro-choir consists of three aisles of almost equal width,[2] which Britton called The retro-choir. " the chantry-aisles," separated from each other by two series of three arches resting on two piers and two half piers of beautiful Early English work, composed of clusters of slender shafts about an octagonal central column, banded at mid-height, with elegant foliage around their capitals.[3] The whole vault is thus divided into nine compartments, which are separated from each other, and intersected diagonally by plain moulded vaulting ribs. An arcade of trefoil-headed arches, with elongated quatrefoils in the spandrels, runs along the lower part of each wall; above which, between two moulded string-courses, is a series of similar quatrefoils, one over the head of each arch. Under the windows this serves as a parapet to a gallery, or passage in the thickness of the walls. The openings to the windows are pairs of lancet arches, standing on this parapet, in front of the windows, which have only one slender engaged shaft at each angle of the jambs.[4]

Facing the east on the back of the wall of the feretory, between the chantries of Fox and Gardiner, is an exceedingly beautiful arcade of nine arches, with richly decorated canopies and pinnacles, resting on a cornice about five feet above the

---

the north side of the clerestory of the choir in Winchester Cathedral," the glass "consists of canopy-work and cherubim. The four figures in the upper tier of lower lights in the easternmost of these three windows are of the same time, and appear to be in their original position. The eight figures and canopies in the upper tier of the two easternmost windows on the south side of this clerestory are likewise of the same date," but they seem to have been "removed from some other windows. All this glass is, I think, of the close of Henry VI.'s reign" (Winston, *u. s.* p. 5.)

Two of these windows were, until recently, whitewashed, to prevent them from casting their glowing hues upon West's picture! This recalls Milner's tale (*u. s.* p. 87) of a proposal to take down the reredos, in order to lengthen the choir of the cathedral; and his exultation in thinking that the attempt to remove that " stay against the inward pressure of the walls and buttresses" would bring the whole down in ruins " on the heads of its presumptuous violators ! "

(1) Willis, p. 49. The ridge rib of the vaulting runs parallel to the side of the presbytery, in the south aisle, which produces a remarkable irregularity in the lierne-work at the eastern end. At the western end, on each side, in the outer wall, is a narrow and low obtuse-arched doorway, with foliage in the spandrels, by which access was originally had to the crypts (see pp. 58, 59); that in the south aisle is still in use.

(2) In fact, the width of the central portion (which was determined by the width of the walls of the crypt of the Norman Lady-chapel) is about thirty feet, and that of the aisles about twenty-five feet. The entire length of this portion of the edifice is about sixty-five feet. The height of the central alley is about forty-five feet ; and that of the aisles, about five or six feet less (Britton, Pl. XXIII.)

(3) Upon the clustered capitals of these piers, in the central portion, stand small single-vaulting shafts ; and on the south side of the arch of the Lady Chapel, below the band of the columns, is a short and slender shaft resting on a corbel, with the characteristic Early English toothed moulding in the hollow beside it. This pier inclines considerably from the perpendicular, towards the south-east, owing to a settlement of the foundation.

(4) Over the doorway, on the south side (see p. 42), is a plain, cinquefoil arch of Purbeck stone, enclosed by an elegant Early English arch, having two cylindrical mouldings, and deeply-cut foliage between them, resting alternately upon them. In the north and the south angles, at the east end of the retro-choir, are trefoil-headed doorways, leading to the turret stairs which communicate with the galleries round the retro-choir and the eastern chapels. The vaulting of the stair is worthy of notice. (Willis, p. 42. See also Arch. Assoc., Winchester Volume, p. 283.)

floor, which is ornamented as richly as the arcade.[1]   The remains of pedestals, two under each arch, may be seen through the whole length of this arcade; and at the foot of each pedestal, on the edge of the moulding, can yet be traced the name of the holy person whose figure was originally placed upon it.[2]   "These tabernacles," says Professor Willis, "are beautiful specimens of Edwardian work, and well deserve study."[3]   Under the centre tabernacle, is a low, arched doorway, which formerly communicated with the crypt below, and is still called the Holy Hole.[4]

The Lady Chapel.

In the centre of the eastern end of the retro-choir is the Lady Chapel, separated from the rest of the edifice by a good Perpendicular screen, with a gallery over it.[5] "The western arch of separation between the Lady Chapel" and the retro-choir, "retains the mouldings of De Lucy, but not in the form in which he left it; for, to accommodate the vault of the fifteenth century, it has been evidently taken down, and reset in the shape of a four-centred arch."[6]   The chapel is divided into two compartments, of which the western one, like the retro-choir, is Early English,[7] and the eastern Perpendicular.   In the former, the lower part is concealed by elaborately carved wood-work with seats, and desks before them, and a gallery above.[8]   A band of panelling runs round the other compartment, just under the

(1) The arches of this arcade are ogee, trefoiled, and double-feathered, enriched with mouldings of very great elegance and beauty; the canopies are boldly crocketted, and adorned with finely-designed and chiselled finials; and the opening is a pointed trefoil. The pinnacles have gables, and are set angularly, so that three rows of crockets and gables (which also are crocketted, and have finials) appear on each pinnacle.

At each end the cornice is carried down beside the piers abutting on the angles of the presbytery, nearly to the ground. It seems to have been restored in several places; and, from the style, the restoration might be ascribed to Inigo Jones, who is known to have employed his skill in this cathedral.

(2) The following are the names which are carved here in Lombardic capitals, beginning at the south end and proceeding to the north :—

"KYNGILSUS REX; S^{CS}. BIRINUS EPS: KYNWALDUS REX; EGBERTUS REX: ADULPHUS REX FILS EJ; ELURED REX : EDWARD. REX SENIOR; ATHELSTAN. REX FILS EJ: S^{CE} MARIA; DOMINUS JESUS: EDRADUS REX; EDGAR REX: EMMÆ REGINA; ALWINUS EPIS : ETHELRED REX; S^{CS}. EDWARD. REX FILS EJ : CNUTUS REX; HARDICNUT REX FILIUS EJUS." (Britton, p. 98.)

There can be little doubt that many of the fragments now collected in the feretory, at the back of this arcade, belong to the series of statuettes which once filled these niches.

(3) P. 51, n.   Britton (ibid.) supposes that this arcade "was originally . . . . the altar screen."

(4) Immediately beneath the cornice, beside this low arched doorway, may be read this distich in large Lom-

bardic capitals, which manifestly refers to the interments in the crypt :—

"CORPORA SANCTORUM SUNT HIC IN PACE SEPULTA
EX MERITIS QUORUM FULGENT MIRACULA MULTA."

In the pavement of this part of the church, and in the aisles of the presbytery, are to be seen most of the glazed and ornamented tiles, which have been preserved to this day. The greater number exhibit the common patterns, but some are of more unusual design. One kind is figured in the "Glossary of Architecture," Pl. CCVII.

(5) On each side of the entrance are three compartments, of five lights each, with open spandrels. The door consists of two leaves, of three wider lights each. There is nothing particularly noteworthy in the design.

(6) Willis, p. 39.

(7) The upper part of the walls, on both sides, shows a splendid arcade of six narrow, pointed arches, each pair being united by a trefoil-headed hood-moulding, like that which runs round the retro-choir. The *alura* extends behind the clustered shafts of these arches. Over the centre is a large quatrefoil composed of four circular openings, united by a moulding round them and a boss in the middle pierced with a trefoil. On each side of it is a plain trefoil moulding (Willis, p. 39).

(8) Each compartment of this splendid work is divided vertically into three parts: the lowest shows the Tudor arch, doubly and triply feathered; the second, an ogee arch, with crockets and finial, and double feathering, and handsome arches in the spandrels and behind it. The pinnacles which divide the compartments rise to the height of these finials. Quatrefoil panelling and pierced

windows;[1] and below it the walls on each side are covered with paintings of the miracles of the Blessed Virgin.[2] On the north side, a doorway, beneath a square hood-moulding, formerly led to "a particular sextry, or sacristy, belonging to

parapet-work are interposed between the upper and the lower part, and the upper is covered with the Tudor flower. The topmost division, which serves as a parapet to the gallery, is plain, the compartments being marked by plain mouldings alone ; and a cornice, ornamented with a running pattern of leaves and fruits, surmounted by open carved work of trefoils, &c., crowns the whole. The front of the desks, and the desk ends, are carved with corresponding designs.

(1) This panelling consists of quatrefoils with shields, &c., divided by sets of three double arches; and under it is an elegant cornice.

(2) In Carter's "Specimens of Ancient Sculpture and Painting" (Pls. XXV. to XXVIII. pp. 27—36), all that remains of these paintings has been engraved, and described by Milner, who refers to that work from his own history, vol. ii. p. 104. More recently, an account of the "best preserved" and "most interesting," with etchings, has been given in the Winchester Volume of the Arch. Assoc., pp. 268—284, Pls. XII. to XV.

There are twenty-four of these paintings arranged in two rows, one above the other. "The architecture and draperies are painted *en grisaille*, but other objects have their local colour, the style of execution closely resembling that of glass painting of the same date." (Arch. Assoc., *u. s.*, p. 269.) "Each subject had an inscription beneath it, giving a full account of the story, with references to the collection from which it was taken; in one or two instances these references are distinct, but in general the legends are defaced." "The subjects have been much defaced . . . and injured by the injudicious application of varnish; those on the north wall are hardly distinguishable, and what remains [is] chiefly modern retouching." (Ibid.)

The subjects, as explained by Mr. John Green Waller in the last quoted work, are the following. The numbers commence on the south side of the altar, and proceed eastward, returning on the north side to the altar from the west.

1. Represents the story of the young man who was won to the monastic life by the miracle of an image of the Virgin bending its finger, so as to prevent his taking off a ring which he had received from his lady-love, and had placed on the finger of the image, that it might not be lost or bent while he played at ball. 2. Tells the story of the protection and honour conferred by the Virgin on the ignorant priest who knew and could sing but one mass, which was in honour of her. 3. Contains the defaced portrait of Prior Silkstede kneeling before the image of the Virgin; out of his mouth a scroll formerly bore the legend, "*Benedicta tu in muli-*

eribus." Under it was an inscription which, when more perfect, might be read thus :—

"SILKSTEDE [PRIOR] JUSSIT QUOQUE SAXA POLITA
SUMPTIBUS ORNARI, SANCTA MARIA, SUIS."

"Beneath this compartment is the piscina, richly coloured, and having at the back remains of a figure consecrating the elements." 4. Depicts the Virgin defending the young Jew who had partaken of the Eucharist, and was thrown into a furnace by his enraged father. 5. Shows Pope Gregory carrying in procession the famous portrait of the Virgin, painted by St. Luke, for the allaying of a fearful pestilence, and the Destroying Angel sheathing his sword. 6. Shows the widow restoring the image of the child Jesus to the Virgin, which she had taken away on the loss of her only son, who was restored to her. 7. Represents the Virgin assisting the woman who when in company with a party of pilgrims to St. Michael's Church, in Normandy, alarmed at the influx of the tide, was taken in labour. 8. Shows the Virgin instructing the builder of a church, which the Emperor Constantine had ordered to be built in her honour. 9. Contains the story of the female devotee of the Virgin, who died without having confessed one particular sin, and was restored to life at the Virgin's intercession that she might perform this duty. "The head of Christ has a peculiar variety of the nimbus, it forms a floriated cross, and is without the circle." 10. Depicts the Virgin, delivering a monk from drowning beside a foot-bridge, and also from two fiends with instruments of torture, who are evidently the ministers of punishment for concupiscence. 11. Represents the fate of the two Brabançons who threw stones at the image of the Virgin. 12. Shows the Virgin delivering some monastic votaries from a storm at sea. 13. Represents the mass of the Virgin, which was celebrated once by Christ himself, with saints and angels to assist him, when the priest of a chapel dedicated to her was unable to do so. The next number, on the north wall, 14. Depicts the restoration of the arm of St. John of Damascus, and the establishment of his innocence of the charge of corresponding with the unbelievers. 15. Shows the Virgin delivering a thief, who had always venerated her, from the gallows, to which his crimes had brought him. 16. Represents the Virgin justifying a clerk of irreligious life, who was her votary, and commanding his burial in consecrated ground. 17. Shows the Virgin assisting a painter who was devoted to her to paint the devil "as ugly as he knew him to be," in spite of all that the devil could do to prevent it. 18. Contains the Annunciation ; under which is the door to the sextry mentioned above. 19. Shows now but the figure of a

K

this chapel," traces of which are visible on the outside.[1] There is a piscina on the opposite side of the altar, which stood on a platform raised three steps above the floor of the chapel. " The vault is a complex and beautiful specimen of lierne-work. The vaulting shafts have capitals and bases of an unusual form, but very rich and appropriate."[2]

Langton's Chapel.

The chapel on the south side of the Lady Chapel was fitted up as a chantry by Bishop Langton, and is called by his name. It is inclosed by a screen of Perpendicular workmanship, which is much defaced;[3] the wood-work round the chapel is exceedingly rich and beautiful,[4] and the vault still more elaborate than that of the Lady Chapel, for the panels between the ribs and liernes are covered with small tracery."[5] At the east end, above the place formerly occupied by the altar, is a row of seven tabernacles over a cornice ornamented with bosses, heads, &c., the whole of which were originally splendidly coloured and gilt. No traces remain of the images which occupied these niches, but it is probable that some fragments might be found in the feretory.

Chapel of the Guardian Angels.

Corresponding in position with Langton's, but to the north of the Lady Chapel, is the Chapel of the Guardian Angels, or the Portland Chapel,[6] which is separated from

knight, but formerly it told how praying to the Virgin had kept a robber-knight out of the clutches of the fiend. 20. to 24. The subjects are so much defaced as to be undiscoverable. The character of these paintings, though "contemporary with the great masters of Italy," "is essentially German or Flemish, bearing a striking resemblance to the painted glass of the time, and the early wood engravings." Some of the compositions, and many of the figures, are very graceful. (Arch. Assoc., Winchester Vol. p. 283.)

(1) In the spandrels of this doorway may be seen the rebus of Prior Hunton.

(2) "On the vault round the two centre keys," says Willis (p. 39), quoting Milner (vol. ii. pp. 103, 104), " one representing the Almighty, the other the Blessed Virgin, we find the following characters and rebuses :— the letter *T*, the syllable *Hun*, the figure of a *ton*, for Thomas Hunton; and the figure *I* for *prior*. In like manner we see the letter *T*, the syllable *Silk*, a *steed*, or horse, and the figure *I*, for *Thomas Silkstede, prior*."

The capitals of these columns have the running pattern of foliage and fruit, and under it, panelling in quatrefoils, &c.

The Lady Chapel is fifty-four feet in length, and rather narrower than the central division of the retro-choir. Each of the smaller chapels measures about twenty-five feet by eighteen (Britton, Pls. I. and xx.)

Beside the altar table in this chapel stands a curious chair or *faldistorium* (Willis, p. 40), in which, according to Gale (p. 35), Queen Mary sat on the occasion of her marriage to Philip of Spain.

(3) On each side of the doorway are five narrow lights

or compartments, trefoiled in the head, and having two " batements" over each. The doorway under an ogee with crockets, &c., occupies the space of three compartments. On the inner side are small buttresses against the lower part, surmounted with figures; the lower part is panelled in several series of arched openings; and along it, both inside and out, runs an inscription consisting of Langton's motto repeated, " LAUS TIBI CRISTE."

(4) Round the base runs a rich series of panels of various patterns; the compartments are divided by shafts of twisted cane-work; in the lower part each shows a Tudor trefoiled arch, doubly feathered, with trefoils in the spandrels, and panels above with the arms of Langton impaled with those of the sees of Winchester and Canterbury. Another series of rich panels with the running foliage and Tudor flower reaches to the under side of the gallery, which is very beautifully panelled also. Along the front of the gallery runs a bold pattern of leaves and fruit; and above it is an exceedingly elegant open-worked parapet, whilst below is a series of obtuse-headed arches, from which formerly depended a series of shields.

(5) "This vault, like the others, has the rebuses of its builders, namely, as Milner (vol. ii. p. 103) explains them, the musical note termed a *long* inserted into a *ton* for *Langton*; a *vine* and a *ton* for his see, *Winton*; a *hen* sitting on a *ton* for his prior, *Hunton*; and a *dragon* issuing out of a *ton*, which Milner declares himself unable to unriddle" (Willis, p. 41).

(6) Milner suggests that this was Bishop Orlton's chantry, "though there is no memorial of him existing here at present" (vol. ii. p. 105).

the retro-choir by a modern iron railing. The Early English arcade of De Lucy's building is continued along the north side of it; in which also is an ambry, with a square-headed trefoil arch, and a stone shelf in it. At the east end are seven canopied niches, similar in style to those of the altar screen.[1] Two plain diagonal ribs cross the vault, which is farther ornamented with medallions, on which are painted, in a very fine style, busts of angels, "the intervening spaces being filled up with stars formed of composition and raised in relief, and the whole arranged together with arabesque-work."[2]

From this general survey and description of the cathedral, we proceed to a notice of the sepulchral memorials of illustrious persons buried within its walls, commencing with the chantries, which are amongst the most striking architectural embellishments of the place.

Beneath the second arch from the choir, on the south side of the nave, is the chantry, or mortuary chapel of Bishop Edington, inclosing the whole space between the piers, with its Perpendicular screens.[3] A doorway on each side, near the western end (as in all these chantries), gives access to the interior, where, on a panelled altar-tomb, lies the effigy of the bishop, *in pontificalibus*, but without a crosier, much broken and defaced. The following inscription, in old English, may be read upon a blue enamelled slip of brass inserted in the chamfer round the edge of the tomb:— *Edington's Chantry.*

> " Edyndon natus : Wills̄ hic est tumulatus :
> Presul prægratus : in Wyntonia cathedratus :
> Qui pertransitis : eius memorare velitis :
> Prouidus & mitis : fulsit cum mille peritis :
> Peruigil Anglorȝ : fuit adiutor populorum :
> Dulcis egenorȝ : pater et protector eorȝ :
> : M : C : tribȝ iunctum : post . L . X . V . sit I punctū :
> Octauo functum : notat hunc Octobris īunctū :"

Farther to the west, on the same side of the aisle, the chantry of William of Wykeham completely fills up the fifth arch from the west end; its pinnacles rising to the level of the triforium gallery. It is a splendid specimen of early Perpendicular work, and has recently been restored at the expense of the two colleges founded by this prelate.[4] Traces of the altar and of a credence table remain at the east end, with an *Wykeham's Chantry.*

---

(1) According to Milner (vol. ii. p. 105, note ‡), their style "seems to bespeak" Bishop Orlton's time.

(2) Arch. Assoc., Winchester Volume, p. 268. This vault is there said to be "a very perfect example of the application of polychromy to architecture."

(3) The architecture of these screens deserves particular attention, because it differs so widely from that of the windows ascribed to this prelate. It is plainly Perpendicular, by the transoms; but the tracery in the heads of the arches is as distinctly Decorated; so that it may properly be ascribed to a period of transition from the Decorated to the Perpendicular style. Each side is divided into six compartments of two lights each, and divided by

a transom. The irregularity of the open-worked battlements should also be noted.

(4) Each side of this chantry is divided into three compartments, of which that in the centre is the widest. Across them, at mid height, runs a cornice, surmounted by a battlement, above which the arches are open, but below they are filled up with mullions and transoms. The central compartment has three smaller two-light compartments, and the side ones two each, and some of them are filled up with stone-work, and the others with iron grating. An ogee canopy (with crockets, &c.) above a cinquefoiled, or septfoiled, and double-feathered arch, crowns each compartment; and behind the canopies is a panelled battle-

elegant piscina beside them; and over them are two series of five richly canopied niches, corresponding with five at the opposite end. The vault is conformed to the outline of the arch, under which the chantry stands, and is richly groined with lierne-work. The effigy of the bishop, *in pontificalibus* complete, lies upon a panelled altar tomb, with three small figures of monks, in the attitude of prayer, at its feet. Round the edge of the tomb, in a chamfer, on a slip of red enamelled brass, is this inscription, in old English :—

> " Willielmus dictus Wykeham iacet hic nece uictus:
> Istius Ecclesiæ Præsul: reparauit eamq3:
> Largus erat dapifer: probat hoc cum diuite pauper:
> Consiliis pariter regni fuerat bene dexter:
> Hunc docet esse pium Fundatio Collegiorum:
> Oxoniæ primum stat: Wintoniæq3 secundum:
> Jugiter oretis tumulum quicumq3 uidetis:
> Pro tantis meritis ut sit sibi uita perennis."

Beaufort's Chantry.

In the retro-choir, on the south side, under the central arch, stands Cardinal Beaufort's chantry, which consists of eight " clustered piers" (four at the east end, and four at the west), supporting a " mass of canopies, niches, and pinnacles, which bewilder the sight and senses by their number and complexity." [1] There is an open screen at the head, or west end, and a closed screen at the east end; panelled screens inclose the narrower openings at the sides, and low panelled balustrades the spaces between the two groups of piers. [2] Fan-tracery of the most elaborate kind covers the vault. Within, upon an altar tomb, lies the figure of the cardinal in the " proper dress" of his ecclesiastical rank. [3] Round it may be seen the place where once was an inscription, of which in Godwin's time there remained this fragment :—[4]

> " Tribularer, si nescirem misericordias tuas."

A recent inscription affixed to the east wall commemorates the restoration of the chantry, in the year 1819, by Henry Charles Duke of Beaufort.

Waynflete's Chantry.

Under the corresponding arch on the north side of the retro-choir is the chantry

---

ment. A stone seat runs round the base. At each angle, on the face of the stone-work joining the sides with the adjacent piers of the nave, are three elegant ogee canopies, arranged vertically, with pedestals for images beneath them.

Several restorations of the paintings and gilding of Wykeham's effigy are recorded; and, very probably, to these restorations may be ascribed what we must note as the dilapidated condition of the countenance of the figure.

This chantry is said to have been erected here, because when a boy Wykeham was daily accustomed to hear mass (called *Pekismass*) celebrated before an altar dedicated to the Virgin, on this spot. (Lowth's "Life of Wykeham," p. 283, Edit. 2.)

(1) Britton, p. 95. Milner (vol. ii. p. 100) states that "a horse-load" of these pinnacles, &c., " has fallen, or been taken down," at the time he wrote. Most of this ruin has, however, now been repaired.

(2) These " screens," which with the " clustered piers," are of Purbeck stone, show the obtuse-headed arch of the later Perpendicular style, and the Tudor-flower battlement. " The low balustrade and the tomb are of grey marble " (ibid.) The place where the altar stood is yet evident; and above it is " a range of niches," despoiled (as all the others in the cathedral are) of the statues which formerly adorned them.

(3) Britton (p. 81) says of this effigy, " we cannot otherwise account for the extreme badness of this statue, than by supposing that it was placed there at a time much later than the building of the chantry; indeed, since the Reformation." [This, however, is quite incredible.] " It seems rather the workmanship of a stonemason, than of a sculptor." See Milner's account of it in opposition to this (u. s.).

(4) De Præsul. Angl., p. 232. Edit. Richardson.

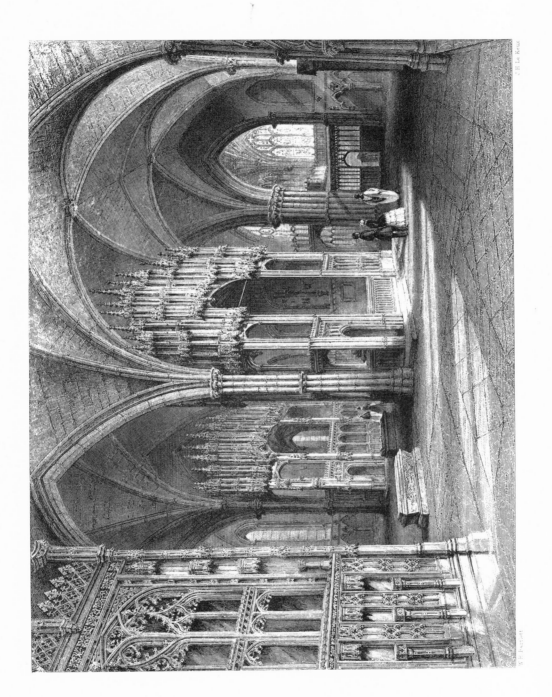

INTERIOR OF WINCHESTER CATHEDRAL.

Beaufort's Tomb

of Bishop Waynflete; which is similar in style to that of Cardinal Beaufort, but still more magnificent. On each side are three flat-headed arches; that in the centre being of the widest span. The east end is closed, but there are narrow open arches on each side of the pier adjoining the west end. Screens surmounted by cornices and battlements fill up these arches to about mid height; and under the central arches the open-work of these screens is carried down lower than under the others, so as to afford a view of the tomb within. The effigy of the bishop, lying upon an altar tomb, represents him *in pontificalibus* complete, and between his hands he holds his heart. Both the statue and the chantry are kept in repair by Magdalen College, Oxford.[1]

Of Langton's chantry mention has already been made;[2] and it only remains to be said, that the large and finely panelled altar tomb of the prelate stands just within the doorway of the screen; and that it has been robbed of the brasses which once adorned it, and were sculptured with his figure, arms, &c.[3]

Bishop Fox's chantry stands at the southern end of the feretory, and is a very splendid monument. The lower part is richly panelled, with niches, canopies, and pedestals; and under a low arch, in the midst of the side, is represented a human figure in the last stage of emaciation, its head resting on a mitre, and its feet upon a skull. The upper part consists of open tracery, with canopies and pedestals intervening; and above the cornice of running foliage, and the Tudor-flower battlements, rise panelled pinnacles of consummate elegance, presenting alternately octagonal turrets and the bishop's recognizance of the pelican.[4] There is no tomb, but the interior shows that it was intended as a chapel solely.[5] The wall over the site of the

Fox's Chantry.

(1) In this "gorgeous mass of architectural and sculptural ornaments," "the designer appears to have exerted his fancy to combine in one object, and in a small compass, an almost countless assemblage of pinnacles, canopies, niches, and sculptured details" (Britton, p. 96). It is constructed of a "fine, soft, white stone, easily worked." The cornice is continued round the interior of the screen, and exhibits grotesque ornaments amongst the bosses. The altar has been removed, but the piscina remains, and three elegant niches at the east end. At the west end is only a single bracket. The groined ceiling exhibits fine tracery and other lierne-work of the most exquisite delicacy. "There does not appear ever to have been an inscription on the tomb," according to Milner (vol. ii. p. 101); but there are traces of a brass in the chamfer round the tomb. Chandler (Life of Waynflete, p. 120) speaks of this chantry as having been dedicated to St. Mary Magdalen. There is a curious ancient lock on one of the doors. The head of the effigy had been so much injured, and so badly repaired, that a new one was substituted for it at the recent restoration.

(2) See p. 66.

(3) The slab of this tomb is of Purbeck marble. In the floor to the east of it may be seen the lid of an ancient coffin, of Purbeck stone.

(4) Richly panelled octagonal buttresses are placed at the corners of this chapel; and similar buttresses divide the sides into four bays. Above the canopies of the lower part is a cornice with foliage, and a plain battlement. A finely-ornamented Perpendicular window, with the Tudor arch, of two lights, with canopies and pedestals on each side of it, occupies the upper part of each bay. Each light is made an arch at the top, and divided into two by a lesser mullion. An embattled transom crosses each pair of lights, at a third of their height; but instead of a second transom, an exceedingly elegant ogee is formed, which reaches nearly to the apex of the secondary arch of the window. Every arch is trefoiled, or cinquefoiled, with flowers on the cusps, and double-feathered; and the ogees are crocketted, with finials. In the spandrels are Fox's badge and motto, and the whole was originally filled with coloured glass. The door to this chantry is very richly carved, with arched and canopied panels.

The repairs of this monument are in the care of Corpus Christi College, Cambridge.

(5) The place for the altar is higher in level than the

altar " is decorated with three large and sixteen small niches," under which is a band with demi-angels holding shields containing the arms of the see, and of Fox, and emblems of the Crucifixion, and this inscription :—

" O sacrum convivium, in quo Christus sumitur."

The ceiling is richly groined ; and behind the altar is a small vestry (used as a lumber closet), accessible by a door on the right side of the altar, " where the ambries belonging to it still remain." [1]

Gardiner's Chantry.

At the north end of the feretory stands the chantry of Bishop Gardiner, of which nothing laudatory can be said. The lower part is panelled, and with the cornice and ornamental work above it are in the Italian style, but the open screens are English. [2] In imitation of Fox's monument, the emaciated figure of the prelate is placed in a long, low, square niche, in the side of the chantry. [3] The site of the altar can be traced within, but there is no tomb. Emblematical figures, after Italian models, representing the Law and the Gospel, or Justice and Mercy, occupy the back of the altar. The ceiling is panelled ; and there is a small vestry at the east end, now used, like the feretory, as a repository for fragments of architectural ornaments, and of sculpture.

The mortuary chests.

The mortuary chests, [4] standing on the parcloses of the presbytery, next demand notice. There are six of these chests, three on each side ; they are made of wood, carved, painted, and gilt " in the *cinque-cento* style ;" and they were the work of Bishop Fox. Beginning from the altar on the north side, and returning to it again on the south, the names painted on the chests [5] are, on the first,—Rex Kyngils, Adulphus Rex ; the second, Kenulphus Rex, Egbertus Rex ; the third and fourth in common,

---

floor of the chantry near the door, and is reached by an ascent of three steps. Fox is said to have used it as a private oratory before his death, which procured for it the name of *Fox's Study* (Milner, vol. ii. p. 97).

The remains of this prelate were found in an oak coffin, beneath the floor of the chantry, during the late restorations.

(1) Ibid., p. 98. This ancient press very nearly fills the vestry.

(2) " Bad Italian and bad English," says Britton (p. 97), with great justice.

(3) The head of this figure has been cut off by some Reformers or Puritans, and the very pavement of the chantry " torn away, out of hatred to Bishop Gardiner" (Milner, vol. ii. p. 99). Milner says (ibid.) that it was reported that " his bones had been removed out of their sepulchre," and that some of them were then to be seen in " a large antique coffer, at the upper end of the chapel." His most recent editor (*u. s.* note ᵃ) assures us that it has been ascertained that the prelate's bones have not been disturbed, and that the bones in the coffin have been decently interred since Milner wrote.

(4) These relics were collected long before Fox's time, for according to John of Exeter (f. 5 b., quoted by Willis, pp. 20, 21), " *tempore Henrici Blesensi translata sunt,*

et propter ignoranciam qui essent reges, et qui essent episcopi, et quod non erant tituli inscripti supra monumenta eorum, predictus Henricus posuit in sarcofagis plumbeis reges cum episcopis, et episcopos cum regibus . . . . permixtos." (See also Rudborne, p. 194 ; Milner, vol. ii. p. 89.)

(5) The complete inscriptions, although not older than Bishop Fox's time, are sufficiently interesting to be inserted here :—

First chest.

" Rex Kyngils, obiit a.d. 641."

" Advlphvs Rex, obiit a.d. 857."

" Kyngilsi in cista hac simvl ossa jacent et
    Advlphi,
Ipsivs fvndator, hic benefactor erat."

Second chest.

" Kenvlphvs Rex, obiit a.d. 714."

" Egbertvs Rex, obiit a.d. 837."

" Hic Rex Egbertvs pavsat cvm rege Kenvlpho,
Nobis egregia mvnera vterqve tvlit."

Third and fourth chests.

" In hac et altera e regione cista reliqviæ
Svnt ossivm Canvti et Rvfi regvm, Emmæ reginæ,
Et Winæ et Alwini episcoporvm."   [" Hac

"RELIQUIÆ CANUTI ET RUFI REGUM, EMMÆ REGINÆ, WINÆ ET ALWINI EPISCOPORUM;" the fifth, EDMUNDUS REX; and the sixth, EDREDUS REX.[1]

There are many other ancient tombs and sepulchral monuments in this cathedral, in addition to those already described, which must be briefly noticed here.

Between the two entrances to the presbytery stands the tomb of the last English monarch interred here, William Rufus. It is a slab of grey marble *en dos d'âne*, raised about two feet from the ground, without inscription or any ornament except a plain rib on each edge.[2]

Tombs of William Rufus;—

Under the central arch of the parclose, on the south side, is this inscription:—

—and King Edward.

"HIC JACET EDMUNDUS REX
EWELDREDI REGIS FILIUS."[3]

On the opposite side of the presbytery is an altar tomb of no very ancient date,[4] partly built into the wall of the screen, and said to be the monument of Bishop John de Pontissara, whose burial-place it probably covers.[5] To the west of the entrance on the same side is a memorial of the sepulchre of Bishop Toclyve.[6]

Tombs of various bishops.

"HAC IN CISTA, A.D. 1661, PROMISCVE RECONDITA SVNT OSSA PRINCIPVM ET PRÆLATORVM SACRILEGA BARBARIE DISPERSA, A.D. 1642."

Fifth chest.

"EDMVNDVS REX, OBIIT A.D. ——."
"QVEM THECA HEC RETINET EDMVNDVM SVSCIPE CHRISTE,
QVI, VIVENTE PATRE, REGIA SCEPTRA TVLIT."

Sixth chest.

"EDREDVS REX, OBIIT A.D. 955."
"HOC PIVS IN TVMVLO REX EDREDVS REQVIESCIT,
QVI HAS BRITONVM TERRAS REXERIT EGREGIE."

On the third chest there was originally (according to Gale, p. 28) this inscription:—

"HIC JACENT OSSA WINÆ EPISCOPI."
"HIC JACET STIGANDVS EPISCOPVS."

and on the fourth (ibid., p. 27) this:—

"HIC JACENT OSSA CNVTONIS ET WILLIELMI RVFI."

"In June 1766, some workmen repairing Winchester Cathedral discovered a monument, wherein was contained the body of Canute. It was remarkably fresh, had a wreath or circlet round the head, and several other ornaments, such as gold and silver bands. On his finger was a ring, in which was set a remarkably fine stone; and in one of his hands was a silver penny" (Archæologia, vol. iii. p. 890). The site of this discovery is not specified, nor are any reasons given for assigning the remains to Canute. The fact is stated on the authority of Edward King, Esq.

It is related that the soldiers of the parliament, when they were masters of the city, ransacked these chests, and scattered the bones about the cathedral. The latest inscription on the third and fourth chests, given above, refers to this, but erroneously assigns the sacrilege to 1642 instead of 1644.

(1) In the year 1797 an officer of militia quartered at Winchester, Henry Howard by name, obtained permission to examine these chests, and found a great number of bones and twelve skulls dispersed amongst them in the most promiscuous manner. A full account of the results of his investigations is contained in Milner, vol. ii. pp. 92 and 93, notes. Nothing new was discovered when the contents of these chests were last inspected, in 1845.

(2) "In the tomb of William Rufus, which was broken open by the rebels in the time of the civil wars, was found the dust of that king, some relics of cloth of gold, a large gold ring, and a small silver chalice" (Gale, p. 27).

(3) This slab was formerly to be seen in Gardiner's chantry (Milner, vol. ii. p. 98); and according to Rudborne (Wharton's Angl. Sacr. vol. i. p. 207), is the memorial of the eldest son of Alfred the Great, who is otherwise unknown.

This inscription, and that on the tomb of Richard, the son of William the Conqueror, are much older than the others which record interments of great antiquity, and may perhaps be ascribed to Bishop Henry de Blois. All the rest, with the exception of the recent inscriptions on the third and fourth mortuary chests, may perhaps be ascribed to Bishop Fox.

(4) The upper slab of this tomb is of Purbeck stone; round it, on the under edge, is a band ornamented with a dancette moulding, having trefoils in the triangular spaces. The lower part of the tomb is divided into compartments, with shields, &c., of the Renaissance style.

(5) "*Sepultus est ex aquilonari plaga majoris altaris*," says Rudborne (ap. Wharton, vol. i. p. 286); and in conformity with this record is the following inscription:—

"DEFVNCTI CORPVS TVMVLVS TENET ISTE JOANNIS POINTES, WINTONIAE PRAESVLIS EXIMII. OBIJT 1304."

(6) Of Bishop Toclyve, Rudborne (*ibid.*) says, "*Sepul-*

Bishop Henry de Blois lies interred in front of the altar,[1] but nothing now marks the exact spot. The same may be said of Bishop Woodlock, who was buried below the steps of the choir.[2]

Bishop Cooper's monument, consisting of a stone with a narrow band of brass running round it, on which was inscribed—

" HIC JACET THOMAS COOPER,
OLIM LINCOLNIENSIS, NUPER WINTONIENSIS, EPISCOPUS,
MUNIFICENTISSIMUS, DOCTISSIMUS, VIGILANTISSIMUS PRESUL,
QUI RELIGIOSISSIME IN DOMINO, OBIIT APRILIS 29, AN. DOM. 1594."

and in the centre a " $\Delta\epsilon\chi\acute{a}\sigma\tau\iota\chi o\nu$ " of Latin hexameters in his praise, by one " W. S.," used to be seen " near the bishop's seat ;"[3] but in Milner's[4] time " seems to have been covered" by it, and is not visible now.

In the south aisle of the presbytery, in the lower part of the screen to the east of the entrance of the presbytery, is an inscription recording the sepulture there of the heart of Bishop Nicholas de Ely.[5] And under the bay next Fox's chantry are two other inscriptions indicating the burial-place of a younger son of William the Conqueror. One of these epitaphs is engraved on the edge of a sepulchral slab, which now forms part of a seat at the base of the screen, and extends under a low many-cusped arch ; it appears inverted, the tops of the letters being outward, and is to this effect :—

" HIC JACET RICHARDUS WILLI SENIORIS REGIS FILI: ET: BEORN: DUX."[6]

Near the wall opposite to Fox's chantry are the traces of a fine brass on a large slab of stone in the floor of the aisle. It was plainly an episcopal monument, and is said to have been that of Bishop Courtenay.[7]

Tomb of King Hardicanute.

In the north aisle, in positions corresponding with the epitaphs of Richard, the son

---

tus est ad aquilonarem partem summi altaris choro proxime." This is the inscription :—

" PRAESVLIS EGREGII PAVSANT HIC MEMBRA
RICARDI TOCLYVE, CVI SVMMI
GAVDIA SVNTO POLI. OBIJT A.D. 1189."

Gale (pp. 30, 31) mentions a "fourth chest," containing the remains of Bishop Elmstan and Kenulph, as having been " formerly on the north side of the wall" of the choir; a "monument" to Bishop "Alfymus," as " on the same wall," above that of John De Pontissara ; an inscription to Bishop Alwin near it ; and, " in the same wall, within the quire," an inscription in five lines to " Queen Emma." Of these nothing is now known.

(1) " *Sepultus est in ecclesia sua coram summo altari*" (ibid.).

(2) "*Ad gradus chori*" (ibid.). Milner (vol. ii. p. 93) records the discovery of his grave, and in it, of "an episcopal ring of solid gold, inclosing an amethyst."

(3) Gale, pp. 86, 87 ; where the *Decastich* is also given. Godwin (p. 239) makes the same statement, and gives both the epitaph on the brass, and the hexameters.

(4) Vol. ii. p. 94. It "was removed on paving the choir with marble" (Wavell, vol. i. p. 74).

(5) The inscription is,—

" INTVS EST COR NICHOLAI OLIM WINTON EPISCOPI
CVIVS CORPVS EST APVD WAVARLEI."

(6) No very great antiquity can be assigned to this inscription, but the other is still more modern, being of the date of the erection of the screens :—

" INTVS EST CORPVS RICHARDI WILLHELMI
CONQVESTORIS FILII ET BEORNIE DVCIS."

It will be observed that an ambiguity in the older epitaph is improved into a blunder in the newer one, the dukedom of Bearn never having been in the possession of the Conqueror, or of any of his sons.

(7) It was formerly called Fox's tomb, but on being taken up by Mr. Howard, in 1797, "there was nothing under it but the arch of the crypt below" (Milner, vol. ii. p. 96, and note †). Milner (ibid. p. 78) conjectures that " the remains of Bishop Courtenay rest" in the Venerable Chapel in the south transept.

of the Conqueror, and of Bishop Nicholas de Ely, are similar memorials of Hardicanute,[1] the last Danish king of England, and of the heart of Bishop Ethelmar de Valence, whose original monument is now restored and built into the wall of the retro-choir, at the north-east angle. The design of this monument is exceedingly rare and elegant, but the upper part of it, and the inscription below it, are quite modern.[2]

All the other ancient sepulchral monuments which existed in the cathedral have now been collected in the retro-choir. Immediately in front of the entrance to the Lady Chapel is the "flat monument of grey marble, without either inscription or ornament upon it, raised about two feet above the ground," which marks the site of Bishop de Lucy's grave.[3] Another large altar-tomb to some mitred ecclesiastic, the slab of which was once covered with a very magnificent brass, stands in front of the Holy Hole, and, according to Milner's conjecture, is the monument of Prior Silkstede.[4] To the south of this tomb is a coffin-shaped one, which bears upon the slab a floriated cross in slight relief, and the head of a mitred ecclesiastic traced by incised lines, and in two hollow chamfers round it, the following inscription :

Monuments in the retro-choir.

"HIC . IACET . WILLELMVS . DE . BASYNGE . QVONDAM . PRIOR . ISTIVS . ECC'E . CVIVS . ANIME . PROPICIETVR . DEVS . ET . QVI . PRO . AÏA . EIVS . ORAVERIT . III . ANNOS . C . ET . XLV . DIES . INDVLGENCIE . PERCIPIET."[5]

(1) "We observe," says Milner (ibid. p. 110), "the figure of a ship, with the following inscription :—

"QVI IACET HIC REGNI SCEPTRVM TVLIT HARDICANVTVS, EMMÆ CNVTONIS GNATVS ET IPSE FVIT. OB. A.D. 1042."

(2) "This stone is coffin-shaped, but of unusual breadth ; upon its surface is sculptured a pointed oval, extending from the head of the slab of its base ; within this oval, and under a canopy, appears the upper part of the bishop's effigy in his episcopal habit ; his uplifted hands holding a heart, and having his pastoral staff resting upon his left arm. Below the figure, and charged with the arms of De Valence, is a shield, which, with some rich foliage, fills up the lower portion of the oval" (Boutell's, "Christian Monuments," pp. 148, 149, and Pl. opp. p. 118).

I am informed by W. S. Walford, Esq., that the arms are not those of De Valence, but those of Hugh de *Lusignan*, Ethelmar's father.

The inscription mentioned in the text is this :—

"CORPVS ETHELMARI, CVIVS COR NVNC TENET ISTVD SAXVM, PARISIIS MORTE DATVR TVMVLO. OB. ANNO 1261."

"On the north side (of the choir), under the stairs which lead to the organ (where Lieutenant Turner's monument now is), was found, some five years since, the heart (as is supposed) of Hugh le Brun, some time prior of St. Swithin's, in a box of tin" (Gale, p. 32). The monument formerly stood here. There was, however, no prior of this name ; and the inscription might have prevented this gross error.

(3) Milner, vol. ii. pp. 102, 133, and note †. The site is determined by Rudborne, in Wharton's Ang.

Sacr. vol. i. p. 286, "*extra capellam B. Virginis humatus est.*" It used to be pointed out as the resting-place of the legendary Lucius, or Lles, the first Christian monarch of Britain, the similarity of the names having occasioned the confusion of the prelate and the king. This was one of the tombs opened by Mr. Howard, who found in it the remains of silken garments and bones, with indications of its having been opened before. There are traces of a metal cross being formerly attached to the slab of this monument.

(4) This tomb measures twelve feet by five feet, and it was regarded as the monument of St. Swithin, until Milner (vol. ii. pp. 105—108) demonstrated the incorrectness of this supposition. Mr. Howard opened this tomb at the time when he was engaged in his antiquarian researches in Winchester, and found the complete remains of a human body, clothed in black serge, with "funeral boots" yet adhering to the bones of the feet. The inner tomb was made with great care, of stone "similar to that used in Bishop Fox's chapel." And, from the appearances described, it is not improbable that if the remains were Silkstede's, they had been removed hither from his chapel in the south transept.

(5) This tomb, and the next but one, formerly stood in the south transept, "near the entrance of [the Venerable] chapel, on the left hand" (ibid., p. 78). The top of this anonymous tomb with the cross on it, was removed to its present position "from the north transept," in front of "the chapel of the sepulchre," and the remainder from the south transept (Milner, ibid. p. 111 ; Britton, p. 85) ; and the other, ascribed to Bishop De Rupibus, was brought hither from the north aisle of the nave, "close to the wall" (Milner, ibid. p. 112). In Arch. Journ. vol. vii.

On the north side of Prior Silkstede's monument stands another coffin-shaped tomb, bearing an elegant floriated cross carved in very low relief upon its surface, but nothing to denote whose remains it originally covered.   Next to it, by the wall of the north aisle, there lies on the ground part of the monumental effigy of a bishop or prior, sculptured so rudely that it seems as if flattened.   In the same aisle, near Bishop Waynflete's chantry, upon a modern base, lies the almost complete effigy of a mitred ecclesiastic, with remarkably disproportioned arms, and having a trefoil arch over its head and a book in its hand, ascribed by Milner to Bishop De Rupibus.[1]

Effigy of Sir
Arnald de
Gavaston.

Between the chantries of Beaufort and Waynflete is now the only ancient military sepulchral effigy in the cathedral.   It is the mutilated figure of a knight in surcoat and a complete ringed armour of the thirteenth century, and having a pointed shield, charged with his arms,[2] suspended by the guige from his neck.   The legs were crossed, the feet resting upon a crouching lion, and the right hand grasped the hilt of the sword ; the head reposes on two cushions, formerly supported by angels.[3]   One side of the tomb, on which this effigy originally lay, is now built into the eastern wall of the Guardian Angels' Chapel.   It is adorned with five elegant Decorated arches, under which are shields bearing the arms which appear on the knight's shield ; those of Peter Gaveston, his son, six eagles displayed ; the arms of England ; those of France, semée of fleurs-de-lis ; and those of Castile and Leon.[4]   It commemorates Sir Arnald de Gavaston, who died in 1302.

Adjoining the north wall, under the window farthest to the east, is an altar-tomb, in the style common during the reigns of the first Stuarts, having on its side two shields, and two tablets, commemorating Thomas Masson, or Mason, who died in 1559, with other members of his family, of the following century.

The remains of Bishop Orlton probably rest in the chapel of the Guardian Angels, but, as we have already observed,[5] there is nothing to indicate the spot.

---

p. 181, is a notice of the tomb of William de Basynge, communicated by the Rev. W. H. Gunner, who ascribes it to the second prior of that name, A.D. 1284—1295.

(1) "It is difficult to determine whether this represents a bishop or a cathedral prior, *if* the former, *and if* it has always continued in the same place, we have no difficulty in pronouncing that it is the monument . . . . of Peter de Rupibus, as it is particularly recorded by him (Mat. Paris), that in his lifetime he chose a humble place in his cathedral to be buried in" (ibid.).

(2) Quarterly, in 1st and 4th quarters, Bearn, two cows passant, gorged with collars and bells ; in 2nd and 3rd quarters, three garbs ; over all a cross.

(3) Gale (p. 32) states that this inscription accompanied the effigy at the time in which he wrote, when, and also in Milner's time (vol. ii. p. 112), it stood "behind the quire on the north side."

" HIC JACET WILLIELMVS COMES DE INSVLA VANA
ALIAS WINEALL."

But the form of this inscription renders it exceedingly suspicious, especially as no trace of it exists now.   During the restorations the shield, legs, and other parts of this figure were made good.

I am indebted to W. S. Walford, Esq., for this satisfactory identification of this monumental effigy.

(4) These arches are cinquefoiled ogees, with crockets and finials, and there are similarly ornamented double-gabled pinnacles between them.   Both ends have been cut off.   The shields are of the same form as that of the knight, and the foliage from which they are suspended is very elegant, and different in each arch.

In the north arch of the north transept, under the east-most window, is a low cinquefoiled, ogee-arched, sepulchral recess, which has been regarded as the original site of this tomb (Walcott's Handbook of Winchester Cathedral, p. 4).

(5) See p. 66.   Richardson (quoted by Britton, p. 83) says that he was buried " *in capella propria*."

Bishops Walkelin and Giffard were buried in the midst of the nave, to the west of the steps to the choir,[1] but no memorial of the exact spots now remains.

On the floor, opposite the eighth arch, is the memorial of Bishop Horne; and more to the north that of Bishop Watson; and between them that of Dean Kingsmill.[2] Close beside the tomb of Bishop Horne, there was in former times the tomb and memorial inscription of a mayor of Winchester, not known to the City Tables. The stone is now in the south transept, and, though fractured, this may be read in old English round its margin—

"Hic jacent Thomas Bowland quodm Maior Winton civitatis qui obiit sexto decimo die Mensis Octobris Anno Dni Millesimo quadringentesimo octogesimo et . . . . na Uxor etrs que obiit xiii° die mensis Octob. anno mill . . . ."[3]

Besides the ancient interments noticed here, almost all the early bishops of Winchester were buried in this cathedral, but the sites of their graves are wholly unknown. The bones of St. Swithin were doubtless lost at the Reformation, when his costly shrine was taken from the feretory, where it had stood so long, and destroyed.[4]

All the monuments and interments hitherto described are earlier than the year 1600; those of the seventeenth century may now be noticed.[5]

Monuments of the seventeenth century;—

Bishop Morley's altar tomb occupies the space between the ninth and tenth piers, on the north side of the nave, opposite to Edington's chantry. The epitaph in Latin is "interesting" (as Milner observes), having been "made by himself in the eightieth year of his age."[6] Over it, on the side of the pier, hang a mitre and crosier.

Bishop Mews (who died in the beginning of the eighteenth century, but may be included amongst the names of that preceding it) lies buried in the Guardian Angels'

---

(1) "*Walkelinus . . . . in navi ecclesiæ ad gradus pulpiti jacet humatus.*" "*Willielmus Gyffarde . . . . sepultus est in medio voltæ in navi ecclesiæ ad gradus pulpiti ad caput Willelmi [Walkelini] episcopi*" (Rudborne, u. s. p. 285).

(2) Bishop Horne died on June 1, 1580, and Bishop Watson on January 23, 1583. Upon the gravestone of the first dean there used to be this inscription:—

"Willielmus Kingsmell prior ultimus, decanus primus ecclesiæ . . . . obit 1548."
(Gale, pp. 37, 38.)

(3) Milner, vol. ii. p. 117, note ‡, reads the name of the wife Editha.

(4) There are traces of two brasses in the central alley of the nave, one near the west door, the other (which was a very splendid one), opposite the sixth pier. In the north aisle are traces of a brass female figure with an inscription near the ninth window, and also of an ecclesiastic near the sixth window; and in the south aisle there was a brass near Wykeham's chantry, and another either of a female or an ecclesiastic near the steps to choir. In the north transept a fragment of a pavement slab bears traces of a floriated cross, with a band round the edge of the stone for an inscription; in the south transept there was a small brass with an inscription; and in the south-east corner two others, one a figure with an inscription, the other a small square, with yet smaller square additions to the corners, set diagonally. In the retro-choir may also be seen traces of the figure of a female, with an inscription.

Milner (vol. ii. p. 16) quotes from Ryves's "Mercurius Rusticus" and Foulis' "Plots of Pretended Saints," this rather exaggerated account of the spoliations of these memorials of the dead by the soldiers of the parliamentary army in 1644:—"Of the brass torn from the violated monuments might have been built a house as strong as the brazen towers of old romances."

(5) For some of these notices we are indebted to Gale, whose work, published almost a century and a half ago, has preserved the memory of many interments and inscriptions, which had else been forgotten.

(6) Gale, p. 67.

Chapel, and has a mural monument on the north side of it, with a crosier and mitre suspended near it.

On the south side of this chapel is the monument of Richard Weston, Earl of Portland. The effigy of the earl in bronze, very finely executed, lies on the top of the sarcophagus, and in four niches in the wall behind it were "busts in marble of certain persons of his family."[1] All the figures have been shamefully injured; one of the niches is vacant, and the bust now occupying another is evidently made up of the fragments of two others.

—in the retro-choir ;—

Against the south wall of the retro-choir, opposite to Beaufort's chantry, is the mural monument of Sir John Clobery. It consists of a full-length figure of the knight, in marble, standing beneath an arch, "ornamented with all kinds of modern military accoutrements and emblems." On the basement is a long inscription in Latin, which, though it ascribes to Sir John Clobery a more prominent part in the restoration of Charles II. than history assigns him, is not without interest and merit.[2]

Not far from this monument is a large slab in the floor, bearing a long inscription in memory of Baptist Levinz, Bishop of Sodor, and prebendary of this cathedral, who died in 1692; and hard by, but nearer to Langton's Chapel, lie buried Frances, Countess of Exeter, who died in 1663; Lord Henry Paulett, who died in 1672; Elizabeth, Countess of Essex, who died in 1656; and Sir Thomas Higgons, who was her second husband, and died in 1692; and James Touchet, Baron Audley, and Earl of Castlehaven, who died in 1700; and west of Sir John Clobery's monument is one erected in memory of Catharine, wife of Prebendary Fulham, who died in 1699.

—epitaph of Alderman Symonds ;—

In the north aisle, near to Waynflete's chantry, is a stone with this inscription, which possesses an enduring interest to this city :—

> "HERE LIETH WILLIAM SYMONDS, GENTLEMAN,
> OF WINCHESTER TWICE MAIOR AND ALDERMAN,
> ALICE HIS WIEF LYES BVRIED BY HIS SIDE,
> THE ONE IN IUNE, IN IVLY TH OTHER DIED.
> ON THE 10TH DAY 1601 SHE,
> ON THE 27TH DAY 1616 HE.
> HIS MERRIT DOTH ENHERITT LIFE AND FAME,
> FOR WHILST THIS CITY STANDS SYMOND HIS NAME
> IN ALLE MEN'S HARTS SHALL NEVER BE FORGOTTEN
> FOR POORES PRAYERS RISE WHEN FLESH LYES ROTTEN."

An inscription in Latin verse on the other side of this chantry celebrates Christopher Perin, who died in 1612; and to the west of it lies Dr. Arthur Taylor, a physician of repute in the city, who died in 1674. Henry Perin, who died in 1694, lies in the Guardian Angels' Chapel; and near it Sarah, daughter of Sir Richard Tichborne, Bart., who died in 1616.

(1) Milner, vol. ii. p. 105.   (2) Ibid., pp. 101, 102.

A monument of greater note and interest than any other of this period may be seen on the floor of Silkstede's Chapel, in the south transept. It is inscribed thus :— —Izaak Walton's epitaph ;—

"Here resteth the body of
MR. IZAAK WALTON,
Who dyed the 15th of December,
1683.
Alas! Hee's gone before,
Gone, to returne noe more.
Our panting Breasts aspire
After their aged Sire,
Whose well-spent Life did last
Full ninety Years, and past.
But now he hath begun
That which will nere be done,
Crown'd with eternall Blisse,
We wish our Souls with his.
Votis modestis sic flērunt liberi."

In the south transept there is also a marble slab inscribed to Dr. William Hawkins, a prebendary of the cathedral, who died in 1691; and in the Venerable Chapel are the monuments of Charles Dingley and Elizabeth, his wife, who died in the years 1700 and 1683, respectively; of Mrs. Mary Young (wife of Colonel James Young), who died in 1683; and of the daughter of Dean Young, who died in 1636. —monuments in the transept ;—

The monument of Sir Richard Harris, who died in 1698, lies near the modern entrance to the crypt, in the north transept. And in the same part of the cathedral may be seen the monuments of several members of the Jewett family; of two minor canons of the name of Taylor, or Taylour; of a daughter of the great orientalist, Pococke; and of Martha Brexton, whose excellence is celebrated in a quatrain of Latin hexameters and pentameters. These all belong to the seventeenth century.[1]

In the nave are the monuments of Prebendaries Gumble (who died in 1676), Wafferer (in 1680), Dayrell (in 1684), Beaumont (in 1687), with his son; Pain, or Payne (in 1689), with his wife; Bradshaw (in 1690); Morley, a near relative of the bishop (in 1696); and Harris, also head master of Winchester College, whose monument is the most conspicuous of all these, and who died in 1700; to whose misdirected zeal the cathedral was indebted for those "sham urns," which formerly so inappropriately occupied the niches of the reredos. —in the nave

Chancellor Say, who died in 1615, is interred in the nave; and Registrars Traffles (died in 1675) and Harfell (in 1680), with two others of his family. Here also lie George Pemerton, who was twice Mayor of Winchester, and died in 1650, with his wife; and Godson Penton, who died in 1700, and thrice occupied the civic chair of this city. Near Bishop Morley's tomb lies Thomas Garrard, a faithful and attached dependent, who died in 1697. These interments are also noted :—Patience Couse, who

(1) Randolph Jewett died in 1675; Anna Jewett, his wife, in 1692; three of their children in 1685 and 1686; Benjamin Jewett in 1691. Minor canons William Taylour and Ralph Taylor died in 1667 and 1687 respectively; Dr. Pococke's daughter, Etheldreda, died in 1698; and Martha Brexton in 1673.

had been married to Christopher Mompesson (died in 1624); Robert Pescod, of the Court of Chancery (in 1633); John Webb, merchant adventurer of London (in 1684); John Forde, son of Sir William Forde (in 1681), with his wife and children; George Popham (in 1687); William Downes (in 1678); Dr. Nicholas Stanley (in 1687), with his wife and son, who also was a physician; and William Smith (who died in 1671), with his wife.[1] The monument of the wife of an organist of the cathedral may be worth copying:—

> "1623: *Feb.* 8.
> " *Organa qui Tēpli pulso, doceoq; Choristas*
> *Isthic sepultam lugeo uxorem bonam."*
> " MARIAM GEORGIUS
> BATH . F. THOMÆ BATH.
> JUXTA SEPULTI."[2]

Remarkable monuments. The two most remarkable monuments of this century, in the nave of the cathedral, are those of Richard Boles, and of the two brothers of Avington. The former is inscribed upon a small brass plate inserted into the pier adjoining Bishop Morley's tomb on the west;[3] the latter is a mural monument with a Jacobean arch, and arms over and about it, under the fifth window from the west end, in the north aisle.[4] Under the eighth window is another Jacobean monument in style still more repulsive to good taste; but happily for the credit of those whom it represents, the inscription is totally obliterated.[5]

(1) Opposite the sixth pier from the west end of the cathedral is a small square stone with the date 1664, a singular monogram; and near to the third pier is another small square stone with the date 1672, and an inscription in two lines round it, but too much defaced to be read.

(2) Wavell (vol. i. p. 77) gives us the following as "an inscription upon an organist," "in the south aisle,"—

> " *Musicus et Medicus, Langton jacet ipse Johannes;*
> *Organa namque loqui fecerat ipse quasi."*

(3) The inscription, which has frequently been printed, is this:—

> " *A Memoriall*

" For this Renowned Martialist *Richard Boles*, of the Right Worshipful Family of the *Bolses* in *Linckhorne Shire*, Collonell of a Ridgment of Foot of 1300, who for his gracious King *Charles* the First did wounders at the Battle of *Edge-hill*. His last Action, to omit all others, was at *Alton*, in this County of *Southampton*, was surprized by five or six thousand of the Rebels; which caused him, there quartered, to fly to the Church with near fourscore of his Men, who then fought them six or seaven Hours; And then the Rebells breaking in upon him, He slew with his Sword six or seven of them, And then was slain himself, with sixty of his Men about him.

> "1641.

" His gracious Sovereign hearing of his Death gave him his high Commendation, in that passionate Expression,

> " *Bring me a Moorning Scarf, I have lost*
> *One of the best Commanders in the Kingdome.*
> " *Alton* will tell you of that famous Fight
> Which this Man made, and bade this World good night;
> His vertuous Life fear'd not Mortalyty—
> His Body must, his Vertues cannot die.
> Because his Blood was there so nobly spent:
> This is his Tombe, that *Church* his Monument.
> " *Richardus Boles Wiltoniensis in Art. Mag.*
> *Composuit posuitq; Dolens.*
> An. Dni. 1689." (GALE, pp. 74, 75.)

(4) The inscription on this monument is as follows:—
" A Union of two Brothers from Avington. The Clerks Family were Grandfather, Father, and Son, successively Clerks of the Privy Seal. William, the Grandfather, had but two sons, both Thomas's, their wives both Amy's, and their heirs both Henry's, and the heirs of the Henry's both Thomas's. Both their wives were inheritrixes, and both had two sons and one daughter, and both their daughters issueless. Both of Oxford, both of the Temple, both officers to Queen Elizabeth and our noble King James. Both Justices of the Peace, both agree in arms, the one a Knight, the other a Captain. *Si Quæras Avingtonum, Petas Cancellum. Impensis Thomæ Clerk of Hide.* 1662." (Milner, vol. ii. p. 124, note.)

(5) Milner (vol. ii. p. 123) states that the epitaph " appears not to have been engraven, but barely painted," and justly condemns the wretched style of the monument.

The most elegant modern monuments, amongst which we include all bearing date Memorial windows. subsequent to the year 1700, are the Memorial Windows, of which there are at present four. At the east end of Langton's Chantry is one, placed there by the present Dean, in memory of his wife. In the head of the window are emblematical figures of the Virtues, and beneath, in two rows, the Healing of the Lame Man at the Beautiful Gate of the Temple; Jesus blessing little Children; the Good Samaritan; Ruth; the Raising of Jairus's Daughter; and the Maries at the Sepulchre. The following inscription, in old English, crosses the window between the two principal series of subjects:—

"MARIÆ GARNIER, FÆMINÆ OPTIMÆ, UXORI CARISSIMÆ, MATRI PIENTISSIMÆ, HANC FENESTRAM ORNANDAM CURAVIT THOMAS GARNIER, LL.D. DECANUS. OB. XIII. KAL. JUNII. A.S. MDCCCXLIX."

Corresponding with this, in the Chapel of the Guardian Angels, is another erected by Dean Garnier to the memory of his brother. In the head of this window are seen the figures of the Evangelists; the principal subjects, arranged as before, are the Miracle at Cana of Galilee; the Baptism; our Lord at Bethany; Moses with the Law; Noah; and St. Paul at Athens; and the following inscription crosses the window:—

"IN HONOREM DEI ET MEMORIAM GUL. GARNIER, CANON ET CANCELL. VIRI PII, PROBI, DONIS BENEFICI; FRATRIS SUI FRATER AMANTISSIMUS."

The other two are in the nave; the first, in the north aisle, next the transept, exhibits the figures of St. Peter, our Lord, St. Paul, Melchizedec, Moses, and David, in two series, with this inscription:—

"IN HONOUR OF GOD, AND IN MEMORY OF DOROTHEA MORLEY, AND HER DAUGHTERS MARIA OGILBY AND HENRIETTA POULTER."

The second is in a corresponding situation, next the south transept, and contains the figures of the Virgin Mary, St. John the Baptist, St. John the Evangelist, Isaiah, Solomon, and Aaron; and this inscription:—

"IN MEMORY OF EDMUND POULTER, CANON OF THIS CATHEDRAL, OF HIS SONS BROWNLOW AND JOHN SAYER, AND OF HIS GRAND-DAUGHTER DOROTHY JULIA POULTER: ERECTED BY BROWNLOW POULTER."

Commencing at the west end of the cathedral, and proceeding along the south side Modern mural monuments. the following mural monuments are seen:—

Under the first window is a monument by Flaxman, with a bas-relief, representing Faith consoling Sorrow, behind which is inscribed—

"THE JUST SHALL LIVE BY FAITH."

It is in memory of Henrietta Maria North, wife of the late Bishop of Winchester, who died Nov. 16, 1796. Adjoining it a small slab commemorates Jane, wife of Charles May, who died Nov. 3, 1840.

Under the next window is now placed the monument of Dr. Joseph Warton, by Dr. Warton's monument. Flaxman, which formerly stood against the pier at the east end of Edington's Chantry.

On a sepulchral cippus, with a lyre above it, is a bas-relief representing Warton teaching a group of three boys. Terminal figures of Aristotle and Homer are in the background; and medallions are on each side of the cippus. The inscription is by Dr. Parr :—

" H.S.Æ.[1] JOSEPHUS WARTON, S.T.P. HUJUS ECCLESIÆ PREBENDARIUS, SCHOLÆ WINTONIENSIS, PER ANNOS FERE TRIGINTA, INFORMATOR, POETA FERVIDUS FACILIS EXPOLITUS, CRITICUS ERUDITUS PERSPICAX ELEGANS. OBIIT XXIII. FEB. MDCCC. ÆTAT. LXXVIII. HOC QUALECUMQUE PIETATIS MONUMENTUM PRÆCEPTORI OPTIMO, DESIDERATISSIMO, WICCAMICI SUI P.C."

Bishop Tomline's monument.

Bishop Tomline's monument is seen under the third window ; it is by Westmacott, and represents, in bas-relief, an angel with an episcopal staff and a book standing beside an altar, on which are the bishop's arms. On the pedestal is this brief inscription :[2]—

" DEPOSITUM REVERENDISSIMI VIRI GEORGII TOMLINE, EPISCOPI WINTONIENSIS."

In the next bay is the monument of Dean Cheyney, the materials and the taste of which are alike, and justly, praised by Milner.[3] The phœnix is seen rising from the flames of an urn, beside which sit Hope and Wisdom ; and on the urn itself is a medallion representing Faith calling the dead man from the tomb at the sound of the last trumpet. A wreath of palms surrounds the whole. Dr. Cheyney died Jan. 27, 1760.[4]

Beside this monument are two others, one to Captain Thomas Robert Fell, of the Bengal army, who died April 1, 1835 ; and the other to the Rev. John Sturges, LL.D., prebendary of the cathedral, and chancellor of the diocese, who died Oct. 2, 1807.

Under the fifth window is a plain monument, with fluted columns, to John Pentone, who died Nov. 24, 1724, and to his wife. And opposite it, affixed to the pier, adjoining Wykeham's Chantry, is a tablet to commemorate the Rev. Christopher Eyre, Master of Winchester College, who died May 9, 1743.

Monument of Bishop Willis.

The great monument of Bishop Willis, by Cheere, fills up the whole of the sixth bay. The figure of the prelate in his robes reposes on a sarcophagus beneath a rich classical pediment, supported by a pile of books, and with its right hand lifted, and its face raised towards heaven. Contrary to custom, the head is placed to the east.[5] This bishop died Aug. 10, 1734.[6]

(1) This assertion is erroneous, for on the floor of the north aisle, near the font, may be read this English epitaph, " Here lie the Remains of the Rev. Joseph Warton, D.D., late Master of Winchester College, and Prebendary of this Cathedral : who died Feb. 23, 1800. Aged 78. See his monument in this Church."

(2) This inscription is repeated on a slab in the floor of the aisle, in front of the monument.

(3) Vol. ii. p. 115.

(4) The following is the epitaph at length :—" *Hic juxta sepultus est Thomas Cheyney, S.T.P. Hujusce Ecclesiæ Deeanus, et Collegii Wintoniensis Socius ; Qui, cum in omni negotiorum genere, sagaci admodum judicio, et rerum usu, prudens, habilis, et fidelis, semper haberetur ; nemo enim ingenia, moresque hominum, aut interius vidit, aut penitius intellexit ; cum principibus viris diu placuisset, et ad altiora feliciter aspirare potuerit ; hic, tamen in otio, et umbratili vita, sed ingenuo, sed literato*

homine vere digna, hic, amicorum commercio frui, et sibi suisque placere maluit ; Donec luctuosa et diuturna valetudine fractus, et ingravescente demum ætate, Deo, bonorum remuneratori, et Supremo Omnium Judici, animam immortalem pie reddidit. Obiit 27° die Januarii,

Anno { *Domini,* 1760. / { *Ætatis,* 66."

(5) Milner (vol. ii. p. 116) says that it is " the most valuable, as well as the most magnificent, mural monument in the whole cathedral." On the other hand, Britton (p. 107) declares that " the judicious artist and critic will seek in vain for beauty in the execution, or the display of taste in the sculptor." Milner also accuses the sculptor of having died of vexation at the blunder he had committed in the disposition of this figure.

(6) Bishop Willis is thus commended in his epitaph : —" *In Memoriam Reverendi admodum in Christi Patris*

Beside the new south doorway are the monuments of the Rev. Richard Cockburn, prebendary of the cathedral, who died Nov. 24, 1831 ; and of Philip Williams, steward to the dean and chapter and recorder of Winchester, who died Oct. 9, 1843.

And in the next bay is Dean Naylor's tablet, bearing the appropriate emblems of Death, Judgment, Time, and Eternity, with the word "MEMENTO." The dean died June 23, 1739.[1] The monument of the Rev. Edmund Pyle, D.D., prebendary of the cathedral, who died Dec. 14, 1776, and of the Rev. Thomas Pyle, also a prebendary, who died July 3, 1807, are placed beside that of Dean Naylor.

The ninth window has, beside the monument of the Rev. Henry Stephens, prebendary, who died April 13, 1739, the tablets commemorating Thomas Woods Knollys, Earl of Banbury, who died March 10, 1793 ; the Countess of Banbury, who died in 1798 ; and (on the eastern side of the window) of General William Knollys, eighth Earl of Banbury, who died Feb. 5, 1818 ; and of some members of his family.

In the next space is the monument of the Rev. Thomas Balguy, D.D., prebendary of the cathedral, who died Jan. 19, 1795 ; an elegant semi-classical design, with an urn, foliage, fruit, &c. And near it is a tablet recording the death of Lieutenant Arthur Francis Maine, before Sebastopol, on Nov. 21, 1854.

The last bay on this side of the nave contains Chantrey's monument of Sir George Prevost, Bart., who died Jan. 5, 1816. Under appropriate military trophies, is seen a female seated beside a tomb, and, conspicuously displayed, this mention of his chief services,—"ST. LUCIA TAKEN," "DOMINICO DEFENDED," "CANADA PRESERVED." A long inscription gives a complete outline of his career. Hard by this is a small tablet, which records the death of the Rev. Edward James, canon of the cathedral, on Sept. 6, 1854.

Monument of Sir G. Prevost Bt.

Crossing now to the north aisle, against the pier opposite to the east end of Edington's Chantry, we see the monument of Bishop Hoadley. Milner[2] justly praises the execution of the medallion portrait of the deceased prelate, and comments severely on the "incongruous association of emblems" beneath it,—the pike surmounted by the cap of liberty, the episcopal crosier, Magna Charta, and the New Testament. The inscription on the tomb is little more than a chronological account of the successive steps of advancement, and the honours which Hoadley enjoyed.

Bishop Hoadley's monument

In the bay opposite this arch, and nearest the transept, are the monuments of Anne Morley, who died Dec. 24, 1787, and an infant ; and of her husband, James Morley, of Kempshot, who died Feb. 22, 1798 ; and of a daughter of Harriett Poulter,

---

Richardi Willis, Episcopi Wintoniensis, Viri ex morum simplicitate, ex animi integritate it verborum fide, ut qui illum optime noverint, ii maxime æstimaverint, propensissime dilexerint ; Patriam, principem, et libertatem publicam unice amavit ; Religionem interea vere Christianam sanctissime coluit, acerrime vindicavit. Nulla temporum varietate debilitari, aut frangi potuit ; in republica, in ecclesia, fidelis, constans, et sui similis. Egregiis

hisce virtutibus instructus, in mediis quos abunde meruit honoribus, felicissime consenuit, donec annorum plenus, obiit, 10 die Augusti, Anno { *Domini,* 1734.
{ *Ætatis,* 71.
Johannes Willis, armiger, filius ejus et hæres, vie memor posuit.

(1) Milner, vol. ii. p. 79.
(2) Ibid., p. 123.

M

whose memorial window is above. On the respond adjoining to the west is a tablet in memory of the Rev. Brownlow Poulter, prebendary, whose death occurred on March 30, 1829.

Henry Bowles, who died Aug. 15, 1815, is commemorated by a tablet under the tenth window from the west end, and near it is the monument of Mathew Comb, M.D., who departed this life Feb. 23, 1748. "It consists of an urn adorned with garlands and flowers, standing upon a sarcophagus, with a pyramid and sepulchral lamps,"[1]—an incongruity of emblems which appears in more than one otherwise appropriate design in this cathedral.

Proceeding westward, under the next window, we find the monument (which is ornamented with fluted columns alone) of the Rev. Charles Woodroffe, LL.D., prebendary of the cathedral, who died Feb. 13, 1726 ; and of Elizabeth, his wife, who died Sept. 6, 1721.

The monument of Sir Villiers Chernocke, Bart., and of Lady Chernocke, occupies the seventh bay from the west. The design represents Justice and Charity beside a funeral urn, over which droops a willow, and is in high relief. The baronet's decease is recorded as happening on the " iii. No. Jun. 1779," and that of his lady on the " xvii. Kal. Sep. 1789."

Opposite the font is the monument of Edward Montagu, who died May 20, 1776 ; and of Elizabeth, his wife, who was the founder of the " Blue Stocking Club," and author of an " Essay on the Writings and Genius of Shakspere." The design of the monument is suitable to the repute of those it commemorates ; and the portion of the inscription referring to the lady is as follows :—" Here lies the body of Elizabeth Montagu, daughter of Matthew Robinson, Esq., of West Layton, in the county of York, who, possessing the united advantages of beauty, wit, judgment, reputation, and riches, and employing her talents most uniformly for the benefit of mankind, might be justly deemed an ornament to her sex and country. She died on the 25th of August, 1800, aged 81." The death of an infant son is also recorded.

Mrs. Montagu's monument.

Beside the window is a monument displaying, in bas-relief, a female figure sorrowing over an urn, by which are military trophies and oriental emblems. It is in memory of Colonel James Morgan (son-in-law to Dr. Warton), who died Oct. 29, 1808.

In the next bay, the fifth from the west end, are the monumental tablets of Andrew Crawford, M.D., who died April 9, 1824 ; and of Mary Anne, the wife of Dr. Littlehales, who died in 1786. In the fourth bay are the monuments of the Rev. Edward Salter, prebendary, who died May 23, 1812, and his widow Delitia, who survived him till May 3, 1833 ; of Katharine Pool, wife of Major Pool, who died in 1779 ; and of her father, Thomas Lacy, who died in 1763 ; and of the Rev. William Hill Newbolt, D.D., minor canon of the cathedral. And under the third window is a tablet to the memory of Mary Anne Gravatt, who died July 29, 1818, and one to

---

(1) Milner, vol. ii. p. 123.

record the death of George Hurst, Esq., of London, in 1783, and of his wife and their sons.

Next the respond between this window and the second from the west end is the monument of Dr. John Littlehales, consisting of a bas-relief of the Good Samaritan, by Bacon, under which is this text, inscribed on the pages of an open Bible:— "THE BLESSING OF HIM THAT WAS READY TO PERISH CAME UPON ME." The epitaph is as follows:—"Near to this place are deposited the remains of JOHN LITTLE- HALES, M.D., fellow of the Royal College of Physicians, London, and formerly of Pembroke College, Oxford. His eminent professional talents, by the blessing of Divine Providence, were successfully exerted, with a generosity so distinguished, and with beneficence to the poor so diffusive and unwearied, amidst a very extended practice, that his decease was an event most deeply regretted and lamented. The principal inhabitants of Winchester and its neighbourhood have erected this Monu- ment as a Public Record of their affectionate gratitude to the Memory of their Friend and Benefactor; but from the SAVIOUR of the World, whose Faith he adorned by a life devoted to Christian Benevolence, he will receive his final Reward. He departed this life the 2nd of January, 1810, Aged 57 years."

Dr. Littlehales' monument.

No other mural monument remains to be noticed in the nave but a small and plain tablet, under the window nearest the Consistory Court, to the Rev. Charles Richards, prebendary, who died Jan. 21, 1833.

In the north transept is the only modern altar tomb, which stands under the western arch of the terminal aisle, and is surrounded by a light iron railing. It is in memory of the Rev. Frederick Iremonger, prebendary of the cathedral and rector of St. John's parish, who died May 11, 1820. The figure of the deceased, in his academical gown, and with a book in his right hand, lies at length on a mattrass or couch, in a placid sleep. It is executed in freestone by Chantrey.

Monuments in the N. transept Prebendary Iremonger's tomb.

Proceeding northward from the entrance to the transept from the nave, we see monuments to the following persons:—the Rev. Thomas Rivers, LL.D., prebendary, who died Sept. 8, 1731, and several members of his family; the Rev. Sir Henry Rivers, Bart., who died July 8, 1851; Elizabeth, wife of Colonel Samuel Wall, of Worthy, who died Oct. 29, 1835,—a very elegant monument, ornamented in imita- tion of Fox's Chantry, with figures of Faith and Charity on either side; Mary Cole, widow of the Rev. Dr. Cole, prebendary, and daughter of the great lawyer Sir William Blackstone, died Jan. 10, 1830; the Very Rev. Dean Rennell, died March 31, 1840; his son, the Rev. Thomas Rennell, a prebendary of Salisbury, died June 30, 1824, and his wife Sarah, daughter of Sir William Blackstone, who died Jan. 29, 1830.

On the north-west pier, opposite the last monument, is one to the memory of Joseph Serres, a Frenchman of the Reformed Church, who died in 1754.

Under the north window in the eastern aisle is the monument of Robert Pescod, Esq., which formerly contrasted its "true Corinthian" columns with the "bad Corinthian" of that anonymous Jacobean monument in the north aisle of the nave;[1] he died Aug. 22, 1725. Beneath the next window, under a Normanesque arch, is the record of the death of the Rev. George Frederick Nott, D.D., on Oct. 25, 1841; and over the entrance to the crypt, at the south end of the aisle, a plain slab in memory of the architect, who was so intimately associated with Dr. Nott in his labours in restoring the cathedral, William Garbett, who died Aug. 31, 1834.

Against the south-east pier is a tablet commemorating the name and death of the Rev. Thomas Watkins, minor canon, on April 9, 1839.

On the wall of the Holy Sepulchre Chapel is the monument of Chaloner Ogle, Esq., who died June 12, 1814; and Catharine, his wife; and near it a small slab bears this elegant inscription :—

> *" Uxori matrique*
> *Ornatissimæ optimæ dilectissimæque,*
> *MELESINA TRENCH,*
> *Obiit viginti septimo die Maii,*
> 1827."

And under the arch of the choir nearest the nave is an elegant and appropriate monument to Lieutenant Frederick McCombe Turner, who died at Bombay, Jan. 14, 1856.

Monuments in the S. transept. Sir Isaac Townsend's monument. In the south transept, beneath the tower arch, stands a monument so large as to be properly entitled a "mausoleum."[2] It is richly, but heavily, ornamented with naval and military trophies, and celebrates in a Latin inscription the memory of Sir Isaac Townsend, K.G., an admiral, and Lord of the Admiralty, who died May 26, 1731. Another inscription, at the back of the tomb (which is accessible by a narrow stair beside it), records the death of Lady Townsend.

On the eastern tower pier is a tablet to the Rev. Matthew Woodford, archdeacon of Winchester, who died in Sept. 1807; and to his sister Mary.

The Venerable Chapel contains monuments to the Rev. Robert Eyre, prebendary, who died Oct. 14, 1722; and to his wife and daughters; to William Eyre, Esq., who died March 7, 1764; to another Richard Eyre, died Feb. 1, 1778; and to his wife Alicia, daughter of Brown Willis; and to Henry Eyre, died Aug. 18, 1830, and his wife and son.

In the next chapel, to the south, is a huge monument (the most conspicuous part of which is a flaming urn), which lauds at length in a Latin inscription the memory of the Rev. John Nicholas, D.D., prebendary of the cathedral, and successively scholar, fellow, and warden of both Wykeham's colleges; who died Feb. 27, 1711.

Monuments in the retro-choir and Lady Chapel. The monument of the Rev. George Turner, D.D., prebendary, who died Oct. 30, 1797, is the only mural one in the retro-choir.

But on the north side of the altar in the Lady Chapel is the fine monument, by

---

(1) See p. 78.   (2) Milner, vol. ii. p. 119.

Chantrey, to the late Bishop Brownlow North. It pourtrays in high relief the prelate kneeling, and in a Latin inscription at great length records his excellences, and his death on July 12, 1820.

Very few of the recently placed floor slabs will require notice; some must, however, be mentioned for their quaintness, such as that which the Rev. Charles Layfield, D.D., and a prebendary, placed by himself, whilst yet living, in the Lady Chapel;[1] and that in the south transept, which, ostensibly to the memory of Madam Mary Davies, really celebrates the valour of Colonel Davies, her husband.[2] *Floor slabs.*

Another, in the north aisle of the nave, in front of that remarkable memorial to the two brothers from Avington, bears this inscription :— " In memory of JANE AUSTEN, youngest daughter of the late Rev. George Austen, formerly rector of Steventon, in this county. She departed this life on the 18th of July, 1817, aged 41, after a long illness supported with the patience and hope of a Christian. The benevolence of her heart, the sweetness of her temper, and the extraordinary endowments of her mind, obtained the regard of all who knew her, and the warmest love of her intimate connexions. Their grief is in proportion to their affection ; they know their loss to be irreparable, but in their deepest affliction they are consoled by a firm, though humble, hope that her charity, devotion, faith, and purity have rendered her soul acceptable in sight of her REDEEMER." *Epitaph of Jane Austen.*

In the south aisle, under the fourth window from the west, the following points out the burial-place of a statesman whose name is not forgotten in political circles :— " *H.S.E. Juxta Parentum Cineres Gulielmus Sturges Bourne, Johannis et Judithæ Sturges Filius, Regibus Georg. III., Georg. IV., Gulielm. IV., et Reginæ Victoriæ, e Secretioribus Consiliis. Ita publicæ, privatæque Vitæ functus est Muneribus, ut honorem sibi et amorem abunde conciliârit. Obiit die Feb. I. Anno Dom. MDCCCXLV. Ætatis LXXVI.*" *Epitaph of William Sturges Bourne.*

---

(1) Milner (vol. ii. p. 121) gives the inscription, and this comment, which requires record here :—

" *Anno Salutis* 1705. *Ætatis Suæ* 58.

" *Carolus hunc posuit lapidem Layfieldus inanem*
Presenti exequias dum parat ipse sibi.
Si tamen hic nolit Deus illius ossa jacere
Tum teneat vacuus nomen inane lapis."

" The occasion of this stone and inscription was, that Dr. Layfield, having new paved the Lady Chapel, prepared, at the same time, his own sepulchre in it, which, however, he never filled. In performing this work there is reason to believe that he destroyed a great number of interesting ancient tombstones, some of which, in a reversed position, form part of the present pavement."

(2) " Here lieth the Body of Madam Mary Davies, Daughter of Jonathan Trelawny, of Trelawny, in the County of Cornwall, Baronett. A Lady of excellent Endowments and exemplary Virtue, of Courage and Resolution above her sex, and equal to the generous Stock whence she sprang. She was Maid of Honour to Mary Princess of Orange, and Relict of Lieut. Coll. Davies, who at the Siege of Namur, mounting the trenches at the head of yᵉ Grenadiers of yᵉ first Regiment of Guards, was the first that threw the fascines (which others used to cover themselves with in theyr attaque) over yᵉ ditch, and with his Men passed it, beating the French out of theyr works, which was a gallant action, and greatly contributed towards the taking of the Towne. In performing of which he received the Wound, of which he dyed ; and gain'd so just an Esteem, for yᵉ Boldnesse and Success of it with the King, that he designed him the great honour of a visit yᵉ morning on wᶜʰ he dyed ; and being informed of his Death, in kind and honourable terms express'd his Concern and Sorrow for yᵉ losse of so Brave and deserving an Officer.

" She dyed the xxiiiith of September, in the year of our Lord MDCCVII."

Near this slab are to be seen the disjointed and displaced fragments of many similar memorials of the seventeenth and beginning of the eighteenth centuries.

Near this monument, between the third and fourth piers, are the sepulchral slabs which cover the remains of Bishop Trimnel, who died in 1723; and Dean Trimnel, his brother, who died six years later.[1]

The Cathedral Library.

Here we conclude our survey of the interior of the cathedral,[2] and proceed by the ancient wooden staircase in the terminal aisle of the south transept, through a doorway just over the entrance from the dark cloister, to the Cathedral Library.

This room is built over the cloister, with a modern roof leaning against the transept wall.[3] This room was built (according to Gale[4]) in 1668; and it is divided into two parts; the larger one, to the east of the lobby, is the Library; and the smaller one, to the west, was originally the Audit House, and more recently the choristers' schoolroom.[5]

The Library is a long, low room, with oaken presses curiously carved, and ornamented with gilded knobs, after the fashion of the latter half of the seventeenth century. It contains a collection of from between three and four thousand volumes,[6] principally on divinity, and the larger part of them the gift of Bishop Morley. These works are accessible to the clergy of the diocese by application to the canon in residence; and a book is kept in which borrowers enter their names and the titles of the books they take. The Bodleian Library Catalogue is used, and there is another catalogue for works not contained in that. There is also a volume in which gifts and bequests to the Library are recorded.[7] Besides the books, there are some exceedingly curious and valuable MSS., among which are—

(1) In the nave, near the second arch on the north side, is the following inscription:—

"*Filio natu maximo*, FRANCISCO GULIELMO TRENCH, *Superstites parentes, Ricardus Chenevix et Francisca Maria, ideo non infelicissumi quod minus abreptum lugent quam in pacem præmissum prospectant; hunc lapidem, desiderii simul et spei monumentum P.C. Quem ipse effugit suis tradidit dolorem. Prid. Id. Januar.* 1841. *Vixit annos* 8."

(2) There is one epitaph in the graveyard which calls for a passing mention. It may be seen in "Notes and Queries," 2nd S., vol. i. pp. 64, 65, and in Pettigrew's "Collection of Epitaphs" (Bohn's Antiquarian Library), pp. 510, 511. The doggrel quartrain on this gravestone is attributed to one Dr. Hoadley, conjectured by the Rev. W. H. Gunner ("N. & Q.," 2nd S., vol. ii. p. 195) to have been a son of Bishop Hoadley, who was chancellor of the diocese, and dabbled in poetry.

(3) Britton (Pl. IX.) has omitted this modern addition to the transept, representing what he supposed the original exterior of the wall to be; but in Pl. XXIV. he gives a section of it, and at p. 100 seems to intimate that the " sloping roof," which now covers the Library, was intended to cover the dark cloister. Milner (p. 78), on the other hand, regards the structure over the cloister as a passage from the dormitories of the monks into the cathedral, used in the nocturnal services.

(4) P. 37.

(5) This school having been discontinued, the room is (I am informed by the present librarian, Mr. Garrett) about to be added to the Library, the additions to the collections of books requiring more space. The doors of this room are formed of parts of the monstrous and gorgeous Jacobean canopy which, until the restorations, concealed the centre of the magnificent reredos.

(6) See Beriah Botfield's " Cathedral Libraries," p. 465, &c.

(7) A note from E. W. Jacob, Esq., of Crawley, informs me, that amongst the scarce and curious pamphlets in this collection are the following:—

" Curiosities of Common Water, or the Advantages thereof in Preventing, and Curing many Distempers:" by John Smith, C.M. 1723; with this motto on the title-page—

" That's the best physick which doth cure our ills
　Without the charge of 'pothecaries' pills."

" Χοιροχωρογραφια : sive Hoglandiæ Descriptio. Plaudite Porcelli Porçorum Pigra Propago. (Eleg. Poet.) Londini. 1709. Pretium 2d."

" Injvncions giuen by the Kynges Maiestie as well to the Clergie as to the Laietie of this Realme." (Black letter.) 1547.

" The third New Yeere's Gift, and the second Protest,

The Vulgate, in three volumes, imperial folio, with splendid illuminations.

"Bedæ Historia Ecclesiastica Gentis Anglorum;" a fair copy, in a hand not later than the eleventh century, and which used to be chained in the church; the place for the attachment of the chain still remaining.

"Liber vocatus Unum ex Quatuor, compositus per Zachariam Chrysopolitanum." An exposition of Anmonius' Μονοτεσσαρον. This book has the chain still attached to its cover.

"Liber B. Mariæ Suthwellie, in quo continentur Revelatio S. Wilfridi . . . . et Historia Frygii Daretis; et Historia Britonum . . . ." This volume was formerly chained in the church.

Another volume contains "Liber Viarum Dei et Revelationum Elizabeth: Versus de Domina: Vita Sancti Edwardi Regis et Confessoris: Vita Sancti Thomæ Cantuar. Archiepiscopi."

"Annales sex Regum Angliæ cum annotationibus per Fratrem Nicolaum Triveth, Ord. Præd."

"Promptorium Parvulorum."[1]

But the most valuable MSS. for the purposes of this History are, in fact, the wreck of the muniment room of St. Swithin's Priory. The greater number of these documents have been preserved from further decay by being mounted in large guard books; others, among which is certainly one unpublished Saxon charter, are deposited in the drawers of a press; and others, again, such as *computi* and rent-rolls, are, it is to be feared, irrecoverably decayed. Amongst these the most generally interesting would be the original Charter of Henry VIII. to the Cathedral, when the Priory was dissolved, and a new order of things established; an old "Rental of yᵉ Mannors belonging to Bp. Winton;" and a "Book of the ancient Clerks remaining within the Mannors of the Priory of the Church of St. Swithin;" and the Chapter-book from 1553 to 1600.[2]

In addition to what has been noted of the contents of the Library, a huge pair of

and the first Proclamation of Outlawry, for this year, 1576, against all the learned Papists in England, Antuuerp, &c." Below is a man blowing a trumpet, on the banner of which is inscribed, "If one trumpet this yeere will not make you learned Papists to auswere! the next year look for two trumpets." And a satirical line engraving of the Pope, &c., follows.

"The Jesuite, the Chiefe if Not the only State Heritique, or the Venetian Quarrell Digested into a Dialogue." 1647.

"Robin's Panegyrick, or the Norfolk Miscellany;" n.d.

"Poems, by H. Travers." 1731.

In this library may also be seen a copy of the "Mercurius Rusticus;" and in vol. iii. p. 144, &c., in the "Countries Complaint at Cathedral Churches," mention is made of this cathedral.

(1) One MS. is inscribed "Libellus Dompni Willi Basynge," and thereby has a great local value.

Another thick and closely-written MS., in double columns, has been commended in the margin, by some old world reader, to the especial attention of those who should come after him. Augustine's Sermons, Jerome's Exposition of Isaiah, Cassiodorus on the Psalms, together with Bede's Martyrology, and the lives of some other celebrated ecclesiastical worthies, are also to be found amongst these scarcely-known treasures.

(2) The preservation of these highly valuable and interesting deeds is due to the zeal of Dr. Nott, and the ability of W. T. Alchin, Esq., now librarian to the Corporation of the City of London, whose Synoptical Indices to the Episcopal Registers of this diocese are a monument of learning and patience; and worthy, from their extraordinary utility, of no less accessible depository than the national museum.

In addition to the documents mentioned in the text, there are two ancient deed boxes more than filled with records fully as interesting and valuable as those which have been preserved in the guard books.

globes by Blaeuw, and a single smaller one, of a much earlier date, may be mentioned; and a collection of ancient coins of some value. One of the tables, also, appears to be as old as the presses and the Library itself.

The Close.

We now proceed to the Close, as that part of the precinct which lies to the south of the cathedral is called. Here are the official residences of the Dean and Canons, and a few private houses; most of them are modern buildings, having been erected (according to Wavell[1]) after the Restoration.[2] Several houses have been removed, and many alterations made in distribution of the grounds, the footways, &c., since the Close was first laid out; and by this means, not only has almost all the old priory been destroyed, but its plan cannot be traced with certainty;—and some buildings of great interest from their associations (such as the house in which Bishop Ken lived when a prebendary, and which he declined to lend to Charles II. for the accommodation of Nell Gwynne) have perished.[3]

Remains of the conventual buildings.
The Cloisters.

The remains of the Monastery of St. Swithin, which have survived to this day, are exceedingly few and fragmentary. The only vestige of the Cloisters now existing is the square space which they, with their inclosed garth, once covered; and this can be traced more clearly on a plan than on the spot, so much has planting and the laying out of this part of the Close altered its aspect.[4] In the absence of the real cloisters, the name has been given to the passage between the end of the south transept and the Chapter-house, and which is most probably, as Milner thought,[5] "Walkelin's original work."

The Chapter-house.

The Chapter-house is in plan a parallelogram; in length nearly equal to the width of the transept, or eighty-six feet; and in width thirty-seven. The entrance from the cloisters (as may now be seen very advantageously) consisted of five semicircular arches, of which the central one is larger than the rest, supported by massive round columns, with capitals like those in the triforia of the transepts. "The arcade on the north side is tolerably perfect," consisting of twenty-four semicircular arches,

(1) Vol. i. p. 83.

(2) On the lead-work of the houses in Dumb Alley (more recently called Dome Alley, probably from its not being known that the old name signified no more than that it was a *cul-de-sac*) may be seen, in addition to the arms of the see, &c., the device of the pomegranate; which was the badge of Catharine of Aragon, and of her daughter, Queen Mary, but can scarcely be regarded as indicating that those houses were built in the beginning or the middle of the sixteenth century.

(3) When Milner wrote, the north-eastern side of the cathedral was concealed by the walls, &c., of the Dean's kitchen garden, which had succeeded to the "Paradise" of Speed's map. In 1850 this was removed, and the interior of the Chapter-house was applied to this use. During the last years (1856, 1857), another alteration has thrown this open to public view, and at the same time a footpath to the east of the Dean's garden has been

closed, so that the grounds of the Deanery extend now, without interruption, to the Lock Pond.

(4) The quadrangle is very distinct in Godson's map, as the south wall was then standing.

Wolcott (Handbook, p. 5) justly declares that the injury done to the cathedral by Waller's troopers, in 1644, was "slight," " in comparison" with the demolition of the cloisters by Bishop Horne, in Elizabeth's time. Yet it appears from Milner's history (vol. ii. p. 136) that the wall of the south cloister, or some part of it, was in existence till 1797. He says that it was four feet in thickness, and that there were in it, besides one wide archway, which "was the entrance from the outquarters into the cloisters," "several arched recesses," half the depth of the wall, " for the purpose of seats," all of which were filled up with modern masonry.

(5) Vol. ii. p. 135. See above, p. 40, note 1, respecting this dark cloister.

with capitals like others to be found in the transepts, and cylindrical shafts, most of which, being completely disengaged, have disappeared. The edge of the base on which these columns stood is chamfered, and has been detected [1] at the south-eastern corner of this area, although no trace of the arcade remains on the south side.

No part of the monastic remains is so complete as the ancient watercourses. Being, in fact, sewers constantly flushed, the drainage of the Close is effected by means of them in the most effectual manner; and it is evident both from their construction, and from a mention of them in Wykeham's Register,[2] that they were intended to perform this office to the old monastery. Entering the Precinct from Colebrook Street, near the east end of the cathedral, the Lock Pond (as it is now called) passes by a slightly bending course to the hatches seen beside the path to the back gate of the Close, whence one arm runs due south, and another, diverging almost at right angles, goes to the second hatches at the end of the Chapter-house. Two branches flow from this point,—one southward, nearly as far as the Dean's Library, and then, turning at right angles eastward, originally in two streams (forming a parallelogram under the great *necessarium*), but now in one stream only, receives the waters of the first-named arm, and falls into the stream from St. Mary's Abbey, which divided the convent grounds from Wolvesey. The other branch passes under the Chapter-house, across the cloister square to the back of the buildings forming its western side, turns southward, crosses Dumb Alley near its entrance, turns again eastward, and when it reaches the open ground of the Close, bending a little to the south, passes under the old post-and-pan stables opposite, and, soon turning once more to the south, leaves the cathedral precinct, and runs along the north side of College Street, and crosses it opposite the end of Commoners.

The ancient watercourses.

From these watercourses, aided by the passage from Wykeham's Register, and the general plan of similar establishments, we may form a tolerably correct notion of the arrangement of the buildings of St. Swithin's Priory. In the external wall of the cloisters, next to the entrance to the Chapter-house is an Early English doorway, with a cinquefoiled head, and shafts of Purbeck marble, within an arch with several bold and elegant mouldings, and having (apparently) episcopal heads as corbels to its hood-mould, and beside it may be seen portions of plain Norman arches, filled up.[3] This doorway was opposite the south cloister, and must have led to the Dormitory and Infirmary; which, in all probability, ranged east and west,[4] and ran back to a considerable distance, for there would not otherwise be room for the accommodation of sixty monks, as the end of the "Prior's Hall" comes nearly as far as this doorway.

Conventual remains east of the cloisters.

(1) I am indebted for this fact to Mr. W. Coles, City Surveyor, who superintended the works at the late alterations made in the Close.

(2) Pars. ii. ff. 178, &c. quoted by Warton, p. 73. "A certain watercourse running . . . . through the middle of the Dormitory, Cloisters, Buttery [cellarer's department], Malt-house [this is a mistake, it should be storehouse],

Kitchen, and the middle of the court, or quadrangle of the said Priory, which course of water is called *Lourte Bourne.*"

(3) These were most probably arched recesses, like those which Milner (*u. s.*) describes as being in the south wall of the cloisters.

(4) Mr. J. H. Parker informs me that he was led to the same conclusion respecting the Dormitory at Chester.

N

Vestiges of the Dormitory and Infirmary.

Very few vestiges of these buildings remain now:[1] the principal are an extension of the south wall of the Chapter-house, in which (at the angle) was recently discovered a narrow oblique window-opening; a little further on the trace of a stone staircase, descending from the south side to the north, and under the wall itself, beneath it, an old lead pipe; still further eastward, a narrow doorway (the upper part of which was destroyed) in the middle of a rude and ruinous semicircular arch springing immediately from the floor-line; a wall parallel to this, and distant southward about the width of the Chapter-house, with an angle in it, chamfered, and having an Early English moulding in the chamfer, and the base of a column of the same period in the angle,[2] and in which appears, a little to the east of the line of the Chapter-house, a segment of a semicircular arch over the branch of the Lock Pond (which line runs from north to south); and, finally, the substructure of the customary huge "*necessarium*," consisting of one perfect row of fifteen arches over the same branch of the Lock Pond (now running at right angles to its former course, under the terrace in the Dean's garden), and part of a second row parallel to it, over the other arm of the same stream which is now stopped up.[3]

The Prior's Hall.

Next, to the south, is the Deanery, which consists in good part of a splendid hall, named by Warton,[4] and by others[5] after him, "the Prior's Hall." "This hall is of the fifteenth century,[6] with a fine roof and windows, but now divided into several apartments. The construction of the roof is simple, but very good; each pair of principals is supported by a wooden arch," with pierced spandrels "springing from corbels carved into heads, some of which appear to be intended as portraits of a particular bishop." "The windows are lofty," of two lights, "divided by a transom," with cinquefoiled arches beneath, and the same in the head of the window, at the apex of which, between two perpendiculars from the two upper arches, is a sixfoil. They "have the customary seats formed in the sill." There are five of these windows on the west side, and another at the south end; and the wainscoting along the lower part of the walls, panelled with the common linen pattern, and a screen richly adorned with many cusped arches, may still be seen.[7]

The present entrance to the Deanery shows "three external arches and a vaulted passage of the time of Henry III. The arches are very acute and without shafts; they were originally all open, forming a sort of vestibule to the house, and was

(1) For the knowledge of all the unpublished facts mentioned here, I am indebted to Mr. W. Coles.

(2) In the Winchester Volume of the Arch. Inst., "Architectural Notes, &c." (p. 6), this angle is figured, and described as "part of the Chapter-house." I have been favoured by Mr. O. B. Carter with the original drawings of these remains, and am thus enabled to correct this mistake.

(3) Mr. Coles has permitted me to copy the plan which he constructed, with views of these remarkable substructures of the conventual buildings; and from these drawings, and personal information, I am enabled to give

this very important addition to the information regarding the plan of this monastery.

(4) P. 75.

(5) Wavell, vol. i. p. 80; Milner, vol. ii. p. 139. The name is adopted in the Winchester Vol., Arch. Inst., "Archit. Notes, &c.," p. 4, from which the description given above is partly quoted.

(6) Milner remarks (vol. ii. p. 139, note ‡) that "there are evident traces in the building of a much higher antiquity than the age which these windows denote."

(7) Wavell (vol. i. p. 80) says that this hall was sixty-five feet long, and twenty-two broad.

probably connected with the cloisters.[1] In the spandrels of the arches are narrow lancet niches, with the brackets for images remaining; and the arches are flanked by the original buttresses on each side."[2]

Most of the modern part of the Deanery was built in the seventeenth century. The massive, black, oaken staircase, and the huge carved tables which adorn the hall, are evidently Jacobean.[3] The Library and some other parts date from the Restoration.[4]

On the opposite angle of the cloister square (which is distinctly traceable, although no portion of the cloisters themselves remain) is another relic of the conventual buildings, consisting of two vaulted apartments, one on the south, and the other on the west side of the square, and joining at the corner. The latter is the most perfect, the shell of the structure, even to the roof, being entire. In the vaulted substructure of this part are three massive round columns, ranged along the centre, with similar responds at the ends, and smaller responds at the sides, all with capitals and bases of undoubted Early English character. The ribs, which divide the vault into eight squares, intersected by diagonals, are semioctagonal. There were three windows on the west side, against which also are three buttresses (in addition to one at the angle), and two opened into the cloister. In the south end was the doorway and a narrow window. Above these may be traced another arch, most probably of a window, replaced by a low square-headed window of later date; and just under the high-pitched eaves is an elegant sixfoil rose window.

Conventual remains at the south-west angle of the cloisters.

Against the middle of the west wall of this vaulted apartment, in a portion of it now used as a kitchen, "are the two stone legs of a table of the thirteenth century, which are ornamented with good bold sculpture and sunk panels; the top at present consists of an oak slab of considerable antiquity, but probably not the original one." "There is no original fireplace or chimney." In one of the other rooms a perpendicular fireplace has been inserted; and "there are remains of early painting on the vault."[5]

In the other building are traces of a vaulted substructure; and at the west end is a good doorway, over which is a singular low window, with shafts supporting

---

(1) This is extremely questionable.

(2) Arch. Inst., Winchester Vol., "Archit. Notes, &c.," pp. 2, 3. Some of the stained glass in the Deanery seems to have belonged to the ancient Priory. Wavell (vol. i. pp. 83, 84) mentions the following pieces in the windows of the Library :—"Three Saints, the arms of King Edgar, or of Edward the Elder [which should be Edward the Confessor, and even these are adscriptitious], of the See, and of William Kingsmill, the first dean." In the windows above the entrance, he says, are "Prior Silkstede's initials, T. S., connected with his usual device of a skein of silk."

Mr. Winston, in his "Short Notice, &c." (*u. s.*, p. 7) merely says, "In the Library at the Deanery are some excellent specimens of heraldic glass, of the time of

James I. and Charles I., in which, however, the decline of the art of glass painting is very apparent."

(3) Wavell (vol. i. p. 83) states that "King James planted a fig-tree in the Dean's garden, which still remains, with an inscription on the wall behind it."

(4) Wavell, ibid.; Milner (vol. ii. p. 139, note †) says, "At the south end of [the prior's] hall is a brick building, said to have been added by Charles II. when he resided at the Deanery, for the accommodation of Mrs. Ellinor Gwynn." This is the fourth residence we have seen ascribed to "poor Nelly" in Winchester. The house she actually occupied was in Colebrook Street, near the back gate of the Precinct.

(5) Arch. Inst., Winchester Vol., "Architect. Notes, &c.," pp. 6, 7.

the arch mould; and beside it, on each side of a low buttress, a narrow window; all of these are Early English.[1] The southmost of these two structures was most probably the basement story of the Refectory; and the other, according to the description in Wykeham's Register, may have been the store-rooms under the Strangers' Hall. The kitchen we conclude to have been further south, on the line of the watercourse, which ran in that direction on the west side of the existing building; and beyond it was an open court or quadrangle; but we do not know whether it was bounded on the south by the exterior wall of the priory grounds, or whether there were (as Milner has represented in his map) any other buildings forming part of the monastery.

Other conventual remains. On the eastern side of the Close is a "curious wooden structure," now the Dean's stables, but formerly one of the halls of the priory. It still has "the original wooden roof of the time of Edward I.," the construction of which is "similar to that of the hall in the deanery, but it is more lofty, and the corbel-heads are of the time of Edward I., representing, as usual, a king and a bishop. The work is, however, of a rude character, more like a good barn roof than that of a hall."[2]

At the west end of the cathedral, almost in a line with the south wall of the nave, is a wall which shows traces of two doorways or windows, and some narrow loops; but it is half buried by the accumulation of earth in the cemetery, and affords no clue to the nature of the buildings of which it formed part.[3]

The high and strong wall surrounding the Precinct on the west and south is in all probability of early date, although it has been so much altered as to possess few distinctive characters at the present day.

Cheyney Court. Hard by the great gate into St. Swithin's Street is the court-house of the episcopal

---

(1) In one of these windows, and in one of those in the contiguous building, within the lancet arch, the actual arch of the window is a flat-headed trefoil.

Mr. Carter's plans, which he has obligingly lent me, show traces of these windows at the eastern end of this vaulted apartment, one of them oblique; and another building adjoining it, and really forming the south side of the cloister. The south wall also seems to have been continued westward; and the east wall of the other building was formerly carried out towards the cathedral.

More extensive remains appear to have existed in this part of the Close in Milner's time, for he says (vol. ii. p. 136), "The refectory stands east and west, and projects beyond the south cloister to the distance of about forty feet. Two long narrow windows, in the style of Henry the Third's reign, are still seen at the east end of the refectory; as, likewise, four round-headed windows, partly blocked up, of Walkelin's work, in its north wall, against which are placed the figures of two large chestnut-trees, carved in hard stone and coloured. This hall was forty-one feet long, twenty-three broad, and nearly forty at its greatest height, being now divided into two stories."

(2) Arch. Inst., Winchester Vol., " Archit. Notes, &c.," p. 8. The flooring of the loft, and the partitions of the stable, make it impossible to see this hall as a whole, " but it must have been originally one large room " (ibid.).

(3) From the character of the mouldings which remain, I conclude that these doorways, or windows, were of the Decorated period. These used to be described as the remains of a college of the time of Constantine the Great (Camden's " Britannia," Holland's Trans., p. 264), which, for the glory of their house, the chroniclers of the Old Minster (Rudborne, ap. Wharton's Anglia Sacra, vol. i. p. 186) said was established here in the first ages of Christianity in Britain. The remains of the great south-western tower of the Norman church was also alleged to be part of this college.

Leland, in his " Itinerary " (vol. iii. fol. 71), notes " a chapelle with a carnary [charnel-house] at the west ende of the cathedrale chirch."

Milner (vol. ii. p. 138) notices " a small ornamented arch " in the south wall of the Slype, which was demolished in one of the alterations of that passage, and which, according to his opinion, " communicated with the buttery."

jurisdiction in the Soke of Winchester, called Cheyney Court. The old barge-boards of this and the adjoining house, and other relics of their pristine condition, are "worthy of notice."[1]

To the east of the Close, and divided from the Precinct by the main stream of the Lock Pond, is Wolvesey,[2] where was formerly the residence of the bishops of Winchester, who now have no house in their cathedral city, nor any nearer than Farnham Castle, in Surrey. The principal entrance is in the road which runs from College Street round the warden's garden to Wharf Bridge; but it is undistinguishable from the gate of the grounds of any ordinary suburban mansion. It is accessible from the Close, also, through a narrow way opening into the path to the back gate of the Precinct in Colebrook Street. On the gateway there are the arms of Bishop Fox, with his name; and on the gate beyond was inscribed "GEORGIUS MORLEY, EPUS, 1670."[3]

Wolvesey.

The palace, of which but a part of one wing remains, was erected by Bishops Morley and Trelawney; and from the views of it in Wavell, and in the margin of Godson's map, as well as from what can be seen of it in Buck's view of the city, it seems to have been sufficiently commodious, and as magnificent as the taste of the times allowed.[4] It is now used as the depository for the muniments of the see, and for the pupils of the Diocesan Training School. The chapel, although much defaced, and in the interior entirely modernised, is the same that was attached to the episcopal residence while the castle was yet standing. It is Perpendicular, but "the exterior of the east end and south side are all that remain perfect," and the work is "poor."[5]

The Bishop's Palace

Of the Castle itself only ruins remain, and those not in such a condition as to afford a very clear notion of the arrangements of its parts. "The walls of the keep, and a great part of the outer walls, are nearly perfect, and of good Norman character." They are very strong, and although inclosed within the line of the city walls, which are tolerably perfect at this part of the quadrangle, "it is evident that they originally formed part of the external defences of the city."[6] "The interior of the castle affords little more than a very picturesque ruin; but considerable parts of the partition walls

Ruins of Wolvesey Castle.

(1) The business formerly transacted in Cheyney Court was far more extensive than it is now; the establishment of the modern police system in the city having taken from it one large department, which made the prison that used to be in St. John's Street a necessary appendage of the court. Little besides manorial business is done here now. The origin of the name of this court has not been satisfactorily explained.

(2) The current etymologies of this name are utterly unworthy of regard. In the absence of all documentary evidence, no better hypothesis respecting its origin can be suggested than this, with which I have been favoured by the Rev. W. H. Gunner, that it means Wolf's Island; a name derived from some possessor in Saxon times.

(3) Wavell, vol. i. p. 84.

(4) Wavell (ibid., p. 86) records this inscription on the front of it, "Georgius Morley, Episcopus, has ædes propriis impensis de novo struxit; A.D. 1684." He also assigns to Bishop Trelawney "considerable improvements;" and adds that when he wrote (before 1773) it was "almost totally neglected."

(5) Arch. Inst., Winchester Vol., "Archit. Notes, &c.," p. 9.

(6) Ibid., ibid.; and plan and views, pp. 10, 11. But the discovery of Roman remains of a domestic character, to the east of these walls (of which I have been informed by the Rev. W. H. Gunner), would seem to be inconsistent with this opinion.

remain, and a part apparently of the refectory, in which is a good Norman arch and window; the rest of the walls are in such a ruinous state that their respective uses can hardly be made out."[1]

Perhaps the most interesting archæological feature in these ruins of Wolvesey Castle is a peculiarity in the masonry of part of the walls, which singularly confirms an incidental mention of a fact connected with its original erection. It was built by Bishop Henry de Blois, in the year 1138; and Giraldus Cambrensis[2] alleges that a considerable part of the materials was obtained by the destruction of the palace built by William the Conqueror within the city, at the north-western corner of the present cathedral cemetery; and, accordingly, "in the place of the course of bonding tiles used in Roman work we have here, apparently for the same purpose of bonding together the rubble wall, a course of stones, long, narrow, and round, resembling closely the shafts commonly used in the jambs of doors and windows, placed lengthwise through the wall, their ends being flush with the masonry."[3] There can be little doubt that these very remarkable bonding stones were originally parts of the Conqueror's palace.

The gate of the castle is yet traceable, facing the north. It is very probable that it communicated (though not in the way in which Milner's map represents it) with Colebrook Street.[4]

Having thus concluded our description of the Cathedral, with its Precinct, before proceeding to notice the churches of Winchester, we will give, in the briefest form possible, outlines of the history of the Cathedral, of the Priory, and of the See, with lists of the bishops, priors, and deans, and an account of the existing cathedral establishment, its revenues, &c.

---

(1) Arch. Inst., Winchester Vol., *u. s.*, p. 9.

(2) "*Domos regias apud Wintoniam, ecclesiæ ipsius atrio nimis enormiter imminentes . . . . vir animosus et audax funditus in brevi raptim et subito nacta solum temporis opportunitate dejecit; et in majorem publicæ potestatis offensam, ex dirutis ædificiis et abstractis, domos episcopales egregias sibi in eadem urbe construxit.*" Giraldus Cambrensis, "Copula Tergemina," cap. xxvii. *apud* Wharton's Anglia Sacra, vol ii. p. 421.

(3) Arch. Inst., Winchester Vol., "Archit. Notes, &c.," **p. 9.** These stones are all of Binstead limestone or Quarr-stone, of which the greater part of the oldest portions of the cathedral is constructed.

(4) Buck's "East Prospect of the City of Winchester" represents much more of the ruins standing than is seen at present; and the relation of the castle to the Precinct and to the city can be better studied in it than in any of the maps; since neither Godson's nor Gale's inserts a plan of the castle, and Milner's plan is "*ad mentem Jo. Milner,*" and only in the direction of the gateway corresponds with the facts,—which is the more to be regretted, as the ruins were more extensive in his day.

ARCHITECTURAL HISTORY OF THE CATHEDRAL.[1]

Into the legendary history of Winchester Cathedral it is not our purpose to enter;[2] and the early part of its authentic history can only be rapidly glanced at here, as we are principally interested in what relates to the existing church.

We cannot doubt that a church was erected on this spot by the first Christian Kings of Wessex, Cynegils and Cenwalh;[3] but nothing further is known respecting it, than that (according to Rudborne[4]) it was dedicated to the "holy and undivided Trinity," and that it became a cathedral church under Hedda, the fifth occupier of this see.

The first historical foundation.

Of the church we learn nothing from any source until the bishopric of St. Athelwold, who appears to have, in part, rebuilt the cathedral, and to have translated the bodies of St. Swithin and other eminent saints buried there, and provided suitable shrines for them.[5]

The second historical foundation.

Rudborne[6] makes mention only of the dedication of the minster in honour of the Apostles Peter and Paul, in the presence of King Æthelred, Dunstan Archbishop of Canterbury, and eight other prelates, on "XIII. Kal." of November (October the 20th, if the date is correct), A.D. 980. Wolstan,[7] a contemporary, describes Athelwold's undertaking at great length, both in his life of the saint, and in his Epistle to Bishop Elphege; but it does not appear from these accounts that he did more than commence the restoration of the original building, for Elphege[8] is

(1) In this section my principal references are to Professor Willis's "Architectural History of Winchester Cathedral," so frequently quoted in the foregoing description of the cathedral; and Britton's work before referred to. Other works will be cited as occasion may require.

(2) The curious in such legendary lore may read in Milner (vol. i. chaps. i. to v.), or in Rudborne (ap. Wharton's "Anglia Sacra," vol. i. pp. 180—189), what will more than suffice for their gratification. Professor Willis has epitomised these legends in the commencement of his first chapter (pp. 3, 4).

(3) "An. 643. This year Cenwalh succeeded to the kingdom of the West-Saxons, and held it thirty-one years; and Cenwalh commanded the Old Church [so called in later times to distinguish it from the New Minster] at Winchester to be built in the name of St. Peter; and he was the son of Cynegils."

"An. 648. This year the minster was built at Winchester, which King Cynwalh caused to be made, and hallowed in the name of St. Peter." (Anglo-Saxon Chronicle, ap. Mon. Hist. Brit., vol. i. p. 311.)

"*Ecclesiam pulcherrimam construxit in Wyntonia,*" says the annalist of Winchester, under the year 639, of King "*Kinewalchus;*" and under 633, he states that

"*Kinegilsus,*" his father, had purposed to build such a church, and also made large preparations for it.

Rudborne (p. 189), and John of Exeter (Willis, p. 4, note i), ascribe the foundation of the church to Cynegils, and say that Cenwalh completed his father's work.

(4) Pp. 190, 192.

(5) Rudborne, p. 223; Willis, p. 9.   (6) Ibid.

(7) Willis, pp. 7—15; Arch. Assoc., Winchester Vol., pp. 364—369.

(8) The particular expressions used by Wolstan are such as these :—"*Magno conamine veterem renovare decrevisset ecclesiam*" (Willis, p. 10, note); and "*Fulcivit, texit, dotavit, eamque sacravit*" (ibid., p. 13, note); which, it must be remarked, is the reading of "the first form of the poem;" in the later form the first two words are replaced by "*fundavit, struxit,*" which do not agree with the scope of the composition.

Athelwold's works appear to have extended from the eastern end some way (but we cannot tell how far) towards the west; and, as it seems, it was part of his plan, for the first time, to elevate the eastern portion of the church on crypts (Willis, pp. 12, 13, and 15, note). He completed sufficient of the cathedral to celebrate its dedication; and he was buried in the southern crypt, which he had constructed (ibid., p. 11, note). But Elphege is strenuously exhorted to carry on his predecessor's design. John of Exeter,[1] however, ascribes to him the entire rebuilding of the cathedral.

It is very noticeable that the annalist of Winchester makes no mention of these great works of Athelwold, but confines his attention to the expulsion of the canons, and the endowments of King Edgar and the bishops.

The third historical foundation. Bishop Walkelyn's rebuilding of the cathedral comes next under notice, and as we ascribe to him the most ancient parts of the existing structure, it will be necessary to show in the most compendious manner the grounds for regarding them as specimens of Norman architecture rather than of Saxon, as they have been designated by writers whose opinions deserve very great respect.

The documentary evidence is more than usually satisfactory, for the Annals are brief and business-like records, and were compiled year by year. From them we learn that, " in the year 1079, Bishop Walkelyn began to rebuild Winchester Cathedral *from its foundations*."[2] They also relate an amusing anecdote of the way in which the bishop cut down and carried off all the timber from Hempage Wood for his works at the cathedral,—the king having given him as much as he could take in " four days and nights ;" and how the king mitigated his anger, and reproached his own unwise liberality and the bishop's excessive greediness at the same time.[3]

" In the year 1093," they tell us, that " on the VI. Ides (the 8th) of April, in the presence of almost all the bishops and abbots of England, the monks came, with the highest exultation and glory, from the old minster to the new one : that on the Feast of St. Swithin they went in procession from the new minster to the old one, and brought thence St. Swithin's shrine, and placed it with honour in the new building ; and that, on the following day, Bishop Walkelyn's men *first* began to pull down the old minster, and that, before the end of the year, they demolished the whole of it, with the exception of one apse and the high altar."[4]

It would seem that these parts also were removed in the course of the next year, for the Annals say, that in it " the relics of St. Swithin, and those of very many other saints, were discovered beneath the altar of the old minster."[5]

From these records it is plain, not only that Walkelyn rebuilt the cathedral, but that he did so leaving the church of Athelwold's erection still standing : and there is a curious confirmation of this in two notices of the site of the chapel erected over St. Swithin's grave, which in his humility he caused to be placed opposite the western

so especially commended for his share in the construction of the crypts, that it is plain they were not finished by Athelwold (ibid., p. 13).

Wolstan's description of St. Elphege's organ, and of the towers, and of the great golden weathercock at the summit of the building (ibid., p. 14; Arch. Assoc., Winchester Vol., pp. 366, 367), may be referred to as illustrations of his style ; the extravagant inflation of which renders so much abatement, in estimating the value of the terms he employs, needful.

(1) Willis, p. 10, note. The plan of the crypts is ascribed to Athelwold by this writer, in such a way as to imply the non-existence of any before his time.

(2) Annales Wintonienses, ap. Wharton's " Anglia Sacra," vol. i. p. 294.

(3) Ibid., p. 295. The roof of the south transept bears testimony to the great store of wood which Walkelyn possessed. (See p. 55, note 2, above.)

(4) Ibid., ibid.

(5) Ibid., pp. 295, 296.

end of his cathedral,[1] but which in Rudborne's time was to be seen "opposite the north door of the nave."[2]

Description of Walkelyn's Church.

Walkelyn's Church extended eastwards a little way into the present retro-choir, and the Lady Chapel reached to the end of the retro-choir. The eastern end of the church, and that of the Lady Chapel, were apsidal, and "two small eastern towers flanked the apse of the presbytery."[3] The western end presented a very different aspect from that familiar to us, being flanked by two huge, nearly square towers (measuring sixty feet from east to west, and almost fifty feet from north to south), by which the entire breadth of the west front was extended to a hundred and twenty-eight feet. Between them appeared the gable of the nave and the grand entrance of the church.[4]

From this towered western end to the eastern apse of the Lady Chapel, beneath and amongst Wykeham's and others' later work, traces of the original Norman structure are abundant. And as it is upon the character and materials of these portions that the advocates of the earlier date of the erection of the cathedral base their opinion, we must show that these facts are in complete accordance with the statements of the Winton Annalist.

Indications of its being a Norman church.

"The argument from rudeness of workmanship," says Professor Willis,[5] "is best answered by comparing the transept of Winchester with Norman buildings erected in places where no Saxon cathedral stood before, and where, therefore, there can be no supposition of the kind above stated. Thus the masonry of these transepts is not more rude in its tooling, and the width of its joints, than that of Norwich Cathedral, which see was removed from Thetford after the Conquest. Again, the architecture, in design as well as roughness of workmanship, of Winchester transept is nearly identical (even in dimensions) with that of Ely transept, as they would naturally be, as the work of the brothers Walkelyn and Simeon."

It must also be noted that the paintings which remain in the north transept (on the soffits of the arches), and which sufficiently indicate the style and character of the original ornamentation of the interior of the building, are clearly Norman.

---

(1) " *Sed magis occiduo mandat se climate poni*
    Illius illustris, quam sæpe notavimus, aulæ."
This is Wolstan's account (Willis, p. 6, note), and it challenges our acceptance as the statement of one *familiar* with the fact mentioned. This is not the "chapelle with a carnary," which Leland (Itin., fol. 71) saw "at the west ende of the cathedrale chirch."

(2) Rudborne, *u.s.*, p. 203. John of Exeter (Willis, p. 6, note) confirms his statement.

(3) Willis, p. 22. These facts are determined by the crypts described above (pp. 58, 59).

(4) We are indebted to the explorations preceding the Congress of the Archæological Institute held in 1845, at Winchester, for our knowledge of this interesting fact (Willis, p. 23, and "Historical Plan"); the exact character of the structure was not determined till after the dispersion of the Congress; but it is recorded in the Volume of Proceedings, in Mr. O. B. Carter's Plan of the Close (Architectural Notes, &c., p. 2).

It must, however, be noted that very possibly these towers were never finished. We have demonstrative evidence that it was intended to finish the transept by flanking each end with towers, and that the plan was not carried out (see pp. 39 and 51, *supra*); and the completion of so great an undertaking as that of the entire rebuilding of the cathedral may well have been deferred when the structure was sufficiently advanced for the due fulfilment of its sacred purpose. We have clear indications of this fact in the changes of plan regarding the construction of the angles of the transept. (See above, pp. 39, 40, 51, 52).

(5) Pp. 33, 34. Compare Mr. Cresy's statements in his essay on the cathedral (Arch. Assoc., Winchester Vol., p. 368) with regard to this particular characteristic.

And this satisfactorily accounts for the absence of sculptured ornament on the capitals of the columns, which has been pointed out as one ground for assigning the earlier date to these parts of the structure.[1]

In the architectural characteristics of the oldest parts of the cathedral, there is nothing inconsistent with the ascription of them to Walkelyn, whilst there is much that is inconsistent with the hypothesis of their being Saxon remains. Norman ecclesiastical buildings (respecting the exact date of which no doubts can exist) are so numerous in this country that the distinguishing features of this style are as well determined as those of the styles which succeeded it. And universally-admitted Norman examples may be adduced, which correspond precisely with one or another part of the disputed portions of this edifice.[2]

"The plan of the present crypt," says Professor Willis, "is in perfect accordance with that of Norman churches in general. . . . . The identity of the work of the crypt with that of the transept may be shown by a peculiar abacus which is used in the crypt, and also in the column which stands at each end of each transept. . . . . They are distinguished by an abacus so thin that it deserves the name better than any other example I have seen, and by the unusual combination of (in Norman pillars) a round capital with a square abacus."[3]

Absence of indications of Saxon style.

Not only do all the features of the original edifice which have been preserved agree with acknowledged Norman types, but in no part of the building can be found any of those characteristics which, though they belong to an earlier style than any found here, yet cannot, with confidence or certainty, be pronounced Saxon. We find no balustered shafts, no projecting imposts, no triangular arch, no "long-and-short" work, no "rag-work," nor any other distinctive indication of the "Supposed-Saxon" style.[4] It is scarcely possible to imagine a stronger corroboration of the account given by the Annals than this.

Some stress has been laid upon the employment of Quarr-stone, or Binstead lime-

---

(1) Cresy, p. 372. Schnebbelie has engraved two full-length figures which were brought to light in the north transept, in the latter part of the last century; and Milner has supplied descriptive letter-press, to which, however, he does not refer in his "History" (vol. ii. p. 111).

(2) The most cursory inspection of the plates of the "Glossary of Architecture," will supply abundant proofs and illustrations of this assertion. Parallels may be found there to the round columns of the original presbytery (see above, p. 62, note 1), and of the terminal aisles of the transept; to the clustered columns of the remainder of the transepts and of the nave; to the plain, square-edged, circular, and horseshoe arches; to the simple capitals, and the rude abaci; to the windows of the transepts, and the mouldings of the string-courses; the arcade on the gable of the north transept; to the apsidal eastern end, &c. &c. Other examples may be

found in Rickman's "Gothic Architecture," and in Bloxam's useful little work on the same subject. The plates in the last edition of Dugdale's "Monasticon" will supply other proofs. Britton's "Cathedrals," and other works, abound in similar demonstrations. Indeed, it is difficult to find a work on this subject, possessed of any claims to notice, which may not be referred to for the exhibition of Norman types exactly corresponding with the oldest parts of Winchester Cathedral.

(3) Pp. 35, 36. These observations are intended to answer those who ascribe the existing crypts to Athelwold, although they admit the transepts, &c., to be the work of Walkelyn; and they are confirmatory of the history of the rebuilding of the cathedral given above, from the annals of the monastery here. (See Milner, vol. ii. pp. 62 to 65.)

(4) See the "Glossary of Architecture," and Rickman's and Bloxam's works already referred to.

stone, in all the parts of this church which are now under consideration; and the employment of a different material for the tower and its piers has been regarded as conclusive evidence against the Norman character of the former.[1] We shall see shortly that the change of material does truly indicate the different dates of the two portions; but the fact, so recently noted, of the employment of Quarr-stone in Wolvesey Castle (particularly in the "bonding stones," which we saw good reasons to regard as parts of the Conqueror's palace at Winchester[2])—its use in the unquestioned Norman arches in the south transept[3]—its frequent occurrence in the parish churches of the city—and the resort to the Binstead quarries by William of Wykeham for materials when he was rebuilding the church,[4] all show that this test is illusory.

The next event to be recorded in this history is the fall of the great tower, Fall of the great tower which occurred on the "nones" (the 7th) of October, in the year 1107.[5] This disaster was believed by Rudborne, and still more firmly by those who lived at the time when it happened, to be a judgment for the sin of burying in the sacred precinct of the church the body of William Rufus, "who had all his life been profane and sensual, and had expired without the Christian viaticum."[6] William of Malmesbury, in relating this, prudently declines to give a decided opinion, because the accident might have taken place in consequence of the instability of the fabric, even if Rufus had not been buried there.[7]

Rudborne, whilst commemorating the excellences of Bishop Walkelyn, states that "he caused the tower of Winchester Cathedral to be constructed as it is now to be seen;"[8] and, in another place, that "he rebuilt it from its foundation in the midst of the choir on four columns."[9] But in the paragraph in which he speaks of the fall of the tower, he remarks that there is some contradiction in the accounts, for whereas the records of the church ascribe the building of the tower to Walkelyn,—and no mention is made of its fall after his building of it (and it is, in fact, the most strongly built tower in England),—yet Walkelyn died two years before William Rufus, and the fall of the tower is attributed to the unexpiated sins of that monarch—being placed seven years after his death by the Annalist. This difficulty he thus explains— "Walkelyn did not build the tower during his life; but after his death, it having fallen after Rufus was buried beneath it, it was rebuilt out of the great funds which Walkelyn left to the church." And he quotes another writer as agreeing with him in this opinion.[10]

Whether this hypothesis be a sound one or not, the fact cannot be questioned, for

(1) This opinion does not appear distinctly in print, but it is implied in what Mr. Cresy says in his essay (pp. 373, 375, &c.). The junction of the two styles of masonry in the transept is figured in the "Glossary of Architecture," Pl. CVIII.

(2) See p. 94, above.

(3) See p. 53, note 2, above.

(4) Wykeham's Register, Pars. II. ff. 47 b., &c.

(5) Ann. Wint., u. s. p. 297.

(6) Rudborne, u. s. p. 271.

(7) Quoted by Willis, p. 19, note 8.

(8) P. 256.　　　　　　　(9) P. 285.

(10) Rudborne, p. 271; Willis, p. 19; Cresy, pp. 376, 377.

the difference between the masonry of the tower and its piers, and of the compartments in the transepts next it, on each side, and the astonishing massiveness of its piers, give us assurance that it is of later construction than the other Norman part of the church, and that it had fallen and was rebuilt as Rudborne states.[1]

Building of the retro-choir by De Lucy. Next in order of time come the works of Bishop Godfrey de Lucy, including the whole of the retro-choir, and the eastern chapels, with the exception of the terminal compartment of the Lady Chapel.[2] The date of this portion of the edifice has never been questioned. Rudborne accurately describes the extent of this work;[3] and the Winton Annalist records the institution, in the year 1202, of "a confraternity for repairing the cathedral, to last for five complete years."[4] The alteration of the Lady Chapel at a later period has made it uncertain whether De Lucy's Lady Chapel extended farther towards the east than the two chapels flanking it; "from some indications," Professor Willis inclines to the belief that they "were all of the same extent."[5]

This enlargement of Walkelyn's Church appears to have been only the commencement of the work of "repairing" it, for which the "confraternity" of De Lucy was established. But for the remainder we have no documentary evidence to guide our inquiries; and our conclusions, however satisfactory, are in consequence vague. It is quite certain that the arcade over the Holy Hole[6] was constructed about the end of the twelfth century, and that the presbytery[7] was rebuilt by the middle of the fourteenth; and some of the windows in the transepts[8] indicate other alterations made during this period. Professor Willis[9] says "the work must have gone on slowly, and was probably carried up at the expense of the monastery, and not by any particular benefactor, therefore it has passed unrecorded."[10]

Bishop Edington's work. With Bishop Edington we regain some documentary evidence of the history of this venerable fabric. It appears from his will[11] that he had commenced the rebuilding of the nave; and he therein leaves money for the continuation of the work. Milner's

(1) Willis, pp. 29 to 32, 36. The Annals record the building of a tower in the year 1200; but the style of the existing tower is of an earlier period than that; and, probably enough, the reference is to one of the western towers, of which no visible traces now remain. (Ann. Wint., p. 304; Willis, p. 37.)

(2) See pp. 42, 63 to 67, above.

(3) P. 286. Willis quotes the passage more correctly from John of Exeter (p. 37, note).

(4) Ann. Wint., p. 305. "The outside wall," says Professor Willis (p. 78), "was first erected without disturbing the Norman Lady Chapel. Then, this Lady Chapel and the circular aisle and towers of the great apse were taken down, and the piers and vault of the new work erected." At page 41 is a fuller account of this process; and he shows that some time must have elapsed between the commencement and the conclusion of this part of the "repairs."

(5) Pp. 38, 39. (6) See above, pp. 63, 64.

(7) See pp. 40, 41, 59, &c., above. "The apse [of the presbytery] was taken down, and the present polygonal decorated termination substituted, apparently about 1320." "The Norman clerestory and triforium of the remainder of the presbytery, namely, between the apse and the tower, were next taken down, about 1350, under Edingdon." Willis, p. 78.

(8) See p. 40, above.

(9) Pp. 44—46. The history of the progress of this part of the work, contained in these pages, is of great architectural and archæological interest.

To this period must be ascribed the Chapel of the Holy Sepulchre, described above, pp. 55, 56.

(10) Britton (p. 139) ascribes this part of the cathedral to Nicholas of Ely, who was bishop here in the latter half of the thirteenth century.

(11) *Continuatio Hist. Wintoniensis*, Wharton, *u. s.*, p. 317. The passage is quoted from "*Registr. Langham,*" and enters into no detail.

acuteness (as Professor Willis[1] rightly observes) first pointed out[2] the remains of Edington's architecture, which had not been discriminated before his time; and his opinion has been indorsed by all who have written on the subject since he enunciated it.

No account has reached us of the circumstance which called for this undertaking to rebuild the western part of the cathedral. We do not know whether the unfinished state of the Norman towers suggested it, or whether they had become ruinous, and their removal was required for the safety of the worshippers. Nor can we tell whether certain traces of fire and newer timbers, which are clearly visible at the western end of the roof of the nave,[3] tell of any accidental conflagration which made this renewal necessary. We know no more than the bare fact that this front, with some portion of both sides, was rebuilt at this time by Bishop Edington.

Britton[4] ascribes to this prelate the whole of the west front; and Willis[5] the whole, with the exception of the triangular gable above the great window. We think that both these opinions are erroneous; and that whilst the walls and principal parts of the west end are rightly attributed to him, the whole of the tracery of the windows, the fronts of the porches, and much of the panelling, is of later date.[6]

Extent of Edington's work.

(1) P. 59.

(2) Milner, vol. ii. p. 67.

(3) See p. 46, note 1, above.

(4) P. 139.

(5) P. 64.

(6) The characteristics of "Edington's work" are described above (pp. 37, 38, 43, 44, 47) in much greater detail than would be needful, but for the determination of the age of the several parts. Professor Willis (pp. 59, to 65) has described them still more minutely. I shall, therefore, offer here only a *résumé* of the grounds for the statement in the text, together with a few additional facts bearing on the question.

No one can deny that the mullions, transoms, and tracery of all the windows in the west front, of the two windows at the west end of the north aisle, and the one in the south aisle nearest to the west front, are not only Perpendicular, but such as would in any other situation be unhesitatingly pronounced rather late Perpendicular. The comparison of these windows with those of Edington Church, which are unquestionably the work of this prelate, will confirm the doubt respecting the authenticity of these. And the close examination of them will show that, just as in the instance of the windows of the clerestory of the presbytery, tracery of later date has been inserted in the windows, the mouldings of which show them to be of Edington's time.

Professor Willis (pp. 48, 62) insists upon the presence of a flower on the termination of the cusps of the tracery of the windows, and of the panelling, as a test of Edington's work. But not only cannot this test be admitted in opposition to the Perpendicular character of the portions now referred to, but it can be clearly demonstrated to be delusive, by comparing the difference between the "flowers"

at the tips of the cusps on walls of the aisles near the west end, and those on much of the west end itself, which are palpably very rude imitations of the others.

Further, both in the window tracery, and in the panelling of the west end, the arches are almost round-headed, which is not at all the character of those in the panels on the walls of the aisle. And in all the window tracery now in question straight lines frequently occur instead of the delicate curves of arches.

In the south transept at the end of the eastern aisle, is a window filled with tracery almost exactly resembling that in the "Edington windows" of the aisles; and the tracery of the clerestory windows of the presbytery, which as Professor Willis (p. 48) says is Perpendicular, and even late in that style, has the "Edington flower" on the cusps, and is not very much unlike that of the great west window.

The panelling on the front of the porches is also of the kind especially characteristic of the Perpendicular style :—over the west windows of the aisles there may be seen a panelled battlement (level with the gabled top of the "Edington buttress," and corresponding with the "set-off" over the two "Edington windows" on the adjoining side), which has been surmounted by the plain parapet of Wykeham's addition :—and it is very questionable whether the pinnacle at the angle ought to be ascribed to Edington, as it does not differ appreciably from those which are known to be Wykeham's work.

Mr. J. H. Parker informs me, that Mr. Blore was of opinion that the whole of the west end had been rebuilt in the time of Henry VII., but I think there are many valid objections to this supposition.

In the "Chronological Table" in Rickman (p. 239, note) mention is made of this bishop as having "com-

William of
Wykeham's
work.

Next after Walkelyn's, however, William of Wykeham's name is most closely connected with Winchester Cathedral. We have spoken so fully of his work in our description,[1] that we shall need to do no more in this place than recapitulate our former statements, and refer to Professor Willis's copious account of the alterations effected by him, and the manner in which they were accomplished.[2]

All the piers of the nave were cut away or recased, and thus transformed from the Norman to the Perpendicular style; the circular arches were removed, and the present lofty arches erected, the Norman triforia being replaced by the pierced parapets over the arches, which are merely ornamental in their character; and Perpendicular windows were substituted for the plain round-headed Norman windows within the aisles and the clerestories, and lierne vaults thrown over both the aisles and body of the nave.

It is quite certain that all this was not completed at Wykeham's death; and the portions which were left for his successors to complete, appear to have been the piers on the north side of the nave, all the windows,[3] and the upper part of the walls and the vault of the body of the church.[4] But the design and the plan of the operations were Wykeham's, and to him, therefore, this extensive alteration and improvement is justly attributed.[5]

Works of
Bishop Fox,
and Priors
Hunton and
Silkstede.

There are no means of determining exactly when much, which must be placed after Wykeham's time, and before the times of Hunton, Fox, and Silkstede, was done. The next definitively fixed event in our story is the lengthening of the Lady Chapel,[6] by Priors Hunton and Silkstede, "between 1470 and 1524."[7] "The Norman side-aisles of the presbytery were taken down and replaced by the present ones, in imitation of Wykeham's aisles in the nave, by Bishop Fox and Prior Silkstede, between 1500 and 1528. The side screens of the presbytery were also erected in 1524."[8] Most of what we have described as Perpendicular in the former part of this section must be regarded as the work of this period, but we have no means of determining the dates more exactly.

---

menced the alteration of Winchester Cathedral into the Perpendicular style;" but as he died in 1366, and in the table the Perpendicular style is said not to have commenced till about 1377, this statement needs to be guarded.

Edington's chantry (as described above, p. 67, note 3) confirms the conclusions maintained in this note.

The wood-work of the stalls in the choir ought to be ascribed to Edington's time. (See p. 57, above.)

(1) Pp. 37, 38, 44, 47.

(2) Pp. 54 to 74.

(3) Willis, pp. 58, 59.

(4) See p. 46, above.

(5) For a full account of Wykeham's work see Willis, *u. s.*, Milner, and Lowth's "Life of William of Wykeham;" but the mistakes of the latter work should be corrected by the aid of Milner. Wykeham's Registers contain a mine of highly curious and interesting information regarding this subject; and there can be little doubt that the registers of both the earlier and later prelates,—if the invaluable indexes compiled by Mr. Alchin (the learned and obliging librarian to the City of London) were but at hand to render the consultation of them possible,—would elucidate many of the knotty points in this architectural history.

(6) See pp. 42, 64 to 66, above. The style of the external arcade round the lower part of this prolongation of the Lady Chapel, would seem to point to an earlier date, but in the present state of our documentary information we must regard this as of the date given above. And it must be carefully remembered, that whilst an *earlier* style may be, and often is, imitated, the imitation of a *later* style is an absolute impossibility.

(7) Willis, p. 79.   (8) Ibid.

We have not referred in this history to the chantries, the dates of which are manifest; nor to the font, the reredos, and some other parts, whose dates have been given in the descriptive account of the cathedral.[1] Neither will it be requisite to detail the injuries done to the building at the Reformation and during the Great Rebellion; nor to speak of the alterations in the times of the Charleses; because, with whatever zeal directed, they can be as little approved as the destruction accomplished by the Reformers and the Puritans, and since passing notices of both will be found in the preceding pages.[2]

Of the recent repairs and restorations, which were commenced in 1818, and continued through so many years, as their general design was to remove the worst enormities of the Jacobean alterations, and to bring back whatever could be so treated to its pristine condition (although we wholly reject the theory of "restoration"), we must yet speak with respect. And, thanks to Dr. Milner, and to those who with a firmer step and a truer eye have followed in his path, there can be little doubt that the subject of ecclesiastical architecture is now so well understood, and these glorious examples of it so highly appreciated, that neither iconoclast nor barbarian will be suffered to lay ruthless hands on them, nor attempt to destroy what Time would suffer to stand for ever.

Recent restorations.

HISTORY OF THE PRIORY OF ST. SWITHIN.

Rudborne has related at length the history of this monastery until "the times of King Stephen," in his *Historia Major Wintoniensis;*[3] but the first portion, though accepted with implicit confidence by Camden and other general writers, and by Gale, Warton, Wavell, and even by Milner, is entirely fictitious;[4] and its only interest, which it possesses in common with all similar stories, arises from its illustrating a particular phase of the development of monasticism, when such pseudo-histories had to be invented for the purpose of imparting to the establishments a lustre which the institution itself had once possessed, as the embodiment of the religious feeling of the age;—and from its exhibiting the ease and rapidity with which (in uninquiring and unlettered ages) such fictions were accepted and acted upon, as records of historical facts.

Legendary history.

The foundation of the monastery is by Rudborne ascribed to Birinus,[5] the first bishop of Wessex; and the monks are said to have been of the order of

---

(1) See pp. 50, 61, note, &c.

(2) See pp. 56, 57, 61, &c.

(3) Wharton's "Anglia Sacra," vol. i. pp. 177—287.

(4) Tanner, who repeats the statements referred to, does so with the observation, that "they seem to be fabulous." (Nasmith's edit.) Hampshire, xxxv., Winchester.

(5) Rudborne, *u. s.*, p. 190.

St. Benedict, to which Birinus himself belonged.[1] But the silence of the *Annales Ecclesiæ Wintoniensis*[2] regarding a fact of so much moment must be admitted as strong evidence against the authenticity of this account.[3]

These Annals also say nothing of the only other fact regarding this first Benedictine establishment, which Rudborne has recorded[4]—that in the year 867, the Danes, after plundering the city, burst into the monastery, and slew every one of its inmates,[5] by which it was destroyed, after it had existed "two hundred and eighty-seven years."[6]

Secular canons in the cathedral.

In the year after this massacre, Rudborne says that secular canons, with the permission of King Ethelred, took possession of the monastery; but he adds that the permission was reluctantly given, and solely on condition that the secular clergy should relinquish the house and the services of the cathedral, as soon as the original order could be restored.[7]

The reformation of St. Dunstan.

And now, at length, we meet with an unquestionably historical event, and hitherto the occupation of the cathedral by the canons is the only fact respecting which no doubt exists. In the year 964, the reformation, which the great Archbishop Dunstan originated and King Edgar enforced throughout England, was accomplished at Winchester. The charge brought against the secular canons in the Anglo-Saxon Chronicle is very simple, quite credible, and amply sufficient (under the circumstances) to account for the proceedings adopted against them—"they would not observe any *rule*."[8] In the year before the famous St. Athelwold had been made bishop here, and he was as earnest a reformer as Dunstan himself. So the canons

(1) Wharton (*u. s.*), in a note, quotes from the *Annales Breves Wintonienses* (Cott. MSS. Galba. A. 15), the statement that Birinus appointed a monk from Monte Cassino, named Benedict, as head of the monastery.

(2) Wharton's "Anglia Sacra," vol. i. pp. 288—314.

(3) The late Mr. Kemble, whose researches into the history of these times were profound and universal, in his "Saxons in England" (vol. ii. p. 457), states that he does not remember to have seen it shown, "that Winchester was ever a monastic establishment" before the reign of Edgar. A very strong confirmation of these doubts is supplied by Rudborne himself, who, when treating of what he represents as the revival of monachism in this place, in quoting the *Historia Aurea* of Winchester, for a description of the sensual sloth of the secular canons, and the substitution of monks from Abingdon in their place, extends his extract so far as to include this sentence :—"*Itaque usque tunc in gente Anglorum non erant monachi nisi in Glastonia et Abendonia.*" (P. 218.)

(4) Ibid., pp. 205, 206. Rudborne names only Girardus Cornubiensis, and Vigilancius, as his authorities for this statement.

(5) No account of this attack upon Winchester is found in the Saxon Chronicle, nor in any of the chronicles contained in the first volume of the *Monumenta Historica Britannica*. It was in the year 860 that the Danes stormed Winchester, but nothing is said, in the record of this event, of a massacre of monks.

Rudborne, after assigning this event to the year 867, says that it happened "in the second year after the death" of St. Swithin, which introduces a new ground of doubt; for St. Swithin died in 862 (as shown by Kemble in the Cod. Dipl. 285, 287, 288, &c.; the date of the A.-S. Chron. is 861), and, two years after his death, the Danes were engaged in other parts of the country, and not in the neighbourhood of the capital of Wessex.

The *Annales Breves Winton.* give 873 as the date of this alleged massacre; whence Wharton thinks it may have occurred in 871. (Anglia Sacra, vol. i. p. 206, note).

(6) Here again is a demonstrable error; for, accepting the date 867, and taking Rudborne's date of Birinus' first coming into Wessex, 635, we have a period more than fifty years shorter than that which has been given to this establishment.

(7) Rudborne, p. 206. These statements wear such an improbable air, as greatly to weaken the credibility of that which they were intended to confirm.

(8) A.-S. Chron. Ann. 963. The *Annales* (*u. s.* pp. 289, 290) bring far heavier accusations against them. "*Frequentationem chori, labores vigiliarum, et ministerium altaris vicariis suis utcunque sustentatis relinquentes, et ab ecclesiæ conspectu ne dicam Dei plerumque absentes septennio, quicquid de præbendis percipiebant,*"

were summarily expelled, and in their place a choir of monks from the Benedictine monastery of Abingdon (of which Athelwold had been abbot) was introduced.[1] Three of the secular canons, according to the "Golden History,"[2] took the cowl along with the new comers, and the rest "were without fixed habitation, wandering over the whole island."[3]

Brithnoth was appointed prior of the new establishment, and a system of rules was drawn up at Winchester, it is said by Dunstan, and promulgated, under the sanction of the authority of the king, and of the synodical council (at which they were presented), as the *Rule* for the Benedictine monasteries in England;[4] and the priory was called *Ealdan Mynstre*,[5] to distinguish it from the adjoining establishment, which was named *Niwan Mynstre*.

locis et modis sibi placitis absumebant. Nudus fuit ecclesia intus et extra; . . . . vix inveniretur unus . . . . qui vel pauperem pallam aut calicem quinque solidorum conferret altari." And even these are exceeded by what is said in the *Historia Aurea*, quoted by Rudborne (*u. s.* p. 218), — *"nefandis moribus implicati,"* — *"repudiantes uxores quas illicite duxerant, et alias accipientes, gulæ et ebrietati jugiter dediti."* But the non-observance of a "rule" was the gravest of all charges in the eyes of the Benedictine reformers, and the existence of every species of irregularity of life and duty was (they held) involved in that unpardonable fault. These other accusations may have been true, but the assertion of them by the annalist, and by Wolstan, cannot be admitted as evidence in support of them.

The Annals (*u. s.*) represent Edgar as attempting the reform of Winchester by giving the canonicates to the vicars of the canons, who had been performing the services of the church for them, and as compelled to resort to severe measures by finding the new canons guilty of the same, and even worse, neglect of their duties. Athelwold is represented as acting with similar hopeful forbearance.

(1) Chron. Mon. de Abingdon, vol. i. p. 348. Rudborne (pp. 217, 218), in relating this event, which he treats as Athelwold's work principally, and as a restoration or revival of the ancient order here, introduces this miraculous incident. The canons, being desirous of retaining their former position, had assembled in the refectory to hear the decision of the king, and of Archbishop Dunstan, Athelwold also waiting with them, when *" divinitus vox de imagine crucifixi in muro collocata regiis auribus pariterque Archipræsulis intonuit sub hac forma, cæteris omnibus hoc ignorantibus,—' Absit hoc ut fiat! Absit hoc ut fiat! Judicastis bene, mutaretis non bene!'"* which, of course, confirmed the resolutions of the two who heard the words, who immediately decided against the seculars. Milner, who does not relate this in the historical part of his work, but in his notice of the refectory (vol. ii. pp. 136, 137), and, then, with the expression of some doubt, says that these words were "inscribed under the crucifix," together with two Leonine

verses, importing that those words had at some time been uttered by it.

(2) Quoted by Rudborne, *u. s.*, p. 218.

(3) William of Malmesbury, lib. ii. cap. 8. This writer, in his *De Gestis Pontificum*, relates that some of the expelled clerics attempted to poison Athelwold, whom they regarded as the author of their loss and degradation; and that he escaped the consequences of their malice only by a miracle.

(4) Dugdale (Monasticon, vol. i. p. xxvii., &c., edit. Caley, &c.) gives a copy of this "*Concordia Regularis S. Dunstani Cantuar. Archiepiscopi;*" and therein it is stated that this *Rule* was decreed by the "*Synodale Concilium Wintoniæ*" summoned by King Edgar. But there is no date to it, nor any signatures to enable us to determine when this council (which does not appear in the ordinary lists) was held.

Several charters in the Codex Diplomaticus (Nos. 512, 599, and 610) refer to this installation of monks in the place of canons in Winchester; but Mr. Kemble has marked the first as of doubtful authenticity, and the other two are not dated. The last (which is quoted by Rudborne, pp. 218—220) accuses the secular canons as vehemently as the annals quoted above; and it contains distinct regulations for this monastery, as, for example, the following :—"*Post unius episcopi obitum, alter ex eadem monachorum congregatione, qui dignus sit pontificatus ordine fungi, et non aliunde eligatur.*"

The editors of the last edition of Dugdale's Monasticon have placed in the appendix (No. xii. p. 213), to the account of this monastery, a charter of Edgar's (No. 523 in Cod. Dipl.) which belongs to Hyde, as the words "*novæ Wintoniensi ecclesiæ,*" and the dedication to St. Peter and St. Edotius (Eudocius), and the mention of Dunketon, Tittlescomb, and Winterburn, ought to have made manifest; and they have appended to this charter, as a note, a quotation from Spelman, relating to the passage I have cited from Rudborne, in a former note, concerning the restriction of monks to the abbeys of Glastonbury and Abingdon, before the time of Edgar.

(5) This name originated with the foundation of the

The date of the first erection of the conventual buildings here is wholly unknown, but it seems not unreasonable to conclude that it was the work of St. Athelwold, the system prevailing (as we have seen) before his time not requiring a monastery. And the renown of this prelate as the rebuilder of the cathedral, and the constructer of the watercourses which still flow through the precinct, may seem to confirm this opinion.[1] None of the other remains still existing are of earlier date than the time of Walkelyn, who appears to have rebuilt the monastery along with the cathedral, or perhaps before it, as the ruins of the chapter-house[2] are by no means late Norman in style.

Henry de Blois, who built Wolvesey Castle, and first collected the relics of saints and royal persons who had been buried in the cathedral,[3] may have carried on Walkelyn's work in the monastery, as he most probably did in the church. And it is certain that Bishop de Lucy altered, or improved, some parts of the building, as there yet exists the doorway to the dormitory,[4] which is in the same style as his work in the cathedral.

We have next to record a feud between the citizens of Winchester and the monks of St. Swithin, in the year 1264, which was most probably the continuation of an intestine contest recorded in the preceding year, and had resulted from the disorganised condition of the entire kingdom, and the sack of the city by De Montfort, in 1262. In this contest the gate of the priory, the monastic buildings near it, and the adjoining city gate, with St. Swithin's Church over it (as it is seen at this day), were burnt, and many of the people belonging to the monastery were killed.[5]

Monastic annals especially abound in matters so trivial as not to merit a place in an historical sketch; and affairs connected either not at all, or by the most slender thread, with the place at which they were recorded; and Winchester had no Jocelin of Brakelond to preserve the picture, photographically minute and accurate, of the interior life of the Priory of St. Swithin; long *hiatus* are in consequence inevit-

---

adjoining *Mynstre* by St. Grimbald; it first occurs in one of Athelstan's charters, dated 931. (Cod. Dipl., No. 353.)

(1) Two charters in the Codex Diplomaticus (Nos. 594 and 1347) relate to the construction of these watercourses, and other changes in this part of the city, which were effected now; and they will richly repay the attention of the inquirer into the topography and history of the old minster and its associated establishments.

(2) See above, p. 88.

(3) See above, pp. 70, 71, and 94.

I have not considered it needful to relate in this "History" all the petty and dismal stories of dissension between the monks and their superiors. The annals of every monastery contain similar accounts, and if they did not, the common experience of mankind would easily supply this inevitable feature in such institutions. Those who wish to read of these quarrels—" *animis cælestibus iræ* "—may consult the *Annales Ecclesiæ Wintoniensis* (ap. Wharton, vol. i.) *passim*.

One illustration alone, I will insert here. It will be seen in the notice of the bishops that Ethelmar encountered great opposition from the monks of St. Swithin, and, in fact, never was properly consecrated as bishop. Nevertheless, when at his death, he sent his heart to be buried here (see above, p. 73) the annalist records, "*juxta magnum altare decenter humatum [est], ubi plurima coruscant miracula.*" When, however, the bishop consecrated in his room had laid hold on one of his creatures, and imprisoned him at Hyde, there happened what the annalist thus relates:—" *Unde exiens per cautelam et fraudem, talia adinvenit falsitatis commenta, quod meritis B. Thomæ Martyris sit a compedibus et carcere liberatus. In cujus signum ipsi compedum annuli apud Cantuariam, ipso eos cum superscriptione offerente, pro ludibrio, ne dicam pro miraculo, reservantur.*" (P. 311.)

(4) See above, pp. 89, 90.

(5) Ann. Wint., pp. 311, 312. This attack was made on the "IV. Non." (or the 4th) of May, 1264.

able. Passing over more than a century, we quote the next paragraphs from the biographer of William of Wykeham.[1]

"In the year 1393, Wykeham held a fourth visitation of the monastery of his cathedral church of Winchester. The principal objects of his inquiry, at this time, were the state and condition of the fabric, and that of the society, both in respect of the number of members and the proper supply of provisions allotted to them. The convent had in former times consisted of sixty monks, but was now reduced to forty-six, and these were but scantily served with provisions, for the priors had for some time converted to their own use the profits of certain estates, which were appropriated to the necessary support of the monks; and this had been the occasion of much discussion between them and their superior. The bishop, by his Injunctions, orders that the number of monks be increased to sixty as soon as may be; and that the prior, for the time being, pay yearly out of his profits forty pounds towards their due support, upon which consideration the monks renounce all farther claim upon him.[2]

William of Wykeham's reforms.

"What success the bishop might have in his endeavours to restore peace to the society we cannot say, but his design of augmenting it to the ancient number, for which, indeed, he had given orders in his former Injunction, seems still to have been ineffectual, for at the time of his death we find it was reduced still lower, to the number of forty-two monks.[3]

"The other object of his inquiry proved a matter of no less difficulty. The fabric of the church was greatly out of repair, and the estates allotted to that use were very insufficient for it. The bishop ordered that the prior, for the time being, should pay a hundred pound a year for seven years ensuing, and the sub-prior and convent a hundred marks in like manner, over and above the profits of all estates so allotted, and all gifts and legacies. Whether it were that their revenues proved unequal to such a burden, or that the necessary repairs required a much larger supply, or that the bishop was not satisfied with providing for a repair only and what was merely necessary, we find that, soon after, he relieved the prior and convent from the whole charge, and, with his usual generosity, took it entirely upon himself."[4]

Only one other event remains to be recorded, the dissolution of this ancient and noble foundation, which occurred after the visitation of 1539. And in 1540 a new charter, dated March the 28th (which may still be seen in the Cathedral Library), reconstituted the establishment, and settled "the site and great part of the revenues" upon "a dean and twelve prebendaries, with six minor canons, ten lay clerks, eight choristers, and other members," and the cathedral was dedicated anew to the Holy and Undivided Trinity.[5]

The dissolution

(1) Lowth's Life of W. W. (2nd edit.) pp. 213—215.

(2) "*Statuta hujus ecclesiæ injuncta per Willm de Wykeham, ep^m Winton^m.*" Harl. MSS. 328.

(3) Quoted by Lowth from "Leger book in the Church of Wint., No. I. fol. 20."

(4) William of Wykeham's rebuilding, or alteration, of the nave of the cathedral has already been described.

(5) Tanner, *u. s.* William Basyng, or Kingsmill, who was prior at the dissolution, is reproached by Milner (vol. i. p. 254) for unfaithfulness to his trust, and to his profession, for having accepted the office of dean under

HISTORY OF THE SEE OF WINCHESTER.[1]

First west
Saxon bishop-
ric.

Omitting, as in the preceding sections, the purely legendary part of this history, we commence with the establishment of a bishopric amongst the west Saxons, at Dorchester, in Oxfordshire, by Cynegils, under St. Birinus, in the year 641;[2] and in the year 683 the body of this prelate, together with the see, was translated to Winchester.[3]

The see
divided.

Christianity now spread so rapidly in Wessex, that the provision thus made was inadequate to the spiritual want of the people; accordingly, in the year 705,[4] on the death of Hedda, the see was divided, and that part including the present counties of Surrey, Sussex, Hampshire, and the Isle of Wight, assigned to Winchester, whilst Sherborne became the see for the remainder of the diocese.[5] Not many years after-

---

the new constitution. Milner also rejoices in finding "reason to think that the greater part of the monks continued firm in their religious engagements;" and he says that the new foundation was endowed with only "a small proportion of the former conventual possessions."

The common seal of the priory of St. Swithin is circular, 3·5 in. in diameter, in the style of the first seal engraved for Edward III., and presents a cathedral west front, having in the central niche St. Swithin *in pontificalibus* (including gloves and rings), seated on a throne, his right hand raised in benediction, and in his left a pastoral staff. In the side niches are St. Peter with key and book, and St. Paul with sword and book, seated on thrones, but not nimbed. Over St. Swithin, in the field, are a sun and a crescent; and there is a candlestick without each side of the canopy. *Leg.*: ✠ S. COMMVNE CATHE-DRALIS ECCE APLŌR′ PET. ET PAVLI ET SCI SWITI, WINTON. It is figured in Dugdale, vol. i. Pl. III. No. 1.

The counter seal, which is also circular, and of the same size as the other, bears a canopy in three compartments, and a trefoil exergue, in which are two three-quarter and two half-length figures of monks praying; whence it is probable that the king in the central compartment of the canopy is a canonized sovereign, and from the devices above his canopy, a species of trefoil and a fleur-de-lis, it *may* possibly be St. Edmund, king and martyr. In the side compartments are a bishop *in pontificalibus*, with staff, and a prior mitred, with his right hand raised in benediction, and a book. Outside the canopies is a lion of England on each side. *Leg.*: FACTVM ANNO GRIE Mᴼ CCᴼ NONAGES′ IIIIᴼ ET ANNO REGNI REGIS EDWARDI XXIIᴼ. It also is figured in Dugdale, *u. s.*

A much earlier seal is also known; it is of the pointed oval form, 3·4 in. by 2·5 in., and presents the figure of St. Peter nimbed, and habited in chasuble, &c., and wearing the archiepiscopal pall, but without a mitre, bearing two keys in his right hand, and a book in his left, resting on his knee. *Leg.* (which is engraved with the tops of the

letters inwards, and on a chamfer, so as to make the impression seem much more sunk than it really is), if perfect: SIGILVM ECCLESIE SCI SWITHVNI EPI.

(1) The arms of the see of Winchester are *gules*, two keys addorsed, in bend, the bows interlaced, the uppermost *argent*, the other *or*, a sword interposed, in bend sinister, of the *second*; pommel and hilt of the *third*; but sometimes the sword is in bend, and the keys in bend sinister, and sometimes there is but one key.

(2) Bædæ Hist. Eccle. in Mon. Hist. Brit., vol. i. p. 179; *Annales Breves Winton.* ap. Wharton, vol. i. p. 193. This was, according to the *Annales* (Wharton, *u. s.*), only a temporary measure,—"*donec conderet ecclesiam tanto sacerdote dignam in regia civitate*,"—which was a very natural thought for those who could not imagine their church in the time of its lowliness and conflict. Even Milner speaks (vol. i. 69) as if these early Saxon bishoprics bore other resemblances, besides that of name, to those of later days.

(3) Annales Breves, *u. s.* "*Sedes episcoporum West Saxonum mansit in ecclesia de Dorcestria per spatium XLII annorum ad tempora Heddæ, qui . . . . sedem transtulit . . . . anno gratiæ DCLXXXIII.*"

(4) Mon. Hist. Brit. vol. i. p. 267, note b.

(5) Cenwalh attempted the division of this extensive diocese in the year 664 (Mon. Hist. Brit., p. 179), introducing a Saxon bishop into Winchester, by name Wini, because he could not understand the foreigner Ægilberht, who had succeeded Birinus. But Ægilberht was highly offended, and Wini, probably, not answering the king's expectations, was expelled in 666 (ibid.), and the see was reunited.

It is a matter of dispute amongst ecclesiastical historians, whether this later and permanent division of the see was accomplished by the authority of Ini, King of Wessex (Godwin, De Præsul., p. 205), or by that of an episcopal synod, as Milner (vol. i. p. 81) maintains, with the aid of William of Malmesbury (Vit. S. Aldhelm,

1.   Seal of Southwick Priory.   3.   Seal of the Prior of St Swithins Winchester.
2.   Seal of the Chapter of Winchester. 1294.   4.   Counter Seal of St Julian or Gods House.
                         5.   Seal of Netley Abbey.

wards, in 711, Sussex was erected into a distinct diocese, the see being fixed at Selsea.[1]

During all this time, and until the "invasion of the north men threw all the established institutions into confusion," the rank held by Winchester in the province of Canterbury was seventh, those preceding it being Lichfield, Leicester, Lincoln, Worcester, Hereford, and Sherborne.[2]

Rank held by this see.

At the commencement of the tenth century occurred the remarkable event of the consecration of seven bishops at one time, which would not, however, have required notice here, had it not been made the ground of a story in after ages, which seemed to show that this country had always been most obedient to the mandates of Rome.[3] One of the bishops thus consecrated was Frithstan of Winchester, and the allegation was that the sees of the west Saxon kingdom had remained vacant (in part owing to the Danish invasions, but, of course, more in consequence of the culpable neglect of the king, whose authority in this matter is thus incidentally admitted) for seven years, and that the pope had threatened to excommunicate the king if they were not immediately filled.

Frithstan consecrated bishop.

But, as Milner[4] judiciously remarks, "there are some chronological difficulties concerning the vacancy in question;" and, in fact, it appears that the division of the see of Sherborne into four parts afforded the ground for the most wonderful portion of this story, and that Winchester was not left vacant at all, Frithstan being appointed at once to succeed Denewulf.[5]

After the loss of Normandy, in the reign of Henry VI., it became extremely inconvenient to allow the Channel Islands to remain attached to the see of Coutances, the bishops of which were now, of course, hostile to England. Henry VII., with his accustomed prudence, obtained a bull from Pope Alexander VI.,[6] separating those islands from the see of Coutances, and attaching them to that of Winchester. But from some cause which is not specified by those who have related this transaction, the transfer was not effected until the year 1565, when the spiritual authority of the French bishop was definitively terminated in Jersey, and the adjacent islands, and they were annexed to the see of Winchester.[7]

The Channel Islands annexed to the see.

---

ap. Wharton, vol. ii. p. 20); but the question is of little interest, since it is well known that the ecclesiastical pretensions, which Milner thus seeks to support, were the growth of a subsequent age. "The privileges and rights conceded to the clerical body," says Kemble ("Saxons in England," vol. ii. p. 376), "were granted by the king and his *witan*, and enjoyed under their guarantee." And he specially mentions "the formation of sees" as being under the control of the king, and refers to the case of Cenwalh's division of that of Winchester, between Ægilberht and Wini, in illustration of these facts.

(1) Bædæ Hist. ap. Mon. Hist. Brit., p. 268.
(2) Kemble, *u. s.*, pp. 361, 362.
(3) Britton, pp. 34, 35.   (4) Vol. i. p. 104.
(5) Wharton (vol. i. pp. 209, 210, note) has discussed

at length "the chronological difficulties" referred to by Milner, which assuredly are formidable enough. But the facts with which my story is concerned are sufficiently simple and authentic. According to the Anglo-Saxon Chronicle, Denewulf died in 908, and Frithstan succeeded in 909 (Florence of Worcester assigns these events to 909 and 910), and by charters (Cod. Dipl. Nos. 342, 1086—1090) it appears that, at the earliest, Frithstan succeeded Denewulf in 908.

(6) This bull is dated XIII. Kal. Febr., A.D. 1499, in the eighth year of Alexander's pontificate, which corresponds with 20th Jan., 1500. It is given in Warner's "Collections for Hampshire, &c.," vol. iv. pp. 195, 196. See also Rymer, tom. xii. p. 740.

(7) Warner, *u. s.*, p. 159. Magna Britannia, vol. ii. p. 891.

Thus in its present extent it includes the counties of Surrey and Hampshire, with the Isle of Wight, and the islands on the coast of Normandy, commonly called the Channel Islands; but some alterations are now proposed by the ecclesiastical commissioners, which, if effected, will be noticed subsequently. There were long conflicts for precedence, maintained by the occupants of this see in former times,[1] which have ceased to be of interest now, since it has been determined that it should rank third after the archbishoprics of Canterbury and York, the sees of London and Durham alone taking the precedence.[2]

The prelacy of the Order of the Garter is one of the privileges of the bishops of Winchester, and is said to have been so ever since its foundation by Edward III.[3]

BISHOPS OF WINCHESTER.[4]

St. Birinus, as we have related above,[5] was the first bishop of the West Saxons; but although the erection of the cathedral at Winchester is ascribed to him, his see was Dorchester, in Oxfordshire. He occupied it from 635 to 650, and, on his death, Ægilberht, a native of France, was appointed by Cenwalh as his successor. But Cenwalh, being unable to understand the language of Ægilberht, during his absence in 664, divided the see; and leaving Dorchester and the northern and western parts of the kingdom to him, made Winchester the see of a new bishopric for the southern and western parts of Wessex, over which he set a Saxon named Wini,[6] who was thus the first bishop of Winchester. Ægilberht, however, refused to recognise this proceeding of Cenwalh, and retired to France, where he soon became Bishop of Paris. This see he would not relinquish, when, a few years afterwards, he was invited by Cenwalh (who had expelled Wini in 666) to return; but he recommended his nephew, Leutherius, or Eleutherius, as his successor, who was consecrated in the year 670. Wini is said, after his expulsion from Winchester, to have bought the see of London of Wulfhere, King of Mercia. In 676 Leutherius died, and was succeeded by Hedda,

who, in the year 683, translated the see to Winchester, and thus was the first of the succession of bishops which has remained to the present day.[7]

---

(1) In Reg. Pontissara, ff. 181vo and 182vo, may be seen some statements of the claims put forward by the bishops of Winchester, in olden times, upon this subject. See also Annal. Wint., *u. s.*, p. 294.

(2) This was recognised by act 10 and 11 Vic. c. 108, by which the see of Manchester was created, and it was enacted that the bishops of Winchester, like those of London and Durham, and the two archbishops, should always have a seat in the House of Lords.

(3) See Cassan, vol. ii. pp. 289, &c., and the authorities there referred to.

(4) In addition to the authorities quoted before, I have used Dugdale's Monasticon (last Edit.); Godwin, *De Præsulibus Anglicæ*; and Cassan's "Lives of the Bishops of Winchester," in this section.

(5) See p. 108.

(6) Ibid., note 5.

(7) Dugdale, vol. i. p. 191. **Of these early bishops,**

A.D. 683—705.[1] St. Hedda (Haedde, Headdi, or Eddi).   He had been a monk, St. Hedda, and was Abbot of Streoneshalh (Whitby) when called to the bishopric of the West 683—705. Saxons.[2]

705—744.[3] Daniel succeeded to the see of Winchester, Aldhelm being set over Daniel, Sherborne.   In 721 he visited Rome, and finally resigned his bishopric, and retired 705—744. to Malmesbury, where he died in the year 745.[4]   He was the author of several historical works, which are known only by report.[5]

744—754.[6] Hunferth (Hunfrith, Humfredus).

754—* *.[7] Cyneheard.

* *—790.[8] Æthelheard.   In 790 this prelate was translated to the metropolitan see of Dover.

790—* *. Ecgbald.

After 793.[9] Dudda.

About 799.[10] Cyneberht (Kinebertus).

Wini, Leutherius, and Hedda, were buried at Winchester, and the relics of St. Birinus were translated thither at the removal of the see.

(1) Mon. Hist. Brit., pp. 179, 267.   The Anglo-Saxon Chronicle places St. Hedda's death under the year 703; but Bede's date is distinct and circumstantial, and was no doubt derived from the successor in the see, from whom he states that he had received information (Hist. Eccl. Præfat.; Mon. Hist. Brit., p. 107).   It is, moreover, supported by the date of an unquestioned document in the Codex Diplomaticus, No. 52.   Three charters of Ini (Nos. 45, 46, 997), bearing date 699, 701, but marked by Kemble with his disparaging asterisk, have the signature of Daniel amongst the witnesses.

It is greatly to be lamented that the learned editor of this invaluable work was not spared to publish the list of bishops, &c., which he promised in the last volume of the Codex; in this, and many other instances his minute and accurate information would have cleared up the difficulty which we must be content to leave unresolved.

(2) Rudborne, u. s., p. 192.   St. Hedda was buried in his cathedral, or rather in the graveyard beside it, as Ussher (p. 59; quoted by Cassan, vol. i. p. 306) states, —"in pyramide saxea, quondam nobiliter exsculpta."   Numerous miracles were wrought by the dust of the spot on which he died, according to Pecthelm, Bishop of Withern (Bede, u. s., p. 268).   His anniversary was the 7th of July, which may consequently have been the day of his death.

(3) This is the date of the A-S. Chronicle, which we have no means of confirming or correcting, unless a doubtful charter (No. 94) in the Cod. Dipl., which bears Daniel's signature under date 745, should be considered sufficiently good evidence to invalidate it.   The chronological difficulty in this instance arises from the fact that the chronicle and other authorities say that his death took place forty-three years after he was made bishop,

which would seem to countenance those charters which we referred to above, noted by Kemble as unauthentic.

(4) A-S. Chron., sub ann.

(5) Milner (vol. i. p. 81) quotes " Harpsfield, Cressy, Godwin," and gives the titles from the last, "De rebus provinciæ, Australium Saxonum gesta, De Vita Ceddæ Episcopi, De rebus Vectæ Insulæ" (Godwin, Richardson's Edit., p. 205).

(6) A-S. Chron., sub ann.

(7) The year of Cyneheard's death and Æthelheard's accession is not given in the A-S. Chronicle; Dugdale (vol. i. p. 192) and Godwin (p. 206) state 780; Wharton, in his notes to Rudborne (u. s. p. 195), evidently in error, states 754, and Cassan (vol. i. p. 109) follows him.   In one MS. of Florence of Worcester, in a later hand, this event is assigned to the year 788 (Mon. Hist. Brit., p. 546).   Milner (vol. i. p. 83) assigns to him an episcopate of twenty-six years.

(8) A-S. Chron., confirmed by Cod. Dipl., No. 159. Godwin and Dugdale (after Gale) say 794, but Dugdale (p. 82) states that he was consecrated as metropolitan in 793.

(9) We find Ecgbald's signature attesting a charter of Offa in the year 793 (Cod. Dipl., No. 163, marked with an asterisk).   This name of Dudd occurs in the list given by Florence of Worcester (Mon. Hist. Brit., p. 619), and in William of Malmesbury, but Rudborne (p. 195) spells the name Und; and, according to Godwin (p. 206, note), it is also spelt Cud.   Dugdale (vol. i. p. 192) places him in 796-7.

(10) In this year, according to the A-S. Chronicle, he went to Rome.   His signature is seen in the charters of Cenwulf of Mercia (Cod. Dipl., Nos. 1020 and 192), dated 799 and 806; but Kemble reasonably doubts the authenticity of the latter, as he also does that of a charter of Beorhtric of Wessex (No. 180), dated 801, in which Cyneberht's name appears.

About 803.[1] Alhmund (Ealhmund).

About 824.[2] Wigthegn.

829 ?—833.[3] Hereferth (Herefrith).

833. Edmund.[4]

833—852.[5] Helmstan (Elmstan).

And now we enter upon a less uninteresting portion of this succession, for the next name we have to record is that of the world-renowned—

852—863.[6] St. Swithin (Swithhun, Swithun). This eminent saint was a native of Winchester, and was born early in the ninth century,[7] and chose the ecclesiastical life. Having been ordained by Bishop Helmstan, he was made by King Egbert tutor to his son Ethelwolf.[8] His name appears, with the description "*diaconus*," as witness to a charter of Egbert's,[9] in the year 838. In 852[10] he was consecrated by Archbishop

(1) He was present at the Council of Cloveshoe, in this year (Gale, p. 93). His name occurs in charters Nos. 183, 185, and 1024 (Cod. Dipl.), dated 803, and Nos. 190 and 191, dated 805. Charter No. 1024 is signed by Wigthegn, *presbyter*, in subordination to Alhmund.

(2) He sat in a council at Cloveshoe in this year (Gale, p. 93). Wharton (vol. i. p. 195, note) says he also sat in the Council of Chelsea, 816. His name occurs in charters Nos. 207, 218, 220, 223, 1031, 1033, 1035—1039 (Cod. Dipl.), bearing various dates from 814 to 828. By the confusion of the name of this bishop with that of Wigbryht, Bishop of Sherborne about the same time, Godwin and others have made him accompany Archbishop Wulfred to Rome, in 812. The A-S. Chronicle, in the year 833, records the death of " Hereferth and Wigthen, two bishops," which has generally been regarded as truly relating the death of Hereferth, Wigthegn's successor, but as introducing Wigthegn's own name by some unaccountable mistake. Rudborne (*u. s.*) substitutes the name of Sighelm, Bishop of Sherborne, for Wigthegn, but he does so, as Godwin (p. 333) remarks, "*mendose*," since there was no bishop of that name at Sherborne till much later. And it deserves to be noted that charters Nos. 1035, 1037, 1038, and 1039 are signed both by Bishop Wigthegn, and by Bishop Hereferth, which indicates a lack of satisfactory information on the subject.

(3) This bishop made his profession of faith, &c. (still extant in Regg. Cantuar.), to Archbishop Wulfred, who died in 829, according to the A-S. Chronicle, but there is a charter (No. 227, Cod. Dipl.) signed by him in 831. His death is recorded (as stated in the preceding note) in the A-S. Chronicle.

It will be evident from several of these notes that the dates of the A-S. Chronicle require correction, but the means do not yet exist for making the attempt with confidence. (See " Introductory Remarks, &c.," to Mon. Hist. Brit., vol. i., and "Introduction" to Kemble's Codex Diplomaticus.)

(4) He made his profession of faith, &c., to Archbishop Ceolnoth, and nothing more is known of him.

(5) The signature of this bishop is appended to charters Nos. 233, 240, 252, 1044, 1048 (Cod. Dipl.), varying in date from 833 to 848. Godwin's date for his death, on the authority of Florence of Worcester, is 837 (p. 206) ; but it is evident, as Wharton (*u. s.*, p. 202, note) asserts, a mere mistake. Dugdale (p. 192) repeats this error. Rudborne's date (p. 202) is 852, which the charters amply confirm.

Excepting the few facts (chiefly valuable for the chronology of this list) mentioned in these notes, there is nothing to be recorded of these bishops but that all of them from Ecgbald were buried in the cathedral at Winchester, "*tres primi* . . . . *in cripta* [which is either a mistake, or else relates to the final resting-place of their remains] *sub D. Genetricis altari ; reliqui vero quatuor in navi ecclesiæ*" (Godwin, p. 206, note). The bones of Bishop Helmstan formerly shared a mortuary chest with those of his remote successor " Kenulph," according to Gale (pp. 30, 31 ; see above, p. 72, note).

(6) Rudborne, p. 203. St. Swithin's death is placed in 861 by the A-S. Chronicle, and by Florence of Worcester in 862. Cod. Dipl., No. 1059, supports Rudborne's date. It may be observed that some of the discrepancies between the dates of the deaths of some bishops, and of the consecration of their successors, may be accounted for by the occurrence of a vacancy, which was no unusual event, and would not be deemed worth recording. The signature of St. Swithin occurs in charters Nos. 265, 270, 271, 273, 283—286, 1050—1056, 1058, and 1059 (Cod. Dipl.), ranging from 851 to 863 in date.

(7) A.D. 826 say some (Godwin, p. 207, note), but certainly in error.

(8) Flor. Wigorn. (Mon. Hist. Brit., p. 548).

(9) Cod. Dipl., No. 1044. It is worthy of remark that an appendix to this charter, dated in the following year, 839 (or the first of Ethelwolf's reign), is signed by Helmstan, and also by " *Suithhunus episcopus*."

(10) Rudborne, p. 202.

Ceolnoth ; and his profession of faith is recorded in Rudborne.[1] No more popular bishop had adorned the see of Winchester, and the record of his works grew by degrees to be one of the richest portions of the Legend. Lantfred's "Life of St. Swithin," which may be seen in the British Museum,[2] contains some invaluable sketches of the condition, both material and spiritual, of these distant times. The well-known weather proverb associated with his name, is said to have originated in a great rain which happened on the occasion of the translation of his relics from the humble place he chose for their repose, into the choir.[3] The ascription to him of much both of local and national moment,—such as the erection of the bridge over the Itchen, at Eastgate,[4] and the procuring the grant of tithes to the church from Ethelwolf,[5]—is a proof of the great influence which he exerted upon his age. The costly shrine "of plate, silver, and gilt, and garnished with stones," in which his bones were enshrined, when it was no longer thought fitting to imitate his virtues, was part of the spoil given up to the king at the Reformation.[6] St. Swithin was one of the tutors of the great Alfred.

863—871.[7] Alhferth (Ealhferth, Ealhfrith), who is said to have been translated to Canterbury under the name of Ethelred.[8]

871—879.[9] Tunbriht (Tunberht, or Dunbert).

879—909.[10] Denewulf. This bishop was originally, it is said, a herdsman, whom Alfred became acquainted with when, in his most disastrous condition, he was hiding in the woods of Somersetshire ;[11] and it was his wife who scolded the king so heartily for suffering her cakes to be burnt on the hearth. He was a vigorous coadjutor of Alfred in his religious and ecclesiastical reforms.

Denewulf, 879—909.

909—931.[12] Frithstan (Frythestan). He resigned his see in the latter year, and died in 932.

(1) Rudborne, p. 203.

(2) MSS. Reg. 15, c. vii., contains two versions, one in prose, the other in verse, of this interesting work.

(3) Brand's Popular Antiquities. Of the place which he chose for his burial mention has been made above, pp. 96, 97.

(4) See above, p. 20.

(5) Kemble, in his "Saxons in England," vol. ii. pp. 480, &c., has, at great length, discussed this "so-called grant" of Ethelwolf, basing his remarks upon the ancient charters themselves, and the genuine Anglo-Saxon laws ; and he concludes that "the opinion that Ethelwolf made the first legal enactment on behalf of tithe in this country" is "entirely unfounded." See also Lappenberg's "England under the Anglo-Saxon Kings" (Thorpe's translat.), vol. i. pp. 198, 199.

(6) Dugdale, vol. i. p. 202.

(7) This is Godwin's (p. 207) date for the supposed translation of this bishop to Canterbury. His signature appears in charters Nos. 295, 300, 302, 1061, and 1062 (Cod. Dipl.), the only specified dates in which are 868 and 869 ; but Kemble places the last one between 871 and 877. The charter No. 297, dated 868, in one copy

presents the signature *Alcuuinus Uuyntoniensis episcopus*, but there appears no clue to the error.

(8) Godwin (pp. 48, 208). Dugdale (pp. 83, 192) makes the same statement. The name of Ethelred, as archbishop, occurs in charters No. 301, &c., but not before 871, and not, that I can perceive, in any charter along with Ealhferth.

(9) Charter No. 1063 (Cod. Dipl.) relates to this bishop, and is dated 877. Florence of Worcester (Mon. Hist. Brit., p. 560) gives us the year of his death.

(10) These dates are clearly made out by the charters Nos. 1086 and 1087 (Cod. Dipl.). The A-S. Chronicle places his death one year too early.

(11) According to a story related by Florence of Worcester (*u. s.*), but not fully credited by him. Asser does not mention it. See Pauli's "Life of Alfred" (Bohn's Edit.), pp. 101—103, 151, respecting Denewulf.

(12) By comparing charters Nos. 1102, 1103 (Cod. Dipl.) we learn that Frithstan's resignation occurred between March the 23rd and July the 21st, in 931. Godwin (p. 208) interposes two names, Athelmus and Bertulfus, between Denewulf and Frithstan ; but, as there is no sufficient authority for them, and as the

931—934.[1] Byrnstan (Beornstan, or Brinstanus).

934—951.[2] Ælfheah (Elphege), surnamed the Bald.

The great Dunstan, at this time Abbot of Glastonbury, was invited to this see, but declined it; it was, therefore, given to—

951—958.[3] Ælfsige (Elfsinus, Alfymus), who was translated to Canterbury in the latter year, but perished in the snow on the Alps as he was travelling to Rome for his pall.

958—963.[4] Brithelm (Byrhtelm).

St. Athelwold, 963—984.

963—984.[5] St. Athelwold (Æthelwold, or Ethelwold), the great monastic reformer and coadjutor of the greater St. Dunstan, and the most famous ecclesiastical architect that had appeared in England. He was Abbot of Abingdon when King Edgar raised him to the see of Winchester. Of his works here mention has already been made;[6] besides those, he reformed the New Minster, and converted it also into a Benedictine abbey, and, if Tanner's authorities may be trusted, he did the same with the establishments at Ely, Thorney, St. Neots, Peterborough, and Chertsey;[7] most of these places he also rebuilt; and he further rebuilt and enriched his own monastery at Abingdon.[8]

984—1006.[9] St. Ælfheah (Elphege). He was translated to Canterbury in the year 1006, and was martyred by the Danes in 1012.

1006.[10] Cenwulf (Kenulf).

1006—1015.[11] Athelwold or Brihtwold (Byrhtwold).

1015—1032.[12] Ælfsige (Elfsinus, or Alfsius).

---

charters clearly leave no interval for them, I omit them. In Dugdale (vol. i. p. 193, note) may be seen a further account of the confusion existing in some lists at this period. See also Wharton (vol. i. pp. 209, 210) and Cassan (vol. i. p. 117).

The A.-S. Chronicle gives the year 909 correctly in one copy (Mon. Hist. Brit., p. 383). Frithstan was buried in his cathedral.

(1) This is Godwin's date (p. 209), confirmed by charter No. 364 (Cod. Dipl.); but charter No. 1109 is opposed to it, and gives us the signature of Ælfheah as Bishop of Winchester in 933.

(2) The date of the A.-S. Chronicle, which gives the specific day, St. Gregory's day, or March the 12th; confirmed by charter No. 430 (Cod. Dipl.). He was buried in Winchester Cathedral.

(3) Godwin (p. 210). His name does not occur in the charters after 958. His relics were formerly contained in a mortuary chest in the cathedral (see above, p. 72).

(4) Godwin (p. 210); confirmed by charters Nos. 503, 504, 1247, and 1248 (Cod. Dipl.).

(5) A.-S. Chron. Consecrated on the 1st Sunday in Advent, or III. Kal. Decembr., or November the 29th; died on Kal. Aug., or August the 1st.

(6) See pp. 95, 96.

(7) Tanner's Not. Mon. (Nasmith's Edit.). See these names. Rudborne, p. 218.

(8) Chron. Mon. de Abingdon, vol. i. pp. 344, 345, 348, 349.

(9) A.-S. Chron. Godwin (p. 211).

(10) Died in the year of his consecration according to the A.-S. Chronicle and Florence of Worcester. Rudborne (p. 226) represents him as holding the see for some three years, and Godwin (p. 211) says that he died in 1008, but admits that some authorities are opposed to this opinion.

The relics of this bishop shared the mortuary chest of Bishop Helmstan in this cathedral (see p. 72).

(11) According to the A.-S. Chronicle, Brihtwold became Bishop of "Wiltshire" in 1006; but Rudborne (p. 227) gives the name of Athelwold to Cenwulf's successor. Godwin (p. 211) follows the chronicler. The date 1015 is assigned by Wharton and Godwin (u. s.), and by Dugdale (vol. i. p. 194), who calls this bishop St. Brithwold.

(12) A.-S. Chron., *sub ann.*, confirmed by the Codex Diplomaticus. Godwin (p. 212) states that Ælfsige, or Eadsinus, was translated to Canterbury in 1038, but his editor has indicated the erroneous character of this assertion.

1032—1047.[1] Ælfwine (Alwyn), "the king's priest," as the Anglo-Saxon Chro- Ælfwine, 1032—1047.
nicle calls him. It was this bishop, respecting whom after ages told that King
Edward the Confessor accused his own mother, Emma, of criminal familiarity with
him; and the minstrels and monastic chroniclers expanded the narrative of their
acquittal into the glowing legend of the ordeal, in which the queen walked unharmed
over nine red-hot ploughshares in the nave of the cathedral.[2] He did not enter the
religious life till the end of the struggle for the kingdom between Canute and Edmund
Ironside, and being of high birth and related to Emma, had accompanied her from her
father's court in Normandy, when she came to England to be married to King
Ethelred. It is also stated that he was made bishop at the request of the queen. His
bones were placed by Bishop Fox in the same chest with those of the slandered queen.[3]

1047—1070.[4] Stigand. He was Bishop of Selsea and of Elmham before. In 1052 Stigand, 1047—1070.
he procured the metropolitan see of Canterbury without relinquishing Winchester.
He received the pall in 1058[5] from the antipope Benedict X., and was never regarded
as rightful possessor of the primacy. He was not immediately deposed by William
the Conqueror, but in the year 1070,[6] soon after Easter, a council was held at Winchester, and he was deposed and deprived, and imprisoned in the castle there until
his death, which occurred soon afterwards.

1070—1098.[7] Walkelyn (Walkelinus). He was appointed at a synod held at Walkelyn, 1070—1098.
Windsor on the Pentecost next following Stigand's deposition (May the 23rd), and
was consecrated by Armenfrid on the feast of the Holy Trinity(May the 30th).[8] His
great work was the rebuilding of the cathedral and monastery, which have been
spoken of above;[9] he also, it is said, having commenced as the opponent of the monks,
became a zealous reformer of the Benedictine rule, as it was observed here, and was
celebrated for his monastic piety.[10] He died on January the 3rd, 1098,[11] and was
buried in the nave of his new cathedral.

1100—1129.[12] William Giffard. So long as William Rufus lived, this and other sees William Giffard, 1100—1129.

(1) A.-S. Chron., *sub ann.*; two copies vary two years
in the date of his death, one assigning it to 1045 (Mon.
Hist. Brit., p. 437); the charters Nos. 783, 784 (Cod.
Dipl.) support the date in the text.

(2) Rudborne (p. 238) refers to this legend, which
is related at length in the *Annales* (pp. 290—293).
Wharton, in his Hist. Eng. Poetry, vol. i. p. 89, on the
authority of some MS. he had found in the muniment-
room at Wolvesey, relates that when Bishop Orlton
visited the monastery in the year 1338, a minstrel named
Herbert sang, amongst other ballads, one of the deliverance of Queen Emma from the burning ploughshares.
None of the older historians or chroniclers refer to it;
and the A.-S. Chronicle, under the date of this alleged
miracle, tells us how Edward despoiled his mother of all
her wealth, "because before that time she had been too
hard with him." The whole story is now regarded as
legendary, and yet the fiction of the discovery of the nine

shares, which (the legend said) were buried in the cloisters, has been lately repeated.

(3) See above, p. 70.

(4) Godwin's date (p. 213) is 1069, but as the council
which deposed him was not held till the octaves of Easter
(April the 11th), 1070 (Rudborne, p. 249), his death,
which happened "*paulo postquam*" (Godwin, *u. s.*), must
be placed in the same year.

(5) A.-S. Chron., Mon. Hist. Brit., p. 457.

(6) See note 2, *supra*. He was buried in the cathedral,
and his relics formerly, as it appears, occupied a mortuary chest with those of Bishop Wini. (See above, p. 71.)

(7) Godwin's date (p. 213) is 1097.

(8) Wharton (vol. i. p. 255, note), citing Hoveden;
Dugdale (vol. i. p. 195).   (9) See pp. 96—99.

(10) Rudborne, pp. 255, 256; Milner, vol. i. p. 146.

(11) Godwin, p. 213.

(12) Godwin (ibid.) gives 1107 as the year of the com-

which had been vacated by death remained unfilled; and on the accession of Henry I., the claim of the pope to fill them by capitular election having been resisted, William Giffard, the new chancellor, was appointed Bishop of Winchester. The Archbishop of Canterbury, however, refused to consecrate him, and as Giffard hesitated to receive consecration from the Archbishop of York, it was not until 1107 that the dispute was composed, and the new bishop duly qualified for his office. The works by which Giffard is remembered are the removal of New Minster to Hyde, which will be more fully noticed hereafter; and the erection of Winchester House, in Southwark, as a metropolitan residence.[1] He was buried near his illustrious predecessor on the VIII. Kal. of February (January the 25th), 1129.[2]

Henry de Blois, 1129—1171.

1129—1171. Henry de Blois (or *Blesensis*), who then held the abbacy of Glastonbury, and was invested with legatine authority, was appointed on Giffard's death, and consecrated on the XV. Kal. of December (November the 17th), 1129.[3] He was a man of great energy, " *vir animosus et audax,*" as Giraldus[4] describes him, and he lived in times which developed his real genius, which was that of a soldier and a statesman rather than that of a bishop. How he pulled down the palace built by the Conqueror too near the cathedral to please him, and with the materials erected his unepiscopal castle of Wolvesey, has been related.[5] English history tells at large the part he played in the fatal contests between his brother Stephen and Maud the Empress, and we shall have to notice the evils which Winchester suffered in consequence. We shall speak of his noble foundation at St. Cross subsequently, but many of his charities and benefactions will not come under notice in our work.[6] Amongst his designs, was one for the elevation of his see to metropolitan rank; and the translation of the see of Chichester to Hyde, near Winchester, which was frustrated. It was he who first collected the remains of the canonized and illustrious persons who had been buried in the cathedral, and placed them in mortuary chests, as we have declared above;[7] and there can be no doubt that he otherwise "improved the building of the cathedral."[8] The day of his death is disputed, but Godwin gives the 6th of August, 1171,[9] and he is said to have been buried before the high altar of the cathedral.[10]

Rich. Toclyve, 1173—1189.

1173—1189. Richard Toclyve (of Ivelchester, Topcliffe, or More). Another vacancy occurred at Bishop De Blois' death. At last the monks had *permission to elect* the Archdeacon of Poictiers, Richard Toclyve, who was enthroned on May the 17th, 1173,

mencement of this episcopate, because Giffard did not obtain consecration till then. The A.-S. Chronicle is the authority for the assignment of his death to the year 1129; by the *Annales Wint.* it is placed in 1128.

(1) Cassan, vol. i. pp. 145, 146. See also the authorities he refers to.

(2) A.-S. Chron., *sub ann.*   (3) Ibid.

(4) *Copula Tergemina*, quoted above, p. 94, note.

(5) See above, p. 94.

(6) Cassan, vol. i. pp. 151, &c., details them, and the works he quotes may also be referred to.

(7) See above p. 70, note.

(8) Dugdale, vol. i. p. 195.

(9) Godwin, p. 216, and note t.

(10) Dugdale and Godwin, *u. s.*

The seal of this bishop, which is 3·4 in. long by 2·1 in. broad, presents him at full length, *in pontificalibus*, with his face turned to the right hand, and a very close-fitting mitre. *Leg.* : ✠ HENRICVS DEI GRACIA WINTONIENSIS EPISCOPVS.

His counter seal was an oval Roman gem, bearing the heads of Jupiter and Juno (?).

EPISCOPAL SEALS.

1 & 2 . Richard. Toclyve . 1173 _ 1189 .   6 & 7 . William of Wykeham . 1366 _ 1404 .

3 & 4 . Henry Woodlock . 1305 _ 1316 .   8 . Cardinal Beaufort . 1404 _ 1447 .

5 . William de Edington . 1345 _ 1366   9 . John Langstone, Commissary to Cardl Beaufort . 1420 _ 1425 .

J. Cleghorn, del et sc .

but not confirmed nor consecrated until October the 6th, in the year following.[1] He was appointed justiciary of Normandy in 1176, and one of the justices in Eyre for Hants, Wilts, &c., in 1179. Milner[2] ascribes to him the foundation of the Hospital of St. Mary Magdalen, near Winchester, which will be discussed when that institution is noticed in our work. The time of his death is disputed.[3]

1189—1204.[4] Godfrey de Lucy. This prelate was the son of the chief-justice of England, and was himself a justice itinerant, as well as a dignified churchman, before his consecration.[5] Of his addition to the cathedral full notice has been taken above,[6] and in subsequent pages we shall speak of his improvement of the navigation of the Itchen, and the charter he obtained from King John. He was buried before the entrance to his own Lady chapel.[7]

Godfrey de Lucy, 1189—1204.

1204—1238.[8] Peter de la Roche (de Rupibus), a native of Poictiers, and archdeacon and treasurer of that city; and before that he had served under Richard Cœur de Lion, and been knighted by that king's hand. In 1214 he was made chief-justice of England, and after the death of John his biography is the history of England during those years, as he was guardian of the infant king, Henry III., and regent of the kingdom. Amongst his opponents was the celebrated Roger Bacon. During the suspension of the royal favour, he made a pilgrimage to the Holy Land, and remained absent from the kingdom from 1226 to 1231; and again from the same cause he was absent at Rome from 1234 to 1236. He died at Farnham, on June the 9th, in 1238.[9] He was buried in the cathedral;[10] and of the Dominican convent in Winchester, and the Austin priory at Selbourne, which he founded, we shall speak hereafter. He is said to have been the Grand Master of the Freemasons in England, from 1216.

Peter de la Roche, 1204—1238.

(1) Godwin, p. 216, note.

(2) Vol. ii. pp. 231, &c.

(3) The date in the text, 1189, is that of the monument mentioned above (p. 72). Gervase and Diceto (cited by Godwin, p. 217, note) assign it to January the 2nd, 1188, which, on account of the various modes of computing the commencement of the year, may possibly be the same. Others, but certainly in error, give 1187. He was buried in the cathedral.

His seal is 3·4 in. by 2·2 in., and represents the bishop *in pontificalibus*, between a hand holding a staff headed with a cross pattée, issuing from the dexter side, and a pentacle (or figure emblematic of the five wounds) on the sinister. *Leg.*: RICARDVS DEI GRATIA WINTONIENSIS EPISCOPVS. Counter seal, 1·9 in. by 1·4 in., contains the effigies of Sts. Peter and Paul, standing. *Leg.*: ✠ SVNT MICHI SINT O BONI PETRVS PAVLVSQ PATRONI.

(4) "*Nominatus est a rege apud Pipewell*, 15 Sept., 1189." "*Consecratus Westmonasterii in capella S. Catherinæ*, 22 Octob." (Diceto, quoted in Godwin, p. 217, note.) Godwin's date for the consecration is November the 1st.

(5) Godwin, ibid.

(6) See pp. 42, 63, 100.

(7) See above, p. 73. He died on either the 11th or 12th of September.

The common seal of Bishop de Lucy is 3·5 in. by 2·3 in., and bears the bishop *in pontificalibus*, between the west front of a cathedral (which may have been intended to represent that at Winchester) on the dexter side, and a hand holding two keys addorsed, issuing from the sinister. *Leg.* (if perfect): ✠ SIGILLVM GODEFRIDI DEI GRACIA WINTONIENSIS EPI. Counter seal, 1·7 in. by 1·1 in. Device, apparently, a rock rising from the water between two stars, above it a luce (or pike) head downwards, and behind it a pastoral staff, in fess. *Leg.*: PRESVLIS ET GENERIS SIGNO . . . . CONSIGNORV . . . . TEGO.

(8) "*Sub exitum anni*," says Godwin (p. 217). He was consecrated at Rome on September the 25th, in 1205, and it may be to this date that Godwin refers.

(9) Godwin, pp. 217, 218; Dugdale, vol. i. p. 196. The *Annales Winton.* place his death on "*V. Idus Julii*" (July the 11th). Godwin prefers Matthew Paris' date.

(10) See above, p. 74, and note 1. His common seal is 3 in. by 1·9 in. in size, and on it is his figure *in pontificalibus*, with an appareil down the chasuble. *Leg.*: PETRVS DIE GRACIA WINTONIENSIS EPISCOPVS.

William de
Raleigh,
1244—1250.

1244—1250.[1] William de Raleigh (or Radley).   A period of confusion ensued upon the death of Bishop de Rupibus, the monks of St. Swithin's priory opposing the appointment of the king, William de Valentia, and electing first the Bishop of Norwich, William de Raleigh, and afterwards Ralph Neville, Bishop of Chichester (both of them men in favour with the king) in his stead.   In consequence of this, both these favourites shared the royal displeasure with the refractory chapter, who suffered imprisonment and the loss of their temporalities for the assertion of their independence.   After the death of the king's nominee, in 1239 or 1240, the Bishop of Norwich was again elected by the monks, and the election being confirmed by the pope on September the 13th, 1243, De Raleigh went to Winchester to be enthroned; but, by the orders of Henry, the mayor refused to admit him, and remained unmoved even by a solemn procession in which the bishop elect walked barefooted round the city; who thereupon laid the whole place under an interdict, and left the kingdom. In the next year, however, peace was restored, the interdict removed, and the bishop enthroned on November the 20th, 1244; but he did not long enjoy the episcopate, for in September, 1250,[2] he died at Tours.

Ethelmar,
1250—1260.

1250—1260. Ethelmar (Aylmar, Aymer, Audomar) de Valence, half-brother to Henry III., was elected bishop, the king himself attending the chapter, and by entreaties and threats preventing opposition, but he was not consecrated. In consequence of his oppressive conduct, he was compelled to fly the kingdom in 1258, and a new election was permitted, the monks choosing the chancellor, Henry Wengham, who, however, would not accept the honour. In 1260, on Ascension Day (May the 13th), Ethelmar obtained the papal confirmation, and in the following December he died at Paris.[3]

John of Exeter
1262—1268.

1262—1268.[4] Johannes Exoniensis (or de Exon., or *Gervasii*),[5] was appointed and consecrated in the papal court, near the close of September, in 1262, two elections made by the monks of their priors William of Taunton and Andrew of London being (" *non vitio personæ, sed aliunde quæsita occasione*," say the *Annales*) successively quashed.[6]

(1) According to Wharton (vol. i. p. 307) he was elected by the Chapter of Winchester before being Bishop of Norwich; and it appears that he was " not consecrated there before September the 25th, 1239," which was after certain bulls had been issued prohibiting the election of any one to the see of Winchester who should be offensive to the king. (Godwin, p. 219, note.)

(2) The date quoted in the notes to Godwin (*u. s.*) from " *Obituar. Winton*." is September the 1st, which the *Annales* give as the day of his burial at Tours. The other two dates are St. Giles' day (16th of Sept.), which Wikes gives, and St. Matthew's (21st of Sept.), which is the date of Matthew Paris.

(3) The safe-conduct granted to Ethelmar and others is in Rymer (1st edit.), vol. i. p. 660. The *Annales* give the day of his death, " *Vigilia S. Nicolai, sc. pridie Non. Decemb*." (which should be " Non. Dec.," or the 5th). The burial of his heart in this cathedral is recorded

above, p. 73. Rudborne (p. 286) erroneously says of this prelate, " *cujus corpus ad aquilonarem plagam altaris reconditum est;*" he was actually buried in the church of St. Geneviève, at Paris. Matth. Westm., quoted by Milner, vol. i. p. 188.

(4) Godwin (p. 221) seems to have made some most remarkable errors in his notice of this bishop. He miscalls him " *Oxoniensis*," and places his succession in 1265 (p. 222). The latter error is corrected by his editor in the margin, and in his notes. We follow the *Annales* in both particulars; and Wharton's note, which places (" *ex fide Chronici Dovorensis*") the consecration, " *paulo ante festum S. Michaelis*."

(5) Not of Guernsey, it would appear, but *Gervasii filius* (Godwin, p. 221, note).

(6) Annal. Wint. *sub ann.* Godwin (p. 222) says, " it was said " that his consecration cost him 6000 marks, paid to the pope, and as many to his chancellor.

He was suspended, in 1266, by Ottoboni, the papal legate, because he espoused the cause of the barons against the king, and immediately set out for Rome ; and died at Viterbo in Italy, on the " XIII. Kal." of February (or January the 20th), in the year 1268.[1]

1268—1280.[2] Nicholas of Ely was translated from the see of Worcester by the pope, since John of Exeter had died " *in curia.*" He had held the offices of lord chancellor and lord high treasurer before he obtained this see. He died on the 12th of February, 1208, and was buried at Waverley, but his heart was buried in this cathedral.[3]

1282—1304.[4] Johannes de Pontissara (de Pontys or Pointes) was appointed by the pope, two elections by the monks having been declared invalid because they elected pluralists.[5] He built the college of St. Elizabeth of Hungary,[6] at Winchester, and died at Wolvesey on the 3rd (or 4th) of December, 1304.[7]

John de Pontissara, 1282—1304.

1305—1316.[8] Henry Woodlock (or de Merewelle), Prior of St. Swithin's monastery at the time of his election.

1316—1319.[9] John de Sandale. He had been both treasurer and chancellor of England, and held the latter office during the first year of his episcopate.

1320—1323.[10] Reginald de Asser (Rigaudus de Asserio) was appointed by the pope, the king and the monks having disagreed respecting the election. He died at Avignon.

1323—1333.[11] John de Stratford, who had held high offices in both church and

---

(1) Annal. Wint. *sub ann.*

(2) The date of his appointment was " VI. Kal. Martii" (or February the 24th) ; he was confirmed by the legate on April the 23rd, received by the king " *in crastino Apostolorum Philippi et Jacobi*" (or May the 2nd), and enthroned at Winchester " VI. Kal. Junii" (or May the 27th). (Annales, *sub ann.*, Godwin, p. 222.)

(3) The *Annales Waverleienses* give us the date of his death, which is generally confirmed by the Patent Rolls (Godwin, ibid., note). The inscription commemorating the interment of his heart here is given above (p. 72, note). The seal of this bishop is in size 3 in. by 1·9 in., and shows his figure *in pontificalibus*, the mitre, &c., being richly ornamented between two trefoils. The legend is so much broken that only part of the word WINTONIENSIS is legible.

(4) His consecration at Rome took place near the end of May, 1282 (Rymer, vol. ii. p. 204).

(5) Wharton, Angl. Sacr. vol. ii. p. 315 ; Godwin, *u. s.*

(6) This college will be described subsequently.

(7) Godwin (p. 222, note). His so-called tomb and epitaph are given above (p. 71, note) ; his common seal is 2·7 in. by 1·8 in. in size, and bears the figure of the bishop as usual, below a small fleur-de-lis and a flower. *Leg.* (on a raised ground) : ✠ IOHANNIS DEI GRA WINTONIEN EPISCOPI.

(8) The licence to elect is dated December the 23rd, 1304 (Rot. Pat. 33 Edw. I.) ; the royal assent was received on the 29th of the following January, and the bishop was consecrated on May the 30th, and enthroned on October the 10th (Godwin, p. 223 ; Wharton, vol. ii. p. 316). He died at Farnham, on the 29th (or 28th) of June, 1316 (Wharton, ibid.), and was buried before the entrance of the choir of his cathedral. His common seal is 3 in. by 2 in. in size, and bears the usual episcopal figure under a small canopy, and having a rose of six cusps, inclosing a head, on each side, with the letters H and II (to indicate that he was the second bishop of Winchester named Henry) under them. *Leg.*: FRAT HENRICVS DI GRA WINTONIENSIS EPIS. His counter seal is 2·4 in. by 1·5 in., and bears a canopy divided into five niches, each containing a half-length figure, that of the Blessed Virgin, between two flowers, at the summit, the apostles Peter and Paul in the middle, and beneath them under trefoil-headed niches, with trefoils in the spandrels, two bishops ; at the base is a bishop kneeling. *Leg.*: SIT XPO GRATVS HENRICI PONTIFICATVS.

(9) His election took place in August, 1316 (Wharton, *u. s.*), and he died at Southwark, near the end of October, as it appears (Godwin, p. 22, note), and was buried in St. Mary Overy's church.

(10) Asser was consecrated on the 16th of November, 1320, and died on April the 12th, 1323 (Wharton, *u. s.*).

(11) The dates of the provision and the consecration are the 20th and the 26th of June, 1323 (Wharton, *u. s.*), and he was elected archbishop by the chapter on November

state, was appointed by papal provision, contrary to the king's pleasure; but he was afterwards restored to the royal favour, and in the next reign he had the custody of the great seal intrusted to him, and finally was translated to the see of Canterbury.

Adam de Orlton, 1333—1345.

1333—1345.[1] Adam de Orlton, at that time Bishop of Worcester, was translated to this see by the pope, in opposition to the king's wishes, as he had been engaged in the rebellion of Mortimer, and was implicated in the death of Edward II.; but he was, at last, recognised by the king, and received possession of the see. He was blind for some years before his death.

William de Edington, 1345—1366.

1345—1366.[2] William de Edington (or Edyngdon) was the choice of the king, who effected a compromise with the monks, and made their nominee Abbot of Canterbury. He was highly honoured by Edward, being appointed prelate of his newly instituted order of the Garter, and keeper of the great seal, and, finally, Archbishop of Canterbury. This last dignity he declined, preferring (as he is reported to have said) "the richer manger" of this church to "the higher rack" of the metropolitan see. His works in his cathedral have been described above, and the chantry in which his monument yet remains.[3]

William of Wykeham, 1366—1404.

1366—1404. William of Wykeham.[4] This prelate, the most conspicuous in this long list of men whose names live in history, was born in the autumn of the year 1324,[5] at the village of this county, from which his name is derived. He was one of that large class upon whose energy and intellect the greatness of our country has been reared—the men of humble birth, but solid practical worth and training, who rise to the highest positions in society by means of the very circumstances that seem most adverse in their lot.[6] He early attracted the attention of the lord of the manor of Wykeham, Sir Nicholas Uvedale, who was also governor of Winchester Castle, and by him the young villager was enabled to study at Winchester, afterwards made his secretary, and introduced to Bishop Edington, who also employed him as secretary, and joined with Uvedale in bringing him under the notice of the king.[7]

the 18th, and nominated "*proprio motu*" by the pope on the 1st of December, 1333 (Godwin, p. 106, note). Godwin (p. 224) describes him as "*Legum Doctor*." A seal is ascribed to him, but it is too imperfect to exclude doubt.

(1) His translation to Winchester happened on December the 1st, 1333, and he died at Farnham on July the 18th, 1345 (Wharton, vol. ii. p. 317). Respecting his burial see above, pp. 66, 74.

(2) The appointment was effected by a papal provision, and Edington was consecrated on the 14th of May, 1346. The date of his death is October the 7th (or 8th), 1366. (Godwin, pp. 225, 226; Wharton, *u. s.*)

(3) See pp. 38, 43, 46, 57, 68, 100, &c.

Edington's only known seal is a small circular one of 1·2 in. diameter; its device is the bishop kneeling to St. Catharine under an exceedingly elegant canopy, and his arms, three mullets on a cross engrailed, in base. *Leg.*: SIGILLUM WILLELM WYNTONIENSIS EPI.

(4) For this summary of Wykeham's life I have neces-

sarily most largely relied upon Lowth's work, of which I have used the 2nd edition of 1759. I have also used Mr. Cockerell's paper, "William of Wykeham," in the Winchester Volume of the Archæological Institute, and Mr. Walcott's "William of Wykeham and his Colleges." Other works have been referred to, as will appear by the notes.

(5) "Between July the 7th and September the 27th" is the nearest approximation to minute accuracy that can be made regarding Wykeham's birthday. His father and mother were John and Sibyl Longe, and an uncle is said to have been named Henry Aas (Lowth, App. No. i.) He is sometimes called Perrot, but that was the name of the husband of his niece Alice (ibid.).

(6) Wykeham's motto "MANNERS MAKYTH MAN," is his own manful boast of his lowly but not unhonourable birth, and of the secret of his subsequent advancement.

(7) This was in 1346 (Cockerell, p. 1) or 1347 (Walcott, pp. 7, 8).

W. J. Edwards

WILLIAM OF WYKEHAM.

BISHOP OF WINCHESTER.

After the Portrait in St Mary's College, Winchester,
and the Monumental Effigy in Winchester Cathedral.

Wykeham's architectural knowledge and skill were such as Edward required ; but it is not till ten years later that we find any record of his employment by the king in tasks worthy of his subsequent renown ; he then was made surveyor of the works that were proceeding at Windsor Castle, the general plan of which still bears the traces of his master-mind.[1] He had already received several benefices from the king, which sufficiently attest Edward's estimate of him.[2]

Our space is too circumscribed to permit us to insert the long list of offices and honours which year after year were conferred upon him by his royal master.[3] We can only notice, that although he was described as "*clericus*" in 1352, it was not until 1361, on the 5th of December, that he was admitted as an acolyte ; in the following year, however, on March the 12th, he was ordained subdeacon by Bishop Edington, and on June the 12th he received priest's orders from the hands of the same bishop.

Ordination of Wykeham.

At the end of 1363, Wykeham was made keeper of the privy seal, and not long afterwards secretary to the king—offices of as great mark in the state as the benefices he held were in the church,[4] which will explain what Froissart[5] reported of him—that he " was so greate with the kynge that all thyng was done by hym, and without hym nothinge done ;" and also the sarcasm of the greatest cleric of Wykeham's times, England's reformer before the Reformation, John Wycliffe, that one " wise in building castles" could readily obtain presentations, while so many "pore priests had no benefices." [6]

Two more honours alone were possible for him. On October the 13th, five days after the death of Wykeham's patron, Bishop Edington, the king addressed his *congé d'élire* to the chapter of St. Swithin's, and eleven days afterwards formally approved the choice of Wykeham to fill the vacant see, which had been willingly made in accordance with the royal will. Some delay arose respecting his consecration, the pope wishing it to appear as his own sole act, whilst the king claimed it as his. By the mediation of the Duke of Burgundy, however, this difficulty was removed, and the bull obtained, yet not before the king had advanced his favourite to the office of lord chancellor of the kingdom, in which he was confirmed about the middle of September, 1367.[7]

Wykeham Bishop of Winchester ;

—and lord chancellor.

We shall not attempt to tell the story of his public life, so far as it was implicated in the affairs of which we read in the histories of England. And of those great works by which his name has acquired imperishable glory in Winchester, we have in part already spoken,[8] and partly we shall hereafter speak.[9] A few notes of his personal history is all that we can add.

(1) By patent dated May the 10th, 1356, he was appointed " clerk of all the king's works at Henle, and Yeshampsted ;" and on October the 30th, next following, he was also by patent made surveyor of the works at Windsor. (Cockerell, p. 3 ; Walcott, pp. 11, 12.)

(2) Walcott, pp. 9, 10.

(3) Ibid., pp. 14—29.

(4) Ibid., pp. 22, 23.

(5) Quoted by Walcott, p. 29.

(6) Ibid., ibid.

(7) Ibid., p. 32.

(8) See the preceding part of this section on " Winchester Cathedral, &c." *passim.*

(9) See the subsequent section on " St. Mary Winton College," and the Hospital of St. Cross. New College, Oxford, was also built by Wykeham.

On March the 14th, in the year 1371,[1] Wykeham resigned the seals of his two offices under the crown, and devoted himself wholly to the cares and toils of his spiritual functions; with what earnestness he did so, the noble results which remain to this hour abundantly witness.

Wykeham's
trials;In the last year of Edward III.'s reign Wykeham experienced his first reverse. Notwithstanding his energetic activity, and the extraordinary favour and prosperity which he had enjoyed, with the exception of Wycliffe's satirical remark, we know of no cloud which at any time darkened his way. He seems, however, to have provoked the opposition of the Duke of Lancaster, who was now in the ascendant at court, and used his influence in parliament to procure his accusation of various misdemeanours in the discharge of his high offices in the state, and his condemnation on one charge, with the most iniquitously severe sentence of the sequestration of his episcopal revenues, and banishment beyond twenty miles from the court.[2] This was in the autumn of the year 1377; in the following January Wykeham was expressly exempted from the operation of a general pardon, by which the jubilee of the king's reign was commemorated.

—and restora-
tion to favour.But half a year later we find the sequestration commuted into a fine in the form of the outfit and maintenance at sea of three vessels of war; and on the accession of the young king, Richard II., not only was this fine remitted, but Wykeham's complete innocence was legally declared.[3]

The new reign recalled the bishop to public political life, and his name again occupies a prominent and honourable place in the page of English history. He was once more, too, entrusted with the great seal, and held it from the 4th of May, 1389, to September the 27th, 1391, after which he seems to have retired from public affairs.[4] On a few occasions he appeared in his place in parliament, and joined, but not actively, in the movements of the time; but his last years were mainly spent in the comparative seclusion of his episcopal life, and in the carrying on of those good works which he had commenced; and on the 27th of September, 1404, he died in his palace at Waltham, leaving behind him a name which even yet has not received its full meed of honour.[5] He was buried in the chantry, which he had himself erected in the nave of his cathedral, on a spot hallowed to him by early recollections.[6]

---

(1) The original record of his resignation of office is quoted by Walcott (pp. 43, 44) from Rymer (vol. iii. part ii. p. 181. Rec. Comm. Edit.).

(2) Walcott, pp. 53, 54.

(3) Ibid., pp. 60—62.

(4) Ibid., pp. 72—75.

(5) Wykeham's will is dated July the 4th, 1403; and the codicil appended to it, January the 10th, 1404 (Walcott, p. 92.) Lowth (App. No. xvii.) has given a complete copy of this highly interesting document, and a full abstract of it may be seen in Walcott (pp. 92—96, notes).

(6) Lowth, p. 284.

William of Wykeham's common seal was of the usual pointed form, 3·5 in. by 2·1 in., and exhibits an elegantly designed figure of the bishop under a canopy of the richest tabernacle-work, between two shields, that on the dexter bearing the arms of France and England quarterly, and the other the arms of Wykeham, *arg.*; two chevrons, *sab.*, between three roses, *gul. Leg.*: S. WILLELMI : DE : WYKEHAM DEI GRACIA WYNETON : EPI. His office seal, 2·9 in. by 1·9 in., has a rich canopy containing in chief the Holy Trinity in the middle, the apostles Peter and Paul in two niches, and in base the bishop kneeling. *Leg.* imperfect; only the words . . . . VIC CURA SANCTIS SUSCIPE, can be read. One *secretum*, a circular seal 1·6 in. in diameter, has a canopy of three compartments;

1404—1447. Henry Beaufort, the second son of the Duke of Lancaster and Henry Beaufort, 1404—1447. Catharine Swinford, was Wykeham's successor. He was translated from the bishopric of Lincoln; for being brother to Henry IV., he was raised to the highest rank in the church without a very long course of probation. The pope bestowed the cardinalate of St. Eusebius on him in the year 1426, and he was called the "Cardinal of England." He was four times Chancellor of England; he assisted at the Council of Constance; and commanded, under the designation of legate, the army which invaded Bohemia in 1429 for the purpose of destroying the Hussites. During the minority of Henry VI. the events of Beaufort's life were those of our national history, and, together with the popular estimate of his character, have been made familiar to Englishmen by their great dramatist. He died at Wolvesey on the 11th of April, in the year 1447, and was buried in this cathedral.[1] It is probable that he carried on the work of his predecessor here, but he is better known by his new foundation in connection with the Hospital of St. Cross, of which we shall speak subsequently.[2]

1447—1486. William Waynflete,[3] so called from his birthplace in Lincolnshire, William Waynflete, 1447—1486. where his father bore the name of Patten, or Barbour. He had reached the dignity of Provost of Eton at Beaufort's death, when he was advanced to this see, by the favour of Henry VI.[4] He was lord-chancellor from October the 11th, 1457, to July the 25th, 1460.[5] During the protracted struggles between the Houses of York and Lancaster, he adhered to the fortunes of the latter, but did not take a prominent part in the miserable events of those times. His great work and abiding memorial is Magdalen College, Oxford. And he died at Farnham on August the 11th, 1486.[6]

in the central compartment are in chief the Blessed Virgin, in the middle the bishop kneeling on the dexter side to St. Swithin, who stands on the sinister, and in base the bishop's arms, and St. Peter occupies the dexter compartment, and St. Paul the sinister. *Leg.*: SECRETUM WYLLELMI DE WYKEHAM EPI WYNTTON. Another *secretum*, of the same size, exhibits the Blessed Virgin, between the apostles Peter and Paul, under a rich canopy, beneath whom are the arms of Wykeham held by an angel between the bishop kneeling on the dexter side, and St. Swithin on the sinister. *Leg.*: SECRETUM . . . . DE WYKEHAM EPI WYNETON.

Walcott (p. 36) has also figured Wykeham's archidiaconal seal, which is circular, 1·5 in. in diameter, and shows the Blessed Virgin seated on a throne crowned with the lily, and the infant Jesus on her left arm; under her the bishop's arms; the sides are filled up with bold and elegant tracery. *Leg.*: S : WILLI : DE : WYKEHAM . . . . the rest being illegible.

(1) See above, p. 68.

(2) Beaufort's common seal is 3·1 in. by 2 in., and has a very rich device. In the principal compartments of a triple canopy are the figures of St. Peter between those of St. Paul on the dexter, and St. Swithin on the sinister; in the tabernacle-work over the central compartment are figures of St. Etheldreda and St. Catharine, both crowned;

in base is a three-quarter length figure of the bishop between two shields bearing the arms of Beaufort, France, and England quarterly, within a bordure gobony. *Leg.*: . . . . HENRICI DEI . . . . WYNTONIENSIS EPI. His *secretum* is circular, in diameter 2 in., and bears the arms of the bishop surmounted by the cardinal's hat, the strings and tassels of which fill up the spaces on the sides. *Leg.*: S . . . . ARMOR HENRICI MISERACIONE DIVINÆ CARDINALIS ANGLIE EPI WYNTON.

(3) For this notice I have consulted Chaundler's Life of Waynflete, in addition to the authorities formerly named.

(4) He was elected on the 15th of April, three days only after Beaufort's death. The consecration took place at Eton on the 13th of July, and he was not enthroned till August the 30th, in the year 1448.

(5) Wharton, vol. i. p. 318.

(6) For a description of Waynflete's chantry and tomb in this cathedral see above, pp 68, 69. He was Grand Master of the English Freemasons from 1443 to 1471.

His seal measures 3·1 in. by 2 in., with the device of a rich triple canopy, bearing in the central compartment St. Peter, with St. Paul in the dexter, and St. Swithin in the sinister compartment, and outside each angels in adoration. The figures of the Blessed Virgin and St. Mary Magdalen are above St. Peter, and above the other niches angels in adoration. In base is the bishop with

1487—1492. Peter Courtenay. After a brief vacancy, the see was filled by the translation of the Bishop of Exeter to it by papal bull, dated January the 29th, 1487,[1] the election by the chapter being made in the month following. Courtenay died on September the 22nd, 1492, and was buried in his cathedral.[2]

Thomas Langton, 1493—1500.

1493—1500.[3] Thomas Langton was translated from Salisbury after this see had been vacant for nearly a year. Shortly after being appointed to the see of Canterbury, in the year 1500, he fell a victim to an epidemic disease, and was buried in a chapel of the retro-choir at Winchester.[4]

Richard Fox, 1501—1528.

1501—1528.[5] Richard Fox, translated from Durham. His works in the cathedral have been described above,[6] but his great work is Corpus Christi College, Oxford. He also established a grammar school at Grantham, and in other ways displayed his desire to promote religion and learning. For several years before his death he was blind. He died on the 14th of September, 1528, and was buried in the chantry he had founded in his cathedral.[7]

1528—1530.[8] Thomas Wolsey, the great cardinal, whilst Archbishop of York, held this see (as he had held others) for a short time; but his history cannot properly be related in this place.

Stephen Gardiner, 1531—1555.

1531—1555.[9] Stephen Gardiner. The details of his life belong to the history of England, or rather to the history of the Reformation, and not to Winchester. He was deprived in 1550 (November 27, or April 18, 1551), but on the accession of Queen Mary, in 1553, was restored; and about the same time, August the 23rd, was

his crosier, appearing above a shield with his arms (lozengy, in chief 3 lilies), having on one side the arms of France and England quarterly, and on the other the arms of the see (a sword in bend, surmounted by a key in bend sinister). *Leg.*: SIGILLUM WILLELMI DEI GRA WYNTONIENSIS EPISCOPI.

(1) Godwin, p. 234, note.

(2) See above, p. 72, and note. Courtenay took the degree of D.C.L. at Padua, and was incorporated at Oxford (Godwin, *u. s.*; but Cassan, vol. i. p. 315, says " we find no record of it in the Athenæ or Fasti ").

His seal, which is 3·2 in. by 2·2 in. in dimensions, exhibits a triple canopy, containing in the central compartment, in chief, the Holy Trinity, in the middle the Blessed Virgin, and in the base a partly facing figure of the bishop kneeling. In the dexter compartment is St. Peter, and under him the arms of the see (two keys in saltire, surmounted by a sword, hilt in base in pale), and in the sinister St. Paul, with the arms of Courtenay (3 roundels, over all a label of three points, gobony) beneath him. *Leg.* (on a ribbon, and in Roman letters, the first instance of their resumption): SIGILLV PETRI COVRTENAY EPISCOPI WINTON. This seal appears to be of foreign workmanship, the tabernacle being in real, not isometric perspective.

(3) Wharton (vol. i. p. 319) gives the 24th of June, 1493, as the date of his confirmation by the Archbishop

of Canterbury in the see of Winchester. His death is placed by the same authority " *anno* 1500 *paulo ante* 10 Oct.;" but the editor of Godwin (p. 234, note) quotes a MS. authority, which places it on the 27th of January in that year, and thereupon observes, " *De die igitur mortis incertus hæreo.*"

(4) See above, pp. 42, 66, 69.

(5) Godwin, at p. 234, states the year 1500, hypothetically, as the date of Fox's translation to Winchester, but at p. 753 (and in the *Index Chronologicus*) he gives 1502 as the date. The earlier date is confirmed by Wood; but Surtees, in his History of Durham (quoted by Cassan, vol. i. p. 346), states that the date was " the festival of St. Faith, Oct. 6, 1501."

(6) See pp. 40, 41, 59—63.

(7) See above, pp. 69, 70.

Cassan (vol. i. pp. 342, 343) gives a list of the various honours and offices which Fox held during his life, and they clearly attest the favour of Henry VII. to him.

(8) He was appointed by papal provision on February the 8th, 1528, and installed (by proxy) April the 11th in the following year. The date of his death is November the 29th, 1530.

(9) Godwin (p. 236), Dugdale (vol. i. p. 199), and Wharton (vol. i. p. 319), say that the see remained vacant for nearly four years; but Godwin's editor, in a note, states (on the authority of " MS. Lowth and *Regist. Cant.*")

made lord chancellor. He died at Whitehall on the 12th of November, 1555, and was buried in his own chantry at Winchester.[1]

1551—1553.[2] John Poynet (or Ponet) was translated to Winchester from Lincoln on the deprivation of Gardiner. He fled the kingdom on the accession of Mary, and died at Strasburg on April the 11th, 1556.[3]

1557—1559. John White, translated from the see of Lincoln on the death of Gardiner, was deprived on refusing to take the oath of supremacy, after the accession of Elizabeth, and imprisoned for his excessive zeal against her. He was the last of the Romanist bishops, and died on the 11th of January, after his deprivation.[4]

John White, 1557—1559.

1561—1580. Robert Horne was raised to this see on the 16th of February, 1561.[5] His destruction of the cloisters of the cathedral has been spoken of in a former page.[6] He died at his palace in Southwark on the 1st of June, 1580, and was buried at Winchester.[7]

Robert Horne, 1561—1580.

1580—1583. John Watson, consecrated on September the 18th in the former year, died on the 23rd of January in the latter.[8]

1584—1594. Thomas Cooper (*Couperus*), translated from Lincoln, and confirmed in the see of Winchester on the 23rd of March, 1584 (1583, o. s.). He died on April the 29th, 1594, and was buried in his cathedral.[9]

Thomas Cooper, 1584—1594.

1595. William Wickham, translated from Lincoln January the 7th, and died at Southwark on June the 12th following.

1596. William Day, D.D. (*Cantab.*), consecrated on the 25th of January, died September the 20th.

1597—1616. Thomas Bilson, D.D. (*Oxon.*), translated from Worcester to this see, being confirmed in it on the 13th of August in the first-mentioned year. He died on June the 18th, 1616.

that Gardiner was consecrated on November the 27th, 1531, and quotes Rymer (vol. xiv. p. 429) to show that the temporalities were restored on the 5th of the month following; and he was consecrated (says Cassan, vol. i. p. 537, after Wood) the same day.

(1) See above, p. 70.

Gardiner was an LL.D. of Cambridge. His common seal measures 3·5 in. by 2·7 in. It exhibits a canopy of debased work, under which, in the centre, is St. Swithin nimbed, and above him a figure of the Trinity; on the dexter side St. Peter, on the sinister St. Paul, each under a shell canopy. In base, encircled with the garter, and surmounted by a mitre, are the arms of the see, impaling those of Gardiner (of Glemsford, Suffolk, Biog. Brit., quoted by Cassan, vol. i. p. 442), on a cross, a cinquefoil, between four griffins' heads erased. *Leg.* (on a ribbon): s. stephani permissione divina : winton: epi.

(2) The exact date of his translation was March the 23rd, 1551 (1550, o. s.). Godwin, p. 237.

(3) Those who are curious respecting the passions of the time of the Reformation may be gratified by the account of this prelate, and of Gardiner, contained in Milner's History (vol. i. pp. 261, 265, &c.).

Poynet was D.D. of Cambridge, and Grand Master of the English Freemasons for 1552.

(4) The date of the *congé d'élire* was July the 16th, 1556; but the temporalities of the see were not restored until May the 30th in the next year. (Godwin, p. 238; Cassan, vol. i. p. 545.) He was D.D. of Oxford.

White's seal, which is 3·2 in. by 2·2 in. in size, has for its device Jacob blessing the sons of Joseph (the name of ephraim remains behind one of them), and beneath it, within a garter, and surmounted by a mitre with long strings, the arms of the see impaling White,—party per chevron embattled, three gilliflowers slipped. *Legend* defaced, but it bore a date in Arabic numerals.

(5) Godwin, p. 238.   (6) See above, p. 88.

(7) See above, p. 75, and note.

He was D.D. of Cambridge, and his seal, which measures 3·4 in. by 2·2 in., bears the device of Jonah and the whale. There are rocks in the sea, on one of which is a city, and clouds in the sky, one bearing the date 1568. In base are the arms of the see impaling Horne,—three bugle-horns with strings.

(8) See above, p. 75 and note. He was M.D. of Oxford.

(9) See above, p. 72. Cooper was D.D. of Oxford.

1616—1618. James Montagu, D.D. (*Cantab.*), translated from the see of Bath and Wells on June the 26th, 1616 ; died on the 20th of July, 1618.

1619—1626. Lancelot Andrews, D.D. (*Cantab.*), translated from Ely on February the 18th in the former year ; died at his palace in Southwark on September the 25th, in the latter year.[1]

1627—1631. Richard Neile, D.D. (*Cantab.*), translated from Durham on the 10th of December in the year first mentioned, and from Winchester to the metropolitan see of York on the 19th of March, 1631. He died on the 31st of October, 1640.[2]

1632—1645. Walter Curle, translated from Bath and Wells on November the 16th, 1632, held this see until the surrender of Winchester to Oliver Cromwell on October the 5th, 1645. He died either in 1647 or 1650 ; his works in the cathedral have been noticed above.[3]

1660—1662. Brian Duppa, D.D. (*Oxon.*), Bishop of Salisbury, was translated to this see on the 24th of September, after the restoration of Charles II., and the establishment of the Church. He died on the 26th of March, 1662.

1662—1684. George Morley, D.D. (*Oxon.*), translated from Worcester on May the 14th in the first mentioned year, died at Farnham Castle on the 29th of October, 1684, and was buried at Winchester. His commencement of an episcopal palace at Wolvesey, and his foundation of a cathedral library have been commemorated above ; the Widows' College which he built and endowed near his cathedral remains to be noticed.[4]

1684—1706. Peter Mews, LL.D. (*Oxon.*), translated from Bath and Wells on November the 2nd, 1684 ; died at Farnham Castle, November the 9th, 1706.[5]

1707—1721. Sir Jonathan Trelawney, Bart., D.D. (*Oxon.*), translated from Exeter the 24th of January, 1707 ; died on July the 19th, 1721.[6]

1721—1723. Charles Trimnell, D.D. (*Oxon.*), translated form Norwich August the 19th in the former year ; died at Farnham Castle August the 15th, in the latter year, and was buried in Winchester Cathedral.[7]

1723—1734. Richard Willis, translated from Salisbury November the 21st, in 1723 ; died at Winchester House, Chelsea, August the 10th, in 1734. He was buried in his cathedral.[8]

1734—1761. Benjamin Hoadly, D.D. (*Cantab.*), translated from Salisbury on the 26th of September, in the year first named ; died at Chelsea on April the 17th, in 1761.[9]

(1) Andrews was the head of that school of divines in the English church which maintained *Catholic* doctrines (properly so called), of which Laud was the most conspicuous defender. His name and renown has been revived in late years, with the revival of Anglo-Catholicism.

(2) The date of his *election* to Winchester is given in the text ; he was confirmed in the see on the 7th of February following. He held in succession no fewer than six sees.

(3) See p. 35, note.

(4) See pp. 86, 87, 93. His tomb is described above p. 75.

(5) Mews is buried in the Guardian Angels' Chapel at Winchester (see above, p. 75). This bishop commanded the artillery of the king's army at the battle of Sedgemoor, having been a soldier before he took orders.

(6) Trelawney completed the palace at Wolvesey, and caused the throne to be constructed, which was removed in the late restorations and repairs. (See above, pp. 57, note, 93.)

(7) See above, p. 86.

(8) See above, p. 80.

(9) His monument in the cathedral is noticed above, p. 81.

THE R^T REV. BENJAMIN HOADLY.

Bishop of Winchester.

1761—1781. John Thomas, D.D. (*Oxon*), translated from Salisbury in the former year; died May the 1st, 1781, and is buried in his cathedral.[1]

1781—1820. The Hon. Brownlow North, D.C.L. (*Oxon.*), translated from Worcester; died July the 12th, 1820. He was buried in the cathedral.[2]

1821—1827. Sir George Pretyman Tomline, Bart., D.D (*Cantab.*), translated from Lincoln in July, 1820; died in September, 1827.[3]

1827——. Charles Richard Sumner, D.D., translated from Llandaff.[4]

PRIORS OF ST. SWITHIN'S, AND DEANS OF WINCHESTER.[5]

Before the reformation effected in St. Swithin's by St. Athelwold, the canons who (as we have seen)[6] occupied the monastery, and most probably had done so from its first establishment,[7] were under the rule of a superior called *Decanus*;[8] but only two names have been determined by the industry and research of Wharton out of all who bore this office during the period from about 639 to 964, when the canons were expelled,—Oswald, afterwards Archbishop of York, and canonised; and Swithin, afterwards bishop here, and also canonized.[9] The first prior was introduced from Abingdon by Athelwold, as we have said in a former page.[10]

(1) The floor slab commemorating this prelate is in the south aisle of the nave, in front of Dr. Balguy's monument. (See above, p. 81.)

(2) See above, pp. 84, 85.

(3) He was buried in the cathedral. (See p. 80.)

(4) A few ancient seals of commissaries of Bishops of Winchester may be described here.

1. Seal of John Langton, commissary to Cardinal Beaufort in 1420 and 1425. Oval, but not pointed; 1·1 in. by 0·9 in. St. Catharine with sword and wheel, and the commissary on the sinister side praying to her. *Leg.*: VIRGO DIVINA CLEMENS SIT MICHI KATERINA.

2. Seal of commissary to Cardinal Beaufort, 1437. Form and size like the last. The commissary is represented praying to the Blessed Virgin Mary. Device protected by a border of rush plaiting, but the legend has perished.

3. John Denton, commissary to Bishop Waynflete, 1450. Size 1·9 in. by 1·3 in. Under an elegant canopy is a fine figure of the bishop. In base the arms of the see; a sword and a key in saltire, and in chief a mitre with labels. *Leg.*: SIGILLUM COMMISSARIATUS . . . . PET W . . . . EPI.

4. Pointed oval; 1·9 in. by 1·1 in. Under a tall perpendicular canopy a figure of the Blessed Virgin Mary. *Leg.*: SIGILLUM COMISSARIJ WYNTON.

5. Vicar-general and commissary of Bishop Mews. Size 3·4 in. by 2·3 in. In base a shield with the arms of Mews,—three pales on a chief, three cross-croslets. Seated above is St. Peter with a monstrous key, on the dexter; and St. Paul with a sword on the sinister. *Leg.*: (in Roman letters) SIGIL . VICARIJ . IN . SPUALIB⁵ . GENLIS . ET . COMᴵ . Dᴵ . EPI . WINTᴺ.

(5) The authorities for this list are Wharton's Anglia Sacra, vol. i. pp. 323—325; Dugdale, *u. s.*; and Gale, with others incidentally referred to.

(6) See above, p. 104, note.

(7) Wharton's opinion fully agrees with that which I have expressed above (p. 104, note) regarding the nature of the original foundation here. "*Mihi enim*," says he (*u. s.* p. 323), "*tantum non constat canonicos sæculares ecclesiam Winton.a prima fundatione incedisse, usquedum ab Ethelwoldo episcopo, anno circiter 963, injuriæ expulsi sunt.*"

(8) Wharton, *u. s.*; Godwin, p. 660. See also the authorities quoted by them.

(9) The authority for the former name is Eadmer, who wrote a life of Archbishop Oswald, and for the latter Rudborne, who (p. 202) says that he was, when chosen bishop, "*Præpositus Wyntoniensis, qui modo dicitur Prior monachorum.*" The Codex Diplomaticus affords us no light here. (10) P. 105.

Priors of St. Swithin's.

After 964—970. Brithnoth.[1]

970—1006. Brithwold.[2]

1006—1023. Ælfric.[3]

* *—1065. Wulfsig.[4]

1070—1082. Simeon, brother to Bishop Walkelyn, and assistant in his great work of rebuilding the cathedral.[5]

1082—1107. Godefridus, an epigrammatist, a volume of whose epigrams is amongst the Cottonian MSS.[6]

1107—1111. Gaufridus I.

1111—1114. Gaufridus II. He had been treasurer of the monastery, and was author of the "Life of St. Modwenna, Virgin."[7]

1114—1120. Eustachius.

1120—* *. Hugo.[8]

* *—1126. Gaufridus III.

1126—1130. Ingulphus.[9]

1130—1135 or 1136. Robert I.[10]

* *—1171 or 1173. Robert II.[11]

1171 or 1173—1175 or 1176. Walter I. He wrote lives of William Giffard and Henry de Blois, Bishops of Winchester, which Rudborne quotes.[12]

* *—1187. John.

1187—1214. Robert III. (or Fitzhenry).[13]

1214—* *. Roger.[14]

* *—1239. Walter II. Died November the 10th, in the latter year.[15]

1239—1243. Audrey I.[16]

(1) Brithnoth was made abbot of Ely in 970. (Wharton, vol. i. p. 323.) His name occurs amongst the witnesses of charters in the Codex Diplomaticus after that year.

(2) Wharton (ibid.) admits that the grounds on which he places this name in his list are very slight. There is great confusion between different persons bearing this name; this one was raised to the see of Wilton or Winton, in 1006. See also Godwin, pp. 211, 335.

(3) Ælfric was elevated to the see of York in 1023. (Godwin, p. 661.)

(4) Wharton derives this name from a copy of the Annals of Winchester, which he refers to (p. 324) as "Chron. breve Winton. vetus." Dugdale (vol. i. p. 200) speaks more positively than Wharton allows himself regarding the right of his name to be in this list.

(5) In the year last mentioned he was advanced to the abbacy of Ely, where he rebuilt the cathedral, and died November the 20th, 1093.

(6) Vitellius, A. 12. (Wharton, vol. i. p. 324.)

(7) The first Geoffrey was deposed by Bishop William Giffard; the second became Abbot of Burton, and died on August the 2nd, 1151.

(8) The authority for these names is a MS. copy of Annales Winton. (Cott. MSS. Vitellius, E. 17.)

(9) Dugdale (vol. i. p. 201) inserts this name and the next, omitted by Wharton.

(10) Robert I. was made Bishop of Bath and Wells; but Godwin (p. 368) calls him only a monk of Lewes, and does not notice this statement of Dugdale, nor does his editor.

(11) Robert II. became Abbot of Glastonbury; the first date is the Glastonbury date, the second that of the Winton Annals. Whether he immediately succeeded Robert I. is not known.

(12) He became Abbot of Westminster.

(13) The confirmation of Robert III. as Abbot of Burton is extant in Rot. Pat. 15 Johan. par. 1 m. 5; but the Annals of the monastery have taken no notice of him, probably (as Wharton, u. s. thinks) because he held the office for so short a time.

(14) Inserted by Dugdale (u. s.).

(15) According to the obituary of Canterbury, quoted (u. s.) by Wharton.

(16) This prior was intruded upon the monastery by Henry III., for the purpose of accomplishing his design

1243—1247. Walter III. was not regularly elected, and, being excommunicated by the bishop, resigned in the latter year.

1247—1249. John de Cauz (de Calceto or Chauce).[1]

1249—1253. William de Taunton.   The date of his appointment was February the 10th, 1249.   He was deposed from the priorate by Bishop Ethelmar in 1253, and appealed to the pope, from whom he received " the ring, mitre, and crosier, with other honours."[2]   *The first "mitred prior."*

1253—1261. Andreas II. de Londonia.   He obtained his confirmation from the pope, " *vi nummorum*," says Wharton ; resigned his office on July the 12th, 1258, and was re-elected the same day, " *vi minarum*," and was finally compelled to resign in 1261.[3]

1261—1265. Radulfus Russel.[4]

1265—1276. Valentinus, resigned " *medio anno* 1267," was restored on the 3rd of July of the following year, resigned again in 1276, was restored on August the 1st, and finally deprived on December the 3rd of that year.[5]

1276—1278. John de Dureville.

1279—* *. Adam de Farnham, excommunicated for disobedience on July the 10th, 1282, and absolved on August the 31st following.

* *—1284. William de Basyng I.[6]

1284—1295. William de Basyng II.[7]

1295—1305. Henry Woodlock (or de Merewell).[8]

1305—1309. Nicholas de Tarente.[9]

1309—* *. Richardus de Enford.[10]

* *—1349. Alexander Heriard.[11]

of procuring the see for his wife's uncle William, Bishop of Valentia, respecting which see above, p. 118.

(1) Chosen Abbot of Peterborough in the latter year.

(2) Annales Winton., *sub ann.* 1254. But Milner (vol. i. p. 187, whom the recent editor of Dugdale follows) states that he was " honourably restored " (which seems not to have been the case, for the Annals, in 1256, speak of him as " *quondam prior* "), and that the privilege of the mitre, &c., " was to descend to his successors,"— which the Annals do not say, but which, nevertheless, appears to be correct, as the seal of the prior represents the prior mitred.   (See above, p. 108, note.)

This prior was made Abbot of Middleton in 1256, and in 1261, on February the 3rd, the chapter at Winchester elected him to succeed Ethelmar in the see, but their choice was not confirmed by the pope.   (See above, p. 118.)   The seal of this prior is 2·3 in. by 1·4 in., and shows St. Thomas (?) with a spear in his right hand, and a book in his left ; on each side are two keys addorsed ; the field is diapered ; above the head of the saint is a slight canopy, and under the bracket on which he stands is a head.   *Leg.*: . . . . . LLI P . . . . SWITHVNI WINTONI.

(3) Wharton, *u. s.* Dugdale, however, *u. s.*, over-looking the *Annales Wintonienses*, ascribes this account " to no better authority than that of Prynne," and rejects the whole, except the statement that Andreas ceased to be prior in 1261, or 1262.

(4) He died on July the 8th in the latter year.

(5) Wharton (*u. s.*).   He succeeded Prior Russel on the 21st of July, 1265.

(6) He died on April the 3rd, 1288.

(7) Confirmed August the 25th, 1284; died May, 1295.

(8) Elected June the 6th, 1295; elected Bishop of Winchester in 1305.   (See above, p. 119.)

(9) Confirmed July the 29th in the former year ; died in July of the latter year.

(10) Confirmed August the 25th.

(11) The date of his appointment, and that of the death of his predecessor, are unknown.   He was in office in 1332, as the register of Hyde Abbey (Cott. MSS. Domitian H. 14, fol. 214) shows.   Dugdale (who gives his name Heriard, *u. s.*) places his death in 1349.

The seal of this prior measures 3 in. by 1·9 in.   Under a small canopy, which has a shield of the arms of England on the dexter pier, and the arms of the priory (or see)—a key in bend, surmounted by a sword (with the hilt in chief) in bend-sinister ; on the sinister pier a figure of the prior wearing a jewelled mitre, his right hand raised in benediction, and a book in his left.   There

1349—1361. John Merlaw (or Merlow).[1]

1361—1384. Hugo de Basyng.[2]

1384—1394. Robert de Rudborne.[3]

1394—* *. Thomas Nevyle.[4]

* *. Thomas Shyreborne.[5]

* *—1450. William Aulton.[6]

1450—1457. Richard de Merleburgh.[7]

1457. Henry Berle.[8]

1457—1470. Robert Westgate.[9]

1470—1498. Thomas Hunton.[10]

1498—1524. Thomas Silkstede.[11]

1524—* *. Henry Broke.[12]

* *—1539. William Kingsmill (or de Basyng) was the last prior and the first Dean of Winchester.[13]

Deans of Winchester.

1540—1548. William Kingsmill, D.D.[14]

1549—1553. Sir John Mason, Knt.[15]

1554—1559. Edmund Steward, LL.D.[16]

are two keys at his right knee, and a sword at his left. The field is diapered with a trellis, having roses in the openings. Outside the canopy are the letters R S D on the dexter side, and I R E on the sinister. *Leg.*: . . . . RI PRIORIS ECCLESIE CATHED . . . . AN . . . . SWYTHVNI WYN . . . . His *secretum* is oval, but not pointed, 1·2 in. by 1 in. The device is included in a rose of tracery of six points, is divided by two lines in fess into three parts ; in chief five billets (?) saltierwise ; in fess a mitred head between a key and a sword, both in pale ; in base two lions rampant. *Leg.*: ✠ S' ALEXANDRI PRIORIS WYNTONIEN SECRETVM.

(1) This name does not occur in Wharton. His seal is very rich, and is 3 in. by 1·9 in. in size. The canopy is in the richest style of decorated canopy-work ; in the central compartment is the prior in benediction, his mitre, and the clasped book in his left hand also, jewelled. On the dexter side the arms of France and England quarterly ; and on the sinister the arms of the priory (?) —a key in bend surmounting a sword in bend-sinister. *Leg.*: . . . . FRATRIS . . . . AWE PRIOR ECC . . . . ERAL SCI SWITVNI WINT . . . .

(2) Dugdale gives us these dates, and states that on the death of John Merlaw, William Thudden was elected ; but the bishop refused to confirm the choice, and Hugo de Basyng was elected. (Milner, vol. ii. p. 147.)

(3) These dates are given by Dugdale (*u. s.*). He was D.D. (Milner, vol. ii. p. 147.)

(4) He died after October, 1404 ; but it is not known when. He was a D.D. also (ibid.).

(5) Dugdale inserts this name, but gives no date with it.

(6) He was prior in 1444 (Wharton, *u. s.*), and died on the 10th of January (ibid.).

(7) He had been treasurer (Milner, *u. s.*, says, "cellarer") to the monastery.

(8) Wharton alone gives this name, on the authority of "*Regis. Coll. Winton.*"

(9) This name and that of Prior Hunton do not appear in Wharton's list ; and it is probable that Westgate's name ought not to be in the list, for we have a seal of his as sub-prior and keeper of the altar of St. Mary in the cathedral. It shows a trefoil-headed canopy ; above, the half-length figure of St. Swithin, and the sub-prior in prayer below. *Leg.*: SIGILLVM SVP PRIORIS STI SWITHVNI WINTONE. It is taken from a deed of 22 Henry VI., but the seal is evidently much earlier.

(10) Of Prior Hunton's works in the cathedral mention has been made above (see p. 66).

(11) Prior Silkstede was no mean benefactor of the cathedral ; his improvements, &c., have been described above (see pp. 53, 64, 65).

(12) Wharton does not include this name. Prior Broke was a D.D. ; he was living in 1535, but the date of his death is unknown.

(13) Kingsmill was prior in the year 1538, but nothing is known of the date of his appointment. Respecting his resignation of the priorate on November 15th, 1539, and accepting the office of dean here, see above, p. 107, note 5.

(14) His appointment as dean is dated March the 28th, 1540. The date of his death is taken from the inscription on his tomb, given by Gale (p. 37).

(15) He was a laic, and was installed on the 9th of October, 1549 ; he resigned his office in 1553.

(16) Installed on the 22nd of March in the former year. Probably resigned in consequence of the accession of Elizabeth.

1559—1564. John Warner, M.D.[1]

1565—1572. Francis Newton, D.D.[2]

1572—1580. John Watson, M.D. In the latter year he was elevated to the see of Winchester.[3]

1580—1588. Lawrence Humphrey, D.D.[4]

1588—1599. Martin Heton, D.D. Raised to the see of Ely on February the 3rd in the latter year.[5]

1599—1609. George Abbot, D.D. Raised to the see of Lichfield and Coventry on the 3rd of December in the latter year.[6]

1610—1616. Thomas Morton, D.D. Consecrated Bishop of Chester July the 7th, 1616.[7]

1616—* *. John Young, D.D.[8]

1660—1665. Alexander Hyde, LL.D. Consecrated to the see of Salisbury, December the 3rd, 1665.[9]

1666—1679. William Clark, D.D.[10]

1679—1692. Richard Meggott, D.D.[11]

1693—1721. John Wickart, D.D.[12]

1721—1729. William Trimnell, D.D.[13]

1729—1739. Charles Naylor, LL.D.[14]

1739—1748. Zachary Pearce, D.D. Consecrated Bishop of Bangor in the latter year.[15]

1748—1760. Thomas Cheyney, D.D.[16]

1760—1769. Jonathan Shipley, D.D. Raised to the see of Llandaff in the latter year.

1769—1804. Newton Ogle, D.D.[17]

1804—1805. Robert Holmes.[18]

1805—1840. Thomas Rennell, D.D.[19]

1840——Thomas Garnier, D.C.L.

(1) October the 15th, 1559, is the exact date of his appointment, and he died on the 21st of March, 1564.

(2) The precise date of the appointment is March the 21st, 1565, which *may be* the same as that of the death of his predecessor, as there is a continual confusion between the Old Style and New Style in all the lists extant.

(3) Admitted February the 14th in the former year. (See above, p. 125.)

(4) Admitted October the 24th in the former year; died February the 1st in the latter (or in 1589, N. s.).

(5) Installed March the 20th, 1588 (or 1589, N. s.); and, similarly, the date of his removal may be 1600. He died July the 14th, 1609.

(6) Admitted March the 6th, 1599 (or 1600, N. s.). He was finally raised to the see of Canterbury, and died August the 4th, 1633.

(7) Admitted January the 3rd, 1610. He died September the 22nd, 1659.

(8) Installed on the 8th of July.

(9) Installed on August the 8th, 1660; died August the 22nd, 1667.

(10) Installed on the 1st of February.

(11) Installed October the 9th.

(12) Installed January the 14th.

(13) Installed February the 16th.

(14) Installed May the 7th in the former year; died June the 23rd in the latter year.

(15) Installed August the 4th.

(16) Installed March the 25th, 1748; died December the 27th, 1760.

(17) Installed October the 21st.

(18) Installed February the 22nd.

(19) Installed December the 9th, 1805; died March the 31st, 1840. The principal part of the panelled woodwork in the south transept is the work of this dean. (See p. 53, note 2, above.)

LANDS AND OTHER POSSESSIONS OF THE CATHEDRAL AND PRIORY OF ST. SWITHIN'S.

First endowment of the cathedral.

Before the foundations of the original cathedral were laid, Cynegils of Wessex had arranged for the endowment of it with the magnificent gift of "all the land surrounding Winchester, extending from the city to a distance of seven *leucœ* on every side."[1] This was the manor of Chilcombe, or Barton, which, after the lapse of above twelve hundred years, is now in the possession of the dean and chapter. It was the first of a long series of similar presents, almost all of which preceded the Conquest, and respecting many of which we possess, in the "*Codex Diplomaticus Ævi Saxonici,*" charters of the highest interest and value.

Domesday Book.

The most complete account of these possessions of the church of Winchester is contained in Domesday, an abstract of which, with notes and such additions as are needful, we now give, postponing, however, for the present such notices of the places in this county as may be desirable, and must be included in the topographical account of each, and referring to other county histories for full accounts of the others.

Lands of the bishop in Hampshire.

We commence with the "land of the Bishop of Winchester" in the survey of Hampshire.[2] Here, in *Falelie* (now Fawley) Hundred, Walkelyn is said to hold, as

---

(1) *Annal. Wint.*, apud Wharton's "Anglia Sacra," vol. i. p. 288. The particulars of this grant will be given under the head of Chilcombe, at the beginning of the next division of this Topographical Description. In a subsequent page of the present division I shall collect whatever information I can respecting the Soke of Winchester.

(2) Domesday Book, vol. i. ff. 40, 40 v₀.

It may be interesting to compare the following catalogue of the possessions of the cathedral a hundred years earlier, contained in a charter of Æthelred, given in the *Codex Diplomaticus* (No. 642). "Æstuna IIII; æt Afintuna V, and æt Ufintuna V; æt Ticceburnan XXV; to Cylmestuna V; to Stoce V; to Brombrygce, and to Oterburnan V; to Twyfyrde XX; to Ceolbandingtune XX; to Hnutscillingæ V; an hund hida to Ciltancumba [which the charter also says is to be reckoned 'on eallum thingon for ane hide']; to Hysseburnan, and to Hwitcyrcan hunendlyftig hida; to Uferantune XL hida; to Cleran X; to Alresforda XL; to Crawelea II læs XXX; to Wudatuna XX; to Aclea X; to twam Polhæmatunan X; to Myceldefer X; to Endefer X; æt Abbotesdun X; to Crundelan L; æt Beonytlege X; to Drocelesford XVII; æt Byrhfuutan, and æt Hafunt X; to Fearrham XXX; to Wealtham, and æt Myceldefer L; other healf to Falethlea. Thæt is ealles fif hund hida and ehta, and hund seofontig hida."

Upon this charter Kemble (Saxons in England, vol. ii. p. 494, note) remarks, "The estate of Chilcombe alone is reckoned at one hundred hides, or at least three thousand acres, which they succeeded in getting rated to the

public burthens at one hide only; but the whole of their estates in Hampshire appear to have comprised no less than five hundred and seventy-eight hides, which at a very low estimate of the hide amount *to seventeen thousand three hundred and forty acres*—a very pretty provision for one chapter."

From a yearly statement respecting the condition of the manors of the priory for the years 1390—2, in the Cath. Lib. Winton., I give the following complete list for those years:—" Crundale, Sutton, Hanyton, Wotton, Wonsyngton, Thurmound's, Berthona, Selkstede, Litleton, Houghton, Michelmersh, Stoktone, Euforde, Ouertone, Aultone, Whitchurche, Husseborne, Chilbolton, Estone, Mapuldurham, Worston."

With these may be compared the following lists of manors granted to the new establishment by letters patent and charter:—" Barthona Prioris, Crundale, Sutton, Whitchurche, Manydon, Lyttleton, Chilbolton, Wunsyngton, Sylkestede, Westmeon, Nutshylling, Mylbroke, Morecourte, Abyngton, Exton, Haddyngton, Bransebury, Henton, Upsombourne, Wymauston, and Shypton Bellynger," in Hampshire; with "Hame, Hynyton, Overton, Alton, Wroughton, Stoketon, Pateney, Westwode, and Langefyssched juxta Endeford," in Wiltshire; and Bledon in Somersetshire. Another list follows, different in some respects from the former, and entitled in the margin "*feod. milit., escaet., releuia, cur. let., vis. franc. pleg., cat., wainat., &c.*" "Barthoua Prioris, Sparsholte, Wyke, Fulflud, Compton, Sparkeford, Chylcomb,

part of the possessions of the bishopric, *Alresforde*, assessed at forty-two hides[1] (with its subdivisions *Sudbertune*, and *Bieforde*) ; *Chelmestune* (now Kilmistun), assessed at five hides ; *Tuiforde*,[2] assessed at fifteen hides, and another manor there at five hides ; *Estune*,[3] assessed at six hides ; *Stoches*[4] (now Bishop's Stoke), at five hides. In *Bitelesiete* (now Buddlesgate) Hundred, he held *Crawlie*, assessed at six hides and a half ; in *Waltham* Hundred, *Waltham*[5] (now Bishop's Waltham), assessed at twenty hides, although there were thirty ; in *Overetune* Hundred, *Overetune*,[6] assessed at forty-one hides (with *Bradelie* as a subdivision in it) ; in *Menestoches* (now Meonstoke) Hundred, six hides and a virgate in *Mene*[7] (now Meon) ; and *Stoches* (now Meonstoke) assessed at seven hides ; in *Fernham* (Fareham) Hundred, *Fernham*,[8] assessed at twenty hides, though there were thirty ; in *Broton* Hundred, *Chingescamp*, half a hide ; in *Ticefelle* (now Tichfield) Hundred, *Mene*[9] (or Meon) ; and *Benedlei* (or Bentley), assessed at eight hides ; and *Burnewic*, of the king in fee, which was not " *de episcopatu*." In *Mantesberge* (now Bountisborough) Hundred the bishop had *Edintune*, assessed " *pro nichilo ;* " *Walde*[10] (now Wield), assessed at ten hides ; and *Abedestune* (now Abbotston), at nine hides ; in *Maneberge* (now Mainsborough) Hundred, *Candevre*, ten hides ; in *Sumburne* (now King's Sombourne) Hundred, *Houstune*[11] (now Houghton), assessed at sixteen hides ; and in *Esselei* (or Eastley) Hundred, *Tistede*, seven hides.

In this county the following lands were " *de victu Monachorum Wintoniensium*." In *Falmere*, or *Falelie* (now Fawley), Hundred, *Ciltecumbe*,[12] assessed at one hide ; and *Avintune*,[13] assessed at five hides ; in *Bitelesiet* (now Buddlesgate) Hundred, *Notesse-*

Lands of the Priory of St. Swithiu in Hampshire.

Ovyngton, Morested, Brykesdun, Wynhall, Otterbourne, Crundale, Yately, Crokam, Dypnall, Bramshutt, Haldershutt, Halley, Swantropper, Flete, Bownest, Charlecote, Fryfolke, Baghurst, Hanyton, Fabyans, Marvyns, Thurmonds, Hursley, Oxenbridge, Deane, and Lovynton," in Hampshire ; with shops, &c., in several parishes in Winchester and the Soke, and the ferm of the borough of Whitchurch. (Rot. Pat. 33 Hen. VIII. p. 9, and charter in Cath. Lib. Winton.).

(1) Alresford was one of the earliest possessions of the see, being the gift of Cenwalch about A.D. 639. *Annal. Wint.* It also occurs in the list of the bishop's manors in the *Taxatio Ecclesiastica*, p. 215.

I shall not give any references to the charters in the *Codex Diplomaticus* relating to places within the county, since the charters will be examined and compared when the several places are treated of subsequently.

(2) This place is named in the *Tax. Eccl., u. s.*

(3) This is found in the list of manors belonging to the priory, in the *Tax. Eccl.*, p. 213.

(4) This occurs in the *Tax. Eccl.*, p. 215.

(5) Waltham is found in the list referred to in the preceding note.

(6) This manor was the gift of Edward the Elder (see *Annales, u. s.*) ; and it is named in the *Tax. Eccl., u. s.*

(7) Edward the Confessor bestowed both the Meons

upon Winchester at the time of his mother, Queen Emma's miraculous deliverance from the burning ploughshares, according to the *Annales.* (See *Ann.* 1043.) But they were the gift of Bishop Alwyn, according to Rudborne (p. 235). This discrepancy between the only authorities for these gifts must be noted, and also the very remarkable fact, that neither charters nor chartularies support the statements of the annalist and the chronicler respecting these alleged gifts. William the Conqueror is said by the latter authority (p. 248) to have taken both of them away. *West Men* is, however, found in the list of manors belonging to the priory in the *Tax. Eccl.*, p. 213.

(8) In the list in *Tax. Eccl.*, p. 215, this is ascribed to the bishop.

(9) See note 7, above.

(10) This name is in the list of the bishop's manors in *Tax. Eccl.*, p. 215.

(11) This was one of the nine manors said to have been given by Queen Emma on the occasion referred to above (Rudborne, p. 235). It appears in the list of the manors belonging to the priory in *Tax. Eccl.*, p. 213.

(12) This was the first endowment of Winchester Cathedral. It appears in the list of the prior's manors as *Bertone*, in *Tax. Eccl., u. s.*

(13) The gift of Edgar (*Annales*, ann. 959), and contained in the list of the *Tax. Eccl.* (p. 213), and the Augmentation Office Roll.

linge[1] (now Nutshalling), assessed at five hides; and *Cilbodentune*[2] (now Chilbolton), also assessed at five hides; in *Evingare* Hundred, *Witcerce*[3] (now Whitchurch), thirty-three hides, including *Frigefolc* (now Freefolk) and *Windenaie* ;[4] *Eisseburne*[5] (now Hurstbourne Priors), thirty-eight hides; and *Clere*,[6] assessed at seven hides and a half. In *Corondel* (now Crondal) Hundred they had *Crundele*,[7] forty hides, including *Ticelle, Cove, Beddeleie, Sudtune*[8] (now Sutton), and *Ferneberga* (now Farnborough) ; *Drocheneford*[9] (now Droxford), in a hundred of the same name (not now in existence), assessed at fourteen hides, and including *Benestede ;* and *Polemtune*[10] (or Polhampton). They held *Essentune*[11] (now Exton), in *Menestoch* Hundred, assessed at eight hides ; *Alwarestoch*[12] (now Alverstoke), assessed at ten hides ; and *Ordie*, three hides ; in *Bertune* (now Barton Stacey) Hundred, *Wenesistune*[13] (now Wonston), seven hides ; and *Brandesberee*[14] (now Bransbury), four hides. In *Manebridge* Hundred, *Stanham*,[15] three hides, was " *de vestitu monachorum ;*" and they had also *Melebroc*[16] (now Millbrook), five hides ; and *Hentune*[17] (now Southampton), assessed at the same quantity. They held in *Rodbrige* (now Redbridge) Hundred one virgate in *Falegia* (now Fawley), the remainder of two hides being at this time afforested. In *Clere* Hundred, *Eccleswille* (now Itchingswell) was theirs, and it was assessed at seven hides and a half ; and *Hanitune*[18] (now Hannington), assessed at six hides and a half, and two parts of a virgate ; in *Odingetone* Hundred, *Odingetone*,[19] two hides ; in *Portesdone* Hundred, half

---

(1) Bishop Tunbriht (Rudborne, p. 206) gave this to the church ; and it is found amongst the prior's manors, in *Tax. Eccl.*, *u. s.*: and also in the Roll of 33 Henry VIII., in the Augmentation Office, given in Dugdale, vol. i. p. 217.

(2) This was one of Athelstan's gifts to Winchester (*Annales*, ann. 924). The *Tax. Eccl.* contains it at p. 213.

(3) The gift of Edward the Elder (*Annales*, 901), and mentioned in *Tax. Eccl.* (ibid.).

(4) Probably " Widehaye," the third manor given by Alwara for the soul of her husband, Leowin (Leland's *Collectanea, u. s.*).

(5) One of the gifts of Edward the Elder (*Annales*, ann. 901) ; and mentioned in *Tax. Eccl.*, p. 213.

(6) The gift of Cuthred (*Annales*, ann. 735) or Agelwyn (Leland's *Collect.*, vol. ii. p. 429), and included in the list of the bishop's manors in *Tax. Eccl.*, p. 215.

(7) Leland (*u. s.*) ascribes this gift to St. Elphege. It occurs amongst the manors of the priory in *Tax. Eccl.*, p. 213.

(8) Ethelred is said to have given this manor to the church here (*Annales*, ann. 979) ; it was one of the manors of the priory when the *Tax. Eccl.* was compiled (p. 213).

(9) This was bestowed on Winchester Cathedral by Egbert (*Annales*, ann. 800), but it is included amongst the manors of the bishopric in *Tax. Eccl*., p. 215.

(10) According to Rudborne (p. 235), this was one of the nine manors, by the gift of which Alwyn testified his

gratitude at the demonstration of his innocence by Queen Emma's deliverance.

(11) Leland (*u. s.*) says that Alwara bestowed this manor, with the next which occurs in the text, and another, on Winchester, "*pro anima Leowini viri sui.*" It is one of the prior's manors in *Tax. Eccl.*, p. 213, and is found in the Roll of Henry VIII. from the Augmentation Office.

(12) See the preceding note. " Alwarstok " is inscribed in the list of manors belonging to the bishop (*Tax. Eccl.*, p. 215).

(13) Amongst the manors of the priory, under the spelling " Wonsyngton " (?), *Tax. Eccl.*, p. 213 ; and in the Augmentation Office list, as " Wymanston " (?).

(14) One of the nine manors given by Queen Emma (Rudborne, p. 235), and included in the list in *Tax. Eccl.* (p. 213), and in that in the Augmentation Office (Dugdale, *u. s.*).

(15) One of the nine manors given by Bishop Alwyn (Rudborne, p. 235).

(16) Another of Alwyn's manors (ibid.), and included in the list in *Tax. Eccl.*, *u. s.*, and in that from the Roll in the Augmentation Office. (Dugdale, *u. s.*)

(17) Another of Alwyn's gifts (*u. s.*). It is in the Augmentation Office list.

(18) This name is found in the list of the prior's manors in *Tax. Eccl.*, p. 213.

(19) One of Alwyn's manors (*u. s.*), which occurs in the list in the Augmentation Office.

a hide in *Borehunt;* in *Cillei* Hundred, *Odetune*[1] (or Wotton), twenty hides; in *Boseberg* (now Bosmere) Hundred, *Helinghei*[2] (now Hayling Island), four hides; *Brochmatune* (now Brockhampton), also four hides; and *Havehunte*[3] (now Havant), seven hides.

"In and around the New Forest," in *Rodbrige* Hundred, Walkelyn held the remainder of those two hides which the monastery had in *Falelie;* and in *Boure* (or Boldre) Hundred, *Truham*,[4] two hides and a half, and *Sclive*, three hides, belonged to the abbey. *Lands in the New Forest.*

There was also in the Isle of Wight, in *Cauborne* (or Calborne) Hundred, which was part of *Bouecomb* (or Bowcombe) Hundred, *Cauborne*,[5] assessed at seventeen hides, belonged to the monastery.[6] *Lands in the Isle of Wight.*

---

(1) Occurs as "Wotton" in *Tax. Eccl.*, p. 213.

(2) This was the gift of Alwyn, or of Queen Emma, for the spelling of the names in Rudborne (p. 235) does not enable us to decide.

(3) Given by Ethelred (*Annales*, ann. 979), and found in the list of manors belonging to the bishop in *Tax. Eccl.*, p. 215.

(4) This was the gift of Cuthred (*Annales*, ann. 735). It is misspelt "Druca" in Wharton (see *Cod. Dipl.*, No. 1007).

(5) This manor, then reckoned at thirty hides, was given to the church by Egbert (*Annales, ann.* 800).

(6) In the account of the endowments of this cathedral contained in Rudborne, and the *Annales Wintonienses* (as compared with the lists in the *Taxatio Ecclesiastica*), we find the following possessions in Hampshire, which are not recorded in Domesday. The corrupt spelling renders it difficult to identify many places, but opportunities will occur subsequently of correcting errors and supplying omissions.

From the *Annales* I collect these names, ann. 639, *Wordia* (or Worthy), given by Cenwalch;—683, thirty hides in *Ewerlande* (or Yaverland) "*in Vecta insula*," and fifty in *Bresdinga* (or Brading), given by Ini;—735, forty hides at *Muleburna*, in the Isle of Wight; twenty-five at *Banewada*; and twenty-two at *Witthingeham* (or Whippingham) given by Cuthred;—800, forty-two hides at *Scaldeblota* (or Shalfleet), and the "*villae*," *Wordia* (or Worthy), and *Beddintona*, which Leland, *u. s.*, calls "Bedhampton," and under which, in *Cod. Dipl.*, No. 606, we find *Cyslesdene* (now Chiseldon), *Tenhric* (Tendridge), and *Lace* (Lake), given by Egbert;—901, ten "manentes" in *Stoka* ("Stoce be Hysseburna," Cod. Dipl., No. 1077), given by Edward the Elder;—924, *Eismeresworda* (called "Hamerysworde" by Rudborne, p. 212, and "Armereworth" in *Tax. Eccl.*, p. 215, "Æscmeresweorth," in *Cod. Dipl.*, No. 1110, now Ashmansworth), given by Athelstan;—959, ten hides at *Itinstoka* (or Itchenstoke), by Edgar;—979, a hide and a half at *Celsehord* (in the *Codex Diplomaticus*, No. 626, "Celcesora," now Cald-

shot); and *Ginnahetche* ("Ginanhecche" on the Darent, *Cod. Dipl.*, No. 640), by Ethelred.

To this list we may add from Rudborne (p. 235), *Mychelmeryshe* (contained in the list of the prior's manors, *Tax. Eccl.*, p. 213), which was one of Queen Emma's nine; and (p. 241) "privilegium quoddam vocatum *Godbegete*" (called in the Augmentation Roll "*Libertas de Goodbigate*," of which mention has been made above, p. 16, note), given by Edward the Confessor (but which in *Cod. Dipl.*, No. 1291, is said to be the gift of Ethelred). Half a "piscary" at *Potelaia* (Botley) was given to the priory by Bishop Gyffard (p. 278).

Leland (*Collect.*, vol. ii. pp. 428—430), in his list of *Fundatores principales*, professedly condensed from Rudborne, in addition to these, supplies these benefactions:— "*Alfstanus dux, filius Ethelredi, dedit ecclesiæ Winton. Merden* (in Hursley) *et Eggebyri* (in St. Mary Bourne);" "*Wolwynus monachus Wintoniensis dedit ecclesiæ Winton. manerium de Butermere ;*" "*Dominus Simon de Winton, miles, contulit Winhale ecclesiæ Wintoniensi.*"

In the *Taxatio Ecclesiastica*, besides those named above, we find in the list of priors' manors (p. 213), *Litleton* (which was, and is, part of Chilcombe or Barton manor); and *Mapelderham;*—and in the list of episcopal manors (p. 215) there are *Scameldon* (which is "Hamuldon" in the list of 1647, and may be Hambledon) *Stocten cum Hamelettis de Welde, Alreford, Sene Hampton, Heyworth* (two of which places have occurred above), *Crowell* (now Grewell?) *Wolveseye; Waltham* has *Byterne* (now Bittern) associated with it; *North Waltham* is associated with *Drekenesfote* (or Droxford); and to *Clere* are assigned as hamlets, *Newinton* (now Newtown), *Bydihaie* (or Woodhay), *Armereworth* and *Estmieswill* (which we have seen above), and *Burclere*.

The Roll 33 Henry VIII., Augmentation Office, supplies us with the names of *Shipton Bellinger* (or "Berenger"), *Morecourte* (in North Baddesley), *Hursley* and *Oxenbridge*, "*Shorumham juxta Soborton*," *Upsomborne* manor, "*Civitas Winton. cum Soca*," and *Deane*. [But

Besides all these possessions within the limits of our county, there are the following entries in Domesday of estates belonging to the see or the priory in other counties, which must be briefly noticed.

Lands in Surrey.

In Surrey,[1] *Ferneham* (now Farnham) belonged to the bishop. *"Sanctus Petrus semper tenuit."* It was assessed at sixty hides, one of which lay within the limits of Hampshire.[2]

Lands in Berkshire.

In Berkshire[3] we find *" de victu monachorum" Olvricestone,*[4] assessed at ten hides; and *" de episcopatu" Harwelle,*[5] also ten hides; *Bristowelle*[6] (properly *Brichtwelle,* now Brightwell), assessed at the same amount. There were lands in *Walengefort* (valued at sixteen pounds and twenty-five pounds respectively) pertaining to these manors.[7]

Lands in Wiltshire.

Wiltshire[8] contained a longer list of names. Amongst the bishop's lands was *Duntone*[9] (now Downton), the history of which, as dimly discerned in the *Annales* and the charters in the *Codex Diplomaticus,* shows that the spoliation of the church was by no means a thing unheard of in these realms before the Reformation.[10] It is not easy to

---

But the additions of the most unquestionable authority are those from the charters in the *Codex Diplomaticus,* which I give without comment, merely for the purpose of completing this synopsis of the territorial possessions of the cathedral and priory of St. Swithin's before the Reformation. They are *Allændune* (No. 593); *Drethecumb,* in the Isle of Wight (No. 599); *Tadanleage* (now Tadley, Nos. 603, 1092, 1094); *Ticceburn* (now Titchbourne, Nos. 604, 1088); *Beowyrthe* (now Beauworth, No. 604); *Ufinctune* (now Ovington, No. 604); *Porteceaster* (now Porchester, Nos. 608, 1085); *Hefesylling, Hortun, Ceoliglond, Oselbirig* (now Owselbury), *Oterburne* (now Otterbourne), and *Hundetun* (now Hound? all in No. 609, and the last repeated in No. 1096); *Brombrygce, Aclea* (now Oakley?), and *Byrhfunt* (No. 642); *Spæresholt* and *Eppelhyrst* (No. 1007).

The account of church lands belonging to this see sold during the time of the civil wars, contained in Gale (pp. 29—33, Cassan's reprint), and also in Dugdale (latest edition, where it is printed from the Rawlinson MS. B. 236, in the Bodleian Library at Oxford), adds one or two names to this long catalogue; the manor of *Adderbury, Longwood* warren, *Willersley* warren, the manor of *Morton,* the manor of *Cold Henleigh* (in Whitchurch), and that of *Upton* (which may be the same as Hoddington).

The list of 1647 adds *Gosport,* and *Owre* (Ore) may be added from the Patent Rolls, cited by Gale; with *Drayton* in St. James's, near Winchester, from charters in Cath. Lib. Winton.

(1) Domesday, vol. i. fol. 31.

(2) From charter No. 994, in *Cod. Dipl.,* it appears that this manor was the gift of Ceadwalha of Wessex, in the year 688, but Kemble has marked it with an asterisk. Charters Nos. 1058, 1093, 605, 607 also refer to this manor, and, with the exception of the last, state its extent as sixty *cassati* or *mansæ.* All but Nos. 1058 and 607

mention (in various modes of spelling), along with *Fearnham, Beonetleh* (now Bentley), in Hampshire; and the list of episcopal manors (*Tax. Eccl.,* p. 215) contains these two names together. Bentley is, in these charters, said to contain ten *cassati.*

Fermesham (said by Kemble to be Frensham) is by Charter No. 610 (*Cod. Dipl.*) said to have been restored by Edgar; and *Hwitanleage* (which Kemble considers to have been Witley, if it be not Widley in Hants) is shown, in No. 1007, to be the gift of Cuthred.

The *Taxatio* (*u. s.*) mentions *Esschere* and *Su'werke* as other possessions of the bishop in the county of Surrey.

(3) Domesday, vol. i. f. 58.

(4) In *Tax. Eccl.* (p. 191) *Wlfrithestone,* belonging to the prior.

(5) In *Cod. Dipl.* (No. 1273) *Haranwylle.* It occurs in the list of episcopal manors (*Tax. Eccl.,* p. 215).

(6) This is included in the list of the bishop's manors (*Tax. Eccl., u. s.*), and in a valuation of the episcopal estates in 1647. It was the gift of Ethelwulf (*Annales,* ann. 837).

(7) In Berkshire two hides at *Apeltune* were the property of the monastery (*Cod. Dipl.,* No. 949), and a hundred *" manentes"* at *Ceolesig* (now Cholsey), *Hacceburn* (now Hagburn) and *Bæstlæsford.* *Wergravys* (one of Queen Emma's nine manors, Rudborne, p. 235), called *" Weregue cum hamelettis"* in *Tax. Eccl.* (p. 215), was taken away by William the Conqueror (Rudborne, p. 248).

(8) Domesday, vol. i. f. 65 v°.

(9) In *Tax. Eccl.* (p. 215) it appears to be intended by *Donington cum hamlettis;* but it is not found in the list of the Augmentation Office Roll, or of the parliamentary valuation in 1647.

(10) This splendid manor (or rather manors) was the gift of Cenwalch, about the year 639 (*Annales,* ann., and *Cod. Dipl.,* No. 985); and it is spoken of as "restored" to the church by Edward the Elder in 908

ascertain its hidage, but in the time of Edward the Confessor it seems to have been assessed at ninety-five hides.[1] To the bishop also belonged *Fontel*[2] (now Fonthill Bishop's), assessed at ten hides; and *Fifhide*,[3] at five hides.

The remainder were "*de victu monachorum;* they were *Awltone*[4] (now Alton), twenty hides; *Hame*,[5] ten hides; *Westwode*,[6] three; *Elendune*,[7] thirty; *Clive*,[8] ten; *Wemberge*[9] (now Wanborough), nineteen; *Enedford*,[10] thirty; *Ovretone*,[11] fifteen; and *Stottune*,[12] ten; most of which may easily be identified.[13]

Tantone (now Taunton) was the chief episcopal possession in Somersetshire,[14] with its long list of lands that paid certain "*denominatas consuetudines*" there,—*Talanda*

Lands in Somersetshire.

(*Cod. Dipl.*, No. 342); by Edred in 948 (ibid. v., and *Cod. Dipl.*, No. 421), Edgar in 953 (Rudborne, p. 219, and *Cod. Dipl.*, No. 599 and 610), Ethelred in 979 (*Annales*, *sub ann.* 997, *Cod. Dipl.*, No. 698), and it was confirmed (vainly as it appears) by Egbert in 826 (*Cod. Dipl.*, No. 1036), and Athelstan in 932 (ibid., No. 1108). And in Domesday we read,—"*tempore Regis Edwardi gelda-verunt pro C hidis tribus minus; Duæ ex his non sunt epis-copi, quia ablatæ fuerunt cum aliis tribus de æcclesia et de manu episcopi, tempore Cnut. regis.*" From the charter of Edward the Elder it appears that Bishop Denewulf had alienated this estate to the king for his lifetime.

(1) It consisted properly of the two manors of *Dun-ton*, containing fifty-five hides, and *Ebblesburn*, contain-ing forty-five. By the efforts of J. Y. Akerman, Esq., Secretary to the Society of Antiquaries, the original boundaries of this great tract of country have been made out very successfully, and he has exhibited the results of his researches in a map (Archæologia, vol. xxxv. Pl. IX.) accompanying a very full and lucid description. The traces of this grant extend more than twenty miles in length. Kemble has marked the copy of Cenwalch's charter (No. 985) with his depreciatory asterisk.

(2) This was given to the church by Earl Ordlaf (*Cod. Dipl.*, No. 1076), and, having been alienated or lost, was restored by Edgar (ibid., No. 610).

(3) One of Queen Emma's nine manors (Rudborne, p. 235).

(4) The gift of Egbert (*Annales*, ann. 800, *Cod. Dipl.*, No. 1035, which gives the true date, 826); and in another charter (No. 1070) it (or some part of it) ap-pears as the gift of Ceolwen for the good of her husband's soul. In *Tax. Eccl.* (p. 192) this appears amongst the estates of the prior; it also occurs in the Roll in the Aug-mentation Office (*u. s.*).

(5) Given by Wulfgar (*Cod. Dipl.*, No. 353), and be-longing to the priory in the time of Edward I. (*Tax. Eccl.*, p. 192).

(6) The gift of Queen Emma for the soul of Hardi-canute (*Annales*, ann. 1042); it was restored by Bishop Toclyve (Rudborne, p. 286), and occurs in the Augmen-tation Roll.

(7) A charge on the church here is named in *Tax. Eccl.*, p. 190.

(8) Leland (*u. s.*) says that this was the gift of Bishop Henry de Blois; but Rudborne (ap. Wharton, p. 285) attributes to him the gift of "*Elme*," a word easily mis-taken for Clive, or *vice versâ*. *Clive Pypard* is a pos-session of the prior's in *Tax. Eccl.*, p. 192.

(9) The gift of Ethelwulf in 854 (*Annales*, ann. 837, and *Cod. Dipl.*, No. 1053). The original charter (or a very early copy of it) of this gift is in the Cathedral Library (A. 1.). Kemble's copy is from the *Codex Win-ton.* The quantity of land is said to be xx[ti] *mansæ*; and the endorsement identifies the spot as that "*quæ modo Hynyton dicitur.*" It is, therefore, the *Hyneton* of the *Taxatio* (p. 193), and perhaps the *Hynxton* of the Aug-mentation Office Roll.

(10) The gift of Athelstan, on the 16th of December, 934 (*Annales*, ann. 924, and *Cod. Dipl.*, No. 1110). The name occurs as *Eneforde* in *Tax. Eccl.*, p. 185, and in the list of the Augmentation Office, with the addition "*reservatum pro rege.*" *Langfischedide*, in the Aug-mentation Roll, was part of this manor or another name for it.

(11) Possibly the manor given by Edward the Elder about 910 (*Cod. Dipl.*, Nos. 1092, 1094), rather than that mentioned above (see p. 133, and note 6). This Wiltshire *Ovretone* belonged to the prior in the time of the *Taxatio* (p. 192), and is included in the Roll in the Augmentation Office.

(12) In *Tax. Eccl.* (p. 186) called *Stoktone*, and in the Augmentation Roll *Stocheton.*

(13) Besides these manors, the *Taxatio* (p. 193) informs us of *Netherwerston*, in this county, belonging to the prior. And the Augmentation Roll adds *Wroughton*. Rudborne (p. 286) says that Bishop Toclyve bought *Cnoel* (now Knoyle), and gave it to his church; and it occurs in *Tax. Eccl.*, p. 215. From the *Codex Diplomaticus Cisel-denu*, or *Ceolseldene*, with *Sweores holt* (identified by Kemble with Chiselden, Nos. 1069, 1077), *Lidgerd* and *Ebingtune* (No. 1076), may be added to this part of the list; with *Stoce juxta Scealdburnan* (Stoke by Shalbourn, Nos. 598, 600, 1082, 1084), *Pateny* (now Patney), men-tioned in *Tax. Eccl.* (p. 185), which occurs in *Cod. Dipl.*, No. 949, *Norton* (*Tax. Eccl.*, p. 215), and *Brottune* (now Broughton).

(14) Domesday, vol. i. f. 87 v°.

T

(now Tolland), *Acha* (Oake), *Holeforde* (Holford), *Ubcedene* and *Succedene* (the two Cheddons), *Maidenobroche*, *Laford*, *Hilla* and *Hela* (which "*non poterant a Tantone separari*"), *Nichehede* (Nynehead), *Nortone* (Norton), *Bradeforde* (Bradford), *Halsa* (Halse), *Hafella* (Heathfield), *Scobindare*, *Stocha* (Stoke), and *Baweberga* (Bagborough); altogether amounting to fifty-four hides and a half, and half a virgate; to which two hides in *Lidiard* and *Lega* were added.[1] *Pipeminstre*[2] (now Pitminster) reckoned at fifteen hides; and *Rintone*[3] (now Rimpton) five hides, also belonged to the bishop. *Bledone*[4] (now Bleadon) fifteen hides, was "*de victu monachorum.*"[5]

Lands in Herts. In Hertfordshire, one manor named *Chodrei*, in *Odesei* Hundred, assessed at five hides, lay "*in dominio ecclesiæ S. Petri, Wintoniensis.*"[6]

Lands in Bucks. In Buckinghamshire we find two manors; the first, *Wicombe*, assessed at nineteen hides, was "*de victu monachorum;*" the other, *Evinghehov* (now Ivinghoe), was "*in dominio ecclesiæ S. Petri, Wintoniensis.*"[7]

Lands in Oxfordshire. Two are mentioned in Oxfordshire, *Witenie* reckoned at thirty hides; and *Edburgberie* (now Adderbury), fourteen hides and a half, *de ecclesia.*[8]

Lands in Cambridgeshire. The last possessions of the Bishop of Winchester recorded in Domesday lay in Cambridgeshire; they were *Mordune*, reckoned at eight hides; *Cloptune*, three hides

---

(1) This valuable estate was given to the see by Frithsgytha, queen of Ethelheard of Wessex, in 737 (*Annales*, ann. 721); and Ethelheard added four *mansas* in *Withiglea*, and three in *Cearn* (for salt-works), to his queen's gift (*Cod. Dipl.*, No. 1002, but it has an asterisk prefixed). Ethelwulf, in 854, augmented it by "*VIII. manentes*" at *Risctune* (now Rushton), and as many "*in Sloce æt Orceard*" (now Stoke and Orchard; *Cod. Dipl.*, No. 1051); he also added, in the same year, a vast tract of country, containing a hundred and thirty-three *manentes* (or hides) and ten more at *Bruna* (ibid., No. 1052). Bishop Denewulf, in 904 (ibid., No. 1082), procured the confirmation of the liberties of this noble domain by the gift of twenty "*manentes*" to Edward the Elder (ibid., No. 1084). Athelstan confirmed Ethelheard's grant in 938 (ibid., No. 374)); and a further confirmation was granted by Edred in 947 (ibid., No. 1157). Yet in 978 we find Edgar restoring the liberties and rights of the church here (Rudborne, p. 219, and *Cod. Dipl.*, Nos. 598 600, 610, and 717). *Hylle* was given by Canute in 1033 (*Annales*, ann. 1035; *Cod. Dipl.*, No. 750). In No. 897 of the *Cod. Dipl.* is a document in Saxon which illustrates the statement in Domesday of the *consuetudines* paid at Taunton. *Crawcumb*, the gift of Githa (*Annal.* 1053), was part of this manor (*Cod. Dipl.*, Nos. 598, 600). *Taunton cum hamlettis* is found in the list of episcopal manors in *Tax. Eccl.*, p. 215.

(2) The gift of Emma for the soul of Hardicanute (*Annales*, ann. 1042); but according to the charter (No. 774, *Cod. Dipl.*) the gift of Edward the Confessor for his own soul.

(3) Given by Alfred (according to the *Annales*, ann. 872) for the augmentation of Taunton. *Taunton* and *Rympton* are both named in the valuation of episcopal lands in 1647.

(4) The gift of Githa in 1053 (*Annales, sub ann.*); but of Edgar, long before, according to Charter No. 587 (*Cod. Dipl.*): it is said to belong to the prior in *Tax. Eccl.* (p. 204), and it occurs in the Augmentation Roll.

(5) The *Codex Diplomaticus* adds the names of *Cumbtun* (now Bishop Compton, No. 598), and *Bananwyll* or *Banewilla* (now Banwell, Nos. 598, 600, 1084). The Augmentation Roll contains the name of *Lovington*, which is in Somersetshire, but it occurs in no other list.

(6) Domesday, vol. i. f. 133.

(7) Ibid., fol. 143 vº. Both these manors are enumerated by Rudborne (p. 235) amongst the nine presented by Queen Emma. And in the *Taxatio* (p. 215) they both occur as *Enigho cum suis hamelettis*, and *West Wycumbe*. *Hrisanbeorgan* (now Monks' Risborough), in this county, was bequeathed by Ælfgyfa, in 1012 (*Cod. Dipl.*, No. 721).

(8) Domesday, vol. i. fol. 155. *Wytneye* is one of the nine manors which Rudborne (p. 235) says Alwyn gave on the occasion of Emma's deliverance; and the Charter No. 775 (*Cod. Dipl.*) contains the gift of it from Edward the Confessor to Alwyn. *Eadbyrgebyrig* appears by Charter No. 722 (ibid.) to have been given to the church by Æthelstan Ætheling. It is the subject of No. 768 also. In the *Taxatio* (p. 215) they appear as *Watteneye cum hamlettis de Crodebreggs, Crawell, et Hayle* (now Curbridge, Crowley, and Hailey), and *Eadbubur cum hameletto de Bodycot* (now Bodicott). We have stated above (see p. 136, note) that Adderbury is in the parliament list of episcopal lands in 1647; *Witney* is also there.

and a half; *Abintone* (now Abington), two hides and a half, and half a virgate; and *Basingborne* (which retains its name), one hide and two virgates and a half.[1]

No other possessions are recorded in this survey, but in the various authorities referred to in the notes there are many other estates mentioned as belonging, or having belonged, to the Bishop of Winchester or St. Swithin's Priory. For the sake of giving all possible completeness to this view of the ancient wealth of this see, we give them below with such illustrations as we can afford. Did any accessible account of these church lands at the present time exist, the comparison of it with these particulars would throw great light upon the ancient topography of many places which is now involved in the greatest obscurity; but it would not in every case afford such light, since by enfranchisement, exchange, sale, and spoliation, the possessions have undergone so many changes.[2]

Much curious information respecting the temporalities of the see in former times *Knights-fees.* may be gathered from the accounts of the knights-fees held by the bishop, of which several are in existence, but they are too long to be quoted here.[3]

When William of Wykeham was bishop there were "ten or twelve different castles, *Episcopal* manor-houses, or places of residence, properly accommodated to the reception of [the *palaces.* bishops] and their retinue"[4] belonging to the see. One of these, or its ruins, at Wolvesey, has already been noticed;[5] others will be spoken of in subsequent parts of this work; but some, as Winchester House, Southwark; Farnham Castle;[6] the castle

---

(1) Domesday, vol. i. fol. 190. The land at *Mordune* seems to be part of Æthelstan Ætheling's bequest (*Cod. Dipl.*, No. 722). It is possible that three hides at *Madanlega*, said by the *Annales* (*sub ann.* 959) to have been given by Edgar, were in the county of Cambridge, at Maddingley (*Confer Cod. Dipl.*, No. 588).

(2) In Middlesex, the *Annales* (*sub ann.* 979) say that Ethelred gave this church "*duas piscaturas apud Brendefordam cum una virgata terræ.*" This grant is recorded more authentically in Charter No. 1291 (*Cod. Dipl*).

In Dorsetshire, according to Charter No. 891 (*Cod. Dipl.*), Edward the Confessor gave to the Old Minster, *Portland*, and all that lay around it; or as Rudborne (p. 235) has interpreted it, making it Edward's atonement for his false accusation of his mother and Bishop Alwyn, "*tria maneria Portland, Wykhelewele, et Waymuthe;*" which Leland (*Collectanea, u. s.*) changes into *four*, dividing the second into *Wike* and *Hollewele.* The *Annales* (ann. 1043) record the gift of *Portland*, but names the two Meons as the remainder of the self-inflicted fine. Leland (*u. s.*) has also this statement, "*Athelwoldus dux contulit Wik ecclesiæ Winton.*"

One of the manors stated by the *Annales* (ann. 1043) to have been granted to the church was five hides at *Wrockeshalle*, in the Isle of Wight; it is a subject of Charter No. 768, where the name is spelt *Wroccesheale.*

There are a few remaining, which, owing to the corrup-

tion of their names in the authorities, and the imperfection of our *Indices Villares*, we cannot identify, nor even assign to any particular county. These are three gifts of Edgar, recorded in the *Annales*, ann. 959, *Breonduna*, thirteen hides; *Aderingfelda*, two hides; and *Thecca*, seven hides; a gift of Edgyva's contained in Leland's list (*u.s.*), *Dorkinham*; and *Birchefelde*, one of Queen Emma's nine manors, or, according to Rudborne (p. 235), *Bergefeld; Elme*, said by the last-named writer (p. 285) to have been given by Bishop De Blois; two, *Yenes* and *Kynton* (Kingston?), in the list of bishops' names in *Tax. Eccl.* (p. 215); and *Morton* (if this be not intended for *Mordune*) in the parliament list of 1647.

(3) In particular, I would refer the reader to the list in the Hyde Abbey Register (Harl. MSS. 1761) fol. 77 v°, 78 v°, entitled, "*Feoda militum quæ tenentur Episcopo Wynton. infra episcopatu et alibi.*" Cassan (vol. ii. pp. 312—315) has printed a list from the Black Book of the Exchequer, with which he was supplied by Sir Richard Colt Hoare; but it contains only the names of the holders of the fees, and not of the localities of them.

(4) Lowth's Life (Cassan's reprint, p. 211).

(5) See above, pp. 93, 94

(6) For notices of both these palaces see Manning and Bray's "History of Surrey." Barclay's Brewery now occupies the principal part of the site of the former of these episcopal residences.

at Taunton, &c., cannot be described in this work. At present the only residences of the Bishops of Winchester are Farnham Castle, and Winchester House, in St. James's Square, London.

Ecclesiastical patronage.

The ecclesiastical patronage of the bishop, and of the dean and chapter, within the county of Hampshire, with which we are chiefly interested, will be noticed under the several parishes. But we must refer our readers to other sources for information regarding that which lies beyond its limits.[1]

Treasures of the cathedral.

In conclusion, we must briefly mention "the inventory of the cathedral church" given by the prior and convent to Cromwell at the period of the dissolution.[2] Amongst the treasures then relinquished to the king were these :—"The nether part of the high altar, being of plate of gold garnished with stones, the front above being of broidery-work and pearls, and above that a table of images of silver and gilt, garnished with stones;" "above the altar, a great cross and an image of plate of gold," similarly garnished; "in the body of the church, a great cross and an image of Christ, Mary, and John, being of plated silver partly gilt" (which was the gift of Stigand, whilst Bishop of Winchester); St. Swithin's shrine of "plate silver," with many other shrines; relics of saints covered with plate of gold; crosses, chalices, and other church utensils, vestments, &c., in almost countless store; and "a book of the four Evangelists written all with gold, and the outer side of plate of gold."

The splendid gifts of King Canute, and particularly his own royal crown, which he is said to have hung up over the high altar, as a substantial and abiding reproof of those who knew not the legitimate boundaries of flattery, must not be forgotten here; nor should it be unrecorded that the great Survey of the kingdom, called Domesday, now in the chapter-house at Westminster, was once preserved in the treasury at Winchester.

Such, in their high and palmy state, was the wealth of the famous Cathedral and Convent of St. Swithin's.

---

(1) All sufficient information relating to the present day may be found in the "Clergy List" for the current year. Other sources are pointed out in Sims' "Manual for the Genealogist, &c." (p. 416, &c.). In Hyde Abbey Register, before referred to (fol. 78 v°, 79 v°), is a list thus entitled,—"*Hic continentur omnes ecclesiæ in Episcopatu Wynton. quas Episcopus Wynton. debet confere.*"

Vast stores of the most curious facts connected with this subject are contained in the Registers of the diocese, though for want of such indexes as Mr. Alchin has compiled, they can be used only cursorily.

(2) It is printed in Wavell (vol. i. pp. 23—31); in Dugdale (vol. i. pp. 200, 201); and in Strype's Memorials of Archbishop Cranmer (p. 24).

CATHEDRAL ESTABLISHMENT AND REVENUES.

No record has survived respecting the number of secular canons, which constituted the establishment here, before the reformation of St. Athelwold; neither have we any satisfactory account of the number of monks which was regarded as the complement after that event. We hear casually of an increase of the number,[1] and of the number falling short;[2] and it would seem that the complete "choir" was considered to comprise sixty monks, but that this number was seldom reached.

Establishment before the Reformation;—

At the Reformation, the new charter of Henry VIII. (referred to above[3]) determined the extent and the members of the new establishment, which was made to consist of a dean, twelve prebendaries, twelve students (six at Oxford, and as many at Cambridge), twelve petty canons, twelve lay vicars, ten choristers, a master of choristers, a gospeller, a "pisteller," two sextons, two butlers, two cooks, one porter, two bell-ringers, twelve poor men (who had grown decayed in his majesty's service), a steward, and an auditor.[4]

and at the Reformation.

The present establishment, when conformed to the provisions of the act of parliament 3 & 4 Vic. c. 113, will consist of the dean and five canons,[5] together with four minor canons (one of whom is precentor, and another epistoller), an organist, eight lay vicars, a master of choristers, with ten choristers, the librarian, two vergers, three clerks, twelve bedesmen, and one porter.

Present establishment.

In addition to these may be mentioned, as officially connected with the cathedral, the chancellor of the diocese, and the apparitor; the registrar, the deputy-registrar, the steward, and the chapter-clerk; the treasurer, the surveyor, and the wood and land surveyor,—some of which offices, however, are frequently (as at present) combined.

We possess three statements of the revenues of the see, and of the cathedral, which it may be interesting to compare with each other. The first is found in the "*Taxatio Ecclesiastica*" of Pope Nicholas IV., about the year A.D. 1291. It is there stated that "*Episcopus Winton. habet in bonis spiritualibus et temporalibus,*" £2977 15s. 10d.;[6]

The revenues of the See and the Cathedral.

(1) Bishop Walkelyn is said to have "improved the church at Winchester in respect to the religion and numbers of the monks," as well as in other things (*Annales,* Wharton's Anglia Sacra, vol. i. p. 296).

(2) See the account of William of Wykeham's "Visitations," in Lowth's Life of Wykeham, and above, p. 107. There were forty-two monks when Thomas Nevyle was prior, but only thirty-five under Silkstede. (Milner, vol. ii. pp. 147, 148.)

In the "*Valor Ecclesiasticus*" (vol. ii. pp. 23, &c.), we find the following titles of office-bearers in the monastery, attached to each of which is the name of the officer at the period of the dissolution, and the value of the office :—*Prior, sub-prior, hordarius et coquinarius, precentor, camerarius, custos operum, elemosinarius,* *sacrista, anniversarius, infirmarius, gardinarius, hostillarius,* and *custos capellæ Beatæ Mariæ.*

(3) See above, p. 107.

(4) The students, butlers, and cooks, have formed no part of the establishment for many years.

(5) There are at the present time (1858) seven canons, five canonries having been already suspended. Honorary Canons are founded by the Order in Council, No. 97. (Eccl. Commis. Engl. Orders in Council, vol. ii. p. 173.)

(6) P. 215. The total of the revenues of the see, as shown by the Cottonian MS. of this *Taxatio,* in which the details of all the manors are given, differs from the gross sum, which alone is inserted in the MS. in the Exchequer, by a few pence only, being £2977 15s. 7½d.

while the sum-total of the revenues of the Prior of St. Swithin's, as collected from the several pages over which the entries are scattered, is £893 15s. 9d.[1]

The next is contained in the "*Valor Ecclesiasticus*" of Henry VIII., the survey for which was made soon after the year 1535. At this time, it is said, "*Episcopatus . . . . valet clare*," £3385 3s. 3½d., and as "*summa totalis clari valoris*" "*Prioratus*," we find £1507 17s. 2¼d.[2]

And in the Report of the Commissioners on Ecclesiastical Revenues in 1835, we find the third. In Table I. of this report the net income of the Bishop of Winchester is given as £11,151; and, in Table II., the average net income of the dean and chapter as £12,783.[3]

The annual income of the Bishop of Winchester will, on the next avoidance, be limited to £7000 per annum,[4] and the first-fruits and tenths are commuted for an annual payment after the rate of £1 17s. 6d. per cent. on that sum.[5]

---

(1) Pp. 185, 186, 190—193, 204, 213. The last page contains the revenues of the priory from the manors in Hampshire alone, the sum-total of which is £701 0s. 7d.

(2) Vol. ii. pp. 23, &c. But the total of episcopal income, as stated therein, is not the sum of all the particulars; I have, therefore, corrected it. The tenths are estimated at £388 10s.

Dugdale (vol. i. p. 191) gives the value of the bishopric as £2793 4s. 2¼d.

Bacon, in the "*Liber Regis*" (p. 917), gives the value of the first-fruits of the bishopric, at the date of his account, as £2873 18s. 1¾d.; as does Ecton's "*Liber Valorum*," with the sole alteration of ½d. for ¾d.; but by Lloyd's "*Thesaurus Ecclesiasticus*," published in 1788, the first-fruits are estimated at £3193 4s. 7½½d. The tenths paid into the Office of First-fruits and Tenths have always been, as estimated in Bacon (*u. s.*), £250 14s. 7d.

Bacon also states (*u. s.*) that by a return made in the 34 Hen. VIII., by Bishop Gardiner, the dean appears to have had a clear annual income of £99 13s. 9d.; twelve prebendaries, £31 6s. 8d. each; and twelve minor-canons, £140 in all; the sub-dean having £31 6s. 8d. over and above the rest. The sum-total of the revenues assigned to the new establishment by the charter of Henry VIII., was £1585 14s. 5d.; and the total of charges under the same charter was £1571 16s. 10½d.

The "total of present rents and profits" of the episcopal estates in 1647 is stated at £3251 0s. 1d.

(3) Pp. 6, 7, and 24, 25. In the Appendix, No. 7, to the Second Report of the Church Inquiry Commissioners, the total of stipends and dividends enjoyed by the dean and chapter is stated to be £9139 18s. 2d.

(4) See 6 & 7 Wm. IV. c. 77, § 1, and Order in Council of August 25, 1851.

(5) See Order in Council of Nov. 27, 1852. (Eccl. Commis. Engl. vol. viii. p. 412.)

ADDITIONS AND CORRECTIONS

TO

"THE CATHEDRAL AND ITS PRECINCT, &c."

Cathedral Yard (p. 35).—The following statement of the boundaries of the *cœmiterium* occur in a charter in the Cathedral Library (vol. i. No. 120), dated 1340. "*A quadam porta vocata la Munstreyate, versus Altum Stratum civitatis Winton. prout quidam murus antiquus vocatus Murus Constabularius, se extendunt [sc. 'bunde et limites'] usque la Gyehall juxta Ecclesiam S. Laurencii; et exinde ecclesiæ S. Mauricii; et exinde per quoddam antiquum fossatum vocatum Temple dich usque rivulum de la Posterne.*" Another copy exists in the Hyde Abbey Register (Harl. MSS., 1761), fol. 75 v°, and along with it this statement of the same boundaries :— "*Ab angulo infra portam de Minsteryate usque ad domum quæ fuit Willelmi de Ismongere, et ab illa domo usque fabrica de la Wolleselde, et exinde versus Altum Stratum civitatis usque portam quæ vocatur Thomasyate, et exinde linealiter usque fossatum vocatum Temple dich, juxta ecclesiam S. Mauricii, et sic linealiter per fossatum usque riveram de la Postere.*"

Boundaries of the Cathedral Yard.

The chief value of these statements, however, lies in their elucidation of the topography of the city. Thus we learn that the Guildhall, or Woollen Hall, occupied the site of the existing Mechanics' Institute, and that beside what is now Great Minster Street ran a wall called the Constabulary Wall. Market Street was *Thomas Gate* (a name which occurs as *Thomes Iete* in *Liber Winton.*, p. 534) ; and from that point to the stream now passing under the houses on the west side of Colebrook Street (which, perhaps, from its entering the precinct near the Postern Gate, was called *de la Posterne*) ran the ancient ditch, which I conjecture to have been originally one of the system of watercourses of New Minster, and was called Temple Ditch, from Willielmus de Templo, who held almost all the ground adjacent on the north side (Chartulary of St. Denys, fol. 120). There were houses along both sides of the yard.

The Slype (p. 35).—The passage on the south-west corner of the cathedral, with the Latin directions inscribed on the adjacent wall, were the work of Bishop Curle's time, or 1632 (Milner, vol. ii. p. 132).

The western front (p. 37).—At the apex of the arch of the great western window the heads of the three central lights are, in fact, obtusely triangular, and the feathering has, in consequence, a remarkably awkward appearance.

The exterior of the cathedral.

The Dean and Chapter have recently commenced the restoration of this fine front in stone [summer, 1858].

The north side of the Nave (p. 38).—It is not at all difficult to detect signs of the insertion of the late Perpendicular tracery into the Transition, or Decorated window openings of the Edington windows, both here and in the west front. The pinnacle at the angle of the aisle differs in one respect only from the others, which are undoubtedly Wykeham's work,—it is a little more solid or less elegant in its dimensions. All the pinnacles are surmounted by slender iron rods, four-forked at the top. The buttresses of the clerestory are plain Perpendicular ones, not flat Norman.

The roofs of the Nave and Presbytery (p. 39).—The great height of these roofs, by which the proportions of the tower. as seen from either north or south, are grievously marred is conclusive against their being original. The ridge of the roof of the nave rises even above the stringcourse of the tower on which the arches stand (compare p. 46, note). This circumstance, and its bearing on the architectural history of the cathedral, was pointed out to me by the Rev. C. Walters.

The Clock (p. 39).—This was formerly in the gable of the south transept.

The transept.   *The Transept* (pp. 39, 40).—The moulding of the stringcourse round the lower part of the transept is not " alternate," but indented billet moulding (Glossary of Architecture, " Mouldings, Norman").

The corbel tables of the clerestory of both north and south transepts are genuine Norman work, and there are plain traces of Norman arches in the wall of the clerestory of the presbytery adjoining the south transept.

The Dark Cloister (pp. 40, 88).—A closer inspection of this passage convinces me that originally there was no vault over it, but that it was an open way from the cloisters to the infirmary, which lay to the east of them. I am indebted to the Rev. Canon Carus for pointing out to me the evidences of this, and of the very recent date of the lean-to above this cloister, particularly in the three broad buttresses built up from the ground within the area of the Chapter-house, to sustain the weight of the books in the library above. The wooden staircase in the terminal aisle of the transept, for access to the library, is coeval with it.

Langton Chapel (p. 42).—There are traces of a floriated arch in the arcade round the exterior of this chapel. The shafts of the middle and lower arcades, which stand at the angle of the chapel, are completely disengaged.

The interior of the cathedral.   *The Nave* (p. 44).—Attached to the eighth pier from the western end, on the south side, there was, until the latter part of the last century, a stone pulpit, but no trace of it remains now. (Gale, *passim;* Wavell, vol. i. p. 60; Milner, vol. ii. p. 76.)

The recess beneath the arch on the south side, nearest the tower pier, at the back of the stalls of the choir, is separated from the aisle (above the floor of which it is raised a step or two) by a screen of six open two-light compartments in the upper part, and ironwork in the interstices, with a door in the eastmost of the central compartments. The style is plain Perpendicular, but I cannot learn its original position (if it be genuine), nor when it was placed here.

At the south-western angle of the south-western tower pier is a Norman column, not coming down to the floor. The adjoining Wykehamised shafts are altered at the level of its abacus, which is on a line with the spring of a blind arch at the northern end of the Chapter-house opposite to it.

Norman remains west of the Tower (p. 49).—It should have been noticed that all these shafts are so much out of the perpendicular as to suggest some considerable dilapidation of this part of the cathedral, in justification of the extensive alterations planned by Edington and accomplished by Wykeham. (See Willis, p. 66, note.)

Chapels in the Cathedral (p. 53).—Milner (vol. ii. p. 111, note) says, " The site of about twenty altars may still be ascertained in this cathedral, but that was probably far from being the whole number of them." He has marked as many sites on his plan, but some of them (as for instance those in the north transept) can scarcely be accepted without more satisfactory evidence.

The transepts.   *The Transepts and their Chapels* (pp. 53, 54).—In the southmost chapel on the eastern side of the south transept (which is now used as a workshop, &c.) is a huge old coffer, such as might, in the olden time, have been the repository of the muniments of the Priory; and the " screen " next the terminal aisle is now of stone.

The letters on the frieze of Silkstede's Chapel are arranged thus :—T ʜᴏ MA s S, so as to present, by one of the conceits fashionable in his time, his own initials and the first two letters of his celestial patroness most prominently; and probably by the remaining letters of his christian name to suggest " *Hominum Salvatrix*," as the character of the Blessed Virgin. There are traces of mural paintings under the window.

In the screen before the Venerable Chapel there are only *seven* pinnacles, but there are *eight* compartments in the upper part of it, and the accessory compartment on the right hand is larger than that on the left.

In the north transept, at the lower part of each pier of the third arch from the tower, on the east side, is a fine Early English canopy rising from the ground, with plain shafts and capitals, ogee arch, trefoiled and double feathered, with crockets and finial. The vaulting shafts of this compartment spring from figured capitals; those on the east side are two angels, and the figure in the north-west corner has a chess-board, or abacus, in its hand.

Chapel of the Holy Sepulchre (p. 55).—The "large arched openings" of the compartments of this chapel are now filled with glass.

Choir, Stalls, &c. (pp. 56, 57).—Some of the pinnacles of the woodwork in the choir appear, *The choir.* on close inspection, to be as old as the gabled canopies, but others are plainly newer, being very clumsy, and having the appearance of bad imitations.

The Bells (p. 58).—Four of these bells bear the date 1734, the other four are dated 1742, 1772, 1804, and 1814 respectively.

The Crypts (pp. 58, 59).—The south-western part of the main crypt is divided from the remainder, and is entered by the original stair from the western extremity of the south aisle of the presbytery, as well as from the open air. This entrance from the " Water Close" (so called because the branch of the Lurte Bourne, which crosses it, was till recently an open stream; see Godson's Map) was constructed by Bishop Fox when he closed the way through the Holy Hole (Milner, vol. ii. p. 61).

Presbytery (p. 59).—On the north door, and on the spandrels of the doorway, are the *The presbytery.* letters H. B., of Bishop Fox's date, at the earliest, and accompanied by Renaissance ornaments.

Above the screens, and serving as a sort of base for the mortuary chests, there is a wide frieze with ornaments of the same style as the chests.

The Reredos (pp. 60, 61).—There is an open gallery across the top of the altar screen, and around the feretory at the same level.

St. Swithin's Shrine (p. 61).—One of the casualties which befel this *palladium* of the cathedral and monastery deserves record,—" *Anno* 1241. *Feretrum S. Swithuni fractum est flabello de turri cadente.*" (*Annales*, sub. ann.) Another entry in the same chronicle may be inserted here. " *Anno* 1248. *V. Cal. Junii, sc. die Ascenscionis, cecidit flabellum de turri S. Swithuni quando classicum vespertinum pulsabatur, et fere contrivit unum monachum.*"

The tower mentioned in the first of these accidents was plainly one of those at the eastern end of the Norman presbytery. (See above, p. 97.) But it is not so evident which tower is intended by " St. Swithin's Tower."

The Retro-choir (p. 63).—The pressure of the exceedingly wide vault of De Lucy's work, *The retro-choir.* which has too small buttresses to resist the thrust, has forced the wall and the piers adjoining Langton's Chapel considerably out of the perpendicular. It has been sufficiently secured, however, and no further inclination is to be apprehended.

The Tabernacles in the Retro-choir (p. 64).—The names inscribed along the chamfer below the pedestals in these tabernacles are incorrectly given by Britton in several particulars. The following is an accurate copy :—

" KINGILSVS REX ; SCS BIRINVS EPC̄ ; KINEWALD′ REX ; EGBERTVS REX ; ADVLPHVS REX ; ELVRED REX FILI′ EI′ ; EDWARD′ REX SENIOR ; ATHELSTAN′ REX FILI′ EI′ ; SCA MARIA ; DOMINVS JESVS ; EDREDVS REX ; EDGARVS REX ; EMMA REGINA ; ALWYNVS EPC̄ : FTHELRED′ REX ; SCS EDWARD′ REX FILI′ EI′ ; CNVTVS REX ; HARDECNVT′ REX FILI′ E′ ."

The Holy Hole (p. 64).—This entrance to the crypts was closed by Bishop Fox (Milner, vol. ii. p. 61).

The chantries.

Wykeham's and Beaufort's Chantries (pp. 67, 68).—These chantries were dedicated, Wykeham's to the Blessed Virgin Mary, and Beaufort's to the Salutation.

Fox's Chantry (p. 69, note 5).—From a copy of a letter addressed to Dean Rennell, respecting the opening of this prelate's tomb in 1820, it appears that the earth was supposed to have accumulated above the original floor of the chantry to the depth of three feet which was removed at this time. The "ledger" of the tomb was broken, and in the grave were found the fragments of a slab of Purbeck stone, on which had been painted the Coronation of the Virgin. No ring was found in the tomb, and the crosier was of wood, but carved in an exceedingly elegant design. In a small leaden box between the feet of the body there was a document, from which it appeared that the day of Fox's death was the 5th of October, 1528. A facsimile of this record, with a drawing of the head of the crosier, and (unfortunately) only a restoration of the painted slab of stone, by J. Cave, are in the Cathedral Library.

The mortuary chests.

Mortuary Chests (pp. 70, 71).—The inscriptions on these chests have been at various times partially renewed, but so carelessly that the most ignorant errors have been committed, and the inscriptions on the opposite sides of the same chests are never exactly alike.

Tombs of Bishops (p. 71).—Amongst the relics of these episcopal interments may be mentioned four ancient gold pontifical, or ecclesiastical, rings, discovered during the restorations in the cathedral, and now in the possession of the Very Rev. the Dean of Winchester, which were exhibited by him at the congress of the Archæological Institute held here in 1845. (See *Catalogue of Antiquities*, in Winchester Vol. of Arch. Inst., p. xliii.)

Arms of Hugh de Lusignan (p. 73).—These arms, as they appear on this monument, are merely—barry of the unusual number of eighteen; the arms of the sons of De Lusignan were the same, with various differences.

Effigy of Sir Arnald de Gavaston.

Monument of Sir Arnald de Gavaston (p. 74).—The effigy on this monument, as may be seen by comparing it in its present condition with Mr. Blore's excellent sketch of it in Britton (Pl. xxvi.), has suffered considerably from the restorations which were committed in the cathedral thirty years ago. The shield, in particular, has lost so much of its original character that the bearings should be studied in the corresponding escutcheon on the tomb.

A complete account of the identification of this monument was read by Mr. Walford at the meeting of the Archæological Institute, June 4, 1858. The evidence of the burial of Sir Arnald in Winchester Cathedral has been printed (Sussex Archæol. Colls., vol. ii. p. 97). The only escutcheon occasioning any difficulty is the three garbs, which may be a species of canting arms, alluding to the first syllable of the name *Gabaston* (which is a barony in Bearn) quite as plainly as many which are allowed to bear this character do. The cross is intended to be plain, and seems to be used only to separate the quarters, as in the *signum* of Alphonso IV. of Castile and Leon. (See Report of Mr. Walford's Paper, Gent. Mag., July, 1858; see Journal of Archæol. Assoc., vol. i. pp. 216—223, for Mr. Planché's paper on this monument; and vol. xii. pp. 94—96, for an account of the name "Petrus Gauston," discovered by Mr. F. J. Baigent, cut twice on the edge of the slab on which the effigy lies.) There are other scratchings on the edge of this stone, and there was, in all probability, an inscription in a chamfer round the tomb, or along one side of it.

Memorial window.

Memorial Window (p. 79).—The southern window in the west front of the cathedral has been converted into a memorial window to ten officers (amongst whom were Col. Handcock and Capt. Hedley Vicars), and five hundred and twenty-seven non-commissioned officers and soldiers belonging to the 97th, or Earl of Ulster's Regiment, who fell during the war of the Crimea. At the apex of the window are the arms of England; in the compartments below, in three rows, are Victory, St. Michael, St. George, Peace; Joshua, Gideon, David, Jonathan; Ethelbert, Egbert, Ethelred, and Alfred the Great. The panels under the window on each side of the door contain the names of the officers, and a summary of the number of the men, to whose memory the window has been placed here.

Monuments in South Transept (p. 84).—On the west wall, under the southmost of the two **Recent monuments.** transferred arches inserted there, is a fine white marble monument representing Victory, with military trophies and emblems, in memory of Col. Yea, Col. Mills, two officers, two quartermasters, one surgeon, and five hundred and fifty-nine soldiers of the 7th Royal Fusiliers, who fell in the Russian war, erected by their brother officers and successors in the regiment.

And at the north end of the Chapter-house, in the aisle next the choir, is a mural monument to General Sir John Campbell, Bart., who fell in the attack on the Great Redan at Sevastopol, on June the 18th, 1855. The names of the numerous engagements in which he bore a part are inscribed beneath.

Remains of the Chapter-house (p. 88).—The Chapter-house appears to have been originally **The Chapter-house.** open to the cloister; and probably it was lightened by a window in the east end. The roof was no doubt one with a high pitch. There must have been steps from the level of the arches at the west end down to the floor of the cloisters. The bases of these columns are worthy of note from their great simplicity or rudeness, some incised lines drawn round one of them being the only attempt at ornament or finish.

Milner (vol. ii. p. 135) states that the Chapter-house was destroyed in 1570, for the sake of the lead with which its roof was covered. On the north side the ledge, on which the roof originally rested, still remains.

Conventual remains east of the Cloisters (p. 88).—The closeness of the end of the Prior's **Conventual remains.** Hall to the entrance to the dormitory is not so great as represented in the text, but still too great to allow a sleeping apartment for sixty monks to have stood there, with its length lying north and south.

Conventual remains on the west side of the Cloisters (p. 91).—Milner (vol. ii. p. 136) describes "a doorway with a pointed arch," as visible when he wrote, at the south-western angle of the cloisters, "which led into an inclosed lavatory." And he speaks also of "a stone staircase, not many years ago taken down, which led into a spacious vestibule, standing north and south, and thence into the refectory."

Other conventual remains (p. 92).—Some traces of old walls (possibly, however, transferred from some other spot) may be seen on the eastern side of the Close.

Milner (vol. ii. p. 139) places the "*officinæ monachorum*" on the south side of the quadrangle which adjoins the refectory on the south. His authority, however, is only Rudborne's account (p. 185) of the imaginary monastery, built, according to the legend of the place, after the cessation of Diocletian's persecution; and that it cannot have been founded on the facts of Rudborne's time is evident from his placing the "*domus necessariæ*" there, which we know were to the east of the cloisters.

From one of Warton's notes to his "Description," printed by Sir Thomas Phillipps, Bart. (p. 15, referring to p. 100, of the work), it appears that during the priorate of Alexander Heriard, about 1340, the monks were possessed of certain "*viridaria*" and "*deambulatoria*" outside the wall of the city, to the east of Kingsgate; and they prayed the Archbishop John Stratford to obtain the king's permission for them to have an "*arcum*" or "*cancellum*" across the wall and the street that passed under it, from their close, called *Mirabell*, to those places, that they might not have to go through the public streets when they wished to visit them. (*Reg. Vet. S. Swithuni.*)

To the north of the presbytery, in the wall which forms the boundary of the precinct and the cemetery, next to the road round the cemetery into Colebrook Street, is the moulding of an early Decorated archway, having an elegantly curved finish instead of a corbel.

In this part of the area belonging to the monastery there stood, in Rudborne's time (p. 209), "*versorium, cum gardino sacristæ,*" "*bracinum, cum gardino imfirmorum.*"

Precinct wall. *The wall of the Precinct* (p. 92).—For about fifty yards in this wall, in St. Swithin's Street, near the top, may be seen a series of small square embrasures.

The Priory: its dependencies in Winchester (p. 92).—Here I should have mentioned two hospitals or infirmaries, within the limits of Winchester, which were dependent on this priory. The first was outside Westgate (*Liber Winton.*, p. 548); and the second without Kingsgate, and was afterwards known as the *Sustern's Spital* (ibid., p. 561). These will be spoken of subsequently.

The tower. *Rebuilding of the great Tower* (pp. 99, 100).—Mr. Cresy states that "where the great crypt unites with the tower it is very evident that additions have been made to the walls subsequent to their original erection, and at the time when the great tower was erected. . . . . The junction of the Norman and Saxon [or say the earlier and later Norman masonry] is well defined. (Arch. Assoc., Winchester Vol., p. 369.)

Traces of fire in the roof at the west end (p. 101).—Milner (vol. ii. p. 68, note) regards the cause of these indications as having occurred, "most probably, within the last three centuries," but he gives no reason for this rather vague and unsatisfactory opinion. Clearly, the fire must have happened after the roof was completed, which was subsequent to Wykeham's death in 1404; but I know of no record of any conflagration. In the text referred to above, the roof of the nave is spoken of as the original Norman construction; but see above, p. 46, note, and addition to it.

Wykeham's work. *Wykeham's Work* (p. 102).—"*Novam fabricam incessit die Mercurii proxima post festum Omnium Sanctorum anno regni regis Ricardi II. octavo decimo*" (MS. Coll. Winton., quoted by Lowth). That is, on the 3rd of October, 1394, Wykeham commenced the reconstruction of the cathedral, which was carried on without interruption till the day of his death.

"Master William Winford" was architect or mason; "Dominus Simon Membury," clerk of the works, or "supervisor and paymaster;" and "Brother John Wayte," controller of the work on the part of the prior and convent (Wykeham's Will, and "Short Notice of Painted Glass, &c.," Arch. Inst., Winchester Vol.).

Celebrated inmates of the priory. *Celebrated inmates of the Priory* (p. 103).—Although the relation of the bishops to the canons who formed the establishment here before the time of St. Dunstan is not very clearly ascertained, it seems certain that they held an official position not greatly unlike that which they afterwards occupied when they were reckoned the abbots of the convent. Accordingly, we reckon amongst the celebrated inmates of this monastery those bishops who especially distinguished themselves in letters, arts, &c.

Ægilberht (bishop, 650—664) is said by Milner (vol. ii. pp. 144, &c.) to have been "a person of great eloquence and learning."

St. Hedda (bishop, 683—705) was "author of certain books and letters addressed to St. Aldhelm, and to other bishops, which Malmesbury, who had seen them, allows to have considerable merit as compositions" (ibid.).

Daniel (bishop, 705—744) was a writer of history, &c. (See above, p. 111, and note; Milner, vol. i. p. 81.)

Æthelwulf (King of Wessex, 836—857), before his accession to the throne, was "a member of this religious community" (Milner, *u. s.*), and is said to have been a subdeacon in it (Rudborne, p. 200).

Alhferth (bishop, 863—871) was raised to the see of Canterbury, it is said, in the latter year, under the name of Ethelred.

St. Oswald, dean of the establishment here (before 938, according to Wharton, vol. i. p. 323), became Bishop of Worcester, and ultimately Archbishop of York.

Brithnoth (prior, after 964) was raised to the abbacy of Ely, in 970.

Ælfsige (bishop, 951—958) was translated to the see of Canterbury in the last named year.

Lantfred (misnamed Lamfrid, flourished 980) wrote an account of the miracles of St. Swithin, an early copy of which is in the British Museum (MSS. Reg. 15 C. vii.; it contains two versions, one in prose, the other in verse). Milner (*u. s.*) says that he was "called, by excellency, the Doctor."

St. Elphege (Ælfheah, bishop, 984—1006) was raised to the see of Canterbury in the latter year.

Wolstan, "cantor of the cathedral, and a famous poet" (Milner, *u. s.*), wrote a life of St. Athelwold, which was addressed to St. Elphege, before 1000.

Elstan (or Leovingus), made Bishop of Wells in 1008, and raised to the see of Canterbury in 1013.

Alfric (or Putta, prior, 1006—1023), raised to the see of York in 1023.

Alfwold, who was Bishop of Sherborn from 1041 to 1058.

Aldred, made Bishop of Worcester in 1046, and raised to the see of York in 1064.

Stigand (bishop, 1047—1070) was raised to the metropolitan see of Canterbury in 1058.

Simeon (prior, 1070—1082), made Abbot of Ely in the last named year.

Godefridus (prior, 1082—1107), an epigrammatist, "who is so highly extolled by Malmesbury" (Milner, *u. s.*).

Robert (prior, about 1130—1135), became Bishop of Bath and Wells.

Robert (prior, about 1170), "removed to the abbacy of Glastonbury" (ibid.).

Walter (prior, about 1171—1175), "translated to Westminster, of which he became the first mitred abbot." "The two latter left valuable histories relating to this cathedral, which are cited by Rudborne" (ibid.).

"Geroald, the first abbot of Tewkesbury, who returned to St. Swithin's, and there ended his days" (ibid.).

Richard of Devizes (1191) wrote a life of Richard I., and a chronicle of English history, the MS. of which is in the library of C. C. Coll., Cambridge (No. cccxxxix.).

Johannes de Calceto (prior, 1247—1249), made Abbot of Peterborough.

Godfrey de Lucy (bishop, 1189—1204).

John le Devenish (1345), "a relation of the founder of St. John's House . . . . being chosen by his merit to fill the episcopal chair, and being obliged to yield that station to Edington, was made Abbot of St. Augustine's at Canterbury" (ibid.).

William of Wykeham (bishop, 1366—1404).

Henry Beaufort (Cardinal of England and bishop, 1404—1447).

John of Exeter (flourished 1431), author of the history of this priory, which Wharton (vol. i. p. xxvi., &c.) calls the epitome of Rudborne (Willis, pp. 1, 2).

Thomas Rudborne (flourished 1440), the author of the *Historia Major Wintoniensis*.

The authors of the *Annales Ecclesiæ Wintoniensis*, of the *Annales Breves Wintonienses*, and some other similar chronicles.

Thomas Langton (bishop, 1493—1500), elected Archbishop of Canterbury.

Thomas Silkstede (prior, 1498—1524) "was not only distinguished for his skill in architecture . . . . but also for his learning, of which he left proofs in certain writings relating to his own profession, which were committed to the press" (Milner, *u. s.*).

Richard Fox (bishop, 1501—1528).

Thomas Wolsey (cardinal and bishop, 1528—1530).

St. Athelwold's
reforms.

Reformation of St. Athelwold (p. 104).—An incidental confirmation of the novelty of the introduction of *monks* into Winchester may be found in the Charter, No. 922, of *Codex Diplomaticus.*

One exceedingly suspicious circumstance of this reformation is thus noticed by Kemble (Saxons in England, vol. ii. p. 461, note): " I regret to think that many of the Saxon charters, which pretend to the greatest antiquity, were forged on occasion of this revival, to enlarge the basis of the restored foundations."

Condition of the precinct before the reformation of St. Athelwold (p. 106, and note).—The Charter, No. 582, in the *Codex Diplomaticus,* distinctly affirms that before this time the residences of the canons were not so secluded as was deemed needful under the matured conventual system.   In it Edgar says, " *habitaculum Uetusti monasterii . . . . ut cænobitæ inibi degentes a ciuium tumultu remoti tranquillius deo seruirent honorifice, magna dilataui cautela ; spaciumque omne . . . . contiguum, dissipatis sæcularium domunculis, in honore, &c. . . . . æterna largitus sum hæreditate.*"   And he assigns this reason, " *Ut spacium omne muris vel sepibus complexum uti dedi sanctis monasteriis* [for the charter refers to the *Niwan Mynstre,* and to *Nunna Mynstre,* as well as St. Swithin's] *perpetualiter deseruiat.*"   And Charter No. 1347 records the exchange effected by St. Athelwold, of twelve " *mansas* " at " Mordune," for two " *jugera ruris et riuum quod terræ adjacet, intra amplitudinem quam præsul muro usque ad monasterium complexus est.*"

Rudborne (p. 204) ascribes to Athelwold, about 857—860, the first fortification of the conventual precinct.   " *Iste Ethelbaldus, instigante sanctissimo Swythuno Cœnobium Vetus munivit contra hostiles Danorum incursus.*"   But we hear of this from no other source.

Dissolution of
the monastery.

The Dissolution (p. 107).—The site of the monastery, with the exception of Wolvesey, which was reserved to the bishop, was granted to the dean and chapter of the new establishment (Rot. Pat., 23 Hen. VIII., p. 6) ; and certain manors and benefices out of those possessed by the prior and convent (ibid., 33 Hen. VIII., p. 9), which are noticed under the head of " Lands, &c.," above.

Annexation of the Channel Islands to the See of Winchester (p. 109).—The exact date of the order by which this union was effected is March the 11th, 1568.   (Jacob's " Annals, &c.," pp. 244, 248.)

Present extent of the Diocese (p. 110).—On the recommendation of the ecclesiastical commissioners (Third Report, pp. 7, 8), the borough of Southwark, and the parishes of Battersea, Bermondsey, Camberwell, Christchurch, Clapham, Lambeth, Rotherhithe, Streatham, Tooting, Graveney, Wandsworth, Merton, Kew, and Richmond, in the county of Surrey, have been transferred to the diocese of London, and the parish of Addington to that of Canterbury.

Rank of the See (p. 110).—In the time of William I., as it appears from Rudborne (p. 254), Winchester ranked next after London.

Bishop Eleutherius (p. 110).—The Saxon name of this prelate, according to Kemble (Cod. Dipl., No. 11), was Liuthari, the names in the text being the monkish Latinizations of it.

Bishops of
Winchester.

Bishops of Winchester (pp. 110, &c.).—Since the completion and printing of this section, the very valuable work of Mr. Stubbs, " *Registrum Sacrum Anglicanum,*" has appeared ; the following notes are taken from it to render my account of the episcopal succession in this see as complete as possible.

Mr. Stubbs places the consecration of *Birinus* in the year 634, on the authority of Bede and the A-S. Chronicle ; and, on the authority of Bede, the consecration of *Wini* to Winchester, in 662, and his removal to Dorchester in the year following.

Hedda's name is said to appear in charters in the Codex Diplomaticus ranging from 676 to 701, but, as the numbers of the charters are in no case given, I have no means of verifying these statements.

Daniel,—his subscriptions range from 705 to 737.

Those of *Hunferth* from 747 to 749; the termination of his episcopate is not dated.

Cyneheard's name is found in charters dated 755 to 759, and one doubtful one of 766.

Æthelheard's and *Ecgbald's* consecrations are placed between 766 and 778; the name of the former appears in the list of metropolitans in the year 793; and the subscriptions of the latter are assigned to the years 778 to 781.

The consecrations of *Dudda* and *Cyneberht* are placed between 781 and 785; and the subscriptions of the latter are said to range from 785 to 801.

Alhmund is placed at 802.

Wigthegn's consecration is dated between 805 and 811, and his death in 833 or 836; his earliest subscription is said to occur in 811. "Wigthen and Herefrith seem to have divided the administration of Winchester, the latter perhaps acting as coadjutor" (p. 13, note).

Hereferth,—date of consecration 825; his signatures occur in 825 and 826, and his death 833 or 836.

Edmund is also called *Eadhun;* his consecration is dated between 833 and 836, and his subscriptions from 836 to 838.

The consecration of *Helmstan* is placed in 838, and his name is said to occur between that year and 841.

The death of *St. Swithin* is placed on July 2, 862, and his signatures are said to range between 858 and 862.

Alhferth (who is called *Alfred*) is placed at 862, and his last signature is dated 871.

Tunbriht (called *Tumbert*) is consecrated between 872 and 877.

The death of *Denewulf* is placed at 908, and the signatures assigned to the years 882 to 904.

The death of *Frithstan* is dated Sept. 10, 933, and his subscriptions 909 to 929 (or 939, in Appendix VIII.).

The subscriptions of *Brinstan* are assigned to 931—934, and his death is dated Nov. 1, in the latter year.

Those of *Ælfheah* range from 933 (934 App.) to 951.

Ælfsige is said to have been translated to Canterbury in 959, and his first signature to occur in 952.

Brihthelm's consecration is dated 960, and his subscriptions 960—961.

The subscriptions of *St. Athelwold* range between 964 and 984.

St. Ælfheah is also called *Godwin;* his signatures are dated 985 to 1005. Oct. 19 is given as the day of his consecration; Nov. 16, 1005, as that of his translation to Canterbury; and April 19, 1012, as the day of his martyrdom.

Cenwulf's consecration is placed in 1005, so that his episcopate occupies parts of two years.

The subscriptions of the second *Athelwold* extend from 1007 to 1012; and *Brihtwold* is Bishop of Ramsbury from 1005 to 1045, as evidenced by subscriptions to charters.

The second *Ælfsige's* episcopate is dated 1014—1032, and his subscriptions 1014—1033.

Ælfwine's death is dated Aug. 29, 1047, and his name is found in charters varying from 1033 to 1046.

Stigand's name is found in charters dated from 1047 to 1053 (App.).

Aug. 11 was the day of *William Giffard's* (or de Giffard's) consecration.

The day of the death of *Henry de Blois* is Aug. 8.

Richard Toclyve's death is said to have happened on Dec. 22, 1188.

Sept. 1 is the date of the death of *William de Raleigh.*

Ethelmar is said to have been consecrated on May 16, and to have died on Dec. 4.

Bishops of Winchester.

The consecration of Ethelmar's successor, who is called *John Gervais,* is placed on Sept. 10, 1262.

John of Pontoise was consecrated at Civita Vecchia, on June 14, 1282.

The date of *John Sendale's* consecration was Oct. 31.

John Stratford died Aug. 23, 1348.

The exact day of *Wykeham's* consecration was Oct. 10, 1367.

Beaufort did not succeed Wykeham till 1405.

Waynflete's consecration took place on July 30.

Langton's death is placed at Jan. 27, 1501.

The year of *Wolsey's* accession was 1529 (N. S.).

Dec. 3 is given as the day of *Gardiner's* consecration.

John White succeeded Poynet in 1556.

The year of Bishop *Watson's* death was 1514 (N. S.).

The day of *William Wickham's* death was Jan. 11.

Richard Neile was translated to Winchester in 1628.

Walter Curle died in 1647.

The year of Bishop *Tomline's* translation is 1820, and the day of his death Nov. 14.

For notices of suffragan bishops see Appendix V. of this *Registrum Sacrum.*

Episcopal seals.

Seal of Bishop Henry de Blois (p. 116, note 10).—A figure of this seal is given in the Journal of the Arch. Assoc., vol xi. Pl. 19, from an impression preserved amongst the muniments at Titchbourne, in which the bishop appears full-faced, and in the attitude of benediction. In some minute particulars this sketch differs from casts which I have seen; and, if it may be relied upon for details, this impression seems to be in a very unusual state of preservation.

Bishop Woodlock's seal (p. 119, note 8).—In Mr. Baigent's account of this seal (Jour. Arch. Assoc., vol. xi. p. 294) the legend differs from any cast I have seen. Mr. Baigent names the two bishops, in the lower part of the counter seal, St. Birinus and St. Swithin.

Date of Bishop Fox's death (p. 124).—From a memorandum found in his tomb when it was opened in 1820, the day of this prelate's death appears to have been October the 5th.

The superiors of the monastery before St. Athelwold's reform (p. 127).—Milner (vol. ii. p. 144 *bis*) adds the name of Helmstan, who was *præpositus* in the reign of Egbert, to those of Swithin (*præpositus* in the time of Ethelwulf) and Oswald, *decanus.* He does not specify his authority, and I do not find his name in the *Codex Diplomaticus.*

In Charter No. 922, *Codex Diplomaticus,* mention is made of a "*decan*" in both *Ealden* and *Niwan Mynstre,* after the change effected by St. Athelwold.

Treasures of the Cathedral (p. 140).—"Athelwold, Bishop of Winchester, in a famine, sold all the rich vessels and ornaments of the church to relieve the poor with bread, and said, 'There was no reason that the dead temples of God should be sumptuously furnished, and the living temples suffer penury.'" Bacon's "Apophthegms."

THE CHURCHES AND CHAPELS IN WINCHESTER.

In the reign of Henry I., according to former historians of this city, Winchester was "enriched with three royal monasteries, besides other religious houses of less note, and an almost incredible number of parish churches and chapels."[1]

Milner, who complains of those works which preceded his as "defective and erroneous, omitting what ought to have been recorded, and supplying the deficiencies with fables,"[2] has in his Appendix (No. VII.) given a list of no fewer than *ninety-two* such churches and chapels, including twelve belonging to various religious communities; and he has added, in a note, this astonishing remark:—"N.B. In making out the above list from different registers, the utmost care has been taken that the same church should not be mentioned twice; hence all such have been omitted, as, by their titles or situations, are not clearly distinguished from others of the same name. This and other circumstances lead us to believe that the number of churches and chapels was *much greater than those here enumerated*, especially before the destructive civil war in King Stephen's reign."[3]

Wavell, on the other hand, in his Appendix (No. I.), after giving a more modest list of sixty-four (exclusive of the religious houses), adds, "it is possible that some of these churches may have been mentioned twice under different names;" and, further, this reasonable caution, "we are not to imagine that all the churches and chapels which appear upon our list existed together;" and he concludes by supposing that "the medium between sixty-two and forty-seven may bring us nearer to the truth."[4]

Now the entire area within the city walls being only about one hundred and thirty-eight acres[5] (omitting from our consideration all churches in these lists which are said to be situated without the walls), if Milner's statement be correct, there must have been sixty-five churches within the *enceinte* of the city, or very nearly one to each two acres; or, if Wavell be correct, forty-eight churches, or one to a little less than three acres throughout the city, which is more than "almost incredible"— from the nature of the case, it is absolutely impossible.[6]

The earliest list, which professes to be complete, is that contained in Pontissara's Register, entitled thus:—"*Iste sunt ecclesie et capelle omnes in Episcopatu Wyntoniensi existentes.*" It contains the names of forty-eight (or forty-nine, including the "*Capella de Wyke*") churches, which must have been situated within the area which Milner

[marginal notes:] Milner's list of Winton churches. Wavell's list. List in Pontissara's Register.

(1) Milner, vol. i. p. 157. See also Wavell, vol. ii. p. 47.

(2) Pref. p. x.

(3) Vol. ii. p. 309, note.

(4) Vol. ii. pp. 242, 243.

(5) See above, p. 15, note 1.

(6) Mr. Smirke, in a paper upon "Winchester in the Thirteenth Century" (Archæol. Journal, vol. vii. p. 380), says cautiously, but emphatically, "There is some ground for suspecting that the number of churches has been somewhat overrated." And "Dr. Milner would compel us to conclude that Winchester, under Henry I., was the rival of Rome itself in excessive development of ecclesiastical architecture."

would call Winchester, but of these only twenty-nine were within the walls of the city.[1]

List in the *Taxatio Ecclesiastica.*

In the *Taxatio Ecclesiastica* of Pope Nicholas IV.,[2] which included only such benefices as were of more than the yearly value of six marks of silver, only nineteen churches are named, and only eight of them were situated within the city, whilst of those eight five are inserted solely because of a "*Pensionaria*" in them, and of one of them it is said, "*non habet parochiam.*" The exceedingly scanty number in this list explains the real character of these churches, and renders the coexistence of so many as are contained in the list in Pontissara's Register quite comprehensible.

Bishop Orlton's list.

A copy of the list given in the *Taxatio Ecclesiastica*, but made in Bishop Orlton's

(1) Reg. Pontiss. ff. 156 b, *et seq.* But it must be observed that the date of the matter immediately adjacent to this catalogue is 2776 (in the pontificate of Nicholas of Ely) ; and from fol. 155 to fol. 166 v°, before and after it, the whole of the entries are of an earlier date than Pontissara (some as early as King Edgar !), and appear to have been transcribed into this register from some earlier one, now lost. This list, therefore, is at least as old as the episcopate of Nicholas of Ely, and may be still older. The following are the churches and chapels of Winchester contained in it. They are all called *chapels*, for some reason which is not very apparent : —

Capella Sancti Petri extra portam orientalem.

C. S. Johannis super montem.
C. Omnium Sanctorum in vineis.
C. S. Nicholai extra Kinggate.
C. S. Valerici.
C. S. Martini in Vico Pergamenorum.
C. S. Michaelis extra Kinggate.
C. S. Petri de Albo Pane.
C. B. Mariæ de Kalendis.
C. S. Petri extra portam australem.
C. S. Margaretæ.
C. S. Pauli.
C. B. Mariæ in Tannerstrete.
C. S. Georgii.
C. Omnium Sanctorum.
C S. Michaelis in Alwardstrete.
C. S. Rumbaldi.
C. S. Martini in Alwardstret.
C. S. Mariæ ultra portam orientalem (which is conjectured by the Rev. W. H. Gunner to be an error for *occidentalem*).
C. S. Bonifacii.
C. S. Petroci.
C. S. Nicholai extra murum.
C. S. Nicholai juxta pisces.
C. S. Clementis.
C. S. Mariæ in Cemiterio.
C. S. Johannis de Edera.
C. Omnium Sanctorum in Bokstrete.
C. S. Michaelis in Judaismo.

C. S. Martini in Garstret.
C. S. Martini in Wodestret.
C. S. Martini de Fossato.
C. S. Swithuni super Kinggate.
C. S. Mariæ juxta Goldestret.
C. S. Johannis de Hospitali.
C. S. Pancracii.
C. S. Swithuni in Muldworstret (in error for *Suldworstret*).
C. S. Petri in Colebrokestret.
C. S. Stephani.
C. S. Petri de Macellis.
C. S. Jacobi de albo monasterio.
C. S. Bartholomæi.
C. de Wyke.
C. de Walle (this is, *B. Mariæ de Valle*).
C. Anastasii.
C. S. Mauricii.
C. S. Maria de linea tela.
C. S. Laurencii.
C. S. Martini a Wynehat.
C. S. Fidis.

(2) P. 210. The following are the names of these churches and chapels:—

Ecclesia de Wylehale.
E. S. Johannis de Monte.
E. S. Petri de Chusulle.
E. S. Jacobi.
E. S. Fidis.
E. S. Anastasii est Pensionaria in.
E. B. Marie de Valle cum Capella de **Wyk**.
E. S. Bartholomæi in atrio de Hyde.
E. S. Stephani.
E. S. Laurencii.
E. S. Georgii.
E. S. Mauricii.
E. S Petri de Albo Pane est Pensionaria in.
E. S. Michaelis in Judaismo est Pensionaria in.
E. de Buckestrete est Pensionaria in.
E. S. Rumbaldi est Pensionaria in.
* C. S. Geretrudis non habit parochiam.
* Domus S. Crucis.

time, exists in the muniment room of St. Mary Winton College; appended to which is a second list containing, "*Ecclesiæ in villa Wynton. non taxatæ*," twenty-six in number, which, with the three contained in the list of *Ecclesiæ taxatæ*, makes the total of those within the walls of the city twenty-nine, as before.[1] It is difficult, however, to accept this catalogue as complete, since it does not contain all the original churches at present existing.[2]

From various sources we collect that there existed within what Milner regarded as the limits of Winchester, at different dates, in addition to those contained in these authorities, some twenty or twenty-two other churches or chapels;[3] together with the cathedral church, the church of Newminster or Hyde Abbey, that of St. Mary's

Total number of churches at any time existing in Winchester.

(1) An incorrect copy of this is given in Lowth's "Life of Wykeham," but I have been favoured with a correct copy by the Rev. W. H. Gunner, from which the following extracts are made:—

* "Ecclesia S. Elizabethe" is said to be the same as "E. S. Stephani."

"Ecclesiæ in Villa Wynton non taxatæ."

* Capella S. Trinitatis.
E. de Colebrokstret.
E. S. Joannis de Hospitali.
E. B. Mariæ in Tannerstret.
E. S. Pancratii.
E. S. Joannis de Edera.
E. S. Martini iu via carnificum.
E. S. Michaelis extra Kyngate.
* E. B. Mariæ de Walda.
E. S. Ruwoldi.
E. B. Mariæ de Kalender.
* E. S. Laurencii.
* E. S. Laurencii de Parchmentstret.
E. S. Petri in Marcellis.
E. S. Clementis.
* E. S. Alphegi.
E. S. Petroci.
E. S. Michaelis in Judaismo.
* E. S. Salvatoris.
* E. B. Mariæ extra *portam borealem.*
E. S. Margaretæ.
E. S. Petri de Albo Pane.
* E. S. Andreæ.
* E. S. Nicholai de Goldstret.
E. Omnium Sanctorum de Goldstret.
E. B. Mariæ in atrio S. Swithuni.

(2) St. Swithin's over Kingsgate is not included in this list (possibly because it had not yet been rebuilt, after its destruction by the citizens, in their riotous attack on the priory in the year 1264; see above, p. 106), and others which are found in the list in Pontissara's Register, and also in episcopal registers after Orlton's time, are absent. St. Laurence's seems to be repeated, also, which still further lessens the worth of this list. Those marked with a *, twelve in number, are not found in the older catalogue.

(3) St. Gregory's is mentioned in Charter No. 1087

(*Codex Diplomaticus*), as well as a "*wind cyrice,*" which may mean a ruined church.

"Ecclesia super portam," which must be Eastgate, is mentioned in Liber Winton., p. 555.

E. S. Egidii cum capella (but what chapel does not appear) occurs in Pontissara's Register, fol. 107.

Cap. S. Katerinæ, a dependency of Chilcombe, but inserted here because Milner includes it (ibid.).

E. S. Patricii (ibid.).

"Oratorium S. Katherinæ infra clausum suum in Parochia S. Georgii" (Reg. Asserii, fol. 29 b, from Mr. Alchin's Indexes).

E. B. Mariæ, Northgate (Reg. Edington, *Pars* II.), or "supra portam borealem" (Reg. Wykeham, *Pars* I.); if this be not the "E. B. Mariæ extra portam borealem" of Orlton's list, quoted above (note 8).

E. S. Bartholomæi infra muros (Reg. Waynflete, *Pars* II.), unless this be a clerical error in Mr. Alchin's Index, from which I take it.

"St. Peter in Whitebred, sometimes the Church of St. Paule" (Tarrages, fol. 5 vº).

St. Leonard's Church (ibid., fol. 34 vº).

"Parish of Fulfloude" (Inquis. Non., p. 106), but this may be the parish of St. Anastasius; it is not that of Wyke, nor of St. Mary in the Vale, for they occur in the same record as distinct from it.

Rectoria S. Thomæ (*Valor Ecclesiasticus*), which Milner (vol. ii. p. 212) says was built on the site of the Church of St. Petrocus.

"The Chirche of Our Ladye in Burdonstrete;" with those of "St. Johan de Port Latyne, in Bukkestrete;"

"St. Martyne in Mynestrestrete;" and

"St. Margaret in Garstret." (Ruined Churches, &c., from Archives in the Tower, Cole's Coll. vol. xxix. p. 456, &c., printed with many errors; Archæologia, vol. i. pp. 91—95; Wavell, vol. ii. pp. 243—251.)

St. Margarett's Church in the High Streete; if it be not that in Gar Street (Trussell, fol. 28 vº, 29).

St. Barnaby (ibid.).

St. Martyne's in the High Streete (ibid.).

St. Buttolphe (ibid.).

St. Dunstan's (ibid.).

St. Mary Magdalen's in Calp Streete (ibid.).

Abbey, those of the monasteries of the Franciscans, Dominicans, Carmelites, and Hermits, that of the Friary of St. Peter,[1] the chapel of St. Mary Wynton College, that of the Hospital of St. Mary Magdalen, that of the Sustern's Spital, the chapel of Wolvesey, and that within the castle; in all thirteen. If to them we add the new churches of the Holy Trinity and St. Thomas, and the chapels of the barracks, the county jail, the hospital, and the union-house, we obtain a total of a hundred and two,—higher than Milner's, but including all the churches of whose existence at Winchester, at any time during nearly a thousand years, we have any record.[2]

Existing parish churches.

There are now in the city and borough of Winchester nine parish churches— St. Lawrence, St. Maurice, St. Swithin, St. Thomas, St. Michael, St. John the Baptist, St. Peter Cheesehill, St. Bartholomew, and St. Cross; and one district church, Holy Trinity. Some parts of the parishes of Week, Winnall, and Chilcomb, are included by the boundary of the borough, but they will not be noticed in this part of the work; and the chapels of St. John's Hospital, St. Mary Winton's College, &c., will be spoken of in connection with the institutions to which they belong, as the chapel at Wolvesey has been in a former page.[3]

(1) Reg. Woodlock, fols. 19, 191 b., from Mr. Alchin's Indexes.

(2) This total of one hundred and two is thus obtained: in the list in Pontissara's Register are forty-nine; in the *Taxatio,* and Orlton's list, twelve not found in the former list; twenty-two are given in note 3 on the preceding page; there are thirteen monastic and other churches and chapels named in the text, two new recently-built churches, and four chapels.

It must be remembered that several of these are known to have occupied successively the same sites; and there is great reason to believe that several of the others have, through variations in the descriptions, been mentioned twice. And to these sources of error must be added the accidental, or wilful, mistakes made by those who have transcribed the lists, &c., referred to. In a future page, I shall specify the sites of all these churches, as far as I shall then be able to determine them. This will be of some service as a means of correcting these lists. I subjoin a list of churches derived from a MS. "Visitation of Hampshire," for 1543 (fols. 20 v°, 21 v°), in the British Museum (Add. MSS. 12,483); the names of the officiating clergymen are given.

Ecclesia Sancti Laurencii.

E. S. Mauricii.

E. de Ode [B. Mariæ de Ode or Walda].

E. S. Georgii.

E. S. Petri de Chesell.

E. S. Johannis.

E. S. Michaelis.

E. de Kyngesgate [S. Swithuni].

E. S. Bartholomæi.

E. S. Petri in Colebroke.

E. S. Petri in Macellis.

E. S. Clementis.

E. Omnium Sanctorum.

E. Kalend [B. Mariæ in Kalendis].

Domus Elemosynarius S. Johannis.

E. de Weke.

And to them I add Domus S Crucis.

Trussell, in 1644 (*u. s.*), says that of "ffiue and thirty distinct p̄ishe churches," "att this day only six [St. Lawrence, St. Maurice, St. Peter Colebrook, St. Swithin, St. Thomas, St. Clement] are frequented; the seaventh [St. Mary Kalendar], having for the space of ffortye yeares and upwards been apparent to bee the highest rooft p̄ish churche in Europe, ffor by all this tyme, yt hath had no other cover but the skyes." The worthy alderman contrasts the few then existing churches in the city with the many that formerly existed in the whole district.

For an account of the condition of these churches about twenty years later, see the reprint of a rare tract in the Winchester Vol. of Arch. Assoc., pp. 105—115.

(3) See above, p. 93.

CHURCH OF ST. LAWRENCE.[1]

This church stands just within the opening from Great Minster Street into High Street, on the eastern side of the way; and is so completely surrounded by the adjoining houses that the only portion of it visible is the western side of the tower and the summit, which has been carried up above the level of the roofs.[2]

It consists of a nave[3] and a western tower only, without either chancel, porch, or vestry; and owing to repeated rebuildings and repairs,[4] has preserved none of its original features—the oldest parts, which are the Decorated window in the tower, the north doorway (now disused), and the east end, being about the age of Wykeham.[5]

The interior is now perfectly plain, the walls being merely plastered, and the roof being a timbered one of the simplest kind. Until recently, also, the building was lighted by the great east window alone, but there is now a skylight in the roof, near the west end. A small gallery (which is dimly lighted from the tower) contains a harmonium; and this, as well as the pulpit, the pews, the five bells, &c., is modern.[6]

The east window is a large and plain early Perpendicular one of five lights,[7] and

The Church.

(1) Wavell, whose notions on the subject appear to be exceedingly misty (vol. i. p. 179), followed by Milner (vol. ii. p. 215), calls St. Lawrence the "mother church" of Winchester, but they offer no satisfactory evidence that it was so. Wavell supposes that it "enjoyed its privileges free of taxation," but the *Taxatio Ecclesiastica* of Pope Nicholas (p. 210) charges it 12*s.*, as being assessed at £6. The list of churches not taxed, however, seems also to contain it (see above, p. 155, note).

In the "Account of the Churches of Winchester," in 1660, reprinted in the Winchester Volume of the Arch. Assoc. (p. 107), "the bishop is said formerly to have performed the ceremonies of his instalment" at "Kalendar's Church," which, at least, shows that no peculiar rank was attributed to St. Lawrence' by its employment for this purpose. The present Bishop of Winchester was inducted, or installed, at St. Lawrence' Church.

(2) There was evidently, when the present church was first built, an entrance at the western end of the north side, the doorway of which still remains (though it now only serves as a closet for the use of the sexton), opposite which, high up on the south wall, a large fresco of St. Christopher was discovered during the last repairs.

The east end can be seen from the small yards in the rear of the houses next it.

(3) The dimensions of the nave are about 50 feet by 40 feet, and it provides 200 sittings.

(4) Wavell (vol. i. p. 180) has preserved this "Memorandum" of one extensive rebuilding:—"The names of the founders and builders of the churche called Sainte Lawrence within the cittie of Winchester, which was done and performed by Thomas Levee, Christian Cornishe, Harrie Cornish, Julian Buckhurst, and John Buckhurst,

in the year of our Lord God, 1449." Of this complete reconstruction, most probably the east window, and the window in the tower, respecting which Mr. J. H. Parker (Arch. Instit., Winchester Vol., Archit. Notes, p. 12) remarks that they "may be of the time of Wykeham," are the still existing memorials.

Ball, in his "Descriptive Walks, &c." (p. 87), says, but erroneously, that it "appears to have been entirely rebuilt in 1674" (Wavell, ibid.).

It has been subjected to a complete restoration during the last few years.

The tower was repaired and "newly covered with lead, A.D. 1680" (Wavell, vol. i. p. 181), and has also participated in the recent renovation.

From the "Account of the Churches of Winchester," before quoted (pp. 108, 111, 112), it appears that before the civil wars this church was one of two "in best repair of any in the city;" but that it was, in 1660, "made a school, wherein are taught the children of the city, whose coming up and down, it may be, spurns up some old pavements;" and from it "a few boards of ruinous seats" had been taken to repair St. Thomas' Church.

(5) Arch. Inst., Winchester Vol., Architect. Notes. &c. p. 12.

(6) There was formerly a side gallery, "erected by the Rev. Mr. Cotton, in the year 1765, then rector of the church, for the use of his scholars." (Wavell, *u. s.*). It was removed about twenty-five years ago.

The date on the oldest bell is 1621.

(7) The two lights on each side of the central one in this window are made into arches.

It is exceedingly probable that this window has not escaped the hands of the restorers, but it has sufficiently

over it is a very small quatrefoil opening, now filled with coloured glass. On the south side of the altar is a long obscurely cinquefoiled niche, and in the adjacent south

The Font. wall, a plain obtuse-headed piscina.[1] The bowl of the font (which is Early English or Transition Norman) is square, with no other ornament than a series of shallow cinquefoiled panels, and originally stood, there can be no doubt, upon a central shaft with four smaller ones at the angles, as it does in its present restored condition. "In the belfry is the parish chest, which is ornamented with the linen pattern of the time of Elizabeth."[2]

The Monuments. A memorial window is the most elegant and conspicuous monument in this church. In the central light of the east window is a figure of the Good Shepherd, with this inscription—"And when he hath found it, he layeth it on his shoulders rejoicing," over which are figures of angels and the Evangelists, and under it one of St. Lawrence. Along the lowest part of the window is inscribed :—

" IN MEMORIAM RICHARDI LITTLEHALES, ARMIGERI, HANC FENESTRAM PIA SOROR MARIA LITTLEHALES,
DONUM DEDIT, A.D. 1849."

There are thirteen mural tablets in the church and the tower (none of peculiar merit), commemorating former residents of the well-known names of Wavell, Lyford, Serle, &c. ; Richard Gosnell, mayor, who died April the 13th, 1718; and John Wilkes, Esq., of Milland House, near Liphook, in this county, who edited the *Encyclopædia Londinensis*.[3]

The Parish. The extent of the parish of St. Lawrence is very small. The boundary is drawn from the north-east corner of the church, straight to High Street; it passes up Parchment Street, along St. George's Street (but formerly, as it seems, included a parallelogram on the north side of it,[4] which it now does not), and St. Peter's Street, to High Street again; from the eastern side of the Town Hall it passes a little way to the south, then eastward to Little Minster Street, and along that street; it returns by the boundary of the Cathedral Yard to the middle of the square, enters a little passage on the opposite side of the way, and then by a few *échelons* to the middle of the south side of the church itself.[5]

preserved its original features to tell its age. From its great size compared with the building, it would seem to have been constructed after the blocking up of the windows which must formerly have existed in the sides of the church.

(1) From this piscina it would appear that there never was a distinct chancel to this church, which thus seems to have preserved to the present day the plan of its original construction in very remote times.

(2) Arch. Inst., Winchester Vol. (*u. s.*).

(3) See Wavell and Ball (*u. s.*).

The floor slabs, which were taken up during the recent alterations, were replaced according to the requirements of the masons; and the mural tablets were also removed; few of these monuments, therefore, occupy their original

places. Some of the ledgers were not laid down again at all, and may be seen in the chamber of the tower, with some mural monuments that were displaced at the same time.

The living is a rectory of the annual value of £56, in the gift of the Lord Chancellor.

There are no registers earlier than 1760, all the old ones having been stolen in that year (Census Report, 1831).

(4) See Godson's map.

(5) I have traced this boundary by Gale's excellent modern map of the city and borough.

There is a fragment of the ancient topography of the city, which incidentally receives very interesting elucidation by means of this parish boundary. When Bishop Henry de Blois pulled down the *Domus Regis*, erected by

CHURCH OF ST. MAURICE.

This is a fine modern structure, situated on the south side of High Street, exactly The Church. opposite Middle Brooks, erected in 1842, and consisting of a nave with a chancel and two aisles, and a vestry.[1] The former building did not occupy so large an area, there being between it and High Street a row of low shops, which partly hid it from view. These have been removed, and the north side of the church is almost level with the general line of the street. The south side, which would be a great ornament to the part of the Cathedral Yard which it stands near, is concealed by mean buildings. The only remaining portion of the old church is the square tower, the upper part of which is of the fifteenth century, but the lower part is much more ancient, as it has a plain Norman doorway in it.[2] There is a public footway through this tower, and through the western end of the church, which was originally the "church path" from the street.

There are three galleries, along the front of which texts of scripture are inscribed; and in that at the western end the organ stands.[3] The pulpit and reading desk are placed in the centre of the nave, just in front of the altar.

The east window is filled with coloured glass, but the only figures in them are the well-known sacred symbols, the lamb and cross, the dove, &c. &c. The font is "good," and "there are some remains of a fine decorated screen worked up into an altar rail, and a fine chest of the fifteenth century."[4] It has five bells, and also a smaller, or saint's bell, now called the "*Tang*."[5]

William the Conqueror near St. Lawrence' Church, and used the materials in building his Castle of Wolvesey, he gave the site of the palace to this church (Dugdale, vol. ii. p. 428). It is probable that this gift was the almost quadrangular piece to the north of the cathedral yard, and to the east of the church. The Surveys, it is true, always speak of this *Domus Regis* as being in High Street, but from various circumstances, and particularly from the *marginalia* of the time of Elizabeth, in the MS. Tarrages of Winton. (quoted so often in the Topographical Description of the City, above), we know that the Surveys of High Street included the property next adjacent on each side of it.

(1) The old church consisted of a nave and a south aisle, and, according to the testimony of Wavell (vol. i. p. 191) and Milner (vol. ii. p. 217), which is confirmed by information I have received from Mr. Henry Moody, there was at an earlier time a north aisle also; the piers, which resembled those of St. Thomas' old church, showing in the north wall. The time of the removal of this aisle is unknown; Ball (p. 179) surmises that it was "taken down shortly after the dissolution." Milner calls the general style of the structure "Ornamented Gothic." Next the altar, on the north side, according to

Wavell (p. 192), there was a window which he conjectured "to have been erected much about the Norman Conquest, or at the original building;" and he states (p. 194) that the piers were "in the same style of St. Thomas." Milner also (*u. s.*) speaks of a north porch in the Norman style, but what he refers to is not known.

(2) In this tower it an ancient stone vertical sundial, consisting of a plain circle merely, and having the hour lines marked from eight A.M. to four P.M. only; Arabic numerals being used. In Wavell's time this tower was of "a very mean appearance, being covered with tiles, as it came by process of time to decay on the roof." It seems to have been repaired in 1613, and once bore that date on the south side. (Wavell, *u. s.*, p. 193.)

(3) This organ was given to the church by the Marquis of Carnarvon, in 1736, and subsequently enlarged by subscription.

(4) Arch. Inst., Winchester Vol., *u. s.*, p. 12.

(5) On the first is inscribed

"SANCTE CLETE ORA PRO NOBIS;"

on the tenor, "Give God the glory, 1610;" on the second, "Prayse the Lord, J. W. 1609;" and on the fourth, "I. N. 1639," and other initials. One of these

The Monuments.

There are two monumental brasses; one of which, dated 1612, commemorates, in very decent Latin verse, the untimely death of the four infant children of John Bond, once a person of some consideration here. The other is as follows :—

"FRIDESWIDE, FIRST WIFE TO CHARLES NEWBOULTE, CITIZEN, AND TWICE MAIOR OF THIS CITIE OF WINCHESTER, WAS BY HER SECOND HUSBANDE, GEORGE JOHNSON, MINISTRE OF GOD'S WORDE, AND ONE OF THE MASTERS OF THE COLLEDGE, LAYED IN THE GRAVE, AND COVERED WITH THE SAME STONE OF HER FORMER HUSBANDE, BY WHOSE SYDE LYETH THEIR DAUGHTER, DULCIBELLA JOHNSON; SHE LIVED RIGHT CHRISTIANLY WITH THE FIRST XIIII., AND WITH THE LATTER XXI. YEARES, BEING OF THE AGE OF LIII. SHEE CHEAREFULLY EMBRACED A BITTER DEATH, IN ASSURANCE OF A BETTER RESURRECTION, JULY XXVII., ANO DO. MDCXXVI.

"AND IN REGARDE OF HUMANE FRAILTY MIGHT SAY—

"BETWIXT TWOOE STAYES AT LENGTH I FELL TO THE GROUND,
FROM ME THE LAY, I FROM THE CHURCHMAN FELL;
WHOSE SHALL I BE AT THE LAST TRUMPET'S SOUND?
NOR CHURCH NOR LAYMAN'S, FOR IN HEAVEN DWELL
NOR WIFE NOR HUSBAND; BUT ALL TRIUMPH THERE.
ALL BEAR PALM BRANCHES, AND ALL CROWNES DO WEARE.
HER VERTUES AND HER HUSBAND'S LOVE CONTENDE
WITH THIS HARD BRASSE, WHICH SHALL HAVE THE LAST ENDE."

Wavell[1] gives the inscriptions on two other brasses in memory of Alicia Pescod, 1624, and Jane Entwesle, 1697.

Amongst the mural monuments is one to Richard Wavell, 1779, the author of the "History of Winchester," to which we so frequently refer; and one which for its quaintness deserves insertion here :—

"TO THE MEMORY OF WILLIAM WIDMORE; HE WAS (WHICH IS MOST RARE) A FRIEND WITHOUT GUILE, AN APOTHECARY WITHOUT OSTENTATION. HIS EXTENSIVE CHARITY IN HIS PROFESSION ENTITLES HIM TO BE CALLED THE PHYSICIAN OF THE POOR. LET OTHER INSCRIPTIONS BOAST HONOURS, PEDIGREES, AND RICHES, HERE LIES AN HONEST ENGLISHMAN, WHO DIED THE 19TH DAY OF JUNE, 1756, AGED 63."

Another of an earlier date we also give :—

"POST TENEBRAS SPERO LUCEM.

"BEHOLD HERE LIETH THE CORPS OF HIM THAT WAS AN AUNCIENT WIGHT,
WHOE LYVED FOWER SCORE YERES AND NYNE, JOHN MYCHELBORNE HE HIGHT.
THIS MAN WHEN SEAVENTENTH DAY WAS COME OF LATEST MONETH SAVE ONE,
DEPARTED FROM THAT LINGERINGE LIF, WHICH HERE HE HAD OF LONE.
IT WAS THE LATEST DAY OF LIF WHICH HE DID HERE RETEYNE;
IT WAS THE FIRST OUR NOBLE QUEENE BEGAN HER EIGHTENE RAIGNE.
A MAN OF GOOD AND HONEST FAME AND EKE OF GENTLE BLOOD;
NOT VOYD OF SKYLL, AND COUNSELL SAGE, TO DO HIS COUNTRY GOOD.
OF SUSSEX SOILE BOTH BORNE AND BRED, BELOVED OF ECHE MAN SOE,
THAT NONE OF HIM CAN SPEKE BUT WELL, NO NOT HIS MORTAL FOE.
SO THAT ALTHOUGH HIS CORPS FULL COLDE IN EARTH BELOWE DOTH LYE,
YEAT GOD NO DOUBBT HATHE PLAST HIS SOWLE IN HEAVEN THAT IS SOE HYE.

"NOV. 17. ANO. DI. 1575."[2]

bells belongs to St. Peter's Colebrook. (See note 1, p. 161.) Wavell (u. s.) says that in the vestry of the old church was "an image of St. Michael, which formerly stood upon the pulpit, but was removed some time after the Reformation." He also speaks of "the remains of some elegant painted glass, exhibiting the portrait of St. Michael, and probably . . . . the representation of his miracles," in the great east window.

(1) Vol. i. pp. 195, 196.

(2) St. Maurice is a rectory, of the yearly value of £135; the Bishop of Winchester is patron. The registers, which relate to St. Mary Kalendar and St. Peter's Colebrook also, are stated, in the Census Report (1831), to commence in 1575, and to be deficient between 1609 and 1653; but there is a register of marriages commencing in 1528, and one of burials in 1538.

The extent of this parish, though not equal to that of St. Thomas, was, until the **The Parish.** erection of Holy Trinity Church, very considerable, since it included the parishes of St. Mary Kalendar, and St. Peter Colebrook, and it still comprises the greater part of them.[1] The old boundary of St. Maurice' parish proper commenced with the wall of the cemetery, a little west of the entrance opposite Market Street, which it followed eastward,[2] nearly to the postern entrance in Colebrook Street, from which point it proceeded northward, almost in a straight line (really following the boundary of St. Mary's Abbey precinct), to the middle of High Street, down which it went eastward to the point, now the corner of Eastgate Street,[3] and thence to the north, as far as where the old wall crossed the brook that flowed through Buck Street. It followed the road along the North Wall as far as the boundary of Whitebread Mead, and then turned to the south along that boundary, and midway between Upper and Middle Brooks, nearly to St. George's Street,[4] where it turned at right angles to the east, into Middle Brooks, thence proceeding along the street,[5] and up St. George's Street, and then by Upper Brooks, but just behind the houses on the east side of the way, to High Street, and along it almost to the east end of the pent-house, and thence straight across to the wall of the cemetery.

The boundary of the parish of St. Mary Kalendar[6] is the same as this from the north wall to the wall of the cemetery, along which it goes westward to the boundary of St. Lawrence' parish, which it coincides with, as far as the middle of St. George's Street, whence it proceeds northward, in an almost straight line, nearly half way to the North Wall, and along the road to the east side of Whitebread Mead.

(1) The "Account of the Churches of Winchester," quoted above (pp. 111, 112), tells us that "the Church of St. Maurice hath, by order of union, the parishes of Calendar and St. Peter Colebrook united to it."

The condition of "Kalendar's Church" (p. 107) is said to be infamous, standing as it did "in the High-street and principal place of the whole city," the nuisance of which deserves something more than the "sharp reproof" which "a judge of assizes, before the window of whose lodging" it stood, was "remembered" to have administered to the city. Four bells, said to belong to this church, were found in the castle when taken by the parliament's forces, and were redeemed by the committee of the county, and by them given to the city to be disposed of as they should think fit.

St. Peter's in Colebrook is said (p. 108) to be "an inconsiderable little place, no use of it for about these fourteen years [since 1645, that is to say], extremely untiled, the covering almost gone; grass, nettles, weeds growing in the body of it." The "three bells belonging to it," by the consent of the parish, were "disposed to the churchwardens," and one of them was "joined to four others" in St. Maurice' Church before the others were sold (p. 112).

(2) Mr. Moody informs me that the boundary ought to run due east from the gate of Cathedral Yard, opposite Market Street, so as to include Bishop Morley's College and part of the cemetery. But as this piece was the old Temple ditch (see above, p. 143), I have thought it better to follow Godson and Gale in my text.

(3) These boundaries are traced as before by Gale's map. The comparison of them with the lines in Godson's map shows that the abbey boundary was marked by a watercourse, and that, before the alteration of the eastern part of High Street, the parish of St. Maurice included the great watercourse that ran along the south side of the way to St. John's House, and thence proceeded along another watercourse to the point in the city wall named above.

(4) In Godson's map the boundary turns sharply to the west as far as Upper Brooks, and, encompassing a house there, returns midway between Whitebread Mead and St. George Street.

(5) This piece, which seems taken out of St. Maurice' parish and added to St. Mary Kalendar, marks the site of St. George's Church.

The extent of the district assigned to Holy Trinity Church will be given subsequently.

(6) This parish was united to that of St. Maurice in 1682; the original MS. containing the assent of the Corporation is now in the Museum in this city.

The parish boundary of St. Peter Colebrook[1] coincided with the eastern boundary of St. Maurice' parish, and proceeded along the precinct wall, from near the postern, to the wall of the city next the Weirs, including the houses, but excluding the footpath, as far as the bridge, where, turning a little way towards the west, it followed the line of the ancient wall to the point where it crossed the old Buck Street brook, and there joined St. Maurice' boundary again.[2]

The friary, or fraternity of St. Peter, in this Church of St. Maurice, and the College of St. Mary Kalendar, will be noticed subsequently under another division.

CHURCH OF ST. SWITHIN.[3]

The Church. Formerly there were churches over North-gate and East-gate,[4] as well as over Kings-gate, but this is the only one which has remained to recent times. The gate itself has been described above;[5] the church, which is the superstructure of the entire gate, is a curious but not very ancient building.[6] It consists of a plain room, measuring about 40 feet from east to west, by 16 feet from north to south. At the east end is a modern window, with stained glass representing Christ standing at the door; on the south side are two much smaller, square-headed, two-light windows, the head of each light being cinquefoiled; and one on the north side. The window at the west end is original, and is divided into three lights by straight mullions, without any transoms or foliations.[7] In the north wall is a small Tudor-arched niche, with the arms of the see under it;[8] and at the west end is a good octagon, panelled font, half of which is built into a recess in the wall.[9]

The ascent, which is on the north side, and at the west end, is modern; as is the small belfry with its two bells.[10]

---

(1) This parish was never expressly united with that of St. Maurice.

(2) The space left between the city wall and the river, on each side of East-gate, was a procession-way (see above, pp. 20, 21). The long narrow strip belonging to St. Peter's Colebrook parish lay between the walls and the precinct of the Dominican monastery, as far as the old line of Buck Street.

(3) The ancient and correct form of this name is Swithun. Having as a rule adopted the spelling of the Census Report, I can only regret that the debased form of this truly venerable name has been adopted therein.

(4) See above, p. 25, note 1.

(5) See above, p. 25.

(6) Mr. J. H. Parker (Archit. Notes, &c., in Win-chester Vol. of Arch. Inst., p. 13) says it has been "re-built in the sixteenth century."

(7) The east window was formerly exactly like this at the west end.

(8) Ball (p. 141) says that there were the remains of an inscription in his time. The colouring of this niche has been restored recently.

(9) Archit. Notes, &c., *u. s.*

(10) In the year 1264, as related above (p. 106), this church was destroyed in a riotous attack made on the priory by the citizens, and it seems not to have been rebuilt even in Bishop Orlton's time. (See above, p. 155, note 2.)

From the parochial registers (as I learn by the kind-ness of the rector, the Rev. W. H. Gunner), it appears

The parish extends from the Close gate, along the wall of the precinct, nearly as The Parish. far as Symond's Street; it then crosses to just beyond the old city wall, and proceeds thus by the inner edge of the old ditch, almost to Kings-gate, when it turns at right angles southward to Canon Street, down which it turns again, crosses Kingsgate Street, and by a course with one double angle in it, reaches the college walls at the back of the old school-room, so as to include the greater part of Commoners: it then returns to the north, crosses College Street, and turns down it eastward, almost to the point where the Lurte Bourne issues; and returns again, along the city wall westward, till it comes opposite the Close gate, from the front of which we set out.[1]

In connexion with this church there used to exist, as we learn from Waynflete's Registers,[2] a Gild of St. Thomas.

CHURCH OF ST. THOMAS.

This noble modern structure[3] stands on the west side of Southgate Street, just The Church. beneath the hill on which the Barracks stand. It consists of a nave and chancel with aisles, a north transept, and a fine tower and spire in place of a south transept. The style adopted is the geometrical variety of the Decorated, with the exception of the piers and arches of the nave, which are imitations of those of the old church.[4] The

that between March, 1634, and April, 1635, " the church was downe," and, in consequence, the baptisms in the parish were performed in St. Michael's Church.

The " Account of the Churches of Winchester," quoted before (p. 108), also speaks of it, in 1660, as " ruinous" and " unfit for a congregation of the city to meet in;" in consequence of which one " Mr. Rich. Love" contrived to get the parish united to St. Michael's, and let this church by lease to one Robert Allen, who was as careless respecting the decencies of life as he was regarding the sanctity of the place, as he had " his wife delivered of children at one end thereof, and a hogsty made of the other."

St. Swithin is a rectory, and the present patron is the Lord Chancellor; but, according to an entry in Edington's Register (as I learn from the Rev. W. H. Gunner), the church was in his time in the patronage of the Archdeacon of Surrey. The value of the benefice is £80 per annum, the Ecclesiastical Commission having granted £21 per annum to augment the stipend; and there is a pension of £3 13s. 4d. paid yearly to the rector from the Woods and Forests.

The registers commence in the year 1562.

(1) Gale's map is here again our authority; the only

difference between it and Godson's is, that the latter does not carry the boundary so far to the east down College Street.

The boundary of this parish, without the walls, may perhaps be regarded as indicating the extent of the possessions of the Priory of St. Swithin there; the Sustern Spital seems to have stood on the site of Commoners, and the *viridaria* and *deambulatoria* (see above, p. 145) may have been between it and the gate: at least, the line there shows the limits of the parish of Allsaints in the Vineyards.

(2) *Pars* I. fol. 14*.

(3) This church was erected during the years 1845 and 1846, from the plans of E. W. Elmslie, Esq., at a cost of £8060 14s. It was consecrated on the 16th of April, 1847.

The tower and spire, which are 172 feet high, were not completed until February, 1857, and cost £1644.

(4) The old church of St. Thomas (which was at first dedicated to St. Petrocus) stood in the midst of the graveyard in St. Thomas' Street, and consisted of a nave, chancel, and south aisle; " the north aisle having been destroyed, and the arches [which were pointed and ornamented with the zigzag moulding] walled up." Mr.

pulpit is of stone, and there is a very handsome brass lectern, and an organ placed on the floor at the west end, without a case, but ornamented both brilliantly and appropriately in polychromy.

The reredos is diapered in polychromy with great elegance and richness of design ; and the east window, which is of five lights, is filled with stained glass, exhibiting in the upper centre the symbol of the Trinity, and in the lower part, in three rows, St. James the Greater, St. Peter, St. James the Less, St. Paul, St. Andrew ; St. Bartholomew, St. Matthias, St. Thomas and St. Clement, St. Simon, St. Jude ; St. Matthew, St. Mark, St. Philip, St. Luke, and St. John.

The Monuments.

The mural monuments,[1] seventeen in number, were almost all removed from the old church, and commemorate names formerly well known in the city—Imber, Woodward, Gauntlett, &c. ; a more modern one has been erected in memory of Captain Barlow ; and one, quite recent, records the worth of the late Rev. George J. Cubitt.

The Parish.

In tracing the boundary of this parish,[2] which comprises not only all that remains of the city, but also some portions without the walls, we commence at the point where the parish of St. Swithin crosses the city wall in St. Swithin's Street, and proceed along the wall of the precinct to Little Minster Street, thence along the boundary of

---

J. H. Parker considers it to have been " of the time of Richard I.," and says that the [round] pillars and capitals of the nave were " remarkably good examples of that period ;" the foliage with which they were ornamented being " very elegant and free, with more of the character of the work of the thirteenth century, though here used with Norman work." The chancel (which had " a south aisle or chapel attached "), he says, was of a subsequent date, and the windows were " insertions of Perpendicular work." (Winchester Vol. of Arch. Inst., Archit. Notes, &c., p. 18 ; Winchester Vol. of Arch. Assoc., pp. 479—481.)

Wavell (vol. i. p. 187, &c.) says " the tower is low and mean, being covered at the top with tiles ; but in its pristine state it was more spacious and lofty, and contained five bells, which have since been disposed of : the church, however, is exceeding neat, and the largest of the kind in Winchester." The altar, he adds, " is lofty and elegantly ornamented ;" and " at the west end " " is an handsome gallery, erected A.D. 1733, by Thomas Baker [which ought to be Barton], Esq., as appears by his arms and initials on the front."

From the " Account of the Churches of Winchester " in the year 1660, (already so often quoted), it appears that this church, and especially the chancel, was in a very ruinous condition at the time, and was not used for religious worship. Two bells had been taken away and sold (" because the steeple was small and weak, unable to bear more than one bell left in it "), and the money left in the churchwardens' hands.

There were two bells in the old church, which, being unintentionally included in the agreement with the builder

of the new church, were taken by him ; and for ten years the bell of the new church was of an unusually primitive character, being no more than a steel bar suspended so as to sound when struck by a hammer. There is now one fine toned large bell.

(1) Amongst the monuments in the old church, according to the account of Wavell (*u.s.*) and Ball (p. 143), was this, which may be deemed worthy of record here, " at the east corner of the south aisle :"—

" BEATI MORTUI QUI

R.   B.

OBIIT 23° MARTII, A° Dⁿⁱ 1573.

CUM . SEPTEM . DENOS . ET . QUINOS . VIXERAT . ANNOS . URBIS . VENTANE . CLARO . BIS . MUNERE . MAJOR . BURTONUM . RAPIUNT . CRUDELIA . FATA . RICHARDUM . CONJUX . JONA . MANET . CELEBS . WILIHELMUS . ET . HERES . JANAQ ; NATA . PATRIS . CHARI . SUA . PIGNORA . VIVENT .

IN DOMINO MORIUNTUR."

There were also floor slabs commemorating Peter Symonds, " who built and endowed the almshouse at the north-east of this church ;" John Purdue, twice Mayor of Winchester ; and another John Purdue, " the honest college woodman." (Wavell, vol. i. p. 189.)

There are sittings for 1000 persons in this church, of which about 300 are free.

The registers do not commence till 1678. (Census, 1831.)

The living is a rectory, in the gift of the Bishop of Winchester, and valued at £145 per annum.

(2) I follow Gale's map here, as before, comparing it with Godson's.

St. Lawrence's parish to St. George's Street, and thence by the boundary of the parish of St. Mary Kalendar to the north wall; along this it proceeds westward (but diverges from it to exclude the block of houses between the old line of Jewry Street[1] and the present street running to North-gate) to Hermit's Tower, and then southward, still following the line of the wall, till it nearly reaches the middle of Tower Street, when it turns at right angles, and crosses the old ditch[2] and Sussex Street, and, bending a little to the south, touches the angle of the ground on which the Union-House stands; it follows the line of the south wall of this house, crosses Oram's Arbour to the old City Ditch (now filled up and converted into a roadway), turns again southward, but before reaching the Romsey Road stretches suddenly to the west, so as to cross it opposite the soldiers' burial-ground, from a little to the south of which it returns obliquely eastward to St. James' Lane, and follows it nearly as far as Southgate, where it again takes a southward direction along the footpath beside Painter's Fields, almost halfway to the site of St. Faith's Church, and there passes eastward to the high road, and returns nearly to the city gate; then, with another bend eastward, crosses Canon Street, so as to exclude some houses on the side next the city wall,[3] and follows that to its junction with the boundary of St. Swithin's parish.

CHURCH OF THE HOLY TRINITY.

This new church stands at the north end of Middle Brooks, in the plot of ground to the east of that named in the maps Whitebread Mead. It consists in a nave,[4] with aisles, and an octagonal bellcot with an acute spire, to the east of the centre of the roof. The style adopted is Decorated throughout, and it is a very good copy of some of the most elegant examples of it. The east and west windows (which are each of five lights) are filled with coloured glass.

The interior is lofty and light, the effects of the piers and arches of the

The Church.

(1) Godson does not notice this divergence. Can this be the last vestige of the original *Judaismus*, or Jewry, which was, of course, extra-parochial? Or is it the parish of St. Mary's *"extra"* or *"supra portam borealem?"*

(2) The extra-mural portion of this parish appears to include the parishes of St. Leonard, St. Martin, St. Mary, St. Valery, and St. James. The intra-mural portion will be considered when the sites of the formerly existing churches are discussed. Here, however, it may be stated that the parishes of St. Martin and St. Petrocus were added to that of St. Elphege, by Wykeham (Reg. *Pars* II. fol. 353 b., &c.); and that both St. Elphege's and St. Clement's parish were afterwards united with that of St. Thomas, as the church of St. Petrocus was called when rebuilt.

(3) In Godson's map the boundary here excludes the City Ditch as far as the south gate.

(4) The east end is so constructed that the window-arch could be converted into a chancel-arch, and a true chancel added to the nave, if it should be desirable to enlarge the church. It now contains 900 sittings, of which 600 are free.

The entire cost of the site was £900, and of the structure, £4500, which was principally defrayed by subscription. The endowment, amounting to £3333 6s. 8d., was given by the present incumbent, the Rev. G. A. Seymour.

The architect was Mr. Woodyer, of Guildford; and the church, which was commenced in February, 1852, was consecrated in July, 1854.

aisles being exceedingly good, and the walls are richly decorated with passages of Scripture.[1]

The District.   The district assigned to this church is taken from the parishes of St. Maurice and St. Mary Kalendar, and is bounded by a line drawn along St. George's Street, Silver Hill, and Lower Brooks (excluding the houses next those streets), crossing by Ford's Buildings to the wall of St. John's Hospital, and thence southward to High Street.[2]

CHURCH OF ST. MICHAEL.

The Church.   We now leave the city, and enter the Soke.   This church stands at a little distance from the road, on the western side of Kingsgate Street, being reached by a narrow flagged footway, which passes along the south side of the church to Culver Close,[3] upon which the churchyard of St. Michael abuts.

The church is now an almost square structure, in what has been called the "modern Perpendicular" style;[4] the principal remains of the original building[5] being the north wall (which was raised at the time it was altered), and the tower at the south-west angle, which is "plain Perpendicular work, with the pyramidal tiled roof common in this part of the country."[6]

There is a gallery at the west end, and a small organ; and the east window has modern coloured glass in it.

(1) The living is a perpetual curacy, in the gift of the bishop, of the value of £100 per annum.

(2) See above, p. 161. The Order in Council authorizing the formation of this district is dated March the 10th, 1855. I am indebted to the Rev. G. A. Seymour for most of these particulars.

(3) The way to the church from Kingsgate Street was formerly through the premises of Mr. William Coles (as I am informed by him), and along the east side of Culver Close; the present more convenient access is of recent date.

(4) Archit. Notes, &c., *u. s.*

(5) Wavell (vol. i. pp. 204, 205) gives the following account of the old church :—" It consists of two handsome aisles and a good tower . . . . The aisles are divided by round pillars, and are almost of the same dimensions, the south of the two being the largest. At the east end of this aisle stands the altar, which is very neat, under a window retaining the remains of some painted glass, exhibiting the figure of King David on the top, under whom is the Virgin Mary with our Saviour in her arms, with MARIA, being part of an inscription, under the whole. Over the altar is a square room or vestry . . . . Access was had to this place by means of a flight of steps, the extremity of which is now closed by a large buttress on the north side of the church . . . . This room is now entirely closed up, and can only be discerned through a couple of very narrow windows at the south end."

"This room," says Ball (p. 216), "has been destroyed, and the space occupied by it thrown into the height of the chancel."

The door in the middle of the south side was originally that under the south porch. That in the south side of the tower was removed from some other part of the old church.

The last rebuilding of this church occurred in 1822; the date 1582, on the south side of the tower (Wavell, *u. s.*), may relate to an earlier renovation.

In the south side is "a curious ancient sundial of the earlier part of the thirteenth century, as is evident from the character of the foliage at the angles" (Archit. Notes, &c., *u. s.*). It has crosses at the end of the hour-line for noon, and (as I conclude from the angles they make with the meridian line, for there are no numerals to denote the hours) for those of 9 A.M. and 5 P.M.

Many pieces of Binstead limestone (which may perhaps be regarded as relics of an earlier structure) may be seen in the sides of the tower.

(6) Archit. Notes, &c. (*u. s.*)

There are five bells, and on the tenor is this inscription :—

"GOD IS OUR GUYDE. 1610."

Within the church are thirty-one mural monuments, bearing such names as Beeston, Charker, Strickland, Martin, Meggs, Taylor, Shipman, Soden, and Oades ; and fourteen similar tablets have been inserted into the outside of the walls. Several floor slabs of the seventeenth and eighteenth centuries may be seen in the aisles of the church, evidently displaced from their original position ; and in the church passage there are others. An ancient coffin-lid, with a cross in outline on it, has been used as a modern memorial for two several persons.[1] *The Monuments.*

The boundaries of this parish coincide with those of St. Swithin and St. Thomas, on the north and west, from Commoners to the southmost point reached by the boundary of St. Thomas' parish on the Southgate Road. From the latter point, the boundary of St. Michael's parish proceeds but a very little way further south, and then turns at right angles, and, with one small interruption where it crosses Kingsgate Street, proceeds due east to the river, along the nearest arm of which it goes to the south-west limit of the college grounds, the line of which it follows till it meets St. Swithin's boundary.[2] *The Parish.*

CHURCH OF ST. JOHN THE BAPTIST.

This church is in the East Soke, at the upper part of St. John's Street, and from its situation is called St. John on the Hill. It is the most interesting of the churches of Winchester, and consists of a nave and chancel, not divided by any arch, with north and south aisles to each, and a square tower at the west end of the south aisle. Its proportions are very peculiar. The length along the centre of the nave and chancel is fifty-five feet, but the east end being made to conform to the line of the street, instead of being at right angles to its length, the north wall is sixty feet long and the south wall no more than fifty. The central alley is fourteen feet wide, but each of the aisles is seventeen feet eight inches in width.[3] *The Church.*

The oldest parts of the church are the arches (three on each side) and piers separating the aisles from the central alley ; they are said to be of the time of Richard I.[4] The walls, as is evident from the original corbels of the roof, are Early English. There is "a good Early English window of four lights, with a foliated circle in the head, and quatrefoils in the heads of the sub-arches."[5] There are two wooden

---

(1) See Wavell and Ball (*u. s.*) for copies of some inscriptions.

This living is a rectory, in the gift of the bishop, and of the value of £104 per annum. There are no registers of earlier date than 1634 (Census 1831).

(2) Traced by Godson's and Gale's maps.

(3) These details are taken from the plan of the church in Archit. Notes, &c. (*u. s.* p. 17).

(4) Ibid., p. 13.

(5) Ibid., pp. 15, 16. Traces of two windows of this period were discovered during the late repairs in the north wall of the nave.

screens with wide, open, ogee arches in the upper part, and banded shafts, enclosing the sides of the chancel, which are of the fourteenth century, Decorated; and some good bench-ends of the same period.

All the rest of the church appears to be Perpendicular, of a not very late date. There is a tall screen, which runs quite across the nave (at right angles to its length, not parallel to the east end), and "part of the rood-loft remains, with the passage through the walls on both sides. The staircase to the rood-loft is [but not "perfect"] in a turret on the south side, with doors inside and outside: this turret is an addition of the fifteenth century, and the outer doorway a still later insertion; there seems to have been a passage through for the priest."[1]

The Tower.

"The tower . . . . is of the fifteenth century, very good, and built chiefly of masses of hard chalk, faced internally as ashlar-work, and cased on the outside with flint and stone dressings." The stairs are a very good specimen of the excellence of this building material. "The tower arch is deeply recessed, and has a succession of bold ogee mouldings continuous to the ground."[2]

On the south side of the chancel is "a Perpendicular piscina, with a niche of singular form, and a single sedile," with a squint through it from the south aisle. There is also a niche under the east window of the south aisle; and on the south side of the north aisle a square ambry, and a squint looking from the chancel towards a plain, wide, arched recess on the north side, which is supposed to be the Easter sepulchre. There is another niche in the north aisle, just outside the screen, and there are brackets beside the east window. At the east end, on the outside of the church, between the chancel and the south aisle, is a niche; and at the opposite end, close beside the window of the north aisle, another smaller one; and there is a bracket outside the south aisle of the chancel.[3]

"The font is octagonal, panelled;[4] the pulpit of Perpendicular wood-work; the front of the gallery is ornamented with some good old bench ends;" the stalls in the chancel appear to have been cut away; but the old, plain, timber roof has been preserved.[5]

Mural Paintings.

During the recent repairs, some exceedingly interesting frescoes were discovered in this church. At the west end of the north wall was a representation of the Judgment, in three compartments, the lowest showing the dead rising from their graves; the central one the Archangel Michael weighing the souls, and the blessed being conducted to the left hand by St. Francis, whilst a huge and hairy devil dragged off

(1) Ibid., pp. 13, 14. These screens were, according to Wavell (vol. i. p. 213), "ornamentally painted."

(2) Archit. Notes (u. s.), p. 16. Wavell states (u. s.) that the clock was "said to be given by King Charles II." Its dial "appears on the south side of the tower."

(3) These niches and brackets are particularly noticed, because they furnish us with some notions of the amount of ornamentation bestowed on this church, and of the varied devotion of those who frequented it.

(4) In the course of the late repairs, in levelling the floor of the church, the bowl of the old Norman font was found; it was square, and had been broken into two pieces. It was removed by the contractor as his rightful perquisite.

(5) The organ in this low gallery is modern; and the marble flooring of the chancel quite recent. A vestry was erected at the west end, with an entry from the tower, when the last alterations were made.

the children of perdition in the opposite direction;[1] and in the uppermost division, our Lord, seated, showed his five wounds, and the Blessed Virgin Mary, kneeling beside him, bared her breast to enforce her intercession : two angels held the instruments of the Passion ; the Apostles sat six on each side, and at each end was an angel blowing a great trumpet.

Next, over one of the windows now stopped up, was a figure of our Lord, seated in a circle, with the emblems of the Evangelists, two on each side, and lower down, beside the window arch, two angels censing.

Between the two windows were the Crucifixion, in which St. Francis with a book in his hand, and another cowled and tonsured figure, occupied the places of the Virgin and the Apostle John ; and the martyrdom of St. Andrew.

Over the point of the next stopped window (along the arch of which ran an elegant flower pattern) was an angel holding out two crowns ; and farther to the east, just over the screen, the Blessed Virgin with the infant Jesus seated on a throne. Small crosses flory, &c., filled up the spaces amongst these figures. An angel kneeling and censing was painted over against the arch of the window near the east end of this wall ; but there were no paintings found on the other side of the window.[2]

On the north side of the altar was represented the martyrdom of St. Thomas-à-Becket ; and on the south wall, not far from the door, was the customary gigantic figure of St. Christopher. There were also other paintings of a later date.[3]

Fragments of old stained glass still remain in several windows,[4] and in the central east window is a full-length figure of St. John the Baptist, which, together with the new mullions, &c., was presented in good part by the Rev. F. Swanton.

There are five bells, of which the tenor is plain, but the others are variously inscribed ; on the first (which is cracked) is—

" FEARE GOD." " LOVE THY GOD, AND OBAYE THY PRINCE." " ANNO DOMINI 1574." " JOHN COLE, BELL-FOUNDER ;"

on the second is—

" SANCTE PETRE ORA PRO NOBIS ;"

on the third—

" GIVE GOD THE GLORY. RB. 1606."

on the fourth—

" GOD IS MY HOPE. . RB. 1606."

Beneath the recess, which has been called the Easter sepulchre, is a large altar tomb, " the sides of which are ornamented by panels, with shields bearing the emblems

The Monuments.

(1) This part of the subject was damaged, " a singing gallery " having once been erected in this part of the church. (Arch. Assoc. Journal, vol. ix. p. 7.)

(2) A full account of the discovery of these frescoes, and of the subjects, with coloured engravings of them all, by Mr. F. J. Baigent, will be found in the Journal of the Archæological Association, vol. ix. pp. 1—16, Pl. III.—VI.

(3) I am indebted to the Rev. Francis Swanton, the present perpetual-curate, and to Mr. James Masters, churchwarden of the parish, for this and other valuable

information respecting St. John's Church, which I have largely used in this account of it.

(4) Wavell says (vol. i. p. 212) that the " painted glass " " in the east window of the middle aisle " " seems to have represented the miracles of St. John, and has now the visible portrait of that saint." Ball (p. 192) says, " the whole of the windows preserve some remains of the rich glass with which they were formerly adorned." Mr. Baigent (u.s.) mentions part of a figure of the Saviour, a shield with the emblem of the Trinity, &c. &c.

of the Crucifixion," and the letters S and I (or T) interlaced; but in the chamfer round the edge of it there was originally a slip of brass with an inscription. Nothing is now known respecting it.

On a stone slab is this inscription :—

"ORATE : P̲ : AIᾹ : ALICIE : NUP̲ : VXORIS : WILLI : GERNEYS : "

In the central alley of the nave is the trace of a brass inscription, and another is seen in the tower; but the brasses have both been lost.

The mural monuments are not very numerous, and commemorate the names of Brereton, Knapp, Earle, Leversuch, Wake, Beacham, Moss, Lyne, Blackmore, and Deverell. Among the floor slabs (which were much displaced during the recent alterations, some of them being taken away) are several which record interments of members of the Gosnell family.[1]

The Parish.

The boundary of the parish is conterminous with that of St. Peter Cheesehill, from East-gate to the farthest point of the fence of Palm Hall, from which it proceeds a short way to the east, and then at right angles northward, to the farther side of the old London Road, and there turns to the west again; and shortly diverging from it, assumes a westerly direction, so as to meet the line of St. John's Terrace (formerly called Beggar's Lane), in about the middle of it. Along this lane it goes nearly to the end, and then crosses westward again to the river, up which it is drawn to the next diverging streamlet, when it turns along it to Tumbling Bay, and thence at right angles along the cut nearest the city walls, to the rivulet which flows through Middle Brooks, which it follows as far as the north wall, and thence proceeds by the line of the ancient walls to East-gate.[2]

(1) See Wavell (u. s., pp. 215, 216) for a deplorable account of the state of things in this parish, about the middle of the last century.

The registers of baptisms in this parish commence in the year 1595; those of marriages, in 1610; and those of burials, in 1611. There is also "a book for St. John and St. Peter Cheesehill" commencing in 1578.

In the parish chest is kept a book of churchwardens' accounts, commencing in 1550, and containing very curious and valuable materials for a minute history of the church.

This living is a perpetual curacy, in the gift of the Bishop of Winchester, of the value of £82 per annum.

Milner (vol. ii. p. 228), referring to "MS." as his authority, speaks of "the charities formerly annexed to this church." And Mr. Baigent (u. s., p. 2) says that the north aisle, probably, belonged to a confraternity, and was called the "Chapel of Our Ladye," the services in which were maintained by certain tenements, &c., given by John Thomas in the year 1527, which property being overlooked in the general confiscation of chantry lands, &c., in the time of Edward VI., has now come into the possession of the parish.

(2) Traced by the help of Gale's map, (with which Godson's agrees in every particular), and the Ordnance map.

CHURCH OF ST. PETER CHEESEHILL.

The Church.

This curious structure also stands in the East Soke, in the street after which it is named, Cheesehill Street.[1] It is "a small church of singular ground plan," being thirty-seven feet long, by nearly forty feet wide. It has "no distinct chancel,[2] and a south aisle only, which has no side windows; on the north side there is one small Perpendicular window, which is evidently an insertion. The three arches of the south aisle are transition Norman, supported by massive round pillars, having moulded capitals. The tower stands at the south-east angle, outside of the aisle," and is covered with a pyramidal tiled roof; "the lower part is Norman, and there is a singular window of Early English character in the ringing-loft, square on the outside, divided by a shaft, and having a pointed segmental arch within."

"At the east end of the church are three good Perpendicular windows, and at the end of the aisle two rich niches in the Decorated style, one in the east wall, the other in the north; the material of this is chalk, but the sculpture is particularly good. At the west end are two Decorated windows, and there is a plain Early English doorway in the north wall." At this end there is also "a Decorated doorway, now blocked up."

The Font.

"The font is late Norman, square, of Petworth marble, with shallow panels and detached shafts. In the east windows are some pieces of painted glass, consisting chiefly of good borders of the fifteenth century." "On the ridge of the roof are good open crest-tiles. There are some good early corbels to the roof in the aisle."[3]

There is a gallery on each side of the church; and in the north gallery is a window, or opening, closed by a shutter, by which persons in the adjoining house can participate in the service of the church without leaving their home. There is also a small organ.

On the tenor bell is inscribed—

"SANCTA MARGRETA ORA PRO NOBIS;"

the inscriptions on the other two do not require notice.

The Monuments.

There is, or was,[4] one brass in this church bearing the inscription—

"ORATE PRO AĪE MARGARETE UUEDALE;"

and seven mural monuments, recording the names of Cooke, Long, Ekersley, Standfast, Stevenson, and Earle.[5]

(1) See above, p. 26, note 5, for some notice of this name.

(2) Wavell (vol. i. p. 210) says the altar "is separated from the south aisle by a wooden screen, or partition, of great antiquity; and another of the same kind is likewise continued across the whole east end of the church, by which means it has the appearance of a double chancel." Part of this screen remained when Ball wrote (p. 189).

(3) Archit. Notes, &c. (*u. s.*), pp. 19, 20.

(4) Ball, p. 189.

(5) This living is a rectory, of the yearly value of £100 (the income having been augmented by Order in Council, at the suggestion of the Ecclesiastical Commission, vol. ii. p. 134), and the patron is the Lord Chancellor.

The register of baptisms commences in 1606; that of marriages, in 1597; and that of burials, in 1595 (Census 1831).

The Parish.

The boundary of this parish, commencing at East-gate, follows the line of the old city wall, southward, as far as the entrance to Wolvesey, where it crosses the path, and coincides with the fence of the meadow opposite, as far as Blackbridge (or Wharfbridge), where, crossing the river, it goes up Wharf Hill, and along the old road to Alresford, until it comes to the point where the fence of the land attached to Palm Hall touches it; from this point it returns westward along the fence of Palm Hall, turning northward along its western front as far as the footpath, which it then follows down the face of St. Giles' Hill, and so along Bridge Street to East-gate.[1]

CHURCH OF ST. BARTHOLOMEW HYDE.

The Church.

On the left-hand side of the way, originally leading to Hyde Abbey, from Hyde Street, without North-gate, stands this curious old church, which consists of a nave, chantry chapel,[2] and tower, with a later south porch, and a recently erected chancel.[3] The oldest parts of the structure are Norman, and we may note particularly the fine south doorway in that style[4] (which has been recently restored), and the capital to the arch of the chantry chapel,[5] as indications of this.

The Early English trefoil-headed lancet windows of the nave "appear to be in their original positions."[6] On the east side of the chantry is a blind two-light window, of a little later date, but still Early English, filled with early Perpendicular tracery.[7] The north window of the chantry is an elegant two-light transition Early English

(1) This is traced by Gale's map, and the Ordnance map, as prepared for the use of the Tithe Commission. Godson carries the boundary from East-gate along the weirs, by the edge of the river, and between the two streams to Blackbridge; and instead of following the footpath down St. Giles' Hill, carries it straight from the northern fence to the old London Road.

(2) The raised site of the altar against the east wall shows that this was a chantry, and not a transept. Wavell (who calls it the "chancel") says that "the Powletts" were buried under it (see below, p. 173, note 4), and the chantry-priest may have been maintained by that family.

(3) It is not known at what time the original chancel was destroyed, but Wavell (vol. i. p. 201) tells us that an unsuccessful attempt was made to rebuild it "in the time of Bishop Trelawney," or the beginning of last century. I have been shown by the present vicar, the Rev. William Williams, a sketch of the church, showing its condition about that time, when a cottage occupied the site of the chancel, and was attached to the eastern end of the church. The former chancel may have extended further to the east than the present one, as there are foundations there. Its windows, according to Wavell (ibid.), were

Norman, but we must not implicitly rely on this statement.

Wavell (ibid.) says that the altar all this time stood against the north wall of the chantry, which "is truly disgusting; it is attended with every inconvenience, being out of the view, as well as hearing, of the greater part of the congregation." I am, however, informed by the Rev. William Williams, that it stood against the east wall when he became vicar. The commandments were inscribed on the wall at the east end of the body of the church (Wavell, ibid., p. 202; Ball, p. 211), which appears to show that before the space had been required for pews, the communion table had been placed there.

(4) The tympanum and some of the capitals are modern, but the rich mouldings of the arch, cheveron, lozenge, and alternate billets, with one or two of the capitals, are ancient. The inner arch of this doorway is plain stilted Norman.

(5) This arch, with shafts supporting it, appears to have been perfect in Wavell's time (u. s.).

(6) Archit. Notes, &c. (u. s.).

(7) Mr. J. H. Parker (ibid.) regards this window as not belonging to the place it now occupies.

or Decorated window; and on the west side is a blind lancet window, which appears to have been inserted there.

There are two other windows in the nave, debased Perpendicular, but in arch-moulds of earlier date. There are niches in the splays of the nearest of these to the chancel; and outside, near the south porch, is a trefoil-headed Early English niche, "probably a piscina," which must have been brought from some other place.[1]

The tower is low, with chequer-work on the sides, and "may be of the period of the dissolution of the abbey. The font is of the thirteenth century, octagon, with shafts, but very plain."[2]

Of the three bells only one can be used at the present time; on one is this inscription :—

"SANCTEA NICHOLAE . . . . ORA PRO NOBIS;"

with what appears to be the name of the maker.

The gallery and the organ are both modern.

There remains the vestige of an early brass, which consisted of a demifigure and inscription, above an escutcheon.[3] Another of later date is thus inscribed :—

The Monuments.

"SUM PULVIS QUI CARNE FUI VESTITUS AMŒNA
DISCE TUOS CASUS HAC QUI DISCURRIS AMICE
EDMUNDUM DIXERE MEUM POORE NOMEN, ET, ILLUD
EXTINXIT SUPREMA DIE, MENS VIVIT IN ÆVUM.
1599."

The oldest mural monument bears this remarkable inscription :—

"HERE LIETH THE BODY OF EDW. NORTON, GENT., OF TISTED AND AVINGTON HOVSES DE-SCENDED, WHO HAD 2ˢ A DAY PENCION FOR HIS GOOD SERVICE BY SEAE IN ANO D̄N̄I 1588, WHO DESESSED 10° IVLII, 1600."

There are eleven other mural tablets, recording the deaths of persons of consideration, bearing the names of Bradburne, Deane, Lyford, Richards, Clarke, à Paisy, and Hesseltine, of whom the last two were vicars of the church.

On one of the floor slabs is this, which is worthy of insertion here :—

"IANVARIE XIIIIth, 1640.
LET MEN DETRACTE,
SAY WHAT THEY CAN,
HEE LIVD AND DYED   GENT.
AN HONEST MAN.   ROBERT POORE
FVI NON SVM . ESTIS NON ERITIS
VALETE ET GAVDETE."[4]

From the river Itchen to near Hermit's Tower, at the north-west angle of the city, *The Parish.*

(1) Wavell's theory (*u. s.*) was that the existing church "was built . . . . out of the ruins of Hyde Abbey;" but it is unquestionably Norman; yet, fragments from the abbey may have been used to repair it, or may have been built into its walls, as other pieces have been into all the walls near the site of the ruins.

(2) Archit. Notes, &c. (*u. s.*).

(3) Wavell (vol. i. p. 203) gives the inscription on a brass, which may have occupied this place :—

"HIC JACET ISABELLA HOCLEY, MATER EDWARDI HOCLEY, ARTIUM MAGISTER ET TUNC VICARII ISTIUS ECCLE. QUE

OBIIT VIII. DIE MENSIS FEBRUARII. ANO D̄N̄I MILL° CCCCLXXXIII. CUJUS ANIMA PROPICIETUR DEUS."

(4) "Under this chancel [that is, the chantry chapel] is a very large vault belonging to the Powletts, and contains the reliques of several of that ancient family, to whose memory there are several inscriptions on the ground" (Wavell, vol. i. pp. 202, 203). None of these inscriptions are known now.

The earliest registers commence in the year 1563. This living is a vicarage, of the annual value of £100 (the income having been augmented by the Ecclesiastical

the boundary of this parish is conterminous with those of St. John on the Hill, St. Maurice, St. Mary Kalendar, and St. Thomas; it thence diverges (leaving a small space between it and the wall), and turns to the north for a short way, and, with a slight bend, joins the Andover Road, along which it proceeds for about a mile, and then returns by a somewhat circuitous sweep to the Itchen, one or other stream of which is the eastern boundary of the parish.[1]

ST. PETER'S CHAPEL (ROMAN CATHOLIC).

Revival of Roman Catholic worship.

Near the middle of St. Peter's Street, on the western side, is a good plain Norman arch, which once belonged to the hospital of St. Mary Magdalen,[2] and now serves as a gateway to the Roman Catholic chapel, which is dedicated to St. Peter. The renewal of the ancient worship in this city was effected by Roger Corham, who, soon after 1667, having built himself a house[3] a little to the south of the gateway just spoken of, celebrated divine service in it according to the ritual of Rome, even before the Act of Toleration was passed. Subsequently, it appears, there was a detached building in the garden behind the house, which was used as a chapel; and Milner has recorded the alteration of it, for the purpose of rendering it more commodious, in the years 1759 and 1784.[4]

The Chapel.

The existing building was erected by Dr. Milner in 1792, and is described at considerable length in his History.[5] It is a small chapel, and, very remarkably, lies so little in the customary position, that what should be the east end is almost due south.[6] It was exceedingly elegant, and even ornate when first built, but much of the original ornamentation has now disappeared. In addition to which, Gothic ecclesiastical architecture has of late been so critically and minutely studied, that what was in Milner's day a most praiseworthy attempt to follow the old models, is now found to fall very far indeed behind them.[7]

The entrance is by a porch (which was formerly of wood, but has recently been

Commission, Orders in Council, vol. ii. p. 78), and the patron is the Lord Chancellor.

(1) Traced from Gale's map, and the Ordnance map, as before.

(2) See above, p. 22, note 3.

(3) This house stood a little back from the street, having a garden, or courtyard, with a low wall in front of it, between it and the street. I am indebted to the Rev. Ignatius Collingridge for the sight of a sketch of this house, and for other information, of which I have gladly availed myself.

The present house is quite a modern one. In his text (vol. ii. pp. 213, 251), and in his Ancient Ichnography

of Winchester, Milner places the church of St. Peter in Macellis, on the site occupied by his own chapel. But this is completely erroneous, the site of this church being next the street, between the Royal Oak Passage and St. George's Street. (See above, p. 22, note 1.)

(4) Milner, vol. ii. p. 251.

(5) Ibid., and pp. 252—266.

(6) This neglect of orientation is very remarkable in Dr. Milner. In the Church of England it prevailed until that revival of the study of Gothic architecture, of which Rickman's work was certainly the sign, and to no small extent the cause also.

(7) Within the gateway may be seen " certain capitals

BISHOP MILNER.

The Original in the Posession of the Rt Rev: Dr Ullathorne.

rebuilt in stone) on the east side of the north end, immediately opposite the gateway; and in the porch is the long Latin inscription commemorating the generosity of George III. (who permitted a number of refugees from the first French revolution to occupy the King's House in this city), which was removed hither from that house when it was converted into barracks.[1]

It is lighted by six windows on the east side, and two others, with a quatrefoil window between them, in the north end, all of which were originally filled with painted glass, those in the side exhibiting "the most renowned saints or kings who heretofore flourished in Winchester." There are two galleries, one "a private gallery, over the sacristy," at the south end; the other, at the north end, containing the organ.

The reredos is painted in imitation of panel-work, and the altar-piece is a copy of Raphael's Transfiguration. On the west wall is a series of paintings "in chiaro-oscuro," the subjects being taken from the Scriptures; and originally every surface and nook exhibited some holy symbol or sacred text; for a full account of which we must refer to Milner's great work.[2]

Behind the altar is the sacristy, in which is "kept an old processional cross, now newly painted, which before the Reformation belonged to the neighbouring parish church of Barton Stacey, likewise an ancient cope, &c."[3]

and, bosses of groins, collected from the ruins of Hyde Abbey," "a bust from the fortifications of the ancient castle," and a huge flattish boulder, weighing nearly two tons, which Dr. Milner imagined to be the upper stone of a cromlech, and had it brought hither from Upper Brook Street, where it used to lie against the wall of a blacksmith's shop (Milner, vol. i. pp. 7, 8; vol. ii. pp. 253, 254). It is evidently one of the drift boulders, which abound in the valley of the Itchen, and of which a full account will be given in the General Appendix, under the head of "Geology."

(1) Milner, vol. ii. p. 201; Ball, pp. 198, 199.

(2) Dr. Milner is the most eminent of those who have held the office of priest in St. Peter's Chapel, which he did from 1779 to 1803, when he was consecrated Bishop of Castabala, and appointed Vicar-Apostolic of the Midland district. He died in 1826, in the seventy-fourth year of his age. His "History of Winchester" was his principal work; he also wrote on the "Ecclesiastical Architecture of England," and the "Modern Style of altering Ancient Cathedrals;" and communicated several valuable papers to the Society of Antiquaries (of which he was a Fellow), which are printed in the "Archæologia" and "Vetusta Monumenta;" and to Carter's "Specimens of Ancient Architecture;" and supplied the article on Gothic Architecture in "Rees's Cyclopædia." His other writings are principally controversial; and he was one of the most indefatigable and successful pioneers of archæological study and research in England.

The Rev. Thomas White, who entered on this mission in 1810, and died in 1826, was an eminent classical scholar, and his sermons, which were edited after his death by Dr. Lingard, attest the elegance of his English style. The Rev. Ignatius Collingridge is the first missionary rector of St. Peter's.

(3) A figure and full description of this cross will be found in the Winchester Volume of the Arch. Assoc., pp. 466, 467.

The number of sittings in this chapel is in round numbers 300.

CONGREGATIONAL CHURCH.[1]

History of the
Congregation.

No records of the existence of a congregation of dissidents from the Church of England, anterior to the Restoration, have been preserved; but after the enforcement of the Act of Uniformity mention is made of one, with a Bartholomean, the Rev. Samuel Tomlyns, M.A., of Trinity College, Cambridge, who had been ejected from the neighbouring parish of Crawley, as its pastor;[2] and it is stated, but on no surer ground than tradition, that his congregation assembled in a private room in Cheesehill Street.

At a later period another Bartholomean, the Rev. Samuel Sprint, also of Trinity College, Cambridge, and ejected from South Tidworth in this county, appears to have preached here, but he resided near Andover, and his services could have been only occasional.[3]

The first meeting-house, which occupied the site of the present Primitive Methodist Chapel in Parchment Street, was erected soon after 1700, when the Rev. —— Davison, the son of a Bartholomean (his father[4] having been ejected from the living of Norgrave, Gloucestershire, in 1662), was pastor.

In 1808 this meeting-house was rebuilt as it at present exists, and it continued to be the place of worship for the Independents in Winchester until 1853, when the present chapel was erected.

The Chapel.

The site of this new chapel is in Jewry Street, on part of the area of the former county jail. It has a good appearance from the street, having a triple lancet window (filled with coloured glass), and three doorways below, in the Early English style. The interior is an oblong octagon, with a gallery all round, behind the piers of the arches which support the roof. In the centre of this is a lantern, which makes the whole structure exceedingly light and pleasing in its general effect.[5] A good organ

(1) For the historical account of this congregation I am indebted to the kindness of Joshua Wilson, Esq., of Tunbridge Wells, and the Rev. William Thorn, who has been pastor of it since 1826.

(2) Palmer (vol. ii. p. 8) states that Mr. Tomlyns continued to preach here for nine years, "exposed to great hardships and difficulties on account of his nonconformity." After the Edict of Toleration he became minister of a congregation at Andover. "He was," says his memorialist, "a good critic in Greek and Hebrew, and an excellent textuary; a man of great gravity and wisdom, and a good casuist. He was mighty in the Scriptures, for his head, memory, heart, and tongue were full of them; and he had a general reputation as a scholar, a preacher, and a divine."

(3) Palmer (vol. ii. p. 24) says of him, "He was of a pacific, healing, catholic spirit, a complete scholar, a very useful preacher, and one of strict piety, of wonderful

modesty and humility, and, therefore, contented to live in an obscure corner." "His carriage was such as recommended him to the good esteem of all the neighbouring gentry in these parts."

It was not at all unfrequent in those troublous times for one minister, especially if he was a man of learning, as most of the ejected ministers were, to preach on alternate Sundays to two congregations lying at some distance apart from each other; this was the case with the Rev. Thomas Bridge, who being ejected from the living of St. George Tombland, Norwich, was minister of dissident congregations at Norwich and Yarmouth for many years.

(4) See Palmer's Nonconformists' Memorial (vol. i. p. 547).

(5) The architect, W. F. Poulton, Esq., of Reading, has, with great ingenuity, constructed this building with a thoroughly ecclesiastical appearance and character, yet not so as to parody an ancient church. The roof is

occupies part of the gallery at the end of the chapel, and the pulpit stands immediately in front of it. The number of sittings provided is about 700, which could be increased to 1000.

A residence is provided for the minister, whose stipend is augmented by the rental of a house similar to, and adjoining the *manse.* Apartments are provided for the chapel-keeper over the school-house at the back of the chapel.

There are also in Winchester a few other chapels of dissenters. The Wesleyan Methodists have one in Parchment Street, at the corner of St. George's Street; it is a plain unobtrusive building, containing sittings for 160. The Primitive Methodists occupy the chapel which once belonged to the Independents; it is in Parchment Street, opposite the County Hospital, containing sitting room for 350. In Silver Hill, on the north side, is the small Baptist chapel, built on a spot on which it is said John Wesley once preached in an empty lumber warehouse. It has sittings for 250.

Other congregations have at various times existed, for short periods, in Winchester, but have now disappeared.[1]

Other Dissenting Chapels.

carried up to the lantern on a double series of plain hammer beams, and the front of the galleries is open iron-work.

Under the side galleries are passages to the schools behind, which will be described in a subsequent page.

The greater part of the cost of erecting this chapel with the school-rooms, &c., in the rear of it, amounting to about £5000, was defrayed by the Rev. William Thorn, and members of his family.

(1) A congregation formerly occupied the Hyde House school-room, and at another time a house in Upper Brooks. There was once, also, a New Jerusalem congregation in Southgate Road.

THE

COLLEGE OF ST. MARY WINTON;

AND

THE SCHOOLS, LIBRARIES, AND MUSEUM OF WINCHESTER.

———◆———

St. Mary's
College.

WILLIAM of Wykeham's College is, in local importance, second to the cathedral only, and on this account, as well as because of its educational character, which would place it next in order after the ecclesiastical institutions of the city, we now direct attention to it.[1]

Its site :—

This renowned college, the most ancient of all the existing foundation schools in England, stands on the south side of the city, without the walls, between the two streams which flow through the cathedral precinct.[2] The entrance is in College Street, which runs eastward from Kingsgate; and the grounds extend from Kingsgate Street, on the west, to Blackbridge (or Wharfbridge), on the east; and on the south, as far as the Old Barge River.[3] It is thus secluded from all the din and stir of Winchester, and screened by it on the north from the winds that sometimes sweep along the valley, whilst it is open to the water meads, that stretch in perennial green to St. Cross and Twyford, and overlooked from a short distance by St. Catharine's down, which Wykehamists have designated " Hills."[4]

(1) Besides the works of Warton, Wavell, Milner, &c., I have made more or less use of Walcott's " William of Wykeham and his Colleges," Cockerell's " William of Wykeham " (printed in Winchester Vol. of Arch. Instit.), Crabb's account of the college (in Ackerman's " History of the Public Schools of Winchester," &c.), Lowth's " Life of Wykeham," Tanner, &c. I have also the pleasure of acknowledging obligations to the Warden, the Rev. W. H. Gunner, J. D. Walford, Esq., M.A., and the Rev. Mackenzie Walcott, for assistance and information, which have greatly enhanced the value of personal observation and books.

(2) These are the Lurte Bourne, and what might be named Athelwold's Bourne. (See pp. 10 and 89 above.)

(3) They extend as far as Blackbridge, being bounded by the road from College Street thither; thence the boundary follows the course of the old river (inclosing the whole precinct of St. Elizabeth's College) to the first hatches below the college mill, and thence proceeds by an irregular line, westward, to Kingsgate Street, and along it to the north as far as St. Michael's Passage; opposite to which it returns eastward to the watercourse I have called Athelwold's Bourne (thus including the precincts of the Carmelite monastery), which it follows to College Street. This brook makes two great bends in its course here round the ancient boundary of the Sustern Spital, on the site of which Commoners now stands, which will be spoken of shortly. (Gale's and Godson's Maps.)

(4) See above, p. 9, note 3.

WINCHESTER COLLEGE.

(from the Warden's Garden)

Its original plan is very simple.[1]   The collegiate buildings are all arranged —and plan.
round a quadrangle (measuring a hundred and fifteen feet from east to west, and a
little less from north to south), between which and the highway on the north is a
forecourt (nearly sixty feet across), surrounded by the storehouses and offices indispensable, in the old times, to such an establishment, and the stables; while to the
south of the quadrangle, immediately adjoining the chapel, stand the cloisters (about
a hundred and fifteen feet square), with an oratory, which was not the work of the
founder, and apparently formed no part of his design.

A very few alterations have been made in this plan, and all of them have been
necessitated, or suggested, by the alterations in the social and domestic condition of
England since Wykeham's day.

No effort was made by the founder to relieve or adorn the front of the buildings,
which occupy the whole length of the site (nearly three hundred feet) next College
Street; partly because being without the *enceinte* of the city, it needed, in such a
century as the fifteenth, something of the strength of a fortress; or for the sake of
the privacy requisite to a place of study; but more because it was not the custom of
architects like Wykeham, under any circumstances, by decoration, to impart to mere
offices an importance which they were not in themselves entitled to.   It displayed no
more than a few small stanchioned windows, and the image of the Blessed Virgin in
a tabernacled niche over the arched gateway.[2]

The Warden's House now forms the eastern side of the forecourt, an Elizabethan   The Warden's
structure, with oaken-panelled rooms and carved mantelpieces, built by Warden   House.
Harmar, in 1597, as the initials and date formerly on the front next College Street
showed; but in parts of much more modern date.   A fine gallery in the upper floor
contains portraits of Wykeham, and of all the wardens from Elizabeth's time, with
the exception of one or two.[3]

On the west side of this court are the warden's stables, with a yard before them;
and between them and the gateway, on the north side, are various offices, with the
brew-house and the porter's lodge.   The door next "the inner buttress of the gateway
leads to the bursary."[4]

(1) Cockerell, Pl. II.

(2) There are some modern sash windows at the east
end now, which part is substantially buttressed, and
there formerly were (as may be seen in all the ancient
views) two small oriels, one on each side of the gateway,
above.   The arch of the entrance, which is in a low
square tower, is a wide four-centred arch with plain
mouldings, and the heads of Wykeham himself and King
Edward III. (as it is believed) for corbels.   The founder's
arms are sculptured on the central boss of the vaulted
ceiling of the gateway.

(3) The warden's house is built partly on the site of
the storehouses for flour and malt, &c. (Cockerell, p. 17,
and Pl. II.), and partly in front of them, thus reducing the
area of this forecourt.

"That part which fronts the garden," or the eastern
portion, "was erected at the expense of Warden Nicholas,
in the year 1692, and greatly repaired by . . . . Warden
Lee in the year 1767."   "The north front of the second
quadrangle loses much of its intended effect by means of
another part of these lodgings, built A.D. 1613." (Wavell, vol. i. 90, 91.)

In one of the great mantlepieces the date 1615 is
visible, and the whole building was "newly fronted in
1832—1833, by Mr. Repton." (Walcott, p. 189.)

The examinations for the Heathcote prize used to be
held in the gallery mentioned above; and it is said that
there is a curious hanap, with a cross of the sixteenth
century, in the warden's possession. (Ibid.)

(4) Ibid.; Cockerell, *u. s.*

A A 2

The inner
gateway.

Immediately opposite the outer gate is the entrance to the quadrangle, through an archway similar to the former, but under a higher tower, and having over it three tabernacled niches containing the figures of the Blessed Virgin, the Angel Gabriel, and William of Wykeham. The room in the tower is now used as the Election Chamber, where the annual examination of the candidates for admission into New College, Oxford, takes place.[1]

The inner front of this second gateway tower is also ornamented with three niches containing the same figures as are seen on the outer front, which are executed with great freedom and excellence. The domestic buildings round three sides of this quadrangle, or inner court, are of two stories, and all the windows are square headed, with hood-moulds and corbels appropriate to the uses assigned to the several parts.[2] The entrances to the several chambers and offices are good plain pointed arches, with corbels of various designs. The lavatory, which was formerly covered by a curious penthouse, is near the middle of the west side.[3] On this western side are the kitchen and offices connected with it,[4] in the passage to which is painted the emblematic picture of "The Trusty Servant," so well known to visitors. It represents the servant in a closely-buttoned blue vest and bands, with the head of a pig, the ears of an ass, and the feet of a deer; a padlock on his mouth, his right hand held up open, his left hand filled with kitchen utensils, a sword by his side, and a buckler on his

The " Trusty
Servant."

(1) This chamber, with one apartment to the west of the gate, and the whole range on the east of it, was originally the warden's lodge, and the rest of the range westward was occupied by two masters and a fellow. (Cockerell, *u. s.*). But the growth of the institution and the progress of society, together, have rendered such changes as I have noted indispensable.

(2) These windows are now all modernized; they were originally of two lights, with cinquefoiled heads and transoms.

Amongst the corbels may be noticed "the psaltery and pipe at the entrance to the refectory, the master and scholar, the iron bound chest, the soldier, and the clerk." (Walcott, p. 194.)

The eastern side of the quadrangle was originally assigned to the fellows of the college, and "casements were added in their chambers, in 1540, by Warden More." (Walcott, p. 195.)

The seventh chamber, on the ground-floor, at the western end of the south side (under the hall or refectory), was, with the passage beside it, the original school-room. The windows are arched, of two lights, and have wide stone seats in the sills; and, as in other chambers on the ground-floor, a huge beam, supported in the middle by a square post, crosses the ceiling.

The furniture of all the chambers is of the simplest character, but amply sufficient for the health and comfort of the boys, each of whom has a bed to himself. And the great fireplaces, with blazing wood fires whenever

the season requires it, and over each a light in its *functior* (as the candlestick is named here), are evidences of the attention paid, from the very first, to the physical well-being of the scholars. Formerly the beds were mere bundles of straw. The flooring of the chambers and the oak bedsteads were the gift of Dean Fleshmonger. (Walcott, p. 197.)

In all the chambers the names of various former scholars, with the dates of their leaving the school, are painted on black tablets in groups over the beds; and it is with deep emotion and interest that even the casual visitor sees amongst them some which have since become familiar to all lips as household words, or hears the traditions of each chamber, such as (for example) that of "the bloody hand" in the seventh chamber, which is, in fact, merely the cognisance of a baronet.

(3) Carter's "Memorials;" Ball's Walks, p. 154. It had originally some kind of porch in front of it, as the wall above it shows. The more recent one was excessively incongruous with the building, and has very properly been removed. Washing apparatus and an abundant supply of water is now provided in the chambers; but formerly the boys washed themselves here, in all seasons, *sub dio*.

(4) Cockerell (pp. 17, 18) states that these have "undergone much change through the interpolations of the warden, Watson, who in 1540 built what are called *aisiamenta*, easements, for the convenience of the masters and fellows."

left arm. The founder's arms are painted beside him, and beneath is an inscription in Latin verse, with an English translation.[1]

The Refectory.

A flight of stone stairs from the south-western corner of the quadrangle gives access to the refectory, over the seventh chamber (which was the original school-room,) and the passage to the present school, which will be noticed subsequently. It is a noble hall, nearly sixty-three feet long by thirty wide, wainscoted, and with a finely groined oak ceiling, and a dais, raised by two steps, at the upper end.[2] It is lighted by three lofty two-light windows on the south side, and two on the other.[3] The tables are placed along each side;[4] and in front of the screen which separates the buttery, &c., from the hall at the lower end, stands the "tub" for the broken meat, which is given to the poor.

In the same line with the refectory and seventh chamber, and projecting beyond the range of the kitchen and offices to the west, on the ground floor, is the cellar, with a vaulted ceiling supported by a central pillar, from which the groining ribs spring. Above it is the buttery, on the level of the hall; and over it the audit room, which is paved with Dutch tiles, where may be seen some fragments of tapestry of the

(1) The following are the inscriptions beneath this curious painting :—

" EFFIGIEM SERVI SI VIS SPECTARE PROBATI,
    QUISQUIS ES, HÆC OCULOS PASCET IMAGO TUOS.
PORCINUM OS QUOCUNQUE CIBO JEJUNIA SEDAT,
    CERVUS HABET CELERES IRE, REDIRE, PEDES.
LÆVA DOCET MULTUM TOT REBUS ONUSTA LABOREM,
    VESTIS MUNDITIEM, DEXTERA APERTA FIDEM.
DAT PATIENTEM ASINUS DOMINIS JURGANTIBUS AUREM ;
    HÆC SERA CONSILIUM, NE FLUAT, ARCTA PREMIT.
ACCINCTUS GLADIO, CLYPEO MUNITUS, ET INDE
    VEL SE VEL DOMINUM QUO TUEATUR, HABET."

" A TRUSTY SERVANT'S PORTRAIT WOULD YOU SEE,
THIS EMBLEMATIC FIGURE WELL SURVEY.
THE PORKER'S SNOUT NOT NICE IN DIET SHOWS ;
THE PADLOCK SHUT, NO SECRET HE'LL DISCLOSE ;
PATIENT, THE ASS, HIS MASTER'S RAGE WILL HEAR ;
SWIFTNESS IN ERRAND THE STAG'S FEET DECLARE ;
LOADEN, HIS LEFT HAND APT TO LABOUR SAITH ;
THE VEST, HIS NEATNESS, OPEN HAND, HIS FAITH ;
GIRT WITH HIS SWORD, HIS SHIELD UPON HIS ARM,
HIMSELF AND MASTER HE'LL PROTECT FROM HARM."

This figure, it appears, has been more than once repainted, and its present style is that of the beginning of last century. About a hundred years earlier, also, it was similarly restored ; a *Compotus* of the year 1637, showing that thirteen shillings was then disbursed, " *Pictori pingenti Servum et Carmina ;*" but the original painting was most probably made in the sixteenth century, for the verses appended to it are apparently the production of Dr. Christopher Johnson, head master of the school between 1560 and 1571, being found in " a small MS. volume of Latin verses in the library of the college," " mixed up with

pieces unquestionably" his (the Rev. W. H. Gunner, in "Notes and Queries," 1st S., vol. vi. p. 417) ; and Sir Frederic Madden has shown (Ibid., pp. 12, 13), by a quotation from a treatise of Cognatus (or Cousin, who was secretary to Erasmus), entitled " *De Officio Famulorum,*" that a figure resembling this in all its essential features, and called, like this, " the Trusty Servant," was, at that time, commonly painted in halls in France.

(2) Dean Fleshmonger, in 1540 (Walcott, p. 200), gave the wainscot which now lines the walls ; immediately before that time they were adorned with tapestry, the gift of Archbishop Warham. (Ibid.)

The corbels of the groining ribs are the busts of kings and prelates alternately, and "the middle of the roof is raised higher than the rest of it," and was a sort of lantern with louvres to ventilate the hall, and under that part most probably stood a charcoal fire. (Milner, vol. ii. p. 164 ; Cockerell, p. 20.)

The wardens, masters, fellows, and other officers, occupy the dais on grand occasions ; grace is sung there, and there also the *Domum* is sung by the scholars.

(3) These windows are quite Perpendicular in style, and are divided at mid-height by transoms. In the window next the head of the room, on the north side, are the arms of England, and of the Marquis of Winchester.

(4) Until quite recently, only the old square flat trencher was used, and all the table furniture was of the same primitive order, but the comfort and cleanliness of modern crockery, &c., have now been judiciously and most advantageously substituted for the archaic contrivances which had been handed down from the time of Wykeham itself. Even the blackjacks, in which the ale was served, have recently disappeared from the hall.

fifteenth century, exhibiting a portion of the story of David and Abigail,[1] and some of a later date. Its furniture consists of some high-backed settles, an ancient locker, the "founder's hutch," or coffer, with three locks, the *functior*, which is used in all the chambers as a candlestick, &c.[2] A spiral stair in a turret at the corner next the refectory communicates with all this floor, and with one yet higher, now a mere lumber-room.[3]

The Chapel.

The chapel and the muniment tower occupy the remainder of the south side of the quadrangle and the adjoining part of the east side. The archway of the porch of the chapel is of the same character as the others surrounding this inner court. Six massive buttresses (in pure Decorated style), and one at the angle of the muniment tower, support the walls on the north side; there are two at the east end, and eight (according to the plan) on the south side. The parapet is plain; and the turret stair, giving access to the muniment rooms, is in the inner angle next the chapel.

The interior dimensions of the chapel are ninety-three feet long, by thirty in width, and the vaulted ceiling is nearly sixty feet high,[4] in which admirable proportions its beauty in great part now consists. The tracery of the windows in the sides closely resembles that of Wykeham's windows in the cathedral (which are of later date), but there are transoms at mid-height, which makes them more decidedly Perpendicular in character.[5] The east window, which is of seven lights, shows a greater advance towards the maturity of that style, but there is still only one transom across the lower part.[6] All these windows are richly adorned with stained glass (the east window being a "Jesse window"), which has recently been restored.[7]

Originally there was a richly carved reredos beneath the east window, some

---

(1) The costume of the figures plainly indicates the date of this arras. There are two Latin couplets, explanatory of two scenes, worked in these fragments:—

"*Jurare David tremuit in Nabal vindicare*
Armigeros admonuit stultum extirpare."

"*Abigail percipiens ineptiam mariti*
Graui David cupiens benigne reniti."

It may formerly have adorned the chapel. (See note 3, p. 181.)

(2) Cockerell, p. 20.

(3) This room, which is lighted by three small windows, is said to have been the library. "The floor is in plaster." Mr. Cockerell (p. 20) considers it difficult to suppose that the books catalogued in the founder's lists were deposited here.

"The door and bolt are of the date of the building." (Ibid.)

(4) Cockerell, p. 18.

(5) The arches of these windows are not (like those in the cathedral) segments, but are complete, and of an exceedingly good and elegant form. There are three lights in each, and the mullions are carried through from top to bottom, the head of the centre light being bisected by a smaller mullion, over a transom, crossing it a little lower than the points of the arches, which are made at the heads of the lateral lights.

(6) The mullions in this window are carried from top to bottom also, and the three lights on each side of the central one are made into an arch, the tracery in which very closely resembles that of the other windows. The upper part of the central light is bisected, and in the head is a very irregular quatrefoil.

(7) The windows of the south side of the chapel contain figures of Isaiah, David, Jeremiah, Daniel, Hosea, Amos, St. Peter, St. Andrew, St. James the Great, St. John, St. James the Less, St. Thomas, St. Martin, St. Athelwold, St. Edward, St. Leonard, St. Oswald, St. Giles, St. Stephen, St. Anne, and St. Mary Magdalen; and those on the side, the figures of Joel, St. Mary, Haggai, St. Thomas, Zephaniah, St. Swithin, Ezekiel, St. Dunstan, Zachariah, St. Birinus, Obadiah, St. Christopher, St. Matthew, St. Edmund, St. Simon, and St. Jude, St. George, St. Augustin, St. Wolstan, and St. Lawrence. (Walcott, pp, 221, 222.)

In the east window the prostrate figure of Jesse occupies the lower part of the three central lights; on the right hand are the figures of King Richard II. and the founder

part of which can still be seen, and a row of stalls along each side of the chapel; but they were removed in 1681 by Warden Nicholas, and the modern carved wainscoting, which now surrounds the interior, substituted for them. The floor of black and white marble is the work of the same period. The ceiling, with its fan-tracery of wood (of which style it is probably a very early example), was, happily, out of the reach of this well-intending but mistaken improver.

At the western end of the chapel there is an ante-chapel, separated from the larger chapel by a screen of the same style as the wainscoting; over which, it appears, the roodloft originally was; and on the south side of this ante-chapel is Warden Thurburn's Chantry, on the bosses of the vaults of which are the arms of the founder, and the arms and rebuses of various benefactors.[1] The south window was given by the scholars and commoners as a memorial of affection to the Rev. Charles Wordsworth (now bishop of St. Andrew's), when second master.[2]

Thurburn's Chantry.

himself, and on the left hand King Edward III. and the Salutation; in the next series the central light contains the figure of David; those on the right hand, Absalom, Nathan, and Elisha; and those on the left Ammon, Samuel, and Elijah; and in the series next beneath the transom are Solomon, in the central light, Abia, Jehoshaphat, and Micah to the right of him, and Rehoboam, Ara, and Isaiah to the left. Above the transom the central light contains the figures of the Blessed Virgin and Infant Jesus, and above this the Crucifixion; whilst on the right hand, in three tiers, are the figures of Hezekiah, Joash, Amos; Zerubbabel, Manasseh, Daniel; St. John, Jeconiah, and Malachi; and on the left are those of Joram, Jotham, Jeremiah; Ahaz, Josiah, Ezekiel; the Blessed Virgin, Zedekiah, and Zachariah. In the tracery of the central light above the Crucifixion are St. Peter and St. Paul, and the Resurrection.

The figures of Simon Membury, clerk of the works; William Wynford, the mason; with the carpenter and the glazier, are introduced at the head and feet of Jesse.

All this glass, with the exception of about half-a-dozen small fragments, is modern, but it is pronounced by Mr. Winston (Arch. Inst. Winchester Vol., "Short Notice," &c., p. 4) to be "a very good copy of the old."

Bishop Lowth, when a scholar here, wrote as a school imposition a poem upon this Jesse Window, which was published in a miscellany called "The Union," in 1729, and is reprinted in Wordsworth's "College of St. Mary Winton" (pp. 77, &c.)

(1) "The thurible for Thurburn; a capital C, with tapers *in saltire*, for Chandler; three sugar-loaves for Hugh Sugar; a beacon and tun for Beckington." (Walcott, p. 222.)

In this ante-chapel stand some of the stalls, which were removed from the chapel by Warden Nicholas. Here also Wykeham ordered a copy of the statutes of the college to be set up.

(2) This memorial window (which, happily, comme-

morates not the dead, but the living) contains, in the first light, St. Paulinus, and beneath him the administration of Holy Baptism; in the second, St. Clement, with a bishop catechising; in the third, St. Peter, with our Lord's charge to that apostle (after Raffaelle) beneath; in the next, St. Cyril, and the rite of confirmation; and in the last, St. Augustin, and the administration of the Eucharist. The following is the inscription crossing the window at the base:—

"BAPTIZATOS CATECHESI, PASTOR, MAGISTER, PER CONFIRMATIONEM ET S. EUCHARISTIAM ET AD OMNIA CŒLESTIA, MEMORES GRATOSQUE DISCIPULOS DUCEBAT."

(Walcott, pp. 224, 225.)

Part of the glass which formerly adorned the windows of this chantry is at the present time in the windows of the library. The subjects are described by Wavell (vol. i. pp. 96—99) to this effect:—the arms of Wykeham, Beckington, and three others; a bishop in his robes, supported by two other bishops; and an archbishop, mitred, with his cross, and two chaplains praying, to represent the consecration of Wykeham; the Blessed Virgin, and a student at his devotions, with these words on a scroll from his mouth—

"FELIX PRECATRIX MIHI SIS PRECOR AUXILIATRIX;"

St. Anne teaching the Virgin, with a female praying, and this inscription on a label—

"O MIHI PER NATUM VITAM PRECOR ANNA BEATUM;"

a representation of God the Father with the Saviour in his arms, and under them two men praying at a table, and these inscriptions on scrolls at their mouths—

"PER MORTEM NATI QUI MUNDUM VIVIFICASTI,"

"SIMUS SALVATI PETIMUS QUOS IPSE CREASTI;"

and the following inscription—

"ORATE PRO, ANIMA MAGISTRI WILLĪ DENSFORD, QUONDAM SOCII PERPETUI HUJUS COLLEGII, QUI OBIIT

The Tower.   This chantry is now divided into two parts by a wall, built in the hope of preventing the destruction of the tower, to which the western half serves as the basement story, and which rises conspicuously above all the buildings of the college, with its square-headed windows, and panelled battlements, and pinnacles, all in good Perpendicular style. The buttresses are gabled in imitation of Wykeham's; and the turret of the staircase, covered with a small plain spire, supplies the place of the north-east pinnacle.[1]

The organ, which fills the arch of the easternmost window on the north side, was "built by the elder Harris, and improved by Green;" the eagle was presented by some of the college prefects in 1848, and the font by the present head master, Dr. Moberly; the altar-piece by Le Moyne, representing the Salutation, was the gift of Dr. Burton, a former head master; and the two double-gilt silver candlesticks were given by Christopher Eyre, formerly second master of the college.[2]

The Muniment   A door on the north side of the chapel, near the altar rail, conducts by a spiral
Room.   stair to the muniment room, a highly interesting place to the antiquary, for there, in oaken presses (ornamented with the familiar linen-pattern) of the date of the founder, and in coffers that may be still more ancient, are arranged in perfect order and preservation a most magnificent series of bulls, rolls, and charters, &c., relating to the college, and to its possessions;[3] and with them (it is said) such relics as "the travelling-case" for Wykeham's mitre, and the locker for his copes.[4]

This chamber is fireproof, and the windows are closed by the original iron-bound shutters. The ceiling is vaulted, and "the springers present an archbishop in benediction, a bishop, and a king, and over the door a guardian angel. Bosses of oak-leaves and roses alternately, carved with great taste and *subtilité*, enrich and cover the junction of the ribs."[5]

Under this chamber is a room, which was formerly the repository of the plate and vestments belonging to the chapel. There is in it a curious wooden platform,

---

OCTAVO DIE DECEMB. ANN. DM. 1476. CUJUS ANIME PROPICIETUR DEUS."

Part of another inscription contained only the words, "AGNETIS UXORIS EJUS;" and across the whole width of the window, at the base, was this, which had partly perished—

". . . . HULYN, A.M. . . . SCHOLA GRAMMATICALI HUJUS COLLEGII ET PRO ANIMABUS PARENTUM ET AMICORUM EORUNDEM."

(1) The window of the ringing loft is square-headed, with two lights and a transom, so as to be divided into four small cinquefoiled arches. The belfry story is ornamented with cinquefoiled arches under square hoodmoulds, resembling an arcade, some of which are pierced with quatrefoils, &c., for sound holes.

"At the period of the Reformation " . . . . the lower part of the north wall of the oratory, or basement story,

of this fine tower was weakened by cutting two arches through it, in consequence of which the tower exhibited such signs of being in danger of falling, that in 1671, and again, and more effectually, in 1777, some new substructure was attempted. But only one bell out of the five, which compose the peal, is ever used, for fear of destroying the tower. (Walcott, pp. 223, 224.)

(2) Walcott, pp. 216, 221, 224.

"Amongst the organists occur the names of Thomas Weelkes, B. Mus, author of 'Madrigals,' George King, ... John Reading [to whom we are indebted for the music of the *Domum*, the *Hymnus Matutinus*, and the College Grace], John Bishop, Kent, Fussell, G. W. Chard, and Dr. Wesley." (Walcott, p. 216.)

(3) The whole of this splendid collection has been examined and calendered by the Rev. W. H. Gunner.

(4) Cockerell, p. 19.

(5) Ibid. The lowest windows in this portion of the

with steps to it, which may have been the place for a watcher; and there are indications of an opening directly into the chapel, beside the altar.[1] There is another chamber over the muniment room; and the turret containing the stair, rises boldly above the leads of the chapel.

South of the chapel and the tower are the cloisters, the side of which is not *The Cloisters.* parallel to the wall of the chapel (the orientation of which is nearly the same as that of the cathedral), but more nearly due east and west. The length of each side of the square is about a hundred and twelve feet, and the length of each side of the included cloister-garth about eighty-four feet.[2] The tracery in the open three-light window arches round it (nine on each side) is very good Perpendicular, resembling Wykeham's other work in the cathedral and college. The roofs are of plain segmental-arched timber.[3]

In the middle of the square of the cloisters stands the Library, which was originally *The Library.* a chantry chapel, with a chamber (probably meant for a *scriptorium*) above it.[4] There are two three-light windows on each side of this chapel, and one of five lights at each end, the entrance being beneath an elegant square hood-mould, which fills up almost all the lower part of the west window.[5] "It is thirty-six feet in length, and eighteen feet in breadth. The roof is richly groined, and springs from responds; upon the bosses are carved shields charged with the arms of Henry VI. and John of Gaunt, the Cardinals Beaufort and Stratford, and Bishop Beckington."[6]

Few libraries of no greater extent than this can boast so many literary and historical treasures; and they have recently been rearranged in new presses, which are in harmony with the purpose and style of the place; and it is the desire of the Warden and the Fellows that literary men should know and avail themselves, as far as is practicable, of the rarities which have been transmitted to their care.[7]

---

chapel are of three lights; those in the muniment room, and the chamber above it, are of two lights, and all are of a plain but elegant and quite early Perpendicular design.

(1) I am indebted to the Rev. W. H. Gunner for information respecting this room, which has commonly been called the "sacristy."

(2) See Cockerell's plan, Pl. ii.

(3) The plain parts of the stonework in the cloisters bear many incised names of former scholars, amongst which we read with interest those of "Tho. Ken, 1646;" "Francis Turner, 1655;" "Tho. Warton," &c.

(4) This is the opinion of the Rev. W. H. Gunner. Mr. Cockerell thinks it may have been "the dormitory and cell" of the chaplain; but his lodgings were at the west end of the north side of the quadrangle. (Wavell, vol. i. p. 128.)

(5) The stained glass in the window at the west end is modern; in the east window is the glass from Thurburn's Chantry. (See note 2, p. 183.)

(6) Walcott, p. 241.

(7) An account of the rarer books and MSS. contained in this library was published in the *Literary Gazette* of December the 29th, 1855, from which I take the following notes:—

Amongst the earliest MSS. are some Anglo-Saxon charters, which appear not to have been printed by Kemble in his Codex Diplomaticus; and there are royal charters from the Conqueror to Charles II. There is a volume of letters of the time of Queen Elizabeth, containing some written by that sovereign. Besides a copy of the Taxatio Ecclesiastica of Pope Nicholas, there is a Taxatio of the Diocess of Winchester alone, of Bishop Orlton's time. A roll of the household expenses of William of Wykeham possesses great interest. Two rolls ascribed by Bishop Bale to Roger Alban, a Carmelite of London, contain the history of the world from the creation, in two divisions, sacred and profane. There are also a commentary of Paschasius Radbertus on Jeremiah; a Latin translation of the Antiquities of Josephus; "*Liber Smaragdi,*" a collection of passages from the early Fathers; Peter Comestor's "*Historia Scholastica;*"

The roof of the *scriptorium* is of plain timber, supported by beams springing from corbels carved with angels bearing shields. On each side there are four windows, and one at each end.[1]

Monumental Brasses of Wardens in the chapel.

At the same time that Warden Nicholas removed the stalls from the chapel, he took up the ancient brasses from before the altar, and put them in the ante-chapel, where those which remain still are. Some of these are very fine, but most of them are worn, and a few are placed so as to be in part concealed by some stairs, &c.; but others have been taken away or destroyed. The most conspicuous among them are (or were) those of John Morys, the first warden of the college :—

"HIC JACET MAGISTER JOHES MORYS, PRIMUS CUSTOS ISTIUS COLLĪI, QUI OBIIT DIE UNDECIM MILLIA VIRGINUM [October 21st], ANNO DNĪ MILLESIMO CCCCXIII, ET ANNO REGNI REGIS HENRICI QUINTI PRIMO, LITERA DOMINICAL. A. CUIUS ANIME PROPICIETUR DEUS."

Of Robert Thurburn,[2] his successor—

"CUSTOS ROBERTUS THURBERN COGNOMINE DICTUS,
EN MORIOR CERTUS, CUI NON PARCIT NECIS ICTUS,
SPES MEA, VERA QUIES, BONE JESU, SUSCIPE GRATUM
QUEM TRECENA DIES RAPIT OCTOBRIS VERE STRATUM.
ANNO MILLENO DOMINI C QUATER SOCIATO
ET QUINQUAGINTA MORIOR, BONE CHRISTE, JUVATO,
DEPRECOR ORERIS PRO ME CUSTODE SECUNDO
DISCAS LEGE PARI, CUSTOS, NON CREDERE MUNDO."

Higden's "*Polycronicon;*" MSS. of some of Roger Bacon's works; the Offices of the Blessed Virgin; the Legend of St. Thomas-à-Becket; the Story of Prince Arthur; one of the Wicliffite translations of the Scriptures; a MS. of the Vulgate of the thirteenth century, &c., &c.

Amongst the early printed books is perhaps the finest copy known of one of Caxton's rarest volumes, "The Lyf of Saint Katherine of Sene;" two, at least, Wynkyn de Worde's, one in the original oak binding, &c.; "an extraordinary collection of old English poetry, rich in pageants and masks;" one of the earliest pieces of James I., not contained in the collective edition of his works; a unique copy of one of George Wither's productions, &c. Besides these, there is a rich collection of "theology, particularly of the period of the Reformation; Bibles in all languages, and of all dates, concordances, lexicons, and fathers of the church; the works of Purchas, Hakluyt, &c." Raleigh's "Briefe Description of the Newe-founde Lande of Virginia," "one of the rarest of all rare books;" an absolutely unique copy of an unfinished edition of Polybius, by the Rev. Mr. Williams, every other copy of which was destroyed; with others of both ancient and modern times, valuable from their usefulness, as those I have here named are from their rarity or curiousness.

Besides the books and MSS., there are some relics of great curiosity and interest preserved here, such as Wykeham's finger ring.

"A catalogue of books belonging to the College of St. Mary, Winchester, in the reign of Henry VI.," from a MS. register in the Library itself, has been printed by the Rev. W. H. Gunner in the Arch. Journal, vol. xv., pp. 59—74. It is a paper of very great general archæological and literary value.

(1) Cockerell, p. 21.

The windows of this oratory "were formerly ornamented with curious painted glass," says Wavell (vol. i. p. 130), which has been long since destroyed. All that remained legible near a hundred years ago, or upwards, were the following :—In one window, the picture of a bishop writing in a book; under him, ". . . . S. EPŪS . . . ." In another window, a bishop writing as before, with "ROBERTUS LINCOLNIENSIS." In another window are two doctors writing; under them, ". . . . DOCTOR . . . ." Under the whole, "MATILDÆ QUONDAM UXOR JOHANNIS FROMOND LEGAVIT COLLEGIO WINTON. CYPHUM HARNESIATUM CUM ARGENTO DEAURATUM VOCATUM . . . ."

On one of these cups was engraved—

"HE SHALL HAVE CRYSTES BLESSING TO HIS DELE WHOSO OF ME DRINKETH WELE."

(Ibid. p. 129.)

"This chapel was converted into a library, A.D. 1629, [chiefly by the munificence of] Robert Pink, Warden" [of New College, Oxford]. (Ibid.)

(2) Wavell (ibid. p. 116) says of this brass, and of those of Wardens Cleve, and Stempe, Fellows Vole, Walynford, and Fraunces, and Warden Bouke, "these . . . . were torn off long since . . . . are preserved. Some of them do not at present appear;" and they are now, as I am informed, in all probability, lost.

Of Michael Cleve, the fifth warden, on four roundels of brass, which formed the corner pieces of the monuments, first, the figure of St. Michael, with—

" SATRAPA CŒLORUM MICHAEL CUSTOS PARADISI
SORTEM JUSTORUM CUSTODI DA MICHAELI ;"

on the second, St. John, with this inscription—

" MORE VOLANS AQUILÆ SCRUTANSQ3 ABSCONDITA VERBI
CŒLESTIS PATRIÆ REQUIEM CONFER MICHAELI ;"

on the third, some arrows, with—

" CUI SEBASTE DEDIT NOMEN CONFOSSE SAGITTIS
PRÆSTA· PERPETUE MICHAELI GAUDIA LUCIS ;"

on the fourth, under a figure praying to the Blessed Virgin—

" VIRGO FACTA PARENS DUM CONSENTIS GABRIELI
SERVO SANCTA TUO NATUM PLACA MICHAELI."

Of Bishop White, the ninth warden, with a long epitaph[1] composed by himself, in Latin verse, and placed in the chapel in anticipation of his death, which proved to be a mere cenotaph; for, living in the troublous times of the Reformation, it was his lot to be extruded from his office, and imprisoned; then raised to the see of Winchester, from which, also, he was ejected, and again imprisoned; and, finally, he "died in obscurity, and was buried, by his own desire, in the cathedral," without any record of the spot.[2]

Of Warden Stempe, the eleventh in the series, thus inscribed :—

" THOMÆ STEMPE CUSTODIS IN HOC COLLEGIO UNDECIMI, LLD[ris] ET SACRÆ THEOLOGIÆ MUSICESQ3 LAUDE CLARISSIMI, EPITAPHIUM.

" QUI JACET HIC CUSTOS VIGINTI QUATUOR ANNOS
PRÆFUIT, ET QUI SIT SI LEGIS ISTA, SCIES.
VOCE MANUQ3 MODOS DIDICIT FORMARE CANOROS,
ADDIDIT HUIC LINGUAS RHETORICAMQ3 PUER.
GRANDIOR AD LEGES CIVILES IBAT, IN ILLIS
DOCTOR, ET HUIC JUDEX NON SINE LAUDE FUIT.
PRESBYTER IN SACRIS SCRIPTURIS PLURIMUS HÆSIT,
QUAS POPULO ACCEPTAS, PLAUSIBILESQ3 DEDIT.
QUID MEMOREM VITA QUAM SE CONSTANTER IN OMNI
PRÆSTITIT, ET FLUXAS QUAM PROPE SPREVIT OPES."
" OBIIT NONO DIE FEB. 1581."

Of Dr. Love, the fourteenth warden, with an inscription commemorating his excellence, learning, and honours, "composed," says Milner,[3] "by the regicide Nicholas Love," the warden's son, and "breathing a spirit of piety, though tinctured with Pagan mythology, and of veneration for the college, and the old founders of it, which we should not expect from a writer of his character."

---

(1) Wavell (ibid. pp. 110, 111) gives this at length, but incomplete, "above half the inscription being covered with a pew."

(2) Milner, vol. ii. p. 143.

(3) Ibid. Milner's censure is hypercritical. See the inscription in Wavell (*u. s.* pp. 105, 106).

Of Dr. Harris, Love's successor, who died on the 11th of August, 1658, of whom the inscription states, that—

"IN DIFFICILI SÆCULI ILLIUS ÆSTUARIO PER VARIAS TEMPESTATES NAVIM CUI PRÆFIC-
IEBATUR, CUM DEO REXIT ET SOSPITAVIT, NEC TAMEN SÆCULA QUIBUS USUS EST COLUIT,
SED SÆCULORUM DEUM."

Also of an unknown warden,[1] the inscription belonging to which is lost, but on a scroll at his mouth is written—

"CUM NON POSSITIS FRATRES EVADERE MORTEM ME . . . ."

And one of John Bouke, Warden of New College, Oxford, who died March the 2nd, 1442.

Mural Monuments of Wardens in the chapel. There are also four mural monuments of Wardens Braithwaite, Cobb, Coxed, and Golding, the eighteenth, nineteenth, twenty-second, and twenty-third in the series, who died in the years 1720, 1724, 1757, and 1763, respectively.[2]

Monumental Brasses of Fellows and others in the chapel. In addition to these three are (or were[3]) brasses commemorating the following fellows of the college :—William Walynford, who died in 1339 ; John Cleir, 1421 ; John Wyllynghall, 1432 ; John Frances, and Nicholas North, 1445 ; William Nyghtyngale, 1467 ; John Beckynton, 1473 ; John Wyght, 1494 ; Thomas Lyripin, 1509 ; Thomas Ashburn, 1516 ; John Barrat, 1523 ; Thomas Basset (who was also sub-warden), 1555 ;[4] Dr. John Leffe, 1557 ; and Thomas Vole, the last, to this effect :—

"EPIT. T. VOLE OLIM SOCII.
"UT VOLUS IN MONTEM DÑI VOLAT ORE VOLENTI
CHRISTO FUNDE PRECES CHRISTUM QUICUMQ3 PRECARIS."
"OBIIT X DIE AUGUSTI, AN. 1558."

There are also brasses to Henry Kesewyk, "*specialis amicus hujus Collegii*," 1409 ; John Bedell (Mayor of Winchester), and of Johanna, his wife, 1498, and 1497 ; and of William Exule, 1521.

Other Mural Monuments in the chapel. Mural monuments commemorate William Wither, who died 1656 ; Humphrey May, 1657 ; Richard Osgood, 1684 ; and John Taylor,—Fellows ; Thomas Cheyney, 1724 ; John Burton, 1766 ; and Henry D. Gabell, 1824,—Head-masters ; William Madgwick, "*perliteratus concionator*," 1623 ; and Charles B. Henville, 1849.

The Crimean Monument. But the most striking monument is one recently erected to the Wykehamists who fell in the Crimean war, the inscription of which was written by the present Warden. It consists of a plinth with an arcade of five Early English arches on the west side of the porch to the chapel ; the shafts of the columns are of richly polished marble, and

(1) Wavell, vol. i. pp. 111, 112.

(2) Wavell (ibid. pp. 120, 121, 125, 127) gives the inscriptions on these monuments in full.

(3) I am informed by the Rev. W. H. Gunner, that great numbers of these brasses, and of those belonging to the cloisters, are not now to be found.

(4) The lines on this brass were written by C. Johnson, and may be inserted here on that account :—

"HIC BASSETE JACES NULLO MEMORANDUS IN ÆVO
SI TUA IN HÆREDES GRATIA SOLA FORET,
NUNC QUID ME GRATIS VICECUSTOS ESSE SCHOLAREM
JUSSERIS, HOC GRATIS PRÆSTO TIBI OFFICIUM.
TEQ3 LEGENT ALII UT TUA (QUANQUAM O) FACTA
SEQUANTUR,
ET MONITI DICANT: OPTIME, VIVE DEO."
"C. JHONSON POSUIT. MDLXI."

the capitals are angels, with the words " FAITH, VIRTUE, KNOWLEDGE, TEMPERANCE, PATIENCE, CHARITY ;" and along the base, in large Lombardic characters—

" HE IS NOT A GOD OF THE DEAD, BUT OF THE LIVING, FOR ALL LIVE TO HIM."

The two arches on each side are occupied with the names of those who are commemorated; and in the central arch is this inscription :—

" THIS PORCH HAS BEEN PREPARED AND BEAUTIFIED BY WILLIAM OF WYKEHAM'S SONS, AS A SACRED SHRINE, IN WHICH THE MEMORIES OF THEIR THIRTEEN BRETHREN WHO DIED IN THE WAR OF THE CRIMEA, A.D. 1854-5, MAY BE PRESERVED FOR AN EXAMPLE TO FUTURE GENERATIONS. THINK UPON THEM THOU WHO ART PASSING BY TO-DAY, CHILD OF THE SAME FAMILY, BOUGHT BY THE SAME LORD ; KEEP THY FOOT WHEN THOU GOEST INTO THIS HOUSE OF GOD ; THERE WATCH THINE ARMOUR, AND MAKE THYSELF READY BY PRAYER TO FIGHT AND TO DIE, THE FAITHFUL SOLDIER AND SERVANT OF CHRIST, AND OF THY COUNTRY."

The monuments in the cloisters are very numerous, and consist for the most part of brasses and tablets, now inserted into the walls.[1]

There are brasses in the west cloister commemorating the following Fellows :— William Laus, who died 1417 ; Edward Tacham, 1422 ; William Ball, 1471 ; John Taknell, 1494 ; Thomas Ryve, 1523 ; Thomas Beche, 1531 ; John Dolber,[2] 1560 ; William Adkins, 1561 ; Edmund Hodson,[3] 1580 ; Thomas Jones,[4] 1585 ; Thomas Davison,[5] 1586 ; and Thomas Geffres, 1615.

Monumental Brasses of Fellows in the cloisters.

In the south cloister are brasses to Richard Bowman,[6] 1464, and John Curtoys, both Fellows ; in the east cloister, to John Gilbert, John Grewaker, and Richard

---

(1) Warton and Wavell print, with various errors, all the inscriptions existing in the cloisters in their time. A collection of those " of the period immediately subsequent to the Reformation " was communicated to " Notes and Queries " (2nd Series, vol. ii. pp. 195, 196) by the Rev. W. H. Gunner.

Two ancient, but undated, inscriptions are engraved on the sides of two buttresses of the west cloister :—

" HIC JACET WILLMUS WILLKOK."

"ORATE PRO AIA JOHIS LEYERE."

(2) As some of these inscriptions are both interesting and curious, I insert a few specimens.

This lies at the entrance to the cloisters :—

" EPI. M. JO. DOL. SOCII.
DEFUNCTI 3. APRILIS, 1560.
CLAUSTRI PRO FORIBUS DOLBERUM CERNE SEPULTUM,
UMBRARUM ASSESSOR, JANITOR ILLE LOCI EST:
NON MALUS ILLE FUIT, QUI VERBA NOVISSIMA DIXIT,
O BONE CHRISTE, PRECOR TE MISERERE MEI.
SANCTORUM ASSESSOR, VEL CÆLI JANITOR UT SIT,
FUNDE PIAS CHRISTE, LECTOR AMICE, PRECES."

(3) " EDMUNDE HODSON, CLERKE AND FELLOW OF THIS COLLEGE,
" DIED THE VII. OF AUGUST, 1580.

" WHOSO THOU ART, WITH LOVINGE HARTE,
STANDE, READE, AND THINKE ON ME ;
FOR AS I WAS, SO NOWE THOU ARTE ;
AND AS I AM, SO SHALTE THOU BE."

(4) " EPITAPHIUM THOMÆ JONES IN LEGIBUS BACHILERII QUONDAM HUJUS COLLEGII SOCII.

" HIC JACEO, JUVENIS, PRIMUM CIVILIA JURA
QUI DIDICI, QUI IDEM SACRA SECUTUS ERAM ;
QUI VITAM MORBIS VARIIS, GRAVIBUSQUE PEREGI ;
TANDEM PER TE (MORS) HOC REQUIESCO LOCO ;
JURA MIHI MULTUM, PLUS PAGINA SACRA PLACEBAT ;
NEMPE FUIT MORBIS HÆC MEDICINA MEIS.

" DUM VIXIT SEPE IN ORE HABUIT, SATIS DIU VIXI,
SI DNO SATIS. OBIIT 16. DIE SEPt ANO DNI 1585."

(5) " THO. DAVISON, OBIIT 20 JULII, 1586.
" HIC NUNC DENIQUE DAVISONE PUTRES ;
TRIGINTA SOCIUS PERENNIS ANNOS ;
VIVENS, IPSE TIBI NIMIS SEVERUS ;
EXPIRANS, ALIIS SATIS PROFUSUS."

(6) Wavell (vol. i. p. 150) gives this name and date in a note, with " MS. W. N." appended, apparently as his authority ; as does Warton also.

Skynner, 1514; John Dere, 1532; Thomas Lark,[1] 1582; and Robert Watton, 1596, —all of them Fellows; and in the north cloister, to John Clerke,[2] 1571; John Scott, 1575; and George Flower,[3] 1578,—likewise Fellows.

Ledgers or tablets in the west cloister also record the burial of these Fellows:—John Boles, 1610; John Marshall, 1670; Thomas Colnet, 1679; Joseph Cox, 1680; Anthony Rous, 1681; Charles Emes, 1703; Richard Barker, 1716; and John Oglander, 1814: in the south cloister, Henry Hendyg, 1433;[4] Jonathan Cooke, 1574; Stephen Cooke, 1666; Henry Banks, 1672; John Chalkhill, 1679; Charles Scott, 1762; Charles Blackstone, 1813; and Harry Lee, 1838: in the east cloister, Rice Price, 1782; Daniel Williams, 1788; John Ballard, 1789; Benjamin Jeffreys, 1799; and John Penrose Cumming, 1810: and in the north cloister, Robert Beely, 1634; Lancelot White, 1642; William Terry, 1657; Thomas Harris, 1642; John Marshall, 1670; and Henry Sissmore, 1851.

A brass in the west cloister commemorates Richard Dean, the thirteenth headmaster, who died in 1484.

In the west cloister there are also the following monuments: a brass to William Clyffe,[5] first chaplain of Fromond's Chantry, 1433; and another to Thomas Emes, chaplain of the college, 1629;[6] with a ledger to William Emes, organist of the chapel, 1637; and another to John Bishop, a more distinguished organist, 1737.

The south cloister shows brasses to John Fylde, 1507; John Hopkyns, "*conductitius*," 1514; Richard Cole, "*conductitius*," 1519; and Maurice Morrys, chaplain, 1523: and tablets to Christopher Badger, 1635; Mariott Stopes, 1673; and Thomas Welsted ("*quem calculi ictu mors prostravit*"), 1676; to Owen Phillips, "*Hostiarius*" (whose name, cut in the stone sill of the cloister arch, may yet be seen nearly opposite his monument), 1654; to Joshua Cook, chaplain, 1648; and William Trenchard, 1713.

Monuments to William Turner,[7] chaplain, 1644; and to Walter Garrett, and Jane, his wife, 1737 and 1738, are in the east cloister.

Side note: Other Monuments of Fellows in the cloisters.

Side note: Other Monuments in the cloisters.

(1) "EPITAPHIUM MAGISTRI THOMÆ LARKE NUPER, SOCII ISTIUS COLLEGII. OB. 16 MAII, 1582.

"QUI PREMOR HOC TUMULO, DICOR PRÆNOMINE THOMAS,
  COGNOMEN FUIT DULCIS ALAUDA MIHI.
BIS SEPTEM MENSES, TER SEPTEM PRESBYTER ANNOS,
  HIC COLUI, CUJUS NUNC FRUOR, ORE DEUM."

(2)   "EPITA. JO. CLERKE.
"CLAUSUS JOANNES JACET HOC SUB MARMORE CLERKUS,
  QUI FUIT HIC QUONDAM PRESBITER ET SOCIUS,
IN TERRA ROSEOS SOLITUS STILLARE LIQUORES,
  IN CÆLO VIVIS NUNC QUOQUE GAUDET AQUIS.

  "OBIIT Xº DIE MENSIS JUNII, 1571."

(3) "EPITA. GEORGII FLOWER, IN ARTIBUS MAGISTRI.
"ECCE GEORGIUS HOC FLORUS SUB MARMORE DORMIT.
FLORUERAT, SED FLOS ILLE CADUCUS ERAT.

BIS SEPTEM SOCIUS VIX HIC TRANSEGERAT ANNOS,
  MORS PEDE QUUM PULSAT, FLORUS UT HINC ABEAT.
  "OBIIT 18º DIE NOVEMBRIS, Aº 1578."

(4) Wavell (*u. s.* p. 143, note) supplies this date, which is not inserted on the brass.

(5) "ORATE PRO AĪA DŃI WILLĪ CLYFFE, PRIMI CAPELLANI ISTIUS CAPELLE, QUI OBIIT XXIIII DIE MENSIS MARTII, AN. DŃI MCCCCXXXIII. CUIUS AĪE ꝒPICIETUR DEUS."

(6) Another brass, partly destroyed, shows the following:—
"PRAY FOR THE SOUL OF EDWARD . . . . NEW COLLEGE OF WYNCHESTER . . . . OF SEPTEMB. THE YEARE OF OUR LORD . . . ." (Wavell, *u. s.* p. 137).

(7)   "GULIELMUS TURNER,
  "HUJUS COLLEGII CLERICUS; OBIIT 14º
  "DIE MARTII, ANNO DOMINI 1644.   ["OLIM

In the north cloister are brasses to Philip Derenee, chaplain, 1578 ; and John Gray, 16 — : and other monuments to George King, organist, 1665 ; and to William Windham, 1678 ; James Beach, 1740 ; and John Bingham, 1768,—all of them scholars at the time of their death.

Our survey of the ancient buildings of the college terminates here ; we now proceed to the modern buildings. The School-room, which is the most important of these, forms the south side of a small court lying to the west of the cloisters. It is a plain brick building, erected in the year 1687, at the expense of the Wykehamists ; and is ninety feet in length, by thirty-six wide, and lighted by six large windows on the north side. The entrance is in the middle of the same side, and over it is a bronze statue of the founder, by Cibber, the sculptor, who presented it to the college.[1]

The interior is lofty and well proportioned ; round the cornice of the ceiling (which is divided into compartments, and ornamented with garlands) are the arms of the following principal contributors to the building fund :[2]—Bishops Ken, Morley, and Turner ; William Pierpoint, Earl of Kingston ; Charles Pawlett, Earl of Wilts ; Wriothesley Baptist Noel, Viscount Campeden ; Wardens Nicholas and Beeston, and Dr. Harris. The walls are covered to half their height with dark wainscot, and a bookcase, with the stove in front of it, stands opposite the entrance. The seat of the head-master, and those occasionally occupied by the warden and sub-warden, are on the right-hand side of the bookcase ; the second master's seat is on the left ; and the seats of the lower masters are on the north side of the room. Across each end of the room are three rows of seats, one above another ; and four rows of benches, with cross seats, on which the "scobs"[3] (or boxes for study, &c.) are placed, extend the whole length of the building, except in front of the entrance.

In the centre of the upper part of the wall, at each end, is a tablet ; on that at the west end are depicted a mitre with a crosier, and beneath them "AUT DISCE ;" lower still, a sword, with a pen, inkhorn, &c., and under them "AUT DISCEDE ;"

The School-room.

" Disce aut Discede."

" OLIM CANTICA (MUSICÆ PERITUS)
DULCI VOCE DEDISTI, ET ARTE MULTA :
AT NUNC LONGE, ANIMA POLIS FRUENTE,
EDIS DULCIUS, PERITIUSQUE."

(1) " Under the statue is this inscription :—

' M.S. GULIELMI DE WICKHAM, EPISCOPI WINTONI-ENSIS, COLLEGII HUJUS FUNDATORIS, STATUAM HANC E METALLO CONFLANDAM, ATQUE HEIC SUMPTU SUO PONEN-DAM CURAVIT, EX CONJUGE AFFINIS SUA, CAIUS GABRIEL CIBBERUS, STATUARIUS REGIUS, MDCLXXXXII.' "
(Wavell, vol. i. p. 160).

Colley Cibber, son of the sculptor, and Poet-laureate, of "Dunciad" renown, tells a good tale of his father and this statue. "Being, by my mother's side, a descendant of William of Wickham . . . . my father, who knew little how the world was to be dealt with, imagined my having that advantage would be security enough for my success, and so sent me simply down thither without the least favourable recommendation or interest, but that of my naked merit, and a pompous pedigree in my pocket." He was, of course, not elected ; but, " the experience which my father then bought at my cost, taught him, some years after, to take a more judicious care of my younger brother, Lewis Cibber, whom, with a present of a statue of the founder, of his own making, he recom-mended to the same college. The statue . . . . was so well executed, that it seemed to speak for its kinsman. It was no sooner set up than the door of preferment was opened to him." (Quoted by Walcott, pp. 231, 232.)

(2) Lists of the contributors, with the amounts of their contributions, are given by Warton, Wavell, Walcott, &c. Warden Nicholas' was the most splendid gift, being £1477 11s. 9d., and the whole sum was £2599 18s. 9d.

(3) " Scob " is one of the words peculiar to St. Mary Winton College, and is merely box (bocs) reversed.

and at the base a four-twigged Wykehamical rod, and " MANET SORS TERTIA, CŒDI."
That at the opposite end is inscribed, " TABULA LEGUM PÆDAGOGICARUM," and contains
a series of Latin precepts relating to the general conduct of the scholars.[2]

The mathematical master has a room at the western end of the school-room,
adjoining to which is the Præfects' library, given by the late Archbishop Howley,
the lavatory, and a room for the use of the fourth book, or class.

The Play-ground. Behind the school-room, to the south, is the college meadow, which is the
playground for the scholars, who have a tennis or fives-court against the south wall
of the school-house itself; and to the west of this meadow, and separated from it by
The Infirmary. one of the brooks before mentioned,[3] is another meadow, in which stands the Infirmary,
built by Warden Harris in 1640, and enlarged by the addition of the south or
garden front, by the Rev. John Taylor, a Fellow of the college in 1775.[4]

College Meads. College Meads are bounded on the east by Non-Licet Gate, which communicates
with the College Mill, and the road leading to Black-bridge.[5]

(1) Christopher Johnson has explained this table to
signify that the rewards of learning are the dignities of the
church; that the professions of arms and the law are
open to those who prefer to stop short of those higher aims
(Milner, however, considers both sword and inkhorn
emblematical of expulsion); and that if neither of these
aims please, then there remains the rod as the only possible reward (Wordsworth's "College of St. Mary Winton,"
p. 26). The place for administering correction by the rod
is most appropriately beneath this tablet.

(2) The "Table of Laws," as it at present appears, is
the work of Bishop Huntingford; the differences between
it and the older, or original version, are noted in *italics.*

" IN TEMPLO. Deus colitor. Preces cum pio (*devoto*)
animi effectu peraguntor. Oculi ne vagantor. Silen-
tium esto. Nihil profanum legitor.

" IN SCHOLA. Diligentia quisque utitor. Submisse
loquitor secum, Clare ad præceptorem. Nemini mo-
lestus esto. Orthographice scribito. Arma scholastica
in promptu semper habeto.

" IN AULA. Qui mensas (*mensam*) consecrat Clare pro-
nunciato. Cæteri respondento. Recti interim (*omitted*)
omnes stanto. Recitationes Intelligenter et apte Dis-
tinguuntor. Ad mensas sedentibus Omnia decora sunto
(*quies esto*).

" IN ATRIO. (*In Atrio, oppido, ad montes.*) Ne quis
fenestras Saxis pilisve petito. Ædificium neve inscribendo,
Neve insculpendo deformato. Neve operto capite, Neve
sine socio, Coram magistris incedito. (*Wholly omitted.*)

" IN CUBICULIS. Munda omnia sunto. Vespere stu-
detor. Noctu quies esto (*Noctu dormitor. Interdiu stu-
detor. Solum cubiculorum verritor. Sternuntor lectuli.
Munda omnia sunto. Per fenestras nemo in atrium
Prospicito. Contra qui faxit Piaculum esto.*)

" IN OPPIDO, AD MONTEM. Sociati omnes incedunto.
Modestiam præ se ferunto. Magistris ac obviis honesti-
oribus, Capita aperiuntor (*Genua flectuntor*). Vultus,

gestus, incessus, Componuntor. Intra terminos apud
montem Præscriptos Quisque se contineto (*omitted*).

" IN OMNI LOCO ET TEMPORE. Qui Plebeius est
Præfectis obtemperato. Qui Præfectus est, Legitime im-
perato. Is ordo vitio careto (*omitted*). Cæteris specimen esto (*omitted*). Uterque a pravis omnibus Verbis
factisque (*mendaciis, ostentationibus, jurgiis, pugnis, et
furtis*) abstineto. (*Togam, cæterasque vestes, nec dis-
suito, nec lacerato. Patrium sermonem fugito, Latinum
exerceto.*) Hæc aut his similia Qui contra faxit (*omitted*).
Si quando deferantur Judicium damus.

" Feriis exactis nemo domi impune moratur (*omitted*).

" Extra collegium absque venia exeuntes tertia vice
expellimus (*omitted*)."

(3) See above, p. 178, note.

(4) Walcott, p. 261. " Upon it were carved the
words, 'SUMPTIBUS HARRISII FUIT ÆDIFICATA BETHESDA.'
Originally, the word BETHESDA, in Hebrew letters, was
inscribed over the doorway, between the arms of Wykeham,
and of Warden Harris (Wavell, vol. i. p. 169). Over the
windows, on the east side, this legend still remains :—

' VOTVM AVTHORIS PRO PVERIS.
JEHOVAH, QVI SANITATIS AVTHOR EST VNICVS, NOXIA,
PRECOR, .
OMNIA A VESTRIS CAPITIBVS ARCEAT AC REPELLAT.'
" And on the west, this sentence :—
' VOTVM PVERORVM PRO AVTHORE.
' CVBANTIS IN LECTO LANGVORIS EXTREMVS COR EIVS
ET ARTVS JEHOVAH CVRET, FOVEAT AC SVSTENTET.' "
(Ibid.)

" A house, in which the society might take refuge during the time of the plague, was built at an early period of
its history, in the hamlet of Mounsberle, or Moundsmere,
in the parish of Preston Candover " (Walcott, p. 261).

(5) In Godson's map, College Mead is divided into
two parts by a hedge running east and west.

The old wall, which separated the Mead from the ground

To the west of Wykeham's College stands Commoners, which is the residence of the Commoners. head-master, and of the scholars who are not on the foundation. The present building was erected in 1840 and 1841, by the College and the contributions of old Wykehamists, amongst whom Dr. Williams, Sir William Heathcote, Bart., Bishop Wordsworth, Lord Eldon, and a contributor who appears under the initials A. B., were the most munificent.[1] It consists of two quadrangles; the principal one, on the north, has the master's house next College Street (the front of which is faced with squared black flint and stone); the west side contains the servants' hall, with dormitories above it, and in the court nineteen small studies for the scholars; the east side is formed by the warden's stables; and the south side comprises the tutors' rooms, the infirmary, and other dormitories. The second quadrangle is open to the south, and the east wing contains the hall, and the west the refectory.[2] There is a separate playground for the Commoners, a meadow adjoining Domum Wharf, beside the Itchen.

Strictly connected with the college, although not included within its grounds, are The Domum Tree, and the Maze. the "*Domum* Tree," which formerly grew on the east side of the river below Blackbridge, at Domum Wharf, and the Maze, cut in the grass on the summit of St. Catharine's Hill;—both of them, it is true, of recent interest compared with the college itself, but rendered antique to the present generation by a legend, which has supplied, or suppressed, all reliable information respecting them.[3]

of the Carmelites, on the south, was built by the College in 1410, and its course may still be traced in dry weather across the grass. The present wall was built in 1554, after the Dissolution, of the materials obtained by pulling down St. Elizabeth's College. The following inscriptions in this wall refer to the land which was originally that of the Carmelites, the college ground, and the property of the cathedral.

On the eastern wall :—

" SOLUM ECCLESIE IN OCCIDENTALI PARTE HUJUS MURI AB HOC ANGULO."

On the western wall :—

" IN OCCIDENTALI PARTE HUJUS MURI SOLUM COLLEGII EXTENDIT SE."
" SUPER TENEMENTŪ ECCLESIE CATHEDRALIS WINTON.
" 1554."

(1) The entire cost of New Commoners was £25,000. The ground required for it was taken from Fellows' Meads.

(2) "Memorials of Winchester College." "Old Commoners was built by Dr. Burton, and formed an irregular quadrangle. On the west side were the head-master's house, an excellent ball-court, and the upper and lower cloister galleries, built over a small cloister; on the north was 'Wickham's' buildings, containing the hall of the juniors, various dormitories, and the residence of the tutors; on the south were upper and lower conduit galleries, part of the ancient 'Sustern Spital,' and divided into dormitories above, and below into apartments for the matron, and three 'Continent Rooms,' or sick bays. On the ground floor, to the west of the inner entrance, were the 'Hatches,' from which the bread (or *sines*) and cans of beer (called *jorams*) were issued; the kitchens, &c., opening into a small court containing a dormitory known as 'New Room.' On the other side were the prefects' and the tutors' studies. . . . . The entrance gate stood where the west gate of modern Commoners is at present. Parallel with the east side of the court, and to the southward of the tutors' studies, was the dining hall; and above it was a set of sleeping rooms, upper and lower hall galleries. On the westward of the hall was the conduit." (Walcott, pp. 183, 184, note).

Dr. Burton was head-master from 1724 to 1768, and he bequeathed the house he had built for himself, with portraits of some favourite pupils, to his successors. (Ibid., pp. 358, 359.)

(3) The legend tells that, "once upon a time," during the Whitsuntide vacation, one of the scholars was left at the school, as a punishment for some extraordinary offence; and that he vainly endeavoured to beguile the misery of his solitude by cutting the maze in the turf on the hill, and by composing the Latin ode, "*Dulce Domum*" (which will be found in a subsequent page); but that he pined away, and died beneath the "*Domum Tree*," singing that thrice-renowned song. The original tree has long since perished, but another has been planted in its stead. Beneath it the *Domum* used formerly to be sung, at the end of "long half."

Neither the ode nor the maze can be traced farther back than the latter part of the seventeenth century;

Government of the College.

Until recently, the government of the college has been carried on in as strict conformity to the statutes, originally appointed by the founder, as was possible after the Reformation; but, in consequence of the changes which mere lapse of time had brought in, an ordinance was framed, in 1857, by "the commissioners appointed for the purposes of the statute, 17 & 18 Vict. c. 81," modifying the regulations then in force; and in accordance with it the college is now governed.

The Society.

By the original statutes, the whole society consisted of a warden, seventy scholars, ten secular priests as fellows, three chaplains, three clerks, sixteen choristers, a school-master (called *Informator*), and an under-master (called *Hostiarius*).[1] The scholarships are, by the new ordinance, increased to a hundred, and, in addition to them, twenty exhibitions of fifty pounds a year are created. There are now also six sub-preceptors, and teachers of French, German, writing, and drawing; an organist,[2] and a master of choristers, together with the steward, surveyor, servants (all of them male, no female being admissible except when she had, through age, become *rugosa*), and porters,[3] who (as well as the Commoners) formed no part in the plan of the founder.

The Warden and Fellows.

The duties of the warden and masters are indicated with sufficient clearness by their names; those of the fellows,[4] according to Wykeham's design, related to the performance of the frequent services in the College Chapel; but as most of them were put an end to at the Reformation, the fellowships are now sinecures, and are in most instances held by clergymen who have vicarages in the patronage of the college, in augmentation of their benefices. Honorary fellowships have been made lawful by the new ordinance.

The Scholars.

Scholars[5] are now admissible between the ages of ten and fourteen years, and are open to all who can pass an examination "differing in difficulty for candidates between

---

but the composer of the former, and the constructor of the latter, are alike wholly unknown. Besides these, some mention ought to be made of "Dalmatia," "Double Hedge," "The Pot," "Newbridge" and "Tunbridge," and the "Waterman's Hut,"—places and names endeared to Wykehamists by remembrances which grow ever more sacred as years pass away.

(1) Harpsfield, who was a Wykehamist, first pointed out the mystical reason for the particular number of the scholars, "*qui sacrum septuaginta discipulorum numerum conficit.*" (*Hist. Eccl. Anglic.*) But Milner expounds the subject more fully, and shows "that the warden and ten priests, who were perpetual fellows, represented the college of the Apostles, Judas Iscariot, of course, not being represented; that the head-master and second-master, with seventy scholars, denoted the seventy-two [the reading of the Vulgate, which the founder, of course, followed] disciples, that the three chaplains and three inferior clerks marked the six faithful deacons; Nicholas, one of that number, having apostatised, has therefore no representative; finally, that the sixteen choristers represented the four greater and twelve minor prophets" (vol. ii. p. 155).

The new ordinance provides for the reduction of fellowships to six, and the application of the emoluments of the suppressed fellowships to certain scholarships and exhibitions.

(2) In the time of C. Johnson, one of the three clerks was organist.

(3) Formerly, many "servile offices" were performed by the scholars. The task of "making their own beds, and keeping their chambers clean" was abolished by Bishop Trelawney in 1708.

(4) The fellows used to live, three together, in each upper chamber, on the eastern side of the quadrangle (see above, p. 180, note). The head-master and the "*hostiarius*" had the west chamber in the northern side of the quadrangle, and the three clerks the adjoining chamber in the western side (Walcott, p. 195). Six chambers were then allotted to the scholars, and one to the choristers.

(5) For most of the information respecting the school itself I am indebted to J. D. Walford, Esq. I must also acknowledge my obligations to Mr. Wells, who has for many years conducted the business of the Bookseller to the college, Mr. D. Nutt.

ten and twelve, and those between twelve and fourteen." The exhibitions are open to all boys under fifteen years of age, and are tenable during the whole period of the exhibitioner's stay in the school, unless vacated by his subsequent election to a scholarship, or forfeited by misconduct. The qualifications required both for exhibitions and scholarships are determined by the electors, and have been so regulated as very highly to raise the standard of attainments amongst the scholars.[1]

The grammars in use in the school are *Græcæ Grammaticæ Rudimenta*, Oxford The Grammars. (Wordsworth's Greek Grammar) ; and King Edward VI.'s Latin Grammar ; and these are the only educational works invariably employed.[2] The scholars rise in the school in proportion to their progress. They are divided into six classes, known in the school as Sixth Book, Senior Part Fifth Book, Middle Part Fifth, Junior Part Fifth, and Senior and Junior Parts Fourth Book.[3]

Eighteen of the head boys in the school are invested with authority in the school, The Præfects. and assist in it as private tutors, under the title of præfects,[4] or Præpostors. Of these, ten are " in full power," and act in the place of the masters, in their absence. Special offices are borne by some, as Præfect of Hall, Præfect of School, Præfect of Chapel, Bible Clerk, *Ostiarius*. The system of " fagging " remains in force, but it is entirely altered from what it was in olden time, and regulated so as to be a source of advantage to both parties in this school-boy *clientela*.[5]

(1) " The names of the best of the candidates are arranged upon a roll, but only so many of these as are required to supply the vacancies that may occur during the ensuing year are admitted scholars, and in the order in which the names stand upon the roll." " Their character, and their pecuniary circumstances, as far as made known to the electors," are also taken into account in the making up of the roll. (Printed Notice.)

Candidates are examined in elementary religious knowledge, English dictation, arithmetic, Latin composition, both verse and prose, and in construing and parsing in Greek and Latin.

" Founder's kin," or descendants from the family of William of Wykeham, formerly enjoyed special privileges in all elections at the college, but these privileges were abolished by the new ordinance, and actually ceased in 1858.

The average number of vacancies during the last ten years has been between thirteen and fourteen.

The result of these new regulations is seen in the fact that the great majority of the scholars are in the higher classes in the school ; and that sometimes there is no lower class at all.

(2) As in all public schools, great attention is given to various species of composition, both in English and Latin, and to exercises which qualify for public speaking.

The ordinary tasks in Latin composition are in prose, verse, or " metre " (that is, any metre beside hexameters and pentameters). A " *vulgus* " is a Latin epigram of four lines, and is an exercise of the juniors ; a " varying,"

a similar composition of greater length, which is expected from the seniors.

Recitations and declamations, in English and Latin, are practised at certain parts of the year.

Encouragement has been given lately to mathematical study, but as a member of the University of Oxford, St. Mary Winton College could not be so unfaithful to its traditions as to follow the sister University too closely.

Still less could it be expected that natural science should be encouraged, but it is cultivated by some among the scholars.

(3) The scholars receive their schooling, board, and lodging free, with one black cloth gown yearly, but are chargeable for instruction in modern languages, præfects' tuition (before they reach the sixth class), books, &c., the amount of which charges varies from £15 to £30 *per ann.*

The exhibitions are for boys not on the foundation, and are to assist in defraying their school expenses.

In the yearly roll the choristers are inserted as the second class.

(4) Small payments are made to the præfects in acknowledgment of their services as tutors.

(5) This portion of the discipline of our public schools, which in former times called forth such merited expressions of abhorrence, has been so greatly humanized within the last quarter of a century—*responsibility* being imposed on those who are permitted to exercise authority, and menial service provided for menial duty—that it may now be regarded as one of the most beneficial features of these peculiarly English institutions. It is by thus

School-terms. Each session is divided first into " short half " and " long half;" the former including the time from October to Christmas, and the latter that from Christmas to July. It is also divided into " Common time," extending from October till Easter; " Easter time," the six weeks from Easter till Whit Sunday; and " Cloister time," the remainder of the " long half;" but the last week is called " Standing up week," from the recitations which are delivered then by the lower half of the school.[1]

Daily routine. The daily routine of the scholars' life is at present nearly as follows. After " first " and " second peal," in the summer, they rise and attend chapel from six A.M. to half-past six; in winter three-quarters of an hour later. School begins at half-past seven. Breakfast is served at eight; on Sundays at nine o'clock. School is resumed at nine, and continued till twelve. At a quarter past one P.M. they dine, after singing the beautiful Wykehamical grace; the choristers acting as servitors. From two o'clock till four, school again; and on Mondays and Wednesdays from half-past four till six; on Tuesdays, Thursdays, and Fridays there is what is called a " half-remedy;"[2] and on Saturday, after school from three to five, comes chapel. At six they have tea; " toy-time "[3] follows, from seven o'clock until prayers at half-past eight; and after a slight supper, the scholars retire to bed at nine, except the præfects, who have the privilege of remaining up till ten.[4]

Sunday services. On Sunday morning prayers are read in the college chapel at eight; at half-past ten the scholars hear the Litany and sermon at the Cathedral; and at five in the evening there is another service in the chapel, when the warden or the head-master preaches. The scholars who have been confirmed are expected to partake of the sacrament regularly, but are not compelled to do so.[5]

" Leave-out," " Hills," &c. Except when " leave-out " is obtained, the scholars are strictly prohibited from going beyond the walls of the college; and the " bounds " of the " leave-out " are rigidly defined. But " Hills " (as the daily visit to St. Catharine's Down is entitled), and

carrying on the government of the school, by the agency of the scholars themselves, who learn by turns to obey and to rule, and at all times to exercise such self-command, and to guide their conduct by constant reference to an ideal of character, which is the very *genius loci*, that these *gymnasia* prove such admirable preparatives for the duties of the higher walks of life.

Two of the junior scholars are appointed " rod-makers," for this symbol of absolute authority is still borne by the head-master, and occasionally used also; but in this respect also the humanizing influence of the times has not been without effect, and corporeal chastisement is now the appropriate punishment for base faults only, and it is inflicted so as to cause more disgrace than pain, and without the offensive proceedings formerly adopted.

(1) Walcott, pp. 239, 240.
(2) See below, p. 197.
(3) " Toys " are similar to the " scobs," but are in the chambers.
(4) Christopher Johnson's poem (" *De Collegio*, &c.")

supplies us with a complete sketch of the school duties in the time immediately succeeding the Reformation. They rose at five (v. 34), and at half-past five chapel service began (v. 45); at six school commenced (v. 58), and the tasks were opened with prayer (v. 60); each morning in the week had its special engagement (v. 100), and those for Wednesday and Thursday were " morning hills " (v. 116), whilst Friday was flogging morning (v. 162); nine was the hour for breakfast (v. 195), and school was resumed at eleven (v. 203); dinner was served at noon (v. 206); at half-past three there was another, but a light repast (v. 239), which was immediately followed by lessons (v. 241); at five the scholars went " circum " (v. 245); supper followed (v. 246), and at eight, after attending evening service, all retired to rest. From the statutes a similar picture of the daily round of duty, before the Reformation, might be derived.

(5) Bishop Ken's " Manual of Devotions," composed expressly for the scholars of Winchester College, is still used here.

bathing at the lock, under the charge of the præfects, and the fine open College Mead as a playground, render this restriction no barrier either to health or enjoyment.

Holidays are not unfrequent. Every saint's day is one, in addition to which there *Holidays.* is the "remedy"[1] (as a time of relaxation from the routine of the school is termed), and the "half-remedy," during which the modern languages, drawing, and other branches of study not included in the original *curriculum,* are attended to; and when, under the direction of the præfects, in "Books-chambers," private study is carried on.

Founder's Commemoration is a "public day," and so are the days of the quarterly *Public Days.* visits from the Fellows; but the nearest approach to "Gawdy Days" is at election time, when, on the six last Saturday evenings before "Evening Hills," the *Domum* is sung; and the fine old Latin hymn, "*Jam lucis orto sidere,*" on the morning of breaking up, after chapel (as it is also before the winter holidays); and the Warden and Fellows dine in hall, and the grace is sung with unusual solemnity and effect; and, all the anxiety of election over, the *Domum* Ball (under the stewardship of the superannuates) terminates the academical year.

Each year the following prizes are open to competition :—" Two gold medals for *Medals and* Latin or English prose or verse, alternately; and two silver medals for a Latin or *Prizes.* English speech," given by the Queen. The Say and Sele prizes of books, " given successively by Lord Rivers, the Earl of Aylesbury, and the Duke of Buckingham." The Maltby prizes of books, instituted by the retired Bishop of Durham, in 1841, for Greek iambics; and in 1854 for a Latin essay, and for English verse. The Duncan prizes, established by Philip Bury Duncan, Esq., for mathematics, in 1841, and for reading, and for an English historical essay, in 1855.[2]

And there are the following scholarships and exhibitions for the advantage of *Scholarships* superannuates :—" The Goddard and Pitt scholarships, founded in 1846 in grateful *and Exhibi-* remembrance of the services of Dr. Goddard," head-master from 1793 to 1810, and by *tions.* contributions from the Pitt Fund; the Winton College exhibitions of £50 each, and tenable for four years; the Fox and Burton exhibitions (founded in 1742 by E. B. Fox, and Dr. Burton), of the same amount, and for the same period; and Sir Villiers Chernocke's exhibitions, £25 each, tenable likewise for four years.[3]

School life in Commoners is necessarily the same as that in the college in most *Commoners.* things; but the boys are not subject to many domestic Wykehamical regulations, and in some respects enjoy greater liberties.

(1) The symbol of the "remedy" is a ring given formally to the Præfect of Hall. This ring has for its "posy," "COMMENDAT RARIOR USUS;" but formerly it was inscribed "POTENTIAM GERO, FEROQUE." (Wordsworth, p. 13, note.)

(2) Walcott, pp. 238, 239. The Maltby and Duncan prizes are personal presents given annually by Dr. Maltby and Mr. Duncan.

The Heathcote prize was given from 1832 to 1846 by Sir William Heathcote, Bart., of Hursley, and consisted of thirty guineas worth of books; it was discontinued when the Goddard and Pitt Scholarships were founded.

(3) Walcott, p. 239. There are three Goddard scholarships and one Pitt scholarship. The number of Winton College exhibitioners in the roll for 1858 was eight, and that of the Fox and Burton exhibitioners, three. "Archdeacon Cobden's Exhibition at Trinity College, Oxford, of £50 a year is included in the Winton College Exhibition" (ibid).

" Dulce
Domum."

Although there is thus an inevitable distinction between the scholars and Commoners, yet many things conspire to produce a family spirit, or *esprit de corps*, pervading both sections of this scholastic community ; and perhaps of all symbols of that spirit none is so well known, nor so effective, as the famous Wykehamist song, *Dulce Domum*,[1] on which account we do not hesitate to introduce it into this account of St. Mary College, Winton, from the text in Bishop Wordsworth's work.[2]

" DULCE DOMUM.

" Concinamus, O sodales !
 Eja ! quid silemus ?
  Nobile canticum,
  Dulce melos, domum,
  Dulce domum resonemus.
Chorus. Domum, domum, dulce domum,
  Domum, domum, dulce domum,
  Dulce, dulce, dulce domum,
  Dulce domum resonemus !

" Appropinquat, ecce, felix
 Hora gaudiorum !
  Post grave tædium
  Advenit omnium
  Meta petita laborum !
Chorus. Domum, domum, dulce, domum, &c.

" Musa, libros mitte, fessa ;
 Mitte pensa dura ;
  Mitte negotium,
  Jam datur otium,
  Me mea mittito cura !
Chorus. Domum, domum, dulce domum, &c.

" Ridet annus, prata rident ;
 Nosque rideamus ;
  Jam repetit domum
  Daulias advena ;
  Nosque domum repetamus !
Chorus. Domum, domum, dulce domum, &c.

" Heus, Rogere ! fer caballos !
 Eja ! nunc eamus !
  Limen amabile,
  Matris et oscula,
  Suaviter et repetamus !
Chorus. Domum, domum, dulce domum, &c.

" Concinamus ad Penates ;
 Vox et audiatur ;
  Phosphore ! quid jubar,
  Segnius emicans,
  Gaudia nostra moratur ?
Chorus. Domum, domum, dulce domum,
  Domum, domum, dulce domum,
  Dulce, dulce, dulce domum,
  Dulce domum resonemus."

Relation to
New College,
Oxford.

Winchester College, having been intended by its founder as a high school and preliminary place of instruction for his earlier foundation at Oxford, now called New

(1) This song used to be sung before the Whitsun holiday, at Domum Wharf, and at the College Gate.

(2) I am indebted to a friend, Wyndham Kent, Esq., for the following translation of this famous song, which has so happily caught the spirit, as well as the meaning and the measure, of the Latin, that I am bound to impart it to my readers. It was written before I knew that Bishop Wordsworth had given a translation, which, like it, may be sung to Reading's rich harmony :—

" SWEET HOME.
" Sing together, dear companions ;
 Sing a sacred measure ;
  Ring out the chime, brothers ;
  Measure the time, brothers ;
  Give the day to joy and pleasure !
Chorus. Home ! home ! sweet home !
  Home ! home ! sweet home !
  Sweet home ! sweet home !
  Give the day to joy and pleasure !

" Lo ! the happy hour approaches,
 Bringing home and gladness ;
  School went so wearily ;
  Home smiles so cheerily ;
  Home repays us all our sadness.
Chorus. Home ! home ! sweet home ! &c.

" Leave, my weary Muse, thy task-work ;
 Leave thy books and learning ;
  Labour and sorrow, Muse,
  Leave till to-morrow, Muse ;
  Home and freedom are returning.
Chorus. Home ! home ! sweet home ! &c.

" Laughs the year, and laugh the meadows ;
 All should laugh together ;
  Home flits the swallow now,
  Home let us follow now,
  Thro' the shining summer weather.
Chorus. Home ! home ! sweet home ! &c. [" Roger !

College, many of the original statutes regulated the admission to that college of those scholars of Winchester College who desired to prosecute their studies at the university, and who were most deserving of the privileges which Wykeham's munificence had provided there. And at the present time, by the new ordinance, six scholars, either from the school or from Commoners, are to be admitted yearly.[1]

The examinations commence on the Tuesday next after St. Thomas-à-Becket's day, the 7th of July.[2] On that afternoon the Warden and two of the Fellows of New College (chosen, year by year, for the purpose, and designated Posers, or Supervisors) arrive at Winchester College, and are received at the gate with three orations in Latin, delivered by scholars selected by the Head-master. On the next morning they are conducted to the election-chamber, where, in the presence of the Warden, Sub-warden, and Head-master of Winchester College, they examine the Præfects and other senior scholars; and on Thursday evening make out a roll of the admissions, arranging the successful candidates in the order of their merit.[3] After this, the examinations for scholars to fill up the places of the superannuates, and for exhibitioners at Commoners, take place; and the successful candidates are entered in a roll in the order of their merit, which also regulates the admissions.[4] *The Examinations.*

The Bishop of Winchester is Visitor, and has supreme jurisdiction, under the statutes and the ordinance; and under him, by the new ordinance, considerable power is vested in the Warden and Fellows.[5] *The Visitor.*

There is satisfactory evidence of the maintenance of a school in connection with St. Swithin's Priory at Winchester long before the Conquest; for not only do we *Early history of Winchester College.*

"Roger! man! bring out the horses!
Quick! we would be going;
Oh, for the lovely place!
Oh, for the mother's face!
Kisses sweet once more bestowing.

Chorus. Home! home! sweet home! &c.

"Sing of home and happy greetings;
Sing a sacred measure!
Morning star! why delay?
Sing, brothers! wake the day!
Day of home-delight, and pleasure!

Chorus. Home! home! sweet home! &c."

(1) In former times, the number to be admitted varied year by year, according to the vacancies, which were, on an average, about nine in two years (Walcott, p. 192).

(2) The examinations and elections formerly took place in September (Wavell, vol. i. p. 172).

(3) Under the old statutes, in making out the roll, two of the founder's kin were placed at the head, and the rest in order of seniority, or according to merit.

Founder's kin had also the privilege of not being superannuated till the age of twenty-five; and when elected to New College were fellows at once; but all are superannuated now at the age of eighteen, and cannot succeed to any vacancy in New College after they have attained the age of nineteen.

Since there are now at every examination more deserving candidates for the university than there are scholarships in New College, exhibitions are granted to a certain number of those who stand next on the roll, after those who are admitted to New College, to enable them to prosecute their studies in either Oxford or Cambridge.

(4) According to the old regulations, two of the founder's kin were first elected by a majority of votes; and the rest were nominated in order by the six electors—the Warden of New College, the Warden of Winchester College, the Senior Poser, the Junior Poser, the Sub-warden of Winchester College, and the Head-master. The new ordinance has not only abolished the special privileges of founder's kin, but also abrogated the statutes which enjoined regard to the place of the scholar's birth, &c., and other regulations, which had become unsuitable through the social changes brought about by the lapse of time since the foundation of the college.

(5) The Warden of New College and the Posers used, at their annual visits, to make inquiry regarding violations of the statutes, to hear complaints, &c.; but they are now relieved of this part of their duties.

read of King Egbert's intrusting his son Ethelwulf to the care of Bishop Helmstan (by whom he was placed under the instruction of St. Swithin, who was then prior),[1] and of Alfred's being placed by his father Ethelwulf (when he had succeeded to the kingdom) under St. Swithin's care,[2] but we incidentally meet with the mention of "a scholar of Winchester (*Wintoniensis alumnus*)" in a life of St. Athelwold,[3] which is an indisputable proof of the existence of a school here.

The "High Schole;"—

Besides which, we know that Bishop Henry de Blois specifically included in the hundred poor, to be received and fed daily at the Hospital of St. Cross, "thirteen of the poorer scholars of the Great Grammar School of Winchester, sent by the schoolmaster."[4] Jordan Fantosme (*Jordanus Fantasma*), the poetical chronicler of Henry II.'s Scottish expedition, and chancellor of the diocess of Winchester, was also master of this school.[5] William of Wykeham himself was educated in it.[6] But the most conclusive evidence is contained in a Survey of the City in the very beginning of the fifteenth century, where specific mention is made of "the High Schole."[7] And it is highly probable that there were other schools in connection with the other monastic establishments in Winchester.

—its site.

The site of the principal school was formerly unknown, and was conjectured to be that of the College of St. Mary Winton,[8] but from the joint evidence of the Survey of the City, made a few years after Wykeham's death,[9] and the Chartulary of the Priory of St. Denys, near Southampton,[10] it appears that it stood near Minster-gate, or in the present Symond's Street, not far to the south of the lane leading into St. Thomas' Street.[11] But nothing is known of the sites of any other school in Winchester.

Wykeham's first school.

In the year 1373 the first step was taken by William of Wykeham towards the

---

(1) Rudborne, p. 199.

(2) Ibid., p. 207.

(3) Chron. Monast. de Abingdon, vol. ii. p. 255. This being the first occasion on which I have referred to the volumes published by the Master of the Rolls, under the general description of " *Rerum Britannicarum Medii Ævi Scriptores*, or, Chronicles and Memorials of Great Britain and Ireland during the Middle Ages," I may be permitted, generally, to commend the design, and to recommend the volumes to those who are interested in either topographical or historical studies, in their largest scope. The two volumes comprising the Chronicle of the Monastery of Abingdon will be found of especial interest to the Hampshire archæologist.

(4) Lowth (2nd edit.), p. 77.

(5) Francisque Michel, who edited Fantosme's poem for the Surtees Society, has determined this fact. See also Wright's " *Biographia Britannica Literaria*, Anglo-Norman Period."

(6) Ibid., 13. See above, p. 120.

(7) Tarrages, f. 30.

(8) Lowth, p. 196; Milner, vol. ii. p. 154. In the preceding page, and in his first volume (p. 21), Milner, following the most fabulous portion of Rudborne's History (Rudborne, p. 185), states that "a temple of Apollo, the deity of literature, stood near the site of the present college, when this first part of Britain entered into the list of civilised provinces."

This story is not very clear in itself, and it has the further incumbrances to belief, that it is entirely unsupported by unquestionable authority, and that it is wholly opposed to the evidence of the documents which record the purchase of "the site of the present college" by William of Wykeham.

(9) Tarrages, f. 30. "A tenement of the Priory and Convent of St. Swithin's, called the high schole," and "a garden of the Priory and Convent of St. Swithin's, in the weste parte of the Highe Schoole."

(10) In f. 117 mention is twice made of the house of Jordanus Fantasma, as situated in "Menster Stret," which was the present Symond's Street, with part of St. Swithin's Street and Little Minster Street (as it is now called).

(11) Now the garden of C. M. Deane, Esq., as I am informed by the Rev. W. H. Gunner.

establishment of the College. It is very probable that the High School had fallen into decay; and it certainly might be greatly improved by so zealous a promoter of learning as Wykeham. Three years before this he had commenced his splendid foundation at Oxford, and there is no doubt that an essential part of his plan was a renovated High School at Winchester. Accordingly, in the year just named, he engaged Richard de Herton, for two years, (himself, or by a satisfactory substitute,) to instruct diligently in grammatical learning as many poor scholars as he should send to him for that purpose, but no others without his leave. He also appointed an under-master to assist De Herton; and at Michaelmas the school appears to have been opened with its full complement of seventy scholars.[1]

He obtained a Bull of Licence to found a college here, from Pope Urban VI., in 1378;[2] and the king's licence in 1382;[3] and in this latter year, on October the 20th, he signed the charter of foundation, " by which he nominated Thomas de Cranlegh warden, admitted the scholars, and gave his college the name of ' Seinte Marie College of Wynchester.' "[4] *The Charter of Foundation.*

Deserting the old school, Wykeham now provided lodgings for his new establishment in the parish of St. John on the Hill, in which church he directed them to attend vespers, complines, matins, and the other hours and masses on Sundays and Saints' days, and to chant and sing devoutly as it became them.[5] And by the year 1386 he had purchased from the prior and Convent of St. Swithin's, " two medes, called Dumer's Mede and Otterbourne Mede, lying between the Sustern Spytal and the gardens and closes of Kyngesgate Strete on the weste, and the gardens and closes of the Carmelite friars on the south; and a certain house of the said prior and convent, called " Le Garite, and the path leading to Prior's Barton on the east.[6]

On March the 26th, 1387, at nine o'clock in the morning, the first stone of the new college was laid; and at the same hour, on March the 28th, 1393, the warden and society made their solemn entry into it, chanting psalms in procession.[7] *Commencement of the College;—*

The first nomination of Fellows, five in number (although ten was already fixed as the full number), took place in 1394, and the chapel was finished and dedicated in

---

(1) Lowth, pp. 95, 96, 183, and note, and Appendix VII.

(2) June the 1st, 1378 (ibid., p. 183, note).

(3) Ibid., p. 195, note.

(4) Ibid., p. 195.

(5) Ibid., Appendix X.

(6) Milner, vol. ii. p. 154. Both Walcott (p. 115) and Cockerell (p. 14) say " a messuage attached to Dumer's Mede, containing an acre and a half;" and then they tell a story of a tailor, named Thomas Devereux, claiming in pretended right of his wife " the three acres, Dumer's Mede."

Otterbourne Mede contained three acres.

These " medes " (or at least Dumer's Mede) were the " *viridaria* " and " *deambulatoria*," spoken of above, p. 147.

Milner, and all who have followed him, have designated

the house on the east of Wykeham's purchase " *La Carité;* " but the Rev. W. H. Gunner has discovered that it really is *Le Garite*. In another document it is called *Priourgarryt*. Standing at the end of the solitary path to the Barton, it was, very probably, as the name signifies, a warder's or watchman's lodge; and certainly was not, as Milner suggested, an hospital.

The whole site was not obtained till 1392, when Wykeham procured two separate grants and instruments from the king, for the inclosure of a piece of waste land twelve feet in width, and extending along nearly the whole front of his purchase, two hundred feet, from the prior and convent; together with a small piece containing one rod, belonging to Sustern's Spital, and lying at the north-western angle of his former purchase (Cockerell, p. 14).

(7) Lowth, p. 196.

—its comple-tion.

1395, when (as Lowth supposes) the other Fellows may have been appointed;[1] and the royal charter in 1396, which confirmed the founder's enactments and regulations,[2] completed the establishment of St. Mary Winton College.   So long as such confirmations were needful, this charter appears to have been ratified by all the sovereigns of England, in succession, down to Charles II., with the exception of Queen Mary.[3]

In the succinct history of the college, which alone our space and plan allow, none but the great events, and those which have most remarkably affected its fortunes can be spoken of.   For royal visits, and those of scarcely less illustrious personages, we must refer to the portion of " William of Wykeham and his Colleges," which is devoted to this institution ;[4] and there the curious reader will find some record of those episodes in the history of our public schools, which have become so completely things of the past—rebellions of the scholars against the authorities of the school.[5]

The Refor-mation.

At the Reformation, after the forced exchange of much of its original property,[6] the very existence of the college was endangered, in the year 1545, by the statute of 37 Hen. VIII. § iv.   The death of Henry and the accession of Edward VI., however, saved it; and in 1547, by the statute 1 Edw. VI. § xix., it, with Eton and the colleges of Oxford and Cambridge, was especially excepted from the general forfeiture of the chantries and similar endowments, which furnished the means for the foundation of the schools which date from that period.[7]

Of the manner in which the change from the faith and services of the Catholic Church to those of the Reformed Anglican Church was effected, a few vestiges may be traced in the list of Wardens and Head-masters between the years 1531 and 1560.[8]   And in the first year of the reign of Edward VI., " Injunccions " were laid

(1) Lowth, p. 197.

(2) This charter is given at length in Mr. Walcott's work (pp. 126—130), where also are recited various letters patent, &c., relating to the possessions of the college (pp. 123, 130, 134).   And in Nasmith's " Tanner " a fuller list of them may be found (*Not. Mon.* Hampshire, xxxv. 8).   See also Dugdale's *Monasticon*, last edition, vol. vi. p. 1381.

(3) Walcott, p. 134.

(4) Ibid., pp. 136—140, 143—145, 153—158, 170, 173—176, 185.

One royal visit which Mr. Walcott has not mentioned may be briefly spoken of here.   It is the visit of Edward VI., on September the 5th, 1552, in the course of his progress through the county of Hampshire.   The only record of it now known consists of two MS. copies of a book of verses in Greek and Latin, one preserved in the British Museum (King's MSS. 12 A. xxxiii.), and the other in the Library of New College, Oxford (No. 340).   The Latin verses, and a notice of all that is known of this visit, will be found in pp. 150—152 of the Camden Society's volume, " Literary Remains of King Edward VI.," edited by John Gough Nichols, Esq., to whom I am indebted for this information.

(5) Walcott, pp. 147—149, 176—178.

(6) It was by this exchange that the college acquired the precinct of the White Friars' Monastery, which extended from the river-side on the south of Otterbourne Mead to Kingsgate Street.   Beside this, the college received the sites of the monasteries of the Dominicans and the Franciscans within the city, and of the Austin Friars without Southgate (Tanner, *u. s.*).

At the same time Thomas Lord Wriothesley sold to the college, for £360, St. Elizabeth's College and precinct, which he had received from the crown.   And, according to the conditions of the purchase, as the warden and fellows were unwilling to convert the church into a grammar school, it was pulled down (Walcott, p. 150).

(7) Ibid., pp. 146, 147.   " An important act of royal favour " towards this college, as well as those of Eton and the Universities, in 1540, by which they are exempted from a species of " spiritual taxation," which was levied in the province of Canterbury, is recorded in Walcott (p. 150), from Wood's History, vol. ii. Pt. I. Bk. i. p. 70.

(8) See below, pp. 204, 206.   The use of Grotius' "*De Veritate*, &c.," as a text book for catechetical instruction, is another of these vestiges.

on the college concerning the reading of the Bible in Hall, the disuse of "untrewe and superstitious anthemes," the adoption of Protestant prayers, &c.[1]

Through the next great social convulsion which England experienced, the Puritan Rebellion, Wykeham's college passed with complete safety. There were "two sons of Wykeham" in the victorious party at the time of extreme danger to the college:[2] Colonel Nathaniel Fiennes, a fellow of New College, and one of the founder's kin.; and Nicholas Love, son of Warden Love, and one of the six clerks in Chancery. To one or both of these, the grateful Wykehamists have ascribed the exemption of the college from such wanton sacrilege as that of which Waller's horse-soldiers were guilty in the cathedral; and, probably, it was to the former of them that the college was most indebted, for it is upon record that a present of £29 5s. 6d. was made to the soldiers under his command;[3] and he is said to have placed a guard at the college gates, and thus to have prevented all harm to the society of which he could not forget that he was a member.

The Great Rebellion.

This college has in late years experienced many changes from the reforming influence of the times. Many customs and usages which had become quite obsolete in English society, and unsuited to the spirit of the age, have been quietly abandoned for others more befitting such an institution in the present century. And by the authority of Parliament some important alterations in the statutes have been made. by which the objects proposed by the great and benevolent founder are far more effectually secured than could have been the case had the letter, merely, of his regulations been observed.[4]

Recent changes.

The series of wardens commences with John Morys; Thomas de Cranlegh,[5] whom Wykeham appointed by his charter of foundation, not being included.

List of Wardens.

1. John Morys, M.A.; admitted March the 28th, 1393; died October the 21st, 1413.[6]

2. Robert Thurburn, M.A.; admitted December the 10th, 1413; died October the 30th, 1450.[7]

3. Thomas Chandler, D.D.; admitted November the 30th, 1450; made Warden of New College, February the 22nd, 1454.[8]

4. John Baker, D.D.; admitted July 2nd, 1454; died, 1487.[9]

(1) Wilkin's Concilia, vol. iv. p. 8.

(2) Milner, vol. ii. p. 156, note.

(3) "1643. *Dat. militibus M^{ri} Fines,* 29 : 5 : 6." (Walcott, p. 172.)

(4) These changes have been especially brought about by the new "Ordinance," so frequently referred to.

(5) The date of his appointment, as given above (p. 201), was October 20th, 1382; he was removed to the wardenship of New College, 1389, and died Archbishop of Dublin in 1487.

The dates and particulars of the wardens and headmasters are principally derived from Mr. Walcott's work, and from Carlisle's "Endowed Grammar Schools."

(6) Buried in the chapel of the college (see above, p. 186).

(7) Also buried in the chapel, to which he added a chantry (see above, p. 183). He is commemorated as a benefactor of the college, having bestowed certain vestments upon this chapel, and bequeathed some books and silver cups to this college (Walcott, pp. 223, 352).

(8) Warden Chandler was also Master of St. Cross, and he died Dean of Hereford, in 1490.

(9) To Warden Baker, Christopher Johnson attributes ("*si laus est*") the invention of the quadruplicate Wykehamical rod (Walcott, p. 352). He held a prebend in Lincoln Cathedral.

5. Michael Cleve, D.C.L.; admitted 1487; died, 1501.[1]

6. John Rede, D.D., head-master of the college; admitted November the 18th, 1501; elected Warden of New College, September the 20th, 1520.[2]

7. Ralph Barnacke, D.D.; admitted December the 18th, 1520; resigned October, 1526.[3]

8. Edward More, B.D., head-master of the college; admitted November the 11th, 1526; died 1541.[4]

9. John White, D.D., head-master of the college; admitted January the 13th, 1541; consecrated Bishop of Lincoln, April the 1st, 1554.[5]

10 John Boxall, D.D.; admitted October the 29th, 1554.[6]

11. Thomas Stempe, D.C.L.; admitted November the 21, 1556; died February the 9th, 1580.[7]

12. Thomas Bilson, D.D., head-master of the college; admitted March the 11th, 1580; consecrated Bishop of Worcester, June the 13th, 1596.[8]

13. John Harmar, D.D., head-master of the college; admitted July the 8th, 1596; died September the 13th, 1613.[9]

14. Nicholas Love, D.D., head-master of the college; admitted October the 29th, 1613; died September the 10th, 1630.[10]

15. John Harris, D.D.; admitted September the 30th, 1630; died August the 11th, 1658.[11]

16. William Burte, D.D., head-master of the college; admitted August the 28th, 1658; died July the 3rd, 1679.[12]

17. John Nicholas, D.D., Warden of New College; admitted July the 23rd, 1679; and died 1711.[13]

18. Thomas Braithwaite, D.C.L., Warden of New College; admitted March the 24th, 1711; died July the 23rd, 1720.[14]

(1) Buried in the college chapel (see above, p. 187).

(2) Warden Rede was also Master of St. Cross, and of St. Mary Magdalen Hospital. He was one of the tutors of Prince Arthur, the elder brother of Henry VIII., and died a canon of Lincoln in 1521.

(3) He was appointed to the wardenship by Bishop Fox, the fellows having allowed their right of nomination to lapse to him.

(4) He was also a canon of Chichester, and was buried in the college chapel.

(5) Warden White was translated to Winchester in 1556 (see above, p. 125, and note); his epitaph is in the college chapel, but he was buried in the cathedral (see p. 187 above).

(6) Warden Boxall was one of Queen Mary's Secretaries of State, and, after other valuable preferments, received the Deanery of Chichester. He was deprived and imprisoned on the accession of Elizabeth, and died in obscurity in 1587.

(7) He was buried in the college chapel, and the date of his death is recorded, 1581 (o. s. ?). He held a canonry in Winchester Cathedral, and a prebend in Lincoln.

(8) Translated to the see of Winchester in 1597 (see above, p. 125).

(9) Warden Harmar was Regius Professor of Greek at Oxford from 1585 to 1590, and was afterwards a canon of Winchester. He was buried in the college chapel. We are indebted to him, through Alderman Trussell, for the final version of the legend of Colbrond the Dane (see above, p. 33).

(10) Warden Love was a canon of Winchester, and was buried in the college chapel (see p. 187 above).

(11) He was Regius Professor of Greek at Oxford from 1619 to 1622, and was afterwards a canon of Winchester. He was also elected a member of the Assembly of Divines; and was buried in the college chapel.

(12) Warden Burte held a canonry in Winchester Cathedral, and was buried in the college chapel.

(13) He was canon of Winchester, and of Salisbury.

(14) Buried in the college chapel (see above, p. 188).

Wardens.

19. John Cobb, D.C.L., Warden of New College; admitted August the 8th, 1720; died November the 25th, 1724.[1]

20. John Dobson, D.D., Warden of New College; admitted December the 17th, 1724; died January the 2nd, 1729.

21. Henry Bigg, D.D., Warden of New College; admitted January the 23rd, 1729; died 1740.

22. John Coxed, D.C.L., Warden of New College; admitted August the 18th, 1740; died May the 26th, 1757.[2]

23. John Purnell, D.D., Warden of New College; admitted 1757, but refused admission by Bishop Hoadley.[3]

24. Christopher Golding, D.C.L.; admitted June the 29th, 1757.

25. Harry Lee, D.D.; admitted December the 26th, 1763.[4]

26. George Isaac Huntingford, D.D.; admitted December the 5th, 1786; died April the 29th, 1832.[5]

27. Robert Speckott Barter, B.C.L.; admitted May the 18th, 1832.

In the list of head-masters, Richard de Herton, who was appointed by Wykeham when he first took the High School of Winchester into his own hands,[6] and John Westcott,[7] who succeeded him, are not introduced; the series begins with—

List of Head-masters.

1. John Milton, 1394.
2. Thomas Rumsey, 1395.
3. John Pole, 1407.
4. Thomas Rumsey, 1414.
5. Richard Darcey, 1418.
6. Thomas Alwine (or *Walweyne*), 1424.
7. William Waynflete, 1430.[8]
8. Thomas Alwine, 1442.
9. William Ive, D.D., 1445.[9]
10. John Bernard (or *Barnarde*), 1454.
11. John Grene, 1460.
12. Clement Smith, M.A., 1464.
13. Richard Dene (or *Dean*), M.A., 1466.[10]
14. John Rede, B.D., 1484.[11]
15. Robert Festham, M.A., 1490.[12]

---

(1) Warden Cobb also was a canon of Winchester; and was buried in the college chapel.

(2) Buried in the college chapel.

(3) Walcott, pp. 350, 351.

(4) Wardens Golding and Lee were buried in the college chapel (see above, p. 188).

(5) Consecrated Bishop of Gloucester, 1802; translated to the see of Hereford in 1812.

(6) See above, p. 201.

(7) Milner, vol. ii. p. 167.

(8) Consecrated Bishop of Winchester in 1447 (see above, p. 123, and note).

(9) Chancellor of Sarum, 1470.

(10) Buried in the college cloisters (see above, p. 190).

(11) Afterwards sixth warden of the college (see above, p. 204).

(12) Died in 1522.

Head-masters

16. William Harman (or *Horeman*), M.A., 1495.[1]
17. William Farlington (*Forelington* or *Derlington*), M.A., 1502.
18. Edward More, B.D., 1508.[2]
19. Thomas Erlisman, M.A., 1517.[3]
20. John Tychiner (*Towchener, Tuchyner,* or *Twychinere*), M.A., 1526.[4]
21. Richard Tuchiner (or *Twychinere*), M.A., 1530.
22. John White, D.D., 1537.[5]
23. Thomas Baylie, B.A., 1542.
24. William Evered, M.A., 1547.
25. Thomas Hyde, M.A., 1552.[6]
26. Christopher Johnson, M.D., 1560.[7]
27. Thomas Bilson, D.D., 1571.[8]
28. Hugh Lloyd (or *Floyd*), D.C.L., 1580.[9]
29. John Harmar, 1588.[10]
30. Benjamin Heyden, D.D., 1595.[11]
31. Nicholas Love, D.D., 1601.[12]
32. Hugh Robinson, D.D., 1613.[13]
33. Edward Stanley, D.D., 1627.[14]
34. John Pottinger (or *Potenger*), B.D., 1642.[15]
35. William Burte, D.D., 1653.[16]
36. Henry Beeston, D.C.L., 1658.[17]
37. William Harris, D.D., 1678.[18]
38. Thomas Cheyney, D.D., 1700.[19]
39. John Burton, D.D., 1724.[20]
40. Joseph Warton, D.D., 1766.[21]

(1) He was head-master of Eton College before his appointment at Winchester, and he died in 1535.

(2) Afterwards eighth warden of the college (see above, p. 204).

(3) Head-master of Eton College, 1511.

(4) Prebendary of Chichester, 1532.

(5) Afterwards ninth warden of the college (see above, p. 204).

(6) He was Canon of Winchester in 1556, and in 1558 retired to Douai, where he died in 1597.

(7) Johnson was a Wykehamist, and one of the most distinguished of the head-masters of Winchester, being a physician and philosopher, but principally owing to his great facility in Latin verse. Besides the specimens given above (pp. 188, &c.) in his epitaphs, there are his distichs on the wardens and masters, printed by Wills, 1573; and his poem on the school itself, which Bishop Wordsworth has printed. He died in 1597.

(8) Afterwards twelfth warden of the college.

(9) Canon of St. Paul's; died in 1602.

(10) Afterwards thirteenth warden of the college, and Bishop of Winchester.

(11) Died Dean of Wells in 1607.

(12) Afterwards fourteenth warden of the college.

(13) Died in 1655. He held various preferments, but was "a zealous presbyterian" (Walcott, p. 358).

(14) Canon of Winchester; died in 1662.

(15) Resigned on account of Puritanical innovations, and died in 1659.

(16) Afterwards sixteenth warden of the college (see above, p. 204).

(17) Canon of Winchester, and subsequently Warden of New College; died in 1701.

(18) Canon of Winchester; Regius Professor of Greek at Oxford.

(19) Canon of Wells; died in 1724.

(20) Died in 1774.

(21) Died in 1800. He was Professor of Poetry at Oxford, and Canon of St. Paul's; and was one of the great literary notabilities of the last century.

41. William Stanley Goddard, D.D., 1793.[1]

42. Henry Dison Gabell, D.D., January 24th, 1810.[2]

43. David Williams, D.C.L., January 15th, 1824.[3]

44. George Moberly, D.C.L., 1836.[4]

From the long roll of eminent Wykehamists, we select a few of the more conspicuous names, for the purpose of indicating the high place occupied by this institution amongst the public schools of England.[5]

ARCHBISHOPS.—William Warham (*Cantuar.*), Hugh Ynge (*Dublin*), Charles Cobb (*Dublin*), William Stuart (*Armagh*), William Howley (*Cantuar.*).

BISHOPS.—William Waynflete (*Winton.*), Richard Fox (*Winton.*), Thomas Beckington (*Bath and Wells*), John Kingscote (*Carlisle*), John Russell (*Lincoln*), Richard Mayhew, or Mayo (*Heref.*), Thomas Janyn (*Norw.*), Robert Sherburn (*Chichester*), William Knight (*Bath and Wells*), John Holyman (*Bristol*), John White (*Winton.*), James Turburville, or Trobylfylde (*Exon.*), John Merricke (*Sodor and Man*), John Underhill (*Oxon.*), Thomas Bylson (*Winton.*), Henry Rowlands (*Bangor*), Arthur Lake (*Bath and Wells*), Alexander Hyde (*Sarum*), William Bue (*Llandaff*), Francis Turner (*Ely*), Thomas Ken (*Bath and Wells*), Charles Trimnell (*Winton.*), Thomas Manningham (*Chichester*), Philip Bisse (*Hereford*), Henry Downes (*Derry*), Henry Egerton (*Hereford*), William Bradshaw (*Bristol*), George Lavington (*Exeter*), Robert Lowth (*London*), Henry Bathurst (*Norwich*), Thomas Burgess (*Sarum*), Isaac Huntingford (*Hereford*), Edward Maltby (*Durham*), Richard Mant (*Down and Connor*), John Banks Jenkinson (*St. David's*), Charles Wordsworth (*St. Andrew's*), T. S. Townsend (*Meath*).

DIVINES AND SCHOLARS.—William Grocyn (tutor of Erasmus), John Stanbrugge (author of "An Accidence"), William Fleshmonger (Dean of Chichester), Nicholas Udall, Thomas Bedell, John Philpot (the Martyr), Thomas Hardyng, Thomas Martyn, Thomas Neile, Christopher Johnson, Nicholas Saunders, Thomas Stapleton, John Fowler, Henry Garnet, John Lloyd (translator of Josephus' "*De Maccabeis*"), John Owen (Latin epigrammatist), John Hoskyns, Thomas James (author of Catalogue of the Bodleian Library), Thomas Lydyatt, William Twisse, John Reinolds (Latin epigrammatist), John Harman (classical scholar), Henry Bold (Latin poet), Nicholas Lloyd (author of a classical dictionary), John Potenger (translator of Tacitus' "*Agricola*"), John Norris, Robert Woodward (Dean of Sarum), Edward Holdworth, Christopher Pitt, Joseph Spence (author of "Polymetis"), Gloucester Ridley, Sir

(1) Canon of St. Paul's, and of Salisbury; died in 1847.

(2) Died in 1831.

(3) Now Warden of New College, Canon of Winchester, and Vice-Chancellor of Oxford.

(4) Fellow of Baliol College, Oxford.

(5) I am principally indebted to Mr. Walcott's carefully compiled "Roll of Distinguished Wykehamists;" and my list has been most obligingly revised by Mr. Walcott himself. There is a list in Carlisle's "Endowed Grammar Schools," and another very brief one in Milner (vol. ii. p. 167).

Where any possibility of doubt might exist respecting the person intended, some clue for the identification of the name has been added; but, in general, the names have occupied, and that worthily, a large space in the eye of the world.

James Stonehouse, Bart., William Dobson (translator of "Paradise Lost"), James Hampton (translator of "Polybius"), Richard Chandler (author of "*Marmora Oxoniensia*"), Michael Wodhull (translator of "Euripides"), John Sturges, William Shipley (Dean of St. Asaph), John Lempriere (author of the "Classical Dictionary"), Sydney Smith, George Frederic Nott (editor of the Poems of Surrey and Wyatt), Moyle Sherer (biographer of the Duke of Wellington), Thomas Arnold (Head-master of Rugby), Richard Ford (author of the "Handbook for Spain"), Augustus W. Hare (one of the authors of "Guesses at Truth"), Walter Farquhar Hook (Dean of Chichester), William Sewell (Professor of Moral Philosophy, Oxon.), John Jebb (author of "Letters on the State of the Church"), Christopher Wordsworth (Canon of Westminster), Hugh Seymour Tremenheere (Inspector of Schools), George W. Ward.

POETS.—George Coryat (author of "Crudities"), Thomas Leyson, Thomas Flattman, Thomas Otway, John Phillips, William Somerville, Edward Young, Christopher Pitt, William Whitehead, William Collins, Charles Dibdin, John Ring (translator of "Dulce Domum"), William Crowe, Robert Holmes, William Lisle Bowles.

MEN OF SCIENCE.—Andrew Borde (physician to Henry VIII.), William Musgrave (Sec. R. S.), Anthony Addington (physician to George III.), George Williams (Radcliffe librarian), William Buckland (Dean of Westminster), C. G. B. Daubeny (Professor of Chemistry, Oxon.).

HISTORIANS AND ANTIQUARIES.—Robert Talbot (annotator of Antoninus' Itinerary), John Harpysfelde (author of "*Historia Anglicana Christiana*"), John Rastall (author of "*Anglorum Regum Chronicon*"), John Pitts (author of "*De Illustribus Angliæ Scriptoribus*"), Sir Thomas Browne, John Ecton (editor of "*Liber Valorum*"), John Warneford (Camden Professor of History), John Chernocke (author of "*Biographia Navalis*"), James Ingram (translator of the Anglo-Saxon Chronicle), Bulkeley Bandinel (editor of Dugdale's *Monasticon*), F. C. Penrose (author of "Athenian Architecture").

NAVAL AND MILITARY OFFICERS.—Adm. Sir Richard Goodwin Keats, Adm. Sir John Borlase Warren, Adm. Henry Raper, Gen. Sir Robert Wilson, Gen. Sir James Charles Dalbiac, Gen. Lord Seaton, Gen. Sir Andrew Barnard, Gen. Sir Alexander Woodford, Gen. Sir R. Wilson, Capt. Sir R. J. M'Clure.

STATESMEN.—Henry Howard, Earl of Northampton; Sir Henry Wotton; Sir Benjamin Rudyerd; Sir Thomas Ryves; Richard Zouch (writer on International Law); Nathaniel Fiennes; Sir Edward Herbert; Anthony, Viscount Falkland; Anthony Ashley Cooper, Lord Shaftesbury; Arthur Onslow; Sir James Eyre; Charles Wolfran Cornwall; James Harris, Earl of Malmesbury; Henry Addington, Viscount Sidmouth; Charles Bragge-Bathurst; William Sturges-Bourne; Sir George Henry Rose; Sir Robert Harry Inglis; Sir William Goodenough Hayter; Robert M. Rolfe, Lord Cranworth; Charles Shaw-Lefevre, Viscount Eversley; Sir Francis T. Baring; Henry Labouchere; Frederic Twisleton, Lord Say and Sele; Sir William Page Wood; Sir Alexander Malet; Edward Cardwell.

The cricket matches with Eton (which have risen to the rank of an institution in these schools) are played at Eton and at Winchester alternately. The curious in these matters will find ample details of the victories of the Wykehamists in the journals especially devoted to such records, from the first in 1825 to those of the current year; and to those authorities we refer them.[1]

Cricket matches.

From the "*Valor Ecclesiasticus*," it appears that the gross revenues of the college in the time of Henry VIII. amounted to £710 8s., and the net revenue was £628 13s. 6d.;[2] with this may be compared the statement of the steward before a committee of the House of Commons, in the year 1818, that the income for the preceding year amounted very nearly to £15,000.[3]

Revenues.

(1) Mr. Walcott has loyally consecrated a page (183) of his work to a synopsis of the victories of the Wykehamists up to 1851; but the details (which are of chief importance) must be sought elsewhere.

(2) Vol. ii. pp. 4, 5. The particulars of the annual expenditure may interest Wykehamists of the present day. "*Custos*, £22 18s. 8d.; *Socii*, £74 4s. 2d.; *Pædagogus*, £11 18s. 5d.; *Suppædagogus*, £4 9s. 4½d.; *Cantarista*, ex fundacione Johannis Fromond, £6 13s. 4d."

(3) Parliamentary Reports, 1818, vol. iv. p. 132.

The following papers (in addition to those already quoted) relate to the college, and serve to complete its history :—

Archæological Journal, vol. viii. pp. 79—87, "Extracts from the Bursar's Accounts, preserved among the Muniments of Winchester College." Vol. x. pp. 235—239, containing Inventories of Plate given to the College and Chapel by William of Wykeham and other benefactors, from the Muniments of the College. Vol. xvi. pp. 166–73, "The Will of John Fromond, Benefactor to Winchester College."

These were all contributed by the late Rev. W. H. Gunner, whose name has so frequently appeared in these pages—yet not so frequently as to express the obligations under which I have gladly lain to the sound archæological scholarship, and the generous and earnest spirit of my lamented friend, whose too early death not I alone, nor my work, have to deplore.

The Eton Latin and Greek Grammars were formerly those of Winchester as well; and earlier still, of course, *Donatus* (see above, p. 125).

In "Notes and Queries" (1st S. vol. viii. p. 298), Mr. Walcott says that there are libraries for the Commoners and the scholars, with books for general reading, under the charge of the Senior Commoner Præfect and the Præfect of Library, severally, who lend, on application, to the juniors.

For the water-supply of the college, see above, p. 27, and note 4. It dates from Waynflete's time.

The Sub-warden and Bursar are fellows, the former of whom is annually appointed to the office.

A. Alsop is stated by Warton (additions printed by Sir Thomas Phillips, Bart., p. 7) to have written the epitaphs on Wardens Braithwaite and Cobb, mentioned above, p. 188.

The school for the choristers is in College Street, near the college, and the boys are clothed and boarded there, and receive a sound English education; but they are no longer eligible to scholarships, as formerly they were.

The ancient Seal of the College is a pointed oval, measuring 2·8 in. by 1·8 in. In the centre is a rich double canopy, having a shield with Wykeham's arms on each side, and under it seated figures of SS. Peter and Paul. Above it, under another double canopy, is represented the Salutation, the Blessed Virgin standing, and a label inscribed with the words "AVE MARIA," proceeding from the angel's hand. In base is the founder, half-length, full-faced, *in pontificalibus*, praying, beneath an arch; and in a niche on each side is the head of a saint. Across the seal, between this and the upper compartment of the device, is "WILLELM EPS FŪDATOR." *Leg.* "SIG : CŌE : COLLEGII : VOCATI : SCE : MARIE : COLLEGIE OF : WYNCHESTRE : PPE : WYNTŌ."

The Arms of the College are those of the See of Winchester, impaling Wykeham's.

For many other interesting facts respecting the college I must refer to Mr. Walcott's work, and to the "Memorials of Winchester College,"—a fine work, the letter-press to which was written by Mr. Gunner; and end my account with the "Thanksgiving for the Founder," as at present used on commemoration-days.

"O, ETERNAL GOD, the Life and the Resurrection of all them that believe in Thee, always to be praised as well for the Dead as for those that be Alive, we give Thee most hearty Thanks for our FOUNDER, WILLIAM OF WYKEHAM; and all other our Benefactors, by whose Benefits we are here brought up to Godliness and the Studies of good Learning; beseeching Thee that we, well using all these Thy Blessings to the Praise and Honour of Thy Holy Name, may at length be brought to the Immortal Glory of the Resurrection, through Jesus Christ our Lord. *Amen.*"

HYDE HOUSE SCHOOL.

Hyde House School.

Amongst the private schools in Winchester, the Hyde House School only requires particular mention. It was founded in 1851 by Dr. Behr (who had been the German master at Winchester College), with whom, since 1855, the Rev. E. Firmstone has been associated. It is divided into the Military, the General, and the Town Schools; and its present number of scholars is about a hundred and twenty, of whom about thirty are intended for the army, and the remainder for the universities, the professions, &c. The military school is conducted in the noble school-house which belonged to Hyde Abbey School, standing a little to the west of Hyde Street; and the other buildings —the playground and tennis-court—adjoin it on the north.[1]

Private Schools.

The Winchester Commercial and Mathematical School in Canon Street, which is in union with the Winchester Diocesan Board of Education, may also be noticed with commendation.

Choristers' Schools.

And here may be mentioned the schools for the choristers of the cathedral, and of the college, the former of which is now associated with the school in Canon Street, just noticed, and the latter is at present in College Street, near the college.[2]

CHURCH DAY-SCHOOLS.[3]

Church Day-schools.

The energetic activity of the friends of education, which has given to Winchester the distinguished position which becomes it as a cathedral city and provincial

---

(1) The Rev. E. Firmstone has obligingly communicated to me these particulars respecting Hyde House School; and has also obtained for me, from the surviving daughter of the late principal of Hyde Abbey School, some interesting facts connected with that distinguished *gymnasium*.

Hyde Abbey School was established about the year 1760, by the Rev. Dr. Cotton, at that time Rector of St. Lawrence, Winchester (see above, p. 157, note 6), under whom, and his son-in-law and successor, the Rev. C. Richards, it attained very great and deserved celebrity (Wavell, vol. i. p. 174, warmly recommends it); and it numbered at one time a hundred and eighty scholars. Mr. Richards retired in 1829, on being appointed a canon of the cathedral, and in the hands of his sons it declined so rapidly, that in six or seven years it became extinct. The school-house (which was built by Mr. Richards) has since seen various changes of fortune (see above, pp. 32, and 177, note 1), but has now reverted to its original use.

Amongst the scholars of this school, the following are the most distinguished:—the late Marquis of Winchester, Lord Charles Powlett, the late Earl of Liverpool, Admiral

the late Lord Lyons, the sons of the late Lord Bandon, Lord Bridport, the sons of Lord Poltimore, the sons of the late Archbishop of Tuam, Dean Garnier and his brothers, the sons of Dean Shipley of St. Asaph, Dr. Gaisford (late Dean of Christchurch), the Rev. Charles Wolfe (the poet), the Rev. Sir Thomas Miller, Bart., George Canning (the statesman), Admiral Walcott, Sir John Sinclair, General Sir Peregrine Maitland, General Sir Edward Barnes, the late Admiral Sir Charles Ogle and his brothers, Sir Willoughby Gordon, the sons of Sir Edward Newingham, of Sir Riggs Falkener, and of Sir Richard Worsley, Sir George Hewitt and his brothers, the late Sir Charles Mill, and Sir John Mill.

In 1828 a small volume was published, entitled "*Musæ Hydenses*," containing prize poems in Latin and English, composed by scholars of Hyde Abbey School, which affords a fair criterion of the excellence of the school. The English poem for 1808 is by Wolfe.

(2) See above, p. 86, for a notice of the Cathedral Choristers' School; and p. 209 for a notice of the College Choristers' School.

(3) For the information I have received respecting

metropolis, received a new impulse in 1846. Before that time there existed the Central School, in Colebrook Street, which was erected in 1812, and can now accommodate five hundred and forty boys, girls, and infants;[1] St. Peter's Parochial School, in Cheesehill Street, erected in 1840, and capable of accommodating eighty children;[2] and one of the schools in Middle Brook Street, which was built in 1844. In 1846, also, there were erected a school in St. Thomas' Street, for St. Thomas' parish; and one for St. Bartholomew's parish, adjoining the churchyard.[3]

At the annual treat of the children of the Central School, in the last-named year, the number of poor children, who were spectators only, seemed so great, that an inquiry from house to house was instituted by the clergy; and it was ascertained that there were in the city 1835 children who stood in need of eleemosynary education; that of those 617 were in the existing church schools, 596 in dames' schools, and 622 in no school whatever. It was impossible to allow such a state of things to continue. At a meeting, therefore, of the Hampshire Society, convened by the Bishop of Winchester, these facts were embodied in a report drawn up by the Rev. N. Midwinter, the secretary; and it was resolved to create a School Building Fund, for the purpose of making grants to the clergy, who should erect schools in their parishes, of £2 10s. for each child the school could provide a place for. This fund was commenced by donations of £100 from the bishop, and £250 each from the dean and chapter, and the warden and fellows of the college; and the result was the erection, in 1848, of a school for boys and girls in Canon Street, for St. Michael's parish; a boys' school in Tower Street, for St. Thomas' parish; and a second school in Middle Brook Street, which is now assigned to the parish of Holy Trinity.

Origin of the educational movement in Winchester;—

Since then, an infant school in 1855, and a model school in 1858, have been added to St. Michael's Schools; a school for girls and infants has been built in St. John's Street for the parish of St. John;[4] and the Central School, and the school-houses

—subsequent efforts.

these schools, I am principally indebted to the Rev. N. Midwinter, Rector of St. Michael's, and Mr. J. W. High, of the Central School, Secretaries to the Hampshire Church School Society. I have embodied in the text the interesting narrative furnished me by Mr. Midwinter, and the dates and details which I have received from Mr. High.

(1) This school should ever be associated with the honoured name of its founder, the Rev. Frederic Iremonger. It is one of the oldest National Schools in the kingdom, and it was long the only school for the children of the poor in the city. Until the formation of the Diocesan Board, and the opening of the Training School, it was for many years the Model School of "the Hampshire Society for the Education of the Poor in the principles of the Church of England." It still retains its general character, children being admitted from any part of the city or suburbs at a nominal payment. The building is quite plain, but is large and well adapted to its

purpose; and there are class-rooms in addition to the ordinary school-rooms, &c. The children of the "Winchester Free School" are taught here.

(2) In 1845 a house was built for the master of this school.

(3) In the report of the Church School Inquiry, 1846-7, is the following return for Winchester:—Central, one boys' school, one girls' school, two teachers' houses; St. Bartholomew's, one parochial school, one infants'; St. Maurice' (now Holy Trinity), two parochial schools; St. Thomas', one charity school, one infants'; St. Peter's, two parochial schools.

(4) "The energy of the Rev. Canon Jacob in giving effect to a bequest of £200 on the part of Mr. Martin Filer, for the endowment of a salaried teacher for St. John's parish, was the main-spring of the efforts which have resulted in the erection of the noble school and teacher's residence" there. (Letter from the Rev. N. Midwinter.)

of St. Thomas', Holy Trinity, and St. Bartholomew's parishes have been enlarged. In St. Michael's parish a teacher's residence has also been erected as "a Thank-offering to Almighty God, in the year of Peace, 1856." The cost of these school buildings may be approximately estimated from the cost of those for St. Michael's parish alone, which has exceeded £1400.[1]

All these schools are Sunday-schools also; and those recently erected are amongst the most ornamental buildings in the city.

BRITISH SCHOOL.[2]

British School.

Immediately behind the Congregational Chapel, and forming an integral part of that building, is the "British Hall," which has the largest school-room in the city. It was erected at the same time as the chapel, and comprises, besides all the needful conveniences for a school, with class-room, lecture-room, &c., a commodious residence for the teachers; and the cost of its erection was £1500. There are two entrances in Staple Gardens, and two in Jewry Street, through passages beneath the galleries of the chapel. It is used as a Sunday-school also, which has been maintained, in connection with the Independent congregation, upwards of fifty years.

Catholic School.

The poor children of the Roman Catholic congregation receive instruction in a small building, which has been appropriated to this use by the Rev. Ignatius Collingridge.[3]

SOCIETIES FOR THE PROMOTION OF POPULAR EDUCATION.

Three societies, which have been established principally for the promotion of education amongst the children of the poor, may be mentioned here, although the sphere of their operations extends much beyond the limits of Winchester.

(1) This tabular view of the church day-schools has been supplied to me by Mr. High:—

School.	Character.	Site.	Date of first erection.	Present accommodation.
* Central	B. G. I.	Colebrook St.	1812	540
St. Peter's. . .	B. G. I.	Cheesehill St.	1840	80
* St. Michael's .	B. G. I.	Canon St.	1848	200
St. Thomas' . .	B.	Tower St.	1848	75
* ,,	G. I.	St. Thomas' St.	1846	150
* Holy Trinity .	B.	Middle Brooks	1848	100
* ,,	G. I.	,,	1844	200
* St. Bartholomew	B. G. I.	Hyde St.	1846	150
St. John's	G. I.	St. John's St.	1857	150

Those marked with an asterisk (*) have been enlarged since their first erection. B., G., and I., signify *boys, girls*, and *infants*.

(2) A small British school was commenced in Upper Brook Street, about ten years ago, under a female teacher only; the present school, which has a master and a female teacher, was opened in 1854.

(3) For about half a century the Benedictine nuns maintained, in their convent in St. Peter's Street, two schools, one for pensioners, the other for poor girls of the catholic congregation. The former of these schools was, at the beginning of this century, supported by many of the best families, but it subsequently fell away consider-

" *The Winchester Diocesan Board of Education,* in connection with the Incorporated National Society," comprises the whole diocese in its sphere of operations, which are principally directed to the training of teachers and the regulation and inspection of schools. It also aids parochial schools by grants of money. The training school is, for the present, carried on in the palace at Wolvesey ; but the dean and chapter have recently given to the board a fine site in the western suburbs of Winchester ; and a new training college for fifty masters is about to be erected upon it.[1] The Hampshire Church School Society is established in connection with this board, and the Commercial and Mathematical School in Canon Street, Winchester, is in union with it. Winchester Diocesan Board of Education.

" *The Hampshire Church School Society* " was established in 1854. The object proposed in its formation " was the extension of the action of the Diocesan Board of Education by the promotion of unity and sympathy among the friends, promoters, and teachers of church schools."[2] And the principal means adopted has been the invitation to an annual meeting of " all persons engaged in the work of church education " in the county.[3] At these meetings opening addresses are delivered ; prizes for essays on subjects connected with popular church education are read, and the prizes bestowed on the successful competitors ;[4] model lessons are given, practical educational questions are discussed, and lectures on local archæological subjects delivered.[5] Hampshire Church School Society.

The happiest results have followed this mode of action, and great activity and earnestness have been imparted to the efforts of all interested in church education throughout the county by means of these meetings.

The " *Hants and Wilts Adult Education Society,* for promoting the education of the adult classes, in union with the Society of Arts," necessarily makes Winchester one of its centres of action, and may therefore be most conveniently noticed here. Its objects are, " 1st, the establishment and assistance of literary and scientific institutions, libraries whether stationary or itinerating, reading-rooms, and evening schools ; and, 2ndly, the encouragement of a spirit of improvement, either by the delivery of lectures and the formation of classes, or by examinations, certificates, and prizes." There are in Winchester the following institutions in union with this society :—St. Maurice' School, Church of England Young Men's Society, Mechanics' Institute, Military Café and Reading-room, and Model and Practising School.[6] The society has a room in Winchester, temporarily, at Northgate. Hants and Wilts Adult Education Society.

---

ably, as similar schools were open in other and more healthy localities, and it was closed in the year 1857, when the nunnery was removed to East Bergholt, in Suffolk.

(1) Some particulars of this new college will be given in an Appendix.

(2) Third Annual Report of the society, p. 9.

(3) The meeting for 1857 was held at Southampton, but all the others have taken place at Winchester.

(4) Prizes have been given annually by the bishop, the dean, and the archdeacon ; and others have been given occasionally.

(5) These lectures, up to the present time, have been on Winchester Cathedral, by the Rev. Dr. Moberly ; on Winchester College, by the Rev. J. C. Chandler, of Witley ; on the History and Antiquities of St. Cross, by the Rev. the Master of St. Cross ; on Netley Abbey, by the Rev. F. W. Baker, of Beaulieu ; and on the *Liber Winton.,* by the writer of this work.

(6) Prospectus of the society, January, 1859.

LENDING LIBRARIES.

Public Library.   The "*Public Library*," established in connection with the Museum, contains about a thousand volumes, which are lent to any person producing a written recommendation from a member of the Town Council. The annual issue is about two thousand volumes.

Mechanics'
Institution.   The "*Mechanics' Institution*, in union with the Society of Arts, &c.," was established in 1835, and has its rooms in the square, at the gate of the Cathedral Yard, on the site which has been at various times the Guildhall of the Wool Merchants, a prison, a corn market, a theatre, and a shambles. The building (which in part belongs to the society, and was erected in 1838, and altered in 1849) has recently been again altered and improved, so that the institution has now a very commodious library, with class and reading-rooms on the ground-floor, and a good lecture-room above them, with apartments for a resident attendant, and librarian, &c.

The library contains above four thousand five hundred volumes, and will, when the new arrangements are completed with the reading-room (for newspapers and periodicals), be open every day till half-past ten o'clock.

Lectures on literary, scientific, historical, and other subjects, or readings, or conversazione, are provided almost weekly, on Wednesday evenings, from September to April. It numbers about two hundred and fifty members.

Other
Libraries.   The "*Church of England Institution*," and the "*Church of England Young Men's Society*," have small libraries in the same rooms in St. Peter's Street. A "*Young Men's Mutual Improvement Society*" is maintained in connection with the Congregational Church.

SOUTH HANTS AND ISLE OF WIGHT BOOK-HAWKING SOCIETY.[1]

Book-hawking
Society.   As this society includes Winchester in its field of work, although properly and most intimately connected with Southampton, we mention it here; both because it is of kindred nature with the societies and institutions spoken of immediately above, and also because its simplicity and effectiveness demand that a most prominent place should be given to its name.

It originated with the present Archdeacon of Winchester, the Venerable J. C. Wigram, and was set in operation by him, in 1851, in the neighbourhood of South-

(1) For information respecting this society I am indebted to the courtesy of the Rev. J. Silvester Davies, of Woolston, Southampton, who is its secretary. I have also used a tract on the subject by the Rev. G. H. Sumner.

ampton.   There are now two flourishing societies at work in the county.   The one before us at this time regularly employs two hawkers, and, according to the last report (for 1858), the total annual sales amounted to £281 30s. 11d.; whilst the subscriptions were no more than £61 10s.   The most gratifying fact respecting this educational agency is, that the great majority of books sold by it are religious works, and the next most numerous class those which are either useful or instructive; merely amusing books selling more sparingly than any others.

THE MUSEUM,

with the Public Library, has now a fine substantial building in Jewry Street, which was the governor's house in the old jail.   It was established in 1847 as "The Hampshire Museum," in the present school-house of Hyde House School, and was maintained by private subscriptions and donations, until in a few years the interest in it had so greatly declined, that the proprietors offered the collection to the Corporation, if the rate-payers would accept it under the provisions of the Public Library and Museum Act.   This offer was accepted, and the transfer effected in February, 1851; and in the following November the new building (in which the curator and librarian has apartments) was completed, and opened freely to the public on three days in every week. It is now supported partly by an annual rate of a halfpenny in the pound, which produces about £100, and partly by subscriptions.

There are in this museum some local curiosities of considerable interest, deposited here by the Corporation; with casts of Hampshire seals, rubbings of brasses, and other archæological remains from the city and county; a small collection of stuffed birds and other animals, and some illustrations of ethnology; but neither its extent, nor the interest generally taken in it, are worthy of Winchester, or of Hampshire.[1]

(1) See " the Second Catalogue of Specimens and Objects exhibited in the Winchester Museum," 1858.

THE

HOSPITAL OF ST. CROSS;

AND

THE OTHER CHARITABLE INSTITUTIONS OF WINCHESTER.

————•————

Site of the
Hospital of
St. Cross.

ABOUT a mile from Winchester, between the Southampton Road and the Itchen, just within the limits of the parliamentary borough, stands the far-famed Hospital of St. Cross.

Like the cathedral precinct and the college, the hospital and its grounds are extra-parochial, but the church is appropriated to the use of the parish of St. Faith, which comprises all the area of the borough lying to the west of the river, below the boundaries of the city parishes of St. Thomas and St. Michael; and on the north extends nearly to Fulflood, where it adjoins the parish of Week; and to the west some way beyond the bounds of the borough.[1] The site of the old church (which was taken down by Bishop Fox in 1509), at the angle where the road from Kingsgate joins the Southgate Road, is still used as a burial-ground for the parish.[2]

Plan of the
hospital.

The hospital buildings are arranged round a spacious quadrangle and a forecourt, the entrance to which is from the north. On the eastern side of the forecourt is the brewhouse, and on the western side are the stables, the kitchen, the larder, &c. The south side is composed of Beaufort's Tower (or gateway), with the porter's lodge on the east, where the doles of bread and beer are still given to all wayfarers; and the hall or refectory of the brethren. On the west of the hall within the quadrangle is the master's house, and the residences of the brethren form its western side; they were continued along the south side also, as far as the church, but at the present time an

(1) The name of this parish was formerly Sparkford, and it consisted of two parishes, Sparkford St. Faith's and Sparkford St. James'. The name is still preserved in the two tythings of Bishop's Sparkford and West Sparkford, which constitute the parish of St. Faith. St. James' was the church called White Minster, which stood near the present Roman Catholic burial-ground on West Hill. (Charters in Cathedral Library, &c.)

(2) The stone screens inserted beneath the arches beside the high altar of the Church of St. Cross, and the bowl of the font there, appear to be the only existing remains of the Church of St. Faith.

The rectory of St. Faith was given to St. Cross by Cardinal Beaufort; and the church having become completely dilapidated (as was the case with so many at that time in Winchester), was taken down in 1509.

ST CROSS.

From the River Itchen.

W. H. Bartlett.

A. Willmore.

iron railing alone divides it from the park. The church stands at the south-eastern angle, and an ambulatory, or cloister, with the infirmary over it, extending from the north transept to the porter's lodge, forms the eastern side.

To the south of the buildings is the park, and close to the church the cemetery; on the east is the Master's garden; and on the west are the gardens of the brethren, and another garden belonging to the Master. To the north of the hospital, beside the high road, is a small village, which has sprung up, in the course of centuries, apparently in consequence of the charity.

The architecture[1] of the outer gate presents no features requiring remark, but the entrance to the quadrangle is by a noble gateway and massive tower, quite worthy of the name of Beaufort. The arches are good, four-centred arches, rather flat, but well moulded, without shafts, and the outer one has rich spandrels with shields. Three string-courses beneath the stories of the tower are ornamented with bosses, alternately busts[2] and foliage. A plain square-headed window, of two lights, and divided by a transom, on each front, lights what is called the "Founder's Chamber." The upper story, on the outer side, displays three elegantly tabernacled niches; and in that on the left there still remains the figure of the cardinal kneeling in prayer.[3] Only one niche[4] appears on the side next the quadrangle, and it is now empty. The chamber is lighted by several small windows on the south front and sides.

Beaufort's Tower.

The parapet is quite plain, as is the string-course beneath it, but the buttresses have gables with crockets and finials. A handsome octagonal turret at the south-west angle, accessible by a low arched doorway from the quadrangle, contains a spiral stair, and rises boldly above the roof, giving "much character to the outline."[5] The vault of the gateway is richly groined, the central boss displaying "fruit and foliage in the shape of a cross." On the eastern side is the porter's lodge, in the wall of which one of the masters, Robert Sherburne, has inserted his favourite motto, " DILEXI SAPIENTIAM," with his initials and the date, 1503.

(1) I have found the essay "On the Architecture of the Church and Hospital of the Holy Cross," by Mr. E. A. Freeman, in the Winchester Vol. of Arch. Instit., a very valuable help in my survey and description of this subject. I have also used Britton's "Architectural Antiquities;" Dollman's "Examples of Ancient Domestic Architecture," Part II.; a lecture on "The History and Antiquities of the Hospital of St. Cross," by the Rev. L. M. Humbert, the present Master, to whom I am further indebted for much valuable personal assistance and information. I have also to acknowledge my obligations to W. T. Alchin, Esq. (Librarian to the City of London Library, Guildhall), for the use of his MS. collections relating to St. Cross.

(2) "Amongst them, it is said, are represented the cardinal's father, 'old John of Gaunt, time-honoured Lancaster,' Henry IV., Henry V., and probably also Henry VI., together with his accomplished, undaunted, and unfortunate queen, Margaret. There is also the bust

of the cardinal's predecessor in the see of Winchester, William of Wykeham" (Duthy's "Sketches," p. 278.)

(3) It has been conjectured that the central niche was occupied by the Holy Cross, and that on the left hand by the figure of the first founder of the hospital, Bishop De Blois. (Ibid.)

(4) This niche was originally occupied by a figure of the Blessed Virgin, crowned. Milner (vol. ii. p. 184) has given an absurd local story of its being the figure of a woman with a milkpail on her head, placed there because the foundation of the hospital was suggested to Bishop De Blois by such a woman, whom he casually met in the meadows hard by its present site. This figure, "more than three-quarters of a century" ago, "fell accidentally to the ground, and nearly crushed one of the brethren in its fall" (Ibid.; Duthy's "Sketches," p. 280).

(5) On the southern face of this tower, at the level of the "Founder's Chamber," is a vertical sundial. There is a chimney on the west side.

F F

The church.

The Church of St. Cross is one of the most beautiful architectural studies in England, and it has long enjoyed a corresponding renown.[1] Exquisite examples of every style, from the "Romanesque in all its purity and majesty," through the Transition-Norman and Early English, to "the fully developed Decorated,"[2] are to be seen in it; and in Transition-Norman it is perhaps the most complete and elegant specimen now in existence. It consists of a nave and choir, with aisles, two transepts, a low and massive square central tower, and a north porch. It is "remarkably lofty for its other proportions," being only a hundred and twenty-four feet from east to west, and a hundred and fifteen across the transept, and fifty-three and a half across the nave (interior measurement), whilst the height of the vault of the nave is fifty-seven feet.[3] Its orientation, like that of the cathedral and the college chapel, is a little south of the true east.

**The exterior:—
The east end.**

We commence our survey with the east end, which is the oldest part of the structure. The end of the choir is a high-pitched gable, between two handsome square turrets, rising from flat buttresses, which are so characteristic of the Norman style.[4] A central buttress of the same kind runs nearly to the apex of the gable;[5] and on each side of it is a small round window, or air-hole, for ventilating the roof.[6] Each of these buttresses has a narrower one attached to it, which rises to the spring of the gable. "Just below the gable, and continued round the square turrets, is a string adorned with the billet-moulding."[7] There are three sets of windows in this front, the highest, ranging with the clerestory, are on each side of the central buttress, with plain architraves, jamb-shafts, and sculptured capitals, the imposts being carried out to the buttresses. Those on a level with the triforium are two on each side, perfectly plain, without mouldings of any kind;[8] the lowest row, one on each side, have no jamb-shafts; and the plain arch-mould is carried out horizontally to the buttresses, as in the upper story.[9] The ends of the aisles of the choir are low and plain, with one window in each, like those on the same line in the end of the choir; and two broad flat buttresses near the angles.[10]

(1) The architectural celebrity of the Church of St. Cross commenced, perhaps, when Milner—who most inappropriately called it "a collection of architectural essays"—claimed, with as little reason, for the intersecting arches of its clerestory, the honour of originating "the pointed style" (Milner, vol. ii. pp. 135, 136).

(2) Freeman, pp. 3—9.

(3) Lecture on St. Cross, by the Master, p. 3.

(4) "These turrets are in two stages, of which the upper is adorned with slender banded shafts with capitals" (Freeman, p. 4.); whilst the lower stage exhibits narrow semicircular arches. There is no reason to doubt that properly the upper stage would be completed with a range of semicircular or pointed arches, and each turret surmounted by a pyramidical pinnacle; but no record remains to show that they were ever so completed.

(5) This buttress is narrower within the gable.

(6) The mouldings of these air-holes are perfectly flat, and the inner edge of the outer one is ornamented with nail-heads. These openings are now glazed.

(7) Freeman, p. 4.

(8) "But windows have been inserted of an equally plain character, in the two outer ones with pointed arches, in the inner square-headed" (Ibid.).

(9) No traces of these windows appear on the inside; and as "the inner wall is covered with remains of ancient paintings, it would seem that they must have been destroyed at an early period" (Ibid., p. 5).

A plain string-course runs round all the older parts of the building, at the level of the sill of these windows.

(10) These buttresses have two shallow set-offs, one above and one below the string-course; and the same may be observed of the other buttresses at this end.

"The choir is short, consisting of only two bays, which are, both in the aisle and The choir clerestory, divided by a flat buttress;" and similar flat buttresses appear near the eastern ends of the aisles. "At the angle of the south choir-aisle and the transept is the celebrated triple arch, which has given rise to so many opinions."[1] The three segments are circular, and richly ornamented with zigzag and cable mouldings; the imposts also are channelled, and that in the wall of the aisle is supported by a shaft with a most beautifully sculptured capital.[2] "The roofs of the aisles have been lowered, so that a range of small pointed windows in the triforium appears externally; this gives the clerestory a disproportionate height for a Romanesque building; but the original height of the roofs, reaching to the string underneath the proper clerestory windows, can be clearly traced in the weather mouldings yet remaining against the east sides of the transept."[3] A doorway with an obtusely pointed arch, and richly sculptured capitals and archmoulds, though blocked up, is still to be seen in the north aisle of the choir, near the angle with the transept; and from marks in the wall above and beside it, it would seem to have had at one time a porch over it, and at a later period a lean-to against the transept.[4]

Shallow buttresses divide the transept into two parts, but they are so placed as The transepts. to suggest the probability that the aisles of the body of the church were added, or made wider, after the erection of the first structure by De Blois; and the lower window nearest the aisle, on the east side of the north transept, "is most uncomfortably squeezed in between" the wall of the aisle and the buttress, which strongly confirms that suggestion.[5]

(1) Freeman, p. 5.

It appears most probable that this much-discussed arch was intended for a doorway, for which sufficient space was not afforded between the original buttress of the transept and the wall of the aisle; the half arch in the wall of the aisle was therefore constructed to make the opening wide enough, and to carry the superincumbent mass of masonry. In support of this, it may be alleged that this triple arch formed no part of the original structure, being in the later Transition-Norman style;—that there is an imperfect arch in the interior corresponding with it in position, slightly pointed, "with the embattled moulding," so that it may be regarded as of nearly the same date, or a little later, than the external one;—it is also quite certain that some part of De Blois' hospital was on the south side of the church, and that a cloister occupied the whole space between the choir and the transept (Freeman, p. 5), so that an entrance into the church, although in an eastern wall, was needful;—and I have seen an entrance to a turret stair in one of the South Elmham churches, in Suffolk, similarly constructed. The blocking up of the internal arch, and various other constructions which are of *later* date than this outer triple arch, ought not to be regarded as disproof of its original purpose. A similar arrangement for the priest's door is seen at Little Walsingham, Norfolk (Arch. Inst., Norwich Vol., p. 187). See also the Lecture of the Master (p. 15). There did exist a cloister having a doorway into the church (MS. *penes* the Master).

(2) "The lower windows both of the aisle and transept are unusually short, although the one in the choir most to the west has been lengthened by having the string beneath it cut away, and afterwards again blocked up by masonry" (Freeman, p. 5).

(3) Ibid., p. 7. The alteration of these roofs, and the formation of the windows in the triforium, were the work of John de Campeden. (MS. *penes* the Master.)

(4) Ibid., p. 8.

(5) Mr. Freeman (p. 8) observes that the wall of the south aisle, being of the early period, shows that this opinion is untenable. But though of an "early" period, it is not certain that the south aisle, in its present condition, is of the *earliest*, for the windows in it are far less simple and rude than those (for example) of the triforium at the east end; and there are numerous examples of changes of plan executed during the progress of a building, of which no traces remain but such as are fully as difficult of discovery and interpretation as these. (See above, in the description, &c., of the cathedral, p. 51, note 5.)

The windows to the aisles of the choir, and of the clerestories of both sides of the south transept, and the lower story of the eastern side of the north transept, are all in semicircular arches; those in the north aisle and transept with rich mouldings, the others like the lower series of the east end; but the upper windows in both choir and transept are of a later date than the lower ones.[1] In the north transept the windows of the clerestory are brought down much below the line of the bases of the corresponding windows in the south transept, and serve for the triforium as well; they are lancet-shaped, and have a perfectly simple hood-mould. One of the basement windows at the end of this transept is concealed by the cloister; the other, which is now filled up, is round-headed, with rich zigzag mouldings. At the end of the south transept are "two segmental-arched windows, now blocked up, ranging with the triforium."[2] The original sacristy is below these windows.[3] Traces of some of De Blois' buildings are to be seen here, and in the masonry of the south side of the choir.[4] There is also a small pointed window over the vaulted ceiling in the gable of each transept.

The roof and parapets.

The parapets of the choir and the transept are of the same height, but that of the nave is rather higher; and the ridge of the roof of the nave is higher than those of the choir and the transepts.[5] In the angles next the choir are squinches, which carry the parapet walk across from the choir to the transepts.

The tower.

In the lower part of the tower, between each angle and the slope of the adjoining roof, is a small and plain window of two lights.[6] Above these is a plain string-course, and on each side over it an arcade of five Early English pointed arches,[7] without moulding or shafts, each being divided by a species of transom (or interrupted

---

(1) Freeman, pp. 5, 8. This fact, which might appear inevitable, from the circumstances of the case, here demonstrates that changes in style were proceeding whilst the church was in progress of erection; and that the builders, instead of adhering to the type of the parts already completed, adopted each new fashion as it was introduced. The great picturesqueness and beauty of our choicest examples of ancient architecture, would seem to depend upon this occurrence of different styles in the same structure. And it must be constantly borne in mind, that in the old times, church-builders did not "adopt a style," as our architects do, but used sincerely the style of their day, or improved upon it if they could; and that thus each portion of every building most commonly bears authentic marks of the exact date of its construction.

(2) Freeman, p. 9.

(3) This is a plain room, vaulted with cross-springers, lighted by a single small loop rather than window; and in the wall next the church are three large ambries: all which facts seem to indicate that it was the original sacristy or vestry. The now adjoining room appears to be of more recent date.

Above the present roof, on the end of the transept, however, are traces of two higher gables.

(4) The string-course on the southern side of the choir is "quite flat on its under surface, having had the roof of a cloister underneath it" (Freeman, p. 5).

(5) Mr. Freeman considers the whole of the parapets of the church "a later addition" to it; and is of opinion that the roofs of nave and choir, aisle and transept, were originally "dripping roofs" (p. 7). The roof of the nave was covered with lead by Edington during his mastership; before that time it had been covered with a thatch of straw. The roofs of the choir and aisles were renewed in the mastership of John de Campeden. (MS. *penes* the Master.) On the south side of the nave, near the tower, may be seen traces of the original wall-top.

(6) These windows are Transition Decorated, or Perpendicular; each light having a cinquefoiled head, and a short mullion carried up straight to the arch from the apex of the small arch thus made; and they, as well as the windows in the story above, were the work of John de Campeden. (MS. *u. s.*)

(7) From the inspection of the interior of the tower I have ascertained that these arches were originally open; and that a glazed and shuttered window in the inner wall protected the belfry from the weather.

The clock is on the north side of the tower, in the arch to the west of the window.

string-course) midway between the base and the spring of the arch; and the upper part of the central arch, on each side, is pierced as a plain two-light window. Another string-course marks the base of the parapet.

The nave has three bays, and in it the roofs of the aisles are complete, and *The nave.* rise to the sills of the clerestory windows. The windows of the aisles nearest the transept are late Norman; the second, on the south side, "retains the round arch, but has otherwise Early English features; the third in each aisle is pure Early English," as are those at the ends of the aisles.[1] In the clerestory, on both sides, the two-light windows are good examples of the Decorated style.[2] The north porch, which is vaulted, is Early English; and it has a chamber over it, "lighted by a very elegant little window," which is Transition Early English.[3] The south door is Early English, also.[4]

Although devoid of rich ornamentation, the west end of the body of the church is *The west end.* very fine. Two solid Early English buttresses, with three set-offs, form, together with two flat Norman buttresses at the end of the clerestory, a square turret, on each side, rising just above the base of the gable. The west door is a double doorway of the Early English style, and deserves particular attention on account of its excellence, "and also for the bold and singular variety of the tooth-ornament in its arch mouldings."[5] The great western window stands on a plain string-course, and is of five lights; the central one being rather wider than the others, with splendid geometrical tracery in its head, in "fully developed Decorated."[6]

On entering the church, the eye is immediately struck with the great height of the *The interior.* roof, in comparison with the extent of the structure. No impression of disproportion or want of harmony is, however, produced; but instead, an air of cathedral grandeur is imparted to the interior, which would otherwise be noticeable principally on account of the exceedingly rich ornamentation of its arches and mouldings. In its pristine state, when decorated with colour and gilding, with saintly pictures, and sacred

(1) Freeman, p. 9. The northern window has rich mouldings stopped above the imposts; the southern mere chamfers (ibid., p. 10). Over the window at the end of the south aisle is another very small one, with an ogee arch.

(2) The arches of the lights in these windows are trefoiled merely; and in the heads are circles feathered with six cusps, or else divided into two long quatrefoils. Peculiar interest attaches to these windows, because we learn from the MS. before referred to, that they were the work of Edington. They may, therefore, be cited in proof of the opinion respecting the Edington windows in the cathedral, which I have expressed above (p. 101).

(3) Each light is trefoiled, and in the head is a circle with a cinquefoil. Mr. Freeman (p. 9) calls it Early English, but it is certainly later than the undoubted Early English of this western part of the church.

(4) Similar changes in style are observable in the buttresses. Those (in the aisles) between the first and second windows from the transept are Norman, but the

others are plain Early English in two stages. That nearest the west end, on the south side, is much deeper than the rest; being, indeed, part of the wall of the brethren's houses, removed in 1789.

(5) "The arches of the two openings are of the trefoil shape; the central shaft is a square pier, with the angles chamfered, so as to make it octagonal; the capital is mutilated. In the head is a small quatrefoil, now glazed. The ground has risen so as to hide the basis of the joint-shafts" (Freeman, p. 9).

(6) Each pair of side lights forms, in fact, a large and most elegant lancet-window, with a quatrefoil in the head. The circle occupies the entire head of the window, so that the arch of the central light is flattened. All the lights are trefoiled. Three spherical triangles (two above and one below), six-foiled, with small trefoils in the interstices, fill up the circle. And in the gable is a small plain opening, now glazed, with a pointed arch, over the vaulted ceiling.

legends, few churches of its magnitude or character would be found which surpassed in splendour the Church of St. Cross.[1]

The nave.   The western portion of the nave is substantially Early English, but the bay next the transept is Transition Norman. The three arches on each side are obtusely pointed, with boldly-cut mouldings, all of them being plain in the western arches; and "the first (on each side from the east) springs from a respond forming part of the lantern piers, and like them exhibiting all the features of the Transitional period."[2] The piers are massive and cylindrical, with square bases, and extremely elegant ornaments at the angles, round abaci, and simply moulded or scalloped capitals.[3] Over the points of these arches runs a string-course,[4] on which stand the openings of the triforium;[5] and above them is another string-course, and then the clerestory windows, Decorated, under Early English arches, and with a gallery in front of them, carried through passages in each jamb. The vaulting shafts spring from elegant corbels, placed midway between the two string-courses; and the vault is groined, with moulded ribs. On bosses near the west end, the arms of Beaufort and Wykeham have been subsequently carved.

The font.   The font consists of a plain panelled square Early English bowl of Purbeck marble, on a modern base, and stands under the eastern arch on the north side of the nave.

In the aisles the change of style is also to be observed, and the groining ribs at the eastern ends are richly ornamented. The responds to the piers are pilasters with shafts at the angles, having fluted Norman capitals and corbels at mid-height, from which rise the vaulting shafts of the direct rib of the vault. The hood-mould to the south door (the interior of which is only a segment of an arch) is formed by the string-course which runs round beneath the windows.

The tower.   The piers of the tower are massive, but relieved from all heaviness by slender shafts set in rectangular recesses, two on each side, whilst another shaft springs from a (more modern looking) corbel in the middle of the face of each pier. The tower is still, as it was originally, open to the interior of the church as high as the "solar;" the lower story exhibits on each side "an arcade of four" Early English arches; and in the two outer arches in each arcade are the Perpendicular windows noticed above.[6]

(1) At the present time a rude modern wooden screen, or partition, incloses the portion of the church used for divine service, and greatly mars the effect of the whole.

(2) Freeman, p. 16. Most of these bases have three plinths, and the upper base-mould is a reversed ogee, but the central plinth is wanting in others. The arches have soffits, and not mouldings, beneath. The responds from which the easternmost arches spring are shafts rising from corbels at about their own height from the floor.

(3) The base of one of these piers is simply recessed at the angles. Base ornaments occur in the small vaulting shafts in the choir; and there is an ornamented bracket in the side of the pier near the font

(4) This string is Early English in the western parts of the church, and Norman, or Transition Norman, in the east; and it is carried round the shafts of the tower (or lantern) piers as a band. The point of change in the style is marked by a bunch of foliage. (Freeman, p. 16.)

(5) There is no triforium opening over the arch next the tower; the arches are perfectly plain Early English, with shafts and hood-moulds terminating in corbels. The ascent to these triforia, and the "solar" of the porch, is now by a stair at the north-west corner.

(6) See above, p. 220. The floor of the "solar" rests on short octagonal engaged shafts (double in each angle,

The original windows of the "solar," or belfry, were small cinquefoiled windows in the inner walls, which were glazed and closed by shutters. There are two bells in this chamber, both of them of recent date. The ascent to the tower is in the south-eastern angle, mounting originally from the triforium of the transept, but the stairs there are now ruinated and stopped.

In the transepts we meet with the richly ornamented arches which are so charac- *The transepts.* teristic of this church. The basement windows in the north transept are thus enriched with variously arranged chevron or zigzag mouldings, without shafts; the northern window on the east side "exhibiting a remarkable variety of the beak-head moulding, developed into the complete form of a bird."[1] In the south transept there are shafts in the jambs, and we see the double-cone moulding, and the plaster within the splay is finished with the chevron and scalloped mouldings.[2] The arcade of the clerestory in the north transept has been cut away in constructing the long lancet windows round it, but the opening can be seen near the piers of the tower on each side.[3]

A small door communicates with the ambulatory at the north end, and the traces of an altar are very visible on the east side. The vaulting is pointed, with late Norman mouldings, "rising from corbels with round abaci."[4] A late wooden screen divides the transept from the body of the church, and here at present stands the organ.

In the south transept, at the back of the triple arch noticed above,[5] is an *The south tran-sept.* imperfect pointed arch with flat embattled moulding, but it is blocked up, and several open and shallow rectangular recesses appear instead of the doorway. On the eastern side is a wide recess under a low, flat, pointed arch, springing from imposts with indented mouldings, resting on sculptured capitals. It seems to have formerly covered an altar, and we know that there were in this part of the church altars dedicated to

and three along each side), resting on corbels consisting of grotesque heads.

The "*campanile*" is said to have been repaired in the time of John de Campeden. (MS. *u. s.*)

(1) Freeman, p. 14.

(2) Both the windows next the walls of the aisles of the choir are rather oblique, as if those walls had been built after the plan of the transept was completed, and would otherwise have darkened them.

(3) The triforium arcade on the west side has been made wider, and painted with a plain and late fresco pattern, which can be traced from an arched opening through the north wall of the transept, which is now blocked up; and along the north wall of the nave in the triforium, under the roof of the aisle, where, above the plain pattern consisting of squares of black arranged symmetrically, and connected with diagonal lines, may be still seen a border ornamented with medallions of the heads of figures, now almost obliterated. The wall of the tower pier is cut away, so as to afford a partial view of the altar from this gallery, which I am inclined to regard as intended for the sick brethren; for in Wavell's view of St. Cross (vol. ii.

p. 230) there appears to be a very narrow lean-to against the north end of the transept, and a lower one crossing from it to the infirmary, which would indicate the existence of a descent from this arcade to the infirmary, when that view was taken. The present contrivance of a shutter opening through one of the basement windows into the transept is certainly of Protestant origin; and there is no triforium along the side of the choir whence the celebration of mass could be observed.

(4) Ibid. "There may be seen in the north-east angle the remains of a base connected with nothing at present remaining, and therefore, apparently, the only relic of the first period [of its erection] to be observed in the interior of the church" (ibid.). The vaulting shaft springs from a corbel high up in the angle.

(5) Above the arch of the south aisle of the choir the arch in the triforium is double and pointed, but behind it, in the outer wall, there was originally one wide circular arch, which probably opened into the space above the aisle. A small door through it now communicates with the leads over it. And there is, on the outside, the trace of another door.

St. Ursula and St. Sitha, with the 11,000 virgins, and to St. Stephen.[1]   Another similar, but smaller and lower, recess, with short shafts in the jambs, and richly sculptured capitals, is in the south wall, beside the door of the sacristy.   The ascent to the triforia of the south side of the church, and to the tower, is in the south-western angle.[2]

The choir.   Two pointed arches, resting on massive octagonal piers of much later date, divide the aisle on each side from the body of the choir.[3]   The style of the original piers, with their clustered columns and sculptured capitals, may be seen in the responds.[4] "As far as the original work remains," it is acutely observed by Mr. Freeman, this choir "is Romanesque," or Transition Norman, "with the pointed arch introduced as an arch of construction throughout, while the semicircular form is retained as an arch of decoration."[5]

The triforium.   " Above the pier-arches is the celebrated triforium of intersecting arches, to which Dr. Milner attributed the origin of the pointed style."[6]   It was not until the time of John de Campeden that the segmental arches formed by the intersections of the interlaced semicircular arches of the arcade, on each side of the choir, were pierced.[7]   The form, also, is different from that of the genuine Early English arch ; the primary arches of the arcade being much flattened or depressed ; and the inspection of the roofs of the aisles will show that these openings were not originally intended for windows to light the choir, but to afford a faint light from the choir into the dark passage behind the wall, as in the nave.   At the east end there is a proper triforium,[8] and there the windows were originally round-headed, as may be seen on the outside.   There is another triforium, or passage, beneath the windows of the clerestory, all round the choir ; and the mouldings and details of the interlaced arches of the arcade, and of the window arches, and shafts, &c., of the clerestory are excessively rich and varied, and must, when at first adorned with colour and gilding, have appeared unusually magnificent.

The vault.   Besides all this decoration, the ribs of the groined vault are elaborately moulded ; and the eastern bay having " a double cell," produces " in a slight degree the effect of apsidal vaulting."[9]   The clustered vaulting shafts have now no corbels, but originally they probably had such as may yet be seen in the south transept.

The reredos, &c.   The remains of a finely sculptured and coloured Perpendicular reredos may be

---

(1) MS. in the Master's possession, quoted above These altars were dedicated in 1388.

(2) The corbels to the vaulting shafts are worthy of observation, as the very rudest and simplest possible, short of leaving the blocks of stone wholly unsculptured.

(3) From our MS. we also learn that these piers were constructed in 11 Rich. II. (1387-8). They had been styled Perpendicular by Mr. Freeman (p. 12). The bases of these columns are peculiar, being, in fact, the original bases of the Norman pier, with clustered columns like the tower piers, but altered so as somewhat to conform to the style of the new piers, which had been substituted for the original ones.

(4) Mr. Freeman (p. 12) calls these capitals " Corinthianizing," but there is more of the promise of the Early English clustering foliage in them, than the remembrance of the Corinthian acanthus. Some of the capitals of the shafts to the tower piers, and the responds in the aisles, are still in block, or are merely " boasted " in the first rough outline of the design.

(5) Freeman, p. 11.

(6) Ibid., p. 12.

(7) MS. authority, u. s.

(8) This arcade is accessible from the leads of the aisles only.

(9) Freeman, p. 13.

seen on each side of the modern construction of wood, on the south side of which, at the base of the respond to the pier, is a very elegant altar-shaped credence.[1]   Both pier-arches next the east end are filled up, that in the north side wholly, and the other in part, with rich stone screens and pinnacles, Perpendicular in style, and very probably removed hither from the Church of St. Faith, when it was taken down; but there was always some substantial parclose between the choir and the aisles here, because the aisles were really chapels; and the low wall beneath the tabernacle work on the south side may, perhaps, be the remains of that partition.   The other arches are similarly filled up with low walls.[2]

Few of the original stalls remain, and they are now removed from the choir into the space under the tower, which is now fitted up with pews and other seats, and inclosed from the nave and south transept by a very unsightly wooden partition for the regular parochial service.   In the place of the old stalls are found sixteen of more recent date, with a most elaborate and well-carved Renaissance canopy above them; the pendants of which are demi-figures with labels, &c., females, kings, &c., with other figures in medallions above, and among the ornaments Bishop Fox's well-known pelican, and the arms of the see of Winchester.[3]

The stalls.

On each side of the choir the aisles were made into chapels, that on the north side was in all probability dedicated to the Blessed Virgin Mary.[4]   It is divided from the north transept by a wooden screen of late workmanship, with a small doorway in the middle.   Traces of the altar are very manifest, and there is a very remarkable late

The Lady chapel.

(1) This credence is panelled on the side with trefoiled arches, and flowers on the cusps; at the end is a panel sculptured with an eagle of St. John; and a cornice, with flowers at intervals in it, and a quatrefoil border, run round both sides.

Just beneath the string-course of the triforium is a wooden projecting cornice, apparently the remains of some sort of reredos of that material, earlier in date than the present one.

An altar of alabaster was placed here for the high altar, on the feast of the Annunciation, 1385, and it was consecrated in honour of the Holy Cross, on the feast of St. Vitalis, April the 28th, in the following year.

(2) The tops of the pinnacles being cut off to make this highly ornamented work fit into the arch, shows that it is an insertion, as well as its unfitness for a parclose in so small a church.   The wall on which the part of it in the southern arch rests, was painted over on both sides with a kind of trellised pattern with acorns, which show very plainly through the numerous coats of limewash which Protestant zeal and want of taste have in successive ages bestowed on it; and the same ornament may be traced on the back of the walls which fill up the other two arches, and elsewhere in the aisles.

In the wall on the south side of the altar the piscina and sedilia may be traced, but they are stopped with lath and plaster and apparently painted over.

There is a doorway in the wall on the north side, next the tower pier, which seems to be of the date of that rude parclose.

(3) John de Campeden is recorded in the MS. I have so frequently referred to, as having restored, or repaired, the stalls, sedilia, and benches in the choir, with the painting of the reredos; and of having completed the presbytery near the altar; and inclosed a chapel for a vestry.

The pulpit was the work of William Byflete, Priest of St. Cross, and Rector of Morestead.

The carvings on the canopy in the choir resemble nothing more closely than the figures in the Nuremberg Chronicle, and seem to be of foreign execution.   The date of their erection is plainly signified by the occurrence of Bishop Fox's emblem, and we know that the church must have undergone various alterations at that time.   On the eastern stall, on the north side, are neatly carved the names of all the officials of the hospital and the church in the year 1572.

(4) The existence of a Lady Chapel is proved by the MS. to which I am so much indebted, which notices the construction of the parclose (*interclausum*), and the fitting of this chapel with benches and stalls (*descis*), and particularly with stalls (*descis*) for the thirteen brethren, in the year 1390.

The altar of the Blessed Virgin is also spoken of in connection with one of St. Thomas of Canterbury.

G G

Norman piscina at the foot of the respond of the pier beside it.[1] Above the piscina are two brackets attached to the shafts of the respond; and in the other side, in the angle of the wall, a large bracket, which has the wall cut away behind it, as if it had proved of insufficient width for the image or shrine placed on it.[2]

The south aisle.

It is uncertain to what saint the chapel formed by the south aisle of the choir was dedicated;[3] but the traces of the altar are very distinct, and there is a plain, double, trefoil-headed piscina, with vestiges of sedilia (also with trefoiled heads) beside it in the south wall. Both these chapels or aisles show the same rich chevron, or mascle, moulding, on the window arches, and on the ribs of the vaulting.[4] And both here and in the transepts there are steps within the sills of the windows, which serve " to disguise the shortness of the part actually pierced for light."[5]

Stained glass, &c.

In the great western window is collected together a remarkable assemblage or fragments of ancient stained glass, together with some modern performances (at the charge of a late Master, Dr. Lockman), the intention of which far surpasses the execution.[6] And in every part of the church, but particularly in the choir and under the tower, are to be seen good and ancient encaustic tiles of various patterns, the most effective of which exhibit the motto " HAVE MYNDE," a most suitable precept for a house of prayer.[7] Many traces of wall-paintings yet remain; the most frequent is a trellis pattern with acorns; another, on the inside faces of the piers of the towers, appears to have been some kind of flower-pattern; and occasionally some figures can be very plainly perceived, as at the east end, and in the aisles of the nave.

The ancient monuments.

The most ancient monument was most probably that which was placed under the low recess at the south end of the transept, but all record of it has perished now. In the north aisle of the nave, beneath the window near the transept, the sarcophagus of Petrus de S. Mario, Master of the Hospital in 1289 (who died 1296), is built into the

---

(1) The bowl of this piscina is surrounded by grotesque figures, and stands on a short octagonal shaft, with a square base, ornamented at the angles, and it is attached to the parclose by a small tretoiled arch.

(2) In this chapel stands an old and very plain wooden table, its history and use are, however, unknown.

(3) Mention is made in my MS. authority of a chapel of St. John the Baptist, and the removal thither of a crucifix, with images of the Blessed Virgin and St. John, from a " solar" in the northern part of the nave, which was most probably the porch chamber. An altar of St. John the Baptist is also mentioned, and likewise one of St. John the Evangelist. An altar of St. Catharine is also spoken of as having been consecrated in 1386.

(4) " The arch between the two bays has a plain flat soffit, and springs from a flat pilaster, to the angles of which are attached the shafts whence spring the ribs." And both aisles " open into the transept by arches with very broad soffits, rising from rectangular piers with shafts at the angles, the capitals of which are continued

as a sort of frieze along the inner flat surface " (Freeman, pp. 13, 14).

(5) Ibid.

(6) Mr. Winston, in his " Short Notice of Painted Glass, &c.," in the Winchester Vol. of Arch. Instit. (p. 2), says that there are fragments of Early English and Decorated glass to be seen in the church, as well as much of the Perpendicular period (p. 5).

Wavell (vol. ii. p. 229) says that the words " NICHOLAS BEDFORD " were legible in the west window, and adds, " a window in the east side of the north transept was formerly ornamented in the same style, and still retains an *Ave Maria*, and some fragments, under which is *Orate pro anima Richardi Lusteshall* . . . . Master of this hospital in the year 1346. And in a south window of the cross aisle are these arms, viz., *Gules*, three lions heads passant [probably for jessant], fleur-de-lis reversed, or three eagles quartering barry, and a chief."

(7) The paving of the church, with the chapels and aisles, according to our MS. record, was renewed, or restored, in 13 Rich. II. (1389—90).

wall, under a wide and low arched niche, cinquefoiled and ornamented with crockets and finials, pinnacles, and a square hood-mould. The stone cover of the sarcophagus is quite modern, and the upper part of the monument is of more recent date than the interment.[1]

Most conspicuous amongst the monumental brasses is that of John de Campeden, which now lies under the tower; it consists of a full-length and full-sized figure of the Master in his ecclesiastical vestments, with his hands raised in prayer, and from his mouth two scrolls containing the words— Monumental brasses.

"IHŪ CŪ VENIS IUDICAR̄ NOLI ME CŌDĒPNAR̄;"

and—

"QUI PLASM[AU]ISTI ME MISERERE MEI."

Two small shields on either side of the head contain the emblems of the Trinity and the Passion; and this inscription is at the feet :—

" HIC IACET JOHANNES DE CAMPEDEN QUDĀ
CUSTOS ISTIUS HOSPITALIS CUIUS AĪE P̄PICIETUR DEUS."

And on a fillet round the stone, with roses at the angles, is this inscription :—

✠ " CREDO Q̄D REDEMPTOR MEUS VIUIT & IN NOUISSIMO DIE DE TERRA SURRECTURUS SUM & RURSUM CIRCUMDABOR PELLE MEA ET IN CARNE MEA VIDEBO DEUM SALUATORĒ MEŪ QUEM UISURUS SUM EGO IPĒ & OCULI MEI CONSPECTURI SUNT & NON ALIUS REPOSITA EST HEC SPES MEA IN SINU MEO."

Near this, beneath the full-length figure of a Master, in brass,[2] is the following inscription on copper :—

" ORATE PRO AĪE DN̄I THOME LAWNE RECTORIS DE MOTTYSFOUNT QUI OBIIT NONO DIE MENSIS MAII A° DN̄I M° QUINGENTESIMO XVIII° CUIUS AĪE PROPICIETUR DEUS."

In the nave are the following brasses : on a Petworth marble coffin lid :—

" THE YERE OF OURE LORD M° CCCC° L° AND TWO:
VPPON THE XI DAY IN THE MONETH OF FEBEVER:
THE SOUL OF JOÑ NEWLES THE BODY PASSID FRO:
A BROTHER OF THIS PLACE RESTYNG UNDIR YIS STONE HERE:
BORN IN BEAME [Bearn ?] SQUYER AND S̄UANT MORE YAN XXX YERE:
VNTO HARRY BEAUFORD BUSSHOP AND CARDINAL:
WHOS SOULES GOD CONVEY AND HIS MODER DERE:
VNTO THE BLISSE OF HEVEN THAT IS ETERNALL. AMEN:"

(1) The shafts and capitals of this monument are plain Early English or Decorated, but the panelled and gabled pinnacles, the cusps, and foliage of the crockets and finials, and the quatrefoils of the square hood-mould are much later in style, and look rather like an imitation of Decorated work than genuine Perpendicular. Wavell (vol. ii. p. 232) says that the original inscription "in Saxon [or, as we may interpret, Edwardian] characters," was " HIC JACET MAGISTER PETRUS DE SANCTA MARIA, QUONDAM CUSTOS HUJUS DOMUS." In the Lecture by the Master of St. Cross (p. 20), the following incident respecting this tomb is recorded :—

" It is within the recollection of a respected inhabitant of the village, that the Purbeck marble sarcophagus which contained the body, was accidentally laid open by workmen, and the features of its venerable occupant, after a lapse of more than 500 years, were found entire . . . . But while she gazed, a tremulous motion came over the countenance, and all was *dust* . . . . The habiliments and cope remained, the latter was, as usual, of costly material, interwoven with gold and colours, and for a long time shreds of it were preserved."

(2) The Master of St. Cross considers this figure to be of an earlier date than the inscription.

Under the trace of the brass of a demi-figure :—

"HERE LYETH ELIZABETH WROUGHTON GENTILWOMĀ WHO DEPARTYD THE XXVIIJᵒ DAY OF MAYE
IN THE YERE OF OUᴿ LORDE GOD Mᵒ CCCCᵒ LIᵒ WHOSE SOULE JHŪ P̄DON."

There are numerous traces of brasses here; and one figure of a Master (?), but without any inscription.[1]

In the south transept is the following :—

"ORATE P̄ AM̄ DN̄I WILLM̄I SAŪDRES QUŌDĀ CAPELLANI NOVE FFŪDACŌIS HŪ COLLEGII QUI OBIIT
XXIXᵒ DIE NOUĒBRˢ Aᵒ DN̄I Mᵒ CCCCᵒ LXIIIJᵒ CŪ AĪE P̄PICIET DĒ."

And another commemorates Alexander Ewart, a brother, who died July the 18th, 1569.

In the possession of the Master is the following brass, supposed to have come from the south aisle of the choir :—

" HIC IACET JOHĒS WAYTE FILIUS JOHĪS WAYTE ARMIGĒR ET AGATHE UXORIˢ EIUS QUI
QUIDEM JOHĒS WAYTE FILIUS OBIIT VLTIMO DIE OCTOBRIS Aᵒ DN̄I Mᵒ Vᶜ IJᵒ CUIUS AĪE
PROPICIETUR DEUS. AMEN."[2]

Other traces of brasses may be seen; two inscriptions, preserved by Wavell, are given below.[3]

Some other ancient inscriptions on ledger stones may be preserved here.   In the nave are these :—

" HIC IACET JOHĒS TURKE QUI QUONDAM ERAT FR̄ ISTIUS LOCI NOUE FUNDACIŌIS EDIT. P̄
HENRICŪ EP̄M WYNTON ET CARDINALĒ ANGLIE CUĪ AĪE P̄PICIET DEUS.   AMĒ."

" HIC IACET JOHĒS KNYZTH QUI QUŌDAM ERAT FR̄ ISTIUS LOCI NOVE FŪDACIŌIS EDIT. P̄.
HENRICŪ. EP̄M WYNTON ET CARDINALĒ ANGLIE. CUĪ AĪE P̄PICIET DEUS.   AMEN."

On the top of a stone coffin in the south transept is inscribed, in much later characters, " THOMAS PRESTWOODE, 7 DEC. 1566."

And in the adjacent aisle of the choir are the following quaint records :—

" SUSAÑA LAVRENCE	" GEORGIVS LAVRENCE
VAS CARNE VALENS.	EGO VTI LAVRVS RIGENS.
A FLESH-PREVAILING VESSEL FOVND	I VNDER LY
BEAVTIF'D TO LYE VNDER GROVND.	AS LAVREL DRY.
VIXIT DEC. 13. 1647.	VIXIT OCTOB. 14. 1650.
REVIXIT JAN. 18. 1650."	DEVIXIT SEP. 19. 1651."

(1) Wavell (vol. ii. p. 232) gives this fragment of the inscription formerly belonging to this figure, and states that it was then "preserved in the porter's lodge."

". . . . RWARD DECRETORUM DOCTORIS AC NUPER HUJUS . . . . DIE APRILIS ANNO DOMINI MCCCC NON-AGES TERTIO."   And in a note he refers it to Richard Harward, Master in the year 1489.

This fragment, I am informed by the Master of St. Cross, is not now to be found.

(2) From the Master of St. Cross I learn, that Charles Wayte, Esq., of Appleshaw, near Andover, considers this John Wayte to be an ancestor of his, and a descendant of John Wayte, controller on the part of the prior and convent during Wykeham's works in the cathedral.

(3) In the nave was this—

" HIC JACET DONUS JOHĒS BERTON, QUONDAM VICA-RIUS SCI JOHIS IN SOCA WINTON."

And in the south transept this—

" HIC JACET JOHĒS PREWS, QUONDAM RECTOR EC-CLESIÆ DE MECHELMERSH, QUI OBIIT 13 DIE MENSIS APRILIS, A.D. MCCCCXVIII. CUJUS ANIMÆ, &c." (Wavell, vol. ii. pp. 234, 235.)

Modern monuments.

The following are the most noteworthy modern monuments. In the nave, near the south door, is a handsome mural monument, with a long inscription, to the memory of the Right Honourable Charles Wolfran Cornwall,[1] some time Speaker to the House of Commons, born 15th January, 1735, died 2nd January, 1789; and of Elizabeth, his wife, died 8th March, 1809.

There are mural monuments in the south aisle of the choir, also, to the memory of Mary, wife of the Rev. William Rawlins, Rector of Teversal and Chaplain of the Hospital, died 27th July, 1802; and Robert White, Steward of the Hospital, died 12th March, 1755; and Anne Randal, his sister, died 14th June, 1763.

And in the choir, beside other inscriptions on ledgers, are those which commemorate Abraham Markland, S.T.P., Rector of Meon-Stoke and Master of the Hospital, died 29th July, 1727; his wife Catharine, died 1693; and his sons, George, died 1722, and Abraham, died 1705; also William Lewis, Canon of Winchester Cathedral and Master of the Hospital, died 7th July, 1667.[2]

Other ledgers record the deaths of various members of the Russell, Forder, Churcher, and other families well known in this part of the county.

Returning now to the quadrangle, we may note the general arrangement of the domiciles of the brethren (each of whom has three rooms), amongst which are to be seen some interesting relics of olden times in the heavy and iron-bound oaken doors, and the handles to them, as well as in the chimneys, which are ascribed to Cardinal Beaufort, and are the most conspicuous feature in that range of buildings.[3] The Master's house has been modernized as far as it was possible, by which process it has lost its antique appearance without gaining the aspect of a new building.[4] Some plain panelled oak is to be seen in some of the rooms, and along the cornice in that next the dining room, in large carved letters of the sixteenth century, is this inscription :—

The brethren's dwellings.

The Master's house.

" COMPROBATVM VIRTVS LAVDATA CRESCIT DIGNVS A DIGNIS."

Between the Master's house and Beaufort's Tower lies the most interesting of all

The refectory, &c.

---

(1) Speaker Cornwall occupied the Master's house during some part of Dr. Lockman's mastership.

(2) Duthy (" Sketches," p. 287) has printed these inscriptions at length.

(3) See the Master's Lecture, p. 15; and Dollman's " Examples of Ancient Domestic Architecture," Part II., referred to above.

In 14 Rich. II. (1390-1) eleven chambers and a chapel were constructed for the thirteen brethren, according to my MS. authority.

The watercourse, which is brought obliquely from the " Lock Burn " (not *Lock Pond*, as in Winchester; see above pp. 10, 89, and note), enters the outer gate and crosses the fore-court to the south-west angle, passes under the larder, and round the *outside* of the north and west side of the quadrangle, and in the same manner skirts the site of the old southern range of the brethren's dwellings,

reappearing a little way to the south of the church, running due east until past the level of the east end of the church, where it turns southward to the side of the river. There was most probably a branch through the brewery and under the eastern side of the quadrangle. In ascertaining the original arrangement of the hospital buildings, the course of this streamlet is of the greatest use.

A rent is paid annually to the dean and chapter for the use of this rivulet.

(4) Some painted glass in the gallery, amongst scriptural subjects of no great antiquity, shields of Cardinal Beaufort's and other arms, contains Robert Sherburne's motto—*Dilexi sapientiam*, Bishop Fox's emblem, &c.

The residence originally assigned to the Master was over the gateway (MS. *u. s.*), whence the whole of the establishment could be completely under his eye.

The MS. I have found so valuable, records the conthe domestic portions of the hospital buildings, the refectory, with the kitchen, larder, &c. The hall, which was originally part of the " Hundred-men's Hall,"[1] is raised on a crypt (which shows some good plain groining), and is entered from the quadrangle by a broad flight of steps, under a neat Perpendicular porch. It is rather lofty for its length, which may be accounted for by its having been but a part of the original refectory.[2] There are two windows on the south side, and two on the north looking into the forecourt; they are good early Perpendicular, of two lights, with a plain transom at mid-height, and a large quatrefoil in the head, surrounded by gracefully flowing tracery. There are, in painted glass, in these quatrefoils, the arms of Cardinal Beaufort, surmounted with the hat, and surrounded by its pendent strings, and " the livery-colours of his family," with a motto—" A HONO ET LYESSE."[3]

The high-pitched timber roof, the rafters of which are open at the north-west end, the hearth in the centre of the hall, the dais at the upper end, the long tables and benches, and the rude stair to the chamber in the tower beside it, the panelled gallery with its projecting centre at the lower end, impart an air of quaint antiquity to this hall, which forms no small part of the general interest of the hospital.[4] Opposite the entrance to the refectory is the door to the kitchen, larder, bread-room, and other offices of that description, which form the west side of the forecourt.[5] There is nothing very remarkable here except some painted glass in the passage to

struction, " *in prima camera custodis*," of a new chimney, and of two windows called " Standisshes," " *pro aisiamento Domini Comitis Canciæ*," who resided here when the parliament met at Winchester in 16 Rich. II. (1392-3).

(1) My reasons for hazarding this assertion are the certainty that the building commonly designated as the Hundred-men's Hall (now the brew-house) never was a hall at all; the appearance of architectural features in the windows, and elsewhere, in the present hall, of an earlier date than Beaufort's time; the difficulty (not to say the impossibility) of making out the plan of the hospital in its earlier condition (*i. e.* before the *nova fundatio* of Beaufort), in keeping with the course of the water-channels, and the various incidental notices of the several buildings on any other supposition; and a notice in the MS.—which has proved of so much service in respect to the architectural history of the church—recording the building of a roof by William of Edington, during his mastership, to the hall called Hundred-men's Hall, which is now, says the writer, at a later date, divided into two halls, " *viz.*, *aula Custodis et Familiæ ibidem et aula Hundredmannorum*." It is not surprising that amongst the changes which St. Cross has seen, should be the extinction of the institution of the Hundred-men's charity; the separation of the *Custos* and the *Familia*; and the appropriation, to the former, who no longer lived in the gateway tower, of the Hundred-men's Hall, which had lost its special use, and was converted into the existing Master's house; and to the *Familia* the hall they had formerly shared with the *Custos*.

(2) See the preceding note.

(3) Winston, *u. s.*, p. 6.

(4) The roof is a plain timbered one, and the corbels on which the wall-piers rest are angels with shields. Beneath the wall plate is a series of trefoil-headed panels.

The space under the gallery is divided from the hall by a wooden partition, in which are two doors, and thus serves as a kind of lobby.

On the newel of the stairs to the tower, Bishop Fox's pelican is carved.

There is a German painted triptych fixed on the wall above the wainscoting, on the dais; the principal subject is the Holy Family, in which an angel takes the place of St. John; and St. Barbara and St. Catharine occupy the two lateral compartments. It is an early painting, but is not by Albert Durer.

Several rude articles of furniture are to be seen in this room; amongst them is a wooden chair carved in the Jacobean style, which is exhibited as Cardinal Beaufort's chair; and some old wooden saltcellars, candlesticks, and blackjacks, which receive their full meed of attention from visitors.

(5) John de Campeden is stated in the MS. record of the hospital to have made a *domus lardariæ*. The chambers over the kitchen are too ruinous to be applied to any use now.

There are many other notices of the offices of the hospital in the MS. referred to, but the identification of all the sites would require too much space.

W. H. Bartlett.

R. J. Roberts

HALL OF ST. CROSS.

the kitchen, in which is Sherburne's motto, and the date 1497, in very early numeral characters.[1]

Both the infirmary (or "Nuns' Chambers," as they are called) and the ambulatory *The infirmary, &c.* beneath it have been very much altered from their original condition, for the wood-work and windows are not earlier than the sixteenth century, and the octagonal stair turret and the parapet of the ambulatory are a complete patchwork of brick and fragments of some older buildings. All this part appears to have been altered in the time of Henry Compton.[2]

The brew-house forms the eastern side of the forecourt, and from its rough timber roof, the absence of windows, with the exception of one small two-light window opening into the court, and other signs, it must be adjudged not to have been originally the Hundred-men's Hall, but to have been erected for the purpose which it still so admirably serves.[3] Between it and the outer gate is a porter's lodge, now used as an outhouse. And on the stream of the Itchen, hard by, and forming one of the boundaries of the precinct, there still stands what anciently was the hospital mill, in "Mullesmede," or "Seintcrosmules Mede."[4]

Having thus fully surveyed this most interesting church and the domestic *The history of the hospital.*

(1) This motto is curiously misspelt here, and the quarrel containing the date has been reversed when the window was releaded. (Arch. Journal, vol. vii. pp. 75, 76.)

(2) The joint of a slender-shafted column is built into the breast-wall next the church. The gurgoyles beneath the parapet of the turret could scarcely have been intended for so small a structure. And in front of the central window is a remarkable construction, consisting of a brick pillar, surmounted by a sculptured stone capital, exhibiting Robert Sherburne's initials and motto, &c., over which is a corbel representing some bat-winged monster, and on the summit is a crocketed pinnacle. In the wall at the back of this is a stone bearing this inscription— "HENRICUS COMPTON, EPISCOPUS," which could not be earlier than 1674.

In the "Nuns' Chamber" communicating with the tower, over the fireplace, are Robert Sherburne's initials and motto, and the date 1503 (with a character for 5 nearly resembling the black letter "h," exactly as in the porter's lodge below) carved in stone; and there are some curious old presses, ornamented with panels and the linen-pattern, there.

There stands in the ambulatory a very solid oval table made of a slab of Purbeck marble, mounted on an oaken pillar and tripod, in the Jacobean style, traditionally (but I know not on what grounds) said to have been brought from Winchester Castle.

The earliest notice of this part of the building is in our MS., which states that about 1398, John de Campeden built a stone wall, with doors, from the northern part of the church to the Master's lodgings, or gateway tower.

On the authority of "the cicerone of the hospital,"

Duthy (p. 283) says that "previously to the repairs which took place many years [before he wrote], portions of the old chimneys, similar to those which appear on the opposite side in the cells of the brethren, were then existing, but were on that occasion destroyed."

(3) It is recorded in the MS. belonging to the hospital, that, amongst other works of John de Campeden, he made a new and large furnace in the brewery, also that he rebuilt "*alam lateralem juxta rivum fluminis,*" as a brewery, and repaired the watercourse (*gutter*) through that building. This watercourse is not now known, but the position and construction of the latrinas to the east of the gateway, and the great probability that there was originally a similar structure connected with the infirmary,—for which part of the establishment it would be indispensable,—may be said to establish the fact of its existence.

At the base of the east end of the church, in the northern bay, may be seen the traces of an arch, which cannot have belonged to a crypt, but which might possibly have served for the passage of this eastern watercourse.

"High up, at the eastern [it should be *southern*] end of it," says Milner (vol. ii. p. 183) "there appears to have been a window, by means of which the Master was enabled, from an apartment communicating with it, to inspect the behaviour of this class of poor men." This opening does not seem very ancient, and such a purpose as Milner ascribes to it, is not in accordance with the general mode of conducting such charities in olden time.

(4) MS. *u. s.* John de Campeden repaired the sluices, and added a new part to this mill, which (like the rest of this hospital) had been allowed to fall into decay.

buildings of this ancient institution, we must briefly tell the story of its foundation and its fortunes, which have unhappily been of a very uniform character, from the earliest time until the recent scheme of management approved by the Court of Chancery, which has introduced a new state of things, and of a more auspicious omen.

Legend, as is usual, has been busy with the Hospital of St. Cross, and Milner[1] joyfully quotes Bishop Godwin, as the authority for a story of a monastery existing on this spot, from the earliest ages of Christianity until the time of the Danish invasions, when it perished; for the whole of which there is not the shadow of any authentic evidence. The earliest records of St. Cross are two papal bulls, one given by Innocent II. in 1137; the other by Lucius II. on the 11th of March, 1144, confirming the foundation of the hospital and the various endowments bestowed on it. And it is believed that the actual date of the foundation is the year 1136.[2]

Foundation by Bishop De Blois.

The scheme of the founder, Henry de Blois, then Bishop of Winchester, is contained in an instrument to which (as was not unfrequently the case then) no date is affixed, but which we think may be assigned to the year 1137.[3] This charter delivers to Raymond, Prior of the Knights of St. John of Jerusalem, this hospital, which, says the bishop, "I, for the health of the souls of myself, my predecessors, and the kings of England, have newly (de novo) instituted without the walls of Winchester." And it asserts that the foundation has been confirmed by both royal and papal authority.

Original scheme.

It provides for the reception of "thirteen poor impotent men, so reduced in strength as rarely or never to be able to raise themselves without the assistance of another,"[4] who were to be lodged, clothed, fed, and properly cared for in this hospital continually,[5] another being introduced as soon as any one should have sufficiently recovered his strength to be "dismissed with decency and respect." Besides this,

---

(1) Vol. ii. p. 180.

(2) Copies of the bulls exist in Harl. MS. 1616, as well as in the MS. I have quoted as in the possession of the Master of St. Cross, which are indubitable authorities.

Other authorities, which the reader may be pleased to consult, are Lowth's "Life of William of Wykeham" (2nd Edit.), pp. 73, &c.; Thirty-first Report of the Charity Commissioners (Parl. Papers 1837-8, xxxiv.), pp. 843, &c.; "Notes and Queries," 1st S., xi. 42-44; together with Milner, Duthy, Wavell, &c. There is also a "History of St. Cross" by Henry Moody. But the best popular account is contained in the Lecture by the Master, to which I have already often referred.

Lowth (2nd Edit., p. 73) assigns the foundation to the year 1132,—which date Milner (vol. ii. p. 180) ascribes to Godwin (De Præsul. Angl.),—and cites as his authorities Wykeham's Registers; a MS. in New Coll. Library; and another "penes Dom. Episcopum Wint." Tanner (Mon. xxiv. xxxv. 10) prefers 1132; Wharton (Angl. Sac., vol. i. p. 284) 1136.

(3) This charter is contained in Harl. MS. 1616, and also in Pontissera's Register. The Charity Commissioners' Report, and the article in "Notes and Queries," contain English translations of it.

The Harl. MS. 1616 (fol. 3) records the confirmation of St. Cross to the Hospitallers in the year in which Wolvesey Castle was commenced, 1137. By others this charter is assigned to 1157 ("Notes and Queries," &c.).

(4) Lowth, and all who have followed him, make inability to maintain themselves without charitable assistance the condition of admission for the brethren to the hospital, instead of inability to raise themselves without help (sine alterius adminiculo se valeant sustentare), overlooking the subsequent provision for the discharge of such as shall have recovered health and strength.

(5) "Good wheaten bread to the weight (ad pensum) of five marks daily, with three dishes (fercula) at dinner, and one for supper, and sufficient drink." The good bishop prescribed the best medicine for enfeebled men—generous diet. Dinner and supper were the only meals in the day then.

"a hundred other poor men of good conduct," to be selected from the most necessitous class, were to be received and fed at the hour of dinner,[1] and permitted to take away the remains of both meat and drink when they departed. Other assistance was to be imparted compassionately, " according to the means of the house, to the needy of every description."

Under Henry De Blois' successor, Richard Toclyve, serious disputes appear to have arisen with the Hospitallers, who on IV Id. (or the 10th) of April, 1185, gave up the management of St. Cross to the bishop by a formal deed of surrender.[2] They remained in possession of it, however, for two years afterwards,[3] making repeated appeals to Rome. The hospital was awarded to them by Pope Clement III. in 1187,[4] and on the 16th of September, 1189, Richard I., by royal charter, granted it to them.[5] In the year 1197 the Bishops of London and Lincoln, and the Abbot of Reading, who had been appointed arbitrators by Pope Celestine III., awarded it to the bishop;[6] and yet, two years later, it was again confirmed to the Hospitallers by King John.[7] Disputes concerning the hospital.

Soon after the year 1200, however, this dispute must have been terminated in favour of the bishop, for we find him nominating the masters,[8] and it has so remained without opposition to the present day. The muniments and records were, nevertheless, retained by the Hospitallers, and not given up until 1379, when Robert Hales, Prior of the order in England, delivered them to William of Wykeham.[9] The bishop obtains the hospital.

Owing to these quarrels the original intention of the founder was widely departed from,[10] and the church was not finished till, in 1255, Ethelmar, Bishop of Winchester, aided by others who were interested in the foundation, invited assistance for its completion.[11]

When William of Wykeham was made Bishop of Winchester, one of the first objects of his care was the restoration of this establishment to a healthy condition. The story of the contest which the effort involved him in is too long for our work, but Reforms by William of Wykeham.

---

(1) These men, as not requiring medical treatment, were to have each the same quantity of coarser bread (*grossior panis*), but only one dish, " as shall seem meet according to the convenience of the day," and not so much drink as the others (*ciphus ad certam mensuram*).

(2) Harl. MS. 1616, fol. 27. The original charter is also in the Harleian Collection (43 I. 38). See Mr. John Gough Nichols' account of it in " Collectanea Topographica," vol. iii. p. 174. By this agreement the bishop provides for the increase of the Hundred-men poor to two hundred, and makes certain concessions in return for the surrender. (Harl. MS. 1616, fol. 7v°.)

(3) Ibid., fol. 3. See also fol. 2 for intimations of the appeals to Rome.

(4) Charity Commissioners' Report, *u. s.*

(5) Harl. MS. 1616, fols. 2 v°, 11 v°.

(6) Charity Commissioners' Report, *u. s.*

(7) Rot. Chart., vol. i. p. 16.

(8) The first appointment is that of Alan Stoke, in 1204, according to the MS. *penes* the Master (fol. 50);

Harl. 1616 (fol. 10); and Reg. Winton. (referred to in " Notes and Queries," 1st S., vol. xi. p. 44).

(9) Harl. MS. 1616, fol. 3 v°, &c. Where is also a list of the muniments, each charter, &c., being described by the initial words of the 1st and the 4th lines.

(10) Several of the masters, who, according to Wavell (vol. ii. p. 210), " considered their office in the light of an ecclesiastical benefice, rather than the mastership of an hospital and a place of trust," converted to their own private purposes great part of those revenues, which were designed for pious and charitable uses." And he singles out John de Edyndon (or Edington), nephew to William de Edington, and appointed by him, as one of the worst of these peculators.

It is to be noticed that the early appointments by the bishops particularly specify that the office does not involve the cure of souls (*sine cura animarum*). In the Harl. MS. an inquiry respecting this is recorded.

(11) Ibid., fol. 29 v°. The architectural description of the church given above fully confirms this.

it may be read in the works referred to below.[1]　It must suffice for our purpose in this brief account, to say that he had to contend with three ex-masters, and one in possession of the office, all of whom had been guilty of scandalous malversation ; that it was not until he had exercised all the powers he possessed as a bishop, including sequestration, excommunication, and appeal to the Pope, that he succeeded in bringing the offenders to justice, and in clearing the ground so as to be able to put the charity once more into the form in which the Bishops De Blois and Toclyve intended it to be ; and that he had expended about seventeen years on this business, before he ventured to commit the hospital to the care of John de Campeden, " one in whom he had the greatest confidence, having for many years had experience of his fidelity in affairs of importance."

New foundation of Cardinal Beaufort.

Wykeham's successor, Cardinal Beaufort, " with the consent of the master of that day, Thomas Forrest, and the brethren, established within the precincts a new foundation [*nova fundatio*], termed ' the Hospital or Almshouse of Noble Poverty,' . . . . which was to consist of a warden, two priests, thirty-five brethren and three sisters."[2] This transaction was confirmed by letters-patent from Henry VI., bearing dates 1439 and 1443.　The cardinal's deed is dated January the 3rd, 1445, and his almshouse is distinctly stated to have been " on the western side of the church,"[3] and his " foundation " to have been under the general government of the house.[4]

Common tradition ascribes to the cardinal extensive alterations and additions to the original buildings of the hospital ; most of these have been already noticed, and

(1) Lowth's " Life of Wykeham," *u. s.*; Wavell, vol. ii. pp. 219—226 ; Duthy, pp. 253—255.

In the MSS. already referred to will be found full materials for the history of this critical period in the existence of the Hospital of St. Cross.

But I will give here some passages from documents relating to these troubles, which will afford us some information concerning the mode of living of the inmates of the hospital, who certainly were not neglected, though the masters carried off the lion's share of the spoils. From the examination of Walter de Sevenhampton, steward in the time of John de Edington (Harl. MS. 1616, fols. 21 v°, *et seq*., and 15 v°, *et seq*), it appears that each of the brethren received daily 5 marks' weight of wheaten bread, 1 " *lagena* " (or *galione*) and a half of beer (*mediocris servisie*), a sufficiency of pottage, 3 dishes (*fercula*) at dinner, viz., 1 " *mortrell* " (a little mortar or basin) of " *wastell* " (the best bread) and milk, 1 dish of meat or fish, and 1 other dish of whatever might be provided for the day (*pitancia juxta exigenciam diei*), and 1 dish for supper, so that the food and drink (*cibaria et poculenta*) of each brother amounted daily in value to *three pence*.　On the vigil of St. Lawrence (which was the Founder's Obit) and the six greater feasts (in addition to 1 dish of better meat or fish) they had 4 " *lagenæ* " of better beer amongst them ; and each of the Hundred-hall poor, of whom 13 were " *pauperiores scolares scole gramaticalis ibidem missi*

per magistrum summe scole gramaticalis civitatis Wynton.;" 1 loaf of barley bread (*panem ordei*), 1 dish of pulse, 1 salt fish (*allec*) or 2 " *pilchers*," (or 2 eggs, or 1 farthing's-worth of cheese, Lowth, p. 77), 1 *pocellum* of beer, or (according to the other account) 3 quarts of small (*debilis*) beer ; to which on the feast days was added 3 loaves of wheaten bread and some meat.　On Founder's day 200 poor were entertained ; 100 received each 1 wheaten loaf, pottage, a pottle (*pottelum*) of beer, and 1 dish ; and second 100 half a loaf each.　Besides these there were seven poor persons, who were choristers, and daily received each 1 wheaten loaf, 1 quart of beer, and 1 dish ; when not engaged in the church they " *solebant scolas exercere in dicto hospitali.*"

The whole establishment at this time included the Master (*Custos*) and the 13 brethren, the steward (*senescallus*) " *cum clerico*," 13 " *clerici*," 7 choristers, 4 " *capellani*," 2 servants (*garsiones*), 3 bakers, 3 brewers, 1 cook, 1 " *curtilarius*," 2 " *lotrices*," and 3 " *carectarii*;" 8 horses are also spoken of, and 3 carts.

The grant of the mastership to Geoffrey de Wellesforde (Lit. Pat. 12 Edw. II. m. 25, cited by Gale, Pt. 1.), in 1322, speaks of the " sisters " as well as the brethren in this hospital, but I do not know to whom it refers.

(2) Lecture by the Master, pp. 15, 16.

(3) MS. *penes* the Master.

(4) Charity Commissioners' Report, *u. s.*

respecting one, at least, reasons given for not accepting the tradition regarding it. The specific indication of the site of his almshouses, and the occurrence of the name and motto of Robert Sherburne in the buildings to the east of the gateway, and that of the emblem of Bishop Fox on the stairs leading to the chamber over the gate, from the refectory on the western side, may be regarded as proofs that this tradition is not to be accepted implicitly.

We know also that, in consequence of the troubles of the times in which he lived, *Waynflete's reforms.* the intention of Beaufort was not carried out during his lifetime, and that the triumph of the Yorkists, for a time, completely frustrated his benevolent designs. Even before that, discord and confusion had arisen in the house, and both the old and the new foundations seemed to be in danger of perishing. Bishop Waynflete, therefore, devoted himself to the re-establishment of the hospital, and having procured a charter from King Henry VI. in the year 1455, he, in 1486, by an instrument dated the 2nd of August, remodelled the statutes of the house, and in consideration of the loss of endowments bestowed on it by the cardinal, reduced the numbers on the new foundation to one priest and two brethren, the appointment of whom took place in the following year by Waynflete's successor, Peter Courtenay.[1]

The Reformation appears to have effected but little change in this institution. *The Reformation.* "At a visitation held in September, 1535, by the vicar-general's commissary, Dr. Legh, 'the thirteen brethren are directed to receive sufficient meat and drink, and not money in lieu thereof; one hundred men to be daily fed, but sturdy beggars repulsed.' Also a priest in the house was enjoined to teach the poor men dwelling in it the Lord's Prayer and the Apostle's Creed in English, which the said poor brethren were to rehearse in the church after dinner."[2] The choral service survived the change in the times, for there is a list of "chanters" and "singing men," with the date 1572, carved in the stalls of the choir.[3]

The next event in the history of St. Cross may be related in the words of the old *Destruction of the Register.* Register, the first entry in which, in the handwriting of John Hunt, chaplain, under date September the 23rd, 1676, states that "when Sir Peter Young, a Scotchman, was master of this hospital, which was in the days of King James [about the year 1616], he, living in Scotland, left the management of the concerns of this house to his sonne, Dr. Young, Dean of Winton, who made one Mr. Wright both chaplain and steward. This Mr. Wright dying, his widdow, whether out of fear of being brought to account, or out of obedience to his commands, is uncertain, burnt all his

(1) Ibid.; Lecture by the Master, p. 17; Reg. Waynflete, Pars IIda. fol. 132.

From the *Compotus* of Robert Burell, steward, in 29 Hen. VI., it appears that the distinctive dress of the brethren of the new foundation was a cloak of a deep red colour, with the cardinal's hat embroidered in white silk and silver. The dress of the brethren of the old foundation was then, as it appears, what it is now,—a

black gown with a silver cross potent (as a badge), which was derived from the Hospitallers. (Lecture by the Master, p. 19.)

(2) Ibid., p. 25. "The priest is also forbidden to exhibit relics, images, or miracles in order to obtain money;" and mass is directed to be said for the souls of the founder, the king, and the queen. (Duthy, p. 259.)

(3) Ibid., p. 26. See also above, p. 225, note 3.

papers, and amongst them the Register also, since which time to this there hath been no other bought."[1]

Twenty years after the writing of this record, in the first year of the mastership of Dr. Markland, for the purpose of allaying the disputes which continually occurred between the Master, the brethren, and the officers of the hospital, " there was drawn up from the usages of many previous years, with such alterations as were deemed expedient, a ' custumary' [or *Consuetudinarium*], which was agreed to by the master, brethren, and officers, and ratified by the Bishop of Winchester."[2]

By this instrument, which recited " that upon diligent and strict search made among the records of the hospital, no statutes, nor footsteps of any statutes could be found directing the government thereof,"[3] proceeded to state that the establishment consisted of thirteen brethren, one Master, one steward, and one chaplain. It reduced the number of Hundred-hall poor to twenty-eight poor men and twelve poor women, with two reversioners to succeed to any vacancy caused by death or removal. It further regulated the diet and allowances of the brethren, the stipends of the officers, and placed the whole of the revenues into the Master's hands, out of which he was to bear the whole charge of the house, and to keep the church in sufficient repair, retaining the entire surplus for himself.[4]

Under this " *Consuetudinarium*," which received a few alterations in its details, the hospital was managed until the end of the late mastership.[5] The circumstances

---

(1) Lecture by the Master, pp. 26, 27. This account is commonly improved into the destruction of *all* the statutes, ordinances, charters, and other muniments of the house. (See Duthy, p. 261; Charity Commiss. Report; " Notes and Queries," *u. s.*, &c.) But, in fact, no such destruction ever took place; and there is not merely the MS. I have so largely used to disprove that story, but also a great mass of original records still in the possession of the Master; the Harl. MS. 1616, which is an ancient register; and the charter of agreement between Bishop Toclyve and the Hospitallers, also in the Harleian Collection.

I may remark here that the supposition of a *dispersion* of some of the muniments of St. Cross at this time may possibly involve the history of the *Liber Winton.*, the possession of which has been traced backwards from the Society of Antiquaries to the very Dr. Young who figures in this story; and as it contains Bishop De Blois' Survey of Winchester, it is not unlikely to have been originally amongst the muniments of St. Cross, just as there is still amongst those of St. Mary's College Winton, the only existing copy of the *Consuetudinarium* of the City of Winchester.

(2) Duthy, p. 261.

(3) " Notes and Queries," *u. s.* And yet the Master of the Rolls, in his recent decision, could say that " documents *then* and NOW in their possession contain ample evidence of the original rules and statutes, showing the object and destination of the charity to have been the very opposite to that to which they were about to convert it."

(4) It is not wonderful that the Master of the Rolls should characterize this Custumary as " one of the most extraordinary documents that ever was produced, or relied upon in a court of justice." The distribution of the revenues as settled by it he pronounced to be " in direct opposition to the evidence and documents then in their own custody;" and added, " A more bare-faced and shameless document, in my opinion, than this *Consuetudinarium* could not have been framed; nor could a more manifest, and probably wilful, breach of trust have been committed by the Master and brethren." (Law Journal, 1853, Chancery Cases, pp. 793—809.)

(5) The daily divine services, attendance at which was the sole requirement of the brethren, were in 1744 reduced to one at 11 A.M. on week-days; but there were still to be two services on Sundays, and a sermon at one of them, with other services on the feasts of the church. In 1782 further changes were made, and the custom that four of the brethren should reside out of the hospital, receiving £10 a year, was disallowed. The state of affairs when the Report of the Charity Commissioners investigated them was briefly this:—

The thirteen brethren each received 1s. weekly, and 8s. 5d. quarterly instead of milk, and 8s. quarterly in addition to this, with 2d. " pan money " on Lady Day and Michaelmas Day, and 2d. in the pound on all except copyhold fines, and a black cloth gown yearly, at Christmas. The provisions in hall were on Sunday 3 shoulders of mutton or veal, on Monday a leg and a neck of mutton,

attending the abrogation of this custumary, are so recent that we must refer to the public journals for an account of them. The result of the contest by which it was accomplished was the Scheme for the Interim Management of the Hospital, approved by Orders in Chancery, dated the 22nd of June, 1855, and the 20th of March, 1857.[1]

By this scheme the entire management and control of the charity is committed to fourteen trustees, of whom the Master, the Dean of Winchester, the Mayor of the city (if a member of the Church of England), the Warden of St. Mary's College, and the Vicar of Compton (the adjacent parish), are always to be trustees *ex officio;* the others being nominated by the Scheme in the first instance, and afterwards under the sanction of the Charity Commissioners. The original style of the corporation—" the Master and Brethren of the Hospital of St. Cross "—is to be used by the trustees, as well as its common seal. And, for the first time, a sufficient muniment room has been constructed, in " Founder's Chamber " (as it is called) ; which is now fitted up with all modern appliances for security against thieves, fire, and damp.

The "Scheme."

The principal feature in the management is the suppression of the office of the chaplain, and the appointment of a Master (still by the Bishop of Winchester), who, in addition to the general duties of residing in the hospital, and acting as governor and superintendent (under the trustees), is to be, in fact, at once the chaplain of the hospital and the incumbent of the parish of St. Faith,[2] reading prayers in the church every morning, performing two full services every Sunday, and discharging all the other duties involved in these offices. The annual stipend is fixed at £250, in addition to the residence and the gardens. The number of the brethren is fixed at the

The present constitution the charity.

---

on Tuesday and Thursday boiled beef. Each brother also received 3 quarts of beer a day, and a loaf weighing 1½ lb. On " gaudy days " there were provided 45 lbs. of roast beef, with mince-pies and plum-broth (which is the genuine Christmas pudding), and a jack (or 4 gallons) of beer, and 4*s.* amongst them for beer money. The Master provided a charcoal fire at 5 P.M. on these occasions, and 3 roasted necks of mutton were given the brethren for supper. Besides all this, on " dole days," each brother received two penny-loaves.

The stipends of the steward and the chaplain were £80 each *per annum,* and the chaplain received also £15 for Freefolk, and each of them had 6*d.* in the pound on all except copyhold fines. The steward also received 45 lbs. of roasting beef yearly, and a portion of the mince-pies on gaudy days.

The forty poor men and women of the Hundred-hall received 6*d.* each weekly, or 26*s.* yearly ; and the doles consisted of five sacks of penny-loaves, and after they were distributed, ½*d.* to each applicant.

For the " wayfarers' dole " there was provided daily a " cast " of bread and 6 quarts of beer.

Other details may be seen in Duthy, pp. 261—3 ; in Moody's " History and Description of the Hospital of

St. Cross," pp. 14, &c. ; and in the Lecture by the Master, pp. 30 and 33.

(1) Law Journal (Chancery) Reports, vol. xxii. pp. 793, &c.

(2) A sum not exceeding £80 *per annum* is to be paid by the trustees " to the clergyman for the minister officiating at the Chapel of Freefolk, who shall be nominated by the Bishop of Winchester."

No mention of the union of the parish of St. Faith to St. Cross occurs in the Indexes to the Registers of the Diocese, compiled by Mr. Alchin, to which I have been permitted free access. But in " Notes and Queries," 2nd S., vol. ii. p. 450, a correspondent, under the signature " Oxoniensis," sends a paragraph from a friend's scrap-book, which contains the following (*verbatim*), said to be copied from a MS. signed John Young, Dean of Winchester, who managed the affairs of the hospital for his father, Sir Peter Young, in 1618 :—" *Ecclesia S. Fidis et S. Crux juncta Maias decimus* 1507. *Fox Epus et Custos S. Crucis. Joannes Claymond, Antistes. Ista cœtus confirmabat pro mea auctoritate qui adjungere pot . . . . Joannes Poynet, Primus Episcopus Religionis reformatæ et Patronus; Joannes Incentius, magister.*"

original thirteen of De Blois' foundation,[1] with a weekly stipend of seven shillings each for those already in the hospital, and five shillings for each brother appointed afterwards, and a new cloth gown every Christmas time. It is also provided that the trustees may "abolish the system of supplying the brethren with food," and instead pay them a certain fixed stipend of not less than £30, nor more than £40 *per annum* by weekly instalments, if it shall seem good to them so to do. Twenty poor persons, to be called "the Hundred-hall Poor," are to receive a shilling a week each "for the present;" and in like manner the "Wayfarers' Dole," is "for the present," to be continued;[2] but the trustees are at liberty to abolish it if they shall think fit, and apply the money which would be saved thereby to the increase of the allowance, or the number of the Hundred-hall poor.

The surplus income of the charity is to be invested in the 3 per cent. Consols; and when the amount shall be increased to such a sum as shall make it, in the opinion of the Attorney-General, desirable that a new scheme should be settled for the administration of the charity, he is to apply to the Court of Chancery for that purpose. And it is distinctly specified not only that the present scheme is temporary, but that "it shall in no way prejudice the claim of the Almshouse of Noble Poverty."[3]

The ancient revenues of the hospital.

Full accounts of the revenues of the hospital may be seen in the authorities to which reference has been made continually in the notes. Some slight sketch alone can be admitted here. In De Blois' charter the churches of Fareham, Nursling, Milbrook, Twyford, Hinton Ampner, Alverstoke, Exton, Hurstbourne, Whitchurch, Chilbolton, Woodhay, and Ovington (in Hampshire), Wintney (in Oxfordshire), and Alton and Stockton (in Wiltshire), are enumerated as bestowed on the charity, "with all their appurtenances and appendages," together with the tithes of the demesne of Waltham, and other rents assigned to it in Winchester. Upham, Baughurst, and Farley, were subsequently added to the Founder's endowment.[4]

In the *Taxatio Ecclesiastica* of Pope Nicholas it is assessed at £7 4s. 6d. (upon which the tax is 14s. 5½d.), which was the income of the Master, because all but that sum was for the use of the poor.[5] The value in Wykeham's time was £245 0s. 5d., and the outgoings were £242 15s. 11d.[6]

Cardinal Beaufort's grants to the hospital amounted in yearly value to about £500,

(1) In consequence of the falling off of the funds of the charity, through the costly and continued litigation, the number of brethren had fallen to nine, but it is now raised to the full tale of thirteen.

(2) The porter (who, under the new scheme, is no longer one of the brethren) informs me that as many as thirty genuine wayfarers, for the most part of the class denominated "tramps," daily apply for, and receive, this dole. All visitors, of course, receive it, but their *douceurs* prevent any loss accruing therefrom.

(3) This Scheme is printed by order of the trustees, and though not published, is yet thereby placed under the guarantee of publicity. The concluding observation re-

garding Cardinal Beaufort's foundation (which has been so long in abeyance), is also a pledge that the Hospital of St. Cross has entered on a new and healthful term of existence.

(4) Charity Commiss. Report, *u. s.*; Harl. MS. 1616, fol. 7.

The letters confirming many of these grants, and some others not here specified, are to be found in the last cited authority, fol 2v°, *et seq.*

(5) P. 210; Harl. MS. 1616, fol. 5.

(6) Ibid., fol. 15 v°. In his letter to the Pope, Wykeham estimated the revenue at more than £300 *per annum*. (Lowth, p. 75.)

and although some of them were afterwards alienated, the charity possesses the greater part of them to the present day.[1]

According to the *Valor Ecclesiasticus*, in the 26th of Henry VIII., or 1534-5, the yearly revenue of the hospital was £281 13s. 5d., and the amount expended in the charity £197 9s. 3d., leaving as its value, £84 4s. 2d. But a detailed account, dated eight years earlier, makes the value to be £496 18s. 4½d., and the yearly expenses £406 14s. 1½d.[2]

The greater part of the property now in the possession of the institution is comprised in the original endowment of the cardinal, and much of the rest is contained in the ancient account. The amount of the pensions now received from De Blois' grant is nearly the same as it was in 1526, and the small fee-farm rents from Winchester may probably be referred to the first founder. The aggregate income, according to the Commissioners' Report, was £1088 2s. 9d., or according to another statement the receipts for the year 1835-6 were £1112 7s. 5d.; the disbursements during the same period amounting to £914 16s. 11d., leaving £197 10s. 6d. for the income of the Master. But it must be noted that the amount of fines from 1818 (inclusive) to the date of the report (printed 1837) was £41,558, shortly after which date fines to the amount of £12,000 were received; so that after deducting the yearly average for repairs, and the shares of fines appropriated by the *Consuetudinarium* to the steward, the chaplain, and the brethren, the average annual income of the Master appeared to be little less than £1400.[3]

The first Master to the hospital was Robert de Limesia, whose name appears amongst the witnesses to the grant of Waltham, Upham, &c., by the founder.[4]

Recent revenue.

List of Masters.

---

(1) Lowth, p. 91, note 9. Henry VI. is said to have granted the manors yielding this sum to the cardinal, together with his licence to assign them to the Hospital of St. Cross, for a consideration of 13,350 marks. And the cardinal is said to have added the impropriation of Crondall, and of several other parishes in his diocese and patronage.

Amongst the endowments of the cardinal, which were afterwards taken from St. Cross, were the manors of Henxtridge, Ambresbury, Charleton and Winterbourne Erlys, and the borough of Wilson. (Charity Commiss. Report, *u. s.*)

Waynflete's Decree assigns to the Master, yearly, £4, " *pro labore suo*, &c." (Reg. Pars. II. fol. 132); and Courtenay (Reg. fol. 25) 100s. Other interesting details of the expenses of the hospital are contained in these registers.

(2) This account of the 18 Hen. VIII., derived from a *Compotus* for the year ending Michaelmas, 1526, contains amongst the receipts "*Pensions*" from Waltham, Upham, Exton, Alverstoke, Stockton, Woodhay, Hinton, Nursling, Chilbolton, Milbrook, Ovington, Alton Canons, Farley, and Baughurst, in all £58 5s.; and other receipts from Whitchurch, Owselbury (granted to the hospital, it

is supposed, in the cardinal's time), Twyford, Fareham, Hurstbourne and St. Mary Bourne, Ashton (granted at the same time as Owselbury), Mill of St. Cross, houses in St. Cross, houses in the Soke of Winton and Sparkeford, the Hospital of St. John at Fordingbridge, Free Chapels of Cold Henley, and of Itchenswell, Crondall Rectory, Sutton, Yately, and Aldershott Chapels, the Rectory of St. Faith, and the Chapel of St. James (otherwise called St. James of Henley on the Hill, near Winton, or White Monastery); together with miscellaneous receipts, such as the produce of sales of skins, wood, suet, and the property of a deceased brother, which, with the pensions before spoken of, amounted to £496 18s. 4¼d.

Amongst the payments we find 3s. 4d. to the Priory and Convent of St. Swithin's for the water course. (Charity Commiss. Report, *u. s.*)

(3) Ibid.; Moody's History, &c. The burial-ground of St. James' was sold to the Roman Catholics, in 1800, for £41. (Charity Commiss. Report, *u. s.*)

(4) For the discovery of this name I am indebted to my lamented friend, the Rev. W. H. Gunner, who found it in a copy of De Blois' Charter, either in the Episcopal Registers, or amongst the muniments of the College. His name only appears in the grant I have referred to in the text.

Roger ——— was Master when Bishop Toclyve, in 1185, effected the arrangement with the Hospitallers.[1]

Alan Stoke, appointed in 1204 by Bishop Peter de Rupibus: the first so appointed.[2]

Galfridus de Fernyng, appointed by Bishop William Ralegh.[3]

Humfredus de Millers (or *Mylers*), appointed April the 14th, 1241.[4]

Henry de Secusia, appointed by Henry III., the 14th of April, or 30th of May, 1241.[5]

Stephen de Wotton, died 1275.[6]

Petrus de S. Mario, 1289 or 1290; died 1295 or 1296.[7]

William de Wendelynge (*Wenllyng* or *Welynger*), 6 Kal. January (27th of December, 1295), or 3 Id. (11th of) November, 1296.[8]

Robert Maydeston (or *Maydenstan*), 1310; deprived.[9]

Galfridus de Welleford (or *Walesford*), 1321, or 2 Kal. September (31st of August), 1322.[10]

Bertrand de Asserio, 1322.[11]

Petrus de Galiciano (or *Galesianis*), 1332.[12]

William de Edington (or *Edyndon*), 1334; afterwards Bishop of Winchester.[13]

Raymond Pelegryng (or *Peregrin*); resigned, 1346.

Richard de Lusteshall (or *Listeshill*).[14]

John de Edington (or *Edyndon*), 1346; resigned.

William Stowell, 1366.[15]

(1) Harl. MS. 1616, fol. 4v°.

(2) MS. *penes* the Master of St. Cross, fol. 50, *et seq.* This is stated to be the first name in the records which the compiler of the MS. list had access to, the former Masters having been appointed by the prior of the Hospitallers in England.

(3) Ibid. The appointment is said to have been made on the Feast of Innocents (28th of December), in the 6th of his translation (or 1250), which would place this Master after De Secusia. I have observed the order of the MS. list until further authority is discovered.

(4) Ibid. The year in the MS. is 25 Hen. III. This name occurs much earlier in Dugdale's list; and C. J. Kelly, a correspondent of "Notes and Queries," 1st S., vol. x. p. 473, suggests that he was the Master of the Hospitallers. Duthy (p. 265) calls him Henry de Milers, assigns no date to him, and adds that "he is the first Master of St. Cross on record. (MSS. Records of the Hospital.)" There appears to be some difficulty regarding the name, as the next entry shows.

(5) MS. *penes* the Master, *u. s.* See preceding note.

(6) The name of Thomas de Colchester, 1260, which does not appear in the MS. authorities, interposed between Henry de Secusia and Stephen de Wotton. ("Notes and Queries," *u. s.*)

(7) Both the MS. last quoted and the Harl. MS. give the name of this Master as Petrus de Sancto Mario. The modern inscription on his tomb (for he lies buried in the Church of St. Cross) cannot be appealed to against such authority. There is a discrepancy between different accounts of the dates of his appointment, and his death.

(8) The former date is that of the Harl. MS. 1616, fol. 12v°; the latter that of the MS. *penes* the Master, fol. 50.

(9) Duthy (pp. 265, 266, and note) hypothetically misplaces this Master, and states that he died in 1244.

(10) Harl. MS. 1616, fol. 13.

(11) The MS. *penes* the Master, *u. s.*, gives the date 2nd Kal. September, 1322, which is the date of the preceding Master. Duthy (p. 266) gives the date 1323.

(12) MS. *penes* the Master, *u. s.* It is stated there that this Master was blind.

(13) See above, p. 120. In connection with this appointment, there is recorded in the MS. *penes* the Master, fol. 50, a story of the death of Bishop Adam de Orlton, which differs widely from that related above (p. 120).

(14) According to Mr. Kelly ("Notes and Queries," *u. s.*), this Master was succeeded by Walter de Wetewang, whose appointment was cancelled by the king.

(15) Stowell exchanged the mastership of St. Cross with Lyntesford, his successor, for the Rectory of Burghclere. (Lowth, p. 81.)

Richard de Lyntesford, 22nd of March, 1367.[1]

Roger de Cloune, 1370 ; resigned 1374.[2]

The management of the hospital was now taken by William of Wykeham into his own hands, until the death of Cloune.[3]

John de Campeden, 1382.[4]

John (or Thomas) Forrest, 1426.[5]

Thomas Chaundler, D.D., 1463, Warden of St. Mary's College, Winchester.[6]

William Westbury, 1465.

Richard Harward (or *Hayward*), LL.D., died in 1489.[7]

John Litchfield, 1489.

Robert Sherburne, 1496 ; afterwards Bishop of St. David's, and of Chichester.[8]

John Claymond, before 1517 ; afterwards President of Magdalen and Corpus Christi Colleges, Oxford.

John Incent (or *Innocent*), 1524 ; afterwards Dean of St. Paul's, London.

William Medowe (or *Meadowe*), 1545.

John Leefe (*Leffe* or *Leigh*), D.D., 1557.[9]

Robert Reynolds (or *Rainolds*), D.D., 1557.

John Watson, 1559 ; afterwards Bishop of Winchester.[10]

Robert Bennett, 1583 ; afterwards Bishop of Hereford.

Arthur Lake, D.D., 1603 ; afterwards Bishop of Bath and Wells.[11]

Sir Peter Young, Knt., 18th of January, 1616.

William Lewis, D.D., 1627 ; afterwards Provost of Oriel College, Oxford. **Dis**possessed at the establishment of the Commonwealth.

John Lisle, 1649.[12]

John Cooke, 1657.[13]

Richard Shute, 1660.[14]

William Lewis, D.D., restored after 1660.[15]

(1) Lyntesford exchanged his mastership with Roger de Cloune for the Rectory of Campsall, in Yorkshire. (Lowth, p. 82.)

(2) It is uncertain whether he resigned the mastership or the management of the hospital, but most probably it was the latter.

(3) In the MS. belonging to the Master, Nicholas de Wykeham is said to have been appointed Master on the resignation of Roger de Cloune, and to have resigned the office in 1382; but it appears that he was no more than the agent for his kinsman, the bishop. (Lowth, pp. 88, 89, note.)

(4) Appointed after the 8th of September, on which day Cloune died. Campeden was Canon of Southwell and Archdeacon of Surrey, and is buried in the Church of St. Cross.

(5) He is called John in the Master's MS., and Thomas in the cardinal's charter and will. Henry Edwards ("Notes and Queries," 1st S., vol. x. p. 299) makes two

Masters, assigning 1444 as the date of Thomas Forrest's appointment.

(6) See above, p. 203, note 8.

(7) Buried in the Church of St. Cross.

(8) Mr. Edwards (" Notes and Queries," *u. s.*) dates his appointment in 1491.

(9) He was collated in June, and died in August; and is buried in the Chapel of Winchester College.

(10) See above, p. 125.

(11) Here and elsewhere in the list Milner's History would intercalate names which were never associated with the mastership. (See Duthy, *u. s.*, and " Notes and Queries," *u. s.*) Mr. Walcott also (" William of Wykeham and his College," pp. 347, 413, 434) has added some names to the list, in opposition to the MS. authorities.

(12) Duthy, p. 273.

(13) Milner, vol. ii. p. 24.

(14) Duthy, p. 274.

(15) Buried in the Church of St. Cross.

Masters.

Henry Compton, D.D., 1667 ; afterwards Bishop of London.

William Harrison, 1675.

Abraham Markland, D.D., 1694.[1]

John Lynch, D.D., 1728; afterwards Dean of Canterbury.

John Hoadly, LL.D., 1760.

Beilby Porteus, D.D., 15th of May, 1776 ; afterwards Bishop of Chester and London.

John Lockman, D.D., 22nd of March, 1788.

Francis North (Earl of Guildford), 9th of January, 1808.   Resigned.

L. M. Humbert, M.A., 15th of April, 1855.

THE HOSPITAL OF ST. MARY MAGDALEN,
NEAR WINCHESTER.

From the Hospital of St. Cross, which, in spite of such a chequered history as we have recorded, still preserves so much of its mediæval aspect and character, we pass to that of St. Mary Magdalen, which is now no more than some six plainly built alms-houses, situated on the upper side of Water Lane, in the East Soke.[2]

Original site of the hospital.

The original site of this institution, on the down called after it "Magdalen Hill," may be discovered now by the fragments of ancient tiles, &c., with which it is thickly covered,[3] and is distant about a mile from the city, due eastward, on the road which was till lately the high-road to London.[4]

Early notices of it.

Of its first foundation no record is known to exist.[5]   But the style of architecture of its chapel justifies Milner's conjecture that it was erected by Bishop Toclyve, or during his episcopate.[6]   It is first mentioned in the Register of John de Pontissera,

---

(1) Buried in the Church of St. Cross.

(2) See above, p. 26, and note 2.
I am indebted to the Rev. W. Williams, the present Master of this hospital, for the permission to examine the whole of the deeds, &c., which are the only remains of the muniments of this institution.   This inspection has greatly increased my confidence in Wavell's History of Winchester generally, for I find that in his account of this hospital, of which he was Master, he proceeded upon a careful study of the only original documents which were in existence, having not only copied out all the deeds with great accuracy, but also prepared a series of queries relating to the property of the hospital, &c., which MS. now forms part of the records.

(3) No one can mistake these fragments for those of modern tiles, &c.   Amongst them I picked up one or two

pieces of plain encaustic floor-bricks, and one small piece of the common blue Roman pottery.

(4) The extent of its site is defined in the Ordnance Maps (which have the parish boundaries laid down) as extra-parochial.   "Without the walls of the hospital, adjoining to them, they had sixteen acres of land, which might in some degree supply them with corn ; and they had pasture for 120 ewes and 6 rams " (Wavell, vol. ii. p. 201).

(5) Although there are no registers of Winton diocess before Pontissera's, and his does not record the foundation of this hospital, it is possible that the papal bull confirming it, or some other authentic document relating to it, may yet be discovered.

(6) The style of the remains of the chapel (of which elaborate drawings were made by Schnebbelie, and en-

where it is included in the list of churches of which the Bishops of Winchester are said to have long (*per multa tempora*) been patrons.[1] The next mention of it is in Stratford's Register,[2] where it is called "*Hospitale Leporosorum.*" In the Patent Rolls of Edward III. it is called the hospital of poor infirm persons on the hill (*infirmorum super montem*).[3] Orlton's Registers call the chapel a chantry (*cantaria*).[4]

Under this date we find the following in Trussell's MS. History of Winchester[5] (where the hospital is also called the "*Meason de Dieu*"):—"The House of St. Mary Magdalene [was] founded by Maria de Valentia, daughter of Guido, Earle of St. Pawle of Ffraunce, wief of Adamore de Valentia, Earle of Pembrooke, in the dayes of Edwarde the Third." And although this statement cannot be literally correct, it may be an authentic record of some considerable endowment, or even of a new foundation, no other notice of which has survived.

Trussell's account.

Wykeham, whom we have seen in his cathedral and the convent of St. Swithin, in the grammar school of Winchester, and in the Hospital of St. Cross, a great and effective reformer, was compelled to interpose in the management of this hospital also, and by his trusty coadjutors, John de Campeden, Simon Membury, and John Elmer (his official), to investigate its affairs with a view to the punishment of delinquents.[6] That he succeeded in restoring the institution to a more healthful condition, we may be assured, by finding it amongst those to which he bequeathed assistance in his will,[7] and from the fact that John Fromond, Steward of St. Mary's College under Wykeham, also made its inmates the object of a bequest in his will.[8]

Wykeham's reforms.

In the year 1438 William Waynflete held the mastership of this hospital at the same time that he was head-master (*informator*) of St. Mary's College at Winchester.[9]

At the Reformation, it passed scatheless through the ordeal in which so many institutions of the elder time perished. The certificate in the Augmentation Office states that it was "Founded by the Bishop of Winton, as it is supposed," and that the inmates were to "remaine and continew for ever to pray for the soules of the founders and all crysten soules."[10]

The Reformation.

In the disastrous wars of the Great Rebellion this charity suffered very severely.

The Great Rebellion.

graved for the Essay in *Vetusta Monumenta*, vol. iii.) was that called Transition Norman, which immediately preceded the Early English, and was used during the last quarter of the twelfth century.

(1) Fol. 107 v°. See also fol. 104 v°.

It does not, however, occur in the List of Chapels and Churches quoted above, p. 154, note 1; nor in the *Taxatio* of Pope Nicholas, nor in that of Bishop Orlton's time.

(2) Fol. 13 v°. "*Confirmatio collationis prebendæ ibidem factæ.*" (From Mr. Alchin's Index).

(3) Lit. Pat. 3 Edw. III., cited by Tanner, *s. v.*

(4) Pars. II. fols. 67, 92. It is thus described in the registers of Wykeham and Waynflete also.

(5) Fol. 39.

(6) Vet. Mon., vol. iii., *u. s.*

That Wykeham was forced to resort to energetic measures may be concluded from the fact that instead of "collating" John Melton to the mastership, as had been customary, he "*deputed*" (*deputamus*) him (Reg. Pars. I. fol. 231), thus retaining in his own hands the real control of the charity. This John Melton appears, afterwards, as one of the principal offenders, to punish whom the commissioners named in the text were appointed. (Wavell, vol. ii. pp. 170—177.)

(7) Lowth's "Life of Wykeham," p. 295, App. xlii.

(8) Arch. Jour., vol. xvi. p. 170. "*Lego ad distribuendum inter leprosos B. Marie Magdalene Wynton.*"

(9) Wavell, vol. ii. p. 177.

(10) Ibid., pp. 161, 253.

The king's troops plundered its barns, stole and killed its sheep, burned all the wood-work they could remove, and turned the chapel into a stable for their horses.[1]   It seems, however, to have recovered from this *dragonnade*, for the Masters and almsfolk were residing in it when Charles II. chose the hospital as a depôt for the prisoners taken in the war with Holland, in 1665.   The prisoners, unsupplied with some of the first necessaries of life, consumed for fuel all the wood-work which had been left unburnt by the Royalist troops, or subsequently replaced; and so entirely dismantled and

The destruction of the hospital.

destroyed the whole of the buildings, that after they left, it could not be occupied as an hospital without being rebuilt, and, as this was impossible, it was never inhabited again.[2]

When the almsfolks were thus unceremoniously ejected, and their hospital wantonly destroyed, they were for some time lodged in the city without any "fixed or permanent habitation;" but in 1671 the Master, Dr. Darel, took a lease of some tenements in Colebrook Street,[3] into which they were admitted; and they continued to be the almshouses for the sisters till near the end of last century, when the ruins

Removal of its ruins.

of the old hospital were taken down, and the materials given for the erection of the six almshouses in Water Lane.

The remoteness of the hospital from the city favours the belief that it was originally erected (as is so distinctly intimated in Stratford's Register and Fromond's will) as a leper-house.[4]   But it is very probable that from the first, or in consequence of subsequent benefactions, the admission of other classes of "infirm persons" may have been contemplated.   Its gradual transformation from an hospital to an almshouse is nothing more than has happened to almost every similar foundation; and may be regarded as an inevitable consequence of the other changes which time has wrought.[5]

Its constitution.

Some of the earliest notices of it informs us that it was intended for nine poor brethren and sisters, and a Master;[6] but during the period between the years 1547 and 1562 the number was reduced to eight, which is the present complement.[7]   In the order for their ejection by Charles II. the occupants are called "almswomen;" but this is noted as an error.[8]   The appointments were formerly all made by the bishop,[9]

---

(1) Wavell, pp. 202, &c., 254, &c.

(2) Ibid., pp. 206, 207, 256, 257.   "The estimate of the expense of rebuilding the almshouses was £650; the allowance made by government was £100."

(3) These tenements are in the eastern part of Cole-brook Street, and are marked in Godson's map as Magdalen Hospital.   They are said to have been bought by Dr. Darel, and bequeathed to the charity, but this is a mistake.   The commission for removing the ruins was given in 1788.   (See Wavell, *u. s.*, p. 208; Vet. Mon., vol. iii.; Charity Commiss. Report, 1837, *u. s.*; Milner, vol. ii. p. 232.)

(4) In the same way (to refer to no other examples) there was situated, at about the same distance from one of the northern gates of the city of Norwich, an hospital

for lepers, dedicated, like this, to St. Mary Magdalen. (Blomefield's Hist. Norfolk, vol. iv. p. 440.)

(5) The establishment of a *science* of medicine, by necessitating a totally different method of treatment for the sick, would of itself suffice to explain the transformation of endowed hospitals into "*ptochia*," strictly so called.

(6) The Master is called a "pryst" in Henry VIII.'s time, but in the next reign it appears that there was another, and stipendiary priest, belonging to this society. (Wavell, vol. ii. p. 165.)

(7) Ibid., p. 182.

(8) Ibid., p. 206.

(9) Ibid., pp. 178—180, where several appointments are cited from Wykeham's Registers.

but now the bishop appoints the Master (*quamdiu se bene gesserit*, which is in fact for life), and confirms the appointment of the almsfolks by the Master.[1]

We have no account of the revenues of this charity before the fifteenth year of the reign of Henry VII. The total income is said then to have been £42 7s. 8d.;[2] the "*Valor Ecclesiasticus*"[3] gives the income in the twenty-sixth year of the succeeding reign as £42 16s.; and the certificate in the Augmentation Office, dated in the thirty-seventh year of Henry VIII., as £41 6s. 8d.[4] The payments recorded in the "*Valor*" amount to £25 19s. 9½d., leaving the clear value of £16 6s. 2½d., which would seem to have been the perquisite of the Master. In the Augmentation Office certificate the total of payments is given as £27 17s. 7d., " and so remayneth £13 9s. 4d., whyche the Maister receaveth for his paynes, and repayring of the tenements."[5]

In Wavell's time the income was £88 19s., and the expense £43 5s. 4d., leaving £45 13s. 8d. for the Master, " out of which he keeps in repair the poor people's houses, and the buildings belonging to the hospital on Magdalene Hill [which, however, were in a state of irretrievable ruin], and pays land-tax."[6] The yearly income is now £122 8s. 8d., of which about £50 remains for the Master, in lieu of the residence formerly provided, out of which he has to pay for all repairs, and to meet other incidental expenses.

Each brother and sister of the nine received in Henry VIII.'s time 13s. 4d. each, and eight of them, at " borde wages, at eight pence a weyk a piece," cost the charity £13 17s. 4d.; but since that time Dr. Ebden (a former Master) added 4d. for each recipient weekly, and 6s. 8d. additional yearly; and Mr. Percivall (another benefactor) added £1 per annum, which, with some other perquisites, and the increased value of the estates, have raised the yearly stipend of each of four brothers and four sisters to £5 14s.,[7] two of whom, having no houses, are for the future to receive 2s. a week additional; and there is an annual allowance of 13s. 4d. to an out-pensioner.

These payments, together with the rents of a garden, the steward's fee, &c., make the annual expenditure of the hospital very nearly £65.

(1) Charity Commiss. Report, *u. s.*

(2) Wavell, vol. ii. p. 186.

(3) Vol. ii. p. 4.

(4) Wavell, vol. ii. p. 253.

(5) Amongst the payments was included £6 to the stipendiary priest, which at first was declared forfeit to the king under the Act 1 Edw. VI.; but due representation of the state of the case having been made, it was allowed to the Master, in augmentation of his income from the hospital. (Ibid., pp. 165, 166, 187.)

Amongst the receipts was the sum of 60s. yearly, granted by Edward III., which the city of Winchester had agreed to pay to him for the removal of the Drapery (or Cloth Hall) into High Street. And on the fly-leaves of the copy of the Tarrages of Winchester, in the British Museum (Add. MSS., 6133), is this memorandum :—" The Hospital of Mary Magdalen, by Winchester, doth pay to

ye City yerely quitrent, as by ye accompts of ye hospital at ye tyme of dissolucon of monasteries apperith, 3/7."

(6) Wavell, vol. ii. p 192.

(7) Ibid., p. 193.

I may add here a brief account of the buildings of the hospital, as they are described and represented by Wavell (*u. s.*), and in the *Vetusta Monumenta* (vol. iii.).

The chapel stood nearest the high road, and parallel with it; behind it, and joining it, stood the Master's house, lying north and south; and beyond it again, and joining it, in a line parallel with the chapel, the dwellings of the brethren, eight in number, with chimneys as conspicuously prominent as at St. Cross. There were some other buildings within the precinct-wall, but their sites are unimportant.

Only the chapel and the Master's house remained, even in a state of ruin, at the time when our authorities de-

Its revenues and expenditure.

THE HOSPITAL OF ST. JOHN THE BAPTIST, AND LAMB'S ALMSHOUSES.[1]

St. John's
House, and
Lamb's Alms-
houses.

At the eastern end of High Street, between Busket Lane and Eastgate Street, stands St. John's House, with its chapel;[2] and behind them are twenty-one commodious and well-built almshouses,[3] pleasantly situated in a garden with a large iron gate into the street. And on the opposite side of the way, at the corner of Colebrook Street, is a fine modern building with a tower and gateway,[4] consisting of almshouses for twenty poor persons, and inclosing a very agreeable garden. These are the

scribed them; and the remains of the chapel alone are worthy of special notice. It was a plain rectangular structure, 77 ft. in length, and 35 ft. 6 in. in breadth, and consisted of a central alley, with two aisles divided from it by six pointed Transition Norman arches on each side, springing from short thick cylindrical piers, with scalloped capitals and round abaci. Two of these arches are included in the chancel, and they had square abaci. The responds resembled the piers; and the arches in the aisles, between the chancel and the nave, were much depressed or flattened. The mouldings of all these arches were flat, and painted with floral patterns and scroll-work in black and brown. The west window was an early Perpendicular one with three lights, and under it was the Norman doorway, now to be seen in St. Peter's Street, at the entrance to the Roman Catholic chapel. The windows at the ends of the aisles were mere loops, as is frequently the case in small Norman churches. The east window was Early English, with two lights, and a quatrefoil in the head; at the east end of the aisles were flat-headed windows, in the Perpendicular or late Decorated style, of four or fewer lights. The south door was a plain Transition Norman pointed arch, with shafts and moulded capitals. There was no clerestory. A deep string-course or ledge ran all round the church inside, which was wider under the east window; and there were niches on each side of the altar.

Almost every part of the interior showed traces of painting, and coloured sketches of the most noteworthy, by Mr. Schnebbelie, are in the possession of the Society of Antiquaries. Over the east window were five shields, one bearing the arms of Winchester; on the north side of the altar was a figure of St. Peter *in pontificalibus* and pall, with two keys in his left hand, and in his right a church with a lofty spire. Next was the figure of a bishop, and then one of a warrior in armour, with a shield of the form used in the reign of Edward I. On the south side the figure of a bald man, with a sword in his left hand, kneeling under a canopy; and next it a small figure of an archbishop holding a cross. This also was quite Edwardian in style. On the spandrels were two angels with censers. On the soffits of the eastmost arch of the

north aisle were three paintings; and the central one was supposed to represent the martyrdom of Becket. Blue crosses were painted in many parts of the walls.

There was a wooden gallery of later date under one of the middle arches on the north side of the nave, projecting into the church, which was entered from the upper floor of the Master's house.

The following inscription was to be seen on a brass fixed to the south wall of the chancel:—

"CORPUS JOHANNIS EBDEN, S. T. P. PII ECCLESIÆ CATHEDRALIS WINTON. PREBENDARII DOCTI, HUJUS HOSPITII MAGISTRI REVERENDI, QUI INTER ALIA DONA IN ALIOS CHARITATIS USUS COLLATA 200L. IN AUGMENTATIONEM STIPENDIORUM IBIDEM LIBERE DEDIT; HOC TEGITUR TUMULO. OBIIT 16, NOVEMBRIS, 1614; ÆTATIS SUÆ 98.

"HE THAT BOTH GOD AND GOOD MEN FEAR'D AND LOV'D
WHICH BY EXAMPLE CHERISH'T OR REPROV'D
HEER LYES ENTER'D. HE LIVING WAS, DEAD IS;
A PREACHER WHOM THE CHURCH LOV'D, THE PEOPLE
    MYS;
HIS LIFE FOR LENGTH, LEARNING FOR TRUTH, WAS
    GREATE,
HIS DOCTRINE PURE, HIS DEEDS WITHOUT DECEITE,
AND IN HIS LIFETIME WAS, AND ATT HIS ENDE,
TO RICH AND POORE, A FATHER AND A FREINDE."

(Wavell, vol. ii. pp. 210, 211.)

A gravestone commemorated Mrs. Elizabeth Symonds, daughter of Dr. Ebden, who died Sept. 12, 1695, aged 90 years. (*Vet. Mon., u. s.*)

(1) My account of these institutions is derived chiefly from the Charity Commissioners' Report for 1824, pp. 435, &c., and Appendix, pp. 685, &c.

(2) See above, p. 20.

(3) There are now [1859] actually only thirteen almshouses finished and occupied, but four more are nearly completed, and another four will be added without much delay.

(4) Erected in 1833 (in the "Tudor" style) by the late Mr. O. B. Carter, on the site of some pre-existing hospital or almshouses on the same foundation, as may

Hospital of St. John the Baptist and Lamb's Almshouses, under the management of the trustees appointed by the Court of Chancery.

The history[1] of this charity begins with the foundation, in the year 1289, by John Devenishe, "citizen and alderman of the cittie of Winchester," by licence from Edward I., of an hospital "for the only relief of sick and lame souldyers, poor pilgrims, and necessitated wayfaring men, to have their dyett and lodging ther fit and convenient for one night or longer, as their abilities to travayl gave leave, without any expence or payment therefore." And he is said to have "endowed yt with competent and fayer allowance, and furnished the roomes with bedding and all necessaries for their better accommodation;"[2] making the mayor keeper of the hospital, without a ticket from whom none were "to be admitted entraunce ther." *Foundation of the hospital.*

The return in the Augmentation Office (37 Hen. VIII.) adds to these particulars that the founder intended "to have a priest to sing there for ever, to pray for his soul, and the souls of all Christian men."[3] This foundation is by Trussell ascribed to a descendant of his, named Richard Devenishe, in the reign of Henry VI., who (he says) both founded and endowed the chapel.[4]

It has already been stated[5] that at the dissolution, the hospital falling into the king's hands, the house was by him granted to the corporation, or as Trussell[6] says, "to the maior, bayliffs, and cominaltie of the cittie of Winchester, and their successors," as a public hall for holding the municipal elections and other similar purposes;[7] but *The Reformation.*

be seen in Godson's map. Over the gateway is the trustees' room.

(1) We are indebted to Alderman Trussell (fol. 103, &c.) for this account of the origin of St. John's Hospital. And it is confirmed by the architecture of the east window of the chapel, which is late Early English. The difference between it and the "Rooms" is fully accounted for by the rebuilding of the hospital in 1408. (See below, p. 248, note.) Wavell (vol. i. p. 219) rightly rejects the supposition that it had been founded by St. Brinstau, as based on a mere "conjecture of Leland's," who says (vol. iii. fol. 70), "there is yn the chapelle an ymage of S. Brinstane, sumtyme Bisshop of Winchester; and I have redde that S. Brinstane founded an hospitale in Winchester." Milner, however (vol. ii. p. 223), accepts it as "plain," and adds that "there is some reason for supposing that this establishment became the property, or fell under the administration of the Knights Templars," quoting "Trussell's MSS." as his authority, which contains nothing to justify the supposition. He also (ibid., p. 224) alters the date of John Devenishe's foundation to the reign of Edward II., because Trussell happened to speak of "the suppression of the Templars immediately before it, in the year 1289," on the ground of the generally "erroneous and confused" character of the worthy alderman's chronology. But by this method we arrive at no satisfactory result.

In some guide-books and directories further confusion

is introduced by the substitution of the name of Birinus for Brinstan—most frequently, however, with St. Brinstan's date.

It is worthy of observation, that in Elizabeth's charter it is stated that "the name of this hospital is somewhat obscure and uncertain." (Milner, vol. ii. p. 305.)

(2) In the Black Book of Winchester (fol. 62 v°) is an enumeration of the "*utensilia domus Sci Johannis,*" made in the seventh year of Edward IV. (1467), on occasion of the appointment of an actual *keeper;* the greater part are furniture and books for the chapel, but there are also many pairs of sheets, three blankets, and a few coverlets. Leland says (*u. s.*) that "pore syke people be kept" there.

(3) Charity Commiss. Report, *u. s.*

(4) Trussell, *u. s.*; Charity Commiss. Report, *u. s.* The amount of the endowment, £5 3s. per annum, and its sources,—lands in Little Sombourne, and in Winchester,—are specified in this Report, so that this part of the story is unquestionable; but the episcopal registers, as well as the style of the chapel, prove that it was not now first erected.

Amongst the undoubted benefactors of the original hospital was Mark Le Faire (mayor in 1408, and other years), who gave a part of the George Inn, the King's Head, and his own house, which was under the Penthouse.

(5) See above, p. 20, and note 1.

(6) Fol. 803.

(7) From the Black Book of Winchester (Brit. Mus.

it is also evident, both from the will of Ralph Lamb, and from Elizabeth's charter to the city, that the hospital was not then suppressed.

Lamb's Alms-houses founded.

In 1558, by his will dated August the 17th, Ralph Lamb bequeathed £400 for the purchase of lands to be conveyed to "the Master and brethren" of this hospital, for the purpose of adding to it as many poor as the rents of those lands would maintain, who were to be called "the Alms-folk of Ralph Lamb." And accordingly, an estate called Ratfin (or Rothfen), in Amesbury, Wiltshire,[1] and some small properties in Winchester, were purchased; and six "poor needy persons" established in as many almshouses, with various perquisites in money, coals, and clothing.[2]

Queen Elizabeth's Charter.

The charter of Elizabeth, in the year 1588, after describing this charity as "a certain hospital, with divers lands and tenements . . . . belonging from time whereof no memory of man is to the contrary, founded in pure and perpetual alms, commonly called the Hospital of St. John the Baptist, wherein many poor people are relieved and provided for, as well in victuals as apparel, also with other necessaries . . . . which hospital . . . . always was, and yet is, in the government and custody of the mayor and commonalty [of Winchester], and for the better relief and sustenance of the poor and feeble persons living in the said hospital, divers [other] land and tenements . . . . granted . . . . by one Ralph Lamb and others," ordains that the mayor, bailiffs, and commonalty of Winchester shall be "founders" and "keepers" of this hospital.[3]

Resignation of the Corporation.

Under this charter the affairs of the charity were administered till the year 1829, when the corporation resigned their powers and responsibilities to the trustees appointed by the Court of Chancery. For in the year 1811 a suit was commenced against the corporation for mismanagement and misapplication of their trusts,[4] not only with regard to this hospital, but also to all the other charities which had been

Add. MSS., 6036, fol. 61) I find that assemblies, at which ordinances were passed, were held at "the House or Hospital of St. John the Baptist," at least as early as the sixth year of Edward IV. (or 1466); and it is recorded (fol. 3 v⁰) that in the tenth year of Henry IV. (1408) Mark Le Fayre, being mayor, an order was made that the House of St. John the Baptist should within the year be rebuilt (*de novo*) and covered with lead, the cost being partly defrayed by voluntary contributions, for receiving which collectors were then appointed; and incidentally we learn from Trussell (fol. 103 v⁰), that the use of St. John's House for municipal purposes dates from the recorded foundation of the hospital. "Yt appeereth," says he, "by the booke of ordinances of this cittie [an earlier one than the Black Book], that in the time of Roger le Long, who succeeded John Devenishe in the place [as mayor], that there was an ordinance made that euerye yeer, uppon the next Sunday after Midsomer day (except upon some extraordenarie occation hindered, and that not to bee allowed of but by a generall assemblie),

the maior and his brethren, and all the whole corporacion, with their wives, showld meet att this house at supper, whereat ouer and aboue the rate sett, the maior for the tyme beeing, and hee that was maior the precedent yeere, were to bestowe a couple of ffatt capons; which loue-feast or merry meeting was appoynted to revive the memory of the Devenishes. This meeting is obserued to this daye."

Such an employment of the hall of an hospital, which the corporation regarded as their own property, is not surprising; for in the seventh year of Edward IV. (1467) one assembly is said to have been held in the chapter-house of the Friars Minor.

(1) Since exchanged for an estate called Thruxton Farm, near Andover.

(2) Charity Commiss. Report, *u. s.*

Milner's account (vol. ii. p. 225) affords a remarkable illustration of the real scope of his work.

(3) Ibid., p. 305.

(4) Law Journal (Chancery) Reports, vol. iii. pp. 64—66.

committed to their care; and after a litigation of nearly twenty years the contest was terminated by their surrender.[1]

"Since the transfer of the trusts the revenues of the hospital have been greatly increased;" six poor women, past the age of sixty, receive each 10s. weekly, one ton of coals, and 8s. 4d. (as "shift-money") yearly, £1 every other year for a gown, and 6s. 8d. on All Saints' day; and the remaining inmates of the establishment receive 10s. each weekly.[2]

The property of the hospital consists of Thruxton Farm,[3] a farm at Mitcheldever, and another at Headbourne Worthy, together with about sixty houses, &c. (including the site of the Town-hall), in Winchester; and the income arising from it is about £1500 per annum. The trustees consist of the Bishop of Winchester, the Wardens of Winchester College and New College, Oxford, and five others; and they have a chaplain, a secretary, an almoner, and one or two subordinate officers.

Property of the hospital.

The chapel was disused after the Reformation, and fell into a ruinous condition, but in 1710 it was converted into a school-room for the instruction of sixty poor children, for which purpose it continued to be used until the year 1838, when it was repaired, consecrated anew, and restored to its original use.[4]

The chapel.

CHRIST'S HOSPITAL.[5]

This, which is also called the Blue-coat Hospital, stands in its garden, at the south-western corner of Symonds' Street, opposite the wall of the precinct. It is inclosed by a high wall, and over the iron gate is an inscription containing a short account of the institution.[6] The central portion contains apartments for the

Christ's Hospital.

---

(1) Moody's "Handbook to the Charities of Winchester," with corrections, for which I am under obligation to the author; and also to J. H. Todd, Esq., who is secretary to several of these institutions.

(2) Moody's "Handbook."

(3) See above p. 248, note 1.

(4) Wavell, vol. i. p. 222. He also states that "many of its priests were buried in it," with Ralph Lamb, "and many other people of note."

The following note is from the Winchester Volume of the Archæological Institute (Archit. Notes, &c., p. 13). The "chapel is a building of the time of Henry III. [Edward I. we have seen], with a triple lancet window at the east end, and six single lancet windows on the south side; the two easternmost have trefoil heads. The north wall is blank, being joined to other buildings." "Built into the wall at the back is a head, which is a good piece of sculpture of the fourteenth century, representing our Saviour with a nimbus, and the cross in it." "It was probably the centre of the tracery of a fine window." (Compare Milner, vol. ii. p. 225.) The triple lancet window has externally one hood-mould.

(5) My information respecting this charity is principally derived from the Charity Commissioners' Report, above referred to; and from Mr. Moody's pamphlet on the Charities of Winchester, with additions and corrections as I have before said.

(6) This street, of course, derives its present name from the founder of Christ's Hospital. Its ancient name was "Menstre Stret."

The inscription over the gate is merely—

"Christ's Hospital, founded by Mr. Peter Simonds, of London, mercer, for six old men, one woman, and four boys, who have a plentiful maintenance. He gave also

matron, and for four boys; and there are three residences on each side for the old men, who receive the benefit of the charity. There is nothing particularly noteworthy in the building.

The founder.

Peter Symonds, the founder of this hospital, was born in Winchester, and was a mercer in London. By his will, dated in the year 1586, he bequeathed lands in Essex and Surrey for the purpose of erecting and endowing an hospital for the perpetual maintenance of six poor, old, unmarried men, and four poor young children; and besides the clothing and support of these almsfolk, two poor scholars were to be kept, one at Oxford and the other at Cambridge, out of the rents of these lands.[1]

The management and control of the charity he intrusted to the Warden of Winchester College (for the time being), as "conservator," and to six "gubernators," two of whom were to be citizens who had filled the office of mayor in Winchester, and the other four "the most substantial and honest citizens who had not filled the office," one of which number was to be appointed treasurer. James I., by letters patent, bearing date the 15th of July, 1605, established and organised the hospital as a body corporate.[2] And in the year 1607 the existing almshouse was built.[3]

The new statutes.

New statutes were drawn up, approved by the Corporation of Winchester, and passed under the common seal, on October the 11th, 1793. The particulars of most interest being the allowance to each of the men of £2 12s. per annum, and to the matron, for each of the boys, of £1 6s. per annum, over the fixed weekly and other allowances; the weekly payment, on Friday morning, of 3s. 6d. to each of the men, and the same to the matron for each of the boys, and 5s. for herself; the providing for each of the men, once in two years, a gown of blue cloth, on which was to be fixed the silver badge of the hospital; for each boy a coat, hat, and pair of breeches of the same, and a pair of leather breeches;[4] and for the matron a gown of the same, or £1 2s. instead of it; the enforcing of the daily attendance of the almsmen at the cathedral, morning and evening, except in case of sickness or leave of absence, under penalty of forfeiting 4d. for each default; with the instruction of the boys, and the provision of £10 for each as apprentice-fee on his attaining the age of 14.

ten pounds per ann. to two poor scholars in the universities, and also some other charities."

On the front of the building are the founder's arms, with his name, and the date, 1607.

(1) He directed that the poor men should not be less than 50 years of age; that if they should marry, they should be put out of the hospital, and that the approbation of the mayor and the "twenty-four," as well as of the conservators and gubernators, should be requisite for each appointment. The boys were to be admitted from 7 years of age, and remain till 17 or 18; and a poor woman was to be admitted into the hospital for dressing the provisions for the poor men and boys, washing their clothes, and attending to the boys generally. All necessary food, clothing, &c., was to be provided for the almsfolk; and it was particularly specified that "at supper the old men [were] to have but a small drinking." The poor scholars were to be selected by the Mayors of Oxford and Cambridge respectively, and to receive £5 each per annum.

(2) By the authority of these letters patent, the Mayor and Corporation of Winchester had more power in the management of the hospital; and a draught of statutes for the government of it was drawn up.

(3) The house has been repaired at various times, and especially since the beginning of this century, but it has not lost the general character of the time of its original erection.

(4) Milner (vol. ii. p. 215) observes that the almsmen and boys of this hospital "exhibit the fashion of the dress prevalent amongst the ordinary people at the period of . . . . the reign of James I."

Since that period, the pecuniary value of the endowment having increased[1] (the annual value now falling little short of £800), the allowances have been increased in proportion, and the brethren now receive 8s. 6d. each weekly, and the matron, for herself and the four boys, £1 12s. Each brother also receives 2s. 6d. quarterly, and the matron and boys £1 1s. Coals are provided for all, and £1 1s. is allowed half-yearly for the commemoration of the founder. Additional allowance is made in sickness. The boys are instructed at the Choristers' School, at the cost of £10 a year for each. The apprentice-fee is increased to £30, with £5 for the boy's clothing; and each of the two scholars at Oxford and Cambridge now receives £10 annually.[2]

In addition to all this, £4 is distributed amongst the inmates of the hospital yearly, out of the charity called "*Pemerton's Quarterages.*"[3]

BISHOP MORLEY'S COLLEGE.[4]

On the north side of the cathedral yard, near the entrance from Market Street, stands this college, which was founded in the year 1672 by Bishop Morley, and endowed by him for the widows of ten poor clergymen of this diocese and that of Worcester. It is a plain building, in the form of three sides of a square, and consists of ten distinct residences, and it is enclosed by a wall. Over the gate, at the entrance to the quadrangle, are the arms of the founder, with this inscription :— Bishop Morley's College.

"NOW SHE THAT IS A WIDOW INDEED, AND DESOLATE, TRUSTETH IN GOD, AND CONTINUETH IN PRAYERS AND SUPPLICATIONS, NIGHT AND DAY.

"GEO . MORLEY . EPUS . 1672.
"THE COLLEGE OF MATRONES."

The Dean and Chapter are the trustees of this society, which, having been increased by other benefactions since its foundation, has an income of nearly £800 yearly. The two "Senior Matrons" receive each £77 10s., and the other eight £74 each per annum.

PAROCHIAL CHARITIES.[5]

St. Lawrence.—The poor of this parish receive yearly £1 (less 1s. 10d. deducted for land tax), by the will of Nathaniel Mill,[6] who left £42 annually to the Mayor and Charities of St. Lawrence' parish.

(1) Charity Commiss. Report, *u. s.*; Moody's Pamphlet, p. 40.

(2) One of the estates, which was situated at West Ham, was sold to the Victoria Dock Company, and the proceeds invested in the 3 per cent. Consols.

(3) See below, p. 257.

(4) Wavell, vol. ii. pp. 223, 224.

(5) See Report of Charity Commissioners for 1837, *u. s.*; and Moody's "Handbook of Charities, &c."

(6) Dated 13th of April, 1636.

Corporation of Southampton, out of his lands at Woolston, to be given to twenty poor persons on New Year's Eve; and one portion of it being allotted to the parish of St. Lawrence, is paid yearly to the Rector, and by him distributed.

Another sum of £2 (less 8s. land tax) is distributed yearly in this parish, under the will of Ann Neale,[1] arising from an estate at Huxtable, in Kent; 2s. being given to the clerk, and the remainder divided amongst nineteen poor women.

On every Sunday in the year, immediately after divine service, two shillings' worth of bread is given to six poor people of the parish, who are selected by the churchwardens, which is provided by a rent-charge on certain lands in Martyr-Worthy, in conformity with the will of Edward Grace.[2]

Charities of St. Maurice' parish.

St. Maurice.—The sum of £2 is yearly distributed in this parish by the church-wardens, under the name of "Epiphany money," amongst sixteen poor widows, arising from the investment of a residuary legacy under the will of Barbara Kerby.[3] The principal is now in the hands of the overseers, on the account of the parish (acknow-ledged by a promissory note), who pay interest at the rate of 4 per cent. per annum.[4]

Charities of St. Thomas' parish.

St. Thomas.—On the Sunday after every quarter-day twenty sixpenny loaves are distributed, at the discretion of the churchwardens, amongst the poor of the parish who attend this church, provided by a charge of £2 per annum on three tenements in Jewry Street, under the will of Thomas Brooker.[5] And in the month of November, every year, bread to the value of £5 is distributed among the poor of this parish by the Dean and Chapter, as agents for the representatives of Elizabeth Imber,[6] who left the sum to be so expended, arising out of lands at Bromham, in Wiltshire. Two eightpenny loaves are given to each person.

The "Imber Girls" in this parish are twelve poor children, who are clothed and instructed under the direction of the rector and the churchwardens, by means of a bequest of £24 per annum, left by the before-named Elizabeth Imber.[7]

Charities of St. Michael's parish.

St. Michael.—Four gowns and four coats, of the value of £8, are annually given away at Christmas, at the direction of the rector and the parochial officers, to four poor

---

(1) In 1693.

(2) The annual amount of the rent charge is £5 4s., and the will bears date June the 7th, 1712.

Wavell (vol. i. p. 184) adds from the List of Bene-factors to this church the following:—

"The Rev. Mr. Price gave £100.

"Joseph Perceval, merchant, gave £10 a year for reading evening prayers in the church."

And he speaks of a bequest by Richard Budd, of Lon-don, in 1630, "for tolling the bell at the execution of condemned malefactors."

(3) Dated October the 16th, 1758.

(4) The original amount of this legacy (which was to be put out at interest in the name of the rector for the time being) is unknown. The Rev. John Newbolt, a former rector, used to lay out the interest in the purchase of Bibles and Prayer-books, which he distri-buted amongst the poor. His successor, the Rev. G. Z. Armstrong, when appointed to the rectory, received £42 13s. as the balance of the charity, with which he purchased £50 four per cents. This, being sold at his death, realized £50; and after remaining a short time in a bank in the city, was invested as is stated above.

(5) Dated March the 17th, 1713.

(6) Under the statute 9 Geo. II. c. 36, this bequest was void; but her charitable intentions are, nevertheless, carried out by her representatives. The will is dated 1789, and 1805.

(7) The sum of £1338 6s. 8d. three per cent Consols was invested in the names of the Dean and Chapter, and £24 of the dividends are annually applied as stated above, the remaining £16 being similarly expended in the town of Devizes.

women and four poor men of this parish, in accordance with the will of Samuel Kent,[1] which directed his executors to invest £400 in 3 per cent. Consols, the dividends of which were to be applied in the purchase of these garments. The surplus, in conformity with the same instrument, is laid out in bread, which is distributed on every fourth Sunday after evening service.[2]

St. John.—The oldest charity in this parish, is one which, being left for the celebration of mass in the Lady-Chapel, escaped confiscation at the Dissolution.[3] Seventeen messuages, or lands and tenements, were committed to certain feoffees by John Thomas, in an instrument dated December the 10th, 1577, that the rents and profits accruing from them should be delivered to the warden of the fraternity of the Chapel of the Blessed Virgin, in the parish church, for the celebration of masses, &c., in that chapel. Instead of being taken by the crown, under the Act 1 Edw. VI. c. 14, by some inexplicable accident, it passed into the possession of the parish. There are now eighteen tenements and some other small properties, and some of the former are occupied by poor persons, rent free, whilst the rent arising from the rest is applied to the repairs and current expenses of the church, and the balance carried to the overseers' account.

Charities of John's parish.

"Smith's Gift," amounting to £22 10s. yearly; "Pemerton's Gift,"[4] of £1 10s. yearly; and an annual rent-charge of 13s. 4d. on some premises in Hyde Street, left to the poor of this parish, are now employed in the apprenticing and clothing of poor children, supplying coals to the poor, and pecuniary relief to the sick and indigent. The first of these sums arises from estates at Shalden, and a house in this parish, the proceeds of which Henry Smith (according to a deed of gift executed by his feoffees[5]) bequeathed to the poor of the following parishes, and in these proportions, viz., £11 yearly to the poor of St. John's parish, £10 to those of St. Peter Cheesehill, £5 to those of St. Michael, and £2 to those of St. Bartholomew Hyde. The two last-named parishes appear never to have received any benefit from this bequest, the rents from Shalden having been divided equally between this parish and St. Peter's from the year 1645;[6] and the house in this parish, opposite the church,[7] having been occupied jointly by poor persons from these two parishes.

Another sum of £3 annually is derived from a bequest of the Rev. Mr. Percival, and is paid by the Dean and Chapter to the minister, by whom it is distributed.

(1) Dated June the 10th, 1772. This will was never proved, but in 1815 the administratrix, Josepha Sophia Wheat, purchased with the sum named above £691 3s. Consols, in the names of the then Rector of St. Michael's, and two others; and it now stands in the names of those who have succeeded to the trust.

(2) Bread to the value of £1 is given on each one of twelve Sundays, and on the thirteenth to the value of 14s. 8d., the residue of the income.

(3) See above, p. 170, note 1. I am indebted to Mr. J. Masters for information respecting this parish.

(4) This is received from the trustees of St. John's Hospital.

(5) Dated December the 20th, 1641.

(6) Amongst the records of the parish is an agreement drawn up in this year, between the occupier of the estate at Shalden, and the parishioners of St. John and St. Peter, to the effect above stated. The moiety of the rents received by this parish was formerly merged in the general account of the churchwardens and overseers, but it is now accounted for separately.

(7) This was formerly one of the few ancient houses

Two charities, consisting of the interest of £22, left by Christopher Johnson, and that of £15, left by Bartholomew Smith, (which was formerly distributed amongst the poor by the churchwardens), were terminated near the close of the last century, by the principal sum being placed to the general account of the parish.[1]

Charities of St. Peter's parish.

St. Peter Cheesehill.—This parish receives yearly £22 10s., the moiety of the rent of the estates at Shalden, noticed under the last parish as " Smith's Gift," and £1 10s., " Pemerton's Gift," and 13s. 4d. from the bequest of John Pink, in the same manner,— all which sums are distributed amongst the aged poor by the churchwardens. The parish likewise receives £3 annually, under the will of the Rev. Mr. Percival, from the Dean and Chapter.

There was formerly distributed here, likewise, the interest on £15, received from Bartholomew Smith; but the principal was applied, in 1813, to the rebuilding of the houses opposite the church, which belong to the parish.

Another charity has also ceased; it consisted of a rent-charge of £1 10s. yearly on certain houses and gardens in Cheesehill Street, left by John Bowles,[2] to be distributed on St. Thomas' Day and Good Friday, amongst the most afflicted persons in the parish, each of whom was to have 1s. It is now placed to the churchwardens' account.

The parochial school receives yearly the interest of £100 bequeathed to it by Miss Earle.[3]

There are three houses with gardens opposite the church, two other houses and gardens in the same street, and some tenements in the parish of St. John, the rents of which are received by the churchwardens, and are employed in meeting the ordinary expenses of the church and parish; but the parishioners have no title deeds, although they have long been possessed of the property.[4]

Charities of St. Bartholomew parish.

St. Bartholomew Hyde.—" Pink's Gift,"[5] of 13s. 4d. annually, is received in this parish, and distributed by the churchwardens at Christmas.

The sum of £15 is also distributed by the churchwardens annually, at Christmas,

---

in Winchester, which retained its primitive appearance (see Carter's view of St. John's Street); but it has recently been modernized, having become so ruinous as to threaten to fall.

(1) Moody's " Handbook," p. 57.

Wavell (vol. i. p. 215) states that the list of benefactors is the same as that of St. Peter's parish, " for, as the parishes are united, they receive an equal benefit from donations made to either of the churches." (See below.)

I have not been able to learn anything respecting the union of these parishes, which is here spoken of.

See above, p. 211, note 4, for notice of another charity.

(2) This deed was dated March the 27th, 1612.

(3) The date of this bequest was 1855.

(4) Wavell's account of the " table of benefactors " in St. Peter's Church (vol. i. p. 211) comprises the following, not noticed in the text:—

" Dr. Over, by his will, that two boys are to be sent to the free school in Winchester.

" Mr. Johnson £20.

" George Percival gave £1 10s., paid yearly by the Mayor of Winchester.

" Five shillings given annually to a poor widow by an unknown hand.

(5) " The testator, by his will, dated 14th January, 1642, gave £200, and directed that his executors should purchase either lands or tenements of the clear annual value of £10 10s., or else a rent-charge of that amount to be given to the poor of the several parishes of Mitcheldever, Medstead, Bighton, Bishop's Sutton, Old Alresford, Overton, New Alresford, St. John in the Soke, St. Peter Cheesehill, and St. Bartholomew Hyde; whereof the three latter were to receive the sum of £2 annually." (Moody's " Handbook," pp. 49, 50.)

arising from a messuage or tenement bequeathed for the maintenance of aged persons by Sir George Powlett.[1]

A further sum of £9 is annually distributed in the same manner, which arises from the rental of a field in the parish, in which formerly the sheep fair was held. It is not known how or when the field became the property of the parish, but it has been held that one portion of its rent was given for the poor, and the other for the repairs of the church ;[2] and, accordingly, the above-named sum is appropriated to the poor, and the residue, £5, to the church.

The churchwardens also receive for their general account the sum of £7 yearly, arising from the funded proceeds of the sale of a field near Swan Lane, which was sold to the London and South-Western Railway Company, on the formation of their line ; the sum of £7 10s., the rent of two tenements at Dern-gate ; and £10, the rent of a tenement and garden in Hyde Street.

Congregational Church.—There is an endowment of £5 a year, which is expended for coals and bread, and distributed amongst the poor of this congregation.

Congregational Church Charity.

CHARITIES ADMINISTERED BY THE TRUSTEES OF ST. JOHN'S HOSPITAL.

Burton's Gift.—£50 is annually distributed, in quarterly payments of £1 5s. to each, amongst ten poor persons of the parishes of St. Michael, St. John, and St. Peter Cheesehill, under the will of William Burton,[3] who left to the mayor, bailiffs, and commonalty of Winchester, and their successors, Little Denmark Meadow, the land on which Clifton Terrace, West Hill, now stands, and other property in Winchester ; with instructions to them to distribute £7 yearly amongst one hundred poor people on St. Thomas' Day, and in the Church of St. Thomas, and the residue amongst the poor of the parishes first mentioned. The improved management, and the increased value of the property, have very greatly raised the income of this charity.

Burton's Gift.

William Symonds' Gift.—William Symonds, alderman, who lies buried in the cathedral,[4] bequeathed[5] certain property in Chawton to the mayor, &c., the proceeds

William Symonds' Gift.

---

(1) This will is dated September the 20th, 1631. The original annual value of the bequest is unknown, but the property having become so dilapidated as to be untenantable, was let, in 1732, for the term of 99 years, at £2 10s. per annum, on condition of the lessee's rebuilding the premises, and surrendering them to the parish, at the expiration of the lease, in good repair.

(2) The churchwardens are possessed of an old plan, which shows the division of the field into *church land* and *poor land*.

(3) Dated December the 7th, 1603.

(4) See above, p. 76.

(5) His will is dated July the 26th, 1606. The manner of the bequest is remarkable :—If Thomas Morey the

of which were to be bestowed in quarterly payments on six poor and aged persons of the city, each receiving £3 6s. 8d. yearly. In consequence of the improved management of the charity at the present time, the poor persons now receive £1 13s. 4d. each quarterly.

Ashton's Nobles.—The name of this charity is derived from a quarterly payment of 6s. 8d. each, to fifteen almsfolk, which was formerly derived from the rental of three small houses near the site of St. Clement's Church, amounting to £20 per annum, bequeathed to the city by Thomas Ashton.[1] The rental of these houses is now £24 per annum, and is applied towards the repairs of St. Thomas' Church.[2] The payment is now made from the dividends of the sum of £666 13s. 4d. three per cent. Consols, which appear to have arisen from a further bequest[3] of Thomas Ashton; and also from one of £200 bequeathed by his brother, Richard Ashton,[4] to be applied to charitable uses by him with the approbation of the mayor, the dean, and the warden of Winchester College.

Budd's Gifts.—These consist of 1s. each to eight poor persons, and 6d. to each of twenty-four others, paid weekly on Sunday mornings in St. John's Chapel; together with £1 annually to the rector of St. Maurice for a sermon on the Feast of All Saints, arising from an annual rent charge of £39 16s. 5d. on the lordship and manor of Romsey extra; and one of £36 12s. 1d. on those of River, in Sussex, bequeathed by Richard Budd,[5] who was a native and resident of St. Maurice' parish.

Ashton's Nobles, and Tenements.

Budd's Gifts.

---

younger married the testator's daughter, Jane Symonds, he was to have the property on lease for 99 years, at the yearly rent of £20, which was to be distributed as stated above; but if the marriage did not take place, the whole of the property was to pass into the possession of the mayor, &c., who were directed to expend £4 yearly for wood and coals, to be distributed amongst the prisoners in Winchester jail, and also amongst the poor of the city, and the remainder for the benefit of the six poor persons as aforesaid. It was not proved to the satisfaction of the Charity Commissioners that the marriage did take place; but they found that the property, estimated by them as worth £90 a year, was let on renewable lease of 14 years, at £20 a year, subject to a fine at each renewal. The proceeds were distributed amongst six poor women, each receiving £1 13s. 4d. half yearly, and the fines were carried to the general account of the corporation, and expended for civic purposes.

(1) The date of this will is not known, but it was before 1661, as the "nobles" were certainly distributed annually from that year.

(2) This is in conformity with the directions of Ashton's will, which were that the rents should be applied to the yearly payment of £1 each to these poor persons, and that as they died the rents should be employed in the repair of the Church of St. Clement, which was subsequently destroyed, and the parish united with St. Thomas.

(3) He gave £1100, which Sir Richard Tichbourne owed to him, to be applied (after the death of his wife) to charitable uses by the corporation, and further devised that £200, for the payment of which Sir John Philpot and Sir Richard Tichbourne were bound, should be employed according to the directions of his brother's will. It is added, however, in Moody's "Handbook" (p. 20) that there is no evidence of the money having been received by the corporation.

(4) His will is dated April the 16th, 1624.

(5) His will bears date July the 20th, 1630. His directions were that 1s. should be given weekly at St. Maurice' Church, to each of ten poor men, and 6d. each to twenty others, and to ten poor women so long as they lived, except in case of their unallowable absence from divine service, when the gift should be distributed amongst four persons who did attend. The residue was appropriated to the annual sermon and the expense of collecting the rents.

He also bequeathed, but subject to certain contingencies, property in Wood Street, London, and in Llandeilo Vawr, in Carmarthenshire, for the poor of St. Maurice and the city, and to provide a dinner for the corporation on All Saints' Day; but there was no evidence produced to the commissioners that these contingent legacies had been received.

He further gave £40 to the dean and chapter, that they might allow the great bell of the cathedral to toll

Pemerton's Quarterages.—These are twenty poor men who receive £1 10*s.* each Pemerton's
Quarterages
and Donations quarterly, and a great-coat yearly; £1 is paid to the rector of St. Lawrence for the annual sermon on St. George's Day; after which one hundred and eighty fourpenny-loaves are distributed; £1 is sent to the mayor to be given away by him, and £1 is given to the almsfolk of Christ's Hospital every quarter.[1] All these charities are sustained by the gift by George Pemerton,[2] of property in North Houghton, Long-stock, King's Sombourne, and Stockbridge; only the first of which remains to the trustees, and produces £230 per annum, all traces of the other lands and houses having long ago been lost. He directed that ten poor men (to be nominated for their lives by the corporation) should receive 13*s.* 4*d.* each quarterly, £1 each for a coat at Christmas, and the other payments and gifts just mentioned to be made, but the £1 to the mayor was to be expended in cake and wine for the corporation. The quarterly payment to Christ's Hospital arises from the gift of £60 to the corporation, and is now paid out of a sum of stock invested for that purpose; and he further gave £20 freely to the stock of the city.

In addition to these payments, and in conformity with the instructions and provisions of his will, £3 is paid annually to the overseers of Compton, £2 6*s.* 8*d.* to those of North Houghton, and £1 10*s.* each to those of the parishes of St. John on the Hill, and St. Peter Cheesehill, to be distributed amongst their poor.[3]

Yalden's Gift.—The sum of £1 14*s.* 8*d.*, being the interest of £20 left by Yalden's Gift. Margaret Yalden,[4] at 8 per cent., is annually divided amongst eight poor widows, each of whom receive 4*s.* 5*d.*[5]

Sevier's Gift.—This is an annuity of £10 (less £2 deducted for land-tax), received Sevier's Gift. from the owner of the Saracen's Head Inn, at Salisbury, bequeathed[6] by John Sevier, for the purpose of apprenticing two poor children in Winchester, to which purpose it is applied as often as is possible, the usual premium paid being £15.

Sir Thomas White's Bequest to Poor Tradesmen.—This consists of an annual sum Sir Thomas
White's
Bequest. of £100, bequeathed to the corporations of twenty-four cities and towns (of which Winchester is one), in turn, by Sir Thomas White,[7] who was born at Reading, and

---

for condemned criminals before their execution, and cause a certain prayer to be read to them; but the gift being refused on those conditions, it has remained in the hands of the corporation, who pay the interest of it to the chaplain of the county jail, to supply the prisoners with Bibles and Prayer-books.

(1) See above, p. 251.

(2) He was buried in the cathedral. (See above, p. 77.)

(3) See above, pp. 253, 254, and under the parishes of Compton and Houghton.

(4) By her will, dated October the 27th, 1642.

(5) This was originally bequeathed and paid to the poor of St. Clement's parish, but after the union of St. Clement's with St. Thomas' parish it was extended to the city generally. The payments appear not to have been made before 1659, and then by the mayor and corporation, instead of the minister and churchwardens of St. Clement's.

(6) About the beginning of the seventeenth century.

(7) He was the founder of St. John's College, Oxford, and of the Free School at Bristol, and to the corporation of the latter city he intrusted the fund out of which this annual payment is made. This gift was made about the year 1553 (Blomefield's "History of Norwich," vol. i. p. 269), and the yearly sum is paid on each 24th of August. The loans were specified to be of £25 each, and clothiers were to be preferred as the borrowers. It was also provided that default in using the gift to the donor's intent should disqualify any place from receiving it ever after, but this provision has not been enforced.

became a merchant of London, for the purpose of assisting young freemen with loans, without interest, in those places. It is lent in sums of £50, and a bond with two sureties is required for repayment at the end of ten years.[1]

Tilney's Gift. *Tilney's Gift.*—This consists of £50 bestowed by a deed of gift[2] by Frederick Tilney, to be employed in loans to two freemen of the Guild of Merchants in Winchester for seven years each, without interest, on their giving sufficient security for repayment; and further, of £25, a rent charge, to be paid every fifth year out of a farm in Newnham and Nately Scures, to be employed in the same manner.

City and Soke Boys. *City and Soke Boys.*—There are now taught in the Central School[3] thirty boys, who, in addition to their gratuitous education, receive a suit of clothes yearly, and other advantages. They are known as the children of the "Winchester Free School," which was formerly held in the chapel of St. John's Hospital.[4] This charity was founded by the bequest of William Over, who left[5] the residue of his estate (with the exception of £1 to the mayor and aldermen to drink a glass of wine on the anniversary of his death) for the establishment of a free school for twenty-four poor boys, who were to be instructed so as to be fit for apprenticeship to tradesmen.[6] In 1708 the Court of Chancery ordered the property to be sold, and with the proceeds, amounting to £580, a perpetual rent-charge of £22 was purchased on a meadow and hop-yard at Romsey, which is now paid to the master of the Central School, for the instruction of the boys of the Free School.

Swaddon's Gift. *Swaddon's Gift.*—An annual sum of £4 is received from the rents of property at Great Horwood, Buckinghamshire, in accordance with the will of William Swaddon, D.D.,[7] and is distributed annually at Christmas amongst the poor of the city.[8]

Edmonds' Gift. *Edmonds' Gift.*—This consists of £100 given by Anthony Edmonds "to set the poor on work," which the corporation agreed to do in 1619. The capital of this charity has been accumulating for several years, and now awaits a scheme for its appropriation.

CHARITIES ADMINISTERED BY TRUSTEES APPOINTED BY THE COURT OF CHANCERY.

Symonds' Bread. *Symonds' Bread.*—Every Monday morning there is distributed at the Guildhall 6s. worth of bread amongst twelve poor persons; and on each Good Friday, a sermon is

(1) The first payment was made to Winchester in 1590, the last in 1854; and the total amount received was then £1248.

(2) Dated July the 11th, 1700.

(3) See above, p. 211, and note 1.

(4) See above, p. 249.   (5) He died in 1701.

(6) Over's will prohibited the appointment of a Welshman, Scotchman, Irishman, foreigner, or north-countryman as master, that his scholars might not be corrupted in their youth by a vicious pronunciation, nor taught barbarous English.

(7) The date of the deed of conveyance of the property to trustees is 1624. Besides Winchester, Worcester, Reading, Calne, Aylesbury, and two parishes near Worcester, are also beneficially interested in this charity.

(8) Formerly the payment of this donation was very irregular, and when it was received it was carried to the general account of the corporation.

preached in St. Lawrence' Church, for which the rector receives 6s. 8d., after which the mayor distributes 6s. 8d., in sums of 2d., to forty poor persons. These gifts are provided by a sum of £4 2s., paid yearly in compliance with the will of the founder of Christ's Hospital, Peter Symonds,[1] by the Mercers' Company of London, out of an annuity of £10 bequeathed to them by him;[2] and by the dividends of £406 three per cent. Consols, which were purchased with the accumulated arrears of the payment by the Mercers' Company from 1772 to 1823.[3]

Godwin's Gift.—This consists of a rent-charge of £5 a year on the tenement called the Royal Oak, in the passage leading from High Street to St. Peter's Street, which was given by the will[4] of Thomas Godwin, formerly alderman and mayor of the city, to be divided annually on St. Thomas' Day amongst twenty poor householders of the city who had not received parochial relief.[5] Godwin's Gift.

Alice Long's Gift.—Mrs. Alice Long, of Marwell Hall, bequeathed[6] the yearly sum of £60, arising out of the old South Sea Annuities, of which £30 were to be applied to the relief of poor debtors confined in the city.[7] Alice Long's Gift.

Cawley's Gift.—The yearly sum of £2 3s. 4d. was left by William Cawley, to be paid by the Drapers' Company of London, and distributed in fuel for the poor.[8] Cawley's Gift.

DR. LAYFIELD'S CHARITY.

This consists of the clear annual income of £1307 15s. 5d., invested in 3 per cent. Consols, in the names of nine trustees chosen from the parishes of St. Lawrence, St. Mary Kalendar, St. Swithin, St. Maurice, St. Peter Colebrook, St. Thomas, and St. Bartholomew, which is distributed at the Guildhall on St. Thomas' Day (December Dr. Layfield's Charity.

(1) See above, p. 250.

(2) According to the will of Peter Symonds, leave was to be obtained from the bishop, or the dean, to place his picture in the body of the cathedral, with a small table before it, on which were to be placed twelve penny-loaves of good wheaten bread, which, immediately after the service, were to be given to twelve poor persons at the will of the mayor; except on one Sunday in each quarter, when the bishop, or dean, was to nominate the recipients. The annual sermon he directed to be preached in the Church of St. Mary Kalendar; and, in addition to the 6s. 8d. distributed after it, a dole of penny-loaves was to be given away at Christ's Hospital on St. Peter's day.

Instead of expending the residue thus, however, up to 1772 it was placed to the credit of the general account of the hospital.

(3) When this sum was invested, the balance, amount-ing to £24 7s. 6d., was paid to the conservator and gubernators of Christ's Hospital, because they had, at their own expense, maintained the sermon and the gifts on Good Friday from 1772.

(4) Dated March the 12th, 1732.

(5) The *Liber Intrationum* of the corporation records the origin of the gift, notwithstanding which it was lost for about fifteen years, after which the arrears were paid to the corporation, who distributed them amongst house-holders of the city and borough.

(6) Her will is dated May the 15th, 1834.

(7) This sum is actually applied to the relief of deserv-ing discharged debtors. The remaining £30 was be-queathed to the poor of Owslebury, and will be noticed under that parish.

(8) This charity is recorded in the *Liber Intrationum*. The express provisions of the will were that the company

the 29th), in sums not exceeding £5, to poor persons, widows, or families belonging to the city. It arises from a bequest by the Rev. Charles Layfield, D.D., formerly a Prebendary of Winchester; and this scheme of management has received the approval of the Court of Chancery.[1]

THE CHARITABLE SOCIETY OF NATIVES AND CITIZENS.

The Natives' Society.

This society[2] originated in an annual feast, instituted on August the 26th, 1669, by "natives" of Winchester, for the commemoration of the great plague which had

should pay yearly to the warden and bursars of the college £3 6s. 8d.: of which 13s. 4d. was to be paid for an obit in the Church of Allhallows, 10s. to the Master of St. John's Hospital for blankets, 1s. 8d. to the mayor, and 10d. to each of the two bailiffs of the city, and the same to the warden and bursars of the college, 3s. 4d. to the poor at the time of the obit, and the residue was to be laid out in fuel ("3000 tall woods"), except 3s. 4d., which was to be given to the procurer and distributor of it.

This payment has frequently been suffered to fall into arrears: in 1781 arrears for five years were paid, in 1812 arrears for thirty-one years, and in 1847 arrears for twenty years. On the last occasion the attention of the corporation was directed to the subject by Mr. H. Moody, who received the thanks of that body after the recovery of the arrears. And under the old system of management 13s. 4d. was paid to the college, and the remainder carried to the general account of the corporation.

(1) Dr. Layfield died in 1715, and left one-fourth of his estate for charitable purposes, specifying Winchester as one of the places to be benefited by it. The original amount of the charity, and the mode of its application, are not now known. In 1750, by a decree of the Court of Chancery, the yearly income pertaining to Winchester under Dr. Layfield's will was paid to the churchwardens and overseers of the parishes named in the text, to be applied in apprenticing poor children. Soon afterwards it was wholly neglected, and for very many years nothing was either paid or received on account of it. A Chancery suit was at last the means of recovering the property, with arrears for nearly seventy years, in 1825, when the existing scheme of management was approved.

The following charities are spoken of in the Charity Commissioners' Report, (u. s.), but are now lost:—

Clifton's Gift.—£20 to be lent to a resident of Winchester, given by Robert Clifton in 1578.

Davison's Gift.—£100 given by John Davison in 1586 for apprenticing poor children.

Venables' Gift.—£100 to be lent to three persons in the city, and £33 6s. 8d. to be lent to one in the soke or suburb, given by Richard Venables in 1598.

Archbishop Laud's Gift.—£50 per annum bequeathed by Archbishop Laud out of Barton Farm, near Winchester, for apprenticing poor children. At the Restoration, when the archbishop's will was made known, only £25 could have been received; but Sir John Robinson, Lord Mayor of London, who had derived advantage from the lease of the farm, gave £200, to be applied as the archbishop had directed.

Bishops Horne and Watson's Gifts.—£40 given by the former, and £60 by the latter prelate, "to set the poor on work." These sums were long ago transferred to the dean and chapter.

Cæsar's Gift.—£80 given by Avis Cæsar in 1628, to allow £6 a year to twelve poor persons. On this account, formerly, £6 was distributed every Good Friday amongst the poor, in sums of 4s. to each person.

Dennett's Gift.—£2 12s. yearly rent given in 1637 by Richard Dennett, to be laid out in 1s. worth of bread weekly for thirteen poor persons.

Gaurd's Gift.—£1 annually for the poor of the city, and of the Close, given by Richard Gaurd.

Trinity Bread.—Twelve penny-loaves given weekly to as many poor widows, under the will of Mrs. Brewer, from 1740, out of the lease of the tithes of Owslebury, under the Hospital of St. Cross: discontinued in 1817, when the lease expired.

Wavell's Gift.—£5 yearly left by Gilbert Wavell (1741), £4 of it to be distributed annually in fourpenny-loaves amongst the poor of the city and Hyde, and £1 to be spent in wine by the corporation. Four bakers used to receive £1 13s. 4d. each to supply 100 fourpenny-loaves on every 19th of January, but the distribution fell into arrear, and ultimately the bequest was found to be void under the statute 9 Geo. II. c. 36.

(2) For my account of this society I am indebted to "A Memento of the Natives' Society, Winchester," 1859,

visited the city in 1666,[1] and had committed fearful ravages here in that and the following years. The surplus of " monies received " over " monies disbursed," on account the first feast, amounting to £3 1s., was applied to the apprenticing of a lad to a tradesman of the city.[2] The collections made in subsequent years, after paying all the expenses of the feast, " were either distributed in alms to widows and other indigent persons, lent out in small sums to young tradesmen, or expended in the apprenticeship of poor children."[3] " And it was determined in the year 1806 that all future collections should be appropriated to [the last named] purpose, reserving, however, the power of affording occasional relief to decayed trustees."[4]

The income of the society is derived from annual subscriptions, a collection in the cathedral after the yearly sermon, and " small contributions collected by the stewards." The total of receipts for this year, 1859, presented in the hundred and ninetieth account, is £170 17s. 6d., and the total of payments £145 9s.[5]

The feast is now held annually in September, and the proceedings of the day commence by the trustees and stewards (of whom there are four, two being elected at each feast) assembling at St. John's Rooms, or one of the hotels of the city, at ten o'clock, and marching in procession to the cathedral, with the preacher for the day, the apprentices, a band of music, the society's flags, and a grotesquely attired person, called " the champion,"[6] before them. The band remains outside the church, and the colours are carried no farther than the entrance of the choir. After the service and the sermon the procession returns, and at five P.M. the dinner is served, all the business which the secretary cannot perform alone, being transacted before and after the dinner.[7]

Mention has been made above[8] of the obelisk or monument without Westgate ; it

---

published by the secretary, J. H. Todd, Esq., and to the notice in Moody's " Notes and Essays," pp. 96, &c. I have also used Milner, Wavell, &c.

Milner's account (vol. ii. p. 32) of the origin of the society is derived from the inscription on the obelisk without Westgate, which states that the society was " originally established for the relief of their fellow citizens who happily survived that dreadful visitation, but were reduced by it to the utmost distress." But as the inscription on the " monument " is of later date, and, " strange to say, the original object of the institution is not expressed in their books, the whole of which are still extant " (" Memento," p. 1), I have given the account in the text, which is in conformity with the books.

(1) This is Milner's date (u. s. and p. 207).

(2) At this first feast " 70 natives " paid 2s. 6d. each towards the feast, and £2 9s. 8d. was " received for charity." Including this sum, " there was saved att yᵉ above menconed feast £3 1s.," with which the boy was apprenticed.

(3) In process of time the feast and the charity became so far distinct that " no part of the collection was expended in conviviality except for the necessary refresh-

ment of the apprentices, choristers, and servants." (" Memento," p. 2.)

(4) " Memento," pp. 1, 2.

(5) " Aggregate amount collected from the year 1806 " £8301 9s. " Aggregate number of children apprenticed during the same period," 273. (" Memento," p. 2.)

(6) The champion bears a staff, on which are painted the royal arms, and those of the city, with the date 1669 ; on the left breast of his gown is a square silver badge, having the arms of the city engraved on it, and beneath them " PERTINET AD NATIVOS HUJUS CIVITATIS," and on the front of his grenadier's cap are the city arms and the date of the institution of the society. Of his appointment nothing more can be said than that he is " an ancient and, apparently, emblematical officer." (" Memento," p. 3.)

(7) The cost of these feasts is now defrayed by those who take part in them.

(8) P. 30 and note 5. I may here observe that the inscription on it may possibly be correct, as it only states that the " basis " of the monument is " the very stone on which exchanges were made whilst the city lay under the

was erected in 1758, in accordance with a memorandum, recorded in the books of the society, that "the old Market Cross without Westgate,[1] a remaining monument of the plague, shall be neatly rebuilt, to perpetuate so remarkable an event;" and it was rebuilt in 1821, and repaired in 1851.[2]

THE CHARITABLE SOCIETY OF ALIENS.

It appears that this society[3] originated in what has been called the "exclusiveness" of the Natives' Society. It was formed on the 25th of July, 1720, on the same plan as its predecessor, but with the distinctly expressed object of providing for the children of "aliens" (that is, of persons not natives of the city), and for "aliensborne," residing in Winchester, the means of apprenticeship; and its funds were to be applied "to no other use whatever." But this difference in the constitution of the two societies has long ago completely disappeared, and the only distinction between them is that the feast of the Aliens' Society is now held yearly in the month of October, instead of September.

The amount of receipts in 1858 was £163 19s. 8d., and that of payments £157 19s.; and in 1855 the *Winchester Observer* stated that it had apprenticed nearly seven hundred poor children. In all other respects, what has been said of the foregoing society applies to this.

THE COUNTY HOSPITAL.

This excellent institution originated in an infirmary established here in Colebrook Street by the Rev. Dr. Alured Clarke, a prebendary of the cathedral, in the year 1736, in imitation of those at London, which were then the only ones in England.[4] It proved of such great utility, and prospered so well, that having been enriched by a noble legacy from a Southampton merchant, Richard Taunton by name, Clobery

---

scourge of the destroying pestilence in the year 1669," as it is not likely that such a rigid system of non-intercourse between the city and the country would be enforced in the first stages of the visitation.

(1) This "old market cross" existed (as a "procession cross") in the very beginning of the fifteenth century, being noticed in the Tarrages of the city as "the cross in the corner" (Harl. MS. British Museum, fol. 35);

but it, unquestionably, was not a *market* cross till the time of the plague.

(2) "Memento," p. 7.

(3) My information respecting this society is derived from printed papers obligingly furnished me by Mr. Todd, who is secretary to this, as well as to the Natives' Society; and from Moody's "Notes, &c.," *u. s.*

(4) Wavell, vol. ii. pp. 146, &c.

House,[1] in Parchment Street, was purchased in 1753, and the present fine building erected on its site, and opened for the reception of patients, at Michaelmas, 1759.[2] Wings were added before the end of the last century, and other additions and improvements have been made subsequently, both in the house and grounds, which now extend backwards to Upper Brook Street.[3]

It is capable of accommodating a hundred and twenty patients, and is one of the most commodious and well-arranged and conducted establishments in the kingdom. There is a convenient chapel in the north wing. The total income for the year ending June the 30th, 1858, was £3689 13s. 11d.; and the total expenditure was £3287 10s. 10d. The annual subscriptions for that period amounted to £1855 2s. 6d. During that year 786 in-patients had been admitted, of whom 250 had been discharged cured, and 194 greatly benefited. The out-patients for the same term had been 1132, of whom 388 had been discharged cured, and 149 greatly benefited. The "total number of patients admitted since the foundation of the institution, 18th of October, 1736, was, in-patients 60,539; out-patients, 47,967."[4]

FEMALE ORPHAN ASYLUM.

This asylum is situated in St. Thomas' Churchyard, and was opened on January the 1st, 1816; since which time to 1858, "146 girls have been placed by it in respectable service, and have in general conducted themselves well."[5] It provides for 30 girls, who are admitted at six years of age, but a payment of 4s. (or 5s. if aliens) per week is required for their board. They are instructed at the Central School.

Female Orphan Asylum.

PENITENTIARY, &c.

In Little Minster Street, near the Cathedral, there is a Refuge for penitent prostitutes, which is maintained in connection with the "County of Hants Female Penitentiary," at Southampton.

Penitentiary.

(1) Milner (vol. ii. p. 216) says of this house, "By the Saxon doorway, which is almost all that is left of this habitation, it appears to have been of high antiquity." This relic of the mansion of Sir John Clobery disappeared after the purchase of the last remaining portion of the Clobery property by the Hospital, in 1828. I have been unable to learn anything further about this doorway, which, if (as it may be conjectured) a Norman semicircular arch, might have been a relic of one of the churches in Parchment Street.

(2) Wavell, vol. ii. pp. 146, &c.

(3) The 120th Annual Report, p. 18.

(4) Ibid., pp. 15, &c.

(5) Report for 1858.

An *Anti-mendicity Society* has rooms in the square, where necessitous persons, and those travelling in search of work, may receive shelter and refreshment, instead of being compelled to resort to the Beggars' Lodging-house.

And there is a *Society for the Relief of Destitute Discharged Prisoners* from the City and County Jail.

SAVINGS' BANK, &c.

Savings' Bank. The Winchester Bank for Savings' was established on the 1st of January, 1816 ; and the annual statement for 1858 shows a total of 1911 depositors, 36 charitable societies, and 30 friendly societies. The balance on the general account (including interest) was £69,845 16s. 5d. ; the sums received from depositors during the year amounted to £7426 7s. 8d., and the sums drawn by depositors to £8277 1s. 7d.

Hampshire Friendly Society. The *Hampshire Friendly Society*[2] was founded in 1825, and now includes 1716 benefit members, and 267 honorary members. The funds of the society in the Bank of England amount (in 1859) to £27,746 4s. 1d., and the amount paid in the preceding year, in sickness and at death, as endowments, pensions, and annuities, was £1903 14s. 7d. It has agents in thirty-five districts in the county.

Benefit Clubs, &c. Besides these institutions there are various others of a similar character, such as Freemasons' and Odd Fellows' Lodges, Benefit Clubs, &c. &c.

(1) My information respecting this institution is derived from the Report for 1858.

(2) I have taken the particulars stated above from the Report of the Society for 1859.

THE

MUNICIPAL INSTITUTIONS

OF

WINCHESTER.

———◆———

The Roman city.

W INCHESTER was unquestionably one of the cities of Britain in the time of the Romans,[1] but we have no evidence to connect its subsequent importance with its condition at that early period, in such a way as to make it appear derived therefrom. Its municipal history commences with the times of the Saxons, and though the notices of it are exceedingly fragmentary and imperfect, they are sufficient to indicate the character of its institutions, and to enable us to understand the reason for the distinction it attained in after times.

The Saxon city.

Before the consolidation of the Saxon kingdoms in England, this city was the royal city of the Kingdom of Wessex. The first notice of its domestic constitution after this is contained in the Anglo-Saxon Chronicle under the year 897,[2] where it is said that "many of the most eminent king's-thanes" had died during the three years ending then, and "Beornwulf, the wic-reeve at Winchester," is named as one of them.

Court of Husting.

Another intimation of the municipal condition of Winchester is to be found in the existence there of a Court of Husting, the dignity and celebrity of which all our great jurists attest.[3] As a court of record for the recognisance of debts, it existed until the establishment of the modern County Courts.

(1) It is included in Ptolemy's list of cities under the name of *Venta* (Mon. Hist. Brit., vol. i., Introd., p. xv.); and in the *Notitia Utriusque Imperii* (ibid., p. xxiii.) it appears (according to the opinion of the best critics, ancient and modern) as the residence of an imperial officer, entitled "*Procurator Cynegii, or Gynæcii, Bentensis*." No credit whatever is to be given to the treatise *De Situ Britanniæ*, ascribed to Richard of Cirencester, or to the list of Roman *municipia* it contains—in which Winchester is not included. Trussell's legends, and those of the "City Tables," I of course leave unnoticed.

(2) Mon. Hist. Brit., vol. i. p. 369. The "wic-gerefa" was properly a "subordinate fiscal officer," according to

Mr. Thorpe ("Ancient Laws &c., of England," Glossary, *s. v.*), but he seems frequently to have been the same as the provost, or the port-reeve. (See Kemble's "Saxons in England," vol. i. p. 175.)

(3) Spelman, Somner (Glossary to Twysden's "*Decem Scriptores*"), Cowell, Jacob, *s. v.* The functions of this court are described in 4 Inst. 247; see also "Ancient Laws," &c., pp. 197, note *a*, 200, 217; Glossary, *s. v.* References to other and more venerable authorities may be found in Spelman, &c.

"*Hus-ting*" appears to be in itself no more than a *court* which sat in a *house*, and was so called to distinguish it from the folk-mote, which was held in the open air.

But it is from the "*Liber Winton.*"[1] that the most satisfactory information respecting this period can be obtained : the first survey in it relating chiefly to the condition of the city in the time of Edward the Confessor, though made in the reign of Henry I. ; and the second having been made in the year 1148, and therefore anterior to the charters of Henry II.

Provost, burgesses, and guilds.

The town was governed by a *præpositus*[2] (provost, wic-reeve, or port-reeve), with (perhaps) two *bedelli*[3] (beadles or catchpolls) under him ; and some of the citizens were distinguished as *burgenses*,[4] *burgenses boni*[5] or *meliores*,[6] *boni cives*,[7] and *probi homines*.[8] The last named most probably formed the Merchant Guild,[9] which was a municipal as well as a commercial institution, and, at one time, had a guildhall in Colebrook Street.[10] At a later date, in the year 1148, there was a guildhall in another part of the city.[11] Various "frith-gilds,"[12] no doubt, included all the population, or all

Courts of Husting were granted to London, York, Norwich, Lincoln, &c. (See the authorities quoted above, and Blomefield's Norfolk, vol. iii. pp. 37, *et al.*) It was called at London "*Curia Regis ;*" and Mr. Smirke (Arch. Journ., vol. ix. p. 82) found that some of the court-rolls preserved in the great coffer in Westgate were headed "*Curia domini regis.*"

One fragment of "decayed intelligence" respecting the early municipal constitution of this city I may append to this note, although it is in no way connected with the subject of it. The punishment for felons in Winchester was anciently not hanging, but "*demembratio ;*" for an account of which ferociously cruel infliction I must refer to Selden's notes on Ralph de Hengham's "*Summa Magna*" ("Hengham Magna"), cap. iii. This custom, or (as it was called by a Winchester jury in the time of Henry III.) "liberty," certainly dates from the very earliest period of the establishment of civil law here, before the conversion of the West Saxons to Christianity. That Trussell was acquainted with this remarkable "privilege" appears from Wavell, vol. ii. p. 84, and Milner, vol. i. p. 214. Similar savage punishments have been treated of by J. Y. Akerman, Esq., in a paper read before the Society of Antiquaries, intituled "*Furca et Fossa.*" (Archæol., vol. xxxviii. pp. 54, &c.)

(1) The text of this invaluable record (which is in the possession of the Society of Antiquaries) is printed in vol. iv. of the Domesday Book of the Record Commission. I refer to the pages of this copy here and in other parts of my work, but quote from the MS.

Much valuable information respecting Winchester and other municipalities, collected from the Liber Winton., Domesday, and other authentic sources, will be found in a little work entitled "England under the Norman Occupation," by James F. Morgan, M.A., 1858. Sir Henry Ellis' "General Introduction to Domesday" may also be consulted with advantage.

(2) In the first survey *Adelwoldus* is said to have been *præpositus*, T.R.E. (p. 532), *Warinus* (pp. 532, 535), and *Gefordus* (p. 532) subsequently, and *Ricardus*

"*modo*" (pp. 536, 539). In the second survey *Herebertus* is called *præpositus* (pp. 544, 546). The "*Portreue*" is also named (p. 557).

(3) Two *bedelli*, T.R.E., are named in the Liber Winton., *Wlwardus* (p. 533) and *Aisil* (p. 541) ; two in the reign of Henry I., *Alwinus* (pp. 538, 540) and *Bricthwinus* (p. 539) ; and one, *Erneis*, in the time of Stephen (p. 552). The "*bedellus regis*" is mentioned (p. 543) in connection with "*le Balchus*," which was the prison (compare p. 532). See Sir Henry Ellis' "General Introduction to Domesday," vol. i. p. 247 ; and Kemble's "Saxons in England," p. 339, for the relation of the *bedellus* to the *præpositus*.

(4) Lib. Wint., p. 532. *Burgenses* of Winchester are spoken of in connection with Romsey (Domesday, vol. i. fol. 436), and *suburbani* ("out-burgesses," or burgesses of the Soke) under Basingstoke (ibid., fol. 39).

(5) Lib. Wint., p. 532.

(6) Ibid., p. 531.   (7) Ibid., p. 532.

(8) Ibid., p. 556. These were the *prud' hommes* of a later time. (Arch. Journ., vol. ix. pp. 71, &c.)

(9) In the charters this is called *Gilda mercatorum* and *Gilda mercatoria*, and in the *Consuetudinarium* (Arch. Journ., vol. ix. pp. 70, &c.), *Gilde markande*. It was originally the *Cypmanna-gild*, or, perhaps, "*Ingang burhware*," as at Canterbury (Kemble, "Saxons in England," pp. 309, 335). Tradition ascribed it to King Æthelwulf (in the year 856, according to Milner, vol. i. p. 92), but Trussell (fol. 73) ingenuously confesses, "the origen of [this] corporacon I could neuer yet haue the happynes to find."

(10) "*Et ibi solebat esse hantachensele, ubi probi homines Wintoniæ potabant gildam suam*" (Lib. Wint., p. 556). The name of this guildhall appears to signify "merchants' hall," and affords an early use of the term "*hansa*," which was afterwards so well known.

(11) "*Gihald*" (ibid., p. 545). It was very probably on the site of the present guildhall.

(12) "Ancient Laws," &c., Glossary, *s. v.* Kemble's "Saxons in England," vol. ii. pp. 309, &c

but the *pauperes*;[1] and a guild of knights[2] (young men or "young nobles") had a hall in High Street.[3]

Winchester was a royal mint also, six moneyers being established here by Athelstan.[4]   Five of these offices were abolished by Henry I.;[5] the sixth remained till the reign of Henry III.[6]

The Mints.

The first survey in the *Liber Winton.* (about the year 1125) is intituled, " *Liber de Terris Regis reddentibus Langabulum et Brug' in Winton., sicut solebant reddere tempore Regis Edwardi,*" and contains an account of what King Edward the Confessor " *habuit omnibus modis Wintonie in suo dominico.*"   The first tenement entered in it is said to have been held by the king " *in dominio;*"[7] and two " *mansuræ*" are said, in another place,[8] to be " *de dominio Regis.*"   In High Street[9] and in Staple Garden (then " Bredene Stret")[10] are said to be thanelands (" *terræ Baronum,*" or " *thensium*"). And without Westgate[11] was a tenement called " *Domus Safugel,*"[12] which was held " *in elemosina.*"   We find one case recorded of what seems to be a mortgage amongst

Liber Winton
The First
Survey.

(1) Lib. Wint., pp. 532, &c.

(2) " *Cnihta-gyld,*" or " Sodality of young nobles " (Kemble, " Saxons in England," p. 335).   There were knights' guilds in London (Madox, " *Firma Burgi,*" pp. 23, 24), and in Canterbury (Codex Diplom., No. 293).

(3) The sites of two knights' halls are pointed out in High Street, both on the north side of it, one towards Eastgate, the other near Westgate.   The first is thus noticed, " *Ibi de justa fuit Chenictehalla, ubi chenictes potabant gildam suam*" (Lib. Wint., p. 531); and the other thus, " *Chenictes tenebant lachenictahalla libere de Rege Edwardo*" (p. 533).   These notices are solely owing to the circumstance that the halls were " held of the king," for the first survey comprises only such tenements; other guilds may, therefore, have existed, having halls of their own, which were not amongst the royal possessions in Winchester.   Another guild is, in fact, mentioned in the earliest survey (p. 536),—" *reddebant hominibus DESTreGilda xxxv. d,*" but its actual name has not yet been ascertained.

(4) " Ancient Laws, &c., of England," p. 88.   See also Edgar's Laws, ibid., p. 114.

(5) " *In mercato fuerunt v. monete, que sunt diffacte precepto regis*" (Lib. Wint., p. 534).   The site of these mints was near the present Penthouse in High Street; the other was not in High Street.   The names of five moneyers at Winchester, T.R.E., occur in the Liber Winton.   *Godwinus Socche* " *magister monetarius,*" *Alvinus Aitardessone* (p. 532), or *filius Etardii* (p. 536), *Andrebodus* (p. 533), and *Alestanus* (p. 538), *Wimundus* (p. 532), and *Odo* (p. 537), are named in the time of Henry I.; but in Stephen's reign there were *Sanson* (pp. 544, 545) and *Siward* (pp. 545, 552).   The names of *Godwine, Andreboda, Elfstan,* and *Wimund,* occur on coins struck here (" Notices of the Mint, &c.," by E. Hawkins. Winchester Vol., Arch. Instit., pp. 40, &c.).

(6) Money continued to be struck at Winchester till

this reign.   (Ibid., pp. 38, 43; Ruding, vol. iv. p. 264). But in 1215 John granted this mint, or the rent of it, to Walter de Pavilly, who had been Mayor of Rouen, and had suffered in his cause.   (Rot. Claus., vol. i. pp. 214, 219, 225; Hawkins, *u. s.,* p. 37.)   At Walter de Pavilly's death it was escheated to the king, and remained unoccupied and dilapidated until his death. After the accession of Henry III. it was valued, and let to the city at a yearly rent of £6, as their " *Draperia,*" or Cloth Hall.   But this rent was, with others, assigned to the " ferm " of the city, when the suburb of Hyde was granted to the abbot; and in 1245 (?), the mayor, Nicholas Koppinger, undertook to pay £3 more for this building, if the Drapery was removed into High Street. This was not done then, but the additional £3 was charged yearly, if not paid.   (Arch. Journ., vol. vii. pp. 375, 381; Hawkins, *u. s.,* pp. 37, 38; Madox, " *Firma Burgi,*" p. 19, notes *b* and *p;* Madox, " Hist. Exchequer," 1st Edit., p. 353; Ruding, *u. s.*).   This Drapery was in one of the streets parallel to High Street, perhaps the Square.   (Arch. Journ., *u. s.;* and above, p. 143.)   It had been removed when the " Tarrages " were made (see above, p. 18, note 1), and brought the name of the *mint* with it.

(7) " In demesne " (Lib. Wint., p. 531).

For an account of these tenures, see Sir Henry Ellis' " Introduction to Domesday," vol. i. pp. 230, &c.; Morgan' " England under the Normans," pp. 14, &c.; Spelman's Glossary, and Ducange, *s. vv.*

(8) Lib. Wint., p. 538.   This occurs in the account " *de Terris Baronum.*"

(9) Ibid., pp. 534, 535.   (10) Ibid., pp. 537, 538.

(11) " In frank-almoigne " (ibid., p. 535).   But the " elemosina " seems to have been due to the king—" *reddit regi de langablo . . . . et elemosine viii sol.*"

(12) A house where sea-mews and other sea birds were kept for hawking.

the thanelands.[1]   Both the Bishop of Winchester and the Abbot of New Minster are said to have held "feuds" here in the time of Edward the Confessor, as well as after the Conquest.[2] "Soc and sac" are once incidentally noticed.[3] And some tenants were connected with Basingstoke, Weston (?), Polhampton, and Lasham (?).[4]

Some of the tenements were held freely, both with regard to customs and rent,[5] some were free (in whole, or in part) from the former,[6] but most of them appear to have been subject to all the various "*consuetudines*," or customary payments and services, and to rent also.[7] What these customs were we are clearly informed by the exceptional cases, which are noted. The principal were those named in the title—"*Langabulum*"[8] and "*Brug*';"[9] the others mentioned here are "*Geldum*,"[10] "*Fripene*,"[11]

(1) Lib. Wint., p. 535. "*Habet ibi in vadimonio de terris Herefridi xvii s.*"

(2) "*De feudo Episcopi*" (ibid., pp. 532, 534, 535). "*De feudo Abbatis*" (p. 535). One house the abbot held "*in dominio*" (ibid.).

(3) "*Socca et sacca*" (ibid., p. 541).

(4) "*Domus que pertinuit Basingstoches*" (p. 532) ; "*Terra de Ouettona ;*" "*Domus de Polametona ;*" "*Duæ mansuræ de Lessam*" (p. 538; Morgan, p. 169). The perplexing phrase "*de sapalanda*" (p. 538) may possibly relate to such a connection as this.

(5) "*Libere tenebant de rege*" (ibid., pp. 531, 533).

(6) "*Nullam consuetudinem inde unquam reddidit.*" "*Nullam consuetudinem inde facit.*" "*Nichil consuetudinis reddidit.*" "*Non facit consuetudines.*" "*Nullam consuetudinem inde reddidit præter geldum.*" "*Reddit de langabulo vi d. et nullam aliam consuetudinem.*" "*Est quieta præter watam et geldum*" (ibid., pp. 531, 532, 533, &c.).

In some instances the customs were paid "*per deprecationem præpositorum*" (p. 533) ; in others the tenants had suffered their payments, &c., to fall into arrears, as the following entries show :—"*Tota consuetudo est retro*" (p. 538) ; "*tenet omnem consuetudinem*" (all had been paid in the time of Edward the Confessor) "*quia nichil inde dedit*" (p. 532). It does not appear that we should understand "*debet*," which is used in pp. 537, &c., instead of "*reddit*," as intended to imply that the customs were not paid.

Of two shambles ("*eschamel*") said to be "*in ecclesia que pertinet domui* [*Gotebiete*],'' we are informed (ibid.) that "*unaquaque ebdomada reddebant de consuetudine ii d.*"

(7) "*Tenuit unam domum reddentem omnes consuetudines.*" "*Reddebat*," or "*faciebat*," "*consuetudines*" (ibid., *passim*). In one instance (p. 538) the expression is varied thus—"*Debet langabulum et faciebat omnem consuetudinem.*"

(8) In Anglo-Saxon "*Land-gafol.*'' It was a rent for the ground occupied, and it seems to have been paid not only to the king, but also to the Bishops of Winchester and Worcester, and to the Abbot of New Minster. (Ibid., p. 538.)

A few examples of the amount are given : they are such as 6*d.* (p. 533), 5*d.* (p. 537), 10*d.* (p. 538), 13*d.* (p. 539), 2*s.* 6*d.* (p. 538). Others may perhaps be found, as in p. 537.

(9) In Anglo-Saxon "*Brycg-bot.*" It was one of the three services, "inevitably incident to all landed possessions, and which were consequently known by the name of . . . . *Trinoda necessitas*, and similar expressions" (Kemble's "Saxons in England," vol. i. p. 301) ; and was a contribution for the building and repairs of bridges, and at a later period was called "pontage." In pp. 535, 536, and 539 of Liber Winton. it is spelt "*Brueg*.'' The amount is specified as 4*d.* (p. 539), and together with the landgable as 8*d.* (p. 535).

(10) Ibid., pp. 531, 532, &c. It occurs in the plural (*geldis*) in p. 533. This was the land-tax known to all readers of English history as "Danegeld." Originally levied for the purpose of supplying the composition which Ethelred the Unready made with the Danes in the year 991, it was collected long after the occasion had ceased, to the great oppression of the people, until Edward the Confessor commanded the levy to be discontinued. It was revived at an early period of William I.'s reign ; but such numerous exemptions were granted that it was by no means so productive as it had formerly been. (See Ellis, vol. i. pp. 350, &c. ; Morgan, pp. 13, &c. ; Ducange, Kelham, *s. v.* ; Webb's "Short Account of Danegeld," &c.)

Of one tenant (Lib. Wint., p. 536) it is said, "*non geldat ;*" and of others (p. 535), "*non geldaverunt nisi per breve regis.*" Two tenants are mentioned as paying this impost for their under-tenants, "*homines suos adquietavit*" (or "*adquietat*") "*de geldo*" (pp. 532, 533). In another case the actual occupant paid, "*homines domus geldant*" (p. 533).

(11) Ibid., p. 539. *Frith-penny*, or free penny, which was, I am informed by E. Smirke, Esq., "a casual (or perhaps fixed) payment of 1*d.*, in respect of some franchise attached to the property."

But it has been suggested by G. R. Corner, Esq., and H. T. Riley, Esq., that "*fripene*" is written in error for "*thripene*," "the third penny" ("*tertius denarius comitis*"), the earl's fee, respecting which see Selden's "Titles of Honour," c. v. §§ 1—12 ; Spelman, &c.

" *Venta,*"[1] " *Pascere prisonem,*"[2] " *Wata,*"[3] and " *Avera ;*"[4]—some of which were not incident on tenants in towns alone.

The rent of almost every tenement is stated,[5] the lowest being 2*d.,*[6] and the highest £12.[7] It is remarkable that the rents of all the tenements in the minor streets are low, and that all the highly rented tenements are in the principal street.[8]

From the second survey contained in this record (made in the year 1148) we can glean but few additional facts respecting the municipal institutions of Winchester. The guildhalls have already been spoken of.[9] The possessions of the king are distinguished, and they are found in other parts of the city[10] besides those which are noticed in the first survey. Thanelands also are mentioned in other parts of the city than those in which they were spoken of in the earlier account.[11] The customs rendered to the king are very seldom specified ;[12] but the rents are in all but a few cases[13] fully given,[14] and these constitute the most interesting features in this document, in its relation to the present subject.

The rents payable to the king range from 2*d.* to 3*s.* 4*d.,*[15] but in most instances

The Second Survey.

(1) This was apparently a toll on the sale of goods. (Ducange, *s. v.*) It is thus mentioned—" *de venta regis retinuit c sol.*" (Lib. Wint., p. 532) ; " *unam ventam regis retinuit*" (p. 533).

(2) Ibid., p. 537. "To supply food for the prison," which will be noticed subsequently.

(3) Ibid., pp. 534, 535, &c. It is also spelt " *waita*" (p. 537). This was the service of "watch and ward," as Mr. Smirke has shown in the Arch. Journal, vol. iii. pp. 339, &c. (See also Morgan, p. 168.)

(4) Lib. Wint., p. 533. It is spelt " *aura,*" but there is no doubt of its being the well-known service with plough or cart, classed by Sir Henry Ellis (*u. s.,* vol. i. p. 263) "among the baser services." (See also Spelman, Ducange, *s. v.*; Morgan, pp. 134, 135.)

(5) The word " *renta*" or " *rentis*" occurs (Lib. Wint., pp. 534, 536), although " *reddit,*" &c., are more commonly used. With regard to the tenements outside Westgate (and in one or two other instances), not only what the king received is entered, but also what his immediate tenants received from their under-tenants.

" *Per annum*" is introduced in pp. 531, 535 ; another rent is said to be weekly—"*viii carnifices, unde prepositus solebat habere unaquaque dominica die, viii d.*" (p. 532).

Instances where no rent was paid may be found in pp. 531, 532, 534, 535, &c. No rent is specified in some instances, in which the term " *quieta*" is not used (pp. 533, 537, 538, 539). A few tenements are returned " *dehospitatæ,*" or unoccupied (pp. 532, &c.). The Knights' Hall near Eastgate was held rent-free in King Edward's time : and of the tenants at the time of the survey, it is said (p. 531), " *clamant regem inde ad warantum per ejus breve quod habent.*" The church attached to this tenement was held in the same manner (p. 532).

(6) Ibid., p. 537. (7) Ibid., p. 535.

(8) The total rental of the tenements in High Street is £197 7*s.* 8*d.* ; but the total of those in all the other streets, and outside Westgate, is no more than £12 7*s.* ½*d.*

In addition to the money-rent, in three places (ibid., pp. 532, 535), " *estagium*" (the service commonly called " *convivium,*" " *pastus,*" &c., or the obligation to provide food and shelter for the lord) is mentioned ; and in two others (p. 533) it occurs apparently as a deduction from it—" *præter suum estagium.*"

In one instance alone we meet with a rent not paid in money, " *reddens ei vii solidatas ferrorum pro iii adden'.*" (p. 537). But it is not clear that "horseshoes" are meant, as Mr. Morgan (p. 168) supposes.

(9) See above, p. 266, and note.

(10) For example, in Minster Street. (Lib. Wint., p. 557.)

(11) Ibid., pp. 547 to 553, 555, 561.

Two tenements (pp. 545, 555) are said to be held on the terms declared—" *quamdiu justicia Episcopi voluerit.*"

(12) Landgable alone is noticed, and in three places only. (Ibid., pp. 544, 546, 551.)

One tenement is said to be " *quieta pro servicio suo*" (p. 549).

(13) The exceptions noted arose from lack of the needful information on the part of the compilers of the survey, and are explained with great simplicity, as " *non vult dicere quid reddit inde*" (ibid., p. 548), " *nescimus quid reddit inde*" (p. 549).

(14) The general arrangement of the entries is this,— first the name of the tenant, then that of the lord, next the rent due to him, and lastly the rent received by the tenant from the actual occupiers.

(15) This was for a tenement in Tanner Street. (Ibid., p. 555.) For one in Buck Street, not far from East-

they are 4*d*. or 6*d*. All in High Street are 6*d*., except those paid weekly for stalls, &c.[1] Much higher rents are paid to the bishop, but they vary from 2*d*. to £1.[2] The same observation is applicable to those due to the prior, the Abbot of Hyde, the Abbess of St. Mary's, and the other owners whose names are found here. Sometimes rents were paid by the first tenant to the king, and also to the bishop,[3] or to the bishop and the prior,[4] &c. One tenant, besides his rent to the king, owed to William de Chaisneto "*ospicium, salem, et aquam*,"[5] a service of which we have no mention elsewhere.

Municipal
condition,
temp. Henry I.
and Stephen.

Such is the sum of the information concerning the municipal condition of Winchester in the reigns of Henry I. and Stephen. Tenants held of the king *in capite*; there was neither mayor nor corporation; and there is no intimation of any special liberties or privileges granted by royal charter to any class of the citizens. Yet, in the reign of Henry II., we find reference made in a royal charter to liberties enjoyed in the time of Henry I.;[6] and local tradition resolutely maintains that Winchester received a grant of special privileges from that king,[7] but that unhappily the records perished in one of the frequent conflagrations of those days.[8]

gate (for that street extended eastward to the walls), 2*s*. 6*d*. was paid (p. 556); 1*s*. 10*d*. was paid in two instances (pp. 551, 555); 1*s*. 6*d*. in one case (p. 561); 1*s*. 3*d*. in several (pp. 550, 551, 552, &c.), &c.

(1) "*Regi unaquaque ebdomada ii d. præter xl' m.*": "*Rex habet in unaquaque ebdomada de unoquoque i d. præter xl' m.*" (ibid., p. 543): "*Regi i d. de theloneo præter xl' m.*" (p. 544), &c.

(2) The former sum is found in several parts of the record (ibid., pp. 549, 550, 553, 557), the latter in two instances (pp. 544, 546).

(3) Ibid., pp. 542, &c.

(4) Ibid., pp. 552, &c.

(5) "Entertainment, salt, and water" (ibid., p. 552). Rents not in money are mentioned in this survey, "*ii capones*," "*dimid. libræ piperis*" (p. 553), "*i libra piperis*" (p. 559), "*ii libræ piperis*" (p. 544). The "*bizant*" is named twice (pp. 551, 560) as the amount of rental. Some houses seem to have been let furnished— "*Eva habet inde xvi. s. pro catellis homini illius domus commendatis et pro domo*" (p. 556); "*pro domo et pro ustiliis unaquaque ebdomada viii d.*" (p. 553); "*habet pro ii braciniis et pro domo i m'*" (p. 562).

The term "*renta*" occurs in pp. 546, 553, 554, 555; and "*saisina*" (lawful possession) once (p. 556).

In the first survey pounds, marks of silver, shillings, pence, and half-pence ("*ob*") are named; but in the second we also meet with shillings and pence "*de blanco*" ("*sol.*" or "*s. de. B.*," and "*d. de. B.*"), or of pure, unalloyed silver; and farthings ("*quadr*").

(6) See below, p. 271.

(7) Milner, vol. i. p. 152; Wavell, vol. ii. pp. 44, 45. Both writers refer to Trussell's MS., fol. 73, where a charter of Henry II. is given. Milner, in a note, ex-

presses his belief that this charter ought to be referred to Henry II., but he does not the less confidently repeat Trussell's assertion, which is based on his ascription of it to Henry I.

(8) Milner (*u. s.*) and Wavell (ibid., p. 43), on Trussell's authority, tell us of a terrible conflagration, in which "the Guildhall, with most of the city records," perished. According to Trussell, this calamity befell the city in the year 1112, but Milner (who rather prides himself on his accuracy) states that it was in 1102, and refers to the *Annales Wintonienses* in Wharton's "Anglia Sacra" (vol. i. p. 297), where, however, nothing but this most meagre note occurs:—"*Anno MCII. Londonia bis combusta est. Wintonia semel.*" By the present town-clerk, in the preface to his "Transcripts from the Municipal Archives" (p. vi.), this destruction of the city records is attributed to another fire, which happened in 1181; but the *Annales* (*u. s.*, p. 302) tell us no more than that the mint was consumed in that year, on the night of the Vigil of St. Swithin, "*et egressus inde ignis consumit majorem partem et meliorem Wintoniæ.*"

Mr. Smirke (Arch. Journ., vol. vii. p. 379, note 7) remarks on this subject, "The effect of conflagrations appears to be much magnified by our early chroniclers:" and still more, he might have said, by later local historians. "*Civitas incendio penitus destructa* must often be taken to mean only that a bad fire happened in it."

There is no doubt that we have lost many early records relating to Winchester, but the fact that Trussell transcribed Henry II.'s first charter from the original, and that in the British Museum there still exists the Black Book of Winchester, and the original copy of the survey made in 1416, seems to point out a very different cause

Proceeding now to the charters granted to Winchester, we find the earliest to be Charters of
Henry II. those of Henry II., which, however, do no more than grant to the citizens of the Merchant Guild, and their property, freedom from every toll, passage, and custom ; or concede the liberties and customs which the citizens possessed under Henry I., restore those which might have been lost during the wars of the preceding reign, and protect merchants who might visit the city.[1] The dates of these charters cannot be accurately determined ; but they were certainly granted in the earlier part of Henry's reign.[2]

In the first year of Richard I. another charter[3] was granted to the Merchant Charter of
Richard I. Guild of Winchester. By it he greatly extended its privileges. None of its members could be impleaded without the walls of the city (with the exception of moneyers and royal servants), *"de ullo placito præter placita de tenuris exterioribus."* It was further granted *"quod nullus eorum faciet duellum,"* and that in pleas pertaining to the crown they might defend themselves (*se disrationare*) according to ancient custom. In addition to toll, they were declared free in fairs and at all other times, at seaports

---

for their disappearance. Some may yet lurk amongst the unknown treasures buried in that vast coffer in the muniment-room above Westgate. (Arch. Journ., vol. ix. p. 82 ; Arch. Assoc., Winchester Vol., p. 29.)

(1) Trussell (fol. 73) gives the text of the first of these charters correctly, with the exception of one error ("*Andalugiæ*" for "*Andegaviæ*") ; but he has created inextricable confusion by his mistakes in the names of the witnesses. There can be no doubt that he copied from the original, for he says (ibid.), "This charter for the character is the neatest that I haue seene, and the antientest, the sight wherof gaue mee occation first in my cursory reeding to obserue what I haue thus expressed."

A copy of it, and of the second spoken of in the text, is to be seen in the muniments of the Guildhall, London (Letter Book, F. fol. 28), in a transcript of a charter of 1 Edw. II. by *inspeximus*. Its insertion there is easily accounted for by the notices of not unfrequent disputes between the citizens of London and those of Winchester respecting customs.

Milner (vol. ii. App. p. 300) has printed the first from Trussell correctly, except that he has omitted "*episcopis*" in the address. The second, both because it is yet unprinted, and also as more interesting, I give here with a few customary abbreviations :—

"*H. Rex. Anglorum, &c., Sciatis me concessisse civibus meis Wyntoniæ omnes libertates et consuetudines, quas ipsi habuerunt in tempore regis Henrici avi mei : Et precipio quod habeant et teneant omnia acata et vadia sua et tenementa sua, secundum consuetudines civitatis ita libere et quiete et honorifice, sicut unquam melius tenuerunt tempore regis Henrici : Et si alique consuetudines injuste levate sunt in guerra, cassate sint : Et quicunque petierint civitatem illam cum mercatu suo, de quocunque loco sint, sive extranei, sive alii, veniant morentur et recedant in salva pace mea, reddendo rectas*

consuetudines, et nemo eas injuste disturbet super hanc cartam meam : Et volo et precipio quod predicti cives mei firmam pacem juste habeant. T. Can. Canc' ; &c. Apud Sarum."

(2) The date of the first charter lies between 1158 and 1162, for the first signature to it is "*Thom. Cancell,*" and Becket held the chancellorship during those years ; the second was granted in 1162 or 1163, for Becket's signature (see preceding note) shows that he had received the primacy, and had not relinquished the chancellorship.

Trussell's version of the names of the witnesses to the first charter is this :— "*Tho : Canturien', Rich. London, Gil. Winton', &c. ;*" and he conjectured that the second signature was that of "*Rich. Foliat.*" The witnesses to the charter, according to the copy in the Guildhall at London, are :—"*Thom. Cancell. Com. Reg'.* [this signature, by a clerical error, is repeated]. *Com. Thoec'.* [which should be "*Gloec'*"]. *Ric. de Hum'. Constab. Gar. fil' Gir'. Camerar. Will' fil' Ham'. Joc' Baillol.*"

It is easy to see how our worthy antiquary might misinterpret "*Cancell.*" "*Canturien' ;*" but the process by which he arrived at the other conclusions is undiscoverable. Gilbert Ffolliott was Bishop of London in 1163, whilst Becket was Archbishop of Canterbury ; but there was no "Rich. Winton." till 1174, nor any bishop of the name of *Richard* at that time, except Richard Peche, Bishop of Lichfield. The most probable solution of the difficulty is, that he misinterpreted the names in the same way as he misread "*Andalugiæ*" for "*Andegaviæ.*" Milner (*u. s.*) can offer no explanation of the palpable mistakes of his authority.

These charters are referred to in charters to Portsmouth, Petersfield, Andover, &c. (Brady, "Historical Treatise of Cities and Burghs," App. pp. 18, 20, 21.)

(3) Printed by Brady, App. p. 45, from Cart. Antiq. R. 30, n. 19 ; and by Milner, vol. ii. App. p. 300.

and elsewhere, in England and beyond the sea in the English dominions, from lastage, and pontage, and from all amerciament except according to their ancient law ; and all their liberties and privileges were secured by empowering the sheriff of Southampton, or the port-reeve of Winchester, to recover any invasion of them by distress at Winchester. Further, "*ad emendandam civitatem,*" they were freed from "*Ieresgieue*" and "*Scotteshale;*" and the privileges conceded by the second charter of Henry II. were once more assured to them.[1]

Charter of John.

This charter was confirmed and extended by John, in the seventeenth year of his reign.[2] The additional privileges accorded to them and their heirs for their faithful service were that the royal mint and exchange, with all the liberties pertaining to them, should remain for ever at Winchester, and that they should have the sites of two mills within the city, at Coiteburi, "*ad emendacionem ejusdem civitatis.*" They were also relieved from liability to distress without the walls of Winchester for any debt to any one, "*unum non sit capitalis debitor vel plegius.*"

Charters of the Plantagenet kings.

Henry III., in the eleventh year of his reign, confirmed this charter almost in the same words.[3] And Edward I., reciting his father's charter, by *Inspeximus,* confirmed it in the eighteenth year of his reign.[4] Edward II., in the first year of his reign, reciting by *Inspeximus* (as it has been stated above) the charter of Henry II., and the confirmation of the liberties of Winchester by Edward I., added his confirmation.[5] A brief of Richard II. is the next in the series.[6] It is addressed "*Johanni de Montagu et sociis suis Justiciariis nostris ad pacem nostram in Com. Suthamton,*" and refers to a charter of confirmation which is not preserved. The only new article recited is, that the citizens of the Merchant Guild should have a return of all royal briefs and summons from the exchequer within the liberties of the city.

In none of these charters are the mayor or the corporation of the city referred to ; the fee-farm is named only in the charter of Edward II. ; and the next, granted

---

(1) "*Duellum*" was "judicial combat," for which, in the case of the members of the Merchant Guild of Winchester, trial by law was substituted. In Madox (Hist. Exchequer, pp. 382, 383) is an account of a duel at Winchester, in the time of Henry III., to decide a charge of robbery.

"Lastage" (*lastagium*) was a custom paid for carrying wares to fairs and markets. "Pontage" (*pontagium*) was a toll for crossing a bridge.

"*Ieresgieue*" (or *yeresgyeve,* according to John's charter) is the English name for the service or exaction known by the names of "*dona annua*" (or "*regia*"), or "*exennia,*" yearly gifts to the king. For this interpretation I am indebted to W. S. Walford, Esq., none of the glossaries containing the word, and Brady's Gloss. (App. p. 40) not being admissible.

"*Scotteshale*" (or "*scotale*"), an exaction the name of which is exactly equivalent to "drink-money."

See Spelman, Ducange, &c., *s. vv.*

(2) Rot. Chart., 17 John. Memb. 4 (Printed by Record Commiss., vol. i. p. 217). Milner (*u. s.,* p. 301) also prints this charter from Trussell, and, after him, dates it 9 John, or eight years too early.

The present "City Mill" (see above, p. 20, note 5) is one of those in Coitebury.

(3) Ibid., 11 Hen. III. par. 1, Memb. 5.

(4) Ibid., 18 Edw. I. Memb. 34.

(5) Munim. Guildh. London, Letter Book, F. fol. 28. He appears to have confirmed these charters again, for in 17 Edw. II. (Rot. Orig., vol. i. p. 281) the payment of 20 marks to the king for confirming certain charters is recorded.

(6) This brief is dated 5 Rich. II., and is stitched to the top of the first folio in the Black Book of Winchester (Mus. Brit., Add. MS. 6036), but there is no reference to it in the text of the MS.

by Henry VI., merely relates to markets and fairs.[1] There was a "confirmation of charters" on the 18th of November, in the 12th Edw. IV. (1472).[2] The incorporation appears to have been first effected by the charter of Queen Elizabeth, under which the civic officers were appointed and acted until the time of the Municipal Reform Act.

This charter,[3] which is dated in the year 1587, recites that Winchester was always an ancient town, having (time out of mind) for its government a mayor, six aldermen, two bailiffs, two coroners, two constables, and other public officers of the citizens and inhabitants of the same city; that lands, &c., with liberties and privileges, had been granted to "the citizens and inhabitants," sometimes by the name of "the mayor, bailiffs, and commonalty of Winchester," &c., and that ambiguities had arisen in consequence of the variety of names; that upon the ground of their prescription and usage, and being desirous to rectify the same, and that they should enjoy more ample privileges, the queen had granted,— *Charter of Queen Elizabeth.*

That it should be for ever a free city, and that the citizens and inhabitants should be a body corporate, by the name of the mayor, bailiffs, and commonalty of the city of Winchester; and that the officers should be of the older, and principal, better, and more honest sort of inhabitants and citizens; and that there should be twenty-four persons of "the better, and more discreet, and more honest sort," to be assisting and aiding to the mayor, to be called "the Four-and-twenty Men." *Incorporation of Winchester.*

Provisions then follow for the election of the aldermen and the twenty-four from the citizens and inhabitants; for holding twice a year the boroughmote court, with leets, law days, and views of frankpledge of the inhabitants and resiants within the city, and all things thereto belonging; and for acquitting and discharging from the suit of the county and hundred courts, to the sheriffs belonging, with quittance from both, the mayor, bailiffs, and commonalty, and their successors, and all the inhabitants. It also provides that no inhabitant nor resident within the city should be impannelled with foreigners upon juries at assizes, &c., unless the cause concerned the sovereign; that the mayor should be clerk of the market, with assize of bread and ale, &c.; that the mayor, bailiffs, and commonalty might establish a guild, or fraternity, of one master and two wardens, of any art used or occupied within the city; and that they, with the assistance of the wardens, might make ordinances for the government of the same, so that they were not repugnant to the statutes of the realm. Subsequent clauses confirmed to the city the property belonging to it, and authorized the mayor and corporation to administer the charities for which they were the appointed trustees, &c., &c.

The renewal of the charter by Charles II. and James II.[4] does not properly belong to this section, as it was only one of the fiscal measures of those sovereigns, and did *The last royal charters.*

(1) Rot. Chart., 27—39 Hen. VI. n. 36.

(2) Black Book, fol. 40 v°.

(3) An English version of this charter is given by Milner (vol. ii., Appendix, pp. 301, &c.); Wavell gives one also (vol. ii. pp. 99—116). The abstract in the text is derived in good part from Merewether and Stephens, "History of Boroughs," pp. 1407, 1408.

(4) "Transcripts from the Archives of Winchester," by C. Bailey, Esq., the present town-clerk, pp. 23, &c.; Milner, vol. ii. p. 38.

not affect the municipal institutions of the city. The last charter was that of George III., in the year 1762,[1] which was merely a grant or release of part of the fee-farm of Winchester.

Traditions of the incorporation of the city. Queen Elizabeth's charter represents the government of the city by a mayor, two bailiffs, &c., as having existed " time out of mind ; " but none of the earlier charters contain the grant of this government. Trussell, who certainly found amongst the muniments of the city many records which are not now known, states[2] that " Winchester was encorporated by the name of maior and burgesses Aº 1182 ; " and again,[3] King John, " to help him to some monye," " did grannt away for euer in fee-farme to sutch places as wowld make purchase therof, the *iura regalia*, &c." " And begynning with the citty of Winchester, hee under his great seale graunted to the cittizens therof (free of the guild of merchants), and their successors for ever, to be incorporated by the name of maior and burgesses, wᵗʰ perpetuall succession, &c." He then says that they were to pay 200 marks at the time, and 100 yearly for ever.

In the absence of existing proof, this statement must be marked as exceedingly doubtful ; for not only are none of these alleged charters now known, but we find that the purport of charters which do exist (as for example, the first of Henry II.[4] and that of John[5]) is exceedingly mistaken or exaggerated, and the statement itself is incumbered with such inconsistencies as these :—although Trussell states that the city had a mayor in the year 1182,[6] it is not till 1184 that the list of mayors (now in the muniment-room over Westgate) commences,[7] and the earliest named by him is in 1187 ; besides this the name he gives, " Roger de Lune," does not occur at all in the City Tables ;[8] and he not only misread the name of the mayor in 1304, Laurence de Anne,[9] " Laurence de Lune,"[10] but seems to have misplaced another mayor, Roger de

(1) Merewether and Stephens, *u. s.*, p. 2160.

(2) Fol. 92 vº, " Ealeuen yeeres and odd monethes," he says, before the incorporation of London. See " *Liber Albus*," Book ii. (Munim. Guildh. London, vol. i. pp. 128, &c.) He dates the " iucorporation," likewise, thus early ; but in that particular he appears to be mistaken. (See Merewether and Stephens, *u. s.*)

(3) Fol. 91 vº. Trussell seems to have found a genuine document relating to the grant of the city in ferm, and to have mistaken its import, as in other instances which we have met with.

(4) See above, p. 271. Trussell, *u. s.*; Milner, *u. s.*

(5) See above, p. 272. Trussell, *u. s.*; Milner, *u. s.*; Wavell (who in all the early history of Winchester seems to have followed Trussell implicitly, adding nothing of his own but mere mistakes), vol. ii. pp. 64, 65.

(6) Fol. 92 vº.

(7) Wavell (vol. ii. pp. 283, &c.) and Milner (vol. ii. pp. 309, &c.) give copies of this list. Wavell (*u. s.*, p. 59) contributes a mistake to this *imbroglio*, and dates the supposed charter of Henry II. in 1187.

(8) Trussell, fol. 92 vº ; City Tables (*u. s.*) " Philip Lubin, 1187." Trussell's statement is as follows :—" In

the Leidger Book in the Councell howse wher the Catalog of Maiors is recorded, I fiud Roger de Lune, 30 Hen. 2. aº 1187, was " [here he commences an interlineation, and continues his statement on the broad inner margiu of his book] " maior, and Io. Russell B. of W., and in aº 32, Roger de Ingpen was M., and Io. le Grace and March' le Warder were Bayliffs." It is on this statement, as I suspect, that Wavell first (see the frontispiece to his second volume), and Milner (vol. ii. p. 167) afterwards, based their account of the first mayor of Winchester, whose name, by a further mistake, they made " Florence de Lunn."

(9) Madox' " Firma Burgi," p. 157. In the " Inquest " (the text of which was printed by Mr. Smirke in the Arch. Journ., vol. vii. pp. 374, &c.), the name of Laurence de Anne occurs more than once amongst the persons paying landgable in Winchester ; and the name is a good county one, derived from the district of which Andover is now the most conspicuous place. The name " Laurenæ de Andevere " occurs later.

(10) Trussell, fols. 105 vº, 106. He makes other mistakes in names in this place, *e. g.* " Holpenett " for " Holepite," " Pytley " for " Nuttly," &c.

Inkepenne, from the reign of Edward I. to that of Henry II.[1] And the City Tables, which, if not compiled by Trussell, were the work of his age, and based upon his history, are demonstrably erroneous or fictitious in all the earlier part of the list of mayors.[2]

The first authentic mention of a mayor of Winchester is in the Patent Rolls of 1 John;[3] and the first name of a mayor authentically recorded is Nicholas Koppinger, probably in 29 Hen. III.,[4] mentioned in a verdict of the following reign. And yet the charters of John and Henry III. speak only of the "*præpositus;*" and in a record which we still possess, of "a full boroughmote" at Hocktide, 53 Hen. III. (or the year 1269), the two bailiffs are named, but not a mayor.

Connected with this subject, and affording incidentally a faint and dubious gleam of light regarding it, is that of the oldest known "seal of the citizens of Winchester."[5] An impression of this seal, attached to an ancient copy of a *Consuetudinarium* of this city, is described by Mr. Smirke;[6] and the seal is assigned by Mr. Way to the reign of Henry III.,[7] which agrees with the tradition recorded by Trussell,[8] that this king first granted to this corporation a common seal.[9] But the possession of a common seal cannot be regarded as evidence of incorporation.

From existing accessible records we cannot trace, with any satisfactory degree of clearness, the progress of the municipality from the "mayor and citizens," addressed in John's letters patent, to the fully developed government in Elizabeth's charter. The aldermen, who rank next after the mayor and the recorder in the last-named instrument, appear not until then to have been included in the governing officers.

Side notes: First record of a Mayor. The Common Seal. The Aldermen.

---

(1) See above, note 8.

(2) The name of Nicholas Koppinger (Arch. Journ., vol. vii. p. 375) does not occur in these lists at all; nor does the name of Thomas Bowland, whose monumental inscription may yet be seen in the cathedral. (See above, p. 75.)

A few other errors may be pointed out here, that the real value of these lists may be known. In 1266 the mayor was one Simon (Black Book, fol 43 v°, his popular name not being given); but the lists give "Ade de Froyle." In 1298 Richard Gabriel was mayor (Madox' Collect., vol. li. fol. 18); the lists give "Jerman Hardy." In 1300 John Tytinge was mayor (Harl. MS. 1761, fol. 35); but a different name is given in the Tables.

Milner has sufficiently exposed the monstrous absurdities of the historical part of these Tables (vol. ii. Appendix, pp. 298, &c.)

(3) Rot. Pat., vol. i. p. 60.

(4) We learn from the "Verdict" (Arch. Journ., vol. vii. p. 375) that the payment of 60s. annually, for the removal of the "Drapery" from the Mint into High Street, was undertaken by Nicholas Koppinger, in his mayoralty; and from the Pipe Roll of 29 Henry III., that this was undertaken at that time, which seems to determine the date of Koppinger's mayoralty.

(5) This seal is ogival in form, and measures 3·2 in. by 2·2 in. The device is an embattled castle with three lofty towers; and the legend reads—" ☒ SIGILL' CIVIVM WINTONIENSIVM." The counter seal is smaller, 1·7 in. by 1·1 in. The legend, in three lines across it, is—" CONFIR—MATIO—SIL'IS." In chief is a cross, and in the exergue a trefoil ornament, and the whole is surrounded by an ornamental border.

Other impressions of the seal are known. It is figured by Milner in the Miscellaneous plate given with his original work, but he has made in connection with it several very remarkable errors, which are exposed and corrected by Mr. J. Gough Nichols, in a paper on the seals of Winchester (Arch. Instit., Winchester Vol., pp. 107, &c.). Milner (vol. i. p. 287, and note) regarded it as "a new seal" granted by Queen Elizabeth, and he misread the inscriptions of both seal and counter seal. It appears that, at the date to which he refers it, "1589," and the letters " A V G," were engraved in the exergue of the seal, and the same date in the chief of the counter seal.

(6) Arch. Journ., vol. ix. pp. 88, 89.

(7) Ibid., plate. "Date, probably *circa* 1240."

(8) Cited by Milner, vol. i. p. 190.

(9) Here Milner is guilty of two mistakes. The in-

"They were local officers of wards or districts, whose functions related chiefly, but not wholly, to the police and preservation of order, health, and cleanliness within their several limits."[1] In the beginning of the sixteenth century, however, they appear as members of the government of the city.[2]

The six wards.

In connection with them, therefore, the division of the city into aldermanries, or wards, which prevailed as early as the commencement of the fifteenth century,[3] may be spoken of. They were—1. The north side of High Street; 2. The south side of that same street; 3. Jewry Street; 4. Tanner Street; 5. Colebrook Street; 6. Gold Street; and 7. Northgate Street, or the Soke Liberty without Northgate and Westgate;[4] but there were only six wards subsequently, that without the walls having ceased to be a separate aldermanry.[5]

The Bailiffs.

The bailiffs were the successors of the "*præpositi*" (provosts or portreeves) of the city. In the beginning of Edward I.'s reign[6] they were elected thus :—the "Twenty-

---

scription, "*Sigillum Civium Wintoniensium*," shows conclusively that when it was made, the city was not incorporated, and therefore could not have (properly) a "*common* seal."

There are two ancient seals still in the possession of the corporation, which, with the *regalia*, are in the custody of the mayor. The first is a circular silver one, 1·7 inches in diameter, and is "one of those which were made early in the reign of Edward II. in pursuance of the statute of merchants [made at Acton Burnell, 11 Edw. I., 1283], which provided such a legal sanction for the recognizance of debts." It is not a seal of the corporation at all, although Milner (orig. edit. Miscell. pl. fig. 12) has engraved it as such, "but one of the king's seals for recognizances of debtors" (Arch. Inst., Winchester Vol., "On the Seals of Winchester City," by J. G. Nichols, Esq., pp. 108, 109). The design is "a bust of the king, beardless and very effeminate in aspect, with a jewelled rim to his robes . . . . before his breast is a lion, and on each side of his head is a castle, the badge of his mother, Alianor of Castille" (ibid.). *Leg.*: ✠ s' edw. reg. angl. ad recogn. debitor. apvd winton.

The other is a gold ring with the arms of Winchester (*Gul.* five castles in saltier, embattled and mured, *arg.* in fess, on sinister side, a lion passant guardant, on dexter side, another, counterpassant, *or*), and, as a posy, "the gift of Edward White; 1600."

The present common seal is a mere office stamp with the city arms, and the legend "Seal of the Mayor, Aldermen, and Citizens of the City of Winchester."

Three other seals, known only by impressions of them, may here be described. The first is circular, 1·2 inches in diameter; device, a triple-towered castle, the central tower having a high-pitched roof; *Leg.*: sigillvm maioratvs wintonie. The next appears to be a more modern copy of this, it is circular also, but 1·1 inches only in diameter; it has the same legend, but the device is a two-towered castle, and from the towers issue two demi-

lions, combattant, supporting a cross. The third is circular, and only ·8 inch in diameter; device, a triple-towered castle; *Leg.*: wintonia.

(1) Arch. Journ. vol. ix. p. 81. The earliest full account of the government of the city which we possess is found in the *Consuetudinarium*, printed and commented upon by Mr. Smirke (ibid., pp. 69, &c.), and in it the aldermen appear as ward-officers merely. The earliest notice of the office in the Black Book of Winchester is 6 Hen. V. (fol. 45), where the alderman of Tanner Street ward is said to have refused to watch on St. John's night. In the same record (fol. 54) the aldermen are required to "present" the default of cleansing the streets in their wards; and only once are any of them spoken of as present at the assembly, and then (fol. 59.v°) quite incidentally. These duties of the aldermen appear in the "Ordinances of the Gild Merchant of Southampton," printed by E. Smirke, Esq., recorder of that town, in the Arch. Journal, vol. xvi. p. 290. Aldermen, who were seneschals, or masters of guilds, are also mentioned. (Ibid., p. 284.) During a visitation of the plague in 1583, the ancient duties of the aldermen were imposed on them. (Transcripts, p. 106.)

(2) Madox' Coll., vol. li. fols. 38, &c.

(3) The "Tarrages of Winton." (Add. M.S. 6133) contain the earliest complete record of this division which I have yet found; they are called "aldermanries" there. In the "Verdict," *temp.* Edw. I., they are not mentioned, although it is quite probable that they existed then. There is no basis whatever for Trussell's statement, copied by Wavell (vol. i. p. 7, and vol. ii. p. 66), that the division of the city into six wards, and the appointment of an alderman to preside over each, were provisions of John's charter; and the statement is an additional reason for regarding the grant of such a charter as extremely doubtful.

(4) Tarrages, &c., fol. 33 v°. (5) Wavell, vol. i. pp. 7, 8.

(6) "*Abbrev. Placit.*," p. 187. 2 Edw. I., Rot. 9.

four" chose four out of their own number, and out of them the commonalty elected one; and the commonalty chose four from amongst themselves, out of whom the "Twenty-four" chose one, and the two thus elected were bailiffs for the year. When the *Consuetudinarium* was drawn up, the mayor and "Twenty-four" selected four "*prud' hommes*" (or members of the Merchant Guild), and the commonalty chose two of them as bailiffs.[1] These officers were called the two peers ("*deus peres*") of the mayor.[2]

The "Twenty-four," who were also the "peers" of the mayor,[3] are called in the *Consuetudinarium*—"*jurez,*" and are said to be chosen from the "*plus prudes homes et plus sages*" in the city, to aid and counsel the mayor in preserving and sustaining the franchise.[4] This body appears, at a very early date, to have attempted to invade the liberties of the other members of the municipality.[5] And in the Black Book of Winchester there are signs of some conflict of authorities, in which the "Twenty-four" were eventually successful.[6]

The "Twenty-four."

The mayor was chosen annually by the "Twenty-four" and the commonalty, in the time of the *Consuetudinarium*.[7] At a later date, two were chosen out of the "Twenty-four," and the retiring mayor selected one of them to succeed him.[8] Until the year 1524, he could not enter upon his office until he had been admitted by the presentation of two of his fellow citizens at the Court of Exchequer, and by taking an oath of loyalty and obedience.[9]

The Mayor.

The franchise of the city was enjoyed in connection with membership of the Merchant Guild; but not only was there (as it has been remarked)[10] "no adequate provision for securing the admission into it of all those who were reasonably entitled

The Franchise.

---

(1) Arch. Journ., *u. s.*, p. 76.

(2) Ibid. p. 81; Arch. Journ., Winchester Vol., p. 20. For the bailiffs' oath on entering office, see Black Book, fol. 40 vᵒ.

(3) Arch. Journ., *u. s.*, pp. 81, 82, note 5; see also passages in Black Book there cited, and others.

The "*Sacramentum de xxxiiii*ᵒʳ" is given in the Black Book, fol. 42.

(4) Ibid., pp. 70, 76.

(5) "*Abbrev. Placit.*," *u. s.*

(6) See, in particular, the oath to be taken by the mayor on entering his office (fol. 22), where is an erasure, and over it, in a later hand, is written (after "the xxiv"), "of the citie," by which the antiquity and importance of the office might seem to be enhanced; and the "semblance of usage" served as "a justification for perpetuating the usurpations which were introduced" (Merewether and Stephens, pp. 906—908).

(7) Arch. Journ., *u. s.*, pp. 70, 76.

(8) 12 Hen. VIII. (Black Book, fol. 52.)

(9) Madox' Coll., vol. li. fols. 38, &c. The reason assigned for exempting Winchester from presenting its mayor to be sworn in according to ancient custom, was

the "*maxima depauperatio, ruina, desolatio, et decasus*" of the city. The oath was, therefore, to be taken at the guildhall at Winchester, before the recorder and other municipal officers. The oath taken in the Court of Exchequer in 26 & 27 Edw. I. is given in the same volume of Madox' Collections, fol. 18, &c. That administered in 1 Hen. VI. is to be found in the Black Book, fol. 22; and at fol. 41 is to be seen "Master Maires othe" in 12 Edw. IV.

The appointment of "chamberlains" is spoken of 16 Hen. VIII. (Black Book, fol. 56 vᵒ); and the "coroners" in the "Verdict," so often referred to (Arch. Journ., vol. vii. p. 374), in the *Consuetudinarium* (ibid., vol. ix. p. 70), and in the 30 Edw. I. (Harl. MS., 1761, fol. 35). The oath of the recorder on entering office, in 12 Edw. IV., is given in the Black Book, fol. 40 vᵒ.

(10) Arch. Journ., *u. s.*, p. 81. In the Black Book are two forms of oath administered to those who enjoyed the franchise in Winchester; the first (fol. 2vᵒ) is "*pro hominibus intrantibus in Gilda Mercatoria,*" the other (fol. 41) was "to swere men to be fre." There is also given the mode of admission to the Merchant Guild *temp.* Hen. VI. (fol. 23).

to it," but it became needful to inflict a fine on those who, being qualified, neglected to take up their franchise.[1]

Common assemblies

The " common assemblies," or Burghmotes, were held at Easter (Hocktide) and Michaelmas, and at the latter the officers for the next year were chosen.[2] The proceedings at these meetings were recorded in the Books of Ordinances,[3] and at an earlier time in the " Black Book," which is now in the British Museum.[4]

" Firma Burgi."

None of the charters before that of Edward II. (as we have already observed)[5] make any mention of the letting of the city " at Ferme " to the citizens, by the king, to whom it belonged : [6] yet it is certain that this was done in the reign of Henry II.,[7] if not earlier still ; [8] that the demise was renewed from time to time ; [9] that it was at some

---

(1) Black Book, fol. 46. In 4 Hen. VII. a fine of 6s. 8d. was inflicted, half to be paid to the bailiffs, and half to the chamber of the city.

Another entry, in the following reign (fol. 53 v°), seems to bear on this subject. " It is agreed that Mr. Lytchfeld shall come into the company if Mr. Meyre and his brethren fynde hyme resonable."

(2) Arch. Journ., u. s., pp. 76, 82. Black Book, passim.

(3) By way of preface to these volumes, which commence with the reign of Elizabeth, a selection of ordinances passed in the preceding reigns, translated from the Latin or Norman-French, in which they were originally written, is prefixed. It is from these volumes that the present town-clerk has taken his " Transcripts," published in 1856.

(4) This MS. is a very irregular and imperfect journal of the proceedings of the assemblies, with other matters, such as wills, charters, records of compositions, &c., inserted. The order of time is not observed with any regularity in the former part of the book, the records in which extend from the reign of Richard II. to that of Edward VI. Reference is made in the margin in one instance to some Books of Ordinances, which were not those now in the muniment-room over Westgate, and also to a book of wills, &c., which is still there. Trussell also refers (fol. 103 v°) to the Book of Ordinances.

(5) See above, p. 272.

(6) Madox' " Firma Burgi," p. 8.

(7) It is mentioned in the Pipe Rolls at least as early as 1157. (Merewether and Stephens, p. 339.) Madox, u. s., " Civitas Winton. Idem Vicecomes (of Hampshire) reddit Compotum de c et xlii li. et xii s. et iiii d. blancis de firma civitatis Wintoniæ." (Quoted from Mag. Rot. 26 Hen. II. Rot. 10, a. m. 2.)

Four years later, " Idem Vicecomes (of Hampshire) reddit compotum de c et iiii li. et ii d. blancis, de veteri firma, et idem de nova firma " (ibid., 2nd Edit., vol. i. p. 331) ; and in the following year, " Will. de Pontearch' reddit compotum de c et quatuor xx et xvii li. vii s. et v d. blancis, de veteri firma ; et idem de nova firma " (Mag. Rot. Pip., printed by the Record Commiss., pp. 36, &c.).

(8) The great difference between the amounts of rent

recorded as due to the king, in the two surveys contained in the Liber Winton. (see above, pp. 269, 270), makes it probable that some change in the tenure had taken place.

(9) Madox (Hist. Exchequer, Edit. 1711, pp. 230, 231) records the demise to the citizens of Winchester, " ut custodes," of their city ; and the payment of £35 19s., in the 5 Hen. III. (1220-1), " de firma civitatis . . . . propter defaltam ponderis, et portæ, et libertatum," quoting Mag. Rot., 5 Hen. III., Rot. 2 b.

In the 20th of the same reign (1235-6), " Rex concessit probis hominis suis Wintoniæ, quod teneant civitatem Regis Wintoniæ ad firmam usque in tres annos " (Rot. Orig., vol. i. p. 2).

For Edward II.'s charter, see Letter-book F. fol. 28, in the muniments of the Guildhall, London.

Madox (" Firma Burgi," pp. 18—20, and notes) gives various examples, from which it appears that the city was let at ferm to the citizens at various times, " quamdiu regi placuerit ;" and that this was particularly the case in the 16 Edw. III., to which the subsequent renewals as late as the reign of James I. referred ; but that the city was still the king's appears from various circumstances. (See Black Book, fol. 8.) Thus, in 2 Edw. I., it was let to Hugo de Dunnton in the same manner. (Rot. Orig., vol. i. p. 23 b.) And many instances are recorded in which, on slight occasion, the city was " taken into the king's hand " (Madox' " Firma Burgi," pp. 157, 161, &c.; Hist. Exchequer, p. 701 ; Rot. Orig., vol. i. p. 138.)

The ferm after 49 Hen. III. (1264-5) was 100 marks yearly, having been reduced in that year from £80 (which before that time it had paid), " propter impotenciam civium . . . . et paupertatem aliorum inhabitantium," &c. (Madox, Hist. Exchequer, p. 231, quoting Hil. Memor., 49 Hen. III., Rot. 7 a.) It appears that this reduction was intended to continue for no more than twenty-one years, and that on the expiration of that term, on the application of the citizens, it was renewed. (Ibid., quoting Mich. Commun., 14 Edw. I., Rot. 2. a., in bund. 13 & 14 Edw. I.) But the best-known example is that which occurred in 30 Hen. VI. (1452), when the citizens addressed to the king that petition and declaration of the ruined state of Winchester, which is printed in Archæ-

subsequent time[1] let in *fee-farm ;* and that the last trace of the original condition of the city was abolished by the charter of 3 Geo. III.[2] "Fee-farm rents," as they are called, are still collected for tenements which became the property of the city, when it was demised to the citizens in ferm.[3]

"The gross revenues of the city (without deducting the king's fee-farm, &c.) The Revenues. consisted of terrages, *i. e.* quit and rack. rents ; the tax on looms ; the tolls paid at the city gates ; the customs on wool, fish, and some other articles brought into the city ; the tax on cattle-dealers, butchers, bakers and retailers of bread, brewers (who, as well as the dealers in bread, were women) ; on non-freemen buying, selling, or keeping shops in the city ; on tanners, dealers in lard and suet, and shoemakers. Some of these taxes were payable by freemen, but generally only by strangers and non-freemen. Besides these, there were the profits of the city fairs, fines, escheats and forfeitures in, or out of, the city courts ; talliages or town-rates raised for special purposes ; and other sources of casual revenue."[4]

According to the Report of the Municipal Corporations Commissioners in 1835,[5] The Corporation in 1835. the officers at that time were the mayor, the recorder, and deputy recorder, or town-clerk, six aldermen, two bailiffs, two coroners, two (or, in fact, four) constables, the Twenty-four Men, and one clerk for recognizances of debt, who was not elected. These were according to the charter of Queen Elizabeth, and to them had been

---

ologia, vol. i. pp. 95, &c. ; Wavell, vol. ii. pp. 243, &c., and elsewhere.

It should be noted here that both John's and Henry III.'s charters granted the mills in Coitebury to the citizens, "*propter emendacionem civitatis*" (see above, p. 272) ; and in the same way the payment of a portion of the ferm was occasionally excused, that the citizens might repair the walls, as, for example, in 2 Hen. IV., in 1400-1. (Black Book, fol. 9.)

Other payments were made to the king, as well as the ferm ; thus we find the ferm or rent for the Chapman's Hall (or Linen Hall), and for the Drapery (or Cloth Hall), accounted for separately. (Madox, "*Firma Burgi*," p. 19, notes ; Hist. Exchequer, pp. 233, 234, 353 ; Rot. Orig., vol. i. p. 51 ; Mag. Rot. Pip., pp. 36, &c.)

And sometimes charges are made on the ferm, as when "the farmer of the city of Winchester paid £20 . . . . to buy a robe for the young king at Winchester fair" (Madox, Hist. Exchequer, p. 251). And to this time, a payment entitled "creation fee" is made annually to the Marquis of Winchester, amounting now to £33 6s. 8d.—the third part of £100—which seems to have been taken as the amount of the fee-farm instead of 100 marks. This, doubtlessly, originated in the "*tertius denarius comitis*" (Selden's "Titles of Honour," referred to above, p. 268, note 11) ; and the record which granted this to the first Earl of Winchester, Saher de Quinci, is still extant (*Cartæ Antiquæ*, K. 1.), but the date of the commencement of the present payment has not been ascertained.

(1) In the time of Elizabeth, the date of the change from "at ferm during the king's pleasure" to "in fee-farm" had been so completely forgotten, that the records refer it to 16 Edw. III., when the demise of the city was specially said to be "*quamdiu regi placuerit*" (Madox, "*Firma Burgi*," pp. 19, 20).

Trussell (as quoted by Wavell, vol. ii. p. 65), according to custom, egregiously misrepresents the facts of the case, making a supposed charter of John (in 1207) one of "incorporation," for which the citizens had to pay 200 marks at once, and for the fee-farm 100 marks annually. (See above, p. 274.) And this is stated as fact in an essay on "Municipal Privileges and Legislation," in the Winchester Vol. of Arch. Assoc., p. 20.

Brady (*u. s.*, p. 89, quoting Rot. Parl. 11 Hen. IV., n. 57) tells us that Winchester was then held in fee-farm, paying 120 marks per annum ; and some part of it was held of the king *in capite*, which would bring the grant of the city in fee-farm very nearly to Edward III.'s reign.

(2) Merewether and Stephens, p. 2168.

(3) These rents amounted in 1859 to £16 6s., having much decreased in the present century.

(4) Arch. Journ., vol. ix. p. 88. Mr. Smirke has thus summed up the statements of the *Consuetudinarium*, which will be noticed more particularly in the next section. Rents, &c., due "to the king were received by the city, as farmer of the crown dues." (Ibid., p. 83, note 2.) Another statement is contained in the "Verdict," referred to before. (Ibid., vol. vii. p. 376.)

(5) Pp. 893, &c.

added the high-steward, a chamberlain, three cofferers, eight auditors, four sergeants at mace, with the beadle, the bell-man, &c.

The freemen were elected, and were sworn of the guild of merchants. The mayor and aldermen constituted a hall or chamber; the mayor, aldermen, and the Twenty-four were an assembly of the Twenty-four; and a common assembly was composed of the members of the corporation, together with the whole body of freemen. Ordinances were regulations passed in such an assembly. And amongst the payments for certain estates belonging to the corporation, were some made annually to the mayor, and called "chicken money," being in lieu of poultry, or capons, which were a common rent-in-kind in earlier times.

The Reformed Corporation. By the Municipal Corporation Reform Act (5 & 6 Wm. IV. c. 76), and the supplemental acts (6 & 7 Wm. IV. cc. 103, 105, &c.), the offices of mayor, recorder, high-steward, town-clerk, and clerk of the peace, and the six aldermen, were left unchanged; but the six wards were abolished, and three, called after the parishes of St. Thomas, St. Maurice, and St. John, respectively, constituted in their stead; the office of bailiff was abolished, and a council of eighteen was substituted for the Twenty-four Men. The style of the corporate body also was changed from "the mayor, bailiffs, and commonalty" to "the mayor, aldermen, and burgesses of the City of Winchester;" and the time of election to these offices altered to the beginning of November.

There are also ten city magistrates, including the mayor, the ex-mayor, and the recorder, with their clerk; a coroner, who serves with two others for the county as well; a city treasurer, and a chamberlain; two auditors, a city surveyor, with four constables, as many town-sergeants, a city-crier, &c., &c.[1]

The Regalia. The regalia and plate of the corporation are not deserving of special notice. The maces are of silver gilt, and were presented by Charles II. During the war between Charles I. and the Long Parliament, in the year 1643, the corporation sold their plate and sent the proceeds to the King:[2] the plate they now possess is of a later date.

The Revenues. The receipts accounted for by the treasurer consist of the city rate, and the watch rate; quit rents and fee-farm rents; market and fairs' tolls; fines on renewal of leases; cash of the treasury on account of police, maintenance of prisoners, and criminal prosecutions; and miscellaneous sums arising from sale of property, fines, &c.; and the payments are claimed under the heads of salaries, prosecutions, police, miscellaneous, &c. The only charities with which the corporation is now concerned are an annual payment to the Hospital of St. Mary Magdalen, on account of Ebden's charity, and one connected with Owslebury.[3] The total of receipts for the year 1859 was £3115 12s. 2d., and of payments £3161 10s.[4]

(1) Winchester Directory for 1860.
(2) Transcripts, pp. 88, 89.
(3) See above, p. 245, and p. 259, note 7.
(4) Treasurer's account to 1st September, 1859. "The

corporation funds are much diminished; the income derivable from them for the last twenty years averaging only about £152 5s. 5d." The city and watch rates average about 9d. in the pound on the assessed rental of the borough.

The boundaries of the municipal borough are the same as those of the parliamentary borough, already described;[1] and the East and West Soke, which were not within the ancient limits of the city and liberty, now form part of the borough for all municipal purposes.[2] The total amount of the assessments to the borough rates is £47,610 10s. 6d.[3]

Mention has been made of the wait-service, anciently rendered by the tenants of some property belonging to the king in Winchester;[4] and the original duties of the aldermen in their wards have also been spoken of.[5] Before the time of the Municipal Reform Act, the four constables (named above amongst the officers of the corporation) were the chief conservators of the peace. But shortly before the passing of that act,[6] in imitation of London and other towns, an efficient police force was organized here, which has been maintained ever since; and now consists of a superintendent, two sergeants, and ten constables, who are maintained at a yearly cost of about £900.[7]

The Police Station is in High Street, near the eastern entrance of Colebrook Street, and was built for the City Bridewell in the year 1800.[8] The ordinary sittings of the magistrates for the city are held twice a week in the Guildhall, but the quarter-sessions and the assizes are held in the County Hall,[9] as well as the County Court for the City and District of Winchester. The city prisoners are now confined in part of the extensive prison erected for both the city and the county in the years 1846—1849.[10]

---

(1) See above, pp. 12, 13. The boundaries of the ancient borough are given at p. 13.

(2) The East and West Soke still continue to be a manor of the Bishop of Winchester. The municipal constitution of the Soke, before its incorporation with that of the city, may be mentioned here. It consists of the East Soke and the West Soke, in each of which a constable was annually chosen. In the former there were also three tything-men (or aldermen) of St. John's parish, St. Peter's parish, and the Vill of Miltand; and as many in the latter, those of Kingsgate Street (which included the Close, and the parishes of St. Swithin and St. Michael), of Hyde Street, and of Sparkeford. There were two Court Leets, corresponding to the boroughmotes of the city, held annually on the Thursday after Hock Monday (or Easter Monday), and on that after old Michaelmas Day. The ordinary Cheyney Court sat every Thursday, except red-letter days, and was for the recovery of debts of persons living in the liberty. (Hampshire Repository, vol. ii. pp. 305, 306. There is also a list of places in the jurisdiction of this court, pp. 306, 307. See above, pp. 92, 93.)

(3) I am indebted to the town-clerk, C. Bailey, Esq., for this and other information respecting the present condition of the corporation.

(4) See above, p. 289, and note 3.

(5) See above, pp. 275, 276. See also "Transcripts," pp. 122, &c.

(6) "Supplement" to Milner, vol. ii. p. 268.

(7) Yearly account of the corporation for 1859.

(8) See above, pp. 18, 19.

(9) This building will be described subsequently.

(10) The earliest notice of a prison in Winchester occurs in the Liber Winton. (p. 532), where mention is made of "*le balcheus regis ubi latrones ponebantur in prisone,*" in the time of Edward the Confessor, but it had ceased to be a prison in the reign of Henry I. The name, however, survived till Stephen's time, for in the second survey (ibid., p. 543) the "*Balchus*" is named. At a later period we find the custody, or "sergeanty" of the prison or gaol ("*prisona,*" or "*gaiola*") in Winchester,—and, probably, within the castle,—recorded as the service by which the manor of Woodcote, in Bramdean, was held of the king. (Rot. de Oblat., p. 18; Rot. Chart., vol. i. p. 126; Rot. Pat., vol. i. p. 226; Inq. post mortem, p. 137; Inq. ad quod damnum, p. 389; Testa de Nevill, p. 237; Rot. Orig., vol. ii. p. 257; Harl. MS., 2087, fol. 225; &c.) Nigel Fitz-robert was *custos* of the "*carcer*" here, in the 30th of Hen. III. (Rot. Claus. 30 Hen. III. m. 6.) In the beginning of Henry V.'s reign the gaol was in Bridney Street (Tarrages, fol. 16 v°), on the site now occupied by the gas-works; and in the reign of James I. it occupied the same spot, apparently, but with a front towards Jewry Street. (Speed's Map, 1611.) The "prison of the west gate" is mentioned in the time of Edward VI. (Black Book, fol. 76 v°.) In

Paving Commission.

The Paving Commissioners are appointed under an act of parliament obtained in the years 1770 and 1807, and the public convenience is well secured by them at an annual expenditure of about £2000.[1] All the drainage of the lower part of the city is still effected by the ancient watercourses, or brooks, described above;[2] the upper part is kept dry by the great inclination of its surface, and by underground drains of modern construction.[3]

Water supply.

A good supply of water is provided by the Waterworks Company (which was established in 1855), from a well upwards of 200 feet deep, on West Hill, near which are sufficient reservoirs, &c.; and two steam-engines are employed to raise and to distribute the water.

Fire Brigade.

There is a fire brigade, consisting of a director, an engineer, and twenty-five firemen; and the city fire-engines are kept at the Police Station, on the Fair-ground.[4]

The Union Workhouse.

On West Hill, within the original limits of the Arbour, is the Union Workhouse.[5] It is a well-constructed building, with the master's house, chapel, &c., in the centre, and three radiating wings, in which is accommodation for 200 paupers. It was built in 1838, and enlarged twenty years afterwards.

the reign of Henry VIII. the "cayge" was removed to the "market place" (now the Square); and a new "pellory" was made, and set on the "cayge" (ibid. fol. 60 v°). This was most probably on the site of the Mechanics' Institution, where a watchhouse and prison were at a later date. (See above, pp. 18, note 2, 214.)

At the end of the last century there were two considerable county prisons in Winchester, besides the City Bridewell spoken of above, p. 19. (See Godson's Map for the site of this in 1750, when it stood further to the east than the Police Station.) One, called the County Gaol, was in Jewry Street, then called from it Gaol Street. It was built in 1777, and was enlarged about twenty years afterwards. The Museum and Public Library were the governor's house, and part of the north wing yet remains in the house of Messrs. Aylward and Blake. (See above, p. 215.) The other, called the County Bridewell, was erected on the site of Hyde Abbey Church whilst Milner was writing his history. It was taken down in 1850, and its site is now built over. (See Gale's Map.) The Cheyney Court prison was in St. John's Street. (See above, pp. 26, note; 93, note 1.)

The present County and City Prison is a fine structure, covering about six acres on the highest part of West Hill; and was erected between the years 1846 and 1849, at a cost of nearly £75,000. It consists of five wings, connected with the chapel in the centre, and has accommodation for 450 prisoners. The debtors' prison is at the south-west corner of the *enceinte*. The residences of the governor and the chaplain are on each side of the entrance in the Romsey Road; and it is maintained at a yearly cost of about £8000. The head-quarters of the county police are on the east side of this building.

In old time the gallows stood at the northern end of the Barditch (or City Ditch), very near the spot where the railway bridge now crosses the Fulflood Road. (Tarrages, fol. 38v°; Godson's Map.)

The judge's lodgings used to be on the west side of Southgate Street; and the house, which in Godson's Map is called Mr. Sheldon's, is now the head-quarters of the Hampshire Militia. Two hundred years ago they were near the east end of the Penthouse. (See above, p. 161, note 1.)

(1) For facts and regulations respecting the paving of Winchester in the 17th century see "Transcripts," pp. 128—130.　　　　　(2) See above, p. 10.

(3) A sanitary inspector is now appointed under the authority of recent acts of parliament.

In the Black Book, and the Books of Ordinances, are numerous ordinances of a sanitary character. They forbid the throwing of woad into the river by the dyers, the throwing of offal into the brooks by the butchers, &c. (Black Book, fols. 4 v°, 8 v°, &c.; Transcripts, pp. 91, &c.) The Court Rolls contain much curious information on this subject. (See Winchester Vol. of Arch. Assoc., pp. 24, &c.)

(4) For regulations respecting fire in the 17th century, see "Transcripts," pp. 123—130.

(5) The new Winchester Union (which was constituted in September, 1858, under Act 20 Vict. c. 19) consists of the Winchester district (or the borough with Week and Winnall), and the adjacent parishes of Avington, Bishopstoke, Chilcombe, Compton, Crawley, Easton East Stratton, Headbourne Worthy, Hunton, Itchen Abbas, King's Worthy, Littleton, Martyr Worthy, Micheldever, Morestead, Owslebury, Sparsholt, Stoke Charity, Twyford, and Wonston. The old Union (constituted under

During the year 1859 there has been raised at Winchester, under the Act 44 ^{Volunteer Rifle Corps} Geo. III. c. 54, a Volunteer Rifle Corps,[1] under the name of the " First Hampshire Rifle Volunteer Company," which musters about 150 men. The uniform, approved by the Lord Lieutenant, is a grey forage cap with green band and peak, grey patrol jacket with green facings trimmed with black braid, and grey trousers with green stripe; the accoutrements are of black patent leather.

Mention has been made above of the Mints which were in Winchester, from the ^{Town-tokens} reign of Athelstan to that of Henry III.;[2] examples of the coins struck here will be described subsequently,[3] together with the town-tokens, consisting of brass half-pence and farthings, struck by order of the corporation in the year 1669 for circulation in the city, when the coining of similar pieces by private persons was prohibited.[4]

Winchester has been represented in parliament from the 11th of Edward I.;[5] and ^{Parliamentary representation} it has always had two representatives. The nomination takes place in St. John's Rooms, and the voting in the County Hall.[6]

Gilbert's Act) consisted of the city and the seven adjoining parishes; and there was a House of Industry in Lower Brook Street.

(1) Some interesting particulars respecting the Winchester Volunteers of "1793" may be found in both volumes of the Hampshire Repository, under the heading " Army."

(2) See above, p. 267, and notes 5 and 6, and p. 272. In addition to the authorities referred to there, see Winchester Vol. of Arch. Assoc., pp. 285, &c.; and Ruding, vol. i. pp. 359, 360; vol. iv. pp. 260, &c. (For the history of the building spoken of above, p. 267, see Rot. Pat., vol. i. pp. 214, 219, 225.)

(3) See " General Appendix" at the end of Volume III.

(4) Transcripts, pp. 176, 177. See Boyne's " Tokens of the Seventeenth Century" for a full account of these, pp. 104, 105.

(5) " Parliamentary Writs, &c." (published by Record Commiss.), vol. i. p. 16.

(6) The following facts may be added here.

There was a confirmation of the charters in the 10th Edward III., for which ten marks were paid as a fine. (Abbrev. Rot. Orig., p. 108 b. See above, p. 272, and note 5.)

In Elizabeth's reign it would appear that some part of the castle was used as a " House of Correction." (Cott. MS., Vesp. F. ix. p. 277.) And in a plan of encampment near Winchester, in the year 1778 (Add. MS., 15,532), the castle is called the " Goal" or gaol.

THE

TRADE AND MANUFACTURES

OF

WINCHESTER.

Former importance of Winchester.

AT the present day Winchester does not rank amongst the great *emporia*, or centres of trade and commerce; and its manufactures are seldom heard of at a distance; but in former times it was one of the most conspicuous marts in Europe;[1] and one article of its manufacture was sufficiently celebrated to be fancifully referred to as the origin of its name.[2]

Trade in the 11th and 12th centuries.

The *Liber Winton.* supplies us with abundant evidence of the mercantile activity of this city in the eleventh and twelfth centuries.[3] The names of most of the streets[4] were derived from trade: thus High Street was "*Cypping*" (or "*Cyp Strœt*"), the Market; Town Street was "*Snithelinga Strœt*," the street of tailors; Jewry Street was "*Scowertene Strœt*," that of shoemakers; St. Peter's Street was "*Alwarene Strœt*," that of mercers; Parchment Street was "*Flescmangere Strœt*," or that of butchers; and Upper and Lower Brooks were "*Scyldwortene Strœt*" and "*Tannere Strœt*," the streets of shieldmakers and tanners.

Amongst the names of the tenants recorded there (which were all personal, not family, names) we also find the following, which indicate the occupations of those who bore them."[5] In the time of Edward the Confessor there are these—goldsmith,

---

(1) "Perhaps the fair of Beaucaire, in Languedoc, was [the] only rival [of that of St. Giles, Winchester] for several centuries." (Hudson Turner's "Domestic Architecture," pp. 115, &c.)

(2) Wintonia, or Vintonia, *quasi a vino*, wine being once a famous product of Winchester.

(3) It will be sufficient in a note to record, on the authority of Böcking, the latest editor of the "*Notitia Imperii*" (vol. i. pp. 49*, 358*), the earliest authentic mention of the manufacturing industry of Winchester. "*Procurator gynæcii in Britannis, Bentensis.*" But in Monum. Hist. Brit. (vol. i. p. xxiii), instead of "*gynæcii*," or textile manufactory, the word given is "*cynegii*," which means "dog-kennel!" Camden attempts to com-

bine these two most dissimilar readings, in his account of Winchester (Holland's Trans., p. 263); but see Mr. Smirke's observations. (Arch. Journ., vol. ix. p. 84.)

(4) Since the account of the ancient names of the streets given above (pp. 21—23, and notes), fresh evidence of charters, &c., has enabled me to ascertain most satisfactorily that in the time of these surveys, Jewry Street, St. Peter Street, and Parchment Street, were respectively named "*Scowertene*," "*Alwarene*," and "*Flescmangere*" Streets, as I have stated in the text here.

(5) That these were personal, and not family names, appears from the fact that many were patronymic, as "*Elmeressore*" (p. 532), "*Filius Wnstani*" (p. 539);

swordsmith, shoemaker, hosier, seller of herrings, seller of soap, parker, and seller of hay.[1] In the time of Henry I. there are these—tailor, baker, cook, smith, butcher, netmaker, barber, tanner, linen-draper, carver (or embosser), old clothes-seller, washer-woman, &c.[2] In Stephen's time, besides these,[3] we find a long list, including mercer, draper (or cloth seller), weaver, fuller, dyer, furbisher, shieldmaker, leather-dresser, saddler, seller of grease, seller of wax, mason, carpenter, painter, miller, farmer, wine-grower, brewer, innkeeper, jester, writer, parchment-maker, physician, &c.[4]

Not long after the date of the earliest survey in the *Liber Winton.*, in the 31st of Henry I. (or the year 1131), the Pipe Rolls show that the fullers and the weavers were incorporated in guilds; and very soon after the date of the second survey, in the beginning of Henry II. (or after the year 1154), these guilds obtained an extension of their privileges.[5] How long these guilds lasted we do not accurately know, but they were certainly in existence in the fifteenth century, as we find mention made of the swearing in of the four "*magistri*" (or stewards) of the weavers' guild, before the mayor,[6] and of the stewards of the fullers' guild.[7] We also find mention of a fraternity of "*cissores*" (or tailors), who held property on St. Giles' Hill in the year 1348;[8] "of the art of corvesers" (or curriers),[9] and of the "mystery of tapeners," and the "mystery of burillers."[10] All these guilds and fraternities were subordinate to, and possibly included in, the Merchant Guild, which has already been spoken of.[11] *(margin: Trade guilds.)*

It is remarkable, however, that we find no mention of halls belonging to any of these guilds. Instead of this there was the "Drapery," or cloth hall, which was called a guildhall,[12] and the "Chapman's Hall," which originally was the hall for the sale of linen,[13] and is never called a guildhall. *(margin: Guildhalls.)*

others local, as "*de Chainesham*" (p. 534), "*de Esperchefort*" (or Sparkeford, p. 535); and others were derived from peculiarity of character or appearance, as, "*Penipurs,*" "*Penifeder*" (p. 536), "*Blachebiert,*" "*Fulebiert*" (p. 541); whilst in a very great number of instances no such name is given at all.

(1) In the original, "*Aurifaber,*" "*Brandwirchte,*" "*Sutor,*" "*Hosarius,*" "*Harengarius,*" "*Savonarius,*" "*Parcherius,*" and "*Fenarius*" (pp. 531, 534, 536, 538, 541, 542).

(2) In the original, "*Tailator*" and "*Parmentarius,*" "*Pistor,*" "*Coquus,*" "*Faber,*" "*Carnifex,*" "*Casier,*" "*Barbitre,*" "*Taneator,*" "*Napparius,*" "*Tornator,*" "*Scrutarius,*" "*Lavandaria,*" &c. (pp. 531, 533, 535, 539, 541). "*Forgie*" (forges or smithies) are also mentioned (p. 534).

(3) For some of them new terms are used, as "*Bulenger*" for "baker" (p. 553), "*Corduanerius*" for "shoemaker" (p. 542).

(4) In the original, "*Mercerius,*" "*Draperius,*" "*Telarius,*" "*Fullo,*" "*Tinctor,*" "*Furbarius,*" "*Scutarius,*" "*Corvesarius,*" "*Sellarius*" and "*Lorimer,*" "*Unctarius,*" "*Cerarius,*" "*Maconus,*" "*Carpenterius,*" "*Pinctor,*" "*Molendarius,*" "*Fundarius,*" "*Vinetarius,*" "*Brachiator,*" "*Lardinarius,*" "*Joculator*" and "*Sannarius,*" "*Scriba*" and "*Scriniarius,*" "*Parcheminus,*" "*Medicus,*" &c. (pp. 542, &c.) "*Bracinia*" (brewing-plants) and "*ustilia*" (looms) are also mentioned (pp. 553, &c.).

(5) Madox, Hist. Exchequer, pp. 233, 323. The payments made by these guilds, year by year, are recorded in the Pipe Rolls, thus—"*Fullones Wintoniæ reddunt compotum de vi. libris de veteri firma annorum præteritorum, Iidem reddunt compotum de nova firma de ci. libris, &c.*" (ibid., 2nd Edit., vol. i. p. 331.) "*Telarii Wintoniæ reddunt compotum de i marco auri pro gilda sua. Fullones Wintoniæ, &c.*" (Mag. Rot. Pip., printed copy, p. 37.)

(6) Black Book, fols. 22, 31, 32.

(7) Ibid., fol. 39.

(8) Ibid., fol. 44. This property was called "*la Suwerexe.*" (9) Ibid., fol. 31.

(10) *Consuetudinarium,* in Arch. Journ., vol. ix. p. 77.

(11) See above, p. 266, and notes.

(12) See above, p. 267, and notes.

(13) In the Liber Winton. (p. 544) it is called "*seldæ*

It is not improbable that the other trades and crafts in Winchester were held together by some sort of guild-organization, for in an ordinance[1] concerning the observance of the Feast of Corpus Christi, in the year 1435, we find them distinctly marshalled thus:—Carpenters and tilers, smiths and barbers, cooks and butchers, shoemakers, tanners and tapeners, plumbers and silkmen, tailors' serving-men, bakers, fishers and furriers, taverners, weavers, fullers, dyers, chandlers and brewers, mercers.[2]

Modern guilds. Under Elizabeth's charter[3] the incorporation of any arts used here was permitted. Accordingly, on the 19th of September, in the year 1580, the shoemakers and cobblers of Winchester were incorporated into one fraternity, and the tailors and hosiers into another;[4] and at a later date, on the 23rd of March, in the year 1690, two other ordinances incorporated the carpenters and the cordwainers,[5] the latter being most probably the subjects of one of the former ordinances, under a politer name. How long these modern guilds lasted is not recorded.

"Trade protection." But the most curious and interesting facts respecting the trade of Winchester in ancient times are those which exhibit the rigid principles of "protection," whereon all the ordinances relating to it were based. In the *Consuetudinarium*, frequently referred to in the section on the Municipal Institutions of the City, we find a perfectly developed system of regulations, so minute and strict that far from wondering at the irrecoverable decline of trade here, we are rather disposed to marvel that it ever flourished at all. The following are specimens of these harassing restrictions :[6]—

Regulations. No citizen might have burells or chalons[7] woven without the walls, under pain of forfeiting either the goods or their value. None but freemen might weave burells, except that each fuller might make one piece of such cloth yearly, and every weaver ("teler") one, towards the king's ferm. The length and breadth of each piece of cloth was strictly fixed. No tapener might work at night, except from St. Thomas' Feast to Christmas; nor any bureller, except from St. Nicholas' Day to Christmas, under penalties. "Regrating"[8] was vigilantly guarded against.

Any one not a freeman buying skins, or undressed leather, forfeited his purchase; and not even a freeman might take them in the same condition beyond the city

ubi linei panni venduntur ;" in the Pipe Roll the ferm of it is accounted for during the reigns of Henry II., Richard I., and John, under the name of "*Chapmanneshale."* It seems to have stood near the present Police Station.

(1) Black Book, fol. 29. An English version is printed in Mr. Bailey's "Transcripts," pp. 67, 68.

(2) These were no doubt the trades and crafts which were followed most numerously at that time. The "brothers of St. Thomas" and "of St. Anne," and the "wives," took part in the procession. The tilers are called felters in the English copy. After them, Silver Hill was called Felters' Street. (City Muniments over Westgate.)   (3) See above, p. 273.

(4) "Transcripts, &c.," by Mr. C. Bailey, pp. 33, &c.

(5) Municip. Corp. Commiss. Report, 1835, *u. s.*

(6) Arch. Journ., vol. ix. pp. 77, &c.

(7) "Burells" were coarse kinds of linsey-woolsey cloth, and "chalons" were coverlets, so called from "Chalons," in France, where they were originally made.

Trussell, who may have known the meaning of the term he employed, speaks often of the great trade in "capping" carried on here, which Milner, not understanding the word, has interpreted as the manufacture of "men's caps") (vol. i. pp. 157, 200). See also Arch. Journ., vol. ix. p. 84, note 3.

(8) An offence now happily unknown : it was, in this instance, the buying of yarn at the place appointed for the sale of it, before the hour of tierce, for the purpose of selling it again in the city.

liberty.   Before the hour of tierce no fishmonger or poulterer might buy for the purpose of selling again.   Victuals once offered for sale within the city might not be taken out of it for sale without the permission of the bailiff.   "Regrating," or more correctly "forestalling," by buying provisions on their way to the city for sale, was punishable by forty days' imprisonment.

Sellers of beasts were to place their beasts in the paddocks outside Westgate from Michaelmas to St. Nicholas' Day, from morning till high tierce, and afterwards in Minster Street, where they were to stand all the rest of the year.   Every baker was obliged to stamp his bread with a peculiar mark, that he might be made to answer for it if it were not according to "the assise of bread."[1]   And the brewers, or alewives, might not brew except according to the assise of beer.   No one not free of the city might open a shop, or buy, or sell within the city without compounding with the bailiffs.

From the "Black Book of Winchester," and the volumes of Ordinances, many other regulations might be collected, as the following examples will show :— *"Ordinances" relating to trade.*

Butchers and fishmongers were to sell at no other places than those assigned to them ; and no host or innkeeper might suffer fish to be sold in his house, under pain of a fine of forty shillings.[2]   No fishmonger might sell his fish otherwise than in public, nor in summer before six o'clock in the morning, nor in winter before seven o'clock.[3]   Fishmongers not resident in the city were to sell "at the cross opposite the Chequers," others at their old stalls under the western pent-house.[4]   Nine butchers'-stalls, near St. Maurice' Church, were to be let only to persons not belonging to the city.[5]   Mercers, grocers, and haberdashers, were subject to similar restrictions.[6]

Efforts seem to have been made to maintain the old trade in weaving and fulling here : no one might deliver cloth to any one in either of these trades who was not an actual resident in the city, under penalty of fine and forfeiture ;[7] and four masters in the former trade were to be chosen yearly to superintend it in all its departments, with authority to punish disobedience to the regulations ;[8] ancient statutes were revived and put in force, but the tenants of the two fulling mills of the city were excused the payment of any rent because they had no work ;[9] and the weavers complained at length, and in due form, concerning the decay of their trade.[10]   This was in the very first years of the reign of Henry VI., which time may be marked as that of the complete and final downfall of the mercantile prosperity of Winchester.

Hawkers might not offer their wares for sale in the street, or from door to door,

(1) This regulation is based on a charter of the 5th of John.   (Rymer's Fœdera, Rec. Com. Edn., vol. i. p. 88.)

(2) Fols. 4 v° and 14.   (3) Fol. 5.

(4) Fol. 31.   The cross opposite (*quorum* for *coram* ?) the Chequers was the existing market-cross; the "Inn of the Cheker" stood where Messrs. Benny and Hayles' shop now is (Tarrages, fol. 7 v°).   The western "pentice" is called the "Fish Shambles" in the Tarrages (fol. 6),

and was above Jewry Street, on the site of Mr. La Croix' and Mr. Warren's houses.

(5) Fol. 27.   These shambles remained till a very recent period.   (See Wavell, vol. i. p. 91.)

(6) Fol. 31.   (7) Fol. 16 v°.   (8) Fol. 22.

(9) Fol. 23.   The present city mill is one of these.

(10) Fol. 25.   The original (?) document is inserted into the book.

under penalties, but, according to ancient custom, were to stand on the east side of Thomasgate (on the site of the present market-house), and sell there.[1]

Ordinance respecting brewing.

One of the most amusing instances of the operation of the restrictive system of trade which prevailed here belongs to a later date—the reign of Edward VI.[2] In the fourth year of that reign " it was agreid that foreasmuche as Robert Bagge . . . . in time of great derthe and scarsitye, had then plentye and abundance of malte redye in his howse to have byn brewed and made in ale for the releiffe and comforte of the kinge's leige people . . . . and would not brewe the same malte, beyinge a comon brewar . . . . but hathe lefte bruaying utterlie, not onlye to the ill example of the reast of victuallers wth in the citye, but also to the extreme famyshement of the kynge's leige people . . . . it is therefore enacted . . . . upon the rife and mature consideracion of the ungentill and unnaturall behavor of the said Robert Bagg . . . . that [he] shall not from hensforthe be admitted to brewe wth in the citye aforesaid, nother any other to his use, &c."

Charges upon trade.

Besides such regulations as these, every mercantile and manufacturing occupation was subjected to numerous charges, which were amongst the chief sources of revenue to the city.   Thus in the *Consuetudinarium* we find the following : [3]—

" Every great loom for making burells pays five shillings per annum towards the ferm of the city."   " Of the small looms for making chalons each turs [4] loom pays to the city ferm twelve pence, and each single loom six pence."   There is one exception to these charges,—if only one cloth were made in a year the looms were exempted. An apprentice put to work at the loom of a tapener paid ten shillings to the king. And there were customs on fish brought for sale into the city, and on the " pesage " or weighing of wool ; tolls charged at the city gates on wool, cheese, butter, &c. ; corn, iron, &c. ; scythes and sickles, tanned leather, madder, wood, ashes, &c., &c. There were other charges on the sellers of fish and cattle, on butchers, on bakers and sellers of bread.   Tanners who had boards in High Street paid a due called " tangable ;" women retailing lard paid " smergable ;" and shoemakers paid " scogable."   Persons going into, or out of the city, had also to pay a toll at the gates.[5]

Prosperity and decline of Winchester.

It was during the twelfth and thirteenth centuries that this city was numbered amongst the most illustrious seats of trade and commerce in England ; for though it

(1) Fol. 7 v°.

(2) Transcripts, &c., pp. 174, 175.

(3) Arch. Journ., vol. ix. pp. 77, &c.

(4) This Mr. Smirke believes to mean " Turkish loom." (Ibid., p. 85.)   They were used in weaving " great " or " double " chalons.   (Ibid., vol. vii. p. 377.)

(5) These tolls at the gates were not all levied by the city ; those at Eastgate " dyd appertayne " to St. Mary's Abbey, which was situated hard by, on the south side of High Street. (Black Book, fol. 82.) There is preserved in the *Abbreviatio Placitorum* (pp. 147, 148) an account of a dispute respecting these tolls, which affords an amusing picture of the olden time.   It appears that from

time immemorial there were three gates by which the country folks (*homines de patria*) brought to the market their carts and waggons, each of which paid a toll of 1*d.* to the king ; and a fourth gate by which horsemen and foot passengers came to the market.   In the 43rd of Henry III. (or 1259) the prior and monks of St. Swithin's blocked up three gates, so that the king lost the toll.   The sheriff of the county, and the bailiffs of the city, were ordered to remove the obstructions to these gates, but were met by certain monks (amongst them one called Roger le Diable) and lay brothers, in ecclesiastical vestments, with lighted tapers, who publicly excommunicated the royal officers. This having been deposed on oath, it was ordered that all

fell far behind London in the number and magnitude of its trade-guilds,[1] and in its ordinary commerce, being situated on a stream which art had rendered navigable for small craft only,[2] yet it had a foreign trade of its own,[3] and its annual fair on St. Giles' Hill was one of the greatest marts in Europe for every species of merchandise.[4] The existence of a royal residence, with a mint, must also have added greatly to its wealth and importance. It suffered severely in the wars of Stephen's reign, but the increased communications with the continent, occasioned by the extensive possessions of Henry II. in France, enabled it to surmount those disasters. In the barons' wars in Henry III.'s reign it was more completely prostrated, having been sacked by the army of the younger De Montfort, in the year 1262. The trade with France had also greatly declined, in consequence of the weakness and folly of John's policy; the mint was abolished; and the energy of the citizens seems to have been broken so thoroughly, that though parliaments were still held here, and, in appearance, affairs proceeded much as before, it never recovered its high position.[5]

For a short time the prosperity of Winchester was revived by the establishment here of one of the ten great marts for the sale of wool, wool-fells, and leather, by Edward III., in the year 1337;[6] at which time the ground behind St. Peter's Whitebread Church, to the north of High Street, between Snitheling and Bridney Streets, was made the site of the storehouses, &c., required by the staple; and the last-named street has retained the memory of this fact to the present day, being still called Staple Garden.[7] In the year 1363, however, the staple was removed from this place to Calais, and with it departed the last remains of the commercial and manufacturing prosperity and fame of Winchester.[8] *Winchester a staple town.*

The modern trade of Winchester has never been of sufficient importance to dis- *Modern trade.*

---

the lands and tenements of the prior and convent should be taken into the king's hand. (See above, p. 106, for another record of this feud between the city and the priory.)

Some of the customs were commuted in the 8th of Henry VI., in the mayoralty of John Gylmyn, for the encouragement of the city, for a payment of £8 yearly. (Black Book, fol. 28 and v°.)

(1) See above, pp. 266, 267, 285, 286, for an account of the guilds of Winchester; and compare Herbert's "History of the Livery Companies of London."

(2) See below, p. 293.

(3) "*Testes Londonia ratibus, Wintonia Baccho.*" (Henry of Huntingdon, lib. i.; Mon. Hist. Brit., vol. i. p. 693.) And to the same effect says Robert of Gloucester (p. 6, Edit. Hearne),

"At London schippes mest, and wyn at Wyncestre."

There is no doubt that this was (as Milner says, vol. i. p. 200) "claret wine." But that Winchester had some name for producing wine is also certain, for in the low, warm district outside Kingsgate we find a church named "All Saints in the vineyards;" and Wongar, or Wunegre,

Street (see above, p. 21, and note 4), where in the time of Stephen lived at least one "*vinetarius,*" or wine-maker, seems to derive its designation from this manufacture.

(4) See below, p. 292.

(5) The historical facts referred to in this paragraph will be found in a subsequent section, entitled "Annals of Winchester."

(6) Stats. of 27 Edw. III. (Stat. at large, vol. i. pp. 275, &c.), 28 Edw. III. c. 14, 43 Edw. III. c. 1; Henry de Knyghton's Chronicle (Savile), p. 2626; Pauli's Geschichte von England, 4to. Band, Ss. 352, 353; Milner, vol. i. pp. 218, 219; Wavell, vol. ii. pp. 86, 87.

(7) See above, p. 23, and note 2.

(8) The seal of the staple of Winchester, like that of the other staples, is circular in form, and 1·8 inches in diameter; it exhibits a shield suspended by a *guige*, with the arms of England, and two dragons as supporters, surrounded by the *Leg.*: ✶ SIGILL ✶ EDWARDI ✶ REGIS ✶ ANGL' ✶ APVD ✶ WYNTON. The counter seal, of the same form and diameter, has the three lions passant guardant, of England, and the *Leg.*: ✶ PRO ✶ LANIS ✶ ET ✶ COREIS ✶ LIBERANDIS.

tinguish it.   An attempt was made in the latter part of the last century to set up a silk manufactory in Colebrook Street, but it did not succeed, and was finally given up.[1]   At present all that distinguishes it from an ordinary provincial town, in this respect, are the steam breweries in Little Minster, St. Swithin's, and Eastgate Streets;[2] the flax-mills in Lower Brooks;[3] with the malting houses in Hyde Street;[4] the greater extent of some of the warehouses, and particularly the provision warehouses;[5] and the existence of six printing offices, in one of which a weekly newspaper, the *Hampshire Chronicle*, is printed.[6]

Markets and Market-place.   High Street itself was the first market-place,[7] and from the earliest times to the reign of Henry VI. the market day was Sunday.[8]   But we find that this was insufficient for the wants of the place, and that the citizens, without licence, availed themselves of any void plot of ground near the principal street to hold other markets in.   Thus, in the reign of Henry I., they used the ground not far from Westgate,[9] on the north side of the street, near the hall of the Knights' Guild, which stood there; and, afterwards, the site of the New Minster, now the Cathedral Yard or Cemetery.[10]   Before the time of Henry VI. another market was established on Fridays, but we have found no trace of its commencement.   This king, by charter, abolished both the Friday and the Sunday market, and appointed that which still continues

---

(1) Milner, vol. ii. p. 49.

(2) These breweries are now carried on by Messrs. Russ & Co., Messrs. Dear & Co., and Messrs. Round & Son.   The first named firm has agents in London.

(3) Messrs. Yates and White are the proprietors of these mills.

(4) Belonging to Messrs. Simonds & Co., Mr. Dear, Mr. Vokes, and Mr. Wyeth.   There are other malting houses in Winchester; in Southgate Street those of Messrs. R. and G. Barnes, and Mr. W. Moody, and some others in the Soke.

(5) Particularly those of Messrs. Aylward and Blake, Messrs. Benny and Hayles, Messrs. Hutchinson and Ewens, and Messrs. Wright and Eames.

(6) This newspaper is printed at the office of Messrs. Jacob and Johnson, in High Street, who are the principal booksellers in the city also: two other printing offices, those of Mr. N. Warren and of Mr. Barclay, have produced some highly creditable book-work.   Mr. Warren is a bookseller also.   The other noteworthy booksellers' shops are those of Mr. Pamplin, in Jewry Street, and Mr. Prouten and Mr. Tanner, in High Street.   The bookseller to the college is Mr. D. Nutt, in College Street.

For other particulars of the present trade of Winchester consult the Winchester Directory, published yearly; and the Post Office Directory, or White's Directory, for Hampshire.

(7) In two Saxon charters it is called "*Cypstræt*" (Cod. Dipl., No. 1291), and "*Cypping*," which is interpreted "*politana nundinationis platea*" (No. 720). In the Liber Winton. the term market-place is especially

applied to the part of the street near the cross (p. 534); but the market-place extended eastward below St. Maurice' Church (see above, p. 287, note 5), and westward as far as Staple Garden Lane (see above, p. 287, note 4).

(8) Besides the evidence of Henry VI.'s charter, we have that of the Liber Winton., which, speaking of dues to the king on account of certain shambles, on the site of the old prison, says (p. 532), "*in illa eadem terra manent viii carnifices, unde præpositus solebat habere unaquaque dominica die viii d.*"

Sunday-trading was, however, very strictly forbidden at a later period.   "*Mandatum Episcopi quod barbitonsores non radant, vel tondeant, aut domum apertam teneant diebus dominicis: item, quod alutarii . . . . se abstineant et shopas suas clausas teneant:—monitio ne mercatores teneant shopas apertas . . . .:—item, ne exerceant mercata . . . .*" (From Mr. Alchin's Index to Reg. II. Wykeham, fols. 253, and vº, 329, &c.)   Butchers might sell till eight o'clock on Sunday morning, and were then to remove all their meat to the interior of their shops, under a penalty of 40s.   (Black Book, fol. 26 vo.)

Other regulations relating to this subject will be found in Mr. Bailey's "Transcripts," pp. 69, &c.

(9) "*Apud iii*ᵉˢ *monasterios allevatum est mercatum, quod non fuit ibi T. R. E. et est super terram abbatis*" (p. 533).   In the Rot. Canc. of the 3rd of John, or 1201, (p. 255), the *Hordarius* of Winchester acknowledges the receipt of 20 marks, and 5 marks instead of a palfrey, for the establishment of a market there.

(10) This was in Edward III.'s time.   (Charters in Cathedral Library.)

to be held on Saturday.[1]   Another market has been held on every Wednesday from the time of Henry VII., at latest.[2]

The cross, which was used till late times as a market-cross, has been described above, with the pent-house, which was employed in a similar manner.[3]   Mention has also been made of the " western pent-house," or fish-shambles,[4] and of the shambles near Godbegot, and in other parts of High Street.[5]   The last of these market-places was disused on the erection of the Market-House, on the eastern side of Market Street, in the year 1772,[6] which building was enlarged, and completely rebuilt in the year 1857, during the mayoralty of Charles Wright, Esq., as the inscription under the *campanile* records.[7]

The Cross, Pent-house, and Market-house.

Of the new Corn Market, with the Cattle Market behind it, mention has already been made :[8] before the Exchange was built, this market was held on the site of the Mechanics' Institution.[9]   The market held outside Westgate during the visitation of the plague, in 1669, has also been noticed.[10]

Corn and Cattle Market.

The fairs of importance at the present day are one for sheep and horses, held on the first Monday in Lent; one for sheep alone, on October the 23rd; and the Cheese Fair, held on the Fair-ground, and along the lower part of High Street,[11] on October the 24th.   These fairs were granted to the city by Elizabeth's charter.[12]

Fairs.

St. Giles' Fair was in ancient times one of the greatest in Europe.   The origin of it, according to Warton,[13] was a grant by William the Conqueror, to Bishop Walkelyn and his successors, of a fair for one day, on the feast of St. Giles (September the 1st), to whom the chapel on this hill was dedicated.   " William Rufus extended it to three days, Henry I. to eight, Stephen to fourteen, and Henry III. to sixteen days."[14]

St. Giles' Fair.

(1) Rot. Chart., 27-39, Hen. VI., n. 36.

(2) Black Book, fol. 45 v°.

(3) See above, p. 17.   (4) See above, p. 287.

(5) See above, pp. 17, 18.   In one of the yearly rolls amongst the city muniments (for 1470), Godbegot is called the " Metehall," and the entrance to St. Peter's Street, " Bocherrowe."

(6) Milner, vol. ii. p. 216 ; Wavell, vol. ii. p. 153. See above, p. 18, for a notice of this market-house (which was standing when that part of my work was prepared) ; it did not extend far back from High Street.

(7) This new market-house extends southward to the road behind Morley's College, and for a short distance along it eastward.   It has a handsome front towards High Street, in the Roman-Doric style, with a square *campanile* over the central compartment, surmounted by a weather vane.   It was opened for public use on the 3rd of October, 1857.   Market Street was considerably widened at this time.

(8) See above, p. 22.   The cattle market, in earlier times, was outside Westgate, and in Minster Street, or probably between Kingsgate and Little Minster Street. (See above, p. 287 ; Arch. Journ., vol. ix. pp. 72, 78.)

(9) See above, pp. 18, 214; Trussell, fol. 73 v°.   See

Godson's Map ; Wavell, vol. ii. p. 55, note.   It would appear from some ancient records (Black Book, fol. 29 v°, &c.) that a general market used to be held on the site of the square.

(10) See above, pp. 261, 262.

(11) It was formerly held in the upper part of High Street, before the present Fair-ground was formed.

(12) Milner, vol. ii. p. 303 ; Wavell, vol. ii. p. 105. They were originally granted for the feast of St. Edward (Oct. 13), with the day before and after it ; and for the Monday and Tuesday of the first week in Lent.   Henry VI., in the charter mentioned above (p. 290), granted the city a fair for the vigil and feast of St. Swithin, and the following eight days, which was confirmed by Elizabeth, but restricted to three days in all.   Moody, in his " Notes and Essays " (p. 33), says that this fair has not been held for many years.

(13) Hist. of English Poetry (Ed. 1840), vol. ii. pp. 55, 56, and note ; Milner, vol. ii. p. 229.

(14) Lit. Claus., vol. i. p. 123.   Sometimes the traders would fain have extended their stay on St. Giles' Hill, but the bishop was strict in preventing it.   (Reg. Pontiss., fol. 29.)

Gale refers to the Exchequer Rolls, 23 Edw. III.,

During the time of this fair the shops in the city were closed, and the transaction of business was strictly prohibited in Southampton, and in every place within the distance of seven leagues from the fair.[1] The mayor, on St. Giles' eve, surrendered the keys of the gates at which the tolls were collected by the city to the bishop's deputy, who retained them till the end of the fair, and collectors were appointed to levy the customs on all merchandise brought for sale. The proceeds were received by the bishop, but portions were allotted to the priory, to Hyde Abbey, to St. Mary Magdalen Hospital, &c.[2]

St. Giles' Hill.   The summit of St. Giles' Hill, now mere down or poor ploughed land, was covered with a town of shops or stalls, some of them temporary, but others of the most solid construction.[3] They were laid out in streets, and we hear of French Street, Flemings' Street, the stalls of the men of Caen, the streets of the men of Bristol, Nottingham, of Cornwall, and of other towns, &c., in England; there were also the Goldsmithry, the Drapery, the Pottery, the old clothes stalls, St. Swithin's Spicery, &c., &c.[4] For the preservation of order a court, called the " *Papilio*," or " *Pavilo* " (for it originally sat in a tent), with officers of its own, was appointed.[5] And the customs of the fair were digested into a " *Consuetudinarium*," which may still be seen in the registers of the diocese.[6]

The importance of this fair naturally culminated with the erection of Winchester into a staple town; and the reign of Henry VI., which was the period of the visible decline of the city, witnessed also the decline of the fair.[7] It is now held on September the 12th (St. Giles' Day, o.s.), chiefly as a cheese fair, but will soon in all probability be completely discontinued.[8]

pars 2, m. 42; 2 Edw. III., *pars* 1, m. 16 *dorso.*; and Rot. Pat., 2 Hen. VI., for several particulars relating to this fair. See also Rot. Chart. 11 Edward II. n. 85. The last charter was granted by Henry VIII. in 1511. (Warton, *u. s.*)

(1) Henry II. (Madox, Hist. Exchequer, p. 251) ordered the purchase of a robe, and of silver utensils for the queen's chapel, at Winchester Fair; and King John (Lit. Claus., vol. i. p. 91) gave orders for the purchase of wax, pepper, and cummin against the winter, at London, or at Winchester Fair.

(2) Warton (*u. s.*) says that in 1471 the receipts of the bishop amounted to £45 18*s.* 5*d.* See Rot. Claus., 10 Edw. II. m. 26, for the share of the prior of St. Swithin's. Safe-conducts were granted to those who visited the fair. (Lit. Pat., vol. i. p. 74; see also Warton, *u. s.*)

There were, of course, frequent collisions between the bishop and the authorities of Winchester, and the men of Southampton, respecting this fair, and the bishop did not find it at all times easy to maintain these extensive privileges. (Abrev. Placit., p. 158; Reg. Pontiss., fols. 195, 196, 201 v°, 202 v°; Reg. Stratford, fols. 62 b, 63 b, 84; Reg. I. Waynflete, fol. 2*, *et seq.*) The citizens of London were somewhat disinclined to submit to the claims

of the bishop, but were compelled. (See Letter Book H., fol. 18, Guildhall, London.)

(3) Cartulary of St. Denys' Priory, Brit. Mus. Add. MS. 15, 314 (fols. 116, &c.); Hudson Turner's Domest. Archit. of England, pp. 115 to 117. The appearance of the fair-ground at Weyhill resembles this. The hackneyed line of Piers Plowman associates the fairs at Weyhill and Winchester.

(4) Ibid., ibid. Warton and Milner, *u. s.*

(5) Reg. I. Orlton, fol. 37 b; Reg. II. Wykeham, fol. 360 b; Reg. I. Waynflete, fol. 4*. For the appointment of bailiffs and *custodes* of the fair, see Lit. Claus., vol. i. pp. 620, 621, 632, 645, 655. See also Letter Book E., fol. 195, in the Guildhall, London.

(6) Reg. Pontiss., fol. 195 v°. See also Cott. MS., Titus A. viii. p. 60 b.

(7) Warton and Milner, *u. s.*

Moody (Notes and Essays, p. 30) observes that this fair used to be frequented by persons who would come " many miles to it, for the purpose of eating roast pork for the first time " in the season.

(8) A curious relic of this famous fair has been discovered quite recently [1860] on the brow of the hill overlooking the city. It is a strong and ornamentally

In consequence of the decline of this fair, that of St. Mary Magdalen's (or Morn) Hill (as it seems) arose.[1] It is still held on the festival of St. Mary Magdalen (o.s.), or the 2nd of August, for the sale of cheese and country produce; but it is not of any importance now, although in Milner's time it was "by far the most considerable of all the fairs held in the neighbourhood of Winchester."[2] *Magdalen Hill Fair.*

Winchester appears to have enjoyed the advantages of an artificial navigable river from very early times. In a Saxon charter of the eleventh century, we find mention of the "new river;"[3] but it is certain that Bishop de Lucy is to be regarded as the original constructor of the navigable stream which now exists, for in the charter granted by John to that prelate, "*de consuetudinibus capiendis pro mercandisis venientibus Wintoniam per aquam de Ichene,*"[4] occurs this expression in explanation of the latter part of the title, "*per trancheam quam dictus Winton. Episcopus fecit fieri.*"[5] The decline of the trade of Winchester caused this canal to be so completely neglected, that when the condition of the city began to revive under the favour of Charles II., it was necessary in good part to reconstruct it; which was done by a company of "undertakers," under authority of an act of parliament. A new act of parliament was procured by the Winchester merchants in the year 1767, by which "the navigation was effectually thrown open to the public."[6] It is now but little used, and is deeply mortgaged, so that it scarcely pays its working expenses. *The navigable river.*

Since the year 1839 Winchester has been connected with Southampton by means of one portion of the London and South-western Railway, which was completed and opened in the month of June; and in May, 1840, the line was opened to London. *The Railroad.*

Between Winchester and London many contests respecting the privileges accorded by their early charters occurred; and more than one arrangement was rendered necessary. The earliest on record are those of the 27th and 32nd of Edward I.; another took place in the 10th of Henry IV.[7] *Compositions regarding customs, &c.*

---

wrought-iron chain, for suspending barrels from a crane, and it is provided with a swivel for more convenient use.

(1) "No mention of it has been discovered in ancient records" (Milner, vol. ii. p. 232, and note).

(2) Ibid. Godson's map, which takes no notice of St. Giles' Hill Fair, gives, according to the custom of that time, a representation of Magdalen Hill Fair as being held opposite the site of the hospital, and marks on the spot a building called "the Fair House."

(3) This charter contains the grant of eight hides at Stanham to St. Swithin's Priory (see above, p. 134, and note 15) in the year 1045, by Edward the Confessor; and in the land-limits occurs this, which shows what the "new river" was—"*of thære ealdan Icenan on ufwyrd thonæ orcerd on tha niwan ea,*" which signifies, "from the *old* Itchen upward to the orchard on the *new* river." (Cod. Dipl., No. 776.)

(4) Reg. Pontiss., fols. 201 and vᵒ. I have the pleasure of acknowledging my obligation to the late Rev. W. H. Gunner for a copy of this charter, which he discovered in Pontissera's register. Trussell found a copy of it amongst the municipal records. See Milner, vol. i. p. 173, and vol. ii. p. 301.

(5) See above, pp. 2, 3, and note 4, and 27.

(6) 16 & 17 Car. II. priv. pet. 13. It was an act for "making divers rivers navigable," and applied to the Test, and the Hamble, as well as to the Itchen. See Milner, vol. ii. pp. 31, 46, 47, and notes.

In Mr. Bailey's "Transcripts" (pp. 86—88) is a copy of a memorial addressed by the city to the Marquis of Winchester, and the other noble and dignified persons belonging to the county, concerning this navigation, and dated 15th Nov., 1660. Another petition, addressed to the Treasury, is also printed there (pp. 89, 90).

(7) The first of these was an "*Allocatio per breve regis,*" and will be found in the Muniments of the Guildhall, London, Letter Book C., fol. 30. The next was a "*Compositio inter cives Wyntoniæ et cives Londoniæ,*" and is contained in the same record, fol. 81. It is also to be found in Trussell, fols. 104 vᵒ, 105; and (printed)

City gates.

Winchester has retained two of its six gates to the present day,[1] the others were removed for the purpose of facilitating access to the market. North-gate and South-gate were removed in 1771;[2] East-gate not till about 1780.[3]

Winchester weights and measures.

The use of the Winchester measure was abolished by the acts of parliament 5 Geo. IV. c. 74, and 6 Geo. IV. c. 12, by which the imperial measure was substituted for it; and the standard weights and measures, which were formerly preserved with the civic muniments, are now placed in the City Museum.[4]

Tradesmen's tokens and signs, and merchants' marks.

The tradesmen of Winchester do not appear to have issued any tokens at the end of the last, or the beginning of the present, century. And the use of signs by tradesmen seems to have been very rare; so much so, that many more are now exhibited in High Street than we have any record of in earlier times:[5] whilst of merchants' marks only one is known, and for the discovery of that we are indebted to accident alone.[6]

Inns and hostelries.

In the Black Book of Winchester,[7] and the Tarrages,[8] we find mention made of the inns and hostelries of the middle ages—such as the " New Inn of Marke le Fayre" (now the George); the " Cheker," and the "Tabard" (opposite the Cross); the " Starre," afterwards the "Kingshed" (opposite the Penthouse); the "Bell" (now the Bell and Crown); the " Hart" (at the entry of Little Minster Street, recently converted into shops), &c. At the present time the principal hotels are the Royal Hotel, the George, and the Black Swan; the Market Inn, the White Swan, the Eagle, &c., are frequented principally on market and fair days.

in Wavell, vol. ii. pp. 79, 80. The third was a " *Compositio*" also, and occurs in Letter Book I., fol 75; the Black Book, fols. 5 vᵒ, 6 vᵒ; and (printed) in Mr. Bailey's "Transcripts," pp. 2—6; and Winchester Vol. of Arch. Assoc., pp. 26, 27.

A composition with the men of Southampton is recorded in the Black Book, fol. 19.

(1) See above, pp. 14, 25. All except Durngate may be seen standing in Buck's " East View of the City."

(2) Transcripts, pp. 9, 10.

(3) I am thus informed by Mr. Moody. Milner (vol. ii. p. 226) speaks of it as having been recently removed when he wrote.

(4) See above, p. 215; Wavell, vol. ii. p. 117. Milner's miscellaneous plate (original edition) represents the most remarkable of these relics.

In the " Laws of King Edgar" (Ancient Laws, &c., of England, vol. i. pp. 270, 271), under the head, " Of Money and Measures," is this injunction—" let one measure and one weight pass, such as is observed at London, and at Winchester."

(5) Near St. Lawrence' Church, but apparently under the pent-house, was a " litle" shop, named in the Tarrages, "Bolehall of the French" (fol. 12), and " Bell-

hall" (fly-leaf), and in the yearly rolls of the city, " Bullehall," which from the Black Book (fol. 76) appears to have been a shop with the sign of the bull stretched from it over the roadway; and in the same book (fol. 37) a great house in High Street is said to have been called " *le Cristofore*." We also meet with frequent mention of a house in Silver Hill called " Whales' bone."

(6) The most careful search I have been able to make has not discovered on spandrel or keystone of doorway, on beam end, glass quarry, tombstone, or even on seal appended to deed or charter, a single merchant's mar. ; but last autumn [1859], in the Lawn, a massive silver ring, engraved with a merchants' mark between the initials H and A, was accidentally dug up. It is now in the possession of the Rev. C. Collier, Principal of the Diocesan Training School, at Wolvesey. I am encouraged by this discovery to hope that others may yet be found. But I account for the extreme paucity of them by the fact that Winchester had ceased to be a place of mercantile eminence before these trade-marks came into general use.

(7) Fols. 13, 18 vᵒ, 31, 71, 75 vᵒ, &c.

(8) Fols. 6, 8, 13 vᵒ, &c. See above, pp. 15, and note 6, 16, &c.

THE

KING'S HOUSE, AND THE CASTLE;

THE THEATRE, &c.

———•———

THE most conspicuous public building within the municipal limits of Winchester The Barracks. is the noble structure at its south-western angle, now called the Barracks, but formerly known as the King's House, which occupies the site of the ancient castle of the Norman kings.[1]

It is extremely difficult to ascertain the original plan of this castle, for we have The Castle; only Speed's small bird's-eye view of the city[2] to guide us; and the condition of the area, and of its immediate vicinity on both sides, has been so greatly altered by the erection of the King's House, and the conversion of that palace into barracks,—by the closing of Bowling-green (or Gar) Street, and the excavation of the railway cutting,—that the only parts of the castle now remaining are its fine hall, with the foundation of a tower below it, and the eastern slope of the great artificial mound on which the royal fortress was built.[3]

This mound was almost three hundred yards long, from north to south; and from —its walls and ditches; east to west, at its greatest breadth, rather less than one hundred yards across.[4]

(1) The most valuable contribution to the history of this castle is Mr. Smirke's paper on "The Hall and Round-table at Winchester," contained in the Winchester Vol. of the Arch. Instit. Milner has given (vol. ii. pp. 193—208) a very full account of it, but, unhappily, he did not avail himself of an opportunity which he had of constructing a good plan of the ruins and foundations which existed in his time; giving us instead a *restoration* of the castle, and some not very correct or intelligible details on his general plan of the city.

(2) In the corner of his map of "Hantshire."

The coloured MS. plan of the city in the British Museum (Add. MS. 11,564) is nothing but an ornamental copy of this plan by Speed. Godson's map, according to the custom of the last century, gives a bad view of the King's House and the hall, and merely notifies the existence of the ruins at the southern end of the area. Only Milner's plan gives any details of the castle,

and his are manifestly incorrect in some important details.

(3) Part of the donjon wall must have been removed even to the foundation when the south wing of the King's House was built. The erection of the various accessories to the barracks has removed many other remains, both at the north and at the south end of the mound. The outer side of the ditch next the city, and to the south, has been levelled; the western ditch was filled up, and the whole area levelled to form a parade ground when the railway was made; and an ascent from within Westgate has been formed by the filling up of the ditch there; but it is probable that a postern gate was constructed there at an early period, if not when the castle was first built.

The materials of the mound were derived in good part from the great ditch all round it.

(4) Measured on Gale's and Godson's maps, compared with Milner, vol. ii. p. 202.

Towards the north it grew gradually narrower, till the eastern and western walls of the castle met at an acute angle ; but the southern end of the mound was broad, and the plan of the walls was very nearly rectangular.[1]   It was surrounded on all sides by a ditch, which was more than thirty yards wide, and as many deep, and reached nearly to Westgate at the northern end.[2]   The line of the eastern wall did not deviate greatly from that of the old city wall, which on this side of Westgate, most probably, originally corresponded (as far as the ground would permit) with that on the north side of it.[3]   And it appears that the south wall of the city was prolonged beyond its original termination, till it joined the south-western tower of the castle.[4]

—its two baileys ;

There were two *ballia* (or baileys), the inner one (called the "*donjon*"[5]) was the smallest, and was bounded by a wall from south-west to north-east (with, perhaps, a ditch beyond it), cutting off the southern extremity of the area.   The entrance was (apparently) through a tower in the middle of this wall, and perhaps by a draw-bridge.   The great gate of the castle, protected by two towers,[6] was in the western side of the outer *ballium* (called the "upper bailey" or "sheriffs' ward"),[7] and there was a barbican opposite it, on the outer side of the ditch,[8] reached by a swing bridge (*pons turneicius*) ;[9] and there was a postern, or sallyport, on each side of this lower *ballium*, not far from its northern extremity.[10]

Many alterations in the walls, towers, and other buildings must have occurred at

(1) Speed's and Gale's maps.

(2) Measured on Gale's and Godson's maps, compared with Milner, vol. ii. p. 203. This was not naturally nor necessarily a water ditch. Milner's opinion, based upon Trussell's statement, is opposed by the existence of the chapel in the ditch outside Westgate, and by the fact that in Elizabeth's reign (as will appear shortly) the ditch all round the castle was let for grazing. Nevertheless, it could be turned into a water ditch, for in Rot. Lib., 25 Hen. III. (quoted in Turner's "Domestic Architecture," pp. 198, 199), we find an order to have the ditch "prepared and flooded." The Tarrages also (fol. 33 v°.) speak of the ditch to the south of Westgate as being "sometimes a garden, but now a water ditch ;" and the late Mr. Hutchinson, Mayor of Winchester, told me that there were hatches by which water could be kept in the ditches, or let off, at pleasure.

(3) See Speed's plan. There is no reason to doubt that before the castle was built the west end of the city retained the form of the original Roman parallelogram.

(4) See Speed's, Godson's, and Britton's plans. Milner's plan does not agree with the data supplied by Godson in this particular, for he has turned the wall by a sudden curve to the north, and connected it with the south-eastern tower of the castle.   In Rot. Lib., 40 Hen. III., quoted by Mr. Turner (pp. 246, 247), is an order "to complete the town wall to a [particular] tower."

(5) Smirke, p. 57 ; Turner, p. 254.

(6) This, however, was not the original entrance, for

the Liberate Roll of 25 Hen. III. (quoted by Turner, pp. 198, 199) speaks of "the works of the new gateway, &c.," and orders the old gateway to be pulled down.

(7) "Shirreveswarde" and "*Warda Vicecomitis.*" Ibid., ibid., and pp. 77, 78.

(8) Milner (vol. ii. p. 202, note *) quotes from Warton the Pipe Roll of Hen. III. in proof of this, "*porta et birbeca in castro Wintoniensi.*" Smirke, p. 72, "*Camera ultra portam castri.*" But we also read of the "path between the castle gate and the barbican." (Turner, p. 247.)

(9) Smirke, p. 72.

(10) Mr. Smirke has given a plan, with sections, of the passages connected with this sallyport at p. 55 of his Essay ; and a plan now in the Grand Jury Chamber of the hall shows the exact situation of them.   They were constructed in the thickness of a wall, which seemed to be of very ancient work ; the descent was from the south, and one branch passed through the foundations of a semicircular tower to the north-west ; the other, at right angles to the descent, led to an opening in the eastern ditch. There were "arrangements for strong doors, bars, &c.," for closing these passages ; "the masonry is very excellent ; the vaulting constructed with a slightly pointed arch ; the whole is in the style of the early part of the thirteenth century." (Arch. Instit., Winchester Vol., p. xviii.) Milner apparently (vol. ii. p. 203) knew of the descent to this sallyport. See also the addendum to the last edition of Milner, vol. ii. p. 208.

different periods, the evidences of which are to be found in the records,[1] and in the ancient foundations of the castle wherever they have been explored;[2] and, in consequence of this, as well as on account of the imperfection and vagueness of the evidence, it would be in vain to attempt any detailed description of it.

At one angle (perhaps the north-western) of the inner *ballium* was the keep, called the "great tower,"[3] which seems to have had a ditch between it and the bailey.[4] There were towers also at the other corners, and close beneath the walls were buildings of a domestic character. In the outer *ballium* stood the great hall, which is still in existence, and must (after this general survey) be described in detail; and domestic buildings, with the various offices, stables, &c., were ranged along the walls, or at the end of the hall; and there was one tower at the northern end, one between it and the gate, and one behind the hall.[5]

We read of four chapels within the castle, dedicated to the Blessed Virgin Mary (called the "great chapel"), St. Thomas the Martyr, St. Judocus, and St. Catharine; there were also chapels of the king and queen, but these may have been some of those four chapels, or mere oratories.[6] Besides the chambers of the king and queen, were others called "*camera picta*," and "*camera Rosamundæ*," "*camera ubi rex natus fuit*," &c.[7]

—its keep, towers, chapels, &c.

(1) Smirke, pp. 66, 68; Turner, pp. 188, 198, 199, 209, 210, 213, 214, 218, 221, 246, 247, 255, 256; Parker's "Domestic Architecture," from Edw. I. to Rich. II., pp. 83, 109, 110.

(2) See the drawing in Grand Jury Chamber of the hall, which shows the foundations discovered when the inclined roadway from High Street to the hall was last thoroughly repaired. Traces of walls of two periods, and on two different plans, are shown; the earliest consisting of a wall with a small semicircular tower, and the sallyport spoken of in p. 296, note 10, under it; and the later of a strong square tower, standing without any relation to the earlier work, except perhaps the sallyport. Milner (see his plan of Winchester) seems to have known of these foundations; he also saw other remains and foundations at the southern end of the castle, and he says (vol. ii. p. 203) that both the north-east and south-east towers "had been altered into a circular, or rather into an oval, form."

(3) Smirke, pp. 75, 76. It seems also sometimes to have been called the "donjon" (Turner, p. 254). Milner notes (vol. ii. p. 203) the greater size of this tower, and adds that it had a "terrace adjoining to it on the inside."

(4) Ibid., p. 75. "*Pons turnerius in introitu magnæ turris.*" Turner (p. 231) quotes from Rot. Lib., 35 Hen. III., an order to "repair the ditch between the great tower and the bailey." There is an order (ibid., pp. 248, 249) from the same records, 41 Hen. III., to "rebuild the great tower, which threatens to fall."

(5) Mr. Smirke's Essay, Speed's plan, and the construction of mediæval castles generally may be referred to

for evidence of most of these statements. See also the plan in the Grand Jury Chamber. The base of the tower at the eastern end of the hall is still to be seen.

(6) Mr. Smirke (pp. 50, 51) remarks that these four chapels only are found in the records of Henry II. to Henry III., inclusive, and adds, "Chapels of the king and queen are occasionally noticed distinctly from the others, but they were evidently oratories for private devotion. Whether they were in fact only portions of the above-named chapels, or were annexed to the private apartments of the palace is not very clear, nor very important."

The chapel of St. Judoc (which was near the great gate of the castle, Turner, p. 231) had originally an apsidal chancel, which was taken down in the 21 Hen. III., and rebuilt in a square form. (Smirke, p. 74.) The minute particulars respecting the construction, ornamentation, and furniture of these chapels, to be found in the extracts relating to them, are exceedingly interesting and instructive.

"The chaplains of St. Mary and St. Thomas received each 50s. per annum . . . . out of monies in the sheriff's hands. The two other chaplains also received small salaries or stipends. The chaplain of St. Judoc was sometimes paid by the citizens, who were then allowed to deduct the payment out of their fee-farm rent" (ibid., pp. 50, 51; see also pp. 69—77; Turner's "Domestic Architecture," pp. 138, 198, 199, 209, 210, 212, 215, 216, 218, 221, 228, 240, 242, 243, 246—249, 255, 256; and J. H. Parker's "Domestic Architecture," from Edw. 1. to Rich. II., p. 83).

(7) Smirke, pp. 57, 69—76. These chambers were almost all painted, and had glass windows, and chimneys,

Some of the towers were called " King's Tower," "*turris Judaeorum*," "St. Catharine's Tower," " Manesiestour," &c.[1]   There was a "*gaiola*" or prison[2] here, and an alms-house ;[3] within the castle walls, also, were more than one " *herbarium*" or garden ;[4] and there were probably two or three wells.[5]   The mews or " hawkheys"[6] in the " Parrok" (or park), which occupied very nearly the site of the present railway-station, was an appurtenance of the castle.

The Great, or County Hall;   Of all these numerous structures one only remains, the great hall of the castle,[7] which, notwithstanding the lapse of so many ages, and the occurrence of so many changes since it was first erected, preserves to a remarkable extent its original characteristics.   It stood, as we have seen, in the outer bailey, adjoining the eastern wall, and nearer the north than the south end of it.[8]   Its length, which lies nearly due east and west, is rather more than a hundred and eleven feet (internal measurement), and its width almost fifty-six feet.[9]   It is divided longitudinally by two rows of elegantly clustered columns (four on each side) into a central portion and two aisles ; each side is lighted by five windows, and there are windows, just under the gable, in each end.   There were originally two entrances under the second windows from the east end, close to the first buttresses.[10]

and various conveniences. There was a cellar beneath the queen's chamber (p. 74). Milner (vol. ii. p. 195 and notes) is not certain whether " Rosamund's Bower," mentioned in some of the notes to Warton's " Hist. of English Poetry," and stated there to be " *in castro Wintoniæ*," was in the castle, or in the supposititious palace in the north-west corner of the city. In his historical part (vol. i. p. 166, and note) he not only states that it was *not* in the castle, but ascribes the building of it to Henry II., although his authority distinctly attributes it to Henry III. (See above, p. 23, note 5.) There are many interesting details respecting the plan, construction, &c., of mediæval domestic buildings contained in the extracts from the records collected by Mr. Smirke as an appendix to his Essay, and in the " Domestic Architecture" of Mr. Hudson Turner and Mr. J. H. Parker.

(1) Smirke, pp. 57, 69, &c. ; Turner and Parker's " Domestic Architecture," *u. s.* Mention is made in the Pipe Roll of 31 Hen. III. of a " *nova turris versus villam*" (ibid., p. 76), which may be either the " new tower," or the " new tower in the bailey towards the town," in Rot. Lib., 30 Hen. III., quoted by Mr. Turner, p. 209. In that of 37 Hen. III., of a " *turris versus beumund*" (Smirke, p. 76). In the Tarrages (fols. 32, 33) we find that the space between Gar Street and Gold Street, below the castle, was occupied by a pasture called " Bemonde," and it is left open in Speed's plan. Mr. Smirke, in a note on the last extract, says " the Beumut or Beumund seems to be the Beaumont or Belmont of some other castles, as at Oxford, &c. A house '*super Beumund*' is also mentioned in a *rotulus de operationibus factis in castro Winton*,' 42 Hen. III. Ministers' Ac-

counts among the Exchequer records." " Manesies" tower is in the later rolls called " Manyson's" (p. 79).

" St. Catharine's Tower " was so called because the chapel dedicated to that saint was in it. (Turner, pp. 247, 254.) It is called the " high tower," and the chapel is said to be " at the top of the castle " (ibid., p. 243.)

The " king's tower " may have been the keep. (See Smirke, p. 75, and compare Turner, pp. 246, 254.)

(2) Smirke, pp. 53, 57, 69, &c. See above, p. 281, note 10.

(3) Smirke, p. 75.

(4) Ibid., pp. 67, 73, 74 ; Turner, p. 190.

(5) Smirke, p. 74. This is not said to be in the " great tower," but there was certainly one there, and another may be seen in the plans in the Grand Jury Chamber.

(6) Ibid., p. 70. See above, p. 31, note 4.

(7) This hall was formerly always regarded as a chapel (Wavell, vol. i. p. 4), and was named by Milner (vol. ii. pp. 195, 203), without any authority, St. Stephen's Chapel; but Mr. Smirke, in his Essay, has completely overthrown this error.

(8) Mr. Smirke (pp. 50, 60) considers that it stood at the east end of the wall dividing the two baileys, but this would scarcely agree with Speed's plan, in which the southern bailey is the smallest. And Milner's plan, which agrees with Speed's, and in this case may be relied on, shows that a tower stood there.

(9) According to the plan constructed by Mr. O. B. Carter. (Smirke, p. 46.)

(10) The views of the hall in Grose's Antiquities, on

Externally there is nothing now to note particularly, beyond the facts that the —the exterior;
buttresses on both sides have been rebuilt at different periods—those on the south side,
certainly, during the "dark ages" which preceded the present revival of the genuine
appreciation of Gothic architecture ;[1] that the window in the eastern gable just
appears above the castle wall, which has been used as the wall of the hall itself; and
that just beneath the window in the west end are the traces of some very flat roofs of
adjoining buildings.[2]

The style of the architecture of the hall, generally, is Early English, and on this —the interior;
account, as well as on the ground of the numerous notices respecting it, in the records,
which will be found in Mr. Smirke's Essay, and in Mr. Hudson Turner's "Domestic
Architecture," it may be ascribed to the reign of Henry III. The windows at the
ends consist of three short lancet windows, combined, and connected by means of their
hood-moulds and attached shafts ;[3] and it would appear that the windows along the
sides were, at first, of the same character,[4] but were subsequently altered to two-light
windows, with banded shafts and plain hood-moulds externally, and furnished internally with stone seats in the sill.[5]

Internally the south doorway consists of the central segment of a very wide pointed
arch, with shafts reaching quite to the haunch ; but on the outside is seen a very rich
and elegantly moulded arch, with shafts almost entirely disengaged, and bell-caps,

Godson's maps, &c., show the north door in its original place. It has been removed to the central bay for the more convenient use of the hall at assizes and elections. Traces of the older doorway are yet visible.

(1) The buttresses on the south side are merely sloping props of masonry, constructed of old materials; those on the north reach to the corbel table under the parapet, and have three set-offs. The records often mention the buttresses (columpnæ) of the hall. From the records it appears that there was an external porch (most probably) to the north entrance, and two posts with a chain, and "lists" (liciæ) before the entrance to the hall from the king's chamber. (Smirke, pp. 56, 75.)

(2) Wavell (u.s.) says that the chapel was "a detached building ;" but the records speak of adjoining buildings to the hall (Smirke, pp. 72, &c.), and these traces remain to show that there were such buildings at the western end.

(3) There are no shafts now attached to the jambs of the western window externally, but it is not to be concluded thence that there never were any.

(4) Mr. Carter's restoration of the exterior of the hall, in the Grand Jury Chamber, one bay of which is given in Mr. Smirke's Essay (p. 44), shows a small Early English arch (as of a niche blocked up, or part of an arcade) on each side of the now existing window, just opposite the haunch of the arch. I have very carefully examined both sides of the hall, in company with the Rev. C. Walters, and though we found but one shaft remaining on the north side, shafts, or the traces of them,

were visible in almost every compartment on the south side; and there is but one to be seen on each side of the windows, almost in the middle of the void space, with the jamb to which it is engaged towards the buttress; and it appeared to us that the space between the shafts on each side of the window-heads, agreed very nearly with the width of the triple lancet window at the end of the hall.

(5) These windows now come down to the string-course, level with the lowest set-off of the buttresses, externally; the heads of the lights are trefoiled, and there are plain transoms at mid height (but this may have been a later addition), a plain pierced and glazed quatrefoil in the head of each window. There are two plain shafts in each jamb in the interior. There are no traces of fixed glazing in the original mullions which remain, but instead hooks for the hinges of glazed casements (verrinæ), which are often named in the records. (Smirke, pp. 47, and note c, 54, 73, &c.)

One specimen has been preserved, on the south side, of the abomination of ugliness, which occupied the place of each of these windows on the north side, from some time after Godson's view was taken till the late restorations under Mr. Carter's directions.

In the interior, between the heads of the windows, there appear circular mouldings, as of small rose-windows now blocked up. In Godson's view, one such window is shown at the extreme east end on the north side; but it is most probable that the mouldings in the interior are merely ornamental, and of recent date.

and fillets on the mouldings,—all in Purbeck stone, some of the shafts consisting of but a single length of the stone.[1]

—the piers, &c.

The piers are of Purbeck stone, and consist of four shafts set round a central one, which is of such a form that each pier looks like a cluster of nine shafts, arranged in square. The bases and abaci are circular, and the arches springing from them are extremely graceful.[2] The roof is of open timber-work, but is of later date than Henry the Third's reign.[3]

King Arthur's Round Table.

For an account of the original ornamentation of the hall, which was very richly decorated with painting and gilding, we must refer to the extracts from the records collected by Mr. Smirke and Mr. Turner. There now remains only the famous " King Arthur's Round Table," " eighteen feet in diameter," suspended against the eastern wall, just beneath the window ; but as the present style of its painting is of no earlier date than Henry the Eighth's reign, its real interest is not very great.[4]

The County Courts.

This hall is now obstructed by the exceedingly uncouth contrivances for inclosing the two courts which occupy the ends of its area. Beneath the hall, lighted by windows in the basement, are cells for the detention of prisoners during trial, and other needful apartments. The new offices stand at right angles to the west end, and were rebuilt when the hall was restored.

History of the Castle.

Fables, but for the most part of recent growth,[5] formerly obscured the history of this castle. The first unquestionable reference [6] to it is in the *Liber Winton.*, where

(1) The original entrance of the hall was, in 37 Hen. III., made wide enough to admit a cart. (Turner, pp. 176, 243.) Purbeck stone is mentioned in a passage from the Liberate Rolls, quoted by Mr. Smirke (p. 94).

(2) Elevations, plans, and sections are given by Mr. Smirke (pp. 46, 49). The columns of the hall are mentioned in the records (quoted ibid., pp. 69, &c.), but the term sometimes signifies buttresses. (See preceding page, note 1.)

(3) Alterations of considerable extent are recorded under Richard II. and Henry VI. (Smirke, pp. 56, 78, 79) ; and the bosses indicate repairs executed in the reign of Edward IV. (Ibid., pp. 48, 56.)

(4) Its real interest lies in the fact that it was repainted (in its present style) to add splendour to the entertainment given there by Henry VIII. to the Emperor Charles V. in 1522. A great red and white (Tudor) rose occupies the centre, round which is inscribed its title ; "the blameless king" is depicted (but in more modern style than Henry VIII.'s) above the rose, and twenty-four rays, reaching to the edge of the board, bear at the end of each the names of the Knights of the Round Table, according to Sir Thomas Mallory's version of the romance.

The earliest mention of this round table as King Arthur's occurs in Hardyng's Chronicle (last Edit., p. 146), but there is some doubt respecting the genuineness of the passage (Smirke, p. 62, note 2). Before that time we

have record of a " Wheel of Fortune," painted by command of Henry III., in the eastern gable of this hall, where the table hangs (ibid., p. 73) ; and of a " *Mappa Mundi*," painted in the same hall three years later. (Ibid., p. 74.) Those who are curious respecting this long-revered, but very spurious, relic of the great hero of European romance, will find a full discussion of its claims to regard in Mr. Smirke's Essay (pp. 61, &c.).

Milner adds to his account of it (vol. ii. p. 204), that it is " perforated with many bullets, supposed to have been shot by Cromwell's soldiers."

(5) They can be traced no farther back than Alderman Trussell's MS. History of Winchester in the seventeenth century. Wavell (vol. i. p. 3, vol. ii. pp. 7—9) has repeated them ; and Milner (vol. i. pp. 53, &c., and vol. ii. pp. 193, &c.) has gravely discussed and rejected them.

(6) Milner (vol. ii. p. 194) holds that it was built by William the Conqueror, and was used in 1070, when Archbishop Stigand was imprisoned, and again, in 1072, when the question of precedency between the Archbishops of Canterbury and York was " ventilated " before being finally determined. But it is extremely improbable that in so short a time after the Conquest as the first of these events, such a strong castle should have been completed ; and it is equally improbable that the same king would erect two royal residences in one city of no greater extent than Winchester ; for we know that William did build, or more probably enlarge, a " King's House"

the destruction of a street outside Westgate is said to have taken place "*quando rex fecit facere suum fossatum;*"[1] and the form of this reference assigns this work to Henry I.[2] A charter of this king, recited and inspected in one of Edward IV.,[3] shows further that this stronghold was in existence in his reign. During the wars of Stephen's reign,[4] and thenceforward in history,[5] we meet with frequent notices of this castle, until in Elizabeth's time, except the "House of Correction," it seems to have been merely a green bush-grown mound, crowned with ruined walls and towers.[6]

Until this reign the custody of the castle had always been committed to a constable, but it was now granted to the corporation of Winchester.[7] By James I. it was bestowed on Sir Benjamin Tichborne and his heirs.[8] In 1645 it was surrendered to Lieut.-General Oliver Cromwell,[9] and, according to the commonly-received tradition, was by him dismantled.[10] It next passed into the hands of Sir William Waller,

near the Church of St. Lawrence. The selection of this spot, and the existence of the Mints here (see above, p. 267, notes 5 and 6), seem to point to the conclusion that the palace of the Saxon kings stood here, and Milner (vol. i. p. 142) appears to have been of this opinion. William, however, did certainly extend, if he did not originally erect, a palace on this spot, for in the *Liber Winton.* (pp. 534, 535) we find recorded the destruction of twelve houses of burgesses, of which part was in the royal demesne, and part in the demesne of the Abbot of New Minster, to make room for the "*domus regis.*" And in Domesday itself (vol. i. fol. 43) there is a record of an exchange effected between the king and the abbot, of some royal property at Alton, and at Clere, for land in Winchester for this "*domus regis.*" Both these passages, with a charter of Henry I. (*Cartæ Antiquæ*, V. No. 21), are by an oversight in Mr. Smirke's Essay (pp. 51, 52, 68) spoken of as if they referred to the castle instead of the King's House. This palace extended from the immediate vicinity of St. Lawrence' Church along by the west wall of the Cathedral Yard to the end of the two Minster Streets, and included the block of houses between them. (See above, p. 158, note 5, and p. 94, note 2.) To this palace, which was (as all such then were) fortified, I refer both the incidents appealed to by Milner. The statement that Stigand was imprisoned in the castle rests upon Rudborne's gloss on the words of William of Malmesbury (Warton, vol. i. p. 210), "*in salva custodia*, i. e. *in castro Wintoniæ*." The Annals (ibid., p. 294) say merely that he was confined "*in Wintoniæ oppido.*" Of the question of precedency, William of Malmesbury (E. H. Soc. Edn., vol. ii. p. 476), quoting, as it seems, the original decree of the first council held at Windsor, says, "*ventilata est autem hæc causa prius apud Wentanam civitatem . . . . in capella regia, quæ sita est in castello.*" And this "*castellum*" I consider to be the "*domus regis,*" of which I have spoken, for the reasons given in this note.

(1) P. 535.

(2) In the first survey contained in the *Liber Winton.*, where the reference to the king is *personal*, it must signify Henry I., by whose order the survey was made, as in that note (p. 534) of the abolition of five of the Mints, "*quæ fuerunt diffacte precepto regis,*" which has always been understood to refer to him; but it is otherwise when the term is employed *generically* merely, as in "*domus regis,*" "*callis regis,*" &c.

(3) Dugdale's Monasticon (last Edit.), vol. ii. p. 445; also quoted by Mr. Smirke (p. 68). The incidental mention of the "*porta castelli,*" the Church of St. James, Westgate, and St. Valery's Street, shows that the gate of the castle at that time was situated very nearly as it is represented in Speed's plan.

(4) Milner (vol. ii. p. 195) has suffered himself to be misled by the reading of the edition of Roger de Hoveden, which he used, and in opposition to Henry of Huntingdon (whom he also refers to), Bromton, Annales Waverleienses, &c., &c., represents Stephen as having entirely rebuilt the castle of Winchester, instead of that at Wilton, in the year 1142. (Smirke, p. 51, note *e*.)

(5) The "Chronological Extracts" appended to Mr. Smirke's Essay (pp. 68—80) contain a very satisfactory series of these notices from the public records. Others may be seen in Turner and Parker's "Domestic Architecture" (*u. s.*). Milner (vol. ii. pp. 195—198) has collected the historical facts which are connected with the castle.

(6) Harl. MS., Titus, B. ii. pp. 242—244; Vespasian, F. ix. p. 277; Smirke, p. 59.

(7) This grant was dated May the 4th, 1559. (Harl. MS., Titus, B. ii. *u. s.*). Mr. Smirke says (p. 58, note *x*) that this was "probably a mere renewal of a preceding grant."

(8) Milner, vol. ii. pp. 2, 3, 198.

(9) Wavell, vol. ii. p. 129.

(10) Ibid.; Milner, vol. ii. p. 198. But Mr. Smirke (pp. 60, 61) suspects that the castle was "dismantled" before this time.

partly on account of his connection with the Tichbornes, but more because of his services in the cause of the Long Parliament.[1]　His son conveyed the hall to trustees for the use of the county,[2] and afterwards sold the remainder of the site to the corporation of Winchester for £260,[3] to whom (with the exception of the hall) it was conveyed in the year 1678.[4]

Building of the "King's House."

The history of the castle ends here, and that of the "King's House" commences, for in the year 1682 the corporation, in the consideration of the sum of five shillings, conveyed the site to Charles II., "to build on as his majesty should think fit."[5]　Here, under the direction of Wren, on March 23rd, 1683,[6] the foundation-stone of the new building was laid, and a magnificent plan was formed of a palace which should eclipse that of the "*Grand Monarque*" at Versailles,[7] but which the death of Charles, when only an insignificant portion of the programme had been executed, prevented from being ever realized.[8]

Some hopes were entertained in the reign of Queen Anne that this noble palace might be finished, and Winchester once more become a regal city.[9]　But in the following reigns it was used as a depôt for prisoners of war,[10] and when the French Revolution broke out was granted to the Romanist clergymen who sought refuge in

The Barracks.

England;[11] and, finally, in 1796 it was converted into barracks,[12] and has, at various times since then, been altered in different ways to render it more completely adapted to this use.[13]　There are entrances to the barrack-yard from the north, outside Westgate; beside the county hall, on the south; from St. James's Lane, and from Southgate Street.

---

(1) Milner, ibid.　Waller's sister was wife of Sir Richard Tichborne, son of Sir Benjamin, to whom James I. had granted it.　This grant was in 1646.

(2) Ibid., p. 34; Smirke, pp. 58, 80.

(3) On May the 2nd, 1656.　(Bailey's "Transcripts," p. 157.)

(4) Smirke, pp. 58, 80.

(5) Bailey's "Transcripts," pp. 155—157; Milner, vol. ii. p. 34.　The conveyance is dated March the 17th, 1683 (N.S.); the assent of the common assembly had been procured in the preceding September.

(6) At that time the king was at Newmarket, as Mr. W. D. Cooper, in his recent edition of the "Savile Correspondence," for the Camden Society (p. 275, note), has shown; so that Milner's statement (vol. ii. p. 34, in which he is followed by Mr. Bailey) that "Charles himself" laid the foundation-stone, is demonstrably incorrect. Wavell (vol. i. p. 6), and Godson in his map, have avoided this error.

(7) The palace was to have had a great dome, thirty feet high, in the central building, two chapels under smaller domes in the wings, and a splendid staircase on marble pillars, which had been presented to the king by the Grand Duke of Tuscany.　Below the palace were to have been the gardens.　The downs to the south and

west were to have been laid out as a park; and from the great eastern gate a broad street, with elegant houses on each side, was to have been carried in a direct line to the west front of the cathedral.　(Milner, vol. ii. pp. 34, 35, 205.　See also an engraving, purporting to be of Wren's design, in the original edition.　Godson has given a less ambitious representation of it on his map.)

(8) Only the central building, and the wings, were completed.　The marble pillars were at last presented by George I. to the Duke of Bolton, who employed them in his seat in Hackwood Park.　(Wavell, vol. i. p. 6. See Buck's View of the Palace, 1733; and the views in Milner and Wavell.)

(9) Milner, vol. ii. p. 199.　It was granted to Prince George of Denmark by the queen, but he died before any alterations were made in the "King's House."

(10) Ibid.　In 1779 the crowded and unwholesome state of the building produced a fearfully malignant disease, which spared neither the prisoners nor their guards and medical attendants.　(Milner, vol. ii. p. 200.)

(11) Ibid.　See above, p. 175.

(12) Ibid., ibid.

(13) Additional stories have been constructed in the building, for the state apartments were originally twenty feet high, and the whole is now lighted with gas.

Before the construction of the railroad there was an airing or parade-ground on The parade-ground. the west side, beyond the ditch ; but when the cutting was excavated, the ditch on that side was filled up to the level of the mound on which the House stands, by which means a very fine parade-ground was secured in immediate contiguity to the barracks, with a platform beside the railroad for the sole use of the troops. The widening of St. James's Lane on the south side has obliterated the ditch there, also ; and the improvement of the access to the County Hall, and to the entrance to the barrack-yard beside it, has filled up the northern end of this huge fosse, of which only some scanty traces on the north-east of the mound now remain.

Within the last few years a handsome building, in some respects resembling the Officers' quarters, &c. "King's House" in style, has been erected at the southern end of the parade for the officers' quarters, and to the east of it another range of buildings for the accommodation of the married non-commissioned officers. Almost all the space between the barracks and Southgate Street has been acquired for various purposes connected with the garrison ; and there are the hospital, the school (which is used as a chapel), &c., &c. The head-quarters of the Hampshire Militia are to the north of the garrison buildings, where the judge's lodgings formerly were.

We may briefly notice here the few remains of the walls[1] of Winchester. When The City walls. Buck's "East View" was taken, and Godson's Map constructed,[2] the entire circuit was nearly complete, and it had not been much broken in upon when Britton's Map was published.[3] But during the recent improvements of the city, consequent upon the formation of the railway, the ground covered by these masses of ancient masonry has been of too great value for them to be suffered to remain ;[4] and except a few fragments altered into modern walls, or concealed by the houses in St. Swithin's Street, along the Weirs, and to the north of Westgate, the part which bounds Wolvesey on the south and east, and some portions of the north wall, are all that survive to show their strength and structure.[5]

During the last century there were on several occasions encampments of troops in

(1) The gates of the city are noticed above in pp. 14, 20, 21, 24, 25, 155, note 3, 294.

(2) The date of Buck's View is 1736, and that of Godson's Map, 1750. Speed's bird's-eye plan in 1611 cannot be confidently relied upon for its details, or it would be of the greatest value, as the walls were nearly perfect at that time. Milner, in his plan, has drawn far too extensively on his imagination for the details of the walls by Wolvesey, where he has added six massive round towers, of which not a vestige ever existed.

The position of Northgate is so irregular that it deserves a little attention. According to the original Roman plan of the place, this gate ought to have been opposite the end of that part of Jury Street which ran direct to the *enceinte* of the city, and is now stopped up. It is remarkable that we find the foundation of a tower at this spot ; and as we know that this gate was destroyed,

and that all this part of the town suffered greatly during the wars of Stephen's reign, it seems most probable that the gate when rebuilt was removed farther to the west than it stood at first.

(3) The date of this map, which was published in a 4to. Supplement of Plans, Views, &c., to the "Beauties of England and Wales," and is very little known, is 1805. It is based upon Godson's map, but represents the state of the city at the date of its publication.

(4) See above, p. 12. Milner, however (vol. ii. p. 46), pathetically bewails the destruction of the "majestic walls of flint and stone," which was carried on in his day. The materials derived from the wall on the north side of Westgate were almost sufficient for the erection of some of the houses which now stand on its foundations.

(5) The remains round the meadow at Wolvesey exhibit the work of several different dates, and in the oldest

Encampments
near Win-
chester.
the vicinity of Winchester. The earliest was that of 7,000 Hessians under Count Isenberg, from July to December, in the year 1756, on the downs between the Basingstoke and the Whitchurch Roads.[1] In the year 1759 the Wiltshire Militia were encamped there; and in the following year the 34th Regiment, together with the Berkshire, Gloucestershire, Dorsetshire, Wiltshire, and Bedfordshire Militia. In 1761 there were encamped, near the site of the Hessian camp, the Wiltshire and the south battalion of the Gloucestershire Militia, the Dorsetshire and the north battalion of the Gloucestershire Militia, the south battalion of the Hampshire, and the Berkshire Militia. Next year the camp was removed to the north of Magdalen Hill, and occupied by the Berkshire, Wiltshire, and west battalion of the Essex Militia, the Lancers, and the two battalions of the Gloucestershire Militia. The last encampment was on this ground from the 1st of June to the 24th of October, in the year 1778; and it consisted of the 30th Regiment, with the West Kent, South Gloucestershire, Lancashire, Staffordshire, Dorsetshire, and Wiltshire Militia.[2]

THE THEATRE, RACE-COURSE, &c.

Hunting,
shooting,
fishing, &c.
Popular amusements and recreation in Winchester, as in almost every other provincial place, are for the most part left to the occasional efforts of non-resident speculators.[3] We have spoken of the Museum, the Mechanics' Institution, and the Public Libraries already.[4] For walking, riding, and driving, the main roads, the foot-paths along the water-meads, and the downs, provide ample room, and the most

portions pieces of Roman brick are tolerably abundant. The rubble-work of the outside is in some parts arranged in the herring-bone fashion.

There are yearly returns of repairs, &c., done to the walls, beginning in the reign of John, amongst the public records; and in the first year of that reign we hear of alterations in the city ditch, so extensive that the house of one Andrew, a clerk, was removed, and he was compensated by the grant of a house in "Sortene," or "Port" Street (now Jury Street), which had been forfeited by Aaron the Jew. (Rot. Chart., vol. i. p. 55 b.; Rot. Oblat., pp. 44, 45.) See above (pp. 24, note 3, and 279, note) for other notices of repairs to the walls.

(1) Wavell, vol. ii. p. 150; Milner, vol. ii. p. 46. Wavell's account of the preparations for invading this country by the French, of the exercises in embarking and disembarking in a fleet of flat-bottomed boats on the opposite coast, and of the excitement occasioned here, might well be mistaken for a page from the history of the Napoleonic war. There was a plan of Winchester,

with the surrounding country, including the camp, constructed by F. W. Baur, an officer of engineers in the Hessian army, and published at this time.

(2) Plans and particulars of all these encampments are contained in Add. MSS., 15,532, and 15,533 of the British Museum.

(3) It may be questioned whether private or municipal enterprise could not, with great advantage to society at large, attempt the regular provision of popular amusement and recreation in provincial cities and towns. Museums and reading-rooms do not nearly meet the whole of the legitimate requirements of the case. Nor do cricket clubs' and rifle corps' practice supply all the deficiency. The casual visits of travelling menageries, equestrian *troupes*, &c., are too irregular, and are not always of such a quality as to afford (except in a way that is not intended) either recreation or amusement. I am compelled to note the deficiency, and I can only very remotely suggest the means of supplying it.

(4) See above, pp. 214, 215.

agreeable diversity. Not Izaac Walton himself could have desired a choicer stream for angling; it is well suited for bathing also; but boating is impracticable. There is fair shooting for those who can indulge in that sport; and three packs of Fox-hounds, and a pack of Harriers, in the season, occasionally meet at no great distance from the city.[1]

The newly established Rifle Corps affords some of the best athletic recreation;[2] and there is a well-supported Cricket Club, and a tolerably good ground on the road *Cricket Clubs.* to Week, just beyond Fullflood.[3] Both the College and Hyde House School have racket-courts and cricket grounds, but to them the public are, of course, not admitted.[4]

In Jury Street, opposite the Museum, stands the Theatre; a little, and rather *The Theatre.* dilapidated building, which was built in 1785, and is now in the hands of a company whose head-quarters are Southampton, and who seldom visit Winchester, leaving their house for the occasional use of amateur performers, who are generally to be found amongst the officers of the garrison.[5]

The Race-course, two miles in length, is on Worthy Down, nearly four miles *The Race-course.* distant from the city. There is generally one meeting in each season under the patronage of the officers of the garrison, but the races are not of extensive interest or renown.[6]

There is a good Bowling-green in the grounds belonging to the White Swan Inn, *The Bowling-green.* outside Northgate.[7]

(1) These are the Hampshire, the Hursley, and the Hambledon hounds; the harriers are kept by a private gentleman. Popular amusements in olden times was provided by ordinances requiring the butchers of the city to furnish bulls to be baited yearly at a stake, which was planted in front of the house of the mayor for the time being. There was afterwards a regular bull-ring, but I do not know the site of it. (See ordinances quoted in Bailey's "Transcripts," pp. 75, 77; and Winchester Vol. of Arch. Assoc., p. 25.)

(2) See above, p. 283.

(3) This belongs to the landlord of the Roebuck Inn, which is situated there.

(4) See above, pp. 192, 210.

(5) Before the erection of this theatre a large room over the shambles, which stood where the rooms of the Mechanics' Institution now are, was used as a playhouse. (See above, p. 18, note 2.) A humorous prologue was written for the opening of this room, by the Southampton and Portsmouth company, by the Poet-Laureate, the Rev. Thomas Warton. Great opposition to the opening

of the present house, we are told, was made by a solicitor who lived on the opposite side of the street. For about thirty years after it was built it had a regular season every summer, and was a "well-paying property."

The earliest notice of the stage in Winchester which I have met with is an ordinance prohibiting the performance of "any more comedies or tragedies within this city," "upon peril of the law," because it tended to "the corruption of youth." (Bailey's "Transcripts," p. 79.)

(6) Races were introduced here, most probably, in the reign of Charles I., and received great encouragement from Charles II. Some ordinances relating to them are quoted in Bailey's "Transcripts" (pp. 77, 78).

(7) There used to be two bowling-greens in Gar Street (which was called Bowling-green Lane): one on the west side, at the south end; and the other on the east side, a little more to the north; another in Staple Garden Lane, between High Street and the lane leading to Tower Street; and a fourth at the end of St. Peter's Street (apparently), next the walls. (See Godson's map, and Buck's "East Prospect.")

APPENDIX

TO

"THE CITY AND BOROUGH OF WINCHESTER."

I. MONASTICON WINTONIENSE.

BESIDES the "Old Minster," or Priory of St. Swithin, already described (see above, pp. 103, &c., 127, &c.), there were in Winchester several other monasteries and religious establishments, some of which enjoyed great renown in their day. A condensed account of them will be given here, on the authority of Milner, Dugdale, Tanner, &c., with the assistance of original registers and chartularies still existing.

New Minster, or *Hyde Abbey*.—During the tenth and eleventh centuries there stood, on the north side of the cathedral church, in the ground subsequently used as its cemetery, a noble monastic house, which was founded by King Alfred near the close of his life, and completed by his son, Edward the Elder, and called "*Niwan Mynstre*" (Dugdale, Anglo-Saxon Chronicle, &c.). Alfred had appointed as the first superior of his new foundation the learned St. Grimbald, whom he had invited from the Flemish convent of St. Omer (Pauli's Life of Alfred) to assist him in his great works, and who had been desirous of returning thither as the close of his life approached.

The church was consecrated to the Holy Trinity, the Blessed Virgin Mary, and St. Peter, and it stood so close to the north side of the church of the Old Minster, that when it had been rebuilt by Walkelyn, there was not room for a man to pass between. (Dugdale, vol. ii. p. 436.) It could not have been a large building, because Athelwold's cathedral (which was much smaller than Walkelyn's) stood between it and the site of the body of the present cathedral. (See above, pp. 96, 97.) Of its form, we only know that, like most Anglo-Saxon churches, and the Old Minster itself, it could not have any transept.

Leland states (Collect. p. 18) that Alfred's buildings were "*domus et capella*," which were erected "*citato opere*," and that the "*templum*" of New Minster was built by St. Grimbald in the course of two years; and that this must be a tolerably faithful representation, we may conclude from King Edward's charter (Harl. MS. 1761, fol. 47), in which he describes his purchase of three acres and three virgates of land of Bishop Denewulf and the canons of Old Minster, and from certain inhabitants, at the excessively high rate of a mark of gold for each foot of it, for the purpose of erecting "*officinas monasterii*," the church being already built and dedicated. The date of this charter, and of the dedication of the church (to which, at the same time, the relics of St. Judocus were translated), is 903; in which year, also, St. Grimbald died.

The extent of Edward's purchase, and of the precinct of the monastery, cannot be ascertained with exactness in every part, but it included nearly the whole of the cemetery (the part lying south of a line level with the end of the transept being most probably included in the precinct of the Old Minster), and the ground between Great and Little Minster Streets; and the monastic buildings were to the north and west of the church. The Temple Ditch

Marginal notes:
- New Minster, or Hyde Abbey.
- The church.
- Its foundation.
- The precinct.

(spoken of above, p. 143) was in all probability a watercourse connected with them. Thomas Gate (ibid.) seems to have been the chief entrance; there was, probably, one to the west of it, which was stopped when William enlarged the royal palace near St. Lawrence' Church (Liber Winton., p. 534); and another to the east of it, through the tower of St. Maurice' Church. (See above, pp. 34, 159.) Edward placed in it a society of canons regular, like that in Old Minster, and translated to the church the bodies of his father and mother, Alfred and Alsuitha; and there he was himself buried.

As soon as Bishop Athelwold had completed the reformation of the Old Minster (see above, pp. 104, 105), he directed his attention to New Minster; and on the same pretexts (for which see the Annales Winton. and Rudborne, Anglia Sacra, vol. i. pp. 218, 289, 290), and under the same authority, in the course of the years 959—966, he ejected the canons, and replaced them by a choir of forty Benedictine monks from Abingdon, over whom Æthelgar, or Algar, was appointed as abbot. In the last of those years King Edgar gave the new society its charter of foundation and constitution, a magnificent copy of which, written in letters of gold, exists in the British Museum. (Cott. MSS., Vespasian, A. viii.; Cod. Dipl., No. 527; Dugdale, vol. ii. pp. 439—441.) *St. Athelwold's reformation.*

New Minster was pitilessly despoiled by William the Conqueror, in consequence (as it is said) of the Abbot Alwyn, uncle to Harold, having with twelve of his choir and a small number of retainers taken part in the fatal battle of Hastings. Part of the lands which were then confiscated were, however, subsequently restored, as we shall see below. It was at this time, also, that William, being desirous of enlarging and strengthening the royal palace in Winchester, gave to New Minster lands in Clere and Alton in exchange for that part of its precinct which lay to the west of the existing boundary of the cemetery. (See above, pp. 158, note 5; 300, note 6.) *William the Conqueror's spoliations.*

In the reign of Henry I., the new cathedral having been built in the place of St. Athelwold's church, grievous disputes arose between the two choirs, for the churches stood so close to each other, that in performing the services and ringing the bells they caused each other (and that not wholly without intending to do so) great annoyance; besides which the watercourses of the abbey seem not to have been well laid out, for instead of a clear current flowing through them, they were filled with stagnant and unwholesome water. (Dugdale, *u. s.*, pp. 429, 436; see above, p. 10.) The king, therefore, built for them a new church and monastery in Hyde Mede, outside Northgate, which they took possession of in 1110, translating thither all their special interments and relics; and the site of New Minster was given to the Prior of St. Swithin's. Its abbots were afterwards honoured with a mitre, and a place in parliament as peers of the realm. (Brown Willis, Mitred Abbeys, xxii.) *Foundation of Hyde Abbey.*

Hyde Abbey, as it was now called, suffered severely in the wars between Stephen and the Empress, having been burnt down in the year 1140 or 1141, in a great conflagration which consumed all the adjacent suburb, together with the church of St. Bartholomew. (Ann. Winton., Anglia Sacra, vol. i. p. 299). It was not rebuilt till forty years afterwards, Henry II., in the year 1182, having commenced its reconstruction, in obedience to the miraculous command of St. Barnabas, to whom the new church was jointly dedicated.

Of the plan of Hyde Abbey we are able to obtain but few and unsatisfactory details. All that remains of the buildings are a good, but not a very early gateway, and some fragments of walls, with a small chamber in one corner, adjoining it on the west; a mass of masonry, probably part of the Abbey Mill, over the Hyde Bourne; some walls to the south of this, "a few small doorways of the fifteenth century, and some fragments of an earlier period built into the neighbouring walls." (Arch. Instit., Winchester Vol., Archit. Notes, &c., p. 12.) There was also a portion of a stone drain uncovered about fifteen years ago. All these remains lie between Hyde Street and the Bourne. On the other side of the stream, *Its plan and remains.*

opposite the bridge over it, stood the church, the last vestiges of which were removed when the New Gaol, or Bridewell, was built there in 1788. From the investigations of Captain Howard, in 1798, the scanty results of which were published in the Archæologia, it would appear that the church had not a transept, and that the chapter-house stood on the north side of the choir, whilst the conventual buildings, on the south of the church, reached nearly as far as the bend of the Hyde Bourne to the east, close by which were the "fish beds" or ponds. The grange of the home-farm belonging to the abbey is situated about half a mile to the north of it, and is still called Abbot's Barton. There is a foot-path leading to it on the Banks of the Hyde Bourne, called Monks' Walk, or Nuns' Walk. (See above, p. 32.)

The Dissolu-
tion. At the Dissolution in April, 1538, Hyde Abbey was surrendered to the king by the abbot and the whole community, and the site was granted to Richard Bethel. It was soon afterwards pulled down; and when Leland visited the place, nothing but ruins remained of this once magnificent monastery. He states that in the "tumbe" of King Alfred and his son, which was "before the High Altare," "was a late found 2 litle Tables of leade inscribid with theyr Names." (Itin., vol. iii. fol. 72.) Architectural monuments, stone coffins, and the relics of the interments of abbots and other office-bearers in the convent have been dug up on the site of the church, at different times, especially at the time of the building of the Bridewell there. (See above, p. 282, note.) Milner (vol. ii. p. 250) informs us that a small stone, with the inscription "*Ælfred rex Dccclxxxi*," was found at this time, and passed into the possession of Mr. Howard of Corby Castle; a cast of it is in the Museum of the Society of Antiquaries. Some of the painted glass, consisting of "coats of arms," was to be seen in the windows of a house next Hyde Street when Browne Willis visited Hyde, in 1723. (Cole's MSS., vol. xxvii. p. 201.)

Abbots of
Hyde. No catalogue of the superiors of New Minster before the reformation of St. Athelwold has been preserved. The following are the names of the abbots after that date:—

After 964—980. Æthelgar (*Algar*); consecrated Bishop of Selsey on May 2nd, in the latter year; translated to Canterbury in 988; died December 3rd, 989 (Stubbs).

980—995. Ælfsige (*Alsinus*).

995—1006. Brihtwold (*Athelwold*); in the last-named year consecrated Bishop of Winchester. (Milner, vol. ii. p. 248; see above, p. 114.)

1006 (?)—1026. Brihtmar; consecrated Bishop of Lichfield in the latter year (Stubbs).

1026—1035. Alnoth.

1035—1057. Alwyn.

1057—1063. Alfnoth.

1063—1066. Alwyn (*Alwy*); killed at the battle at Hastings, October 14th, in the latter year.

1069—1072. Wlfric (*Wulveric*); deposed by Archbishop Lanfranc in the last-named year.

1072—1078. Riwalo (*Rewalanus, Rualdus*).

1078—1088. Radulfus (*Ralph*); on his death, in 1088, "*commisit Rex abbatiam Radulfo Passeflabere capellano suo.*" (Ann. Winton., Anglia Sacra, vol. i. p. 295.)

1091—1093. Robertus de Losinga obtained the abbacy, his son, Herbert de Losinga, having purchased it of the king. At his death in the latter year (Dugdale) Ralph Passe-flabere was again in possession of the abbey, till on the accession of Henry I. he was imprisoned.

1100—1106. Hugh, a monk from the Old Minster.

1106—1124. Geoffrey (*Galfridus*). During his abbacy, in the year 1121, the translation to Hyde took place, the original site of the abbey being abandoned.

1124—1135. Osbert.

1135—1149. Hugo de Lens (*Hugh Schorche-vyleyn*). Dugdale dates his appointment 1112. His surname, "Scorch-villein," is a sufficient testimony to his character, and indicates the reason for the appeals made against him to Rome by his monks. He was abbot when the monastery was destroyed by fire. Bishop De Blois endeavoured at this time (1143) to get Hyde made a bishopric, his own see being raised to an archbishopric. Hugh being at last deposed—

114   1171. Salidus was appointed. The Hyde Register (Harl. MS. 1761) dates his appointment in 1151, and makes the abbacy vacant for several years after his death.

1177—1180. Thomas, Prior of Montacute. In 1175 (Ann. Wint.), or 1174 (Willis); and he resigned in the year last named above.

1181—1222. John Suthill, Prior of Clugny (Willis).

1222—1249. Walter de Astone; confirmed by the king 7th July, 6 Hen. III. (Dugdale).

1249—1263. Roger de St. Walaric; confirmed 27th April, 32 Hen. III. (Dugdale).

1263—1282. William de Wigornia.

1282—1292. Robert de Popham; succeeded on 17th May.

1292—1304. Simon de Caninges; confirmed 26th July, 19 Edw. I.

1304—1317. Geoffrey de Feringes; confirmed by the bishop 23rd Oct., 1304.

1317—1319. William de Odiham.

1319—1362. Walter de Fyfhyde; confirmed by the king 26th June, 12 Edw. II.

1362—1381. Thomas de Pechy (*Peithy*).

1381—1394. John de Eynesham. The dates of these last two appointments are given on the authority of Dugdale (latest Ed.).

1394—1407. John Letecombe.

1407—1414. John London; confirmed 11th June, 9 Hen. IV.

1414—1440. Nicholas Strode. The dates of his appointment and death are not certainly determined (Dugdale, Willis).

1440—1460. Thomas Bromeley (*Bramley*); confirmed 3rd May, 20 Hen. VI.

1460—1471. Henry de Bonvile. The Patent Roll does not notice his appointment till 1464.

1471—1480. Thomas Wyrcestere (*Worcester*); confirmed 6th December, 12 Edw. IV.

1480—1485. John Colyngbyrne.

1485—1488. Thomas Forte.

1488—1529. Richard Hall.

1530—1538. John Salcot (*Capon*). He was created Bishop of Bangor 19th April, 1534, holding his abbacy at the same time; and in April, 1538, he surrendered the monastery to the king's visitors, and the next year, on 31st July, was translated to the see of Salisbury; died 6th October, 1557.

The following seals connected with Hyde Abbey are known. The first is the seal of the chapter. The obverse shows a triple canopy, in the centre compartment of which is St. Peter seated on a throne *in pontificalibus*, with an archiepiscopal mitre, and two keys in his right hand. In the spandrels above the canopy are two angels, *issuing*, with censers, and in the exergue s PETRVS. In the dexter compartment is King Edward holding a church. The space outside is filled with his name, REX EDWARD'. King Alfred is seen on the other side of St. Peter; his right hand is raised in benediction; in his left he holds a sceptre; in the space on the outside is his name, REX ALVRED. The legend, as it has been ascertained by comparing several impressions, reads thus:—SIGILLV CAPITVL(I) (E)CCE SCT PETRI DE HYDA JVXTA WYNTON. Diameter 3·1 inch. On the counter seal, also, is a triple canopy, but with arches of nearly equal height; in the centre is St. Barnabas holding a processional cross in his right hand, and a book in his left; his cloak is fastened at the throat, and a nimbus encircles his head. In the exergue is inscribed s BARNABAS. St. Grimbald occupies the dexter compartment, in the dress of a monk, and holding a book with both hands; outside the canopy is his name, s' GRIMB'. The sinister compartment is occupied by a priest, who holds a head in his hands; his name, as before inscribed, is s VALENT'. The legend reads—HYDA PATRONORVM JVGI PRECE TVTA SIT HORVM. Diameter 3·1 inch. The seal of Nicholas Strode, Abbot of Hyde, is an oblong of 1·0 × ·9 inches. On a shield, within a rose of tracery, are the arms of Hyde—a lion rampant; on a chief, two pairs of keys addossed, wards uppermost. Legend:—* s NICHOLAI ABBATIS DE HYDA. This seal was used by the abbot for Richard Inkpenne, as his seal was better known. The seal of the last abbot is also preserved. It is an oblong of 3·3 × 2·0 inches, and exhibits a rich canopy containing his effigy, with a crown in his right hand; and in base the arms of the monastery. Legend:—SIGILLUM JOHNIS SAULTCOT ABBATIS DE HYDA.

Interments at Hyde Abbey. The most splendid interments at Hyde were Alfred the Great, his queen Alsuitha, his son King Edward, its actual founder, and a younger son named Ethelward; Alfred, son of Edward, with two of his daughters; and King Edwy. The burial of St. Grimbald has already been recorded.

Amongst the notable inmates of the monastery, we find St. Grimbald; Frithstan and Byrnstan, both afterwards bishops of Winchester, and both canonized; Athelgar, who rose to the metropolitan see of Canterbury; Brihtwold, who became Bishop of Winchester; Brihtmar, afterwards Bishop of Lichfield; Walter, afterwards Prior of Bath; and John, a homiletical writer.

Possessions of Hyde Abbey mentioned in Domesday. Following the plan observed respecting the possessions of Old Minster, we take Domesday as our guide in noticing those of New Minster; and here we find the Abbey of St. Peter recorded as possessing twenty hides in *Candevre* (now Brown Candover, formerly called Candover Abbas), including six and a half in *Vdemancote* (Woodmancote), Edward the Elder having originally bestowed on this foundation ten hides in each of the tracts or manors then known by those names; in *Fugelerestune* (Fullerton) one hide, but five in the time of Edward the Confessor, which, with two hides and a half (in Edward's time five hides) in *Lechtford* (Leckford), were the gift of King Edred; in *Miceldevre* (Mitcheldever) rather more than eighty-three hides, which were a hundred and six in the time of King Edward, and were, in fact, the earliest endowment of the founder, and then rated at a hundred "cassates;" the four manors called *Granborne, Draitone, Stratune,* and *Popeham* (now Cranbourne, Drayton, Stratton, and Popham), the gift of King Edward, and containing twenty-one hides and a half in all; in *Ordie* (Abbots' Worthy) seven hides; five hides in *Aultone* (Alton), which, together with Clere, the Conqueror gave to the abbey in exchange for so much of the site of New Minster itself as he required for the erection of his "Domus Regis," as we have noticed above (p. 301, note, &c.); five hides in *Wortinges* (Worting), which it had received from Edmund Ironside; in *Bighetone* (Bighton) seven hides, which before the Conquest had been ten; ten hides in *Betametone* (Bedhampton); three hides in *Lamere* (Lomer, near Bishop's Waltham), the gift of King Ethelred; eight hides in *Warneford* (Warnford); in *Lichefet* (Lichfield) two hides, which Edmund, son of Athelstan, gave; in *Staneham* (North Stoneham) eight hides, given by King Athelstan himself; four hides in *Clere* (Kingsclere), part of the exchanges made with the monastery for the site of William I.'s palace in Winchester; half a hide in *Taceburie* (Tatchbury, near Eling), one of Edward's gifts; in *Anna* (now known as Abbots' Anne) eight hides, which had been fifteen in the Confessor's time, and were also part of the original endowment; and in *Laurochestoche* (Laverstock) little more than six hides, though at an earlier time ten.

In Sussex, twenty-seven hides are recorded as the property of New Minster in *Svesse* (or Southsea), which were twenty-eight in the Confessor's time, but are reckoned by the Annals, which mention the gift of them by King Edgar, as eight only; in *Lewes* (still so named) its rents and dues were rated at twenty pounds a year, but, in fact, amounted to twenty-eight pounds, and included 28,500 herrings; five hides in *Cloninctune* or *Doninctone* (Donnington); and four pence with pannage (or pasturage) for one hog and a half, in *Cicestre* (Chichester).

In Surrey the monastery possessed, in *Sandestede* (Sanderstead), five hides, which were eighteen in the time of Edward the Confessor, and had been bestowed on it by Æthelfleda, King Edgar's wife.

In Berkshire, sixteen hides possessed by the abbey in King Edward's reign, in *Cedeneord* (now called Chaddleworth), had diminished to ten at the time of the Conqueror's survey; and it also held ten hides in *Sotwelle* (Satwell); with rents to the amount of fourteen shillings and four pence in *Walengeford* (Wallingford).

In Wiltshire, at *Maneforde* (Manningford Abbots) there were in Edward's time ten hides belonging to the New Minster, the gift of King Ethelred; and in *Coleburne* (Colling-bourne), at the same date, fifty hides, which Edward, its founder, had bestowed upon it; thirty hides in *Pevesei* (Pewsey), the gift of King Edward; two hides in *Wintreburne* (Winterbourn), which Edgar gave it; and eleven hides in *Chiseldene* (Chisleton) part of the endowment of its founder, and then reckoned at forty cassates; with which were connected rents amounting to four shillings and a penny in *Crichelade* (Cricklade).

In Dorsetshire only *Pidrie* (?), which in Edward the Confessor's time was reckoned at thirty hides, is recorded as the property of the Abbey of St. Peter.

From an account of the lands bestowed on Hyde Abbey by its various benefactors, printed from the Cottonian MS. (Domitian, A. xiv.), in the last edition of Dugdale, we add the following manors:—Edward the Elder's original grant included also *Burchet* (now Burket Farm, near Stratton), four hides and a half; *Northamptone* (Northington) six hides; *Swereuetone* (Swarraton) three hides, a virgate and a half; and another hide at *Sclatstede* (Slackstead, by Hursley) which is added to the half mentioned above at Tatchbury. King Edmund is stated to have given also ten hides in *Bechandever* (Monxton, formerly called Anne de Bec); and Edred fifty hides at *Andever* (Andover), thirty at *Marwell* (Marwell), and ten at *Titlescombe* (Tittlescomb, in Sussex); but this last manor appears by other and better evidence to have been the gift of Edgar. Queen Æthelfleda's grant included also six hides and a church at *Lingedefeld* (Lingfield, in Surrey), and two hides at *Langehurst* (?). And the grant by Ethelred comprised three hides in the island of *Ethameton* (?), four hides at *Badingburne* (?), *Melokedene* (?) three hides, *Esthede* (?) one hide, and the island of *Portesey* (Portsea), *Tredington* (Tratton?) four hides, *Suthingwerke* (Southwark?) two, *Berton juxta Warewell* (Barton Stacey) one, *Wreforde* (?) one, a meadow called *Mune* near *Kingeswell* and *Suwetone* (Monkemede?), and the meadow called *Dennemarke* (lying on the north of Winchester). Emma, the mother of the Confessor, gave thirty hides at *Pidele* (Piddle-Trentehide, in Dorsetshire), as well as other gifts; and Canute five hides at *Drayton juxta Biketon* (Drayton, in Bighton), besides the famous jewelled cross. The Confessor himself enriched it with the manor of *Papeholt* (near Mitcheldever) and the wood called *Ores* (Owers).

Possessions recorded by other authorities.

Subsequent to the date of Domesday we find recorded in the same memorandum the gift by Henry I., of the Hyde, which was afterwards the site of the monastery; *Abbotis Wordia* (Abbots Worthy) with seven hides; *Litelwordy* (Little, or Headbourne, Worthy) and the "liberty" of what is now Hyde Street, concerning which there were endless feuds between the abbey and the city. His queen, Matilda, gave ten hides at *Lamerkestoke* (Laverstoke?).

Earl "Brygwynus" (*Brihtwen*, perhaps,) also is said to have bestowed on it eight hides at *Upwarnford* (Upham, part of Warnford ?) ; Earl "Hugo Portuensis" (Hugo de Port) *Bedhampton* (still so named) with ten hides, and his "dapifer" Robert sixteen hides at *Fidlewerth* (Fittleworth, in Sussex).

The Anglo-Saxon Charter numbered 336 in Kemble's "Codex," and marked by him with an asterisk as being of doubtful authenticity, alleges that Edward the Elder, in addition to the other grants ascribed to him above, bestowed the manor of *Nortone juxta Seleborne* (Norton) containing three hides ; and that of *Durlea* (Durley, near Eling), on the abbey.

The Rolls for the 32nd and 33rd Henry VIII. in the Augmentation Office supply the names of a few more possessions of this abbey. We find there the names of *Abbot's Barton* (north of Winchester) ; *Northbroke Southbroke*, (Northbrook, Southbrook), and *Dottesley* (?), in connection with Mitcheldever ; the rectory of *Benstede* and *Kingesley* (Binstead and Kingsley) ; *Presshaw* (near Bishop's Waltham) ; *Ludshulfe* (in Andover Hundred) named with Tatchbury ; *Heighton* (Heighton in Sussex) ; and *Doughton* (Duncton ? in Sussex).

And, in addition to these, it was seized of various tenements in the city of Winchester, which are detailed in the Liber Winton., and the Survey of 1408 ; and the produce of three days of the fair on St. Giles's Hill.

The value of all the possessions of Hyde Abbey at the Dissolution was £865 18s. 0¾d. ; and the site of the monastery was granted to Richard Bethell.

The original charters relating to Mitcheldever, Chisleton, Pewsey, and Drayton are in the library of St. Mary's College, Winchester. Others will be found printed in Kemble's *Codex Diplomaticus.* Various registers and chartularies are described in the last edition of Dugdale.

St. Mary's Abbey.

Abbey of St. Mary, or Nunnaminster.—This abbey stood between High Street and Colebroke Street, on the spot still known by its name ; but no traces of it are now in existence, except the watercourses and the mill-stream in Colebroke Street. It was commenced before the year 900 by Alsuitha, wife of King Alfred the Great, and was completed by their son, King Edward the Elder ; and was consecrated by Archbishop Plegmund, in honour of the B. V. Mary and St. Edburga, in the year 981 (Ethelwerd's Chronicle). It participated in the great changes which King Edgar and Archbishop Dunstan introduced, and St. Athelwold, Bishop of Winchester, carried out here ; and was subjected, like the others, to the Benedictine rule. The buildings of the abbey were destroyed during the civil war of Stephen's time ; but we have no record of its rebuilding.

The Dissolution.

Its revenues being less than £200 per annum, this monastery was included in the first act of the Dissolution ; but by some means which have not been recorded the abbess was enabled to obtain royal letters patent, dated the 27th of August, 1536, placing the establishment on a new foundation, without greater loss than the manors of Allcannings and Urchfont, which were given to Edward Seymour, Viscount Beauchamp, and his wife. Thus reconstituted it continued for three years longer, and in the last year of the reign of Henry VIII., it was finally dissolved, and its possessions given to John Bello and John Broxholme, the abbess and nuns having small annuities granted them for their lives.

List of Abbesses.

The list of the superiors of St. Mary's Abbey, which commences only with St. Athelwold's reform, is taken from Dugdale, and is at first rather imperfect :—

963. Ethelreda (*Ethelritha*).

— St. Editha. In the reign of King Edgar.

— Beatrix.

1084. Alicia.

1120 (about). Hawysia.

1174. Claritia.

— Agnes. This abbess died on (3 Kal. Sept.) 30 August, 1265.

1265 Eufemia.

1270. Lucia.
1313. Maud Peccam (*Peacham*).
1338. Maud Spine.
1349. Margaret Mollins.
1364. Christiana Wayte.
1365. Alicia de Mare.
1385. Joan Deymede.
1410. Maud Holme.
1442. Agnes Burton.
— C. H. In the reign of Henry VII.
— A. B. In the reign of Henry VII.
1497. Joan.
1527. Elizabeth Shelly, who was the abbess at the Dissolution.

The only distinguished inmate was St. Edburga, daughter of King Edward the Elder, who is also said to have been one of its first superiors.

Its possessions recorded in Domesday are, in Hampshire three hides at *Lis* (now called Lyss), which in the Confessor's time had been five hides; eight hides, which had been ten, at *Froli* (Froyle); one hide, at the earlier date five, at *Lecforde* (Leckford); half a hide, formerly three hides, at *Stoches* (Longstock); two hides at *Timbreberie* (Timsbury); and what had been a hide and a half of land at *Ebintune* (Ovington). In Berkshire it had formerly possessed eight hides at *Coleselle* (Coleshill), which had shrunk to two and a half; and in Wiltshire thirty hides, at *Irchesfonte* (Urchfont) had diminished to twenty carucates; and eighteen hides, a virgate and a half, at *Caninge* (Allcannings), had fallen to fifteen.

The manor of *Icene* (Itchen Abbas), twelve hides in extent, had also formerly belonged to this abbey.

To this list the Roll of 32 Henry VIII., in the Augmentation Office, adds the following :— *Wetham* (Witham, near Andover), *Goddisfeld* (Godsfield, near Alresford), *Shamelhurst* (Shamblehurst, near Stoneham), *Swyndon* (in Gloucestershire), *Hackeborne* (?), *Shipton Moygn'* (Shipton Moigne, in Gloucestershire), *Blandeford* (in Dorsetshire), *Greatford* (in Lincolnshire), *Braseborough* (in Lincolnshire), and *Barnethorpe* (?).

In the will of Athelstan Ætheling (Kemble's Codex Diplom., No. 722) the gift of lands at *Hrytherafelda* (Rotherfield, in Sussex ?) is mentioned; and in the Taxatio Ecclesiastica, the Liber Winton., and the Survey of 1408, other such possessions are noted.

The value at the Dissolution was £179 7s. 2d.

Monastery of the Dominicans, or Black Friars.— This was situated near Eastgate, on the northern side of High Street, between St. John's Hospital and the way under the walls, in the land called Coitbury. Not the slightest trace of it now remains, Eastgate Street and the new houses on each side of it having been constructed over its site; nor can it be discovered in Godson's or Speed's maps, or in Bucke's view, being then replaced by Mildmay House and its pleasure-grounds. It is, however, probable that the watercourses and the parochial boundaries define its precinct, and show where the conventual buildings stood.

Its history is very imperfectly known, but would most probably be found in the muniments of St. Mary Winton College and the Registers of the Diocese. An inventory of the goods in the house at the time of its suppression may be seen in the Public Record Office, amongst the archives lately removed from the Chapter House, Westminster.

This monastery was founded in the year 1230 by Peter de la Roche, Bishop of Winchester, who had before this introduced members of the Dominican order in England. At the Dissolution its site and revenues were granted to the College of St. Mary Winton, and were valued at 20s. per annum.   Leland, in his Itinerary, has confounded the sites of the Dominican and Franciscan monasteries in Winchester.

Monastery of the Franciscans, or Gray Friars.—The precinct of this conventual establishment was bounded by Wongar and Tanner Streets on the west and east, by Buttle's Lane on the south, and the way under the walls on the north.   The precise site of the church and buildings cannot now be discovered, but the foundations of several long walls running from the side of Tanner Street westward have been traced in the garden of C. Wright, Esq., and some part of the precinct wall remains.   In Trussell's time, however, considerable portions of these structures, "built of smooth black flints," remained.   And Milner was able to trace "the foundation of the church in the great garden, between the Middle and the Lower Brook."

It was established here by Henry III., about the same time with the rival order of Dominicans ; and its site and revenues, when it was dissolved, in the 35th Henry VIII., were also granted to St. Mary's College, Winton, in the muniment room of which noble institution lie the records, and materials for the history of this monastery.   The Bishops' Registers, and records lately in the Chapter House, Westminster, contain other documents relating to its fortunes.

Monastery of the Augustine Friars.—On the eastern side of the road leading to St. Cross, just without Southgate, stood this friary, which was founded in the reign of Edward I. ; enlarged in the year 1314 by the addition of "a messuage and piece of land 12 perches long and 6 broad," given by Hugh Tripacy.   The house was rebuilt in the 15th year of Edward III.; but some ground which had been purchased by the friars without a royal license was by a decree of the Court of Chancery forfeited to the king, and by him granted to the corporation of Winchester.   It was valued at 13s. 8d. only at the Dissolution, and given to the College of St. Mary Winton.   The archives before mentioned contain whatever history the monastery may have had ; and the name of its site, "Priory," or "Friary," is the only vestige of it at the present day.

Monastery of the Carmelite, or White Friars.—This was situated in Kingsgate Street opposite the lane now leading to St. Michael's Church ; and its precinct extended beyond the Athelwold Bourne, to the Lurte Bourne, or Barton Mill Stream.   The church and convent most probably stood between the Athelwold Bourne and the street, but they cannot now be traced.

It was founded in the year 1278 by Peter, the rector of the parish church of St. Helen, in Winchester ; and the church was dedicated to the Blessed Virgin Mary.   At the Dissolution it was valued at 6s. 8d. yearly ; and was granted to St. Mary Winton College.   The Infirmary and its grounds, and College Mead, show the exact extent of this establishment. (See above, pp. 178, &c.)

College of St. Elizabeth.—The site of this college was the meadow between the road to Blackbridge and the Old Barge River, which was called St. Stephen's Meadow, from a chapel dedicated to that saint which anciently stood there.   In dry seasons the entire plan of the chapel attached to the college can be traced.   (Arch. Inst., Winchester Vol. "Architec- tural Notes," &c., p. 20.)   The high altar was dedicated to St. Elizabeth of Hungary, in whose honour the college was founded ; and other altars were dedicated to SS. Stephen and Lawrence, and SS. Edmund (king and martyr) and Thomas of Canterbury.

It was founded in the year 1301 by John de Pontissara, Bishop of Winchester, and the "*Ordinatio*" of the institution may be seen in the Registers of that prelate (fol. 32 v°).   It was to consist of a *præpositus*, or provost, six chaplains, all of whom were to be priests ; six clerks ; and six choristers, or *clericuli*.   The regulations of the college were of the kind common to such establishments in the middle ages ; obedience, cœnobitism, abstinence, the

[Margin notes:]
Monastery of the Gray Friars.

Monastery of the Augustine Friars.

Monastery of the White Friars.

College of St. Elizabeth.

almost incessant performance of religious offices, and the exclusion of females from every part of the building, except the chapel and the porch, being sufficient characteristics of the whole.

Besides St. Stephen's Meadow, it possessed lands, &c., in *Bottele* (now Botley), *Kingesclere* (still so called), *Culmestone Gymminges*, or *Gynninges* (?), *Shidefelde* and *Tychefelde* (still so called), and *Nortone Sti Walerici* (?), *Overland* (?), *Crundale* (Crondale), and in Clarendon Forest.

Its value at the Dissolution was £112 17s. 4d.; and it was granted by 35 Henry VIII. to Thomas Lord Wriothesly, and by him sold to the College of St. Mary Winton for £360. In accordance with the conditions of the sale, as it was not made use of for a grammar school for seventy scholars, it was pulled down early in the year 1547.

Sustern Spytal.—This was an hospital on the site of Commoners, on the western side of the college, where a number of professed nuns lived, who received sick persons, and tended them there, or visited them in their own homes. Some remains of it were visible until the building of the New Commoners. It was supported by charity, and apparently had some connection with the Priory of St. Swithin. There is mention of a " *Hospitale* " in the Liber Winton. (p. 559), which stood near " *Chingeta*," and so may have been the *Sustern Spytal*. " Sustern Spytal."

There was also another *hospitale* or *infirmarium* on the hill outside Westgate (Liber Wint., pp. 536, 548), but we have no accounts of it beyond this casual mention.

College of the Holy Trinity.—This was founded by Roger, John, and Richard de Inkpenne, about the year 1318 (Tanner; but Milner says in the eleventh century), for a warden and several priests. It stood, with its chapel dedicated to the Holy Trinity, on the north side of the *litten*, or grave-yard, of St. Mary's Abbey, beside the great watercourse which then ran along the lower part of High Street, to the east of the present Police Station. And it had a " *carnarie*," or charnel-house, under it. It was built, according to Trussell, as a chantry and charnel-house for the city. College of the Holy Trinity.

College of St. Mary Kalendar.—This was connected with the parish so named; little more of it is known beyond its existence, and that its property was granted to the Mayor and Corporation of the city, in the 1st and 2nd Philip and Mary. Some records of its history might perhaps be discovered in the muniments of the corporation, over Westgate. College of St. Mary Kalendar.

Fraternity of St. Peter.—This consisted of a prior and certain friars, or brethren, who were attached to the church of St. Maurice, and performed religious services there. In the " Tarrages " of Winchester, in the commencement of the fifteenth century, mention is frequently made of this " Frarie," showing that it had possessions in various parts of the city. Fraternity of St. Peter.

II. Annals of Winchester.

We present here, in the compendious form of Annals, an account of the more considerable events in the History of Winchester, not repeating the notices of occurrences which have already found a place in any of the preceding sections, nor trespassing into the peculiar province of the general historian, nor entering at all on the legendary history, which in Trussell and Wavell, and even in Milner, occupies so large a space in the earliest period. Milner's copious " History " is our guide, but we have confirmed or corrected him throughout by the original authorities.

The first authentic recorded event is the following :—

A.D. 648. The Church of St. Peter was built and dedicated on the (viii. Kal. Dec.) 24th of November. (Annal. Wint., Cotton MS., Vitelius A. xvii.; see above, p. 95, note 3.) Winchester was certainly from this date the residence of the Kings of Wessex. A.D. 648.

A.D. 764. The city devastated by a conflagration. (Simeon Dunelm.; Mon. Hist. Brit., vol. i. p. 663.)

A.D. 827. Egbert, King of Wessex, crowned *Bretwalda*, or King of all England, in the Old Minster. (Higden, Rudborne, Anglia Sacra, vol. i. p. 199.)

A.D. 855. This year there was a "*witena gemot*" at Winchester (Kemble's Saxons in England, vol. ii. p. 251); and King Ethelwulf gave by charter the tenth part of his land, throughout his realm, for the glory of God and his own eternal salvation. (Anglo-Saxon Chronicle.) William of Malmesbury (*sub ann.*) cites one charter of Ethelwulf's bearing on this transaction, but dated erroneously in 844; and this he says was . . . . "written in Winchester, in the church of St. Peter, before the high altar, ... and then for greater security King Ethelwulf placed the charter on the altar of St. Peter."

For a full account of this event, which is commonly, but wrongly, spoken of as the origin of tithes, see Kemble's Saxons in England, vol. ii. pp. 480—490.

A.D. 860. A large fleet of Northmen came to land, and the crews stormed Winchester. (Anglo-Saxon Chronicle; see above, p. 104, notes 4 and 5.)

A.D. 897. The crews of two Danish ships, which had been cast on shore, were brought to King Alfred at Winchester, and he commanded them to be hanged. (Anglo-Saxon Chronicle.)

A.D. 909. A "*witena gemot*" of Wessex held this year, and most probably at Winchester. (Kemble's Saxons in England, vol. ii. p. 253; Cod. Dipl., No. 1091.)

A.D. 934. On the 28th of May, this year, there was a great mutiny at Winchester "*tota populi generalitate.*" (Kemble, ibid., p. 254; Cod. Dipl., No. 364.)

A.D. 993. A "*witena gemot*" at Winchester. (Kemble, ibid., p. 256; Cod. Dipl., No. 684.)

A.D. 1002. Æthelred the Unready marries Ymma Ælfgiva, daughter of Richard, Duke of Normandy, and gives her Winchester as her "morning gift" or dowry. (Geffrei Gaeinar, Mon. Hist. Brit., p. 815.)

A.D. 1006. In the winter of this year the Danes occupied the Isle of Wight, and sent out their foraging parties to every part of Hampshire and Berkshire, and "then might the Winchester men see an army daring and fearless, as they went by their gates to the sea." (Anglo-Saxon Chronicle.)

A.D. 1013. The citizens submit to Sweyn, and deliver hostages.

A.D. 1016—1020. "Probably between these years was the great "*gemot*" at Winchester, in which Cnut promulgated his laws." (Kemble, *u. s.*, p. 259.) It was held at "the holy-tide of Mid-winter." (Thorpe's Ancient Laws and Institutes, vol. i. p. 358.)

A.D. 1036. Winchester appointed by the "*witena gemot*" of Oxford as the residence of Queen Ymma, with due retinue, to hold Wessex for Hardacnute, whose half-brother, Harold I., was made king. (Anglo-Saxon Chronicle.)

A.D. 1037. "This year was driven out Ælfgiva, King Cnut's relict." (Anglo-Saxon Chronicle.)

A.D. 1040. Queen Ymma returns to Winchester at the death of Harold I.

A.D. 1043. This year, at Easter, April the 3rd, Edward the Confessor was crowned at a "*witena gemot*" held in this city; and in November the king, with his followers, repaired suddenly to Winchester, and despoiled his mother of her lands and treasures, "because she had done less for him than he would, before he was king, and also since;" but they suffered her to remain there. (Anglo-Saxon Chronicle.) According to the Liber Winton. (p. 535), "*Emma regina*" was possessed of a house which is classed amongst the "thanelands," and was not far from Westgate, on the north side of High Street. (See above, p. 115, and note 2.)

A.D. 1053. Here King Edward kept Easter this year, and on the second day of Easter

(April the 12th) Godwin the Earl sat with the king at the feast, and suddenly he sank down by the footstool speechless and powerless, and being carried to the king's chamber, remained so until Thursday, and then died.

A.D. 1066. Queen Eadgitha, relict of Edward the Confessor, who held Winchester by his gift, submits herself to William the Conqueror after the Battle of Hastings. (*De Bello Hasting. Carmen,* Mon. Hist. Brit., p. 868). In Liber Winton. (p. 553) some of the property of "*Edda Regina*" is mentioned.

A.D. 1066.

A.D. 1069. William the Conqueror was crowned a second time at Winchester.

1069.

A.D. 1070. William is said to have commenced the building of his palace here, or rather the enlargement of that of the Saxon kings, who preceded him.

1070.

A council was held here on the Octaves of Easter (April 11th), at which Archbishop Stigand was degraded, and sentenced to imprisonment. (See above, p. 301, note). Other bishops and abbots were deposed at the same time.

A.D. 1072. A preliminary council was held here at Easter (April 8th) for the "ventilation" of the question of precedency between the sees of Canterbury and York.

1072.

A.D. 1076. The Earl Waltheof beheaded on St. Giles's Hill, " on the Mass day of Petronilla" (or the 31st of May), for conspiring against the king, with the Earl Roger, at Norwich.

1076.

A.D. 1086. This year the great survey of the whole kingdom contained in Domesday Book was completed, and the two volumes of the record were placed in the Treasury of the cathedral at Winchester.

1086

PRINTED BY VIRTUE AND CO., CITY ROAD, LONDON.